An Insider's Guide to Academic Writing
A Rhetoric and Reader

Third Edition

An Insider's Guide to Academic Writing

A Rhetoric and Reader

Susan Miller-Cochran

University of Arizona

Roy Stamper

North Carolina State University

Stacey Cochran

University of Arizona

bedford/st.martin's
Macmillan Learning

Boston | New York

For Bedford/St. Martin's

Vice President, Humanities: Leasa Burton
Program Director, English: Stacey Purviance
Senior Program Manager: Laura Arcari
Director of Content Development: Jane Knetzger
Senior Development Editor: Cynthia Ward
Editorial Assistant: Bill Yin
Director of Media Editorial: Adam Whitehurst
Media Editor: Dan Johnson
Marketing Manager: Vivian Garcia
Senior Director, Content Management Enhancement: Tracey Kuehn
Senior Managing Editor: Michael Granger
Senior Digital Content Project Manager: Ryan Sullivan
Senior Workflow Project Manager: Lisa McDowell
Production Supervisors: Robin Besofsky, Robert Cherry
Director of Design, Content Management: Diana Blume
Interior Design: Claire Seng-Niemoeller
Cover Design: William Boardman
Director of Rights and Permissions: Hilary Newman
Permissions Editor: Allison Ziebka-Viering
Text Permissions Researcher: Elaine Kosta, Lumina Datamatics, Inc.
Photo Researcher: Cheryl Dubois, Lumina Datamatics, Inc.
Director of Digital Production: Keri deManigold
Media Project Manager: Elizabeth Dziubela
Project Management: Lumina Datamatics, Inc.
Project Manager: Nagalakshmi Karunanithi
Editorial Services: Lumina Datamatics, Inc.
Copyeditor: Angela Morrison, Lumina Datamatics, Inc.
Indexer: Christine Hoskin, Lumina Datamatics, Inc.
Composition: Lumina Datamatics, Inc.
Cover and Title Page Image: Andrea Tsurumi
Printing and Binding: LSC Communications

Library of Congress Control Number: 2021942484
ISBN: 978-1-319-33492-5 (Paperback Edition)
ISBN: 978-1-319-42130-4 (Loose-leaf Edition)

Printed in the United States of America.

1 2 3 4 5 6   26 25 24 23 22 21

Acknowledgments

Text acknowledgments and copyrights appear at the back of the book on pages 553–55, which constitute an extension of the copyright page. Art acknowledgments and copyrights appear on the same page as the art selections they cover.

Preface for Instructors

We undertook the third edition of *An Insider's Guide to Academic Writing* during extraordinary times for higher education. During a global pandemic that, in many instances, caused educational institutions to make sudden and dramatic changes to their course offerings and instructional methods, we found ourselves reconsidering many of our assumptions about teaching writing. We thought about how to connect with students in meaningful ways from a distance and how to address our students' and our own well-being during a time of uncertainty. In addition to the challenges of the pandemic, we were also writing while our nation experienced much political unrest even as we experienced an important inflection point in the ongoing struggle for racial equality. These trials of the past year have underscored the importance of facts and truth in both our civic and our academic engagements, and they've reminded us of the importance of making every effort to stem the tide of racial prejudice and discrimination in all of its forms, both implicit and explicit.

The circumstances of the last year have informed decisions related to the development of the latest edition of *An Insider's Guide*. Our primary goal remains to help college students, new to the world of higher education, learn the territory, language, skills, codes, and secrets of academic writing in disciplinary contexts. At the same time, we've endeavored in the new edition to incorporate what we've learned about student engagement and online education from the dramatic instructional shifts stemming from the global pandemic, and we've made numerous changes to the text as part of our effort to affirm our commitment to social justice in a more equitable world.

Core Features of *An Insider's Guide*

An Insider's Guide to Academic Writing continues to offer a unique set of resources for helping students develop rhetorical skills that are transferable from first-year composition to other courses and writing contexts. Through the study of writing in academic disciplines, students are also introduced to the kinds of questions explored by different academic communities.

Building Rhetorical Skills through the Study of Academic Writing

We wrote *An Insider's Guide to Academic Writing* out of a need for a text that would effectively prepare students to navigate the reading and writing expectations of academic discourse communities across the curriculum. We recognized that no single book, or course, or teacher could train all students in all the details of scholarly writing in all disciplines. What we aimed to do instead was offer students rhetorical principles that are fundamental to the understanding of texts and then show those principles at work in various domains of academic inquiry, including the humanities, the social sciences, the natural sciences, and the applied fields.

We set out with three key goals: (1) introduce students to rhetorical lenses through which they can view the genres and conventions they will be expected to read and produce in other courses, (2) provide examples of those genres and conventions to analyze and discuss, and (3) include carefully scaffolded writing activities and projects designed to help students explore and guide their production of those genres. Part One lays the groundwork for this disciplinary approach, introducing students to the fundamentals of writing processes and reflection, rhetorical analysis, argument, and research. Part Two provides unique discipline-specific chapters, and if you are using the comprehensive version of the text, Part Three offers readings from each discipline area on high-interest themes.

An Insider's Guide is as flexible as it is comprehensive. Some faculty, for instance, use this approach to support themed courses; they examine how a particular topic or issue is explored by scholars across a range of disciplines. Other faculty situate principles of argument at the center of their course designs and explore disciplinary perspectives and writing in light of those principles. Still others organize their courses as step-by-step journeys through academic domains while attending to the similarities and distinctions in writing practices (rhetorical conventions and genres) of various fields.

Engaging Students with Class-Tested Pedagogy

We designed *An Insider's Guide to Academic Writing* to provide all the resources we wanted when we transitioned the first-year writing program at North Carolina State University to a writing-in-the-disciplines (WID) approach:

- **Writing Projects**—one or more per chapter—offer detailed prompts and guidance for students to practice the skills and moves taught in the chapters. These include literacy narratives, rhetorical analyses, genre analyses, arguments supported by research, and annotated bibliographies, as well as such common academic genres as textual interpretations (humanities); theory response papers, literature reviews, and poster presentations (social sciences); and lab reports and research proposals (natural sciences).

- **"Insider Example" essays** show how students and academics have responded to different writing projects. Annotations point out key features and moves that students can consider for their own writing.

- **"Insider's View" boxes** feature scholars and students from a range of disciplines, discussing their experiences with academic writing. Several of these boxes are excerpted from video interviews that complement the instruction in this book. These videos are available for viewing in the digital platform Achieve.

- **"Connect" activities** prompt students to reflect on what they have learned and practice applying these new insights and techniques. (These were called "Inside Work" in previous editions.)
- **Tip Sheets** summarize key lessons of the chapters.

In addition to chapters with the above features, the comprehensive edition of *An Insider's Guide* offers **a thematic reader with popular and scholarly essays** that can serve as springboards for writing and discussion as well as models of rhetorical moves and disciplinary genres and conventions. The scholarly essays are organized as **case studies**; each case study includes readings from the humanities, social sciences, natural sciences, and applied fields. Through these unabridged essays, students can contrast the form and content of writing across the curriculum, while also getting practice in tackling academic reading. Annotations, headnotes, and post-reading questions provide support.

What's New

We have substantially revised the third edition to improve the online experience, while also adding new content to reflect the diversity of writing and writers. We listened to teachers using the book to learn what works in their classes and how we could do better. Here are the revision highlights:

- **For the first time, *An Insider's Guide to Academic Writing* is available within the Achieve platform.** Achieve with *An Insider's Guide to Academic Writing* offers a dedicated composition space that guides students through drafting, peer review, Source Check, reflection, and revision. Developed to support best practices in commenting on student drafts, Achieve is a flexible, integrated suite of tools for designing and facilitating writing assignments, paired with actionable insights that make students' progress toward outcomes clear and measurable—all in a single powerful, easy-to-use platform that works for face-to-face, remote, and hybrid learning scenarios. Achieve includes the complete e-book and fully editable and assignable pre-built assignments that support key assignments in the book. For details, visit **macmillanlearning.com/college/us/achieve/english**.
- Readings, boxes, examples, and photos have been revised so that **students with a diverse range of identities and experiences** can see that they too belong as "insiders" in academic communities. In the comprehensive edition, more than half of the readings in Part Three are new, bringing in a more contemporary and diverse range of writers and perspectives on matters of identity and writing, love, food, and criminal justice.

- **New Insider Examples** give students models for every writing project in the book. The new examples include an argument analysis, an annotated bibliography, a genre analysis, a poster presentation, a PowerPoint presentation, an IT paper, and a genre analysis in the applied fields. All of the Insider Examples are now annotated to highlight the writer's rhetorical moves.

- **New "Insider's View" boxes** add to the range of disciplines and research areas represented: Dev Bose, Disability Writing Studies scholar, on accessible design; historian Matthew Sakiestewa Gilbert on research in American Indian Studies; Cristina Ramirez, Writing Studies scholar, on genres and styles in the humanities; and vice chancellor Bruce Moses on writing as an administrator.

- **"Inside Work" activities have been renamed "Connect"** to make explicit their purpose of providing opportunities for students to put their learning into action. These activities have been streamlined so that many of them can be completed in a single sitting, either independently or as group work.

- **Added coverage of multimodal writing** can be found in new discussions and examples of poster presentations (Chapter 8) and PowerPoint slides (Chapter 10). A new reading (Jia Tolentino's "The I in Internet") in Chapter 11 of the comprehensive edition offers a writer's account of growing up in multimodal digital spaces.

- Chapters 7 to 9 offer **a fuller treatment of academic genres**. Each genre is structured to include the rhetorical context of and strategies for writing the genre, followed by a Writing Project and Insider Example.

Acknowledgments

We are grateful to the students who were willing to try this approach and, in many cases, share their writing in this book. Their examples provide essential scaffolding for the book's approach, and their honest feedback helped us refine our explanation of various genres and disciplines.

We are also grateful to our colleagues in the First-Year Writing Program at North Carolina State University and the Writing Program at the University of Arizona, who have shared their expertise and ideas about teaching writing in and about disciplines over the years. Without their support and their innovation, we would not have been able to complete this project.

We are indebted to the many skilled and thoughtful instructors who have used and offered feedback on the book. We are truly grateful to you for supporting, through your engaging advice and encouraging criticism, our efforts to make this book the best it can possibly be. For this third edition, we wish to recognize Jessie Blackburn, Appalachian State University; Virginia Crisco, California State University, Fresno; Lourdes Fernandez, George Mason University; Penny Jacobs, Fayetteville Technical Community College;

Debra Knutson, Shawnee State University; Robin Latham, Nash Community College; Will Mayer, Longwood Community College; Jessica Saxon, Craven Community College; and Terri Van Sickle, Craven Community College.

Our thanks also go to the incredible support from our team at Macmillan. First and foremost among that team is Cynthia Ward, our development editor, who has helped us see this revision through to completion and provided insightful suggestions that guided our approach. We are also indebted to Leasa Burton, vice president of humanities at Macmillan, who understood our goals and championed this project from the beginning. We have also received outstanding support and guidance from Stacey Purviance, program director for English, and Laura Arcari, senior program manager. We are also grateful for the work of Ryan Sullivan, who guided the book through the production process with great care. We thank Claire Seng-Niemoeller for creating the superb design of the book, William Boardman for the book cover design, and Vivian Garcia for her marketing and market development efforts. Additionally, we extend our thanks to Daniel Johnson, media editor for the Achieve platform; Bill Yin, editorial assistant; and Hilary Newman, director of rights and permissions. We thank the other contributors who helped in so many ways behind the scenes.

As always, we remain indebted to our friends and families, who provided a great deal of support as we worked on this edition of the book.

Susan Miller-Cochran

Roy Stamper

Stacey Cochran

Bedford/St. Martin's Puts You First

From day one, our goal has been simple: to provide inspiring resources that are grounded in best practices for teaching reading and writing. For more than 40 years, Bedford/St. Martin's has partnered with the field, listening to teachers, scholars, and students about the support writers need. No matter the moment or teaching context, we are committed to helping every writing instructor make the most of our resources—resources designed to engage every student.

How We Can Help *You*

- Our editors can align our resources to your outcomes through correlation and transition guides for your syllabus. Just ask us.
- Our sales representatives specialize in helping you find the right materials to support your course goals.
- Our learning solutions and product specialists help you make the most of the digital resources you choose for your course.
- Our *Bits* blog on the Bedford/St. Martin's English Community (**community.macmillan.com**) publishes fresh teaching ideas regularly. You'll also find easily downloadable professional resources and links to author webinars on our community site.

Contact your Bedford/St. Martin's sales representative or visit **macmillanlearning.com** to learn more.

Digital and Print Options for *An Insider's Guide to Academic Writing*

Choose the format that works best for your course, and ask about our packaging options that offer savings for students.

Digital

- **Achieve with *An Insider's Guide to Academic Writing*.** Achieve puts student writing at the center of your course and keeps revision at the core, with a dedicated composition space that guides students through drafting, peer review, Source Check, reflection, and revision. Developed to support best practices in commenting on student drafts, Achieve is a flexible, integrated suite of tools for designing and facilitating writing assignments, paired with actionable insights that make students' progress toward outcomes clear and measurable. Fully editable pre-built assignments support the book's approach and an e-book is included. To order Achieve with *An Insider's Guide to Academic Writing*, use ISBN 978-1-319-42370-4. For details, visit **macmillanlearning.com/college/us/achieve/english**.

- **Popular e-book formats.** For details about our e-book partners, visit **macmillanlearning.com/ebooks**.

- **Inclusive Access.** Enable every student to receive their course materials through your LMS on the first day of class. Macmillan Learning's Inclusive Access program is the easiest, most affordable way to ensure all students have access to quality educational resources. Find out more at **macmillanlearning.com/inclusiveaccess**.

Print

- **Paperback.** *An Insider's Guide to Academic Writing* is available in paperback in two versions.
  - To order the paperback **comprehensive edition** (subtitle, "A Rhetoric and Reader"), use ISBN 978-1-319-33492-5. To order the paperback comprehensive edition packaged with Achieve, use ISBN 978-1-319-44587-4.
  - To order the paperback **brief edition** that does not have the four-chapter reader (subtitle, "A Brief Rhetoric"), use ISBN 978-1-319-34612-6. To order the paperback brief edition packaged with Achieve, use ISBN 978-1-319-44740-3.

- **Loose-leaf.** This format does not have a traditional binding; its pages are loose and hole-punched to provide flexibility and a lower price to students. It can be packaged with Achieve for additional savings.
  - To order the loose-leaf **comprehensive edition** (subtitle, "A Rhetoric and Reader"), use ISBN 978-1-319-42130-4. To order the loose-leaf comprehensive edition packaged with Achieve, use ISBN 978-1-319-44631-4.
  - To order the loose-leaf **brief edition** that does not have the four-chapter reader (subtitle, "A Brief Rhetoric"), use ISBN 978-1-319-42132-8. To order the loose-leaf brief edition packaged with Achieve, use ISBN 978-1-319-44744-1.

Your Course, Your Way

No two writing programs or classrooms are exactly alike. Our Curriculum Solutions team works with you to design custom options that provide the resources your students need. (Options below require enrollment minimums.)

- **ForeWords for English.** Customize any print resource to fit the focus of your course or program by choosing from a range of prepared topics, such as Sentence Guides for Academic Writers.

- **Macmillan Author Program (MAP).** Add excerpts or package acclaimed works from Macmillan's trade imprints to connect students with prominent authors and public conversations. A list of popular examples or academic themes is available upon request.

- **Mix and Match.** With our simplest solution, you can add up to 50 pages of curated content to your Bedford/St. Martin's text. Contact your sales representative for additional details.

Instructor Resources

You have a lot to do in your course. We want to make it easy for you to find the support you need—and to get it quickly.

- *Resources for Teaching An Insider's Guide to Academic Writing* is available as a PDF that can be downloaded from **macmillanlearning.com** and is also available in Achieve. In addition to chapter overviews and teaching tips, this instructor's manual includes sample syllabi, correlations to the Council of Writing Program Administrators' Outcomes Statement, and classroom activities.

- *Resources for Teaching North Carolina English 112 with An Insider's Guide to Academic Writing* is also available as a PDF that can be downloaded from the Bedford/St. Martin's online catalog at **macmillanlearning.com**. This brief resource complements *Resources for Teaching An Insider's Guide to Academic Writing*, with teaching attention to specific course outcomes and transfer requirements articulated in the 2014 Comprehensive Articulation Agreement between the University of North Carolina and the North Carolina Community College System.

Contents

Part One introduces you to the kinds of writing expectations you will face in college and equips you with core principles and strategies that you can apply to all types of writing. You'll build your skills by practicing strategies for giving and receiving feedback, reflecting on your writing processes, making supported arguments, and engaging in academic research.

3   Reading and Writing Rhetorically 33

4   Developing Arguments 48

5   Academic Research 67

PART TWO   Inside Academic Writing   101

In Part Two you'll look at how writing works in each of the major academic areas. You'll learn how the conventions and genres of different disciplines represent a discipline's shared values. Throughout these chapters, you'll be practicing skills of rhetorical analysis that you can transfer to your future courses and careers.

6 Reading and Writing in Academic Disciplines   102

7   Reading and Writing in the Humanities 122

10   Reading and Writing in the Applied Fields 259

PART THREE ## Entering Academic Conversations: Readings and Case Studies 299

The four chapters in Part Three allow you to practice reading the kinds of popular and scholarly arguments you'll encounter in your courses. The popular sources show how the principles of rhetoric operate in public persuasion. The academic articles are grouped into casebooks that let you see how different disciplines view similar topics through different lenses.

 # 11 Constructing Identity: Writing, Language, and the Self   300

Jimmy Santiago Baca, *Coming into Language*   301

"The language of poetry was the magic that could liberate me from myself, transform me into another person, transport me to places far away."

Jia Tolentino, *The I in Internet*   306

"As a medium, the internet is defined by a built-in performance incentive. . . . [You] can't just walk around and be visible on the internet—for anyone to see you, you have to act. You have to communicate in order to maintain an internet presence."

Robin Dembroff and Daniel Wodak, *If Someone Wants to Be Called "They" and Not "He" or "She," Why Say No?*   309

This 2018 opinion piece from *The Guardian* looks at the debate over gender-neutral pronouns as a matter of accepting or denying a person's identity.

ANDREA TSURUMI

A Guide to College and College Writing

Part One introduces you to the kinds of writing expectations you will face in college and equips you with core principles and strategies that you can apply to all types of writing. You'll build your skills by practicing strategies for giving and receiving feedback, reflecting on your writing processes, making supported arguments, and engaging in academic research.

An Introduction to Academic Writing

This book introduces expectations about writing you'll likely encounter in college and helps you develop a set of tools to complete writing tasks successfully. A main aim of this book is to help you find connections between what you are learning about writing and how that knowledge can help you achieve your personal, professional, and academic goals. To accomplish that aim, we first introduce you to how and why colleges and universities are structured into academic disciplines. We'll explore how your other writing experiences in high school, college, and work might compare to what you will write in college, and we will also discuss what expectations about writing you might encounter in different classes.

Teachers and researchers who study writing have found that students who are effective writers develop strategies for using what they learn in their writing classes in other classes and contexts. Most importantly, they learn how to *adapt* what they have learned about writing to those new contexts, paying attention to the expectations about writing in each unique situation.

As you read through the chapters in this book, certain recurring features will help you build these strategies as you expand your knowledge of college writing:

- *Insider's View* boxes feature scholars and students discussing academic writing. Several of these are gleaned from video interviews that complement the instruction in this book. The videos, which are available for viewing in the digital platform Achieve, offer further insights into the processes and productions of academic writers.

- *Connect* activities prompt you to reflect on what you have learned while trying out new insights and techniques.

- *Writing Projects* offer sequences of activities that will help you develop your own compositions.

    - *Insider Examples* show how writers have responded to different academic writing situations. Annotations point out key features and moves that you can consider for your own writing.

    - *Tip Sheets* summarize key lessons of the chapters.

ANDREA TSURUMI

Your Goals and Your School's Mission

As we get started on this journey, we'd like you to reflect on your goals: academic, professional, personal, or other. What brought you to college? People's reasons for pursuing an undergraduate degree can differ, depending on their interests and what motivates them. Different schools offer different opportunities as well. Some schools and degree programs focus on preparing students for particular careers that they can pursue directly after graduation. Others focus more broadly on developing graduates in a range of different areas who will be active in their communities regardless of which careers they pursue. Still others emphasize different, and sometimes quite specific, outcomes for their graduates. If you have never done so, consider taking a look at the mission or values statements for your university, college, or department. What do the faculty members and administrators value? What are their expectations of you as a student?

For example, the mission statement of Texas A&M University begins by stating:

> Texas A&M University is dedicated to the discovery, development, communication, and application of knowledge in a wide range of academic and professional fields.

This statement shows a broad commitment to a range of academic interests and professions; therefore, students at Texas A&M can expect to find a wide range of majors represented at the university. The mission statement also emphasizes that knowledge discovery is important at Texas A&M, highlighting the school's role as a research-intensive university.

As another example, the mission statement of Glendale Community College in California reads:

> Glendale Community College serves a diverse population of students by providing the opportunities and support to achieve their educational and career goals. We are committed to student learning and success through transfer preparation, certificates, associate degrees, career development, technical training, continuing education, and basic skills instruction.

This statement illustrates Glendale Community College's emphasis on preparing students for careers and serving a broad range of students with specific academic and professional goals.

A third example is the mission statement of Endicott College in Massachusetts, which begins by stating:

> Shaped by a bold entrepreneurial spirit, Endicott College offers students a vibrant academic environment that remains true to its founding principle of integrating professional and liberal arts with experiential learning including internship opportunities across disciplines.

Endicott's mission mentions an emphasis on "experiential" learning, which is evident through the connection of professional experiences with academics and the availability of internships for students. Students who enroll at Endicott College should expect a practical, hands-on application of their learning throughout their coursework.

Of course, different students have different goals and reasons for pursuing undergraduate degrees. Sometimes those goals match the institution's mission fairly closely, but not always. What is your purpose in attending your college or university? How do your personal and professional goals fit within the school's goals and values?

Regardless of your purpose for attending college, the transition to college can be a challenging one. Vincent Tinto, a researcher interested in what helps students succeed as they make the transition to college, has identified and written extensively about three stages that students go through as they adapt to college: separation, transition, and incorporation.[*] At the separation stage, students might feel disconnected to prior communities and commitments, but successful students move through a transition stage and then find a way to connect themselves with new communities in college (incorporation). The separation stage can be very challenging, though, and knowing what resources you have available to you as you make the transition to college can be incredibly helpful.

Connect 1.1   Identifying Your Goals within the Academic Community

Find your school's mission statement (usually available in the "About" page of the school website). As you work through the following questions, think about how the mission of your school might align with your own interests and goals:

- What do you feel you are motivated to learn about? For example, if you had four hours with nothing to do except read and learn about one subject, what would you choose to read about? Or, if you could take only one class right now, but it could be any class you'd like, what would it be? Why?
- What goals do you hope to achieve by attending college?
- What connections do you see between your own goals and the mission of the university? How might the characteristics and mission of your college or university help you achieve your goals?
- What steps could you take to maximize your opportunity to explore your academic interests and achieve your goals?

---

[*]Tinto discusses these stages in "Stages of Student Departure: Reflections on the Longitudinal Character of Student Leaving," *Journal of Higher Education*, vol. 59, no. 4 (1988), pp. 438–55.

Writing within Academic Disciplines

As you enter the college community, you will discover different communities within it, each using writing to share knowledge and build our understanding of the world. When you take courses within these communities, you read and write within these specialized worlds. This book will give you tools and frameworks to meet these diverse and challenging assignments.

An important organizational feature of colleges and universities is the way they are divided into academic and professional disciplines. Depending on the school, this might take the form of departments, divisions, colleges, or other groupings. **Academic disciplines** are, broadly defined, areas of teaching, research, and inquiry that academics pursue. Sometimes these disciplines are listed in broad categories, such as psychology, English, biology, physics, and engineering. Within each academic discipline are more specialized communities of scholars.

At other times, disciplines are listed in more specialized categories that demonstrate the diversity of areas encompassed within higher education: for example, adolescent psychology, abnormal psychology, sociolinguistics, second language acquisition, molecular biology, physiology, astrophysics, quantum mechanics, civil engineering, mechanical engineering, computer science, Victorian poetry, and medieval literature.

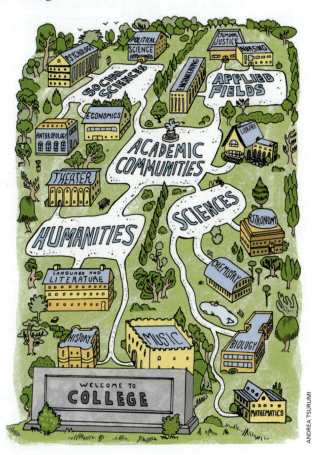

While the specific divisions may differ according to the institution, most college and university faculties are grouped into departments or divisions of some sort, and those groupings usually correspond to similarities in how they approach the world from their disciplinary perspectives. Larger schools are typically further divided into colleges or schools-within-schools, which usually cluster together departments that are related to one another in some way. These groupings often, but not always, fall along common lines that divide departments into broader disciplinary areas of the humanities, social sciences, natural sciences, and applied fields. We use these broader categories when introducing you to different types of academic writing in Part Two.

For the purposes of this text, we're going to explore writing in different disciplinary areas that are grouped together according

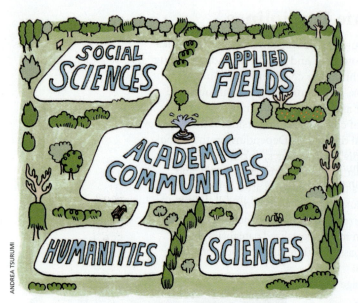
ANDREA TSURUMI

to (1) the kinds of questions that scholars ask in those disciplines and (2) the research strategies, or methods of inquiry, that they use to answer those questions. As mentioned earlier, we've divided various academic disciplines into four broad disciplinary categories: humanities, social sciences, natural sciences, and applied fields. As we talk about these four areas of study and the disciplines associated with them, both here and in Part Two of the book, you'll notice some similarities and differences within the categories:

- Scholars in the **humanities** usually ask questions about the human condition. To answer these questions, they often employ methods of inquiry that are based on analysis, interpretation, and speculation. Examples of academic disciplines that are generally considered part of the humanities are history, literature, philosophy, foreign languages, religious studies, and the fine arts. You'll find examples of the kinds of questions humanists ask — and how they write about them — in Chapter 7.

- Scholars in the **social sciences** usually ask questions about human behavior and society. To answer these questions, they often employ methods of inquiry that are based on theory building or empirical research. Examples of academic disciplines that are generally considered part of the social sciences are communication, psychology, sociology, political science, economics, and anthropology. You'll find examples of the kinds of questions social scientists ask — and how they write about them — in Chapter 8.

- Scholars in the **natural sciences** usually ask questions about the natural world. To answer these questions, they often employ methods of inquiry that are based on experimentation and quantifiable data. Examples of academic disciplines that are generally considered part of the natural sciences are chemistry, biology, physics, astronomy, and mathematics. You'll find examples of the kinds of questions natural scientists ask — and how they write about them — in Chapter 9.

- Scholars in **applied fields** might have their foundation in any one (or more) of the disciplinary categories, but their work is generally focused on practical application. Some disciplines that could fall under the category of applied fields are criminal justice, medicine, nursing, education, business, agriculture, and engineering. Each of these fields has elements that are closely aligned with the humanities, social sciences, and/or natural sciences, but each also focuses on application of that knowledge in specific contexts. You'll find examples of the kinds of questions scholars in applied fields ask—and how they write about them—in Chapter 10.

These categories are not perfectly distinct; they sometimes overlap with one another, and they are debatable. Sometimes you'll find that different institutions categorize certain classes as part of a particular disciplinary area through their General Education requirements, for example. Another institution might list a similar class as meeting a different requirement. You'll see examples of disciplinary overlap in the chapters in Part Two and in the student writing examples there. Regardless, the disciplinary categories of humanities, social sciences, natural sciences, and applied fields are useful for understanding some of the distinctions in the ways academics think and do research. One of the most useful things about understanding distinctions in how different disciplines approach subjects is understanding how they can work together to solve problems.

Connect 1.2 **Understanding Disciplinarity**

Look at your current course schedule. How might you classify the classes you're taking in terms of the four academic disciplines we've described: humanities; social sciences; natural sciences; applied fields? For each class, write for a few minutes about what characteristics of the class cause it to fit into the category you've chosen. Finally, compare your answers with a classmate's.

Entering Academic Conversations

As you think about the writing you will do in college, keep in mind that you are learning how to participate in the kinds of discussions that scholars and faculty members engage in about topics and issues of mutual interest. In other words, you're entering into academic conversations that have been going on for a while. As you are writing, you will need to think about who your audience is (other students? teachers? an audience outside of the academic setting?), who has already been participating in the conversations of interest to you (and perhaps who hasn't), and what expectations for your writing you'll need to follow in order to contribute to those conversations. (We'll have much more to say about the concept of audience in Chapter 3.)

As we explore the kinds of writing done in various disciplinary areas, you'll notice that different disciplines have different expectations for writing. In other words, faculty members in a particular discipline might expect a piece of writing to be structured in a particular way, or they might use specific kinds of language, or they might expect you to be familiar with certain research by others and refer to it in prescribed ways. Each of these expectations is an aspect of the writing conventions of a particular discipline. **Conventions** are the customs that scholars in a particular discipline follow in their writing.

Sometimes those conventions take the form of repeated patterns in structure or certain choices in language use, just to name a couple.

To prepare for writing in varied academic contexts, it might be helpful to think about why academics write. Most faculty members at institutions of higher education explain their responsibilities to the institution and their discipline in terms of three categories: their teaching, their research (which generates much of their writing), and their service (what they do outside of their research and teaching that contributes both to the school and to their discipline). Many academics' writing is related to communicating the results of their research, and it might be published or shared with academic audiences or more general audiences. In fact, a scholar might conduct a research project and then find that he or she needs to communicate the results of that project to a variety of audiences.

Imagine that a physiologist who studies diabetes has discovered a new therapy that could potentially benefit diabetic individuals. The researcher might want to publish the results of her study in an academic journal so that other scientists can read about the results, perhaps replicate the study (repeat it to confirm that the results are the same), and maybe expand on the research findings. She might also want to communicate the results of her research to doctors who work with diabetic patients but who don't necessarily read academic journals in physiology. They might read medical journals, though, so in this case the researcher would need to tailor her results to an audience that is primarily interested in the application of research results to patients. In addition, she might want to report the results of her research to the general public, in which case she might write a press release so that newspapers and magazines can develop news stories about her findings. Each of these writing situations involves reporting the same research results, but to different audiences and for different purposes. The physiologist would need to tailor her writing to meet the needs of each writing situation.

Connect 1.3   **Thinking about Academic Writing**

Look for a published piece that has been written by one of the professors who you have for another class. Try to find something that you can access in full, either online or through your school's library. Some colleges and universities have lists of recent publications by faculty on their websites. Additionally, some faculty members list their publications on personal websites. You might also seek help from librarians at your institution if you aren't familiar with the library's resources. Then write your responses to the following questions:

- What does the professor write about?
- Where was the work published?
- Does your professor appear to be writing for other specialists, or does the audience appear to be nonspecialists?
- What surprised you most about your professor's published work?

Learning to Write in New Contexts

Many of your expectations for writing in college might be based on prior experiences, such as the writing you did in high school or in a work setting. Some students find that writing in college focuses less on personal experience and more on research than writing they've done in other contexts. Some students are surprised to find that writing instruction in college is not always paired with discussion of literature, as it often is in high school. While some colleges and universities use literature as a starting point for teaching writing, many other schools offer writing instruction that is focused on principles of **rhetoric**—the study of how language is used to communicate—apart from the study of literature. (Rhetoric will be discussed in detail in subsequent chapters throughout this book.) As you may have already experienced, many courses require you to write about different topics, in different forms, and for different audiences. Depending on your school, writing program, and instructor, the study of literature might be part of that approach, but you might also need to learn about the expectations of instructors in other disciplines.

Insider's View
Undergraduates Sam Stout, Gena Lambrecht, and Alexandria Woods on Academic Writing

Left to right: Sam, engineering; Gena, design; Alexandria, biology

QUESTION: How does the writing you did in high school compare to the writing you've done in college so far?

SAM: Well, in high school [teachers] mainly chose what we wrote about. And here in college they allow you to write about what you're going to be focusing on and choose something that's actually going to benefit you in the future instead of writing for an assignment grade.

GENA: Well, I thought I would be doing a lot more writing like in my AP English classes, which was analyzing literature and poems and plays and writing to a prompt that talked a lot about specific conventions for that type of literature.

ALEXANDRIA: I expected my college writing to be science-related—doing lab reports and research proposals—rather than what I did before college, in middle school and high school, which was just doing definition papers, analysis of books, and things like that.

Although the approaches toward teaching writing at various colleges and universities differ, we can talk about some common expectations for college-level writing. The Council of Writing Program Administrators (CWPA), a professional organization of hundreds of writing program directors from across the country, published a list of common outcomes for first-year writing courses that has been adapted for use by many schools. The first list of common outcomes was published in 2000, and it has been revised twice since then, most recently in 2014. The purpose of the list of outcomes is to provide common expectations for what college students should be able to accomplish in terms of their writing after finishing a first-year course, but the details of those expectations are often revised to fit a specific institution's context. For example, the CWPA's first outcome deals with "Rhetorical Knowledge" and emphasizes the importance of understanding how to shape your writing for different purposes and audiences. It states:

By the end of first-year composition, students should

- Learn and use key rhetorical concepts through analyzing and composing a variety of texts
- Gain experience reading and composing in several genres to understand how genre conventions shape and are shaped by readers' and writers' practices and purposes
- Develop facility in responding to a variety of situations and contexts calling for purposeful shifts in voice, tone, level of formality, design, medium, and/ or structure
- Understand and use a variety of technologies to address a range of audiences
- Match the capacities of different environments (e.g., print and electronic) to varying rhetorical situations

http://wpacouncil.org/positions/outcomes.html

The statement introduces several specialized concepts and terms that we will describe in more detail throughout the book. You might also notice that the statement doesn't specify what kinds of writing students should do in their classes. It is left up to individual schools to determine what will be most helpful for their students.

Earlier in this chapter, we asked you to reflect on your goals for college. When you put your goals alongside the outcomes listed above, what potential connections do you see? As you compare your goals with the outcomes and the description of the writing course you are currently taking, what opportunities emerge? What might you be able to learn and practice in your writing course that will help you achieve your goals?

Connect 1.4   Understanding the Goals of Your Writing Course

Take a look at the goals, objectives, or outcomes listed for the writing course you are currently taking. You might look for a course description on the school's website or in a course catalog, or you might find goals or learning objectives listed in the course syllabus.

- What surprised you about the goals or objectives for your writing course?
- What is similar to or different from the writing courses you have taken before? →

- What is similar to or different from the expectations you had for this course?
- How do the outcomes for the course align with your goals for writing and for college?
- What does the list of goals for your course tell you about what is valued at your institution?

Writing Project   Profile of a Writer

For this writing project, you will develop a profile of a writer in an academic field or profession of interest to you based on an interview you conduct. Under the guidance of your instructor, identify someone who is either a professor, graduate student, or upper-level student in your major (or a major that interests you) or a professional who works in a career that you could imagine for yourself. You might choose someone with whom you already have a connection, either through taking a class, having a mutual acquaintance, or enjoying a shared interest. Ask the person if you can interview him or her, either in person or through e-mail. Consider the descriptions of different disciplinary areas in this chapter, and write a profile of the writer that addresses questions about his or her writing, such as the following:

- What kinds of writing do people do in your field?
- What is the purpose of the writing you do in your field?
- What writing conventions are specific to and important to your research or work? How did you learn those conventions?
- What kinds of writing do you do most often in your work?
- What was your experience the first time you attempted to do those kinds of writing?
- What expectations do you have for students or new professionals who are learning to write in this field?
- What are the biggest writing challenges you've faced in your work?
- What advice would you give to students who are learning to write in your discipline to help them succeed?

Be sure to follow up your questions by asking for specific examples if you need more information to understand your interviewee's responses. In addition, you might ask to see an example of his or her writing to use as an illustration in your profile. Don't forget to thank the person for taking the time to respond to your questions.

A profile of a writer should do two things: (1) make a point about the person being interviewed (in this case, your point should focus on the person's writing) and (2) include details about the person's experiences that help develop the point.

Incorporate the person's responses into an essay that uses the interview to make a specific point about his or her development and experience as a writer.

....

Insider Example

Student Profile of a Business Professional

Rubbal Kumar, a sophomore at the University of Arizona, conducted an interview with Benu Badhan, a software engineer from India. Kumar is a computer science major, and he interviewed Ms. Badhan to learn more about the expectations for writing in his future profession. Through his interview with Ms. Badhan, Kumar learned that writing is very different for a software engineer than for a computer science major, but the writing he does as a computer science major will still prepare him well for his future career.

Rubbal Kumar's Draft of Interview Questions

1. Why did you choose this specific profession? What interested you in becoming a computer scientist?
2. What is your specific area of expertise in computer science, and why did you choose to specialize in that area?
3. What different types of writing are involved in computer science?
4. Is there any specific set of rules for writing in the IT field? If yes, then how is it different from the kinds of writing students are typically taught in school?
5. Did you face any difficulties in understanding the expectations for writing in computer science? How did you overcome those difficulties?

Rubbal Kumar's Final Essay

Profile of a Writer: Benu Badhan

Benu Badhan is a software engineer at Infosys, an information technology consulting company. She has been working in this field for about five years and her specialty includes software testing: manual testing and automation. She has completed her Bachelors in Technology in Computer Science from the Indian Institute of Technology, Mumbai, and completed her Masters from Delhi University, New Delhi. She worked for two different IT firms, Calsoft and Wipro, before joining Infosys.

> A key point of the profile, followed by examples from the interview

In an in-person interview, she told me that writing expectations in an IT firm are totally different in comparison with college writing. She said, "In college, we had to write 4–5 page essays, but in the workplace there are totally different conventions." At work, software engineers are expected to write programming codes, and along with each programming

> Quotation that emphasizes the differences between college and IT writing

code, they have to explain the function of each line using the comment feature. Comments are the description of the logic used to write the code. Commenting on the code is necessary because a programmer may inherit the features of existing code in his or her own code. Therefore, to transfer code successfully, comments are necessary. In this way, if someone else reads the code, the comments make understanding the logic far easier. She said that comments are the heart of the code because without comments another person cannot easily understand the programming code.

When I asked further about whether college had prepared her for writing comments clearly for her code, she replied that if there had been no college writing then she would have had difficulty. She also said that college writing prepares students to express things clearly and concisely, and this is one of the requirements in the IT field. She said that whether it is college writing or workplace writing, quality matters instead of quantity.

A second key point, which builds from the first one

Apart from writing comments in programming code, another form of writing she engages in frequently is writing email. In order to communicate effectively with colleagues, she mentioned that it is important to have good email etiquette. She said that without good communication skills, a person cannot survive in an IT company. In addition to commenting on code and writing email, there are video conference calls and PowerPoint presentations which demand good communication skills. Sometimes she has to lead projects, so leadership qualities and clear communication with a team are also important. As an example, she described working on an idea proposal with her project group and drawing on skills she had learned through college writing. She is convinced that college writing prepares students for other writing assignments in their careers.

A paragraph elaborating on the second key point with examples from the interview

I learned through my conversation with Ms. Badhan that workplace writing is different from college writing in computer science, but the academic writing we do in college prepares us well for what we will be asked to do in the workplace. The workplace is competitive, so it is important to have good writing skills, communication skills, and leadership qualities, and to be a good problem solver. Through my interview with Ms. Badhan, I learned that in order to be successful in writing in the workplace I must also perform well in my writing in college. While the writing conventions may change in the IT industry, the foundation built in college writing is essential.

The central point of the profile

Discussion Questions

1. Read through Rubbal Kumar's interview questions of Badhan. What was his purpose in interviewing Badhan? What did he want to understand?

2. Was there anything that surprised you in the profile? If so, what was it?

3. If you were going to add a question to Rubbal's interview, what would it be? Why would you add that question?

tip sheet

An Introduction to Academic Writing

- **The institution you attend has a specific focus.** You may find it helpful to identify this focus and understand how it fits with your academic and career goals.

- **Colleges and universities are divided into disciplinary areas.** You might see these areas at your school as departments, divisions, and/or colleges. In this book, we talk about four broad disciplinary areas: humanities, social sciences, natural sciences, and applied fields.

- **Academic writing and professional writing follow unique conventions.** When academics and professionals write, they often follow conventions specific to their writing situations and to their disciplinary and career areas.

- **In college writing courses, we focus on principles of rhetoric, or how language is used to communicate.** This focus will give you skills to adapt to any writing situation.

Writing: Process and Reflection

This chapter has two main purposes: (1) to introduce and discuss the concept of a writing process and (2) to support the development of your reflective writing skills to help you better understand the writing processes that you use. The culminating project for this chapter is a literacy narrative, a genre of reflective writing that can help you develop agency in understanding who you are, see how and why you've come to view writing the way you do, and discover what direction your academic and professional career might take based on what you discover about yourself. This is particularly relevant if you are trying to decide what to major in, what career to choose, or whether the major or career you're considering is the right one for you. Reflective writing emerges as a powerful tool for understanding the values and experiences that have shaped you, as well as how those values and experiences may align with the academic major you are considering.

In Chapter 1, we discussed the Council of Writing Program Administrators' recommended goals for college writing classes. Listed below are their recommended goals related to college students' writing processes, highlighting skills you need to develop an effective writing process and to succeed in college. As you see, they value reflection in writing.

ANDREA TSURUMI

By the end of first-year composition, students should

- Develop a writing project through multiple drafts
- Develop flexible strategies for reading, drafting, reviewing, collaborating, revising, rewriting, rereading, and editing
- Learn to give and to act on productive feedback to works in progress

- Use composing processes and tools as a means to discover and reconsider ideas
- Reflect on the development of composing practices and how those practices influence their work

In this chapter, we will look at what is meant by these goals and offer opportunities for you to explore how they apply to the work you will be doing in college and beyond.

Developing Your Writing Process

When you think about major writing assignments you have written in the past, how would you describe the steps you took to complete them? You will have written a lot of things by the time you reach college, and when you're asked to write a new assignment for a new class, you may find it helpful to think about how you've written most successfully in the past. How many revisions do you usually work through on a major assignment? Do you like to receive feedback from peers, an instructor, a parent, or a tutor as you are drafting? What types of feedback are most helpful to you? If you have to write an assignment that requires multiple days of drafting, or even weeks, what are the steps you use to maintain focus and consistency?

The **writing process** consists of all the steps you use when writing. You might already be familiar with some of the commonly discussed steps of the writing process from other classes you've taken. Often, writing teachers talk about some variation of the following elements of the writing process, each of which offers an opportunity to discover and reconsider ideas:

- **Prewriting/Invention**   Prewriting/invention is the point at which you gather ideas for your writing. There are a number of useful brainstorming strategies that students find helpful in the processes of gathering their thoughts and arranging them for writing. A few of the most widely used strategies are freewriting, listing, and idea mapping:

    Freewriting, as the term implies, involves writing down your thoughts in a free-flow form, typically for a set amount of time. There's no judgment or evaluation of these ideas as they occur to you. You simply write down whatever comes to mind as you consider a topic or idea. Later, of course, you revisit what you've written to see if it contains ideas or information worth examining further.

    Listing is a way of quickly highlighting important information for yourself. You start with a main idea and then just list whatever comes to mind. These lists are typically done quickly the first time, but you can return to them and rework or refine them at any point in the writing process.

Idea mapping is a brainstorming technique that is a favorite among students because it allows you to represent your ideas in an easy-to-follow map. Idea mapping is sometimes referred to as *cluster mapping* because as you brainstorm, you use clusters of ideas and lines to keep track of the ideas and the relationships among them.

- **Research** Sometimes research is considered a separate step in the writing process, and sometimes it is part of prewriting/invention. Of course, depending on the nature of your project, there might be a considerable amount of research or very little research involved. We explore some strategies for conducting research in more detail in Chapter 5.

- **Drafting** At the drafting stage, you get ideas down on paper or screen. You might already realize that these stages don't happen in isolation in most cases; drafting might occur while you're doing prewriting/invention and research, and you might go back and forth between different stages as you work.

- **Peer Review** Writers often benefit from seeking the feedback of others before considering a project complete. This is called **peer review**, which is only one stage in your writing process, so be sure to consider the point at which it will be the most beneficial to you.

- **Revising** At the **revision** stage, a writer takes another look at his or her writing and makes content-level and organizational changes. This is different from the final step of editing/proofreading.

- **Editing/Proofreading** Finally, the writer focuses on correcting grammatical, mechanical, stylistic, and referential problems in the text.

Insider's View
Mathematician Patrick Bahls on the Writing Process

"The more formally recognized genres of writing in my discipline would be research articles or expository articles or reviews of one another's work. Sometimes you'll see technical reports, depending on what area you're working in. Statisticians will frequently write technical reports for folks for whom they're doing consulting or for government work.

"But I think the day-to-day writing, to me, is much richer and often goes overlooked. When you think about the finished product of a five- or six-page research article—I'll look back over the notes that I would've written to generate the work to end up with that article. And even if you only see five or six pages of polished writing, I look back over my notes and see a hundred or two hundred pages of just scribbles here and scribbles there."

Flexible Strategies

While the writing process list described above suggests that writers go through each of the steps in sequence in order to complete a writing project, the process is in fact much more fluid, as you likely know from your own experiences. Depending on the rhetorical context of a writing task, these processes might shift in importance and in the order in which you do them.

Imagine you get a last-minute writing assignment at work. You would progress through these stages rather quickly, and you might not have time for more than a cursory peer review. If you're writing a paper for a class, however, you might be able to do initial prewriting, research, and drafting well before the project's deadline. As we discuss different types of scholarly writing in this text, you might also consider how the writing process for each of these types of writing can vary. For instance, when conducting an experimental study, the research stage of the process will take a significant portion of the time allocated to the project.

If you are rigid, set in your ways, and unable to adapt to a variety of demands, you're going to have trouble. By contrast, if you are flexible and adaptable in your approach to collaborating, writing, and learning more broadly, you will be much more likely to succeed. Everybody brings a different set of experiences to a classroom, and your experiences have gotten you this far, so you certainly have some successful strategies already.

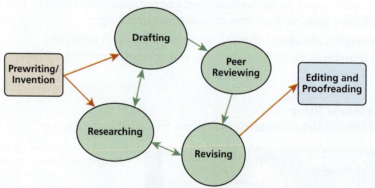

Writers move through multiple stages in the writing process, but the order and importance of stages vary according to the rhetorical context.

Multiple Drafts

By now, drafting is a skill you have probably developed quite well. The hard part about drafting is just doing it. We live busy lives and sometimes put off work until the last minute. For some writing assignments, you might be able to get away with last-minute writing. For more complicated projects, however, you may need to develop your assignment over the course of several weeks or months. A lot of this time may be spent analyzing an assignment sheet, reading examples of the kinds of assignments you're asked to write, brainstorming topics, highlighting or annotating sources you've found to support your points, writing an outline, and drafting. These steps are all part of a well-developed writing process that will be discussed throughout this chapter.

Writers often find it helps to avoid writer's block to think of the first draft as just a rough attempt to formulate ideas. But the work doesn't end with the first draft. Effective writers also take time for **revision** of their drafts, stepping away from the draft for a bit and then coming back to see the draft with fresh eyes (re-vision). At this stage, writers often make changes in the content and substance of their writing, filling in gaps or editing out areas where they are redundant. They might change part of the draft to fit the audience better, or they might reorganize parts of the draft so that it makes more sense to a reader. These kinds of revisions are different from the surface-level grammatical and mechanical changes writers make when editing. While this might seem like a lot to think about as you write, just keep in mind that becoming a better writer takes practice, but developing a writing project through multiple drafts can take your work to a higher level.

Don't be too hard on yourself. Sometimes the expectations for what you have to write can overwhelm you or just aren't interesting to you, and the motivation to stay on task and do a little bit of work each day on an assignment can be hard to come by. The keys are to stay focused, to understand the purpose of the assignment, and to remain as open and engaged as possible.

Connect 2.1   **Reflecting on Your Writing Process**

Describe the most complicated writing assignment you've written prior to this course. It could be for any class, not necessarily an English class.

- What was the class, the topic, and the purpose of the assignment?

- What writing processes did you use to maintain your focus when drafting the assignment? If you're able to name several specific steps you took to maintain your focus while remaining open to improving your drafts, chances are you've developed some good drafting skills.

- Did the assignment require you to be flexible as you worked through the stages of your draft? Were you open to making changes based on feedback? Did you try any new ways of generating ideas or organizing your material or connecting with readers?

Giving and Acting on Feedback

Many of the skills that demand flexibility in writing are demonstrated in peer review activities. **Peer review** is the process of reviewing a peer's writing while a project is in a drafting phase in order to provide feedback to improve the work, or of having your own work reviewed by a peer. When you think of peer review, perhaps you think of fixing grammar, punctuation, and spelling issues—content we would refer to as surface-level improvements. While that kind of feedback is important, equally important is the more variable and flexible feedback that shapes the direction or ideas in a peer's writing. These might be called deeper-level revisions.

Essential too, and often overlooked, is the understanding that giving feedback is itself a skill that is developed in the peer review process, and it is also one that requires flexibility. Often we tend to focus only on the end product of the paper that will be graded, but the skill of giving effective feedback to peers is one that requires excellent social skills, generosity, and intellect. Furthermore, the ability to give constructive feedback to peers is a highly sought-after skill relevant to a variety of careers beyond college. To give effective feedback on someone else's writing, you must be able to read the writing from different perspectives and write comments that will be helpful to the author—this requires flexibility in both your reading and writing.

Giving Productive Peer Review Feedback: A Sample Draft with Comments

Below, you will see a draft of student Jack Stegner's literacy narrative project for a first-year composition class that has been peer-reviewed by one of his classmates. The assignment was to tell a personal story to other students about how the writer changed or developed as a reader, writer, or speaker. Jack's reviewer focused on asking questions about deeper-level issues in his paper:

- **Ideas/Content** Are the writer's ideas clear and fully developed? Does the writer fulfill the main objective of the assignment and tell a story about literacy development?

- **Organization** Is the writing focused, directed, and easy to follow? Where does the essay go off track? Where does the writer need to develop the connection between points?

- **Paragraph Development** Are the ideas in each paragraph clearly linked? Where could the writer provide more information to help the reader understand the point?

If you are doing peer review within the Achieve platform available with this text, then you'll find these kinds of deeper-level issues defined as "draft goals," with accompanying questions to help focus your reading and commenting.

We will discuss the literacy narrative in more detail later in this chapter as an example of reflective writing. As you read Jack's literacy narrative, pay attention to the comments left by his peer reviewer. Do you think these comments will be helpful to Jack as he thinks about how to revise his paper?

You'll notice that the peer reviewer doesn't comment about grammar, punctuation, and spelling matters, and she often phrases her feedback in the form of questions and points to things she would like to know more about. She helps Jack see his own writing through another perspective, which will help Jack develop flexibility in his own writing. This ability to give and receive effective feedback is a skill that can be developed with practice and guidance and is relevant to many careers beyond college.

Jack Stegner's Draft of a Literacy Narrative, with Peer Review Feedback

Orientation to high school was a big thing for me when I was fourteen. I was at one of the best high schools in the country getting ready to start my future life. I was excited yet nervous at the same. I came from a school where I had known kids my whole life and it was different seeing these new faces. I was afraid to talk to anyone since I felt like everyone knew each other. I got my school ID photo taken as I heard a man yelling from the crowd telling freshman to get in line. I looked over and saw this lean man with dark blonde hair and eyes as blue as the sky. As a tiny freshman I was scared to get even close to this man. That was before I realized he was one of the best teachers I would ever have.

I like how you end the paragraph with a surprise. I'm not clear, though, on how this orientation day story ties to the idea of your literacy development.

The next day I walked into my fourth period classroom, and the tall lean man from yesterday was there standing in front of the class. I rolled my eyes to the back of my head saying, "Great, I have to deal with this guy the entire year." The first thing he did was assign us seats, which I wasn't used to, coming from a public school to a private school. He stood in front of the class and said his name was Mr. Alumbaugh and that he was going to be teaching us for the next school year. Then he asked us to write a paper that was due the next day discussing why we decided to go to De La Salle. I left class that day wanting to transfer out. I was already depressed as well not having many friends at the school. I came home crying to my mom saying how I didn't want to go back and how I wanted to go to the high school all my friends were going to which was Northgate. She told me at the end of the year if you still feel the same way we can transfer you out.

Why did this make you want to transfer out? What issues were you having with writing? It would be good to know how you are feeling about your writing at this point.

A few months went by. I was still at De La Salle but still depressed from not having much of a social life. My friend Lauren wanted me to go out with her friend Natalie. We went on a few dates and we started to catch feelings for each other. Although I was her boyfriend and was friends with her friends I still didn't have many male friends. Then one day in English, Natalie was texting me during class when Mr. Alumbaugh saw. He then took my phone

The story of this day is really vivid. The details about how you met Natalie seem to go off track, though.

and started texting Natalie as my whole class was laughing at me. I was so embarrassed being called out and having everyone laugh at me. After class however, my friend till this day as well, Chris came up to me and asked if I could join him and his group for lunch. I was finally invited to something and although I was embarrassed I was happy to be made an example of to get noticed.

Can you connect the story of your growing happiness at school with the story of your reaction to the assignment? I'm not clear how the ideas in this paragraph fit together.

In the Spring, I was conditioning for football and track, had to give my girlfriend attention, and had to juggle school and social life as well. I was starting to become closer with my classmates and actually making friends. I ended up forgetting about my friends at Northgate and even not wanting to go there. I was starting to become happy and realizing that people did care about me and that they did know me. In English, Mr. Alumbaugh assigned us homework to go up in front of the class and just talk about ourselves for two minutes. At first, I laughed, saying to myself "That's too easy of an assignment." When it actually came to writing about it though, I was puzzled and had no idea what to write about. I went to Mr. Alumbaugh's room one day after class ended and asked if he could help me with the

Was this helpful advice? Did you follow it?

assignment. He looked at me smiled and said, "Jack I can come up with a five minute speech about you and who you are. Just write how other people perceive you."

The day of the presentation came and I was calm. It felt like I wrote a pretty good speech about myself, good enough to be confident about speaking it to the class. My name was called up and as I stood there the butterflies came out of nowhere, reminding me of the beginning of the year. I started speaking "Hello my name is . . ." I looked down at my paper when suddenly Mr. Alumbaugh yelled "Stop! Cut!" I was startled. Mr. Alumbaugh said that he could tell I was nervous but I didn't need to look down to see what my name was. The class laughed and I laughed about it, shaking off

I'm interested to know more about what happened to make you so confident. It seems like the only thing your teacher did was tease you and yell at you. What did you learn from him that made you change?

my nerves. He then said, "Go ahead and try again." I read my speech about myself and my goals in life, and I actually got the best grade in the class. Ever since that day in Mr. Alumbaugh's class, I have never been nervous to give a speech to an audience or to a class. He congratulated me personally and we had a great friendship after that year.

You'll notice that the peer reviewer doesn't comment about grammar, punctuation, and spelling matters, and she often phrases her feedback in the form of questions and points to things she would like to know more about. She helps Jack see his own writing through another perspective, which will help Jack develop flexibility in his own writing. This ability to give and receive effective feedback is a skill that can be developed with practice and guidance and is relevant to many careers beyond college.

Responding to Peer Review Feedback

It can be difficult to read feedback from others on your writing, especially if you thought your draft was close to final and your peer reviewers raise big concerns. Responding to peer review feedback is a moment in the writing process that helps you develop flexibility. You are not required to do everything that a peer reviewer suggests, nor do you have to answer every question that is posed. If you have multiple peer reviewers, you might even find that they contradict one another. Your job is to take their feedback seriously, however, and weigh how to respond in a way that improves your project.

Professional writers usually welcome the chance to find out how readers react to their work before it is published, and they use the feedback to see their work through a reader's eyes. They ignore feedback that goes against what they are trying to accomplish, but they use it to focus on places where their readers aren't understanding them or where their readers offer good ideas. Often writers use feedback from peers or teachers to develop a **revision plan**, which maps out the kinds of big picture changes the writer would like to make and the necessary steps to make those changes. For example, after peer review, a writer might see the need for more evidence to support a particular point and make notes about further library research in the revision plan. Having such a plan makes the revision process more manageable and focused.

Connect 2.2   **Giving and Acting on Feedback**

- Reflect on your experiences as a peer reviewer. Did you have a clear sense of what to focus on in the draft you reviewed? Do you think you gave helpful feedback? What did you find most challenging about reviewing someone else's work? What was most rewarding?

- Reflect on your experiences receiving peer review feedback. Were you open to what your readers had to say? Was the feedback helpful to you in revising? If not, what advice would you give to your peer reviewers?

Reflection and Writing

Reflection—and reflective writing—is a powerful tool for understanding your strengths, your weaknesses, and your unique way of seeing the world. Reflection is the act of looking back over experiences in a questioning way in order to create insights. Reflective writing, which can take such forms as diaries, memoirs, blogs, and letters, is writing that processes one's personal experiences and organizes those experiences in a meaningful way. Just as you might use some form of reflective writing to understand and develop a relationship or skill, you can use reflective writing to develop as a writer.

Scholarship in writing studies suggests that the habits of mind most essential to transferring knowledge gained in one context (say this class) to another context (say a senior-level writing-intensive course in your major) are metacognition and flexibility/adaptability. Metacognition is the awareness of one's own thought processes. If your awareness of how you think and process knowledge is highly developed, you'll be able to take knowledge you acquire and more readily draw from that knowledge in another instance. This is where reflective writing is especially helpful because reflective writing improves metacognition.

Reflecting throughout the Writing Process

When you consider your literacy development over the span of your life, it is easy to see marked improvement. When you were a small child, for example, you first learned the alphabet, how to hold a pencil or crayon, and how to make the shapes of letters that would later become words and sentences. What's harder to see are the subtle changes that take place over a shorter span of time, such as a single semester of college. Perhaps you pick up only a few skills: knowledge about when to ask a peer to review your writing, how to insert a direct quotation into a paper, or how to create a graph from data you've collected. Each of these small skills accumulates with others over time to prepare you for the kinds of writing and research that will serve you in a career beyond college.

Reflecting on the progress you are making and the things you are learning can help your overall development as a writer in a couple of ways. First, it helps you feel a sense of accomplishment in what you have learned. Even small steps can accumulate over time to help your writing development in big ways. Second, reflecting on what we have learned can help us discover ways to apply what we have learned and build on it in the future.

As you approach your assignments, look for opportunities to reflect throughout the writing process. Consciously consider the choices you're making and what you're learning as a writer. What are the most challenging parts of the assignment? What do you need direction or help with? What do you like best about your paper? These are just some of the reflection questions that can support your growth as a writer.

Reflecting on Your Story as a Writer

In academic writing classes, the **literacy narrative** is one of the most commonly used reflective genres. A literacy narrative is an essay that reflects on how someone has developed literacy over time. It is a form of reflective writing that draws on the writer's memories and experiences, and as such it is non-fiction. In this context, the word *literacy* means more than the ability to read and write. It also means the ability to communicate and so accomplish things in a specific context or contexts. The purpose of the genre is to reflect on your identity as a literate person, as someone who has or needs to develop a skill. When done well, the literacy narrative makes meaning from experience and helps you to better understand yourself, why you feel the way you do about the skills you have gained, and how to chart a path forward in your life, drawing from the knowledge you have acquired.

A literacy narrative need not be confined to an academic setting. As we've begun to explore, literacy can mean much more than the ability to read and write, and the attitudes we bring to a classroom are informed by thousands of experiences that may have nothing to do with a classroom, teachers, or reading and writing directly. A literacy narrative might encompass the story of how you learned to speak and act as a softball player, YouTube celebrity, or employee at a movie theater. That kind of literacy narrative might explore the slang, codes of behavior, dress, or attitudes that others impressed upon you. Your instructor may have specific guidelines about the kinds of events she wants to see in your literacy narrative. The underlying theme, though, should be literacy (either narrowly or broadly defined), how you came to be literate, and what your feelings and attitudes about literacy are.

Characteristics of a Literacy Narrative

A literacy narrative almost always includes the following characteristics:

1. a main idea (or point) regarding your literacy development
2. scene writing (specific settings with a location and time)
3. use of sensory detail to describe the scenes (sight, sound, smell, touch, taste)
4. the "I" point of view

Effective narratives generally involve a struggle, obstacle, or challenge that you overcame. The struggle could be emotional (shame or anxiety, for example), or it could be physical or situational (perhaps you learned how to read with the help of a single mother who was working two jobs). All struggles appeal to emotions and as such can inspire readers to find persistence, passion, and perseverance, or to overcome challenges.

● **Main Idea**   Probably the most important aspect of a literacy narrative is the guiding principle or main idea of your narrative. This should be something you have a sense of before you get far into the drafting phase of your essay, but it may well develop or change as you write. For some students, it takes writing a full draft of a paper to really begin to see what the main idea is and what point they are trying to make.

The main idea of your literacy narrative should be tied to your identity, how you view literacy, and how your views developed through experiences good and bad. One activity that helps to brainstorm ideas is to list five words that describe your personality.

● **Scenes**   In a literacy narrative, a scene consists of a specific time and location. The bus stop on the morning of your first day of high school, the classroom where you took the SAT, an auditorium stage where you gave a speech, or your kitchen table where an adult helped you learn to spell your name when you were four years old. These are specific scenes. They take place at a specific location over a fairly short amount of time.

An additional word or two about scene length: If the scene you're envisioning takes place over more than a few hours, it likely ceases to be a scene.

Your entire freshman year of high school, for example, isn't a scene. However, one specific lunch period in the cafeteria during your freshman year when you and a friend decided to ditch school would be a scene. The tighter the timeline and location are in your mind, the more vivid the scene will be when you write it.

A literacy narrative written for a college class will usually be between four and ten pages. This affords you the space to describe approximately three scenes from your life that informed how you view reading, writing, language, and education. What would they be? Can you connect the scenes to the main idea you would like to convey about your identity as a student?

● **Sensory Details**   So you decide on a scene. Then what? Writers rely on their five senses—sight, sound, touch, smell, and taste—to describe scenes vividly. To use sensory detail, you absolutely must use your imagination and memory.

Using sensory detail is like painting. The key is to blend your sensory details to create an impression. Make use of as many senses as you can.

Rather than summarize huge chunks of time (your entire middle school experience, for example), decide on three specific scenes with short time spans and fixed locations that paint an impression of who you are, how your views of reading and writing were shaped in an instant of time, and then make use of all the sensory details you can to paint that scene.

● **"I" Point of View**   One of the most commonly asked questions in a first-year writing course is "Can I use the 'I' (first-person) point of view in my paper?" It seems that many college students arrive having been taught contradictory rules about using the "I" point of view for writing in a class. Let's try and clarify this rule for you once and for all.

Use or non-use of the "I" point of view in a paper for a class totally depends on the genre in which you are writing. When writing in the literacy narrative genre, you should make use of the "I" point of view. You are telling your story from your life, and the "I" point of view is the most appropriate point of view to use. In a scientific report, however, it might not always be helpful or appropriate to use the "I" point of view.

Connect 2.3   **Drafting a Scene for a Literacy Narrative**

- Brainstorm a list of at least three specific scenes you could choose from that best illustrate your literacy development.
- Choose one and make notes about where the scene happened (location), how long the scene took place (ideally, between a few minutes and a few hours), who was in the scene, and how the scene helped shape your identity.

The purpose of the literacy narrative is for you to reflect on and tell the story of your literacy development. Effective narratives have a beginning, middle, and end, and a literacy narrative follows a series of connected scenes (perhaps three) that illustrate points regarding how you developed your skills, identity, and views of yourself and others as a literate person.

Your instructor may give you more direction about how to define literacy for the purpose of this assignment, but you could focus on the following lists of questions:

Academic Literacy

- What are your first memories of writing in school?
- How did you learn about the expectations for writing in school?
- Can you think of a time when you struggled to meet the requirements of a school writing assignment? What happened?

Technological Literacy

- What early memories do you have of using technology?
- How do you use technology now to communicate in your daily life? What technologies are most important to you for work, for school, and/or for personal commitments?

Workplace Literacy

- What writing and communication skills are expected in the occupation you aspire to when you graduate? How will you develop those skills?
- Can you think of a time when you encountered a task at work that you didn't know how to accomplish? What did you do? How did you address the challenge?

Social and/or Cultural Literacy

- Have you ever been in a social situation where you didn't know how to act? What did you do?
- What groups do you identify with, and what expectations and shared beliefs make that group cohesive?

In a narrative essay, explore the development of your own literacy. You might do this chronologically, at least as you start writing. Be specific in identifying how you define literacy and how you developed your abilities. In your narrative and analysis, provide examples from your experience, and show how they contribute to the development of that literacy. Ultimately, your narrative should be directed to a particular audience for a particular purpose, so think of a context in which you might tell this story. For example, a student who is studying to be a teacher might write about his early literacy experiences and how they led to an interest in teaching other children to read and write. Or an applicant for a job requiring specific technological ability might include a section in an application letter that discusses her development of expertise in technological areas relevant to the job. Be imaginative if you like, but make sure that your narrative provides specific examples and makes a point about your literacy development that you believe is important.

....

Insider Example

Student Literacy Narrative

The following literacy narrative was written by first-year college student Michaela Bieda regarding her self-awareness that her strengths and skills did not always align well with the expectations that schools, teachers, and peers had about what a "good student" should be. In her literacy narrative, Bieda reflects on the awakening she had through learning her strengths in an academic context and how a teacher contributed to her developing self-awareness of her individuality, her strengths, and her identity. Bieda makes use of all of the aspects of the literacy narrative we've introduced so far: a main idea, scenes, sensory details to describe those scenes, and the "I" point of view.

My Journey to Writing

As a young kid, I struggled a lot in school. I was that student who had a hard time being able to focus and maintain that focus. I was easily distracted, and my eyes and mind would wander rather than listen and watch my teacher. I even fell asleep in class at times either as a result of over-stimulation that I couldn't handle or maybe an underlying depression, knowing I just couldn't cope in a regular classroom or keep up with my fellow students who didn't seem to share my mindset. I remember many a teacher telling my parents, "Micki just doesn't apply herself. She's smart but she's lazy." I wasn't lazy, and I wasn't sure if I was smart or not. I just knew that I couldn't sit still at my desk and do what all the other kids were able to do. Nothing in school held my interest. The traditional way of presenting the three R's didn't hold my attention. I would much rather daydream, waiting to go home and work on my art projects, designing and coloring a world I created. The world of academia had already labeled me ADHD, where I thought of myself as creative. My parents were well aware of the skills I had as well as the ones I didn't have. They thought that by changing schools, I might not resent schoolwork and teachers so much. When I was in 4th grade, I went to another school, but since it was just another private Jewish day school, nothing much was different. "Mom,"

> "I" point of view

> Michaela sets up a problem that leads to the main point.

I complained almost from the first day at the new school, "I've got the same books and the same schedule. All that's happened is that I have to make new friends." The change of schools didn't result in an attitude change for me or a new understanding—and possible appreciation—by my new set of teachers. As they say, "Same old, same old."

A new scene

An important character is introduced.

In 5th grade, I remember sitting at circular tables, waiting for the teacher to come into the classroom. The school principal walked in and announced, "Class, this is Mrs. Crincolli. Please make her feel welcome." As usual, I wasn't really paying attention to the person entering the room, but I did perk up when she had us decorate nametags and stand them up on our desks. Finally! An art project! And it had a practical application! I was thrilled. It meant so much to me to be able to perform a task I knew I could excel at. I loved my nametag, and I have kept it all these years as a tangible marker of my first school success. From that point on, I started noticing how different I felt about going to school. I had never been so excited to see what Mrs. Crincolli was going to ask us to do next. For her part as a caring teacher, she noticed my lack of success on tests yet how good my writing and art projects were. She took the time to work with me to help me find ways to understand and remember the material for tests. I was a tricky learner because, with a mind that tried to absorb a billion things at once, prioritizing one thing to concentrate on took skills I didn't innately have but had to acquire. Mrs. Crincolli helped me to believe that I could learn that skill and then apply it. I can still hear her voice in my head, encouraging me:

Dialogue adds specific detail.

"Give it a whirl, Micki. You can do it."

By the time I hit 8th grade, I had fallen in love with writing, whether formal essays or free-form association. Mrs. Crincolli had also introduced me to the stories and poetry of Edgar Allan Poe. His dark Gothic elements spoke to me, and I tried writing stories and poems—not just emulating him but in my own voice as well. My favorite writing in school was free thought writing. Every day in class, we students had about 10 minutes to write in our journals. We could use the teacher's prompt or just go off on a personal tangent of feeling. Thanks to Mrs. Crincolli, from 5th grade on, I grasped that writing and literature could appeal to anyone needing a creative outlet. Mrs. Crincolli had been so clever in the types of assignments she gave and the books we were assigned to read in class. I always identified something in my life with what I had to write about or the characters and plots I had to follow. The lack of direction and purpose I'd felt before Mrs. Crincolli entered my school life was now replaced by the joy of expressing myself on paper . . . or a screen. I wanted to impress her and the other teachers I had in each successive grade. In each English class I had with Mrs. Crincolli, the way she presented curriculum was so different from the usual textbook approach. Everything she had us students do was interesting, encouraging, and provocative. She had us constantly thinking out of the box, which was something I never thought I could do before she became my mentor.

I became very close with Mrs. Crincolli, spending time after class to help her with her bulletin boards. Eventually during my high school years, I became her Teacher's Assistant. Throughout high school under her tutelage, I learned to appreciate English even more and felt my strength in those skills more than any other class. I remember on more than one occasion, counting pages of younger classes' writing journals. So many of those students just scribbled or wrote random words in order to get the required number of pages completed. I shook my head, sad that these youngsters hadn't yet caught on to the value of journal writing or the joy of exploring oneself through language.

When it came time to graduate from high school, I reflected on the many years I had developed a real relationship with words — using and understanding them — as well as the prize of having a friendship with Mrs. Crincolli. My school, like so many others, had the usual awards ceremony at graduation. Special to my school though was the tradition that each teacher spoke about one student who had made a real impact during high school. I was sitting far in the back of the assembly with my mom as the slide show of our senior class played. All the other students in my class and our teachers sat together, watching this heartwarming video under twinkly lights tangled in the trees. One by one, each teacher walked up to the front of the gathering. When it was Mrs. Crincolli's turn, my mom whispered to me, "I just know she'll talk about you." I wanted that to happen so badly — for her to know and share how much she meant to me and also how much I meant to her. My heart overflowed and so did my tears as she started to talk . . . about ME! She mentioned not only how I had been her student for so many years, but one of the first friends she had at the school — someone who put herself out for a teacher with the only expectation of learning as much as she could. I was so grateful that she understood just how I felt. She was the one, the pivotal one at the pivotal point in my life who made such a difference and such a contribution to me as a person as well as a writer. I don't have to wonder whether she knows how important she is to me or whether she has done her job as a teacher. We both know, and I cherish her and the confidence she gave me to celebrate a creative mind and channel it to positive and productive ends.

> Sensory detail

> The main point of the narrative: Mrs. Crincolli helped Michaela identify her own strengths.

Discussion Questions

1. What would you say Michaela Bieda learned about herself by writing her literacy narrative? What evidence suggests this?

2. What kind of major and career could you see someone with Michaela's strengths going into that would make her happy?

3. What relationships or events from your own life contributed the most to how you see yourself as a student? How did they contribute?

tip sheet	Writing: Process and Reflection

- **You should work to achieve specific goals** related to your writing process during your writing classes:
    - Develop a writing project through multiple drafts.
    - Develop flexible strategies for reading, drafting, reviewing, collaborating, revising, rewriting, rereading, and editing.
    - Learn to give and to act on productive feedback to works in progress.
    - Use composing processes and tools as a means to discover and reconsider ideas.
    - Reflect on the development of composing practices and how those practices influence your work.

- **Revision is an important stage in the writing process.** Feedback from peer reviewers can help writers see their drafts through readers' eyes.

- **Your purpose in using reflective writing is to process experiences** you've had in order to better understand how those experiences shape you and your writing. It is helpful to reflect on what you are learning about yourself as a writer throughout your writing life.

- **A literacy narrative is a reflective writing genre** used to process the experiences you've had that shape your views of reading, writing, and how you communicate with others.

Reading and Writing Rhetorically

You read and write in many different situations: at school, at home, with your friends, and maybe at work. You might, for instance, compose a private reflection about a personal goal in a journal, read a news article and post about it to your followers on social media, record science lab observations for your instructor in a logbook, or make plans with a friend through text messaging. You could probably name many other situations in which you read and write on a daily basis.

But have you ever considered how the experiences of reading and writing are different in these situations? You're performing the same act (reading or writing a text), but elements of the experiences might change from one situation to another:

- the way your text looks
- the medium or technology you use
- the tone that is most appropriate for your text
- the diction, or the particular words you use (or that you avoid)
- the grammar and mechanics you use

Understanding that a writer's choices depend on the specific demands of each writing situation is central to rhetoric, the study of how language is used to communicate. By learning to *write rhetorically* in different academic disciplines, you will gain a deeper awareness of the expectations that your readers bring to the communication and how these expectations inform your decisions about how to shape your own writing. By learning to *read rhetorically*, you will develop the ability to analyze unfamiliar and even difficult texts and become acquainted with the moves that writers make in different disciplines.

ANDREA TSURUMI

Understanding Rhetorical Context

Writing takes place in a **rhetorical context** of four key elements:

- who the **author** is and what background and experience he or she brings to the text
- who the intended **audience** is for the text
- what **topic** (or issue) the author is addressing
- what the author's **purpose** is for writing

Each of these elements has an impact on the way a text is written and interpreted. Consider for a moment how you might communicate about your last job in a text message to a friend in comparison with how you might write about it in an application letter for a new job. Even though the author is the same (you) and the topic is the same (your last job), the audience and your purpose for writing are vastly different. These differences would affect the choices you make as a writer—how you characterize your experience, what details you select to share, your word choice, the format of your communication, and even perhaps the medium through which you choose to deliver it. In turn, how the reader reacts to your writing (with an emoji? with a phone call for an interview?) also depends on the rhetorical situation.

Insider's View
Karen Keaton Jackson, Writing Studies Scholar, on Rhetorical Context

"Purpose and audience essentially shape every decision you will make as a writer. Once you have your topic, your purpose and audience help you decide how you're going to structure your sentences, how you're going to organize your essay, what word choices you will make, and what tone you will choose."

Sometimes writing situations call for more than one audience as well. You might address a **primary audience**, the explicitly addressed audience for the text, but you might also have a **secondary audience**, an implied audience who also might read your text or be interested in it. Imagine you were to write a job application letter as an assignment for a business writing class. Your primary audience would likely be your instructor, but a secondary audience could be a future prospective employer if you also were to write the letter as a template to use when beginning your job search.

In academic settings, these elements of rhetorical context shift as well, depending on the discipline within which you're writing. Consider another example that illustrates how a student's research topic might shift based on the needs of different academic audiences: Imagine a student has decided to research the last presidential election for a school assignment. If the research assignment were given in a history class, then the student might research and write about other political elections that provide a precedent for the outcome of the recent election and the events surrounding it. The student would be approaching the topic from a historical perspective, which would be appropriate for the context of the discipline and audience (a history professor). If the student were writing for an economics class, he or she might focus on the economic impact of elections and how campaign finance laws, voter identification laws, and voters' socioeconomic statuses affected the election. Even though the author, audience, topic, and purpose seem similar at first glance (they're all academic research assignments, right?), the student would focus on different questions and aspects of the topic when examining the election from different disciplinary perspectives and for different audiences. Other elements of the student's writing would likely shift, too, and we'll discuss those differences in Part Two of this book.

Connect 3.1   **Identifying Rhetorical Context**

Think about a specific situation in the past that required you to write something. It could be any kind of text; it doesn't have to be something academic. Then briefly describe the rhetorical context of that piece of writing. Consider the following questions:

- What was your background and role as the author?
- Who was the audience?
- What was the topic?
- What was your purpose for writing?

Understanding Genres

Writing typically takes place within communities of people who are interested in similar subjects and who use writing to accomplish shared goals. They might use similar vocabulary, formats for writing, and grammatical and stylistic rules — these are conventions or customary practices that have evolved within the community. Think, for example, of sports writers who report for newspapers or real estate attorneys who handle sales transactions. In a sense, these writers and their audiences speak the same "language." As you read and analyze the writing of academic writers, we'll ask you to notice and comment on the conventions that different disciplines use in various rhetorical contexts. When you write, you'll want to keep those conventions in mind, paying attention to the ways you should shape your own writing to meet the expectations of the academic community you are participating in. In Part Two, we'll give you the tools to identify conventions in different disciplines.

Academic writing communities — and writing communities at large — also often work in shared genres. **Genres** are approaches to writing situations that share some common features, or conventions, related to form and content. They may be described as categories of writing, such as driving directions, thank-you notes, and résumés, that writers rely on to deliver what their audience needs to know. Cookbook writers, for example, use the recipe genre to guide readers in making a dish. They know readers expect certain content — ingredients, measurements, oven temperatures, and preparation directions — and they typically follow the format of presenting the list of ingredients first and then providing step-by-step directions as a series of directives. Genres evolve, but they help writers by providing a framework so they don't have to start from scratch in every writing situation. In the illustration shown here, cookbook author Johanna Kindvall offers an innovation on the recipe genre by using images instead of words to show a recipe's steps.

Academic writing includes such genres as abstracts, mathematical proofs, research proposals, and lab reports, among many others. If you've ever produced one of these genres as a student, then you would have experience with some of the conventions that make them unique. Lab reports, for example, have a number of conventional features, including standardized headings (like "Methods"

one egg yolk

one oz 70% dark chocolate

one egg white

one tsp sugar

Chocolate Mousse (serves one)

JOHANNA KINDVALL

and "Results") that organize and control the flow of information, and they tend to rely on passive voice constructions to report the actions researchers took as part of their experiment. These are only a couple of the conventional features of lab reports. In the writing project for this chapter, you will be introduced to the academic genre of rhetorical analysis, as well as to the particular form that rhetorical analysis takes in the discipline of English. As we introduce additional academic genres throughout this book, our goal is not to have you identify a formula to follow for every type of academic writing, but rather to help you understand the expectations of a writing situation—and how much flexibility you have in meeting those expectations—so that you can make choices appropriate to the genre.

Insider's View
Moriah McCracken, Writing Studies Scholar, on Genre

"I think my favorite genre still remains what I call the 'handout genre.' Because I do a lot of conference presentation, this is a very particular kind of genre I produce that varies depending even on the conference I'm going to. . . . I also spend a lot of time writing professional development materials for our faculty. Just this week I was making handouts for them that could serve as quick references so they know where to go to find particular kinds of information. . . . I also spend a lot of time creating handouts for parents that try to translate the disciplinary pedagogical work that happens in my field for an audience who may not be familiar."

Connect 3.2   Thinking about Genre

Think back to the rhetorical situation you identified in Connect 3.1, "Identifying Rhetorical Context." What *genre* were you writing in, and how did you learn the expectations of that genre? Identify a few choices that you made because of the genre.

Writing Rhetorically

Writing is about choices. Although genres can provide a framework, writing is not a firm set of rules to follow. There are multiple choices available to you any time you take on a writing task, and the choices you make will help determine how effectively you communicate with your intended audience, about your topic, for your intended purpose. The first step in making writing choices for a project is analyzing the rhetorical context for which you are writing so that your choices will have the effect you intend. You'll think about the following four rhetorical elements:

- **What You, as the *Author*, Bring to the Writing Situation**   How do your background, experience, and position relative to the audience shape the way you write? Understanding what you bring to a writing situation can help you determine how best to represent yourself to your intended audience: Based on your knowledge and past experiences, do you present yourself as an expert or assume the position of someone new to a discussion or a topic? Do you choose to acknowledge explicitly the values and biases that inform your awareness of a topic or issue?

- **Who Your Intended *Audience* Is**   Should you address a specific audience? Has the audience already been determined for you (e.g., by your instructor)? What do you know about your audience? What does your audience value? Understanding your intended audience can help you make critical decisions about how best to shape an audience's experience of your text at every level of your writing: Are you writing for an audience for whom specialized language, or jargon, is appropriate? Do you structure or organize your writing according to the conventional expectations of the audience? Should you employ logical or emotional appeals (or both), based on your intended audience?

- **What Your *Topic* Is**   What are you writing about? Has the topic been determined for you, or do you have the freedom to focus your topic according to your interests? What is your relationship to the topic? What is your audience's relationship to it? Understanding your own awareness of a topic can help you determine, for instance, whether and when you should broaden or narrow your topic scope, the appropriateness of citing source material in your writing, as well as whether or not you should address your audience directly or indirectly.

- **What Your *Purpose* Is for Writing**   Why are you writing about this topic, at this time? For example, are you writing to inform? To persuade? To entertain? Understanding your purpose(s) and the expected outcomes for your writing is critical to achieving your aims and can help to establish your audience and topic. Such an understanding can also assist in shaping the overall tone of your writing, the method through which you communicate, as well as the level of formality in your writing, among other considerations.

In addition to analyzing the rhetorical context of any writing situation, you will also want to think about genre expectations. That is, you'll want to consider if your writing situation is suited to communicating in a specific genre. Should your letter to the local newspaper, for instance, follow the content and form conventions for the genre of a letter to the editor? Of course, you'll always want to keep in mind that some writing choices are more likely to be more effective than others based on the conventions expected for certain situations. Sometimes, too, you might choose to break with conventional or genre expectations in order to make a point or draw attention to what you are writing. Regardless, it's important to consider genre expectations as part of your analysis of any writing situation.

Connect 3.3   **Thinking about Rhetorical Context**

Think back to the rhetorical situation you identified in Connect 3.1, "Identifying Rhetorical Context." Consider that situation more analytically now, using the following questions to expand on your answers:

- As the *author*, how did your background, experience, and position relative to the audience shape the way you created your text?

- Were you addressing a specific *audience*? Was the audience already determined for you? What did you know about your audience? What did your audience value or desire?

- What was your text about? Was the *topic* determined for you, or did you have the freedom to focus your topic according to your interests? What was your relationship to the topic? What was your audience's relationship to it?

- What was your *purpose* for creating a text about that topic, at that time? For example, were you writing to inform? To persuade? To entertain?

Reading Rhetorically

One of the best ways to learn about choices that fit your rhetorical situation and genre is by reading. Not reading simply to absorb what a text says, but reading to analyze how the text says it, so that you can deepen your understanding of the moves that writers make. We want you to *read rhetorically*, paying close attention to the different elements of rhetorical context that help to shape the text and the ways a writer responded to that context. In this book, you will read rhetorically both academic and popular writing, by professional and student writers, and so build your repertoire of strategies for your own writing.

Questions for Rhetorical Reading

When you read a written text rhetorically, you'll study the text to see how it reflects the four elements of the rhetorical situation as well as the genre:

- **Author**   The author's biography may be provided along with the text, or you could do a quick Google search if not. What background, experience, knowledge, and potential biases does the author bring to the text? Does the author use biographical details to establish credibility or connection with the reader?

- **Audience**   Where was this text published, and who are the typical readers for this publication? Is the author writing to other scholars in the field, or does the publication have a general audience of people who are not experts? How much prior knowledge does the audience have, and can you see that reflected in how the author defines terms and provides background knowledge? Does the author seem to assume that the text's audience will agree with the findings or position, or does the author anticipate objections? Are there multiple audiences (primary and secondary)?

- **Topic**   What is the author's topic? How does the author approach the topic, and what kind of attitude does the author assume toward the topic? In what ways does the topic itself contribute to the ways the text is shaped?

- **Purpose**   What does the author hope to achieve? Is the author writing to inform, to entertain, or to persuade? Is the author's purpose stated explicitly, or is it implied?

- **Genre**   Is the author writing in a recognizable genre? Why is the genre appropriate to the needs of the audience and the author's purpose? Does the author alter any of the conventional expectations for the genre? If so, what might be the author's reasoning for doing so?

Noticing rhetorical elements and analyzing an author's choice of genre when you read will help you become a careful and critical reader of all kinds of texts. When we use the term *critical*, we don't use it with any negative connotations. Instead, we use it in the way it works in the term *critical thinking*, meaning that you will begin to understand the relationships among author, audience, topic, and purpose by paying close attention to context.

Reading Visuals

The strategies for understanding rhetorical context and for reading rhetorically are applicable to both verbal and visual texts. In fact, any rhetorical event, or any occasion that requires the production of a text, establishes a writing

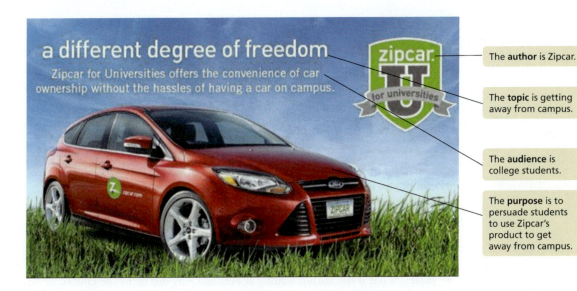

a different degree of freedom

Zipcar for Universities offers the convenience of car ownership without the hassles of having a car on campus.

zipcar.
U
for universities

The **author** is Zipcar.

The **topic** is getting away from campus.

The **audience** is college students.

The **purpose** is to persuade students to use Zipcar's product to get away from campus.

situation with a specific rhetorical context. Consider the places you might encounter visual advertisements, as one form of visual texts, over the course of a single day: in a magazine, on a website, in stores, on billboards, on television, and so on. Each encounter provides an opportunity to read the visual text rhetorically, or to consider how the four elements of author, audience, topic, and purpose work together to shape the text itself (in this case, an advertisement). The Facebook advertisement from Zipcar shown above, for example, creates a specific rhetorical context for an audience of college students. Notice how it employs both written text and images that are specifically targeted to its intended audience.

> ### Connect 3.4   Reading Rhetorically
>
> With the direction of your instructor, choose a verbal or visual text to read and analyze. As you read the text, consider the elements of rhetorical context. Make notes about who the author is, who the intended audience is, what the topic is, and what the author's purpose is for writing or for creating the text. Later in the chapter, we'll ask you to provide evidence for your points and analyze how these elements work together to influence the way the text is written.

Analyzing the Rhetorical Context: A Sample Annotated Text

When you read rhetorically, you analyze a text through a particular lens. When you write in the genre of **rhetorical analysis**, you present the findings of your rhetorical reading to an audience. We'll provide several opportunities for you to conduct rhetorical analyses in this book, since it is one of the ways you will begin to discover the features of writing across different academic contexts.

In a rhetorical analysis paper, the writer uses a rhetorical framework to understand how the context of the text helps to create meaning. One framework you might use involves walking through the different elements of rhetorical context to examine a piece of writing in detail:

- **Author**   What does the author bring to the writing situation?
- **Audience**   Who is the author addressing, and what do they know or think about this topic?
- **Topic**   What is the author writing about, and why did he or she choose it?
- **Purpose**   Why is the author writing about this topic, at this time?

These four components of the rhetorical context function together dynamically. You might analyze the author's background and experience and how he or she develops credibility in the text. Or you could make assertions about the author's primary and secondary audiences based on the author's choices regarding style and language. Although you should focus on one or more of the elements of rhetorical context, you will want to keep in mind that all four of the rhetorical context components function together to shape how someone writes or speaks.

The following text offers an example of what to look for when reading rhetorically. It also serves as the text for the "Insider Example: Student Rhetorical Analysis" at the end of the chapter. The genre is a government letter, one that George H. W. Bush, the forty-first president of the United States (and father of the forty-third president, George W. Bush), sent to Iraqi president Saddam Hussein on January 5, 1991, shortly before the United States, in cooperation with over thirty other countries, launched an assault to expel Iraqi forces from Kuwait. The letter was published by global news organizations a week later. Bush's letter is the kind of document you might analyze in a history or political science class; you'll also encounter contemporary versions of letters and speeches from world leaders in your everyday reading as a citizen. The U.S. military action that Bush warns of came in response to Iraq's invasion and annexation of Kuwait in 1990, and it became a part of the history that is now referred to as the First Gulf War. While the events that precipitated this letter occurred several decades ago, it is a helpful artifact for understanding the complicated power dynamics at play in the U.S. involvement in ongoing events in the Middle East.

Letter to Saddam Hussein

GEORGE H. W. BUSH

Mr. President,

We stand today at the brink of war between Iraq and the world. This is a war that began with your invasion of Kuwait; this is a war that can be ended only by Iraq's full and unconditional compliance with UN Security Council resolution 678.

I am writing to you now, directly, because what is at stake demands that no opportunity be lost to avoid what would be a certain calamity for the people of Iraq. I am writing, as well, because it is said by some that you do not understand just how isolated Iraq is and what Iraq faces as a result.

I am not in a position to judge whether this impression is correct; what I can do, though, is try in this letter to reinforce what Secretary of State James A. Baker told your foreign minister and eliminate any uncertainty or ambiguity that might exist in your mind about where we stand and what we are prepared to do.

The international community is united in its call for Iraq to leave all of Kuwait without condition and without further delay. This is not simply the policy of the United States; it is the position of the world community as expressed in no less than twelve Security Council resolutions.

We prefer a peaceful outcome. However, anything less than full compliance with UN Security Council resolution 678 and its predecessors is unacceptable. There can be no reward for aggression.

Nor will there be any negotiation. Principles cannot be compromised. However, by its full compliance, Iraq will gain the opportunity to rejoin the international community. More immediately, the Iraqi military establishment will escape destruction. But unless you withdraw from Kuwait completely and without condition, you will lose more than Kuwait. What is at issue here is not the future of Kuwait—it will be free, its government restored—but rather the future of Iraq. This choice is yours to make.

The United States will not be separated from its coalition partners. Twelve Security Council resolutions, twenty-eight countries providing military units to enforce them, more than one hundred governments complying with sanctions—all highlight the fact that it is not Iraq against the United States, but Iraq against the world. That most Arab and Muslim countries are arrayed against you as well should reinforce what I am saying. Iraq cannot and will not be able to hold on to Kuwait or exact a price for leaving. You may be tempted to find solace in the diversity of opinion that is American democracy.

Bush's tone and short sentences reinforce the resolve of the U.S. position.

Bush positions the United States as a moral actor by objecting to "chemical weapons" and "terrorist actions."

Bush explicitly identifies a purpose for writing: "to inform."

You should resist any such temptation. Diversity ought not to be confused with division. Nor should you underestimate, as others have before you, America's will.

Iraq is already feeling the effects of the sanctions mandated by the United Nations. Should war come, it will be a far greater tragedy for you and your country. Let me state, too, that the United States will not tolerate the use of chemical or biological weapons or the destruction of Kuwait's oil fields and installations. Further, you will be held directly responsible for terrorist actions against any member of the coalition. The American people would demand the strongest possible response. You and your country will pay a terrible price if you order unconscionable acts of this sort.

I write this letter not to threaten, but to inform. I do so with no sense of satisfaction, for the people of the United States have no quarrel with the people of Iraq. Mr. President, UN Security Council resolution 678 establishes the period before January 15 of this year as a "pause of good will" so that this crisis may end without further violence. Whether this pause is used as intended, or merely becomes a prelude to further violence, is in your hands, and yours alone.

I hope you weigh your choice carefully and choose wisely, for much will depend upon it.

Connect 3.5   **Thinking about "Letter to Saddam Hussein"**

Twitter had not yet been created when George H. W. Bush wrote this letter to Hussein. Imagine, however, that Bush had tried to communicate his message in a single tweet. Write what you think that tweet would be (280 characters maximum). Other than length, what are the most striking differences between the two communications, in your opinion?

Writing Project   **Rhetorical Analysis**

In this paper, you will analyze the rhetorical situation of a text (written or visual) of your choosing. You might want to choose something already published so that you know that the author(s) has finished making revisions and has had time to think through important rhetorical choices. Alternatively, you might choose something unpublished that was produced for an academic, personal, work, or other context. Start by reading the text carefully and rhetorically. Use the elements of rhetorical context—author, audience, topic, and purpose—to analyze and understand the choices the author has made in the text.

In addition to describing the rhetorical features of the article, you will also explore why you believe the author made certain choices. For example, if you're analyzing a blog entry on a political website, you might discuss who the author is and review the author's background. Then you could speculate about the writing choices the author has made and how the author's background might have influenced those choices.

Consider what conclusion you can draw about the text, and highlight that as an assertion you can make in the introduction to your analysis. The body of your paper should be organized around the rhetorical features you are analyzing, demonstrating how you came to your conclusion about the text.

In your conclusion, reflect on what you have found. Are there other issues still to be addressed? What other rhetorical strategies could be explored to analyze the work further? Are there surprises in the choices the author makes that you should mention?

Keep in mind that your essential aim is to analyze, not to evaluate. Additionally, you'll want to keep in mind your own rhetorical situation as a writer. Consider how you'll represent yourself as the author, your purpose for writing, your topic, as well as the needs of your audience.

Insider Example
Student Rhetorical Analysis

The following is a student rhetorical analysis of the letter written from George H. W. Bush to Saddam Hussein. As you read this analysis, consider how the student, Sofia Lopez, uses audience, topic, and purpose to construct meaning from Bush's letter. Additionally, pay attention to how Sofia uses evidence from the letter to support her assertions. These moves will become more important when we discuss using evidence to support claims in Chapter 4.

The Multiple Audiences of George H. W. Bush's
Letter to Saddam Hussein

President George H. W. Bush's 1991 letter to Saddam Hussein, then the president of Iraq, is anything but a simple piece of political rhetoric. The topic of the letter is direct and confrontational. On the surface, Bush directly calls upon Hussein to withdraw from Kuwait, and he lays out the potential impact should Hussein choose not to withdraw. But when analyzed according to the rhetorical choices Bush makes in the letter, a complex rhetorical situation emerges. Bush writes to a dual audience in his letter and establishes credibility by developing a complex author position. By the conclusion of the letter, Bush accomplishes multiple purposes by creating a complex rhetorical situation.

> The introduction outlines the writer's approach to analyzing Bush's letter. She announces her intent to focus on audience and purpose and show that the rhetorical situation is complex.

While Bush's direct and primary audience is Saddam Hussein, Bush also calls upon a much larger secondary audience in the first sentence of the letter by identifying "the world" as the second party involved in the imminent war that the letter is written to prevent. Bush continues to write

> In this paragraph, the writer outlines potential audiences for Bush's letter in more detail.

the letter directly to Hussein, using second person to address him and describe the choices before him. Bush also continues, however, to engage his secondary audience throughout the letter by referring to resolutions from the UN Security Council in five separate paragraphs (1, 4, 5, 7, and 9). The letter can even be interpreted to have tertiary audiences of the Iraqi and the American people because the letter serves to justify military action should Hussein not comply with the conditions of the letter.

In this paragraph, the writer explores the ways Bush is able to align himself with multiple audiences. The writer points to specific references to the international community and other Arab and Muslim countries to support this idea about audience.

Because Bush is addressing multiple audiences, he establishes a complex author position as well. He is the primary author of the letter, and he uses first person to refer to himself, arguably to emphasize the direct, personal confrontation in the letter. He constructs a more complex author position, however, by speaking for other groups in his letter and, in a sense, writing "for" them. In paragraph 4, he speaks for the international community when he writes, "The international community is united in its call for Iraq to leave all of Kuwait. . . ." He draws on the international community again in paragraph 6 and refers to his coalition partners in paragraph 7, aligning his position with the larger community. Additionally, in paragraph 7, he builds his credibility as an author by emphasizing that he is aligned with other Arab and Muslim countries in their opposition to Hussein's actions. Writing for and aligning himself with such a diverse group of political partners helps him address the multiple audiences of his letter to accomplish his purposes.

The writer concludes her analysis by summarizing her ideas about the stated and implied audiences for this letter and how the letter works within a complex rhetorical situation.

While the primary and literal purpose of the letter is to call upon Iraq to withdraw from Kuwait and to outline the consequences of noncompliance, Bush accomplishes additional purposes directly related to his additional audiences and the complex author position he has established. The primary purpose of his letter, naturally, is addressed to his primary audience, Saddam Hussein. The construction of the letter, however, including the repeated mention of UN Security Council resolutions, the invocation of support from other Arab and Muslim countries, and the reference to other coalition partners and the international community, serves to call upon the world (and specifically the United Nations) to support military action should Hussein not comply with the conditions of the letter. The construction of a letter with a complex audience and author allows Bush to address multiple purposes that support future action.

Discussion Questions

1. What does Sofia Lopez identify as Bush's purpose? How does she support that interpretation of Bush's purpose?

2. Whom does Sofia see as Bush's audience? How does she support that reading of the letter?

3. What might you add to the analysis from a rhetorical perspective?

tip sheet

Reading and Writing Rhetorically

- **It is important to consider rhetorical context as you read and write.** Think about how the following four elements have shaped or might shape a text:
    - Who the *author* is, and what background and experience he or she brings to the text
    - Who the intended *audience* is
    - What issue or *topic* the author is addressing
    - What the author's *purpose* is for writing

- **Genres are approaches to writing situations that share some common features, or conventional expectations.** As you read and write texts, consider the form of writing you're asked to read or produce: Is it a recognizable genre? What kinds of conventional expectations are associated with the genre? How should you shape your text in response to those expectations?

- **Writing rhetorically means crafting your own text based on an understanding of the four elements of your rhetorical context.** Specifically, you consider how your understanding of the rhetorical context should affect the choices you make as a writer, or how your understanding should ultimately shape your text.

- **Reading rhetorically means reading with an eye toward how the four elements of author, audience, topic, and purpose work together** to influence the way an author shapes a text, verbal or visual or otherwise.

- **A rhetorical analysis is a formal piece of writing that examines the different elements of the rhetorical context of a text.** It also often considers how these elements work together to explain the shape of a text targeted for analysis.

4

Developing Arguments

Many writing situations, both academic and non-academic, require us as writers to persuade audiences on a particular topic — that is, to develop an argument. When we refer to arguments, we don't mean heated, emotional sparring matches. Rather, we use **argument** to refer to the process of making a logical case for a particular position, interpretation, or conclusion. Of course we all experience and participate in these kinds of arguments around us every day as we decide where to eat dinner with friends, what classes to take, or which movie to download or concert to see. We are immersed in these kinds of popular arguments constantly through advertisements, marketing campaigns, social media posts, and texting with friends, and so we are adept at critically thinking about arguments and persuasion in those contexts.

ANDREA TSURUMI

In academic settings, arguments are frequently more developed and nuanced because the authors are arguing for a particular interpretation or conclusion or action based on the results of research. To make such an argument effectively, academics must develop clear, persuasive texts through which to present their research. These arguments are built on **claims** — arguable assertions — that are supported with evidence from research. The unifying element of any academic argument is its primary or central claim, and although most sustained arguments make a series of claims, there is usually one central claim that makes an argument a coherent whole. Our goal in this chapter is to introduce you to some of the basic principles of argumentation and to help you write clear central claims and develop successful arguments, especially in your academic writing.

Understanding Proofs and Appeals

Aristotle, a rhetorician in ancient Greece, developed a method of analyzing arguments that can be useful to us in our own reading and writing today. He explained that arguments are based on a set of proofs that are used as evidence to support a claim. He identified two kinds of proofs: inartistic and artistic. Inartistic proofs are based on factual evidence, such as statistics, raw data, or contracts. Artistic proofs, by contrast, are created by the writer or speaker to support an argument. Many arguments contain a combination of inartistic and artistic proofs, depending on what facts are available for support. Aristotle divided the complex category of artistic proofs into three kinds of **rhetorical appeals** that speakers and writers can rely on to develop artistic proofs in support of an argument:

- Appeals to **ethos** are based on credibility or character. An example might be a brand of motor oil that is endorsed by a celebrity NASCAR driver. Another example could be a proposal for grant money to conduct a research study that discusses the grant writer's experience in successfully completing similar research studies in the past. In both examples, the speaker's or writer's experiences (as a NASCAR driver or as an established researcher) are persuasive elements in the argument.

- Appeals to **logos** are based on elements of logic and reason. An example might be an argument for change in an attendance policy that reveals a correlation between attendance and grades. The argument relies on logic and reason because it presents a relationship between attendance and grades and draws a connection to the policy, emphasizing how a change in the policy might affect grades.

- Appeals to **pathos** are based on emotions. Emotion can be a powerful motivator to convince an audience to hear an argument. An example might include telling the story of a program that helps homeless teenagers complete high school by finding shelter, food, and social support that enables them to improve their living conditions. Perhaps the program is in need of financial assistance in order to continue helping homeless teens. A story that features one or two specific teens who have come through the program and successfully completed high school would be an example of an appeal to emotion.

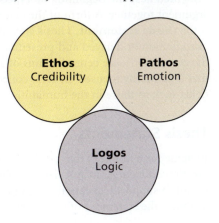

These types of appeals are present in arguments in both academic and non-academic settings. Many arguments, and often the most effective ones, include elements of more than one kind of appeal, using several strategies to persuade an audience. Based on the example above about a program that helps homeless teens, imagine that there is a campaign to solicit financial donations from the public to support the program. Now consider how much more persuasive that campaign would be if other appeals were used in addition to an emotional appeal. The campaign might develop an argument that includes raw data and statistics (an inartistic proof), the advice of civic leaders or sociological experts (ethos), the demonstration of a positive cause-and-effect relationship of the program's benefits in teens' lives (logos), along with a story of one teen, describing how she became homeless and how the program helped to get her back on her feet (pathos). Understanding the structure of arguments, and knowing the potential ways you can develop your own arguments to persuade an audience, will help you to write more effectively and persuasively.

> **Connect 4.1** **Thinking about Rhetorical Appeals**
>
> Choose a text to read that makes a claim. Consider something that interests you—perhaps an advertisement, or even your college's or university's website recruiting page for prospective students. Write about the kinds of rhetorical appeals you notice. Do you see evidence of ethos? Logos? Pathos? Is the argument drawing on statistics or raw data, an inartistic proof?

Making Claims

The unifying element of any academic argument is its primary or central claim. In American academic settings, the central claim is often (but not always) presented near the beginning of a piece so that it can tie the elements of the argument together. A form of the central claim that you're likely familiar with is the **thesis statement**. Thesis statements, whether revealed in an argument's introduction or delayed and presented later in an argument (perhaps even in the conclusion), are central claims of arguments. They are typical of writing that is primarily focused on civic concerns, as well as writing in some academic fields such as those in the humanities.

Thesis Statements

Imagine for a moment that you've been asked to write an argument taking a position on a current topic like cell phone usage, and you must decide whether or not to support legislation to limit cell phone use while driving. In this instance, the statement of your position is your claim. It might read something like this: "We should support legislation to limit the use of cell phones while driving," or "We should not support legislation to limit the use of cell phones while driving." Although there are many types of claims, the statement "We should pass legislation to limit the use of cell phones" is a claim of proposal or policy, indicating that the writer will propose some action or solution to a problem. We could also explore claims of definition ("Cheerleading is a sport") or claims of value ("Supporting a charity is a good thing to do"), just to name a few.

Literary analysis, a genre commonly taught in high school English classes, usually presents a thesis statement as part of the introduction. You may be familiar with a thesis statement that reads something like this: "Suzanne Collins's *Hunger Games* is a dystopian novel that critiques totalitarian regimes and empowers young women who are far too often marginalized and oppressed." This thesis statement makes a claim in support of a specific interpretation of the story. Regardless of the specific type of claim offered, the argument that follows it provides evidence to demonstrate why an audience should find the claim persuasive.

Thesis versus Hypothesis

In an academic setting, thesis statements like those typical of arguments in the humanities are not the only kind of unifying claim you might encounter. In fact, arguments in the natural and social sciences are often organized around a statement of hypothesis, which is different from a thesis statement. Unlike a thesis statement, which serves to convey a final position or conclusion on a topic or issue that a researcher has arrived at based on study, a **hypothesis** is a proposed explanation or conclusion that is usually either confirmed or denied on the basis of rigorous examination or experimentation later in a paper. This means that hypothesis statements are, in a sense, still under consideration by a writer or researcher. A hypothesis is a proposed answer to a research question. Thesis statements, in contrast, represent a writer's or researcher's conclusion(s) after much consideration of the issue or topic.

Consider the following examples of a hypothesis and a thesis about the same topic:

Hypothesis	Thesis
Decreased levels of sleep will lead to decreased levels of academic performance for college freshmen.	College freshmen should get at least seven hours of sleep per night because insufficient sleep has been linked to emotional instability and poor academic performance.

The hypothesis example above includes several elements that distinguish it from the thesis statement. First, the hypothesis is written as a prediction, which indicates that the researcher will conduct a study to test the claim. Additionally, it is written in the future tense, indicating that an experiment or study will take place to prove or disprove the hypothesis. The thesis statement, however, makes a claim that indicates it is already supported by evidence gathered by the researcher. A reader would expect to find persuasive evidence from sources later in that essay.

We highlight this distinction in types of claims to underscore that there is no single formula for constructing a good argument in all academic contexts. Instead, expectations for strong arguments are bound up with the expectations of particular writing communities. If you write a lab report with the kind of thesis statement that usually appears in a literary analysis, your work would likely convey the sense that you're a novice to the community of writers and researchers who expect a hypothesis statement instead of a thesis statement. One of the goals of this text is to help you develop awareness of how the expectations for good argumentation change from one academic context to the next.

Developing Reasons

When writing an academic argument that requires a thesis statement, you can choose how detailed to make that thesis statement. When we introduced thesis statements as a type of claim, we asked you to consider two possible statements on the topic of cell phone use while driving: "We should/should not support legislation to limit the use of cell phones while driving." You can also refer to these two possible forms as *simple thesis statements* because they reveal a writer's central position on a topic but do not include any reasoning as support for that position. When reasons are included as logical support, then you can think about the thesis statement as a *complex thesis statement*.

Consider the following simple thesis statement and supporting reasons:

Simple Thesis	We should support legislation to limit the use of cell phones while driving.
Reasons	They are an unnecessary distraction.
	They increase the incidence of accidents and deaths.

When you combine the simple statement of position or belief with the reasons that support it, then you have a more complex, and fuller, thesis statement:

| Complex Thesis | We should support legislation to limit the use of cell phones because they are an unnecessary distraction for drivers and because they increase needless accidents and deaths on our roadways. |

Although constructing complex thesis statements allows you to combine your statement of position, or your central claim, with the reasons you'll use to defend that position, you may frequently encounter arguments that do not provide the reasons as part of the thesis. That is, some writers, depending on their rhetorical context, prefer to present a simple thesis and then reveal the reasons for their position throughout their argument. Others choose to write a thesis that both establishes their position and provides the reasoning for it early on. An advantage of providing a complex thesis statement is that it offers a road map to the reader for the argument that you will develop.

You also want to be careful not to limit your positions to being only for or against something, especially if you can think of alternative positions that might be reasonable for someone to argue. Often, there are multiple sides to an issue, and we miss the complexity of the issue if we acknowledge only two sides. For example, in light of the usefulness of cell phones for navigation and for emergency situations, you may choose to present a thesis that identifies the complexity of the issue and takes a more nuanced position: *Although cell phones can sometimes be helpful to drivers in a number of ways, including navigating travel routes and in emergency situations, we should support legislation to limit the use of cell phones because they are generally an unnecessary distraction for drivers and because they increase needless accidents and deaths on our roadways.* By acknowledging the complexity of an issue or topic on which they're taking a position as part of the thesis statement, writers can appear more credible and trustworthy.

Connect 4.2   Constructing Thesis Statements

Generate a list of six to eight current social issues that require you to take a position. Consider especially issues that are important to your local community. Choose one or two to focus on for the other parts of this activity.

Next, explore multiple positions. Consider competing positions you can take for each of the issues you identified. Write out a simple thesis statement for those positions. Then list as many reasons as you can think of to support each of those positions. It might be helpful to connect your simple thesis statement to your reasons using the word *because*. This activity can help you to strengthen your argument by anticipating rebuttals or counterarguments. We'll take these issues up in more detail later in the chapter.

Finally, combine your simple thesis with your reasoning to construct a complex thesis for each potential position. Write out your thesis statements.

Supporting Reasons with Evidence

Reasons that support a claim are not particularly powerful unless there is evidence to back them up. Evidence that supports an argument can take the form of any of the rhetorical appeals. Let's look again at the complex thesis from the previous section: "We should support legislation to limit the use of cell phones because they are an unnecessary distraction for drivers and because they increase needless accidents and deaths on our roadways." In order to generate the reasons, the writer relied on what he already knew about the dangers of cell phone use. Perhaps the writer had recently read a newspaper article that cited statistics concerning the number of people injured or killed in accidents as a direct result of drivers using their phones instead of paying attention to the roadways. Or perhaps the writer had read an academic study that examined attention rates and variables affecting them in people using cell phones. Maybe the writer even had some personal knowledge or experience to draw upon as evidence for his position. Strong, persuasive arguments typically spend a great deal of time unpacking the logic that enables a writer to generate reasons in support of a particular claim, and that evidence can take many forms.

● **Personal Experience**   You may have direct experience with a particular issue or topic that allows you to speak in support of a position on that topic. Your personal experience can be a rich resource for evidence. Additionally, you may know others who can provide evidence based on their experiences with an issue. Stories of personal experience often appeal to either ethos (drawing on the credibility of the writer's personal experience) or pathos (drawing on readers' emotions for impact). Sometimes these stories appeal to both ethos and pathos at the same time. Imagine the power of telling the story of someone you know who has been needlessly injured in an accident because another driver was distracted by talking on the phone.

● **Expert Testimony**   Establishing an individual as an expert on a topic and using that person's words or ideas in support of your own position can be an effective way of bolstering your own ethos while supporting your central claim. However, the use of expert testimony can be tricky, as you need to carefully establish what makes the person you're relying on for evidence an actual expert on the topic or issue at hand. You must also consider your audience — whom would your audience consider to be an expert? How would you determine the expert's reputation within that community?

The use of expert testimony is quite common in academic argumentation. Researchers often summarize, paraphrase, or cite experts in their own discipline, as well as from others, to support their reasoning. If you've ever taken a class in which your instructor asked you to use reputable sources to support your argument, then you've probably relied on expert testimony to support a claim or reason already. As evidence for our complex thesis, imagine the effectiveness of citing experts who work for the National Transportation and Safety Board about their experiences investigating accidents that resulted from inattentive driving due to cell phone use.

● **Statistical Data**   Statistics frequently serve as support in both popular and academic argumentation. Readers tend to like numbers, partly because they seem so absolute and scientific. However, it is important, as with all evidence, to evaluate statistical data for bias. Consider where statistics come from and how they are produced, if you plan to use them in support of an argument. Additionally, and perhaps most important, consider how those statistics were interpreted in the context of the original research reported. What were the study's conclusions? Imagine the effectiveness of citing recently produced statistics (rates of accidents) on the highways in your state from materials provided by your state's Department of Transportation.

● **Research Findings**   Writers also often present the findings, or conclusions, of a research study as support for their reasons and claims. These findings may sometimes appear as qualitative, rather than just statistical, results or outcomes.

When selecting the types and amounts of evidence to use in support of your reasons, be sure to study your rhetorical context and pay particular attention to the expectations of your intended audience. Some audiences, especially academic ones, are less likely to be convinced if you only provide evidence that draws on their emotions. Other audiences may be completely turned off by an argument that relies only on statistical data for support. Above all, select support that your audience will find credible, reliable, and relevant to your argument.

Insider's View
Criminologist Michelle Richter on Quantitative and Qualitative Research

"There are a few ways to really look at research. One is more of a quantitative approach. I know one individual in our field who publishes twenty, thirty, many papers a year. Because he's proficient in statistics, he can take the same data set, and run it three, four different times with different research questions in mind. I think it's great. I think it's expedient. But there are limitations. If I told you three out of four women may experience a completed sexual assault or an attempted sexual assault in the course of their lifetimes, does that mean every woman? Does that mean specific women, specific geographic areas, critical age periods? With a lot of the quantitative data, we often have a need for context.

"The other way is the more qualitative. And that's an area that I absolutely love. For me, it's interview based. Sometimes it's very hard to quantify, to put in numerical form. But you do get that background, like why someone decided to drive drunk, or why someone decided to start using drugs at the age of ten. I think that's a really good supplement for the numbers.

"Research that combines the qualitative and quantitative is fantastic. The problem is that it can be expensive; it's time consuming; and there are hurdles with IRB [Institutional Review Board] because you are sometimes asking people directly about things that might be personal or traumatic for them."

Understanding Assumptions

Any time you stake a claim and provide a reason, or provide evidence to support a reason, you are assuming something about your audience's beliefs and values, and it is important to examine your own assumptions very carefully as you construct arguments. Though assumptions are often unstated, they function to link together the ideas of two claims.

Let's consider a version of the claim and reason we've been looking at throughout this chapter to examine the role of assumptions: "We should support legislation to limit the use of cell phones while driving because they increase needless accidents and deaths on our roadways." In this instance, the claim and the reason appear logically connected, but let's identify the implied assumptions that the reader must accept in order to be persuaded by the argument:

Claim	We should support legislation to limit the use of cell phones while driving.
Reason	They increase needless accidents and deaths on our highways.
Implied Assumptions	We should do whatever we can to limit accidents and deaths.
	Legislation can reduce accidents and deaths.

Many audiences would agree with these implied assumptions. As a result, it would likely be unnecessary to make the assumptions explicit or provide support for them. However, you can probably imagine an instance when a given audience would argue that legislating people's behavior does not affect how people actually behave. To such an audience, passing laws to regulate the use of cell phones while driving might seem ineffective. As a result, the audience might actually challenge the assumption(s) upon which your argument rests, and you may need to provide evidence to support the implied assumption that "legislation can reduce accidents and deaths."

A writer who is concerned that an audience may attack his argument by pointing to problematic assumptions might choose to explicitly state the assumption and provide support for it. In this instance, the writer might consider whether precedents exist (e.g., the effect of implementing seat belt laws, or statistical data from other states that have passed cell phone use laws) that could support the assumption that "legislation can reduce accidents and deaths."

Connect 4.4   **Considering Assumptions and Audience**

In Connect 4.3, you considered the most appropriate kinds of evidence for supporting thesis statements for differing audiences. This time, we ask you to identify the assumptions in your arguments and to consider whether or not those assumptions would require backing or additional support for varying audiences.

Begin by identifying the assumption(s) for one of your thesis statements. Then consider whether or not those assumptions need backing as the intended audience for your argument changes to the following:

- a friend or relative

- a state legislator

- an opinion column editor

- a professional academic in a field related to your topic

Anticipating Counterarguments

Initially, it may strike you as odd to think of counterarguments as a strategy to consider when constructing an argument. However, anticipating **counterarguments**—the objections of those who might disagree with you—may actually strengthen your argument by forcing you to consider competing chains of reasoning and evidence. In fact, many writers actually choose to present counterarguments, or rebuttals of their own arguments, as part of the design of their arguments.

Why would anyone do this? Consider for a moment that your argument is like a debate. If you are able to adopt your opponent's position and then explain why that position is wrong, or why her reasoning is flawed, or in what ways her evidence is insufficient to support her own claim, then you support your own position. This is what it means to offer a **rebuttal** to potential counterarguments. Of course, when you provide rebuttals, you must have appropriate evidence to justify dismissing part or all of the counterargument. By anticipating and responding to counterarguments, you also strengthen your own ethos as a writer on the topic. Engaging counterarguments demonstrates that you have considered multiple positions and are knowledgeable about your subject.

You can also address possible counterarguments by actually conceding to an opposing position on a particular point or in a limited instance. Now, you're probably wondering: Why would anyone do this? Doesn't this mean losing your argument? Not necessarily. Often, such a concession reveals that you're developing a more complex argument and moving past the pro/con positions that can limit productive debate.

Imagine that you're debating an opponent on a highly controversial issue like free college tuition. You're arguing that tuition should be free, and your opponent makes the point that free tuition could have the effect of lowering the quality of education an institution is able to offer. You might choose to concede this possibility, but counter it by explaining how varying tuition costs among different kinds of universities contribute to socioeconomic stratification. Though you acknowledge the validity of your opponent's concerns, you are able to make a case that the social damage caused by the current system makes that risk acceptable. That is, you could qualify your position by acknowledging your opponent's concerns and explaining why you feel that your argument is still valid. In this case, your opponent's points are used to adjust or to qualify your own position, but this doesn't negate your argument. Your position may appear even stronger precisely because you've acknowledged the opponent's points and refined the scope of your argument as a result.

Insider's View
Astronomer Mike Brotherton on Counterarguments

"In science, we're really worried about which side is right, and you discuss both sides only to the extent of figuring out which one's right. It's not one opinion versus another. It's one set of ideas supported by a certain set of observations against another set of ideas supported, or not supported, by the same set of observations, and trying to figure out which one is a better explanation for how things work."

Analyzing an Argument: A Sample Annotated Text

One way to understand the process of developing a persuasive argument is to study how others structure theirs. We have annotated the opinion piece below to point out some of the key features of argument that you've just learned about. The author is an inequality researcher at the Institute for Policy Studies, and his essay was published on several news sites in October 2019. In the Writing Project at the end of the chapter, we invite you to find your own text to analyze and annotate, while taking the next step of putting your observations in essay form.

Student Athletes Are Workers; They Should Get Paid

BRIAN WAKAMO

> The author's position is clear based on the article's title.

California has fired the first shot in the fight against the unfair pay practices of the NCAA. The state's new Fair Pay to Play Act, just signed by Gov. Gavin Newsom, allows for college athletes to profit off their own name and likeness.

In other words, if you're a college athlete in California, come January 2023, you can make money off things like the sale of jerseys with your name on them, as well as endorsements and autographs.

The author makes his thesis explicit here: Every state should adopt California's law that "allows for college athletes to profit off their own name and likeness."

The NCAA, which currently bans student athletes from receiving any compensation at all, is angry about the law. And every state should adopt it.

The bill, which passed with overwhelming support and enjoyed the backing of superstars like LeBron James, is a major step toward leveling the playing field (pardon the pun) with the NCAA, which rakes in more than a billion dollars in revenue from college sports.

The bulk of that money comes from television and marketing rights—which means that AT&T Halftime Show during March Madness, which shows all those player highlights, is bringing in the big bucks for the NCAA.

Coaches also hit the jackpot in this system: College football or basketball coaches were the highest paid public employees in 39 states as of 2016. Meanwhile, stories of their players struggling to eat while working near-full work weeks are all too common.

The author makes an appeal to pathos.

The author provides a chain of evidence to support a reason for supporting the new law: "Players are workers, breaking their backs for their bosses and employers to get rich."

NCAA rules dictate that these "student-athletes" are allowed to put only 20 hours a week toward their athletic careers. Yet the NCAA also put out a survey reporting that many of them work at least 30 hours a week, and often more than 40 hours, on their sport.

So, for all intents and purposes, these players are workers, breaking their backs for their bosses and employers to get rich.

The author presents a counterargument in favor of the current system.

Former football star Tim Tebow, who supports the NCAA's ban on paying players while raking in cash for itself, said that the push to pay student athletes comes out of a "selfish culture, where it's all about us."

The author responds to the counterargument by citing a statistic from the Centers for Disease Control and Prevention (CDC).

But when these athletes are significantly more likely to suffer chronic injuries long-term than non-college athletes—the CDC says there are around 201,000 injuries in college sports a year—who really is being selfish? The people risking their bodies, or the ones making money off that damage?

Only a small percentage of these young people risking life and limb even have a chance of making a professional career out of it.

According to the NCAA's own breakdown, only 1.6 percent of football players go on to be drafted into major professional leagues. And for basketball players, it's even lower, with just 1.2 percent of men and 0.9 percent of women going pro.

The author presents another counterargument that favors the current system.

So what good is this system? The NCAA and its defenders say it provides kids with an education, and that's what the whole system is about: they're students first, athletes second. They trot out stats that more than 80 percent of student-athletes end up getting a degree.

But with athletes working full workweeks to train—never mind actually competing—do their schools really care about their education? It's no wonder that story after story comes out about cheating scandals related to players trying to stay academically eligible.

The NCAA even acknowledges it doesn't have a responsibility to ensure education quality.

In short, the NCAA runs a system where athletes destroy their bodies, often don't get a quality education, and struggle to make ends meet, with little chance of going pro—all while the coaches and the NCAA executives make money hand over fist off their labor.

The author sums up his reasons for supporting the California law.

It's a completely exploitative system, where these kids can't even start a side business or win a car in a promotional contest without being punished.

So yes, college athletes should absolutely be paid. The California bill is a starting point, and an important one at that. Let's expand it and allow every student athlete to get paid, in every state and at every college.

The author reiterates his call to support the California law and calls for its expansion.

Connect 4.6   **Thinking about "Student Athletes Are Workers"**

What was the most persuasive point in this essay from your point of view? What was the least persuasive point?

Writing Project   **Rhetorical Analysis of an Argument**

For this project, we ask you to consider the ways in which rhetorical context and appeals work together to create an argument. To begin, choose an argument that you can analyze based on its rhetorical context and the appeals it uses to persuade the intended audience. Then, drawing on the principles of rhetorical analysis from Chapter 3 and the discussion of developing arguments in this chapter, compose an analysis examining the argument's use of appeals in light of the rhetorical situation the argument constructs. These questions will be central to your analysis:

- **Rhetorical Context**   How do the elements of the rhetorical context—author, audience, topic, and purpose—affect the way the argument is structured?

- **Rhetorical Appeals**   Does the argument use the appeals of ethos, logos, and/or pathos, and why?

Keep in mind that a rhetorical analysis makes an argument, so your analysis should have a central claim that you develop based on what you observed through the frameworks of rhetorical context and rhetorical appeals. Make your claim clear, and then support it with reasons and evidence from the argument.

Insider Example

Student Analysis of an Argument

Muhammad Ahamed, a student in a first-year writing class, wrote the following analysis of an argument as a course assignment. He used elements of rhetorical analysis and argument analysis to understand the persuasive effects of the argument he chose.

Rhetorical Appeals in "Letter from Birmingham Jail"

Martin Luther King Jr.'s "Letter from Birmingham Jail" is an important document in the history of the American Civil Rights Movement. The letter, which King began writing after being arrested and jailed in Birmingham, Alabama, in April 1963 for "parading without a permit," is directed at a primary audience of eight white clergymen who argued that the Birmingham protests calling for an end to racial segregation and discrimination were "unwise and untimely" and that they should not occur illegally or in the streets. Instead, the clergymen argued, the issues needed to be debated and resolved in the courts. King offers a forceful response to the white clergymen's position in his letter, and he employs the rhetorical appeals of ethos, pathos, and logos to support the goals, methods, and timing of the Birmingham protests for racial justice.

King uses a number of strategies to bolster his ethos as a writer and powerful voice for racial equality. One of these strategies is the respectful manner in which he addresses his audience of "dear fellow clergymen" throughout the letter. Early on in the letter, King refers to the clergymen as "my friends" and acknowledges that they are "men of good will" whose criticisms appear "sincerely set forth." He maintains a respectful tone throughout the body of the letter, in which he lays out the arguments against the protests put forth by the clergymen and offers his response. The respectful tone of the letter extends through the letter's concluding sections. There, he asks his audience to forgive him if anything in the letter "overstates the truth or indicates an unreasonable impatience," and he concludes the letter by expressing a sincere wish to meet the clergymen, "not as an integrationist or a civil-rights leader but as a fellow clergyman and a Christian brother." King's tone and respectful engagement with his audience support his ethos and would likely further his aim of moving the religious leaders closer to his position.

King further bolsters his own ethos by making specific reference to well-known authorities and established thinkers throughout his letter. On more than one occasion, for example, he provides support for his positions by referencing Socrates: "Just as Socrates felt it was necessary to create a tension in the mind so that individuals could rise from the bondage of myths and half truths to the unfettered realm of creative analysis and objective appraisal, so must we see the need for nonviolent gadflies." King also references T. S. Eliot to support his argument for nonviolent protest

The author establishes the focus of his analysis: King's letter.

The author explains the rhetorical context for King's letter.

The author presents his thesis.

In this paragraph, the author explores one way the letter supports King's ethos: his respectful tone.

In this paragraph, the author explores how King uses references to others' words and ideas to support his own ethos.

as a means to address racial discrimination and to encourage his audience to examine its support of police action, even when that action is relatively nonviolent in nature: "The last temptation is the greatest treason: To do the right deed for the wrong reason." King cites numerous other authoritative sources as well, including Thomas Jefferson and Abraham Lincoln, and these references strengthen his response to the criticism that the actions of the protestors are extreme by situating their actions within the wider history of political and social upheaval in the United States. The history of the United States, after all, is filled with instances of progress that resulted from protests. King's references reveal him as one steeped in knowledge of the past, and they provide support for his authority to defend the actions of the protestors.

> The author provides multiple examples to support his argument.

Perhaps the most powerful way that King bolsters his ethos with his intended audience of fellow clergymen is by demonstrating his knowledge and understanding of the Bible and of the history of Christianity itself. King establishes his own authority as a minister when he reveals his familial connections to the church: "Yes, I love the church. How could I do otherwise? I am in the rather unique position of being the son, the grandson, and the great grandson of preachers." Throughout the body of his letter, King relies on his knowledge of the Bible to provide support for the cause of the protestors. To respond to the clergymen's criticism that the protestors are outside agitators, for instance, King relies on the Bible to support the protestors' actions: "I am in Birmingham because injustice is here. . . . Just as the Apostle Paul left his village of Tarsus and carried the gospel of Jesus Christ . . . to the far corners of the world, so am I compelled to carry the gospel of freedom beyond my own home town." To respond to the clergymen's characterization of the protestors as "extreme," King once again provides biblical precedent for the actions of the protestors. In this instance, he compares the actions of the protestors to Jesus Christ himself: "Though I was initially disappointed at being categorized as an extremist . . . I gradually gained a measure of satisfaction from the label. Was not Jesus an extremist for love[?] . . . Perhaps the South, the nation, and the world are in dire need of creative extremists." Repeatedly, King provides rationales for the positions and actions of the protestors that are rooted in biblical precedents.

> In this paragraph, the author explains how King's strategic references to the Bible and the history of Christianity further support his ethos.

King ends his letter by expressing his worry that the church, which he describes as the "arch defender of the status quo," may lose power to affect people's lives if it chooses not to engage in positive social action and engagement: "But the judgment of God is upon the church as never before. . . . Every day I meet young people whose disappointment with the church has turned into outright disgust." By highlighting his deep familiarity with the Scriptures and choosing biblical precedents as support for the protestors' actions, and by acknowledging his deep concern for the future of the church in the letter's conclusion, King reinforces his ethos and strengthens the power of his arguments to move his primary audience of ministers.

The author concludes this section by highlighting the likely effects of King's strategies on his audience.

King's letter also employs the use of pathos, or emotional appeals, to move his audience. One of the clergymen's criticisms levied against the protestors concerned the timing of the protests. The clergymen felt that the protestors should exhibit more patience as the issues of racial desegregation and justice were litigated in the courts. King responds to this criticism with a powerful emotional appeal comprised of a series of scenes of human suffering that have resulted from racism: "But when you have seen vicious mobs lynch your mothers and fathers at will and drown your brothers and sisters at whim; when you have seen hate filled policemen curse, kick and even kill your black brothers and sisters . . . then you will understand why we find it difficult to wait." King also strategically employs an emotional appeal to criticize the inaction of the church by positing the beauty and majesty of the Southern land against the effects of racial prejudice: "On sweltering summer days and crisp autumn mornings I have looked at the South's beautiful churches with their lofty spires pointing heavenward. . . . Over and over I have found myself asking, 'What kind of people worship here? Who is their God?' . . . In deep disappointment I have wept over the laxity of the church." King's balanced use of emotional appeals would be powerfully affecting for any audience, but this is especially true for his primary audience of ministers who are deeply invested in the life and future of the church.

Throughout this paragraph, the author explores King's use of pathos by providing and commenting on specific examples.

At the heart of King's letter are a series of logical arguments, or appeals to logos, that are driven by the structure of the letter as a series of rebuttals to his audience's objections to the Birmingham protests. One of the clergymen's criticisms was directly related to the illegal nature of the protests. In his response to this criticism, King makes a cogent argument to distinguish just and unjust laws, which he defines as "out of harmony with the moral law." If there are unjust laws, then, his argument is that "one has a moral responsibility to disobey unjust laws," and he relies on St. Thomas Aquinas as an authoritative source to support his contention that an unjust law is really no law at all. King essentially dismantles one of the clergymen's

In this section, the author explores a specific strategy of logical appeals that King employs to support his argument.

objections to the protests by presenting a logical case for reinterpretation of the situation. He also addresses the clergymen's objection to the protests on the grounds that they precipitate violence by appealing to their logic. He explicitly wonders about their reasoning: "But is this a logical assertion?" Instead, King maintains, to stand against the actions of the protestors because they may precipitate violence would be similar to "condemning a robbed man because his possession of money precipitated the evil act of robbery." On multiple occasions, King unravels the logic of the clergymen's position against the protests and offers a clearer, more informed reasoning to favor the timing and methods of the protests.

One of the more soaring logical appeals King makes comes when he considers a future America in which racial discrimination and injustice are vanquished. He argues passionately about the inevitability of the outcome of the protests in Birmingham and beyond, based on the history of the United States themselves, because, as he puts it, the "goal of America is freedom." Since the history of the United States is one of progress toward more freedom, and he can trace that history with specific evidence, then the outcome is clear: "We will win our freedom because the sacred heritage of our nation and eternal will of God are embodied in our echoing demands."

King's "Letter from Birmingham Jail" responds to a specific rhetorical situation. Primarily, it is designed to rebut the concerns of a group of clergymen who resisted the timing and methods of the Birmingham protest for racial justice. To support this purpose, King utilizes the rhetorical appeals of ethos, pathos, and logos. He effectively establishes and bolsters his own ethos as a minister and civil rights activist. He further details a number of scenes that compel his audience to connect emotionally to the experiences of the protestors and to develop sympathy for their cause, and he develops a number of logical counterarguments that have the effect of undermining the clergymen's objections to the protests. Beyond the specific strategies King employs to move his primary audience, however, his text remains a powerful example of persuasion that remains applicable today.

> The author's concluding paragraph provides a brief overview of King's letter and acknowledges its rhetorical strength.

Work Cited

King, Martin L., Jr. "Letter from Birmingham Jail." *The Martin Luther King, Jr. Research and Education Institute*, https://swap.stanford .edu/20141218230016/http://mlk-kpp01.stanford.edu/kingweb/popular _requests/frequentdocs/birmingham.pdf. Accessed 1 Sept. 2020.

Discussion Questions

1. Where does Muhammad Ahamed state his thesis? Why do you think he phrases his thesis in the way that he does?

2. How does Muhammad use logos in his own argument? Why do you think he relies on logos to support his thesis?

3. Which claim(s) do you find most convincing for Muhammad's rhetorical situation? Why?

tip sheet

Developing Arguments

- **Presenting an argument is different from merely stating an opinion.** Presenting and supporting an argument mean establishing a claim that is backed by reasons and evidence.

- **The unifying element of any academic argument is its primary or central claim.** A unifying claim may take the form of a thesis, a hypothesis, or a more general statement of purpose. There are numerous kinds of claims, including claims of value, definition, and policy.

- **Reasons are generated from and supported by evidence.** Evidence may take the form of inartistic proofs (including statistics and raw data) or artistic proofs, including the rhetorical appeals of ethos (appeal to credibility), logos (appeal to reason and logic), and pathos (appeal to emotion).

- **Claims presented as part of a chain of reasoning are linked by (often) unstated assumptions.** Assumptions should be analyzed carefully for their appropriateness (acceptability, believability) in a particular rhetorical context.

- **Considering and/or incorporating counterarguments is an excellent way to strengthen your own arguments.** You may rebut counterarguments, or you may concede (or partially concede) to them and qualify your own arguments in response.

- **Analyzing others' arguments is a good way to develop your skills at arguing,** particularly in an academic context.

Academic Research

M ost of us undertake some kind of research as part of our everyday lives. Imagine for a moment that you have a leaky kitchen faucet you'd like to fix. Unless you're already quite skilled at plumbing work, you may need to consult sources to help you develop a plan to fix the faucet. In this instance, you might consult YouTube videos that demonstrate how a leaking faucet can be fixed, or you might collect information from websites that offer advice about addressing plumbing issues. Or imagine you're in charge of planning a beach vacation with friends. To do so, you may need to consult travel websites to determine the likely costs of the vacation, read reviews of hotels where you're considering staying to help inform the rooms you book, and study maps to determine the best ways to get from one place to another while you vacation. In both of these scenarios, you would be engaging in research. That is, you would be gathering information by examining your own experiences or consulting sources to help you answer questions or accomplish tasks.

Research in the academic context is similar to the kinds of research we conduct in our everyday lives. Students and scholars draw on their own experiences and consult sources to help them answer questions or accomplish tasks. A historian, for example, might study personal journals and newspapers from a particular time to help him understand the social impact of a major historical event. The historian might also consult the work of other scholars who have studied and can provide some insight into the same historical event. Or, before undertaking a series of laboratory experiments to try to answer a question, a biologist may consult the work of other scholars who have already studied the same biological phenomenon. The work of these scholars may inform the biologist's questions as well as the design of her own laboratory experiments. Regardless of their particular research methods, which we'll discuss in more detail in later chapters, these scholars would be engaged in a process of creating knowledge that can be shared with others.

ANDREA TSURUMI

Academic writing, then, is largely focused on sharing the insights that students and scholars gain from their research. The historian might communicate his findings in a new book. The biologist might present the results of her research in a poster presentation at an academic conference or as an article for a peer-reviewed academic journal. Once published, either in the form of a book, a poster presentation, a journal article, or otherwise, the research of these scholars may also become source material for other scholars' research. In this way, these scholars' research would contribute to an ongoing process of creating new knowledge that is the core objective of academic inquiry.

Throughout this chapter, we'll introduce you to some of the basic building blocks of academic research. You'll have the opportunity to consider a research question, to evaluate sources appropriate to that research question, as well as to produce your own researched argument as a starting point for your further participation in academic conversations.

Developing a Research Question

Research projects have all kinds of starting points. Sometimes we start them because a course instructor or an employer asks us to. At other times, we embark on research projects because we want to learn about something on our own. In all these cases, though, the research we undertake typically responds to a question or to a set of questions that we need to answer. These are called **research questions**.

Good research questions are context specific. In other words, a research question that's appropriate for one rhetorical situation may not be appropriate for another. Just as there are various public contexts you encounter on a daily basis for which you may be asked to write an argument, there are also multiple academic contexts in which you may be asked to engage in research. A research question that is appropriate for a literature course in an academic context, for instance, would be quite different from the kind of research question you'd likely ask in a chemistry class. For any research assignment, you want to make sure that you analyze carefully your rhetorical context before undertaking the project. Regardless of your rhetorical context, whether public or academic, there are some general criteria you should consider whenever you're asked to begin a research project or develop a research question.

● **Personal Investment**   Does your question concern a topic or issue you care about? Writers tend to do their best work when writing about issues in which they have a personal investment. Even if you're conducting research in a course with a topic that has been assigned, you should always consider how you might approach the topic from an angle that matters to you or that brings in your unique point of view. Your personal investment and level of interest in the topic of your research can greatly impact the kinds of questions you ask of that topic, but they may also influence your level of commitment to, and the quality of, your research.

● **Scope**   Is your question too broad or too narrow? If a research question is too broad, then it may not be feasible to respond to it adequately in the scope of your research assignment. If it's too narrow, though, it might not be researchable; in other words, you might not be able to find enough sources to support a solid position on the issue. Consider if there's a way you can broaden or narrow your question to an aspect of an issue or topic that is of the most importance to you. When constructing an academic research question, also keep in mind that your question probably should not be answerable with a simple "yes" or "no" response. Good academic research questions typically require more complex and nuanced answers.

● **Researchable Subject**   Is the topic of your research question researchable? Can your question be answered using either primary or secondary research? You'll want to keep in mind that some research questions (as with certain topics and issues) are more appropriate for academic research than others. If a project or assignment you're working on calls for research, and particularly secondary research, then you'll want to formulate a research question that allows you to engage academic source materials to help build your response. This means scholars or other researchers have already contributed to the discussion about your topic in such a way that their contributions might be useful to support your own argument.

● **Feasibility**   Is the scope of the research question manageable, given the amount of time you have to research the issue and the amount of space in which you will make your argument? Most research projects, and especially those you undertake for a class, are bound by deadlines; there's usually a due date for turning over your project to your peers or your instructor for review. It's important to keep in mind the amount of time you have available to collect sources and study them, as well as to draft and revise your project. The scope of your research question can affect the type and number of resources you'll need to study to construct a full answer, so it's important to consider any time limitations you may have for completing your project. Additionally, some writing projects have word or page number limitations, and you'll want to make sure you can fully develop a response to your research question within the bounds of those limitations.

● **Contribution**   Will your response to your question contribute to the ongoing conversation about the issue? A focused research question sometimes comes from reading previously published materials on a topic or issue. If you are able to review what others have already written on a topic before conducting a study or making an argument of your own on that topic, then you will know what still needs to be understood, explained, or debated. In this way, you may identify a gap in what is already known or understood about a topic in order to build a research question that, when answered, could help fill that gap. This is how researchers continue to contribute to ongoing conversations.

Although we can consider the formulation of a research question the first step in any research project, you should note that research, especially in an academic context, is a highly recursive process. In fact, it's quite common for scholars to formulate an initial research question and begin researching only to find that they need to change their initial research question on the basis of actual research. A good research question, then, is one that has been arrived at after much consideration. Sometimes it is developed only after some initial researching has already taken place. Ultimately, though, a good research question provides focus for a research project by explicitly revealing the general topic or issue that is the subject of inquiry. It may also provide, usually implicitly, clues about the kind of research that will be required to answer the question.

Connect 5.1   Writing a Research Question

As you begin your research project, identify a research question that will guide your research and keep you on track. Start by brainstorming a list of possible research questions for ten minutes, and then use the criteria identified above to narrow down your list to a research question that might work for you. If your answer to any of the questions is a definitive "No," then the research question might not be a good choice, or you might need to revise it to make it work for your research project.

Choosing Your Sources

You can gather several different types of sources to respond to a research question. Some of your sources may serve the purpose of simply helping you understand or define your inquiry topic. Other sources may be useful for helping you support or refute another's claims as part of your own argument. Regardless of how your sources are ultimately used as part of your researched argument, you should begin by searching for sources that provide specific evidence to address aspects of your research question. Additionally, you'll always want to keep your target audience in mind as you select your sources, taking into account the kinds of evidence that would likely be most convincing to your audience, whether you are targeting a public or academic audience. Depending on your specific research aims, you must also decide whether you will need to collect primary and/or secondary sources to support your aims.

Primary Sources

Primary sources provide first-hand, or direct, evidence that is useful for supporting an argument. Most research questions require engagement with some kind of primary sources, but the particular forms those sources take in an academic context vary from discipline to discipline.

In a number of academic disciplines, including law, literature, and the arts, for example, primary sources themselves are often the objects of inquiry. If you're making a claim about how to interpret a work of art and you've studied the piece carefully for images and symbols that you discuss in your argument as evidence, for instance, then the work of art is your primary source. Researchers who study the past, like those in the fields of history, may rely on primary sources like newspapers, personal journals, or photographs to provide first-hand evidence to support their conclusions about a particular historical moment.

Scholars in other academic disciplines, including many fields in the social and natural sciences, often rely on data they've gathered from conducting experiments as evidence for their arguments. Imagine a research team that has designed and conducted a survey of people's experiences with a particular social phenomenon, like culture shock. In this case, the results the researchers gathered from their survey are a primary source from which they can provide evidence to answer a research question or support their arguments about the experience of culture shock.

We will delve more deeply into the specifics of research methods in the disciplines in Part Two, but it's important to note that primary sources can take a number of forms. Gathering appropriate primary sources to respond to a particular research question may take a researcher from an archive or museum to a laboratory or library, and it may involve employing any of a number of primary data-collection methods, like interviews, surveys, and experiments to gather first-hand evidence.

Secondary Sources

Based on the scope of your argument and the expectations of your audience, you may also need to engage **secondary sources**, or sources that offer commentary on or description or analysis of primary sources. For example, let's say that your literature professor wants you to offer an interpretation of a poem. You study the poem carefully as your primary source and arrive at a conclusion or claim about the work. But imagine that the assignment also requires you to use scholarly opinions to support your own position or interpretation. As a result, you spend time in the library or searching online databases to locate articles or books by scholars who provide their own interpretations or perspectives on the poem. The articles or books you rely on to support your interpretation are secondary sources because the interpretations were developed by others, commenting on the poem. Likewise, if you cite as part of your own argument the results of a study published by others in an academic journal article, then that article serves as a secondary source of information to you. Some commonly used secondary sources include scholarly books, journal articles, review essays, textbooks, and encyclopedias.

Many of the researched arguments you will produce in college will require you to use both primary and secondary sources as support for your arguments. Even if the main evidence used to support an academic research project comes from primary sources, though, secondary sources can provide you with an overview of what other scholars have already argued with regard to a particular issue or topic. Keep in mind that academic writing and research essentially comprise a series of extended conversations about different issues, and secondary sources may help you understand what part of the conversation has already happened before you start researching a topic on your own, or before you consider entering an established conversation on a topic or issue. Besides revealing what others have already said about a topic, secondary sources may also be useful for providing support for particular claims you might make as part of a broader argument. Scholars often cite the findings and results of other scholars' research to support their own positions.

Connect 5.2   Using Primary and Secondary Sources

Read closely each of the general research questions provided below and consider how each might be researched using both primary and secondary sources. What would those sources be, and how might they offer support to help a researcher respond to the research question?

- What are the effects of food insecurity among students at my college or university?

- What is the meaning of Robert Frost's poem "Stopping by Woods on a Snowy Evening"?

- What are the effects of continuous blacklight exposure on the growth of sunflowers?

Searching for Sources

In Part Two, we discuss collecting and using primary evidence to support claims in specific disciplinary areas or genres in more detail. In the following sections, though, we provide support for collecting secondary sources, which build a foundation for research and writing in academic contexts.

There are many ways to search for sources. Most students today think immediately of the Internet when they consider ways to begin locating secondary sources. No doubt, the Internet can be a highly valuable resource for identifying and collecting potential sources for research projects, both public and academic. When using the Internet to locate sources, however, you should keep in mind that there's a difference between conducting general searches for resources on topics and conducting the kind of narrow and specific searches that will be most useful for academic arguments. How you conduct research on the Internet, including the various online tools you use to search the Internet's vast resources, will impact the volume and appropriateness of the sources you locate for your particular research aims.

For some students, too, the image of a physical library comes immediately to mind when they think of locating sources. No doubt, physical libraries are an excellent resource. In addition to housing any number of possible resources, many libraries also offer workshops on how to locate and use sources effectively, so you should make sure you're knowledgeable about any online or in-person resources offered by your community or college libraries to support your research. For most students engaged in academic research, their institution's library also provides access to more specialized tools to assist in the location of appropriate secondary sources for research projects. In the following sections, we provide a brief introduction to some of the strategies and resources you might use as you undertake your own research projects.

Search Terms and Search Engines

When you search for secondary sources to support the development of a research study or to support a claim in an argument, it's important to consider your **search terms**, the key words and phrases you'll use while you're searching. Let's say, for example, that you're interested in understanding the effects of using cell phones while driving, a topic we explored in Chapter 4. In such a case, you might begin your research with a question that reads something like this:

What are the effects of using cell phones while driving?

The first step in your research process would likely be to find out what others have already written about this issue. To start, then, you might temporarily rephrase your research question to this:

What have others written or argued about the effects of using cell phones while driving?

To respond, you'll need to identify the key terms of your question that will focus your search for secondary sources about the subject. You might highlight some of the key terms in the question:

> What have others written or argued about the effects of using **cell phones** while **driving**?

Let's say you wanted to start by seeing what you could gather from a general search engine such as Google before visiting your library website. If you started by typing "cell phones and driving" into the search bar, your search would return more than 28 million results, from public service ads to news articles to statistics from insurance companies, to name a few. As a result, you may choose to narrow your search to something that emerges as a specific issue, like "reaction time." Doing so reduces the number of hits to 2 million, which is still far too many results to review. The academic sources that might best inform your work will be buried in this overwhelming list of results.

Instead, you might choose to search Google Scholar (scholar.google.com) to understand the ongoing conversation among scholars about your topic. Conducting a search for "cell phones and driving accidents and reaction time" in Google Scholar returns more than 32,000 results:

About 32,900 results

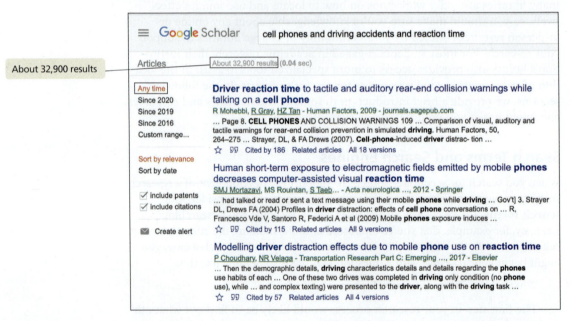

If you take a close look at the left-hand side of the screen, however, you'll notice that you can limit your search in several additional ways. By limiting the search to sources published since 2020, you can reduce your results significantly:

You can continue refining your search until you end up with a more manageable number of hits to comb through. Although the number is still large, thousands of results are more manageable than millions. Of course, you would likely need to continue narrowing your results. As you conduct this narrowing process for your topic of inquiry, you are simultaneously focusing in on the conversation you originally wanted to understand: what scholars have written about your topic. Consider the criteria that would be most meaningful for your project as you refine your search by revising your search terms. Also note that Google Scholar is not the only search engine to work with academic sources; you might also try Microsoft Academic.

Connect 5.3   **Generating Search Terms**

Think of a controversial social issue that interests you. We chose driving while using a cell phone, but you should choose something you would potentially be interested in learning more about. Then follow these instructions:

- What search terms would you enter into Google Scholar or another specialized search engine? List your search terms in the box for Round 1 below, and then try doing a search using your preferred web search engine. How many hits did you get? Write the number in the box for Round 1.

- Now consider how you might refine or narrow your search terms based on the resources you were able to locate in Round 1. Write your new search terms in the box for Round 2. Try the search again and record the number of hits.

- Follow the instructions again for Rounds 3 and 4.   ➔

	Search Terms	Number of Hits
Round 1		
Round 2		
Round 3		
Round 4		

If you were going to write advice for students using web search engines for research, what advice would you give about search terms, based on this experience?

Journal Databases

While more general search engines such as Google Scholar can be useful starting points, experienced academic researchers generally rely on more specialized databases to find the kinds of sources that will support their research most effectively. When you are conducting academic research on a topic of current scholarly inquiry, we recommend that you use these databases to find peer-reviewed journal articles. You may wonder why we don't recommend first scouring your library's catalog for books. The answer is that academic books, which are often an excellent source of information, generally take much longer to make their way through the publishing process before they appear in libraries. Publishing the results of research in academic journal articles, however, is a faster method for academics to share their work with their scholarly communities. Academic journals, therefore, are a valuable resource precisely because they offer insight into the most current research being conducted in a field.

In addition to timeliness, academic journal articles offer credibility. Unlike many general interest publications, academic journals publish research only after it has undergone rigorous scrutiny through a peer-review process by other scholars in the relevant academic field. Work that has gone through the academic peer-review process has been sent out, with the authors' identifying information removed, and reviewed by other scholars who determine whether it makes a sufficiently significant contribution to the field to be published. Work published in a peer-reviewed academic journal has been approved not only by the journal's editor but also by other scholars in the field.

One way of searching for journal articles through your school's library is to explore the academic databases by subject or discipline. These databases usually break down the major fields of study into the many subfields that make up smaller disciplinary communities. Individual schools, colleges, and universities choose which databases they subscribe to. In the following image from North Carolina State University's library website, you can see that the social sciences are divided into various subfields: anthropology, communication & media, criminology, and so on.

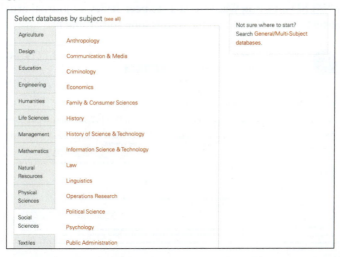

Let's say you need to find information on post-traumatic stress disorder (PTSD) among veterans of the Iraq War that began in March 2003. You spend some time considering the subfields of the social sciences where you're most likely to find research on PTSD: history, sociology, political science, and psychology, for instance. If you choose to focus on the psychological aspects of PTSD, then you would likely select "Social Sciences" and then "Psychology." When you select "Psychology" from the list of available disciplines, typically you'll see a screen that identifies major research databases in psychology, along with some related databases. Choosing the database at the top of the page, "PsycINFO," gains you access to one of the most comprehensive databases in that field of study.

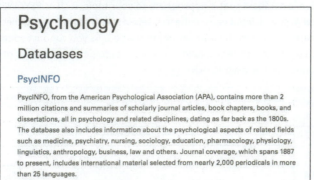

Selecting "PsycINFO" grants access to the PsycINFO database via a search engine—in this case, EBSCOhost. You can now input search terms such as "PTSD and Iraq War veterans" to see your results. Notice that the search engine allows you to refine your search in a number of ways, similar to the criteria that you can use in Google Scholar: you can limit the years of publication for research articles, you can limit the search to sources that are available full-text online, you can limit the search to peer-reviewed journal articles, and more. If you limit your search for "PTSD and Iraq War veterans" to peer-reviewed journal articles available in full-text form online, then the results look something like this:

You can now access the texts of journal articles that you find interesting or that might be most relevant to your research purposes. Depending on the number and content of the results, you may choose to revise your search terms and run the search again.

Connect 5.4   Generating Sources from an Academic Database

For this activity, use the same controversial social issue you relied on to complete Connect 5.3. This time, however, try conducting your search using a more specialized academic database that is appropriate to your topic, such as PSYCINFO or Sociological Abstracts. Input each of the four sets of search terms from Connect 5.3 into the database and record the number of hits yielded. As you conduct your search, using each of the search terms, take a few minutes to peruse the kinds of results that are generated by each search.

	Search Terms	Number of Hits
Round 1		
Round 2		
Round 3		
Round 4		

In what ways are the results of your academic database search similar to those you found from a web search engine? In what ways are the results different? What factors, besides using different terms, could account for any difference in the results?

Evaluating Sources:
Scholarly versus Popular Works

If you use a search engine that limits your results to scholarly journals, you can assume that your sources are reliable. If, however, you are doing a broader search, you'll need to be able to evaluate your sources more carefully. To review, **scholarly sources** are produced for an audience of other scholars, and **popular sources** are produced for a general audience. Scholarly sources have undergone a peer-review process prior to publication, while popular sources typically have been vetted only by an editor.

Examples of Scholarly Sources	Examples of Popular Sources
Academic Journals Most journal articles are produced for an audience of other scholars, and the vast majority are peer-reviewed before they are published in academic journals.	*Magazines* Like newspaper articles, magazine articles are typically reviewed by editors and are intended for a general reading audience, not an academic one.
Books Published by Academic Presses Academic presses publish books that also go through the peer-review process. You can sometimes identify academic presses by their names (e.g., a university press), but sometimes you need to dig deeper to find out whether a press generally publishes scholarly or popular sources. Looking at the press's website can often help answer that question.	*Newspapers* Most newspaper articles are reviewed by editors for accuracy and reliability. However, they typically provide information that would be of interest only to a general audience. They are not specifically intended for an academic audience. A newspaper might report the results of a study published in an academic journal, but it will generally not publish original academic research.

Although it may seem easy to classify sources into one of these two categories, there are sources that fall outside these publication types. In those cases, there are other elements of the source that you can explore to see if the source has the qualities of a scholarly work. Imagine that you locate a study published on the Internet that you think would be a really good source for your research. It looks just like an article that might appear in a journal, and it has a bibliography that includes other academic sources. However, as part of your analysis of the source, you discover that the article, published only on a website, has never been published by a journal. Is this a scholarly work? It might be. Could this still be a useful scholarly work for your purposes? Perhaps. Still, as a writer and researcher, you would need to know that the article you're using as part of your own research has never been peer-reviewed or published by a journal or an academic press. This means that the validity of the work has never been assessed by other experts in the field. If you use the source in your own work, you would probably want to indicate that it has never been peer-reviewed or published in an academic journal as part of your discussion of that source.

Answering the following questions about your sources can help you evaluate their credibility and reliability:

1. Who are the authors?
2. Who is the intended audience?
3. Where is the work published?
4. Does the work rely on other reputable sources for information?
5. Does the work seem biased?

As a writer, you must ultimately make the decisions about what is or is not an appropriate source, based on your goals and an analysis of your audience. Answering the questions above can help you assess the appropriateness of sources.

Connect 5.5   Evaluating Sources

For this exercise, look at an essay that you wrote for a class in the past. Choose one of the sources listed in the essay's bibliography and find it again. Then consider these questions:

- Who are the authors? Do they possess any particular credentials that make them experts on the topic? With what institutions or organizations are the authors associated?

- Who is the intended audience—the general public or a group of scholars? How do you know?   →

- Where is the work published? Do works published there undergo a peer-review process?

- Does the work rely on other reputable sources for information? What are those sources, and how do you know they are reputable?

- Does the work seem biased? How do you know this? Is the work funded or supported by individuals or parties who might have a vested interest in the results?

Summarizing, Paraphrasing, and Quoting from Sources

Once you've located and studied the sources you want to use in a research paper, then you're ready to begin considering ways to integrate that material into your own work. There are a number of ways to integrate the words and ideas of others into your research, and you've likely already had experience summarizing, paraphrasing, and quoting from sources as part of an academic writing assignment. For many students, though, the specifics of how to summarize, paraphrase, and quote accurately are often unclear, so we'll walk through these processes in some detail.

Summarizing

Summarizing a text is a way of condensing the work to its main ideas. A summary therefore requires you to choose the most important elements of a text and to answer these questions: *What* is this work really trying to say, and *how* does it say it? Composing a summary of a source can be valuable for a number of reasons. Writing a summary can help you carefully analyze the content of a text and understand it better, but a summary can also help you identify and keep track of the sources you want to use in the various parts of your research. You may sometimes be able to summarize a source in only a sentence or two. We suggest a simple method for analyzing a source and composing a summary:

1. Read the source carefully, noting the *rhetorical context*. Who composed the source? For whom is the source intended? Where was it published? What issue or topic is the author addressing? What is the author's purpose for writing? Identify the source and provide answers to these questions at the beginning of your summary, as appropriate.

2. Identify the *main points*. Pay close attention to topic sentences at the beginnings of paragraphs, as they often highlight central ideas in the overall structure of an argument. Organize your summary around the main ideas you identify.

3. Identify *examples.* You will want to be able to summarize the ways the writer illustrates, exemplifies, or argues the main points. Though you will likely not discuss all of the examples or forms of evidence you identify in detail as part of your summary, you will want to comment on one or two, or offer some indication of how the writer supports his or her main points.

The following excerpt is taken from the text of Warren E. Milteer Jr.'s "The Strategies of Forbidden Love: Family across Racial Boundaries in Nineteenth-Century North Carolina":

> In an era in which women in general had limited opportunities for work and faced significant wage discrimination, free women of mixed ancestry had to consider the financial security and social standing of potential mates. For a poor woman looking to move up financially, a relationship with a well-established white man who was willing to build a long-term relationship was a promising opportunity. A white man could not directly pass on the benefits of whiteness to a woman of color and her children as he could for a white woman and her children. White enforcement of racial boundaries limited free people of color's access to certain exclusively white networks, therefore limiting a white man's ability to extend his social connections. However, a white man could convey property obtained through connections to these networks and, as long as he lived, he could pass on some of the intangible benefits of being part of middle- and upper-class white social circles.

A summary of this part of Milteer's text might read something like this:

> In "The Strategies of Forbidden Love: Family across Racial Boundaries in Nineteenth-Century North Carolina," Warren E. Milteer Jr. acknowledges that free women of mixed ancestry could improve their social and economic lot by developing relationships with well-to-do white men. He develops this point by identifying parameters that could both potentially support and undermine the advantages of such relationships (615).

You'll notice that this summary eliminates discussion of the specific details about such relationships that Milteer provides. Though Milteer's ideas are clearly condensed and the writer of this summary has carefully selected the specific ideas to be summarized in order to further his or her own aims, the core of Milteer's argument is accurately represented.

Paraphrasing

Sometimes a writer doesn't want to summarize a source because condensing its ideas risks losing part of its importance. In such a case, the writer has to choose whether to paraphrase or quote directly from the source. **Paraphrasing** means translating the author's words and sentence structure into your own for the purpose of making the ideas clear for your audience. A paraphrase may be the same length or even longer than the part of a text being paraphrased, so the purpose of a paraphrase is not really to condense a passage, as is the case for a summary.

Often, writers prefer to paraphrase sources rather than to quote from them, especially if the exact language from the source isn't important, but the ideas are. Depending on your audience, you might want to rephrase highly technical language from a scientific source, for example, and put it in your own words. Or you might want to emphasize a point the author makes in a way that isn't as clear in the original language. Many social scientists and most scientists routinely paraphrase sources as part of the presentation of their own research because the results they're reporting from secondary sources are more important than the exact language used to explain the results. Quotations should be reserved for instances when the exact language of the original source is important to the point being made. Remember that paraphrasing requires you to restate the passage in your own words and in your own sentence structure. Even if you are putting the source's ideas in your own words, you must acknowledge where the information came from by providing an appropriate citation.

To illustrate both inappropriate and appropriate paraphrasing of a passage, let's look at this paragraph taken from William Thierfelder's article "Twain's *Huckleberry Finn*," published in *The Explicator*, a journal of literary criticism:

> An often-noted biblical allusion in *Huckleberry Finn* is that comparing Huck to the prophet Moses. Like Moses, whom Huck learns about from the Widow Douglas, Huck sets out, an orphan on his raft, down the river. In the biblical story, it is Moses's mother who puts him in his little "raft," hoping he will be found. In the novel, Huck/Moses takes charge of his own travels.

The following paraphrase of the first two sentences of Thierfelder's passage is *inappropriate* because it relies on the language of the original text and employs the author's sentence structure even though some of the language has been changed and the paraphrase includes documentation:

> William Thierfelder suggests that Huckleberry is often compared to the prophet Moses. Huck, an orphan like Moses, travels down a river on a raft (194).

By contrast, an *appropriate* paraphrase that uses new language and sentence structure might look like this:

> William Thierfelder notes that numerous readers have linked the character of Huckleberry Finn and the biblical figure of Moses. They are

both orphans who take a water journey, Thierfelder argues. However, Moses's journey begins because of the actions of his mother, while Huck's journey is undertaken by himself (194).

Quoting

Depending on your rhetorical context, you may find that **quoting** the exact words of a source as part of your argument is the most effective strategy. The use of quotations is much more common in some academic fields than in others. Writers in the humanities, for example, often quote texts directly because the precise language of the original is important to the argument. You'll find, for instance, that literary scholars often quote a short story or poem (a primary source) for evidence. You may also find that a secondary source contains powerful or interesting language that would lose its impact if you paraphrased it. In such circumstances, it is entirely appropriate to quote the text. Keep in mind that your reader should always be able to understand why the quotation is important to your argument. We recommend three methods for integrating quotations into your writing. (The examples below follow American Psychological Association style conventions; see "Understanding Documentation Systems" on pages 86–89 for more information about documentation styles.)

1. **Attributive Tags**   Introduce the quotation with a tag (with words like *notes*, *argues*, *suggests*, *posits*, *maintains*, etc.) that attributes the language and ideas to its author. Notice that different tags suggest different relationships between the author and the idea being cited. For example:

   De Niet, Tiemens, Lendemeijer, Lendemei, and Hutschemaekers (2009) argued, "Music-assisted relaxation is an effective aid for improving sleep quality in patients with various conditions" (p. 1362).

2. **Grammatical Integration**   You may also fully integrate a quotation into the grammar of your own sentences. For example:

   Their review of the research revealed "scientific support for the effectiveness of the systematic use of music-assisted relaxation to promote sleep quality" in patients (De Niet et al., 2009, p. 1362).

3. **Introduction with Full Sentence and Punctuation**   You can also introduce a quotation with a full sentence and create a transitional link to the quotation with punctuation, such as a colon. For example:

   The study reached a final conclusion about music-assisted relaxation: "It is a safe and cheap intervention which may be used to treat sleep problems in various populations" (De Niet et al., 2009, p. 1362).

Avoiding Plagiarism

Any language and ideas used in your own writing that belong to others must be fully acknowledged and carefully documented, with both in-text citations and full bibliographic documentation. Failure to include either of these when source materials are employed could lead to a charge of **plagiarism**, perhaps the most serious of academic integrity offenses. The procedures for documenting cited sources vary from one rhetorical and disciplinary context to another, so you'll always want to clarify the expectations for documentation with your instructor when responding to an assigned writing task. Regardless, you should always acknowledge your sources when you summarize, paraphrase, or quote, and be sure to include the full information for your sources in the bibliography of your project.

Insider's View
Karen Keaton Jackson, Writing Studies Scholar, on Plagiarism

"Many students come in who are already familiar with using direct quotations. But when it comes to paraphrasing and summarizing, that's when I see a lot of accidental plagiarism. So it's really important for students to understand that if you don't do the research yourself, or if you weren't there in the field or doing the survey, then it's not your own idea and you have to give credit."

Most schools, colleges, and universities have established definitions of plagiarism and penalties or sanctions that may be imposed on students found guilty of plagiarism. You should become familiar with the definitions of plagiarism used by your institution as well as by your individual instructors.

- Locate a resource on campus (e.g., a student handbook or the website of your institution's Office of Student Conduct) that provides a definition of plagiarism from the perspective of your institution. You may discover that in addition to defining plagiarism, your institution provides avenues of support to foster academic integrity and/or presents explanations of the consequences or penalties for violating rules of academic integrity.

- Locate a resource from one of your classes (e.g., a course website, a course syllabus) that provides a definition of plagiarism from the perspective of one of your instructors.

- Consider what is similar about the two definitions. Consider the differences between them. What do these similarities and differences reveal about your instructor's expectations and those of the larger academic community in which you participate?

Understanding Documentation Systems

Documentation systems are often discipline-specific, and their conventions reflect the needs and values of researchers and readers in those particular disciplines. For these reasons, you should carefully analyze any writing situation to determine which documentation style to follow. You'll find papers that model specific documentation systems in the disciplinary chapters in Part Two. You'll also find more detail on these systems in the Appendix. The three most commonly used documentation systems come from the Modern Language Association (MLA), the American Psychological Association (APA), and the Council of Science Editors (CSE).

Modern Language Association (MLA)

MLA documentation procedures are generally followed by researchers in the humanities. One of the most important elements of the in-text citation requirements for the MLA documentation system is the inclusion of page numbers in a parenthetical reference. Though page numbers are used in other documentation systems for some in-text citations (as in the APA system when quoting a passage directly), page numbers in MLA are especially important because they serve as a means for readers to assess your use of sources, both primary and secondary, and are used whether you are quoting, paraphrasing, or summarizing a passage. Page numbers enable readers to quickly identify cited passages and evaluate the evidence: readers may verify that you've accurately represented a source's intent when citing the author's words, or that you've fully examined all the elements at play in your analysis of a photograph or poem. Of course, this kind of examination is important in all disciplines, but it is especially the case in the humanities, where evidence typically takes the form of words and images.

Unlike some other documentation systems, the MLA system does not require dates for in-text citations, because scholars in this field often find that past discoveries or arguments are just as useful today as when they were first observed or published. Interpretations don't really expire; their usefulness remains valid across exceptionally long periods of time.

Learn more about the style guides published by the Modern Language Association, including the *MLA Handbook*, along with more information about the MLA itself, at www.mla.org.

American Psychological Association (APA)

APA documentation procedures are followed by researchers in many areas of the social sciences and related fields. Although you will encounter page numbers in the in-text citations for direct quotations in APA documents, you're much less likely to find direct quotations overall. Generally, researchers in the social sciences are less interested in the specific language or words used to report research findings than they are in the results or conclusions. Therefore, social science researchers are more likely to paraphrase information than to quote information.

Additionally, in-text documentation in the APA system requires the date of publication for research. This is a striking distinction from the MLA system. Social science research that was conducted fifty years ago may not be as useful as research conducted two years ago, so it's important to cite the date of the source in the text of the argument. Imagine how different the results would be for a study of the effects of violence in video games on youth twenty years ago versus a study conducted last year. Findings from twenty years ago probably have very little bearing on the contemporary social context and would not reflect the same video game content as today's games. As a result, the APA system requires the date of research publication as part of the in-text citation. The date enables readers to quickly evaluate the currency, and therefore the appropriateness, of the research being referenced.

Learn more about the *Publication Manual of the American Psychological Association* and the APA itself at its website: www.apa.org.

Council of Science Editors (CSE)

As the name suggests, the CSE documentation system is most prevalent among disciplines of the natural sciences, although many of the applied fields in the sciences, like engineering and medicine, rely on their own documentation systems. As in the other systems described here, CSE requires writers to document all materials derived from sources. Unlike MLA or APA, however, CSE allows multiple methods for in-text citations, corresponding to alternative forms of the reference page that appears at the end of research reports.

For more detailed information on CSE documentation, consult the latest edition of *Scientific Style and Format: The CSE Manual for Authors, Editors, and Publishers.* You can learn more about the Council of Science Editors at its website: www.councilscienceeditors.org.

Annotated Bibliographies

The **annotated bibliography** is a common genre in several academic disciplines because it provides a way to compile and take notes on—that is, annotate—resources that are potentially useful in a research project. Annotated bibliographies are essentially lists of citations, formatted in a consistent documentation style, that include concise summaries of source material. Some annotated bibliographies include additional commentary about the sources—perhaps a description of their rhetorical context or an evaluation of their usefulness for a particular research project or an explanation of how the sources complement one another within the bibliography (possibly by providing multiple perspectives). Although less common, some annotated bibliographies that are completed as part of a class project may include a brief introduction that identifies a student's research question and/or provides a brief overview of the research or reflection on the annotated sources.

You will want to be careful to follow closely any specific instructions you receive for the construction of your own projects. Annotated bibliographies are usually organized alphabetically, but longer bibliographies can be organized topically or in sections with subheadings. Each source entry gives the citation first and then a paragraph or two of summary, as in this example using MLA style:

Carter, Michael. "Ways of Knowing, Doing, and Writing in the
 Disciplines." *College Composition and Communication,* vol. 58, no. 3,
 2007, pp. 385–418.

In this article, Carter outlines a process for helping faculty across different academic disciplines to understand the conventions of writing in their disciplines by encouraging them to think of disciplines as "ways of doing." He provides examples from his own interactions with faculty members in several disciplines, and he draws on data collected from these interactions to describe four "metagenres" that reflect ways of doing that are shared across multiple disciplines: problem-solving, empirical inquiry, research from sources, and performance. Finally, he concludes that the metagenres revealed by examining shared ways of doing can help to identify "metadisciplines."

For an example of an annotated bibliography in APA style, see the Insider Example on page 90.

Writing Project   Annotated Bibliography

For this assignment, you should write an annotated bibliography that explores sources you've located to help you respond to a specific research question. Your purposes in writing the annotated bibliography are threefold: (1) to organize and keep track of the sources you've found on your own topic, (2) to better understand the relationships among different sources that address your topic, and (3) to demonstrate knowledge of the existing research about it.

To meet these purposes, choose sources that will help answer your research question, and think about a specific audience who might be interested in the research you're presenting. Your annotated bibliography should include the following elements:

- An introduction that clearly states your research question and describes the scope of your annotated bibliography: What led you to your research question? What makes your question important or meaningful? Why does your question need to be answered?

- Three to five scholarly sources (though you may include more, depending on the scope of the sources and the number of perspectives you want to represent), organized alphabetically, from any academic field you believe will help you construct an answer to your research question. If you choose a different organization (e.g., topical), provide a rationale for how you have organized your annotated bibliography in the introduction.

- An annotation for each source that includes the following:
  - A citation in a consistent documentation style. See the Appendix for citation information, but also note that the landing page of online articles often provides the citation elements in various style options.
  - A summary of the source that gives a concise description of the researchers' methods and central findings, focused on what is most important for responding to your research question
  - Relevant information about the authors or sponsors of the source to indicate credibility, bias, perspective, and the like
  - An indication of what this source brings to your annotated bibliography that is unique and/or how it connects to the other sources

Insider Example

Student Annotated Bibliography

The following annotated bibliography by Regan Mitchem, a student in a first-year writing course, is organized according to her instructor's directions, which asked students to provide only their research questions at the beginning of their projects as introductory material. Students were asked to include three to five annotated entries as part of their bibliographies. This annotated bibliography utilizes APA documentation style. It has been annotated to highlight consistent moves the student writer makes across the bibliographic entries. For a complete example of APA paper formatting, including a title page and running head, see the Insider Example on pages 191–98 in Chapter 8.

Benefits of Technology Integration in the Classroom

Research Question: What are the benefits of technology integration in the classroom?

> This student's project assignment asks that students present their research question as the introduction to their projects.

Baylor, B. L., & Ritchie, D. (2002). What factors facilitate teacher skill, teacher morale, and perceived student learning in technology-using classrooms? *Computers & Education, 39*(4), 395–414. https://doi.org/10.1016/S0360-1315(02)00075-1

Baylor and Ritchie (2002), in the article "What Factors Facilitate Teacher Skill, Teacher Morale, and Perceived Student Learning in Technology-Using Classrooms?" explain that a teacher's openness to change and technology-supporting leadership can significantly influence acceptance of technology use, higher-level thinking, teacher technological abilities, and teacher morale.

> The student identifies the researchers' methods.

Baylor and Ritchie (2002) support their claims through a quantitative comparison of 94 classrooms from 12 schools across the United States with varying characteristics related to technology.

> The student notes a finding that may be of particular interest to her research project.

They conclude that "although [they] found that administrators contribute to the positive interactions of technology in a school, of greater importance were teacher attributes" (Baylor & Ritchie, 2002, p. 412). The authors' purpose is to determine how technology can best be supported and utilized in the classroom setting for the benefit of students, teachers, and administrators. The authors write in a formal tone for an audience of administrators and policymakers seeking guidance on the use of technology in schools.

> All bibliographic entries should appear in a consistent documentation style. In this case, it's APA.

Dolch, C., & Zawacki-Richter, O. (2018). Are students getting used to learning technology? Changing media usage patterns of traditional and non-traditional students in higher education. *Research in Learning Technology, 26*, 2038–2055. http://dx.doi.org.prox.lib.ncsu.edu/10.25304/rlt.v26.2038

In their longitudinal study, "Are Students Getting Used to Learning Technology?" which surveyed over 1,000 students enrolled in German institutions of higher education, Dolch and Zawacki-Richter (2018) sought to examine the media use behavior of traditional and non-traditional students. They found that increasing numbers of students enrolling in fully online and technologically blended courses as well as the demand for more digital learning opportunities increasing among non-traditional students. Notably, they indicated "a clearly significant change is the direction towards the use of mobile devices" (Dolch & Zawacki-Richter, 2018, p. 2049). Their study indicates various implications of their findings for higher education settings. The researchers' purpose is to identify trends in student engagement with online media so that institutions of higher education might respond appropriately in their instructional design. They write for an audience of researchers and other educational professionals.

> The student indicates an overview of the researchers' purpose.

Erstad, O. (2003). Electracy as empowerment: Student activities in learning environments using technology. *Young, 11*(1), 11–28. https://doi-org. prox.lib.ncsu.edu/10.1177/1103308803011001073

In his article "Electracy as Empowerment: Student Activities in Learning Environments Using Technology," Erstad (2003) suggests that a balance in traditional teaching and use of technology could open opportunities for independent learning, add a new dimension to communication, and create a more student-centered system for teachers as they facilitate the learning process. Erstad (2003) supports his claims, based on case studies of three schools, to show that the "use of technology gives students tools for empowerment and some possibilities of moving students towards student-centered learning environments" (p. 25). The author's purpose is to encourage the integration of technological opportunities into learning environments so that students are more engaged in their subject material and can better understand their own learning abilities. Erstad (2003) writes in a persuasive tone to address an audience of teachers or education professionals.

> The student offers a general summary of the source.

> The student identifies potential audiences for the researchers' study.

Writing Project   **A Supported Argument on a Controversial Issue**

For this writing assignment, you will apply your knowledge from Chapter 4 about developing an argument and from this chapter on finding and documenting appropriate sources. The sources you find will be evidence for the argument you develop. We ask you to make a claim about a controversial issue that is of importance to you and support that claim with evidence to persuade a particular audience of your position. As you write, you might follow the steps below to develop your argument:

- Begin by identifying an issue that you care about and likely have some experience with. We all write best about things that matter to us. For many students, choosing an issue that is specific to their experience or local context makes a narrower, more manageable topic to write about. For example, examining recycling options for students on your college campus would be more manageable than tackling the issue of global waste and recycling.

- Once you have identified an issue, start reading about it to discover what people are saying and what positions they are taking. Use the suggestions in this chapter to find scholarly sources about your issue so that you can "listen in on" the conversations already taking place about your issue. You might find that you want to narrow your topic further based on what you find.

- As you read, begin tracking the sources you find. These sources can serve as evidence later for multiple perspectives on the issue; they will be useful both in supporting your claim and in understanding counterarguments.

- Identify a clear claim you would like to support, an audience you would like to persuade, and a purpose for writing to that audience. Whom should you talk to about your issue, and what can they do about it?

As you work to develop your argument, consider the various elements of an argument you read about in Chapter 4.

- Identify a clear central claim and determine if it should have a simple or complex thesis statement.

- Develop clear reasons for that claim, drawn from your knowledge of the issue and the sources you have found.

- Choose evidence from your sources to support each reason that will be persuasive to your audience, and consider the potential appeals of ethos, logos, and pathos.

- Identify any assumptions that need to be explained to or supported for your audience.

- Develop responses to any counterarguments you should include in your argument.

Insider Example

Student Argument on a Controversial Issue

The following sample student argument, produced in a first-year writing class, illustrates many of the principles discussed in Chapters 4 and 5. As you read, identify the thesis, reasons, and sources used as support for the argument. Notice also that the student writer, Jack Gomperts, followed CSE documentation conventions throughout his paper, in response to his instructor's direction to choose a documentation style appropriate to the subject of his argument. For a complete example of CSE paper formatting, including a title page and running head, see the Insider Example on pages 241–46 in Chapter 9.

Evaluating Hydration Levels in High School Athletes

Every day, high school athletes across the country put themselves at risk of heat-related injury, and even death, by failing to hydrate properly. Many athletes arrive at practice dehydrated and abandon proper hydration throughout activity. This habit not only puts athletes at an increased risk of injury, but also decreases their performance (Gibson-Moore 2014). Numerous researchers have explored exactly when and how much fluid an athlete needs to maintain proper hydration. Some experimenters focus on which fluids, such as water, sports drinks, milk, juice, or various other drink options, produce the best hydration. The most important factor in making sure athletes maintain hydration, however, is not telling them how to obtain hydration, but rather testing their hydration status. Often, athletes forget or ignore hydration when coaches simply tell them to stay well hydrated. If athletes know that they will undergo testing for hydration every day, they will be more likely to take action to achieve the proper hydration status. Scientists possess dozens of methods for testing hydration in athletes, and urine specific gravity and body mass measurements are the most practical for everyday use. Urine specific gravity requires only one drop of urine from an athlete, and body mass measurements require athletes to step on a scale. In addition, athletes must sign a contract with their school before participating in any athletic event associated with the school. Schools use these contracts to ensure that they are not liable for any injury experienced by an athlete. However, most schools do not include any information about hydration in their contracts, thus exposing athletes to severe risk. Altogether, schools should alter their athletic contracts to include hydration testing for athletes with urine specific gravity and body mass measurements.

> Argument begins by establishing a problem that exists

> Establishes the need for further exploration and action with regard to hydration in athletes

> Establishes a two-part central claim or position of the argument: schools should alter contracts to include hydration testing and they should use urine specific gravity and body mass measurements as the means to test hydration.

Consider the kinds of evidence the writer relies on in this paragraph, including evidence from personal experience. Are they effective? What function does this paragraph serve in the overall structure of the student's argument?

Every year, 10,000 high school athletes in the United States suffer from dehydration (Centers for Disease Control and Prevention 2010). This staggering number only includes injuries that health professionals have diagnosed and does not account for the numerous athletes who suffer from dehydration without realizing it. Personally, I have never witnessed an athlete who was diagnosed with a heat-related illness, but I have seen several athletes suffer injuries that trace back to dehydration. I played on several sports teams throughout my high school career and witnessed a common theme; coaches often tell athletes to stay hydrated, but fail to explain the importance of hydration. At many football games, several of my teammates suffered from cramps caused by dehydration. During my senior year of high school, an athlete collapsed at three of my cross-country meets because of overheating.

How does this paragraph support part of the writer's central position about testing athletes' levels of hydration? What reason is supported here?

The athletes who neglected proper hydration at my school did not do so without consequences. Many of them experienced concussions; at least ten to twelve athletes from various sports at my school received concussions every year. According to Dr. Meehan, "Every time you get [a concussion], there's some effect on the brain that doesn't go away, concussions have a cumulative effect" (Costa 2015). Concussions negatively impact student-athletes for their entire lives, whereas most sports-related injuries do not have detrimental long-term effects. Scientists believe a strong correlation exists between hydration statuses and concussion risks. They have begun to study cerebrospinal fluid, which surrounds the brain and reduces the impact of heavy blows. With less fluid, athletes have a smaller cushion for their brain; scientists believe even a two percent decrease in hydration severely decreases the amount of cerebrospinal fluid (DripDrop 2016).

This paragraph functions to support the writer's reasoning for his central position. What is the reason he presents to support his central claim or thesis?

In addition to concussions, dehydration can also lead to a variety of heat-related illnesses, such as heat cramps, heat exhaustion, heat stroke, or even death. Heat cramps cause involuntary muscle contractions and can be treated by stretching and rehydration. Heat exhaustion causes redness of skin, profuse sweating, nausea, and vomiting, and is treated as a medical emergency by immediate rehydration and applying ice to the core. Heat stroke is the complete inability to thermo-regulate and causes clammy skin, cessation of sweating, dizziness, nausea, and possible unconsciousness. In order to treat a person experiencing these symptoms, medical professionals immediately cool them in an ice bath or transport them to a trauma center (Gallucci 2014). Despite the consequences, many athletes and coaches overlook the problem of dehydration. According to the National Center for Catastrophic Sports Injury Research (2009), 40 high school football players have died from heat stroke since 1995. In addition, they report that dozens of athletes are hospitalized every year for heat-related illnesses, which directly correlates to hydration status. When as many as two thirds of young athletes arrive at practice dehydrated (Southwest Athletic Trainers' Association 2013), it is evident that high school athletic policies must be improved.

> The writer incorporates evidence from statistics.

Once schools recognize the problem of dehydration, there are many possible solutions. Of the various methods, a combination of urine specific gravity and body mass measurements would be the most convenient and effective for daily use. Since urine specific gravity is easy to use and accurate, schools should utilize its capabilities. This system analyzes a drop of urine on the stage of a refractometer to evaluate the level of hydration in the athlete. If the device shows a value between 1.001 and 1.012, the athlete is likely over-hydrated. A value between 1.013 and 1.029 shows proper hydration, and values above 1.030 show dehydration (Armstrong 2005). The device needed to take these measurements can cost anywhere from $60 to $400 (Lopez 2006)—a small price for teams to pay to ensure the safety of their athletes. According to Armstrong (2005), urine specific gravity is the best method to test hydration in an everyday setting because of its reliability, accuracy, and ease of use. Scientists possess several additional methods for testing hydration. These methods, however, are not practical for athletes on a daily basis, although they produce a higher level of accuracy than urine specific gravity. For instance, urine specific gravity loses accuracy as athletes' muscle mass increases. Hamouti et al. (2010) found that urine specific gravity devices falsely classify athletes with high muscle mass as dehydrated far more often than athletes with low muscle mass.

> Provides reasoning to support this particular method of hydration testing

Due to the slightly inaccurate measurements produced by urine specific gravity, coaches should use body mass measurements in addition to urine specific gravity to test hydration. Body mass measurements are even more efficient and less expensive to record than urine specific gravity measurements. In order for coaches to use body mass measurements to determine hydration, they must simply weigh their athletes before and after every practice. If the athletes' mass decreases by more than two percent, they are dehydrated (Armstrong 2005). In addition, if their body mass decreases by more than two percent from the beginning of practice one day to the beginning of practice the next day, they are likely dehydrated.

> Provides further reasoning to support the methods of testing hydration levels in athletes

Ties together issues related to measuring hydration levels in order to support contention that certain steps are necessary

Body mass measurements provide a good estimate of hydration status. Recognizing that the body mass of high school athletes constantly changes due to growth, eating habits, and several other factors, coaches should use body mass measurements in addition to urine specific gravity. They should use urine specific gravity once on the athletes at the beginning of the season, and two to three times randomly throughout the season. This system will provide the coaches with more accurate results than body mass measurements, while not requiring athletes to place a drop of urine on a device every day. This process will ensure the safety of athletes on a daily basis and drastically decrease their risk for illness or death.

The writer acknowledges a potential counterargument. How does he use sources and evidence to refute the counterargument?

Despite the many benefits of hydration testing, some people might disagree with this proposal. Some might argue that regulating hydration status invades the privacy of an athlete and assumes unnecessary control of an athlete's life. I propose that students should decide how much fluid they need, how often they need it, and which drinks best produce hydration. Lopez (2006), Maughan (2010), and Johannsen (2015) all argue for different amounts and types of fluid for proper hydration. These decisions should be left to the athlete since each athlete differs in how much fluid they need for hydration. The schools should only take responsibility for making sure that their athletes are well hydrated. Schools and athletic organizations have put dozens of rules in place to ensure the safety of athletes, like the types of hits allowed in football. If schools have the authority to make rules that protect football players, schools have the power to implement rules and regulations that concern hydration. If implementing hydration regulations can save just one life, schools should do so as quickly as possible. A life is worth more than the few hundred dollars spent on urine specific gravity devices and portable scales. A life is worth more than the slight hassle of taking a few minutes before and after practice to measure athletes' body mass. These rules, however, could have potentially saved the 40 lives that have been lost since 1995 because of heat-related illnesses (National Center for Catastrophic Sports Injury Research 2009). Hydration testing might have prevented several thousand athletes from experiencing heat-related illness every year, or saved dozens of athletes from hospitalization. The slight intrusion on athletes' privacy is well worth saving dozens of lives.

The author identifies another possible counterargument. What evidence is provided to refute the counterargument? Is that evidence convincing to you? Why or why not?

In addition to the intrusion on athletes, some people might argue that coaches already carry immense responsibility, and adding these tests would place a heavier burden on the coaches. However, the coaches' job is to teach the athletes how to improve their play and to keep them safe from injury. The hydration requirements I propose align directly with a coach's responsibility. Although it could be considered a burden to require coaches to measure athletes' hydration status, this burden takes no more than 20 minutes a day to complete. Additionally, these regulations exist in accordance with the coach's job, which is to protect his or her athletes, and enhance the athletes' performance however possible. These tests will help coaches do their job more fully and provide better care for their athletes.

Altogether, hydration should be tested in athletes with a combination of urine specific gravity and body mass measurements because these tests will ensure that athletes are practicing and performing under safe conditions. Dehydration poses a problem in high schools all across America because many teens do not understand the importance of proper hydration. Therefore, they arrive at practice dehydrated, which leads to thousands of injuries a year. I propose that to solve this problem, schools should include a policy in their athletic contract regarding hydration. This policy should require athletes to be subject to three to four urine specific gravity tests throughout the season and two daily body mass measurements. Even though people might argue that these tests intrude on athletes' privacy and place a burden on coaches, the tests are capable of saving dozens of lives. I believe that this insignificant burden is well worth the sacrifice. I further propose that each athlete should be held responsible for determining how he or she can best achieve hydration. While researchers continue to find the best ways for athletes to maintain hydration, schools must take responsibility by implementing regulations to reduce the dangers associated with dehydration in athletics.

> Can you identify other potential counterarguments that might undermine the writer's position here?

> Do any of the writer's proposals, presented in the conclusion to the argument, surprise you as a reader? Why or why not?

> In CSE paper format, the References would start a new page.

> Notice the mix of sources the writer relies upon, both popular and academic, as well as any primary and secondary forms of research.

References

Armstrong LE. 2005. Hydration assessment techniques [Internet]. Nutr Res. [accessed 2016 Dec 9]; 63(6):S40–S54. Available from: https://www.ncbi .nlm.nih.gov/pubmed/16028571

Centers for Disease Control and Prevention. 2010. Heat illness among high school athletes — United States, 2005–2009 [Internet]. Morb Mortal Wkly Rep. [accessed 2016 Dec 9]; 59(32):1009–1053. Available from: https://www.cdc.gov/mmwr/preview/mmwrhtml/mm5932a1.htm

Coe S, Williams R. 2011. Hydration and health [Internet]. Nutr Bull. [accessed 2016 Dec 9]; 36(2):259–266. Available from: http://onlinelibrary.wiley .com/doi/10.1111/j.1467-3010.2011.01899.x/abstract

Costa S. 2015. Just how dangerous are sports concussions, anyway?: Concussions cause the brain to dangerously move back and forth inside the skull [Internet]. Huffington Post. [accessed 2016 Dec 9]. Available from: http://www.huffingtonpost.com/entry/the-truth-about-concussions_us_564a0043e4b045bf3deff7fc

DripDrop Hydration. 2016. Does dehydration increase an athlete's risk for concussion? [Internet]. [accessed 2016 Dec 9]. Available from: http://dripdrop.com/dehydration-increase-athletes-risk-concussion/

Gallucci J. 2014. Soccer injury prevention and treatment: A guide to optimal performance for players, parents and coaches. New York (NY): Demos Medical Publishing. p. 157–159.

Gibson-Moore H. 2014. Hydration and health [Internet]. Nutr Bull. [accessed 2016 Dec 9]; 39(1):4–8. Available from: http://onlinelibrary.wiley.com/doi/10.1111/nbu.12039/full

Hamouti N, Del Coso J, Avila A, Mora-Rodriquez R. 2010. Effects of athletes' muscle mass on urinary markers of hydration status [Internet]. Euro J Appl Physiol. [accessed 2016 Dec 9]; 109(2):213–219. Available from: https://www.ncbi.nlm.nih.gov/pubmed/20058021

Johannsen NM, Earnest CP. 2015. Fluid balance and hydration for human performance. In: Greenwood M, Cooke MB, Ziegenfuss T, Kalman DS, Antonio J, editors. Nutritional supplements in sports and exercise. Cham, Switzerland: Springer International Publishing. p. 105–119.

Lopez RM, Casa DJ. 2006. Hydration for athletes: What coaches can do to keep their athletes healthy and performing their best [Internet]. Coaches' Quarterly. [accessed 2016 Dec 9]. Available from: https://www.wiaawi.org/Portals/0/PDF/Sports/Wrestling/hydration4athletes.pdf

Maughan RJ, Shirreffs SM. 2010. Dehydration and rehydration in competitive sport [Internet]. Scand J Med Sci. [accessed 2016 Dec 9]; 20(3):40–47. Available from: http://onlinelibrary.wiley.com/doi/10.1111/j.1600-0838.2010.01207.x/abstract

National Center for Catastrophic Sports Injury Research (US) [NCCSIR]. 2009. Annual survey of football injury research: 1931–2008 [Internet]. [accessed 2016 Dec 9]. p. 2–29. Available from: http://nccsir.unc.edu/files/2014/05/FootballAnnual.pdf

Southwest Athletic Trainers' Association. 2013. Statistics on youth sports safety [Internet]. [accessed 2016 Dec 9]. Available from: http://www.swata.org/statistics/

Notice the kinds of sources the author uses as support. If he were to conduct additional research for support, what kind of additional sources would you recommend he look to in order to strengthen his argument?

Discussion Questions

1. Whom do you think Jack Gomperts is targeting as his audience in this assignment? Why do you think that is his audience?

2. What kinds of sources does Jack rely on in his argument? How does he integrate them into his argument, and why do you think he has made those choices?

3. Are you convinced by the writer's argument? Why or why not? What would make this argument more persuasive and effective?

tip sheet

Academic Research

- **Research typically begins with a research question, which establishes the purpose and scope of a project.** As you develop research questions, keep in mind the following evaluative criteria: personal investment, debatable subject, researchable issue, feasibility, and contribution.

- **A researcher who has established a clear research focus, or who has generated a claim, must decide on the kinds of sources needed to support the research focus:** primary, secondary, or both.

- **While both scholarly and popular sources may be appropriate sources of evidence in differing contexts, be sure to understand what distinguishes these types of sources** so that you can choose evidence types purposefully.

- **Primary sources are the results of data that researchers might collect on their own.** These results could include data from surveys, interviews, or questionnaires. **Secondary sources include research collected by and/or commented on by others.** These might include information taken from newspaper articles, magazines, scholarly journal articles, and scholarly books, to name a few.

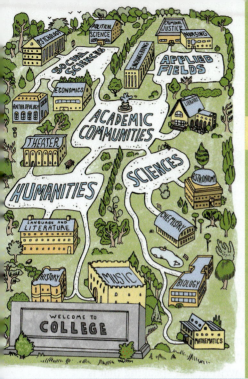

ANDREA TSURUMI

PART TWO

Inside Academic Writing

In Part Two you'll look at how writing works in each of the major academic areas. You'll learn how the conventions and genres of different disciplines represent a discipline's shared values. Throughout these chapters, you'll be practicing skills of rhetorical analysis that you can transfer to your future courses and careers.

Reading and Writing in Academic Disciplines

Now that you have an understanding of the fundamentals of rhetoric, argument, and working with sources, you are ready to analyze and practice writing in various academic disciplines. Keep in mind, though, that we do *not* expect you to master the writing of these communities by taking just one class or by reading one book. Instead, we introduce you to the concepts associated with **disciplinary discourse**, or the writing and speaking that is specific to different disciplines. Using these concepts, you can analyze future writing situations and make choices appropriate to the rhetorical contexts. It's worth noting that such rhetorical awareness may help you enter other **discourse communities**, or groups that share common values and similar communication practices, outside of your college classes as well, both socially and professionally.

ANDREA TSURUMI

As you study writing in the four broad disciplinary areas of humanities, social sciences, natural sciences, and applied fields in the chapters that follow, you'll focus on three defining elements: (1) research expectations, (2) conventions (expectations) of writing, and (3) genres (types) of writing. You'll learn that the conventions and genres of different disciplines are not just patterns to follow; rather, they represent the discipline's shared values. In other words, because scholars in the same discipline might have similar ways of thinking about an issue and what they can contribute to our understanding of it, they follow common ways of researching and sharing their results with others. We'll take a closer look at how values are reflected in such details as what to cover at the start of a paper or how to credit the work of others.

The information we offer you on different academic disciplinary conventions and genres in this book is not necessarily something to memorize, but rather something to view through the frame of *rhetorical analysis*. Ultimately, we want you to be able to look at an academic text and be able to do the following:

- understand the overall rhetorical context of the piece of writing: the author, the audience, the topic, and the purpose for writing
- identify and understand the disciplinary area—humanities, social sciences, natural sciences, applied fields—and make connections to what you know about that discipline
- identify the genre and study the conventions of writing for that genre, including the elements of structure, language, and reference (explained below)

The ability to look at writing through this framework will help you determine and follow the expectations for writing in different courses throughout your college career. It will also help you read the assignments in your other classes because you will understand some of the reasons that texts are written in the way that they are.

Using Rhetorical Context to Analyze Academic Writing

In Chapter 3, we introduced the concept of rhetorical context for analyzing different kinds of writing. Now we want to focus your attention on analyzing the rhetorical contexts of writing in different disciplines. Scholars write for different rhetorical contexts all the time, and they adapt their writing to the audience, topic, and purpose of the occasion. In this chapter, we'll look at two pieces of writing from astronomer Mike Brotherton, a member of the science faculty at the University of Wyoming. Each represents a type of writing that he does on a regular basis. Brotherton writes scholarly articles in his field to report on his research to an audience of other academics—his peers. He also sometimes writes press releases about his research, and these are intended to help journalists report news to the general public.

Analyzing Academic Writing: A Sample Annotated Text

Let's take a look at a press release that Brotherton composed in 2008 to announce his research team's findings on the evolution of galaxies and the black holes at their centers. As you read the press release, which we've annotated, keep in mind the elements of rhetorical context that are useful in analyzing all kinds of writing: author, audience, topic, and purpose. Specifically, consider the following questions:

- How might the fact that Brotherton is both the *author* of the press release and the lead researcher influence the way he wrote the press release? What might have been different if someone else had written the press release after talking to him about his research?

- Who do you think is the *audience* for this piece? Keep in mind that press releases are usually written to the media to encourage them to follow and report on a story. Science journalists often have the background to understand complex scientific topics and translate them for the public, but not all publications have science journalists on staff. What choices do you think Brotherton made that were specific to his audience for the press release?

- How does the *topic* of the press release affect the choices Brotherton made? Would you have made different choices to approach the topic for a general audience? What would they be?

- What is the *purpose* for writing the press release? How might that influence Brotherton's choices as a writer? Do you think he has met that purpose? Why or why not?

Excerpt from **Hubble Space Telescope Spies Galaxy/Black Hole Evolution in Action**

MIKE BROTHERTON

> Identifies the **topic** of the research study and its relevant findings

> Identifies members of the research team, who are all **authors** of the study upon which the press release is based

> Fulfills the **purpose** of a press release by stating the importance of the research project; appears in the first paragraph to make it prominent for the audience

> Provides relevant background information about the topic for the **audience**

JUNE 2, 2008 — A set of 29 Hubble Space Telescope (HST) images of an exotic type of active galaxy known as a "post-starburst quasar" show that interactions and mergers drive both galaxy evolution and the growth of super-massive black holes at their centers. Mike Brotherton, Associate Professor at the University of Wyoming, is presenting his team's findings today at the American Astronomical Society meeting in St. Louis, Missouri. Other team members include Sabrina Cales, Rajib Ganguly, and Zhaohui Shang of the University of Wyoming, Gabriella Canalizo of the University of California at Riverside, Aleks Diamond-Stanic of the University of Arizona, and Dan Vanden Berk of the Penn State University. The result is of special interest because the images provide support for a leading theory of the evolution of massive galaxies, but also show that the situation is more complicated than previously thought.

Over the last decade, astronomers have discovered that essentially every galaxy harbors a super-massive black hole at its center, ranging from 10,000 times the mass of the sun to upwards of 1,000,000,000 times solar, and that there exists a close relationship between the mass of the black hole and properties of its host. When the black holes are fueled and grow, the galaxy becomes active, with the most luminous manifestation being a quasar, which can outshine the galaxy and make it difficult to observe.

In order to explain the relationships between galaxies and their central black holes, theorists have proposed detailed models in which both grow together as the result of galaxy mergers. This hierarchical picture suggests that large galaxies are built up over time through the assembly of smaller galaxies with corresponding bursts of star formation, and that this process also fuels the growth of the black holes, which eventually ignite to shine as quasars. Supernova explosions and their dusty debris shroud the infant starburst until the activated quasar blows out the obscuration.

Brotherton and his team turned the sharp-eyed Hubble Space Telescope and its Advanced Camera for Surveys to observe a subset of these post-starburst quasars that had the strongest and most luminous stellar content. Looking at these systems 3.5 billion light-years away, Hubble, operating without the distortions of an atmosphere, can resolve sub-kiloparsec scales necessary to see nuclear structure and host galaxy morphology.

> Provides a brief overview of the study's methods

"The images started coming in, and we were blown away," said Brotherton. "We see not only merger remnants as in the prototype of the class, but also post-starburst quasars with interacting companion galaxies, double nuclei, starbursting rings, and all sorts of messy structures."

Astronomers have determined that our own Milky Way galaxy and the great spiral galaxy of Andromeda will collide three billion years from now. This event will create massive bursts of star formation and most likely fuel nuclear activity a few hundred million years later. Hubble has imaged post-starburst quasars three and a half billion light-years away, corresponding to three and a half billion years ago, and three and a half billion years from now our own galaxy is probably going to be one of these systems.

> Acknowledges funding support for the research project, giving credit to funding agencies that might also be **audiences** for the journalists' news articles

This work is supported by grants from NASA, through the Space Telescope Science Institute and the Long-Term Space Astrophysics program, and the National Science Foundation.

Insider's View
Astronomer Mike Brotherton on Writing for a General Audience

"It isn't always the case that scientists write their own press releases. Often, there are writers on staff at various institutions who specialize in writing press releases and who work with scientists. I've written press releases solo (e.g., the contribution included here) and in collaboration with staff journalists at the University of Texas, Lawrence Livermore National Laboratory, and the University of Wyoming. Press releases should be able to be run as news stories themselves and contain enough content to be →

adapted or cut to length. The audience for a press release is very general, and you can't assume that they have any background in your field. You have to tell them why your result is important, clearly and briefly, and little else.

"While I don't think my effort here is bad, it is far from perfect and suffers one flaw. Reporters picking up press releases want to know what single result they should focus upon. They want to keep things simple. I tried to include several points in the release, rather than focusing on a single result. Some reporters became distracted about the notion that the Milky Way and Andromeda would someday merge and might become a post-starburst galaxy, which was not a result of my research project. Even though it gave the work some relevance, in hindsight I should have omitted it to keep the focus on the results of my research."

Connect 6.1   **Reflecting on Rhetorical Context**

In his Insider's View, astronomer Mike Brotherton explains some of the specifics of writing a press release and what he sees as the strengths and weaknesses of his own press release. Review the press release with Brotherton's comments in mind, and explain whether you agree with his assessment of it. What advice might you give him for revising the press release?

Recognizing Academic Genres

As you know, different writing situations call for different types of writing, as the example of the press release illustrates. These different types of writing—from short items such as tweets, bumper stickers, and recipes to longer and more complex compositions such as PhD dissertations, annual reports, and novels—are called *genres*. We mentioned genres in Part One, but we want to dive a little deeper here to talk about the kinds of genres you'll encounter in academic contexts and how to analyze them.

Scholars write in many different genres depending on their disciplinary areas, the kinds of work they do, and the situation in which they're writing. You have probably written in several different academic genres in your education already. You might have written a literary analysis in an English class, a lab report in a science class, and a bibliography for a research paper; for this writing course, you may have already written a personal narrative, a rhetorical analysis, a supported argument, or an annotated bibliography. Each of these genres has a distinct purpose and set of expectations that you must be familiar with in order to communicate effectively with your intended audience. In the following chapters, you'll find information about writing in genres that you are likely to encounter as you advance in your studies—such as literary/artistic interpretations, reviews of academic literature, theory responses, observation logbooks, research proposals, lab reports, and memos. The goal is not to make you an expert in every academic genre, but rather to give you the opportunity to practice genre analysis using writing from the disciplines. The skills you will develop through this practice can be applied any time you are faced with a new genre.

Genres are not always bound by discipline, however. Some genres recur across disciplines because writers' purposes can be quite similar even in different fields. For example, you will find the genre of the literature review used by scholars across the curriculum when their purpose is to report on what others have written about a topic. Likewise, when reporting on their own research, many academics follow the IMRaD (Introduction, Methods, Results, and Discussion) format, or a variation of it, to record and publish results, regardless of their discipline. There might be some subtle differences from one discipline or one situation to another, but common elements are evident. Literature reviews and IMRaD-style reports are two examples of common genres of academic writing.

As you read Chapters 7 through 10 on humanities, the social sciences, the natural sciences, and applied fields, pay attention to which genres are repeated and how the conventions of those genres shift or remain constant from one disciplinary context to another.

Connect 6.2   **Reflecting on Academic Genres**

What do you already know about academic genres? What academic genres have you already worked with in high school and college? How did you learn the expectations of those genres?

Using Structure, Language, and Reference (SLR) to Analyze Genre Conventions

Earlier, we introduced two questions that are central to analyzing an academic text:

1. What is the rhetorical context?
2. What conventions are present in the text?

Understanding the rhetorical context is the first step toward understanding how a particular genre works. Knowing the audience and purpose for writing helps us to identify the situations in which different genres occur. To understand fully how a genre works, you must also understand the conventions that are present in the text and whether they follow the expectations for conventions in that genre.

Defining SLR

To understand the conventions that are present in the text, though, we need an additional framework for analysis. The categories of **structure**, **language**, **and reference (SLR)**[*] offer more specific help in analyzing the conventions of genres at a deeper level. Although discourse conventions vary from discipline to discipline, once you understand how to analyze writing through these categories, you can determine what conventions and choices are appropriate for nearly any writing situation.

● **Structure, or Format and Organization** Written texts are often organized according to specific disciplinary conventions. For example, scholars in the social sciences and natural sciences usually organize experimental study reports with an introduction first, followed by a description of their research methods, then their data/results, then the analysis of that data, and finally a discussion and conclusion (IMRaD format, discussed in more detail in Chapters 8 and 9). By contrast, scholars in the humanities tend to write and value essays that are driven by a clear thesis (or main claim: what you are trying to prove) near the beginning of the essay that indicates the direction the argument will take. Scholars in the humanities do not tend, as much, to use headings to divide a text.

● **Language, or Style and Word Choice** The language used in academic writing follows disciplinary conventions. Consider the use of qualifiers (words such as *might*, *could*, *likely*), which are often used in the natural and social sciences to indicate that, while the researchers feel confident in their interpretation of their results, there may be circumstances in which the results would be different. This might be the case, for example, in a study that has a small group of participants (Example: *The positive correlation between the variables* likely *indicates a strong relationship between the motivation of a student and his or her achievement of learning objectives*). When qualifiers are used in the humanities, however, they often demonstrate uncertainty and weaken an argument (Example: *Hamlet's soliloquies in Acts 2 and 4* might *provide an interesting comparison because they frame the turning point of the play in Act 3*).

● **Reference, or Citation and Documentation** The conventions of how scholars refer to one another's work can also shift by discipline. You might already know, for example, that many scholars in the humanities use the documentation style of the Modern Language Association (MLA), while those in the social sciences generally use the style guide published by the American Psychological Association (APA). More citation styles are listed and discussed in the Appendix. Conventions for how often scholars quote, paraphrase, and

---

[*]The SLR concept originated in the following essay: Patricia Linton, Robert Madigan, and Susan Johnson, "Introducing Students to Disciplinary Genres: The Role of the General Composition Course," *Language and Learning across the Disciplines*, vol. 1, no. 2 (1994), pp. 63–78.

summarize one another's work can also vary. We explain the rationale for these differences when discussing documentation in Chapters 7 and 8.

Analyzing Genre Conventions: A Sample Annotated Text

In the next example of Mike Brotherton's work, we'll look at the abstract and introduction to a scholarly journal article that he wrote with several co-authors. If we start with an understanding of the rhetorical context—that Brotherton and his co-authors are writing with the *purpose* of sharing research results and the *audience* of fellow astronomers—then we can move to understanding the conventions that are present in this type of writing. Considering the *structure*, *language*, and *reference conventions* used in the piece provides insight into the way such writing is structured within the sciences—and specifically in the field of astronomy.

As you read the excerpt from Brotherton's co-authored article, notice the structure, language, and reference conventions that we have pointed out in the annotations. The article contains a lot of specific scientific language, and for the purpose of your analysis right now it's not important to understand the concepts as much as it is to recognize some of the elements that make this writing unique from other writing you may have encountered in English classes in the past. Consider the following questions:

- Even though the entire article is not included, what conclusions can you draw about its **structure**? What comes first in the article, and how is it organized in the beginning?

- How would you describe the **language** that Brotherton and his co-authors choose to use in the article? What does it tell you about the audience for the article?

- What **reference** conventions does the article follow? Does the documentation style used for the parenthetical references look familiar? How often are other scholars cited, and what is the context for citing their work? What purpose do those references serve in the article?

Excerpt from **A Spectacular Poststarburst Quasar**

M. S. BROTHERTON, WIL VAN BREUGEL, S. A. STANFORD, R. J. SMITH, B. J. BOYLE, LANCE MILLER, T. SHANKS, S. M. CROOM, AND ALEXEI V. FILIPPENKO

ABSTRACT

We report the discovery of a spectacular "poststarburst quasar" UN J10252–0040 ($B = 19$; $z = 0.634$). The optical spectrum is a chimera, displaying the broad Mg II $\lambda2800$ emission line and strong blue continuum characteristic of quasars, but is dominated in the red by a large Balmer jump and prominent high-order Balmer

The **language** is highly specific and technical.

absorption lines indicative of a substantial young stellar population at similar redshift. Stellar synthesis population models show that the stellar component is consistent with a 400 Myr old instantaneous starburst with a mass of $\leq 10^{11}$ $M_\odot$. A deep, K_s-band image taken in ~0″.5 seeing shows a point source surrounded by asymmetric extended fuzz. Approximately 70% of the light is unresolved, the majority of which is expected to be emitted by the starburst. While starbursts and galaxy interactions have been previously associated with quasars, no quasar ever before has been seen with such an extremely luminous young stellar population.

1. INTRODUCTION

Is there a connection between starbursts and quasar activity? There is circumstantial evidence to suggest so. The quasar 3C 48 is surrounded by nebulosity that shows the high-order Balmer absorption lines characteristic of A-type stars (Boroson & Oke 1984; Stockton & Ridgeway 1991). PG 1700 + 518 shows a nearby starburst ring (Hines et al. 1999) with the spectrum of a 10^8 yr old starburst (Stockton, Canalizo, & Close 1998). Near-IR and CO mapping reveals a massive (~10^{10} $M_\odot$) circumnuclear starburst ring in I Zw 1 (Schinnerer, Eckart, & Tacconi 1998). The binary quasar member FIRST J164311.3 + 315618B shows a starburst host galaxy spectrum (Brotherton et al. 1999).

In addition to these individual objects, *samples* of active galactic nuclei (AGNs) show evidence of starbursts. Images of quasars taken with the Hubble Space Telescope show "chains of emission nebulae" and "near-nuclear emission knots" (e.g., Bahcall et al. 1997). Seyfert 2 and radio galaxies have significant populations of ~100 Myr old stars (e.g., Schmitt, Storchi-Bergmann, & Cid Fernandes 1999). Half of the ultraluminous infrared galaxies (ULIRGs) contain simultaneously an AGN and recent (10–100 Myr) starburst activity in a 1–2 kpc circumnuclear ring (Genzel et al. 1998).

The advent of *IRAS* provided evidence for an evolutionary link between starbursts and AGNs. The ULIRGs ($L_{IR} > 10^{12}$ $L_\odot$) are strongly interacting merger systems with copious molecular gas [$(0.5 - 2) \times 10^{10}$ $M_\odot$] and dust heated by both starburst and AGN power sources. The ULIRG space density is sufficient to form the quasar parent population. These facts led Sanders et al. (1988) to hypothesize that ULIRGs represent the initial dust-enshrouded stage of a quasar. Supporting this hypothesis is the similarity in the evolution of the quasar luminosity density and the star formation rate (e.g., Boyle & Terlevich 1998; Percival & Miller 1999). Another clue is that supermassive black holes appear ubiquitously in local massive galaxies, which may be out-of-fuel quasars (e.g., Magorrian et al. 1998). AGN activity may therefore reflect a fundamental stage of galaxy evolution.

We report here the discovery of a poststarburst quasar. The extreme properties of this system may help shed light on the elusive AGN-starburst connection. We adopt $H_0 = 75$ km s^{-1} Mpc^{-1} and $q_0 = 0$.

Connect 6.3   Gathering Ideas for Analysis

In his Insider's View, Mike Brotherton provides some guidelines for thinking about the conventions of a scientific article through the lenses of structure, language, and reference. Which of his points might help you approach reading a scientific article in your courses?

Writing Project   Genre Analysis

The purpose of a genre analysis is to practice analyzing the rhetorical context and conventions of academic writing so that you have a method of approaching new genres that you encounter in your courses. You will be better able to complete this analysis after reading the following chapters, which provide more detail on academic writing in each of the main discipline areas.

For this project, you might analyze a single piece of academic writing or you might do a comparative analysis of two pieces of writing. For the comparative analysis, you could look at two articles on the same topic, either from different disciplines or from a popular and a scholarly source.

Whether you choose to analyze a single piece of academic writing or do a comparative analysis, start with these questions:

- What is the rhetorical context? Consider the author, audience, topic, and purpose of the article.
- What conventions are present in the text? Consider the structure, language, and reference conventions of the article.

ANALYZING A SINGLE TEXT

Find a full-length academic article in a discipline of your choice, or work with an article assigned by your instructor. Analyze the genre features of the article, considering the choices the writer or writers made. Why did they write the article in the way that they did? How do these genre features work together?

The introduction to your paper should name the article you will analyze, describe what aspects of the writing you will be focusing on, and explain the goal of your analysis—to analyze an academic article in order to see how the writer responds to a rhetorical situation. The body of your paper might be organized around the two guiding questions, or you might focus on one or two of the genre features that are of specific interest in your article. Of course, you can subdivide the features you are analyzing to address specific elements of the larger categories. For example, if you were analyzing conventions of language, you could address the use of qualifiers, the use of first person, and so on, providing examples from the article and commenting on their usefulness for the writer. In your conclusion, reflect on what you've found. Are there other issues still to be addressed? What other rhetorical strategies could be explored to analyze the work further? How effective are the strategies the author used, given the intended audience?

COMPARING SCHOLARLY ARTICLES FROM DIFFERENT DISCIPLINES

Locate two academic articles representing different disciplines. For example, you might find two articles discussing the issue of increasing taxes on the wealthy to deal with the U.S. national debt. You might find one article written by an economist that addresses the impact of the national debt and projects the feasibility of different solutions and another article written by a humanist discussing how the media has portrayed the issue.

Analyze the genre features of the articles using the questions above, and consider the choices the writers made when they wrote the article. You might focus on one genre feature or all three. Formulate a thesis that assesses the degree to which the genre features compare or contrast. Organize your analysis in a way that helps your reader follow the main points you want to make about your comparison. Throughout your paper, develop your comparisons and contrasts by illustrating your findings with examples from the texts. Consider the implications of your findings: What do the conventions say about the values of the discipline? Do not avoid discussing findings that might contradict your assumptions about writing in these two academic domains. Instead, study them closely and try to rationalize the authors' rhetorical decision making.

COMPARING A SCHOLARLY AND POPULAR ARTICLE

Choose a scholarly article and an article written for a more general audience on a common topic. You might reread the discussion of the differences between scholarly and popular articles in Chapter 5 as you're looking for articles to choose.

Once you have described the genre features of the articles using the questions above, consider how the different audiences are reflected in the writing. How do the writers handle specialized vocabulary? How much background knowledge does each writer assume? How much depth and detail does each writer offer? What differences do you perceive in sentence style? For each area of your analysis, look for examples to illustrate your points.

Insider Example
Student Comparative Genre Analysis

Max Bonghi, a first-year writing student, compared two articles from the scholarly casebook on love found in the Long Edition of this book (Chapter 12), with a focus on one aspect of genre expectations (language). He wrote this essay after studying writing in the humanities and natural sciences, which are topics covered in Chapters 7 and 10, respectively.

Writing about Love:

Comparing Language Differences in Two Scholarly Articles

Love is an incredibly difficult word to define, but one could summarize it as an unconditional affection you have toward someone with no limits or drawbacks, while placing your trust into another person that you would do anything for. This broad topic is approached in very different ways in the humanities and natural sciences, as the two academic articles to be analyzed demonstrate. Warren E. Milteer Jr., a historian at the University of South Carolina, looks at sexual and family relationships between white men and women of color during the antebellum period in his essay "The Strategies of Forbidden Love: Family across Racial Boundaries in Nineteenth-Century North Carolina." Through a series of historical examples, active commentary, and thorough discussions, Milteer reveals the creative and mindful techniques that these couples used to navigate a society that publicly refused to accept their relationships. Medical doctors and researchers Donatella Marazziti and Domenico Canale approach the topic of love from a natural science perspective in "Hormonal Changes When Falling in Love," analyzing the complex chemical changes that occur within romantic partners as the first step in long-term pair formation. The researchers report on a study that explored the physiology of falling in love by recording various

> Introduces the common theme and then provides a rhetorical overview of the articles being compared

hormonal levels in twenty-four subjects reported to be in love versus a control group. An analysis of the language features of these two articles reveals the contrasting values of the academic communities for which they were written.

States the focus of the analysis

The differences in how the humanities and natural sciences use language are clear from the start, beginning with the article titles. Humanities articles often employ vivid language, whereas natural science articles are typically plain and purely descriptive. Milteer's humanities article title uses the emotionally charged phrase "forbidden love," which intrigues and engages the reader, and then the subtitle delivers a more specific idea of what the article will be about. Marazziti and Canale use a rather simple title as compared to Milteer. "Hormonal Changes When Falling in Love" gets straight to the point with a phrase that represents the entire premise of the article. The scientists' title is significantly shorter with less abstract and more straightforward words than the historian's. In the historian's title, we can see how the humanities community values the artful use of language, and writers use interesting phrasing to draw readers into their essays. Milteer's title suggests to the reader that they will discover a new way of looking at a piece of American history through his analysis. In the scientists' title, we can see how the scientific community values objectivity and the unadorned presentation of facts. The reader is promised an analysis of quantifiable data that will explain a human phenomenon in terms of body chemistry.

A topic sentence introduces what is being compared in this paragraph.

Each paragraph follows a similar pattern, first discussing the humanities article and then the natural sciences article.

The language features of the two articles at the sentence level also reflect differing genre conventions in the disciplines. Humanities articles tend to include language that revolves around creativity, drama, and bringing attention to an issue. Milteer employs language to create a vivid portrait of the past in his historical essay. For example, when he discusses the dynamics of daily life between white men and women of mixed ancestry, he states that these women "ruled the domestic realm of their households and worked side by side with their white partners to make decisions about other family matters such as finances" (375). He uses dramatic words that highlight the dangers of mixed-race relationships, as when noting that cooperation between the partners was "imperative to their survival" (375). Unlike Milteer's inclusion of vivid phrasing and dramatic terms, Marazziti and Canale stick to more concrete, concise, and specific word choice, as is common in natural science writing. They employ jargon such as "the hypothalamic-pituitary-adrenal (HPA) axis" that has precise meanings within

Quotes are used to support points.

their community of scholars (393). Their sentences often use the passive voice, so that people are "subjects" who are acted upon for the purpose of measurement: "The differences in hormone levels between subjects of the two sexes who recently had or had not fallen in love were measured by means of the Student t-test (unpaired, two-tailed)" (394).

Another related aspect of the differences between the two articles has to do with the celebration versus reduction of language. Milteer and other humanities scholars celebrate the use of language through attention to style. The Milteer article's stylish syntax, diction, and flow take the reader along with the historian as he builds an argument about a particular piece of social history based on his analysis of the evidence. He frames his writing as a contribution to an ongoing conversation about the past when he says that "[s]cholars have shown that familial relationships between whites and non-whites existed despite legal prohibitions, but more work still needs to be completed in order to understand how women of color and white men managed family life in communities that refused to give legal recognition to their unions" (371). Language is central to this work of interpretation, and humanities scholars often communicate their imaginative insights in a way that celebrates language as the expression of ideas. In the natural sciences, on the other hand, writers may attempt to communicate through charts, graphs, images, and numbers rather than words to the extent possible. Marazziti and Canale's article is filled with standard deviations, equations, numerical temperatures, and more. Because natural science articles deliver information in terms of numbers and observations, they can clearly present their findings in a way that seems unbiased. Of course, clarity is a general expectation for all writing, but the desire for clarity in natural science writing can also be linked to the community's shared value of objectivity. The preference to communicate in numbers instead of words is because words can sometimes be open to interpretation. Numbers are more fixed in terms of their ability to communicate specific meaning. For example, the researchers describe their experimental subjects with numeric terms that suggest precision: "They were selected according to the criteria already applied in a previous study (Marazziti et al., 1999), in particular: the relationship was required to have begun within the previous 6 months (mean $\pm$ SD: 3 ± 1 months) and at least four hours a day spent thinking about the partner (mean $\pm$ SD: 9 ± 3 hours), as recorded by a specifically designed questionnaire" (393).

Examining the difference between genre conventions in different disciplines, such as the humanities and natural sciences, offers insights

The conclusion summarizes the analysis and makes a larger point that is relevant beyond the two articles.

into their different values and goals. Comparing two articles on the broad topic of love, we see a historian use language to create a vivid picture of the complex dynamics among a group of mixed-race couples two centuries ago and to make an argument about the effects of institutional racism on these individuals. We see medical researchers use language and numerical data to show their colleagues how they followed scientific processes to gather data supporting the idea that falling in love creates hormonal changes. The humanities and natural sciences disciplines both address significant questions and aim to share their findings through writing, but the form that writing takes is significantly different.

Works Cited

Marazziti, Donatella, and Domenico Canale. "Hormonal Changes When Falling in Love." Miller-Cochran et al., pp. 396–402.

Miller-Cochran, Susan, et al., editors. *An Insider's Guide to Academic Writing: A Rhetoric and Reader.* 3rd ed., Bedford/St. Martin's, 2022.

Milteer, Warren E., Jr. "The Strategies of Forbidden Love: Family across Racial Boundaries in Nineteenth-Century North Carolina." Miller-Cochran et al., pp. 366–83.

Writing Project   **Translating a Scholarly Article for a Public Audience**

The goal of this project is to translate a scholarly article for a public audience. To do so, you will first analyze the scholarly article rhetorically and then shift the genre through which the information in your article is reported. You will produce two documents in response to this assignment:

- a translation of your scholarly article
- a written analysis of the choices you made as you wrote your translation

IDENTIFY YOUR NEW AUDIENCE, PURPOSE, AND GENRE

To get started, you'll need to identify a new audience and purpose for the information in your selected article. The goal here is to shift the audience from an academic one to a public one and to consider whether the purpose for reporting the information also shifts. You may, for instance, choose to report the findings of the article in a magazine targeted toward a general audience of people who are interested in science, or you may choose to write a newspaper article that announces the research findings. You might also choose to write a script for a news show that reports research findings to a general television audience. Notice that once the rhetorical situation shifts, a new genre with unique conventions is often called for. The genre you produce will be contingent on the audience you're targeting and the purpose for writing: magazine article, newspaper article, or news show script.

ANALYZE THE EXPECTATIONS OF YOUR GENRE

Closely analyze an example or two of the kind of genre you're attempting to create, and consider how those genre examples fulfill a particular purpose and the expectations of the target audience. Your project will be assessed according to its ability to reproduce those genre expectations, so you will need to explain, in detail, the choices you had to make in the construction of your piece. Be sure that you're able to explain those choices. In addition to thinking about the audience and purpose, consider the structure, language, and reference conventions of the genre.

CONSTRUCT THE GENRE

At this point, you're ready to begin constructing or translating the article into the new genre. The genre you're producing could take any number of forms. As such, the form, structure, and development of your ideas are contingent on the genre of public reporting you're attempting to construct. If you're constructing a magazine article, for example, then the article you produce should really look like one that would appear in a magazine. Take a look at examples of the genre as models, and consider questions such as these:

- What kind of title does the example have?
- How is information organized in the example?
- How does the example attempt to connect to its intended audience?
- How long is the example? How long are paragraphs, sentences, or other parts of the example?
- Are quotations used? If so, how often? Are they documented? If so, how?

REFLECT ON YOUR CHOICES

Once your translation is complete, compose a reflective analysis. As part of your analysis, consider the choices you made as you constructed your translation. Offer a rationale for each of your decisions that connects your translation to your larger rhetorical context and the conventions of the genre. For example, if you had to translate the title of the scholarly article for a public audience, explain why your new title is the most appropriate one for your public audience.

Insider Example
Student Translation of a Scholarly Article

Jonathan Nastasi, a first-year writing student, translated a scholarly article about the possible habitability of another planet from the journal *Astronomy & Astrophysics* into a press release for a less specialized audience. He condensed the information into a two-page press release for a potential audience interested in publishing these research results in news venues.

Release Date: 18 September 2014
Contact: W. von Bloh
bloh@pik-potsdam.de
Potsdam Institute for Climate Impact Research

Press release formatting is applied here.

Life May Be Possible on Other Planets

Attention-grabbing title

New data shows that a new planet found outside of our solar system may be habitable for life.

The key finding is summarized at the start for a busy audience of reporters.

RALEIGH (SEPTEMBER 18, 2014)—A study from the Potsdam Institute for Climate Impact Research shows that a planet in another solar system is in the perfect position to harbor life. Additionally, the quantity of possibly habitable planets in our galaxy is much greater than expected.

Gliese 581g is one of up to six planets found to be orbiting the low-mass star Gliese 581, hence its name. Gliese 581g and its other planetary siblings are so-called "Super Earths," rocky planets from one to ten times the size of our Earth. This entire system is about twenty light-years away from our Sun. W. Von Bloh, M. Cuntz, S. Franck, and C. Bounama from the Potsdam Institute for Climate Impact Research chose to research Gliese 581g because of its size and distance from its star, which make it a perfect candidate to support life.

Background information is provided for a non-specialist audience.

A planet must be a precise distance away from a star in order to sustain life. This distance is referred to as the habitable zone. According to Von Bloh et al., the habitable zones "are defined as regions around the central star where the physical conditions are favourable for liquid water to exist at the planet's surface for a period of time sufficient for biological evolution to occur." This "Goldilocks" zone can be affected by a number of variables, including the temperature of the star and the composition of the planet.

Simple, non-technical explanation of the research question and methods

The actual distance of Gliese 581g from its star is known; the goal of this study was to find out if the planet is capable of supporting life at that distance. The researchers began by finding the habitable zone of the star Gliese 581 — specifically, the

An artist's rendition of Gliese 581g orbiting its star.

LYNETTE RENE COOK FOR NASA

zone that allowed for photosynthesis. Photosynthesis is the production of oxygen from organic life forms and is indicative of life. In order for the planet to harbor this kind of life, a habitable zone that allows for a specific concentration of CO_2 in the atmosphere as well as liquid water would have to be found.

The scientists used mathematical models based on Earth's known attributes and adjusted different variables to find out which scenarios yielded the best results. Some of these variables include surface temperature, mass of the planet, and geological activity. The scientists also considered settings where the surface of the planet was all-land, all-water, or a mix of both.

Considering all of these scenarios, Von Bloh et al. determined that the habitable zone for Gliese 581g is between 0.125 and 0.155 astronomical units, where an astronomical unit is the distance between the Earth and the Sun. Other studies conclude that the *actual* orbital distance of Gliese 581g is 0.146 astronomical units. Because Gliese 581g is right in the middle of its determined habitable zone, the error and uncertainty in the variables that remain to be determined are negligible.

<aside>
Concepts essential to understanding the results are explained for a non-specialist audience.
</aside>

However, the ratio of land to ocean on the planet's surface is key in determining the "life span" of the habitable zone. The habitable zone can shift over time due to geological phenomena caused by a planet having more land than ocean. According to Von Bloh et al., a planet with a land-to-ocean ratio similar to ours would remain in the habitable zone for about seven billion years, shorter than Gliese 581g's estimated age. In other words, if Gliese 581g has an Earth-like composition, it cannot sustain life. But if the ratio is low (more ocean than land), the planet will remain in its habitable zone for a greater period of time, thus allowing for a greater chance of life to develop.

The researchers conclude that Gliese 581g is a strong candidate for life so long as it is a "water world." According to the authors, water worlds are defined as "planets of non-vanishing continental area mostly covered by oceans."

The discovery of Gliese 581g being a strong candidate for sustaining life is especially important considering the vast quantity of planets just like it. According to NASA's *Kepler Discoveries* Web page, the Kepler telescope alone has found over 4,234 planet candidates in just five years. With the collaboration of other research, 120 planets have been deemed "habitable," according to *The Habitable Exoplanets Catalog*.

"Our results are another step toward identifying the possibility of life beyond the Solar System, especially concerning Super-Earth planets, which appear to be more abundant than previously surmised," say the authors. More and more scientists are agreeing with the idea that extraterrestrial life is probable, given the abundance of Earth-like planets found in our galaxy already. If this is true, humanity will be one step closer to finding its place in the universe.

"[W]e have to await future missions to identify the pertinent geodynamical features of Gl[iese] 581g . . . to gain insight into whether or not Gl[iese] 581g harbors life," write the researchers. The science community agrees: continued focus in researching the cosmos is necessary to confirm if we have neighbors.

The full journal article can be found at http://www.aanda.org.prox.lib.ncsu .edu/articles/aa/full_html/2011/04/aa16534-11/aa16534-11.html.

Astronomy & Astrophysics, published by EDP Sciences since 1963, covers important developments in the research of theoretical, observational, and instrumental astronomy and astrophysics. For more information, visit http://www.aanda.org/.

---

tip sheet

Reading and Writing in Academic Disciplines

- **You should not expect to master the writing of every academic discipline by reading one book,** even this one.

- **It's important to become familiar with key concepts of disciplinary writing in academic discourse communities:** *research* expectations; *conventions* (expectations) of writing; *genres* (types) of writing.

- **Genres are not always bound by discipline, although their conventions may vary somewhat from discipline to discipline.** For example, you can expect to write literature reviews in many different courses across the curriculum.

- **Analyzing academic writing is a multistep process.**
  1. Understand the rhetorical context (author, audience, topic, purpose for writing).
  2. Identify the disciplinary area and what you know about it.
  3. Identify the conventions of writing for that genre, including *structure*, *language*, and *reference* expectations.
  4. Analyze the persuasive strategies if the writer is developing an argument.

- **Remember SLR.** The acronym for *structure*, *language*, and *reference* offers categories that can help you determine genre conventions and choices appropriate for most writing situations. These categories are particularly useful in academic writing situations.
  - *Structure* concerns how texts are organized. *Example:* IMRaD—signifying Introduction, Methods, Results, and Discussion—is a common format in both the social and natural sciences.
  - *Language* encompasses conventions of style or word choice. *Example:* Active voice is typically favored in the humanities, and passive voice is more characteristic of writing in the social and natural sciences.
  - *Reference* concerns the ways writers engage source material, including their use of conventions of citation and documentation. *Example:* Many humanities scholars use MLA style; many social science scholars use APA style.

- **Academic research is important beyond the academy.** Writing that conveys academic research often must be repurposed—translated—for different venues and audiences.

Reading and Writing in the Humanities

Scholars in the **humanities** are interested in, and closely observe, human thought, creativity, and experience. The American Council of Learned Societies explains that humanistic scholars "help us appreciate and understand what distinguishes us as human beings as well as what unites us." To that end, scholars in the humanities ask questions such as these:

- What can we learn about human experience from examining the ways we think and express ourselves?
- How do we make sense of the world through various forms of expression?
- How do we interpret what we experience or make meaning for ourselves and for others?

ANDREA TSURUMI

To understand the human condition and respond to these questions, humanists often turn to artifacts of human culture that they observe and interpret for meaning. These might be films, historical documents, comic strips, paintings, poems, religious artifacts, video games, essays, photographs, and songs. They might even include graffiti on the side of a building, a social media status update, or a YouTube video.

In addition to tangible artifacts, humanist writers might turn their attention to events, experiences, rituals, or other elements of human culture to develop meaning. When Ernest Hemingway wrote *Death in the Afternoon* about the traditions of bullfighting in Spain, for instance, he carefully observed and interpreted the meaning of a cultural ritual. And when historians interpret Hemingway's text through the lens of historical context, or when literary scholars compare the book to Hemingway's fiction of a later period, they are extending that understanding of human culture. Through such examination and interpretation of specific objects of study, scholars in the humanities develop theories that explain human expression and experience or that help us understand further what it means to be human.

In this chapter, we'll often refer to artifacts and events that humanistic scholars study as **texts**. The ability to construct meaning from a text is an essential skill within the scholarship of the humanities. In high school English classes, students are often asked to interpret novels, poetry, or plays. You've likely written such analyses in the past, so you've probably developed a set of observational and interpretive skills that we'd like to build upon in this chapter. The same skills, such as the observational skills that lead you to find evidence in a literary text to develop and support an interpretation, can help you analyze other kinds of texts as well.

Connect 7.1   **Reflecting on Your Experience as a Writer in the Humanities**

What experiences have you already had with the interpretation of texts in the humanities? Have you had to write a formal interpretation of a text before? If so, what questions did you ask?

Research in the Humanities

The collection of information, or data, is an integral part of the research process for scholars in all academic disciplines. The data that researchers collect form the foundation of evidence they use to answer a question. In the humanities, data are generally gathered from texts. Whether you're reading a novel, analyzing a sculpture, or speculating on the significance of a cultural ritual, your object of analysis is a text and the primary source of data you collect to use as evidence typically originates from that text.

Academic fields within the humanities have at their heart the creation and interpretation of texts. A history scholar may pore through photographs of Civil War soldiers for evidence to support a claim. An actor in a theater class might scour a script to develop an interpretation of a character to be performed onstage. And those who are primarily the creators of texts—visual artists, novelists, poets, playwrights, screenwriters, musicians—will have read widely in the field to master elements of style and content to contribute to their art in original and innovative ways. In the humanities, it's all about the text. Humanists are either creators or interpreters of texts, and often they are both.

Observation and Interpretation

To understand research and writing in a specific disciplinary area, it is important to know not only what the objects of study are but also what methods scholars in that area use to analyze and study the objects of their attention. In the humanities, just as in other disciplines, scholars begin with observation. They closely observe the texts that interest them, looking for patterns, meaning, and connections that will help generate and support an interpretation. Humanists use their observations to pose questions about the human condition, to gather evidence to help answer those questions, and to generate theories about the human experience that can extend beyond one text or set of texts.

You probably engage every day in the observation of texts, but you might not be doing it in the systematic way that humanistic scholars do. When you listen to music, how do you make meaning? Perhaps you listen to the words, the chord progressions, or repeated phrases. Or maybe you look to specific matters of context such as who wrote the song, what other music the artist has performed, and when it was recorded. You might consider how it is similar to or different from other songs. In order to understand the song's meaning, you might even think about social and cultural events surrounding the period when the song was recorded. These kinds of observational and interpretive acts are the very things humanists do when they research and write; they just use careful methods of observing, documenting, and interpreting that are generally more systematic than what most of us do when listening to music for enjoyment.

Insider's View
Historian Matthew Sakiestewa Gilbert on Research in American Indian Studies

COURTESY OF MATTHEW SAKIESTEWA GILBERT

"Trained in the field of Native American history, I spend a lot of time studying archival documents such as letters, memos, reports, photographs, and historical newspapers. As a historian, my job is to 'tell and analyze the story,' and I do this by gathering information about certain topics and interpreting their historical and cultural significance. A faculty at a large research university, I publish the bulk of my scholarship in books, journals, and in edited volumes.

"While I am expected to publish as a member of the academy, I am also a member of the Hopi community, and I have a responsibility to make my research meaningful and useful to my people. Since many on the Hopi Reservation do not have access to my academic writings, I created the weblog (blog) *Beyond the Mesas* to reach people back home. It also provides an opportunity for me to engage a broad public audience with my work. For example, sometimes I receive e-mails from young students who stumble across my website as they search for information on the Hopi for their school projects. They occasionally send me short questionnaires to fill out on Hopi history and culture, which I am happy to do.

"Hopi people also regularly engage with my blog. After I published a story about a Hopi runner named Harry Chaca who competed for Sherman Institute in the 1920s, his granddaughter, Cheryl Chaca, read my post and commented about how pleased she was to learn of her grandfather's athletic accomplishments. However, the most meaningful comment came from my oldest daughter, Hannah, who at the time was seven years old. One morning, I heard the words 'If so, please consider...' coming from our living room. I looked around the corner, and to my surprise, I saw my daughter sitting with my iPad on her lap. My blog was open on the screen. When I asked what she was doing, she simply replied, 'I'm learning about Hopi.'"

SKIP BOLENEPA/SHUTTERSTOCK

The Role of Theory in the Humanities

When scholars in the humanities analyze and interpret a text, they often draw on a specific theory of interpretation to help them make meaning. Theories in the humanities offer a particular perspective through which to understand human experience. Sometimes those perspectives are based on ideas about *how* we make meaning from a text; such theories include Formalism (sometimes called New Criticism, though it is far from new), Reader Response, and Deconstruction. Other theories, such as Feminist Theory and Queer Theory, are based more on ideas about how identity informs meaning-making. Still other theories, such as New Historicism, Postcolonialism, and Marxism, are centrally concerned with how historical, social, cultural, and other contexts inform meaning.

These are only a few of the many prominent theories of humanistic interpretation, barely scratching the surface of the theory-building work that has taken place in the humanities. Our goal is not for you to learn specific names of theories at this point, though. Rather, we want you to understand that when scholars in the humanities draw on a theory in the interpretation of a text, the theory gives them a *lens* through which to view the text and a set of questions they might ask about it. For example, they might ask:

- When was the text written, and what major social forces might have influenced the text at the time? (New Historicism)
- What characters exhibit the most power in their relationships to their partners? (Feminism)
- What kinds of tensions does the artifact create for the viewer through its use of shading and lighting? (New Criticism)

Different theories lead to different sets of questions and varying interpretations of the same text.

Engaging with Theory: A Sample Annotated Text

As in other disciplines, scholars in the humanities draw on the work of others to make sure they're contributing something new to the ongoing conversation about a text they're studying. They may also read the work of others to determine if they agree or disagree with previous interpretations of that text. Because of the importance of specific language and detail in the humanities, scholars in the humanities often quote one another's exact words, and they also quote directly from their primary sources. We'll discuss some of the reasons for these conventions, and others, later in the chapter.

In the following example of an interpretation of a text, scholar Dale Jacobs discusses how he constructs meaning from comics. He first presents his theory that interpretations of comics require more complex literacy skills than texts composed only of words (e.g., a novel or short story) because readers of comics must also interpret visual, gestural, and spatial language at work in the panels. He situates his theory in the context of the work of other scholars, quoting directly in a couple of instances. He then illustrates his theory with a close reading of a comic called *Polly and the Pirates*. This excerpt is part of a larger essay aimed at an audience of composition instructors. In it, Jacobs calls on instructors to challenge students to think critically about how they construct meaning from texts. As you read this excerpt from his article, you might reflect on this question: When reading a text, how do you make meaning?

Excerpt from **More Than Words: Comics as a Means of Teaching Multiple Literacies**

DALE JACOBS

COMICS AS MULTIMODAL LITERACY: THE THEORY

If we think about comics as multimodal texts that involve multiple kinds of meaning making, we do not give up the benefits of word-based literacy instruction but strengthen it through the inclusion of visual and other literacies. This complex view of literacy is touched on but never fully fleshed out in two excellent recent articles on comics and education: Rocco Versaci's "How Comic Books Can Change the Way Our Students See Literature: One Teacher's Perspective" and Bonny Norton's "The Motivating Power of Comic Books: Insights from Archie Comic Readers." By situating our thinking about comics, literacy, and education within a framework that views literacy as occurring in multiple modes, we can use comics to greater effectiveness in our teaching at all levels by helping us to arm students with the critical-literacy skills they need to negotiate diverse systems of meaning making.

> Jacobs presents his thesis here: his approach to teaching comics will help students develop critical-literacy skills that they can use to approach multimodal texts.

I'm going to offer an example of how comics engage multiple literacies by looking at Ted Naifeh's *Polly and the Pirates*, but first let me give a brief outline of these multiple systems of meaning making. As texts, comics provide a complex environment for the negotiation of meaning, beginning with the layout of the page itself. The comics page is separated into multiple panels, divided from each other by gutters, physical or conceptual spaces through which connections are made and meanings are negotiated; readers must fill in the blanks within these gutters and make connections between panels. Images of people, objects, animals, and settings, word balloons, lettering, sound effects, and gutters all come together to form page layouts that work to create meaning in distinctive ways and in multiple realms of meaning making. In these multiple realms of meaning making, comics engage in what the New London Group of literacy scholars calls *multimodality*, a way of thinking that seeks to push literacy educators, broadly defined and at all levels of teaching, to think about literacy in ways that move beyond a focus on strictly word-based literacy. In the

> Jacobs identifies how comics employ multiple modes of literacy through their page layout.

introduction to the New London Group's collection, *Multiliteracies: Literacy Learning and the Design of Social Futures*, Bill Cope and Mary Kalantzis write that their approach "relates to the increasing multiplicity and integration of significant modes of meaning-making, where the textual is also related to the visual, the audio, the spatial, the behavioural, and so on. . . . Meaning is made in ways that are increasingly multimodal—in which written-linguistic modes of meaning are part and parcel of visual, audio, and spatial patterns of meaning" (5). By embracing the idea of multimodal literacy in relation to comics, then, we can help students engage critically with ways of making meaning that exist all around them, since multimodal texts include much of the content on the Internet, interactive multimedia, newspapers, television, film, instructional textbooks, and many other texts in our contemporary society.

Jacobs addresses the "So what?" of his theory.

Such a multimodal approach to reading and writing asserts that in engaging with texts, we interact with up to six design elements, including linguistic, audio, visual, gestural, and spatial modes, as well as multimodal design, "of a different order to the others as it represents the patterns of interconnections among the other modes" (New London Group 25). In the first two pages from *Polly and the Pirates*, all of these design elements are present, including a textual and visual representation of the audio element. Despite the existence of these multiple modes of meaning making, however, the focus in thinking about the relationship between comics and education is almost always on the linguistic element, represented here by the words in the words balloons (or, in the conventions of comics, the dialogue from each of the characters) and the narrative text boxes in the first three panels (which we later find out are also spoken dialogue by a narrator present in the story).

As discussed earlier, comics are seen as a simplified version of word-based texts, with the words supplemented and made easier to understand by the pictures. If we take a multimodal approach to texts such as comics, however, the picture of meaning making becomes much more complex. In word-based texts, our interaction with words forms an environment for meaning making that is extremely complex. In comics and other multimodal texts, there are five other elements added to the mix. Thought about in this way, comics are not just simpler versions of word-based texts but can be viewed as the complex textual environments that they are.

Jacobs concludes the introduction to his theory by reinforcing the idea that comics are multimodal and not a simplified version of word-based texts.

COMICS AS MULTIMODAL LITERACY: *POLLY AND THE PIRATES* IN THE CLASSROOM

In this section, Jacobs uses an example to illustrate his theory of how to read comics.

In comics, there are elements present besides words, but these elements are just as important in making meaning from the text. In fact, it is impossible to make full sense of the words on the page in isolation from the audio, visual, gestural, and spatial. For example, the first page of *Polly and the Pirates* (the first issue of a six-issue miniseries) opens with three panels of words from what the reader takes to be the story's narrative voice. Why? Partially it is because of *what* the words say—how they introduce a character and begin to set up the story—but also it is because of the text boxes that enclose the words. That is, most people understand from their experiences of reading comics at some point in their history that words in text boxes almost always contain the story's narrative voice and denote a different kind of voice than do words in dialogue balloons. What's more, these text boxes deviate in shape and design from the even rectangles usually seen in comics; instead, they are depicted more like scrolls, a visual element that calls to mind both the time period and genre associated with pirates. Not only does this visual element help to place the reader temporally and generically, but it, along with lettering and punctuation, also aids in indicating tone, voice inflection, cadence, and emotional tenor by giving visual representation to the text's audio element. We are better able to "hear" the narrator's voice because we can see what words are emphasized by the bold lettering, and we associate particular kinds of voices with the narrative voice of a pirate's tale, especially emphasized here by the shape of the text boxes. Both the visual and the audio thus influence the way we read the words in a comic, as can be seen in these three opening panels.

It seems to me, however, that the key lies in going beyond the way we make meaning from the words alone and considering the other visual elements, as well as the gestural and spatial. If I were teaching this text, I would engage students in a discussion about how they understand what is going on in the story and how they make meaning from it. Depending on the level of the class, I would stress different elements at varying levels of complexity. Here I will offer an example of how I make meaning from these pages and of some of the elements I might discuss with students.

In talking about the visual, I would consider such things as the use of line and white space, shading, perspective, distance, depth of field, and composition. The gestural refers to facial expression and body posture, while the spatial refers to the meanings of environmental and architectural space, which, in the case of comics, can be conceived as the layout of panels on the page and the relation between these panels through use of gutter space. The opening panel depicts a ship, mainly in silhouette, sailing on the ocean; we are not given details, but instead see the looming presence of a ship that we are led to believe is a pirate ship by the words in the text boxes. The ship is in the center of an unbordered panel and is the only element in focus, though its details are obscured. The unbordered panel indicates openness, literally and metaphorically, and this opening shot thus acts much in the same way as an establishing shot in a film, orienting us both in terms

> Jacobs shows how he would use his theory as a lens through which to view the text.

of place and in terms of genre. The second panel pulls in closer to reveal a silhouetted figure standing on the deck of the ship. She is framed between the sails, and the panel's composition draws our eyes toward her as the central figure in the frame. She is clearly at home, one arm thrust forward while the other points back with sword in hand, her legs anchoring herself securely as she gazes across the ocean. The third panel pulls in even farther to a close-up of her face, the top half in shadow and the bottom half showing a slight smile. She is framed by her sword on the left and the riggings of the ship on the right, perfectly in her element, yet obscured from our view. Here and in the previous panel, gestural and visual design indicate who is the center of the story and the way in which she confidently belongs in this setting. At the same time, the spatial layout of the page and the progression of the panels from establishing shot to close-up and from unbordered panels to bordered and internally framed panels help us to establish the relationship of the woman to the ship and to the story; as we move from one panel to the next, we must make connections between the panels that are implied by the gutter. Linguistic, visual, audio, gestural, and spatial elements combine in these first three panels to set up expectations in the reader for the type of story and its narrative approach. Taken together, these elements form a multimodal system of meaning making.

What happens in the fourth panel serves to undercut these expectations as we find out that the narrative voice actually belongs to one of the characters in the story, as evidenced by the shift from text box to dialogue balloon even though the voice is clearly the same as in the first three panels of the page. Spatially, we are presented with a larger panel that is visually dominated by the presence of a book called *A History of the Pirate Queen*. This book presumably details the story to which we had been introduced in the first three panels. The character holding the book is presenting it to someone and, because of the panel's composition, is also effectively presenting it to us, the readers. The gesture becomes one of offering this story up to us, a story that simultaneously becomes a romance as well as a pirate story as evidenced by the words the character says and the way she says them (with the bold emphasis on *dream* and *marry*). At this point, we do not know who this character is or to whom she is speaking, and the answers to these questions will be deferred until we turn to the second page.

On the first panel of page 2, we see three girls, each taking up about a third of the panel, with them and the background in focused detail. Both the words and facial expression of the first girl indicate her stance toward the story, while the words and facial expression of the second girl indicate her indignation at the attitude of the first girl (whom we learn is named Sarah). The third girl is looking to the right, away from the other two, and has a blank expression on her face. The next panel depicts the second and third girls, pulling in to a tighter close-up that balances one girl on either side of the panel and obscures the background so that we will focus on their faces and dialogue. The unbordered panel

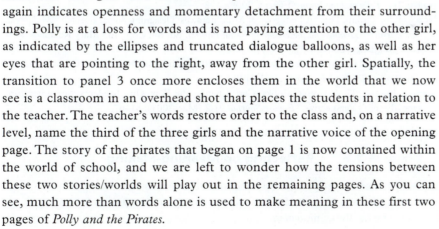

again indicates openness and momentary detachment from their surroundings. Polly is at a loss for words and is not paying attention to the other girl, as indicated by the ellipses and truncated dialogue balloons, as well as her eyes that are pointing to the right, away from the other girl. Spatially, the transition to panel 3 once more encloses them in the world that we now see is a classroom in an overhead shot that places the students in relation to the teacher. The teacher's words restore order to the class and, on a narrative level, name the third of the three girls and the narrative voice of the opening page. The story of the pirates that began on page 1 is now contained within the world of school, and we are left to wonder how the tensions between these two stories/worlds will play out in the remaining pages. As you can see, much more than words alone is used to make meaning in these first two pages of *Polly and the Pirates*.

Jacobs ends his close reading by connecting his observations to his thesis: comics engage multiple modes of literacy to create meaning.

CONCLUSION

My process of making meaning from these pages of *Polly and the Pirates* is one of many meanings within the matrix of possibilities inherent in the text. As a reader, I am actively engaging with the "grammars," including discourse and genre conventions, within this multimodal text as I seek to create/negotiate meaning; such a theory of meaning making with multimodal texts acknowledges the social and semiotic structures that surround us and within which we exist, while at the same time it recognizes individual agency and experience in the creation of meaning. Knowledge of linguistic, audio, visual, gestural, and spatial conventions within comics affects the ways in which we read and the meanings we assign to texts, just as knowledge of conventions within word-based literacy affects the ways in which those texts are read. For example, the conventions discussed above in terms of the grammar of comics would have been available to Naifeh as he created *Polly and the Pirates*, just as they are also available to me and to all other readers of his text. These conventions form the underlying structure of the process of making meaning, while familiarity with these conventions, practice in reading comics, interest, prior experience, and attention given to that reading all come into play in the exercise of agency on the part of the reader (and writer). Structure and agency interact so that we are influenced by design conventions and grammars as we read but are not determined by them; though we are subject to the same set of grammars, my reading of the text is not necessarily the same as that of someone else.

WORKS CITED

Cope, Bill, and Mary Kalantzis. "Introduction: Multiliteracies: The Beginnings of an Idea." *Multiliteracies: Literacy Learning and the Design of Social Futures*. Ed. Bill Cope and Mary Kalantzis. New York: Routledge, 2000. 3–8.

Naifeh, Ted. *Polly and the Pirates* 1 (Sept. 2005): 1–2.

New London Group, The. "A Pedagogy of Multiliteracies: Designing Social Futures." *Multiliteracies: Literacy Learning and the Design of Social Futures*. Ed. Bill Cope and Mary Kalantzis. New York: Routledge, 2000. 9–37.

Norton, Bonny. "The Motivating Power of Comic Books: Insights from Archie Comic Readers." *The Reading Teacher* 57.2 (Oct. 2003): 140–47.

Versaci, Rocco. "How Comic Books Can Change the Way Our Students See Literature: One Teacher's Perspective." *English Journal* 91.2 (Mar. 2001): 61–67.

Connect 7.3   Reflecting on Meaning-Making

Study one of the panels from *Polly and the Pirates* and consider how you make meaning from it. Freewrite for five minutes about your own process for making sense of what the comic means.

Strategies for Close Reading

To develop clear claims about the texts they are interpreting, scholars in the humanities must carefully observe texts to learn about them. Careful observation of a text might involve the kinds of reading strategies we discussed in Chapter 3, especially if the text is alphabetic (i.e., letter-based), such as a book, a story, or a poem. The method that humanities scholars use to engage in such careful observation of a text is often referred to as **close reading**. It's possible to do a close reading of a story, of course, but you can also do a close reading of non-alphabetic texts such as films, buildings, paintings, events, songs, or even multimodal texts, as the preceding example from Dale Jacobs illustrates.

Most college students are highly skilled at reading for content knowledge, or for information, because that's what they are most often asked to do as students. This is what a professor generally expects when assigning a reading from a textbook. As you read such texts, you're primarily trying to figure out what the text is saying rather than thinking about how it functions, why the author makes certain stylistic choices, or how others might interpret the text. As we mentioned in Chapter 3, you might also read to be entertained, to learn, or to communicate.

Close observation or reading in the humanities, however, requires our focus to shift from reading for information to reading to understand how a text functions and how we can make meaning of it. Because texts are the primary sources of data used in humanistic research, it's important for those who work in the humanities to examine how a text conveys meaning to its audience. This kind of work—observing a text critically to analyze what it means and how it conveys meaning—is what we call close reading.

Notetaking Steps

For most of us, when we observe a printed text closely, we highlight, underline, and take notes in the margins. If we're analyzing a visual or aural text, we might take notes on our thoughts, observations, and questions. We might keep a separate notebook or computer file in which we expand on our notes or clarify meaning. As with any skill, the more you practice these steps, the better you will become at interpretation. We encourage you to take detailed notes, underline passages if applicable, and actively engage with a text when conducting your observation. In all cases, we recommend two specific data-collection steps for humanistic inquiry: annotating and developing a content/form-response grid.

● **Annotating**   We suggest that you take notes in the margins for a printed text or on a separate sheet of paper as you read, view, or listen to a text to be interpreted. These notes will draw your attention to passages that may serve as direct evidence to support points you will make later. Additionally, you can elaborate in more detail when something meaningful in the text draws your attention. Jotting down page numbers, audio/video file time markers, and paragraph numbers is often helpful for cataloging your notes. The key is to commit fully to engaging with a text by systematically recording your observations.

● **Developing a Content/Form-Response Grid** We recommend that you develop a **content/form-response grid** to organize the essential stages of your interpretation. The "content" is what happens in the text, and the "form" is how the text's creator structures the piece. In the case of a painting, you might comment on the materials used, the artist's technique, the color palette and imagery choice, or the historical context of the piece. In the case of a religious or political text, you might examine style, language, and literary devices used. The "response" is your interpretation of what the elements you've identified might mean. The grid setup can be as simple as two columns, one for the content/form notes and the second for the corresponding responses.

Close Reading: Sample Annotations and Content/Form-Response Grids

Read the following opening paragraphs from "The Story of an Hour," a brief short story by Kate Chopin published in 1894 that is now recognized as a classic work of American literature. The excerpt includes a student's annotations followed by a content/form-response grid. Notice the frequency of notes the student takes in the margins and the kinds of questions she asks at this early stage. She offers a fairly equal balance of questions and claims.

Heart trouble? I wonder what kind of trouble.

The news of her husband's death is delivered by her sister.

Why would she act differently from other women hearing the same kind of news?

Interesting comparison. The storm-like quality of her grief.

Why is she "exhausted"? Interesting word choice.

Knowing that Mrs. Mallard was afflicted with a heart trouble, great care was taken to break to her as gently as possible the news of her husband's death. It was her sister Josephine who told her, in broken sentences; veiled hints that revealed in half concealing. Her husband's friend Richards was there, too, near her. It was he who had been in the newspaper office when intelligence of the railroad disaster was received, with Brently Mallard's name leading the list of "killed." He had only taken the time to assure himself of its truth by a second telegram, and had hastened to forestall any less careful, less tender friend in bearing the sad message.

She did not hear the story as many women have heard the same, with a paralyzed inability to accept its significance. She wept at once, with sudden, wild abandonment, in her sister's arms. When the storm of grief had spent itself she went away to her room alone. She would have no one follow her.

There stood, facing the open window, a comfortable, roomy armchair. Into this she sank, pressed down by a physical exhaustion that haunted her body and seemed to reach into her soul.

She could see in the open square before her house the tops of trees that were all aquiver with the new spring life. The delicious breath of rain was in the air. In the street below a peddler was crying his wares. The notes of a distant song which some one was singing reached her faintly, and countless sparrows were twittering in the eaves.

There are lots of images of life here. This really contrasts with the dark news of the story's opening.

This student's annotations can be placed into a content/form-response grid that helps her keep track of the ideas she had as she read and observed closely, both for information (*what*) and for ways the text shaped her experience of it (*how*). Notice that the student uses the Content/Form section to summarize the comments from her annotations, and then she reflects on her annotations in the Response section:

Content/Form Notes (*what* and *how*)	Response (*What effect does it have on me?*)
Heart trouble? I wonder what kind of trouble.	There's a mystery here. What's wrong with Mrs. Mallard's heart?
The news of her husband's death is delivered by her sister.	Interesting that a female relative is chosen to deliver the news. A man would be too rough?
Why would she act differently from other women hearing the same kind of news?	I wonder what is special about Mrs. Mallard that causes her reaction to be different. Is she putting on a show? Story says her reaction was "sudden" and "wild."
Why is she "exhausted"? Interesting word choice.	Maybe this has to do with her heart condition or with how physically draining her mourning is.
There are lots of images of life here. This really contrasts with the dark news of the story's opening.	This is a sudden change in feeling. Everything is so calm and pleasant now. What happened?

The purpose of this activity is to construct meaning from the text based on the student's close observation of it. This is an interpretation. We can already see that major complexities in the story are beginning to emerge in the student's response notes—such as the importance of the story's setting and the change that occurs in Mrs. Mallard.

Because content/form-response grids like the one above allow you to visualize both your ideas and how you arrived at those ideas, we recommend using this activity any time you have to observe a text closely in order to interpret its meaning. For a non-alphabetic text, start with the content/form-response grid and use it to log your initial notes as you observe; then reflect later. In the end, such an activity provides a log of details that can help explain how you arrived at a particular conclusion or argument about the text.

Close Reading Practice: Analyzing a Short Story

Now it's your turn. Read the whole text of Kate Chopin's "The Story of an Hour" below, and then annotate the text as you read, paying particular attention to the following elements:

- **Content** What is being said (the facts, the events, and who the characters are)
- **Form** How it is being said (the style, language, literary techniques, and narrative perspective)

A follow-up Connect activity at the conclusion of the story asks you to draw a content/form-response grid like the example above. It's important to take extensive marginal notes (perhaps one or two comments per paragraph) and highlight and underline passages as you read the story. These notes will help shape your content/form-response grid and will strengthen your interpretation. We encourage you to expand on your notes on a separate sheet of paper while you read the story.

The Story of an Hour

KATE CHOPIN

Knowing that Mrs. Mallard was afflicted with a heart trouble, great care was taken to break to her as gently as possible the news of her husband's death.

It was her sister Josephine who told her, in broken sentences; veiled hints that revealed in half concealing. Her husband's friend Richards was there, too, near her. It was he who had been in the newspaper office when intelligence of the railroad disaster was received, with Brently Mallard's name leading the list of "killed." He had only taken the time to assure himself of its truth by a second telegram, and had hastened to forestall any less careful, less tender friend in bearing the sad message.

She did not hear the story as many women have heard the same, with a paralyzed inability to accept its significance. She wept at once, with sudden, wild abandonment, in her sister's arms. When the storm of grief had spent itself she went away to her room alone. She would have no one follow her.

There stood, facing the open window, a comfortable, roomy armchair. Into this she sank, pressed down by a physical exhaustion that haunted her body and seemed to reach into her soul.

She could see in the open square before her house the tops of trees that 5 were all aquiver with the new spring life. The delicious breath of rain was in the air. In the street below a peddler was crying his wares. The notes of a distant song which some one was singing reached her faintly, and countless sparrows were twittering in the eaves.

There were patches of blue sky showing here and there through the clouds that had met and piled one above the other in the west facing her window.

She sat with her head thrown back upon the cushion of the chair, quite motionless, except when a sob came up into her throat and shook her, as a child who has cried itself to sleep continues to sob in its dreams.

She was young, with a fair, calm face, whose lines bespoke repression and even a certain strength. But now there was a dull stare in her eyes, whose gaze was fixed away off yonder on one of those patches of blue sky. It was not a glance of reflection, but rather indicated a suspension of intelligent thought.

There was something coming to her and she was waiting for it, fearfully. What was it? She did not know; it was too subtle and elusive to name. But she felt it, creeping out of the sky, reaching toward her through the sounds, the scents, the color that filled the air.

Now her bosom rose and fell tumultuously. She was beginning to recognize 10 this thing that was approaching to possess her, and she was striving to beat it back with her will—as powerless as her two white slender hands would have been.

When she abandoned herself a little whispered word escaped her slightly parted lips. She said it over and over under her breath: "free, free, free!" The vacant stare and the look of terror that had followed it went from her eyes. They stayed keen and bright. Her pulses beat fast, and the coursing blood warmed and relaxed every inch of her body.

She did not stop to ask if it were or were not a monstrous joy that held her. A clear and exalted perception enabled her to dismiss the suggestion as trivial.

She knew that she would weep again when she saw the kind, tender hands folded in death; the face that had never looked save with love upon her, fixed and gray and dead. But she saw beyond that bitter moment a long procession of years to come that would belong to her absolutely. And she opened and spread her arms out to them in welcome.

There would be no one to live for during those coming years; she would live for herself. There would be no powerful will bending hers in that blind persistence with which men and women believe they have a right to impose a private will upon a fellow-creature. A kind intention or a cruel intention made the act seem no less a crime as she looked upon it in that brief moment of illumination.

And yet she had loved him—sometimes. Often she had not. What did it 15 matter! What could love, the unsolved mystery, count for in face of this posses-sion of self-assertion which she suddenly recognized as the strongest impulse of her being!

"Free! Body and soul free!" she kept whispering.

Josephine was kneeling before the closed door with her lips to the keyhole, imploring for admission. "Louise, open the door! I beg, open the door—you will make yourself ill. What are you doing, Louise? For heaven's sake open the door."

"Go away. I am not making myself ill." No; she was drinking in a very elixir of life through that open window.

Her fancy was running riot along those days ahead of her. Spring days, and summer days, and all sorts of days that would be her own. She breathed a quick prayer that life might be long. It was only yesterday she had thought with a shudder that life might be long.

She arose at length and opened the door to her sister's importunities. There was a feverish triumph in her eyes, and she carried herself unwittingly like a goddess of Victory. She clasped her sister's waist, and together they descended the stairs. Richards stood waiting for them at the bottom.

Some one was opening the front door with a latchkey. It was Brently Mallard who entered, a little travel-stained, composedly carrying his grip-sack and umbrella. He had been far from the scene of accident, and did not even know there had been one. He stood amazed at Josephine's piercing cry; at Richards' quick motion to screen him from the view of his wife.

But Richards was too late.

When the doctors came they said she had died of heart disease—of joy that kills.

Connect 7.4   **Preparing a Content/Form-Response Grid**

Based on your annotations and notes, construct a content/form-response grid modeled after the example in "Close Reading: Sample Annotations and a Content/Form-Response Grid" (p. 134). Be sure to include your responses to the items you identify in the Content/Form column. Remember that in this case "content" relates to what happens in the story, and "form," in the context of a literary text, relates to how the writer makes the story function through style, narrative perspective, and literary techniques.

Once you've completed your close reading, you might pair up with a classmate or two and share your content/form-response grids. When doing so, consider the following questions as part of your discussion:

- What facts or events did you note about the story?

- What did you notice about the ways Chopin shapes your experience of the story? What style or literary techniques did you note?

- What patterns do you see in the notes you've taken in the Form column? What repeated comments did you make, or what elements strike you in a similar way? How would you explain the meaning of those patterns?

As a last step in interpreting Chopin's story, you might draw on the work of other scholars to build and support your interpretations. For example, you might review the notes you made in your content/form-response grid, search for interesting patterns, and then see if other scholars have noticed the same things. You might look for an element of the story that doesn't make sense to you and see if another scholar has already offered an interpretation. If you agree with the interpretation, you might cite it as support for your own argument. If you disagree, you might look for evidence in the story to show why you disagree and then offer your own interpretation.

Structural Conventions in the Humanities

Some writing conventions are shared across different fields in the humanities. Because the kinds of texts humanistic scholars examine can vary so much, though, there are also sometimes distinctions in writing conventions among its various fields. One of the challenges of learning the conventions of a disciplinary discourse community is figuring out the specific expectations for communicating with a specific academic audience. In the following sections, we turn our attention from the nature of research in the humanities to *strategies of rhetorical analysis* that help us examine how scholars in the humanities write about their insights.

Many scholars learn about disciplinary writing conventions through imitation and examination of articles in their fields. Recall that in Chapter 6 we introduced a three-part method for analyzing texts by examining the conventions of structure, language, and reference. Applying this analytical framework to professional writing in the various humanities fields may facilitate your success in writing in those contexts. In this section, we will examine structural conventions—that is, conventions governing how writing is organized. Rather than trying to master the conventions of every type of writing in the humanities, your goal is to understand the general principles underlying writing conventions in the humanities and to practice applying an analytical framework to any writing assignment you encounter.

From your experience in high school, you might already be familiar with common structural features of writing in the humanities. Arguments in the humanities are generally "thesis-driven"; that is, they make an interpretive claim about a text and then support that claim with specific evidence from the text and sometimes with material from other sources that support the interpretation. By contrast, arguments in the social sciences and the natural sciences are usually driven by a hypothesis that must be tested in order to come to a conclusion, which encourages a different structure. First, we'll talk about how humanistic scholars develop research questions and thesis statements. Then we'll turn our attention to a common structure that many students learn in secondary school to support their thesis statements with evidence, which is loosely based on the structure of the thesis-driven argument, and we'll compare it with published scholarship in the humanities.

Using Research Questions to Develop a Thesis

An important part of the interpretation process is using observations to pose questions about a text. From these close observations, humanists develop research questions that they answer through their research. A **research question** in the humanities is the primary question a scholar asks about a text or set of texts. It is the first step in interpretation because questions grow out of our observations and the patterns or threads that we notice. A **thesis statement** is an answer to a research question and is most persuasive when supported by logical evidence. Thesis statements are discussed in more detail in Chapter 4 as the central claim of an argument. It's important to note that developing a research question works best when it is generated prior to writing a thesis statement. Novice writers can sometimes overlook this crucial step in the writing process and attempt to make a thesis statement without formulating a well-realized research question first.

Some of the most important questions for humanists begin by asking, "Why?" Why does George befriend Lenny in John Steinbeck's novella *Of Mice and Men*? Why did Frida Kahlo present a double self-portrait in her painting *The Two Fridas* (1939)? Why did Ava DuVernay open her film *Selma* (2014) with Dr. Martin Luther King Jr.'s acceptance of the Nobel Peace Prize in

1964? To answer such questions, humanistic scholars collect evidence, and in the humanities, evidence often originates from texts.

Many students confess to struggling with the process of writing a good thesis statement. A key to overcoming this hurdle is to realize that a good thesis statement comes first from asking thoughtful questions about a text and searching for answers to those questions through observation.

Examples of Research Questions and Corresponding Thesis Statements

Research Question	What does the recurring motif of Janie's hair represent in her journey throughout Zora Neale Hurston's *Their Eyes Were Watching God?*
Thesis Statement	In Zora Neale Hurston's *Their Eyes Were Watching God*, Janie's hair represents three distinct stages—from innocence to conflict to experience—that parallel her development of identity and voice throughout the novel.
Research Question	What is the significance of light and dark in John Gast's *American Progress?*
Thesis Statement	John Gast's 1872 painting *American Progress* reflects the nineteenth-century American idea of manifest destiny in its depiction of settlers from the east bringing the light of "civilization" to the west.

Once you have carefully observed a text, gathered thorough notes, and developed a content/form-response grid as discussed earlier in the chapter, you will be in a great position to begin brainstorming and drafting research questions. We encourage open-ended questions (*why, what,* and *how*) as opposed to closed questions (questions that can be answered with a *yes* or *no*) as a pivotal step before drafting a thesis statement. Scholars in the humanities often start by asking questions that begin with *why*, but you might also consider questions that begin with *what* and *how*.

Connect 7.5   **Developing *Why, What,* and *How* Questions**

The process of asking questions after conducting a close reading of a text is part of interpretation, and it can help you generate effective research questions to guide the development of a thesis. In this activity, we walk you through developing research questions from your notes on "The Story of an Hour." You could easily follow these steps after observing another kind of text as well.

1. Review your notes on "The Story of an Hour," and develop three questions about the story's content and form using *why* as a starter word.

2. Next, develop three questions using *what* as your starter word. Try to focus your questions on different aspects of the story's characters, language, style, literary techniques, or narrative perspective.

3. Then use *how* as a starter word to develop three more questions. Again, write your questions with a different aspect of the story as the central focus for each—that is, don't just repeat the same questions from your *what* or *why* list by inserting *how* instead. Think of different questions that can help address the story's meaning.

Try sharing your questions with a fellow student and discuss which ones might lead to promising thesis statements to ground an extended interpretation. Effective research questions are ones that can be answered with evidence and not just feelings or emotions.

Developing Effective Thesis Statements

The thesis statement, or the central claim, asserts *what* the author intends to prove, and it may also provide insight into *how* it will be proven. Providing both of these elements in a thesis allows writers to establish a blueprint for the structure of their entire argument—what we describe as a complex thesis statement in Chapter 4. Based on the thesis alone, a reader can determine the central claim and see how the writer intends to go about supporting it.

In the following example, Sarah Ray provides a thesis for her interpretation of Chopin's "The Story of an Hour" that responds to her original research question about the story: "How does Mrs. Mallard's marriage function in the story?" Notice that she includes clues as to how she will prove her claim in the thesis statement itself:

> Through Mrs. Mallard's emotional development and the concomitant juxtaposition of the vitality of nature to the repressive indoors, Chopin exposes the role of marriage in the oppression of one's true self and desires.

Blueprint for how Sarah will prove her claim

Sarah's interpretation of the story, provided as a clear claim

Although it's not uncommon for thesis statements in humanistic scholarship to remain implied, as opposed to being stated explicitly, most interpretations explicitly assert a claim close to the beginning of the argument, often in the introductory paragraph (or, in a longer piece, paragraphs). Thesis statements may appear as single-sentence statements or may span multiple sentences.

Another example of a thesis statement comes from a scholarly article by Christopher Collins, "Final Meals: The Theater of Capital Punishment." Collins explicitly poses a research question: "If food functions as 'a way of getting at some essential truth about each other,' what truths are revealed in the final meals of inmates?" (p. 89). He then provides a plan for how he will develop his analysis of the final meals of inmates as part of the unifying thesis of his article:

> This article analyzes the prisoner's final meals through three perspectives. Dwight Conquergood provides a framework for understanding executions as theatrical performance. Terri Gordon complements Conquergood's work by explaining the final meals within the sacred, the spectacle, and the profane. Finally, Barbara Kirshenblatt-Gimblett provides a method for understanding food as a performance medium. This article aims to achieve an understanding of food as a performance object in order to understand the link between the condemned and the system of capital punishment. (p. 89)

Collins provides a roadmap for how he will develop his argument, building off the scholarship of others to establish his own argument.

Collins offers a clear statement of thesis.

When you develop your own thesis statements, you will want to focus on the content as much as the form. The following checklist will help you determine if you have a strong thesis:

- **Is the thesis debatable?** Claims in the humanities are propositions, not statements of fact. For example, the assertion that "The Story of an Hour" deals with a wife's response to the news of her husband's death is a fact. It is not, therefore, debatable and will not be a very useful thesis. If, however, we assert that the wife's response to her husband's death demonstrates some characteristic of her relationship with her husband and with the institution of marriage, then we're proposing a debatable claim. This is a proposition we can try to prove, instead of a fact that is already obviously true.

- **Is the thesis significant?** Claims about texts should offer substantial insight into the meaning of the artifacts. They should account for as much of the artifacts as possible and avoid reducing their complexity. Have you paid attention to all of the evidence you collected, and have you looked at it in context? Are you considering all of the possible elements of the text that might contribute to your interpretation?

- **Does the thesis contribute to an ongoing scholarly conversation?** Effective thesis statements contribute to an ongoing conversation without repeating what others have already said about the text. How does the claim extend, contradict, or affirm other interpretations of the text?

Connect 7.6   **Drafting Thesis Statements**

Review the questions and responses you drafted in Connect 7.5, "Developing *Why*, *What*, and *How* Questions." Structure your responses to any two of your questions as separate thesis statements, using an "I" statement in the following form:

Template: **By examining** *x* (*x* = the evidence you have found), **I argue that** *y* (*y* = your claim).

Example: **By examining Mrs. Mallard's emotional development and the juxtaposition of the vitality of nature to the repressive indoors in the story, I argue that Chopin exposes the role of marriage in the story to show the oppression of a person's true self and desires.**

Note that some scholars avoid using "I" in thesis statements. You can always edit the thesis statement later to take out "I" if your instructor discourages its use. We find that even if the "I" will need to be changed, it helps when figuring out what you want to say to include yourself in the statement.

- Now test the appropriateness of your claim by asking: Is the thesis debatable? Is the thesis significant? Does the thesis contribute to an ongoing scholarly conversation?

- Once you've analyzed Chopin's story and constructed two separate thesis statements, consider sharing them with a classmate, identifying strengths and weaknesses in both. How is your claim both argumentative and significant? How many direct quotes from the story would help support your points? Which of the two thesis statements offers a more significant insight into the story's meaning?

Thesis-Driven Structural Templates

Many students learn to write academic arguments in primary and secondary school following a template known as the five-paragraph essay. This template places a thesis, or claim, near the beginning of an argument (often at the end of an introductory paragraph), devotes the body of the essay to supporting the thesis, and then offers a final paragraph of conclusion that connects all the parts of the argument by summarizing the main points and reminding readers of the argument's overall significance.

While the premise behind this structure is based on some conventions of the humanities, following the template too closely could get you into trouble. For example, not every thesis has three points to prove. And sometimes an introduction needs to be longer than one paragraph. Instead, we suggest a flexible thesis-driven essay structure that guides the reader through the parts of your argument with appropriate transitional words and phrases.

● **A Flexible Thesis-Driven Template**   The elements of a thesis-driven template that tend to be consistent in scholarship in the humanities are the following:

- Thesis statements generally appear toward the beginning of the argument in an introduction that explains the scope and importance of the topic.
- The body of the argument presents evidence gathered from the text to support the thesis.
- The conclusion connects the parts of the argument together to reinforce the thesis, summarizing the argument's important elements and reminding readers of its overall significance.

A template such as this one can provide a useful place to start as you organize your argument, but be careful not to allow a template to restrict your argument by oversimplifying your understanding of how humanistic scholars structure their writing.

● **Paragraphs and Transitions**   In arguments in the humanities, paragraphs tend to link back to the thesis by developing a reason and providing evidence. The paragraphs are often connected through **transitional words and phrases** (e.g., *similarly, in addition, in contrast, for example*) that guide readers by signaling shifts between and among the parts of an argument. These words and phrases help the reader understand the order in which the reasons are presented and how one paragraph connects to the preceding one. Notice, for example, how Christopher Collins moves between ideas using the transitional phrase "On the other end of the spectrum" (underlined here) in this excerpted section of his article:

> Thomas Grasso, executed by Oklahoma in 1995, wanted Spaghetti-Os. . . . Instead Grasso received a can of Franco-American spaghetti. Grasso complained in his final statement "I did not get my Spaghetti-Os. I got spaghetti. I want the press to know this!" Grasso, in his last words, found it extremely important to communicate that the proper ritual of the final meal, and thus of the execution, was not followed. The final meal request form serves as a behavioral performance of food.

On the other end of the spectrum, some individuals use the request slip as a metaphorical performance. Alyda Faber, drawing on Catherine Bell's *Ritual Theory, Ritual Practice*, discusses the potential political weight of such food performances. . . . The state uses the final meal ritual as an embodied practice that orders and illustrates its sovereignty. (p. 96)

● **Titles**   Scholars in the humanities value the artistic and creative use of language, and titles of their work often reflect that value. In contrast to articles in the social sciences and the natural sciences, which often have descriptive titles that directly state the topic of study and leave little room for interpretation, articles in the humanities tend to have titles that play with language in creative ways, sometimes incorporating quotations from a text in an interesting way. Such titles are meant to engage readers by piquing their interests. Occasionally, such creative titles may have the effect of entertaining an intended audience. Humanistic scholars are also notorious for their love of subtitles. Here are a few examples:

Reforming Bodies: Self-Governance, Anxiety, and Cape Colonial Architecture in South Africa, 1665–1860

Resident Franchise: Theorizing the Science Fiction Genre, Conglomerations, and the Future of Synergy

> ### Connect 7.7   Observing Structural Features in the Humanities
>
> Although we've discussed some common structural features for scholarly articles in the humanities, we'd like to stress that writers might choose to depart from these conventional expectations if they don't serve the writers' particular aims. Find a scholarly article from the humanities, and examine it in terms of these structural features. If the article deviates from the conventions we've described, what might be the writer's reasons?
>
> - **Title**   Does the title seek to entertain, to challenge, or to intrigue the reader?
> - **Thesis**   Can you identify a clear statement of thesis? Where is it located? Does the thesis explicitly or implicitly provide a "blueprint" for guiding the reader through the rest of the paper?
> - **Paragraphs and Transitions**   Look closely at four successive body paragraphs in the paper. Explain how each paragraph relates to the paper's guiding thesis. How does the writer transition between each of the paragraphs?

Language Conventions in the Humanities

Writing in the humanities generally follows several conventions of language use that might sound familiar because they're often taught in English classes. Keep in mind, though, that even though these conventions are common in the humanities, they aren't necessarily conventional in other disciplinary areas.

Descriptive and Rhetorical Language

Writers in the humanities often use language that is creative or playful, not only when producing artistic texts but sometimes also when writing interpretations of texts. For example, you might notice that writing in the humanities uses figurative language and rhetorical devices (similes, metaphors, and alliteration, for example) more often than in other disciplines. Because writers in the humanities are studying texts so closely, they often pay similarly close attention to the text they're creating, and they take great care to choose precise, and sometimes artistic, language. In many cases, the language not only conveys information; it also engages in rhetorical activity of its own.

Active Voice

Writing in the humanities tends to privilege the use of the active voice rather than the passive voice. Sentences written in the **active voice** clearly state the subject of the sentence, the agent, as the person or thing doing the action. By contrast, the **passive voice** inverts the structure of the sentence, obscuring or eliminating mention of the agent. Let's look at three simple examples.

Active Voice: The girl chased the dog.

Passive Voice (agent obscured): The dog was chased by the girl.

Passive Voice (agent not mentioned): The dog was chased.

In the first example, the girl is the subject of the sentence and the person (the agent) doing the action—chasing. In the second sentence, the girl is still there, but her presence is less prominent because the dog takes the subject's position at the beginning of the sentence. In the final sentence, the girl is not mentioned at all.

Now let's look at an example from a student paper in the humanities to understand why active voice is usually preferred. In her interpretation of "The Story of an Hour," Sarah Ray writes this sentence in the introduction, using active voice:

Active Voice: Kate Chopin presents a completely different view of marriage in "The Story of an Hour," published in 1894.

If Sarah were to write the sentence in the passive voice, eliminating the agent, it would look like this:

Passive Voice: A completely different view of marriage is presented in "The Story of an Hour," published in 1894.

In this case, the active voice is preferred because it gives credit to the author, Kate Chopin, who created the story and the character. Scholars in the humanities value giving credit to the person doing the action, conducting the study, or creating a text. Active voice also provides the clearest, most transparent meaning—another aspect of writing that is valued in the humanities.

Hedging

In the humanities, writers sometimes *hedge*, or qualify, the claims that they make when interpreting a text, called **hedging**, even though they are generally quite fervent about defending their arguments once established. In fact, the beginning of the sentence that you just read contains not one but three **hedges**. Take a look:

> In the humanities, writers sometimes *hedge*, or qualify, the claims that they make when interpreting a text.

Each underlined phrase limits the scope of the claim in a way that is important to improve accuracy and to allow for other possibilities. In contrast, consider the next claim:

> Writers hedge the claims that they make.

If we had stated our claim that way, not only would it not be true, but you would immediately begin to think of exceptions. Even if we had limited the claim to writers in the humanities, you still might find exceptions to it. As the original sentence is written, we've allowed for other possibilities while still identifying a predominant trend in humanities writing. Hedging phrases include *they tend to*, *they might*, *it appears that*, and *it is likely to*, along with modifiers such as *some*, *often*, *perhaps*, and *maybe*.

Humanistic scholars hedge their claims for several reasons. The disciplines of the humanities do not tend to claim objectivity or neutrality in their research as other disciplines do, so they allow for other interpretations of and perspectives on texts. As an example, take a look at the opening and closing sentences of the first paragraph of Dale Jacobs's "Conclusion" from his article printed earlier in the chapter:

> My process of making meaning from these pages of *Polly and the Pirates* is one of many meanings within the matrix of possibilities inherent in the text. (par. 16)
>
> Structure and agency interact so that we are influenced by design conventions and grammars as we read but are not determined by them; though we are subject to the same set of grammars, my reading of the text is not necessarily the same as that of someone else. (par. 16)

In these sentences, Jacobs not only hedges the interpretation he offers, but he explicitly states that there are many possible meanings of the text he has just analyzed.

Insider's View
Cristina Ramírez, Writing Studies Scholar, on Writing in the Humanities

COURTESY OF CRISTINA RAMÍREZ

"I've seen a lot of different kinds of writing in the humanities. Personal essays are common, and scholars in my field often relate their work to their personal experience. Humanities scholars will also draw on familial knowledge about their culture and heritage. I've also seen poetry in scholarly writing in the humanities, sometimes on its own and sometimes embedded within a larger scholarly piece that is multi-genre. Other scholars will use song lyrics, recipes, photographs, or other media in their work in a multi-genre approach. I remember a humanities article I read that had a photograph of all of the shoes collected at the Mexico-U.S. border. Using these kinds of media in scholarly work can evoke an emotional response in the reader.

"Writing in the humanities is becoming more accessible, and academics are beginning to understand that they are not only writing to the academy, but they are also writing with and to the communities and people they are writing about. For example, I just wrote a chapter in a book titled *Revolutionary Women of Texas and Mexico: Portraits of Soldaderas, Saints, and Subversives*. All of the chapters in the book are written so that they are very accessible. The language did not sound as academic and jargon-filled as scholarly writing sometimes can; even though the book was published by a university press, it was clearly written for a broader audience, and the language used in the chapters was embedded in the communities that the chapters were written for and with."

Connect 7.8   Observing Language Features in the Humanities

Continue your examination of the article you selected for Connect 7.7, using the questions below as a guide. If the article deviates from the conventions we've described, what might be the writer's reasons?

- **Descriptive and Rhetorical Language**   Is the language of the text meant only to convey information, or does it engage in rhetorical activity? In other words, do similes, metaphors, or other rhetorical devices demonstrate attempts to be creative with language?

- **Voice**   Is the voice of the text primarily active or passive?

- **Hedging**   Is there evidence of hedging? That is, does the writer qualify statements with words and phrases such as *tend, suggest, may, it is probable that,* or *it is reasonable to conclude that*? What is the significance of hedging?

Reference Conventions in the Humanities

Scholars in the humanities frequently cite the work of others in their scholarship, especially when supporting an interpretation of a text. They often quote the language from their primary sources exactly instead of summarizing or paraphrasing, because the exact words or details included in the primary source might be important to the argument.

Values Reflected in Citations

When humanistic scholars cite the work of other scholars, they show how their research contributes to ongoing conversations about a subject—whether they're agreeing with a previous interpretation, extending someone else's interpretation, or offering an alternative one. These citations can strengthen their own argument and provide direct support by showing that another scholar had a similar idea or by demonstrating how another scholar's ideas are incorrect, imprecise, or not fully developed.

As we mentioned in Chapter 5, you can integrate the work of others into your writing by paraphrasing, summarizing, or quoting directly. Scholars in the humanities use all these options, but they quote directly more often than scholars in other disciplines because the exact language or details from their primary sources are often important to their argument.

Take a look at this example from Collins's "Final Meals: The Theater of Capital Punishment." In it, Collins establishes a comparison ("A similar idea") between his own interpretation of prisoners' final meals and the work of another scholar, Bordo, whose ideas on anorexia are explored in a scholarly book by Deane Curtin and Lisa Heldke:

> The final meal serves to reinforce the dichotomy of body and mind through the supposed death of the body and continuation of the mind or soul. A similar idea can be found in Bordo's understanding of anorexia. Bordo notes that starvation of the body is motivated by the dream to be "without a body," to achieve "absolute purity, hyperintellectuality and transcendence of the flesh." The last meal is not a hunger for food as much as it is a gesture towards purity and transcendence of the flesh. (p. 98)

Most scholars in the humanities include references to the work of others early in their writing to establish what the focus and stance of their own research will be. Because abstracts appear in humanities scholarship less frequently than in social sciences and natural sciences research, the introduction to an article in the humanities provides a snapshot of how the researcher is positioning himself or herself in the ongoing conversation about an object of study.

As you read scholarship in the humanities, notice how frequently the text references or cites secondary sources in the opening paragraphs. Here is an example from the beginning of Dale Jacobs's article on teaching literacy through the use of comics (not included in the excerpt in this chapter). Jacobs situates his work historically among work published about comics in the 1950s, and he also references the research of other scholars who had already written about that history in more detail:

> Prior to their current renaissance, comics were often viewed, at best, as popular entertainment and, at worst, as a dangerous influence on youth. Such attitudes were certainly prevalent in the early 1950s when comics were at their most popular, with critics such as Fredric Wertham voicing the most strenuous arguments against comics in his 1954 book *Seduction of the Innocent* (for an extended discussion of this debate, see Dorrell, Curtis, and Rampal).

In these two sentences, Jacobs positions his work within that of other scholars, showing how it's connected to and distinct from it. Also, by citing the work of Dorrell, Curtis, and Rampal, Jacobs doesn't have to write a lengthy history about a period that's tangentially related to his argument but not central to it.

Documentation Styles: MLA and CMS

A few documentation styles are prevalent in the humanities, and those styles highlight elements of a source that are important in humanistic study. Many scholars in the humanities, especially in literature and languages, tend to follow the documentation style of the Modern Language Association (MLA). Scholars in history and some other disciplines of the humanities may rely on the *Chicago Manual of Style* (CMS). When using CMS, scholars can choose between two systems of citations: the notes and bibliography system or the author-date system. In the humanities, researchers generally use the notes and bibliography system, in which numbered footnotes or endnotes are used to cite sources, and then the full publication data for those sources is provided at the end of the paper, in a list alphabetically organized by author. This source list is referred to as "Works Cited" in MLA style and "Bibliography" in CMS.

The values of the humanities are reflected in their citation systems. In MLA, in-text citations appear in parenthetical references that include the author's last name and a page number, with no comma in between; for example: (Miller-Cochran et al. 139). If the author's name is included in the body of the sentence, then only the page number appears in parentheses.

The page number is included regardless of whether the cited passage was paraphrased, summarized, or quoted—unlike in other common styles like APA, where page numbers are usually given only for direct quotations. One reason for including the page number in the MLA in-text citation is that humanistic scholars highly value the original phrasing of an argument or passage and might want to look at the original source. The page number makes searching easy for the reader, facilitating the possibility of examining the original context of a quotation or the original language of something that was paraphrased or summarized.

CMS style also supports looking for the information in the original source by giving the citation information in a footnote on the same page as the referenced material. Additionally, CMS allows authors to include descriptive details in a footnote that provides more information about where a citation came from in a source.

For an example of a paper in MLA format, see Insider Example: Student Interpretation of a Literary Text (pp. 154–60). For a discussion of the elements of citations and Works Cited lists, see "Modern Language Association (MLA) Style" in the Appendix.

Connect 7.9   **Observing Reference Features in the Humanities**

Conclude your examination of the article you selected for Connect 7.7, using the questions below as a guide:

- **Engagement with Other Scholars**   Does the writer refer to other scholars' words or ideas? If so, in what ways? Are other scholars' words or ideas used to support the writer's argument, or do they serve to contrast with what the writer has to say? Does the writer quote directly from other writers?

- **Documentation**   Look closely at examples of how the writer cites the work of other scholars. What form of documentation applies? What type of information is valued?

Genres: Textual Interpretation

Similar to scholars in the social sciences and the natural sciences, scholars in the humanities often present their research at conferences and publish their work in journal articles and books. In some fields of the humanities, books are highly valued, and scholars here tend to work individually more frequently than scholars in the social sciences and the natural sciences. Also, many scholars in the humanities engage in creative work and might present it at an art installation, reading, or exhibit.

In this section, we offer the opportunity to analyze and practice one of the most common genres required of students in introductory-level courses in the humanities: textual interpretation, whether the text is a work of literature, art, film, music, theater, dance, or some other creative form of expression.

What Is the Rhetorical Context for This Genre?

A **textual interpretation** (also referred to as an "analysis") offers a close reading of a text that shows how the elements of the text work together to create meaning. While works of art such as literature, film, music, and visual art have multiple meanings and there is no one "right" interpretation of a text, a strong interpretation is insightful, convincing, and grounded in evidence derived from the text itself.

Students and scholars may compose a textual interpretation to come to a better understanding of a text and how it contributes to a larger understanding of the human experience. In college, students might be writing for their instructor and peers, and using the interpretation to apply what they are learning about the elements of an art form (such as *mise en scene* in film or *meter* in poetry) to a specific work. The writer can assume that their audience has seen, heard, or read the text being interpreted. A **textual interpretation** makes a clear claim about the object of study and may use evidence drawn from the interpretations of other scholars as support.

Strategies for Writing a Textual Interpretation

● **Observe closely and make notes in the way that works best for the medium you are exploring.** As you read, view, listen to, and/or study the text and make notes, consider the ways you are interacting with the text by creating a content/form-response grid: *What* are you learning, and *how* is the text itself shaping your experience of it?

● **Formulate a thesis.** Once your close reading is complete, formulate a thesis (or a claim) about the text. You'll need to provide evidence to support your thesis from the text itself. You might make your reader aware of how your claim about the work is different from that of other scholars, signaling what new insights you bring to the conversation. If you choose to situate your text in a historical context, you will need to do additional research to gather the facts.

● **Remember SLR as you draft and revise.** The Writing Project that follows suggests a structure for your interpretation. Apply what you've learned in this chapter about writing conventions in the humanities as you draft each section of your textual analysis. Focus on developing your interpretation and supporting your points in the first draft, and then use the revision to further clarify your points and work on style.

Writing Project	Textual Interpretation/Analysis

Your goal in this writing project is to offer an interpretation of a text or a set of texts for an audience of your peers. Begin by selecting a text or texts that you find particularly interesting, and then work through the process of close reading described in the chapter.

THE INTRODUCTION

The introductory paragraph of your paper should include information to help the audience understand what your argument is about: the title of the work and name of its creator, a few sentences of background information on the work and/or creator, and a thesis that makes a clear and insightful claim about the meaning of the work.

THE BODY

The body of the argument should present evidence gathered from the text to support the thesis. It should offer an analysis of the work, not simply a summary or description. Select the best evidence from your form/content grid, using quotes, images, paraphrases, and descriptions as appropriate. Each paragraph should make a point that advances the argument, with clear topic sentences and transitions that show the relationships among your ideas.

THE CONCLUSION

The conclusion should connect the parts of the argument together to reinforce the thesis, summarizing the argument's important elements and reminding readers of its overall significance.

TECHNICAL CONSIDERATIONS

Construct a Works Cited page in MLA format that includes the name of the work and any secondary sources you use. Be certain that you include in-text citations throughout your project whenever you quote, summarize, reference, or paraphrase information from source material.

....

Insider Example
Student Interpretation of a Literary Text

In the following essay, "Till Death Do Us Part: An Analysis of Kate Chopin's 'The Story of an Hour,'" Sarah Ray offers an interpretation of Chopin's story that relies on close observation of the text for support. Read her essay below, and pay particular attention to her thesis statement and to her use of evidence. Note how her thesis responds to the question, "How does Mrs. Mallard's marriage function in the story?" Sarah didn't use outside scholars to support her interpretation, so you could also consider how secondary sources might have provided additional support for her claim. ▶

Sarah Ray

Professor Stamper

ENG 101

10 April 2021

Till Death Do Us Part: An Analysis of Kate Chopin's

"The Story of an Hour"

The nineteenth century saw the publication of some of the most renowned romances in literary history, including the novels of Jane Austen and the Brontë sisters, Charlotte, Emily, and Anne. While their stories certainly have lasting appeal, they also inspired an unrealistic and sometimes unattainable ideal of joyful love and marriage. In this romanticized vision, a couple is merely two halves of a whole; one without the other compromises the happiness of both. The couple's lives, and even destinies, are so intertwined that neither individual worries about what personal desires and goals are being forsaken by commitment to the other. By the end of the century, in her "The Story of an Hour" (1894), Kate Chopin presents a completely different view of marriage. Through the perspective of a female protagonist, Louise Mallard, who believes her husband has just died, the author explores the more challenging aspects of marriage in a time when divorce was rare and disapproved of. Through Mrs. Mallard's emotional development and the concomitant juxtaposition of the vitality of nature to the repressive indoors, Chopin explores marriage as the oppression of one's true self and desires.

"The Story of an Hour" begins its critique of marriage by ending one, when the news of Brently Mallard's death is gently conveyed to his wife, Louise. Chopin then follows Mrs. Mallard's different emotional stages in response to her husband's death. When the news is initially broken to Louise, "[s]he did not hear the story as many women have heard the same, with a paralyzed inability to accept its significance"

FORM: Ray uses a common line from marriage vows to indirectly indicate that she will focus on the role of marriage in her interpretation.

CONTENT: Ray clearly states her thesis and provides a preview about how she will develop and support her claim.

CONTENT: In this paragraph, Ray develops the first part of her thesis, the stages of Mrs. Mallard's emotional development.

(Chopin, par. 3). She instead weeps suddenly and briefly, a "storm of grief" that passes as quickly as it had come (par. 3). This wild, emotional outburst and quick acceptance says a great deal about Louise's feelings toward her marriage. "[S]he had loved [her husband]—sometimes," but a reader may infer that Louise's quick acceptance implies that she has considered an early death for her spouse before (par. 15). That she even envisions such a dark prospect reveals her unhappiness with the marriage. She begins to see, and even desire, a future without her husband. This desire is expressed when Louise is easily able to see past her husband's death to "a long procession of years to come that would belong to her absolutely" (par. 13). Furthermore, it is unclear whether her "storm of grief" is genuine or faked for the benefit of the family members surrounding her. The "sudden, wild abandonment" with which she weeps almost seems like Louise is trying to mask that she does not react to the news as a loving wife would (par. 3). Moreover, the display of grief passes quickly; Chopin devotes only a single sentence to the action. Her tears are quickly succeeded by consideration of the prospects of a future on her own.

Chopin uses the setting to create a symbolic context for Louise's emotional outburst in response to the news of her husband's death. Louise is informed of Brently's death in the downstairs level of her home: "It was her sister Josephine who told her, in broken sentences; veiled hints that revealed in half concealing" (par. 2). No mention is made of windows, and the only portal that connects to the outside world is the door that admits the bearers of bad news. By excluding a link to nature, Chopin creates an almost claustrophobic environment to symbolize the oppression Louise feels from her marriage. It is no mistake that this setting plays host to Mrs. Mallard's initial emotional breakdown. Her desires have been suppressed

FORM: Ray primarily uses active voice to clarify who is doing the action in her sentences.

throughout her relationship, and symbolically, she is being suffocated by the confines of her house. Therefore, in this toxic atmosphere, Louise is only able to feel and show the emotions that are expected of her, not those that she truly experiences. Her earlier expression of "grief" underscores this disconnect, overcompensating for emotions that should come naturally to a wife who has just lost her husband, but that must be forced in Mrs. Mallard's case.

Chopin continues Mrs. Mallard's emotional journey only after she is alone and able to process her genuine feelings. After her brief display of grief has run its course, she migrates to her upstairs bedroom and sits in front of a window looking upon the beauty of nature. It is then and only then that Louise gives in not only to her emotions about the day's exploits, but also to those feelings she could only experience after the oppression of her husband died with him — dark desires barely explored outside the boundaries of her own mind, if at all. They were at first foreign to her, but as soon as Louise began to "recognize this thing that was approaching to possess her ... she [strove] to beat it back with her will" (par. 10). Even then, after the source of her repression is gone, she fights to stifle her desires and physical reactions. The habit is so engrained that Louise is unable to release her emotions for fear of the unknown, of that which has been repressed for so long. However, "her bosom rose and fell tumultuously...When she abandoned herself a little whispered word escaped her slightly parted lips. She said it over and over under her breath: 'free, free, free!' ... Her pulses beat fast, and the coursing blood warmed and relaxed every inch of her body" (pars. 10, 11). When she's allowed to experience them, Louise's feelings and desires provide a glimpse into a possible joyous future without her husband, a future where "[t]here would be no powerful will bending hers in that blind persistence with which men

FORM: Ray uses transitions between paragraphs that indicate her organization and connect different ideas.

and women believe they have a right to impose" (par. 14). Her marriage is over, and Louise appears finally to be able to liberate her true identity and look upon the future with not dread but anticipation.

The author's setting for this scene is crucial in the development of not only the plot but also her critique of marriage. Chopin sought to encapsulate the freedom Louise began to feel in her room with this scene's depiction of nature. For example, Chopin describes the view from Louise's bedroom window with language that expresses its vitality: "She could see in the open square before her house the tops of trees that were all aquiver with the new spring life" (par. 5). She goes on to say, "The delicious breath of rain was in the air. In the street below a peddler was crying his wares . . . and countless sparrows were twittering in the eaves" (par. 5). The very adjectives and phrases used to describe the outdoors seem to speak of bustling activity and life. This is in stark contrast to the complete lack of vivacity in the description of downstairs.

The language used in the portrayal of these contrasting settings is not the only way Chopin strives to emphasize the difference between the two. She also uses the effect these scenes have on Mrs. Mallard to convey their meaning and depth. On the one hand, the wild, perhaps faked, emotional outburst that takes place in the stifling lower level of the house leaves Louise in a state of "physical exhaustion that haunted her body and seemed to reach into her soul" (par. 4). On the other hand, Louise "[drank] in a very elixir of life through that open window" of her bedroom through which nature bloomed (par. 18). Because the author strove to symbolize Mrs. Mallard's marriage with the oppressive downstairs and her impending life without her husband with the open, healing depiction of nature, Chopin suggests that spouses are sometimes better off

FORM: When making assumptions about the author's intentions, Ray sometimes uses hedging words—in this case, "seem to."

without each other because marriage can take a physical toll on a person's well-being while the freedom of living for no one but one's self breathes life into even the most burdened wife. After all, "[w]hat could love, the unsolved mystery, count for in face of this possession of self-assertion" felt by Mrs. Mallard in the wake of her emancipation from oppression (par. 15)?

Chopin goes on to emphasize the healing capabilities and joy of living only for one's self by showing the consequences of brutally taking it all away, in one quick turn of a latchkey. With thoughts of her freedom of days to come, "she carried herself unwittingly like a goddess of Victory. She clasped her sister's waist, and together they descended the stairs" (par. 20). Already Chopin is preparing the reader for Mrs. Mallard's looming fate. Not only is she no longer alone in her room with the proverbial elixir of life pouring in from the window, but also she is once again sinking into the oppression of the downstairs, an area that embodies all marital duties as well as the suffocation of Louise's true self and desires. When Brently Mallard enters the house slightly confused but unharmed, the loss of her newly found freedom is too much for Louise's weak heart to bear. Chopin ends the story with a hint of irony: "When the doctors came they said she had died of heart disease—of joy that kills" (par. 23). It may be easier for society to accept that Mrs. Mallard died of joy at seeing her husband alive, but in all actuality, it was the violent death of her future prospects and the hope she had allowed to blossom that sent Louise to the grave. Here lies Chopin's ultimate critique of marriage: when there was no other viable escape, only death could provide freedom from an oppressive marriage. By killing Louise, Chopin solidifies this ultimatum and also suggests that even death is kinder when the only other option is the slow and continuous addition of the crushing weight of marital oppression.

Ray 6

In "The Story of an Hour," Kate Chopin challenges the typical, romanticized view of love and marriage in the era in which she lived. She chooses to reveal some of the sacrifices one must make in order to bind oneself to another in matrimony. Chopin develops these critiques of marriage through Louise Mallard's emotional responses to her husband's supposed death, whether it is a quick, if not faked, outburst of grief, her body's highly sexualized awakening to the freedoms to come, or the utter despair at finding that he still survives. These are not typical emotions for a "grieving" wife, and Chopin uses this stark contrast as well as the concomitant juxtaposition of nature to the indoors to further emphasize her critique. Louise Mallard may have died in the quest to gain independence from the oppression of her true self and desires, but now she is at least "[f]ree! Body and soul free!" (par. 16).

Ray 7

Work Cited

Chopin, Kate. "The Story of an Hour." 1894. Ann Woodlief's Web Study Texts, www.vcu.edu/engweb/webtexts/hour.

- **In the humanities, scholars seek to understand and interpret human experience.** To do so, they often create, analyze, and interpret texts.

- **Scholars in the humanities often conduct close readings of texts** to interpret and make meaning from them, and they might draw on a particular theoretical perspective to ask questions about those texts.

- **Keeping a content/form-response grid can help you track important elements of a text** and your response to them as you complete a close reading.

- **Writing in the humanities often draws on the interpretations of others,** either as support or to position an interpretation within prior scholarship.

- **Arguments in the humanities typically follow a thesis-driven *structure*.** They often begin with a thesis statement that asserts what the author intends to prove, and it may also provide insight into how the author will prove it. Each section of the argument should provide support for the thesis.

- **Rhetorical language, active voice, and hedging are uses of *language*** that characterizes writing in the humanities.

- **MLA and CMS styles are commonly used for *reference*** in the fields of the humanities.

- **Textual interpretation is a common *genre*** in the humanities.

8

Reading and Writing in the Social Sciences

Scholars in the fields of the **social sciences** study human behavior and inter-action along with the systems and social structures we create to organize our world. Their work helps us understand why we do what we do as well as how processes (political, economic, personal, etc.) contribute to our lives. The social sciences encompass a broad area of academic inquiry that comprises numerous fields of study. These include sociology, psychology, anthropology, economics, communication studies, and political science, among others.

Maybe you've observed a friend or family member spiral into addictive or self-destructive behavior, and you've struggled to understand how it happened. Maybe you've spent time wondering how cliques were formed and maintained among students in your high school, or how friends are typically chosen. Perhaps larger social problems like poverty or famine concern you the most. If you've ever stopped to consider any of these kinds of issues, then you've already begun to explore the world of the social sciences.

As a social scientist, you might study issues like therapy options for autism, the effects of racism on people of color, peer pressure, substance abuse, social networking websites, stress, or commu-nication practices and gender equality. You might study family counseling techniques or the effects of divorce on teens. Or perhaps you might wonder (as the authors of examples in this chapter do) about the effects of differing educational environments on student satisfaction and success. Your work would make a difference in peo-ple's lives by informing practices, therapies, and policies that could alleviate social problems.

Whatever the case may be, if you're interested in studying human behavior and understanding why we do what we do, you'll want to consider further how social scientists conduct research and how they present their results in writing. As in all the academic domains, progress in the social sciences rests upon researchers' pri-mary skills at making observations of the world around them.

ANDREA TSURUMI

In this chapter, you'll look at some of the observational methods used by social scientists and see how their ways of researching are reflected in their academic writing.

Connect 8.1   **Observing Behavior**

For this activity, pick a place to sit and observe people. You can choose a place that you enjoy going to regularly, but make sure you can observe and take notes without being interrupted or distracted. Try to avoid places where you might feel compelled to engage in conversation with people you know.

For ten minutes, freewrite about the people around you and what they're doing. Look for the kinds of interactions and engagements that characterize their behavior. Then draft some questions that you think a social scientist observing the same people might ask about them.

For example, if you wrote about behaviors you observed at a public library, you might draft questions such as these: How are people seated around the space in the library? What does the seating arrangement look like? Are some places to sit more popular than others? What different types of activities are people doing in the library? Are people interacting with one another, and, if so, how? How are they positioned when they interact? What do you notice about the volume of their voices? What happens if someone (a child, perhaps) disrupts that volume?

See how many different behaviors, people, and interactions you can observe and how many questions you can generate. You might do this activity in the same place with a partner and then compare notes. What did you or your partner find in common? What did you each observe that was unique? Why do you think you noticed the things you did? What was the most interesting thing you observed?

Research in the Social Sciences

The social sciences comprise a diverse group of academic fields that aim to understand human behavior and systems. But despite the differences in the types of behavior they study and the theories that inform their work, we can link various disciplines in the social sciences and the values they share by considering how social scientists conduct and report their research.

The Role of Theory in the Social Sciences

Unlike in the natural sciences, where research often takes place in a laboratory setting under controlled conditions, research in the social sciences is necessarily "messier." The reason is fairly simple: human beings and the systems they organize cannot generally be studied in laboratory conditions, where variables are controlled. For this reason, social scientists do not generally establish fixed laws or argue for absolute truths, as natural scientists sometimes do. For instance, while natural scientists are able to argue, with certainty, that a water molecule contains two atoms of hydrogen and one of oxygen, social scientists cannot claim to know the absolute fixed nature of a person's psychology (why a person does what she does in any particular instance, for example) or that of a social system or problem (why homelessness persists, for instance).

Much social science research is therefore based on theories of human behavior and human systems, which are propositions that scholars use to explain specific phenomena. Theories can be evaluated on the basis of their ability to explain why or how or when a phenomenon occurs, and they generally result from research that has been replicated time and again to confirm their accuracy, appropriateness, and usefulness. Still, it's important to understand that theories are not laws; they are not absolute, fixed, or perfect explanations. Instead, social science theories are always being refined as research on particular social phenomena develops. The study by Rathunde and Csikszentmihalyi used as an example later in the chapter, for instance, makes use of goal theory and optimal experience theory as part of the research design to evaluate the type of middle school environment that best contributes to students' education.

Research Questions and Hypotheses

As we've noted throughout this book, research questions are typically formulated on the basis of observations. In the social sciences, such observations focus on human behavior, human systems, and/or the interactions between the two. Observations of a social phenomenon can give rise to questions about how a phenomenon operates or what effects it has on people or how it could be changed to improve individuals' well-being. For example, in their social science study "'Under the Radar': Educators and Cyberbullying in Schools," W. Cassidy, K. Brown, and M. Jackson (2012) offer the following as guiding research questions for their investigation:

> Our study of educators focused on three research questions: Do they [educators] consider cyberbullying a problem at their school and how familiar are they with the extent and impact among their students? What policies and practices are in place to prevent or counter cyberbullying? What solutions do they have for encouraging a kinder online world? (p. 522)

Research that is designed to inform a theory of human behavior or to provide data that contributes to a fuller understanding of some social or political structure (i.e., to answer a social science research question) also often begins with the presentation of a hypothesis. As we saw in Chapter 4, a **hypothesis** is a testable proposition that provides an answer or predicts an outcome in response to the research question(s) at hand. Generally, a hypothesis is formed based on prior knowledge, research, or experience that would help the researcher predict the outcome of a study. C. Kerns and K. Ko (2009) present the following hypothesis, or predicted outcome, for their social science study "Exploring Happiness and Performance at Work." The researchers make a prediction concerning what they believed their research would show before presenting their findings later in their research report:

> The intent of this analysis was to review how happiness and performance related to each other in this workplace. It is the authors' belief that for performance to be sustained in an organization, individuals and groups within that organization need to experience a threshold level of happiness. It is difficult for unhappy individuals and work groups to continue performing at high levels without appropriate leadership intervention. (p. 5)

It's important to note that not all social science reports include a statement of hypothesis. Some social science research establishes its focus by presenting the questions that guide researchers' inquiry into a particular phenomenon instead of establishing a hypothesis.

Hypotheses differ from *thesis statements*, which are more commonly associated with arguments in the humanities. While thesis statements offer researchers' final conclusions on a topic or issue, hypothesis statements offer a predicted outcome. The proposition expressed in a hypothesis may be either accepted or rejected based on the results of the research. For example, a team of educational researchers might hypothesize that teachers' use of open-ended questioning increases students' level of participation in class. However, the researchers would not be able to confirm or reject such a hypothesis until the completion of their research.

Connect 8.2   Developing Hypotheses

- For five minutes, brainstorm *social science* topics or issues that have affected your life. One approach is to consider issues that are causing you stress in your life right now. Examples might include peer pressure, academic performance, substance abuse, dating, or a relative's cancer treatment.

- Once you have a list of topics, focus on one that you believe has had the greatest impact on you personally. Generate a list of possible research questions concerning the topic that, if answered, would offer you a greater understanding of it. Examples: What triggers most people to try their first drink of alcohol? What types of therapies are most effective for working with children on the autism spectrum? What kinds of technology actually aid in student learning?

- Now propose a hypothesis, or testable proposition, as an answer to one of the research questions you've posed. For example, if your research question is "What triggers most people to try their first drink of alcohol?" then your hypothesis might be "Peer pressure generally causes most people to try their first drink of alcohol, especially for those who try their first drink before reaching the legal drinking age."

Methods

Research in the diverse fields of the social sciences is, as you probably suspect, quite varied, and social scientists collect data to answer their research questions or test their hypotheses in several different ways. Their choice of methods is directly influenced by the kinds of questions they ask in any particular instance, as well as by their own disciplinary backgrounds. In his Insider's View, Kevin Rathunde highlights the connection between the kinds of research questions a social scientist asks and the particular methods the researcher uses to answer those questions.

Insider's View
Psychologist Kevin Rathunde on Research Questions

COURTESY OF KEVIN RATHUNDE

"I have strong interests in how people experience their lives and what helps them stay interested, engaged, and on a path of lifelong learning and development. I tend to ask questions about the quality of life and experience. How are students experiencing their time in class? When are they most engaged? How does being interested affect the learning process? How can parents and teachers create conditions in homes and families that facilitate interest?

"The fields of developmental psychology and educational psychology are especially important to my work. The questions I ask, therefore, are framed the way a developmental or educational psychologist might ask them. Social scientists from other disciplines would probably look at the same topic (i.e., human engagement and interest) in a different way. My daughter is studying anthropology in graduate school. She would probably approach this topic from a cultural perspective. Where I might design a study using questionnaires that are administered in family or school contexts, she might focus on interviews and cultural frameworks that shed light on the meaning and organization of educational institutions. Although my research is primarily quantitative and uses statistical analysis to interpret the results, I have also used a variety of qualitative techniques (i.e., interviews and observations) over the years. A good question is usually worth looking at from multiple perspectives."

We can group most of the research you're likely to encounter in the fields of the social sciences into three possible types: quantitative, qualitative, and mixed methods. Researchers make choices about which types of methods they will employ in any given situation based on the nature of their line of inquiry. A particular research question may very well dictate the methods used to answer that question. If you wanted to determine the number of homeless veterans in a specific city, for instance, then collecting numerical, or quantitative, data would likely suffice to answer that question. However, if you wanted to know what factors affect the rates of homelessness among veterans in your community, then you would need to do more than tally the number of homeless veterans. You would need to collect a different type of data to help construct an answer—perhaps responses to surveys or interview questions.

● **Quantitative Methods**   Quantitative studies include those that rely on collecting numerical data and performing statistical analyses to reveal findings in research. Basic statistical data, like those provided by *means* (averages), *modes* (most often occurring value), and *medians* (middle values), are fundamental to quantitative social science research. More sophisticated statistical procedures commonly used in professional quantitative studies include correlations, chi-square tests, analysis of variance (ANOVA), and multivariate analysis of variance (MANOVA), as well as regression model testing, just to name a few. Not all statistical procedures are appropriate in all situations, however, so researchers must carefully select procedures based on the nature of their data and the kinds of findings they seek. Researchers who engage in advanced statistical procedures as part of their methods are typically highly skilled in such procedures. At the very least, these researchers consult or work in cooperation with statisticians to design their studies and/or to analyze their data.

You may find, in fact, that a team of researchers collaborating on a social science project often includes individuals who are also experienced statisticians. Obviously, we don't expect you to be familiar with the details of statistical procedures, but it's important that you be able to notice when researchers rely on statistical methods to test their hypotheses and to inform their results.

Also, take note of how researchers incorporate discussion of such methods into their writing. In the following example, we've highlighted a few elements in the reporting that you'll want to notice when reading social science studies that make use of statistical procedures:

- **Procedures**   What statistical procedures are used?
- **Variables**   What variables are examined in the procedures?
- **Results**   What do the statistical procedures reveal?
- **Participants**   From whom are the data collected, and how are those individuals chosen?

In their study, Rathunde and Csikszentmihalyi report on the statistical procedures they used to examine different types of schools:

> The first analysis compared the main motivation and quality-of-experience variables across school type (Montessori vs. traditional) and grade level (sixth vs. eighth) using a two-way MANCOVA with parental education, gender, and ethnic background as covariates. Significant differences were found for school context (Wilks's lambda = .84, $F(5, 275) = 10.84$, $p < .001$), indicating that students in the two school contexts reported differences in motivation and quality of experience. After adjusting for the

Variables examined, participants or populations involved in the study, and statistical procedure employed— MANCOVA, or a multivariate analysis of covariance—are identified.

Results of the statistical procedure are identified.

covariates, the multivariate eta squared indicated that 17 percent of the variance of the dependent variables was associated with the school context factor. The omnibus test for grade level was not significant (Wilks's lambda = .99, $F(5, 275) = .68, p = .64$) indicating that students in sixth and eighth grade reported similar motivation and quality of experience. Finally, the omnibus test for the interaction of school context x grade level was not significant (Wilks's lambda = .97, $F(5, 275) = 2.02, p = .08$). None of the multivariate tests for the covariates—parental education, gender, and ethnic background—reached the .05 level. (p. 357)

● **Qualitative Methods**   Qualitative studies generally rely on language, observation, and reporting of individual human experiences to reveal findings in research. Research reports often communicate these methods through the form of a study's results, which rely on in-depth narrative reporting. Methods for collecting data in qualitative studies include interviews, document analysis, surveys, and observations.

We can see examples of these methods put into practice in Barbara Allen's "Environmental Justice, Local Knowledge, and After-Disaster Planning in New Orleans" (2007), published in the academic social science journal *Technology and Society*. In this example, we've highlighted a few elements in the reporting that you'll want to notice when reading qualitative research methods:

- **Method**   What method of data collection is used?

- **Data**   What data are gathered from that method?

- **Results**   What are the results? What explanation do the researchers provide for the data, or what meaning do they find in the data?

- **Participants**   From whom are the data collected, and how are these individuals chosen?

| |
Participants — | Six months after the hurricane I contacted public health officials and research-ers, many of whom were reluctant to talk. One who did talk asked that I did
Data-collection method: interview — | not use her name, but she made some interesting observations. According to my informant, health officials were in a difficult position. Half a year after the devastation, only 25% of the city's residents had returned; a year after the storm, that number rose to about 40%. Negative publicity regarding public
Data, followed by explanation or meaning of data — | health issues would deter such repatriation, particularly families with children who had not returned in any large numbers to the city. The informant also told me to pursue the state public health websites where the most prominent worries were still smoking and obesity, not Hurricane Katrina. While the information on various public health websites did eventually reflect concerns
Data — | about mold, mildew, and other contamination, it was never presented as the health threat that independent environmental scientists, such as Wilma Subra, thought it was. (pp. 154–55)

. . .

About five months after Hurricane Katrina, I received an e-mail from a high school student living in a rural parish west of New Orleans along the Mississippi River (an area EJ advocates have renamed Cancer Alley). After Hurricane Katrina, an old landfill near her house was opened to receive waste and began emitting noxious odors. She took samples of the "black ooze" from the site and contacted the Louisiana Department of Environmental Quality, only to be told that the landfill was accepting only construction waste, and the smell she described was probably decaying gypsum board. I suspect her story will be repeated many times across south Louisiana as these marginal waste sites receive the debris from homes and businesses ruined by the hurricane. The full environmental impact of Hurricane Katrina's waste and its hastily designated removal sites will not be known for many years. (p. 155)

> Participant

> Explanation or meaning of data

● **Mixed Methods**   Studies that make use of both qualitative and quantitative data-collection techniques are generally referred to as mixed-methodology studies. Rathunde and Csikszentmihalyi's study used mixed methods: the authors report findings from both qualitative and quantitative data. In this excerpt, they share results from qualitative data they collected as they sought to distinguish among the types of educational settings selected for participation in their study:

> After verifying that the demographic profile of the two sets of schools was similar, the next step was to determine if the schools differed with respect to the five selection criteria outlined above. We used a variety of qualitative sources to verify contextual differences, including observations by the research staff; teacher and parent interviews; school newsletters, information packets, mission statements, and parent teacher handbooks; summaries from board of education and school council meetings; and a review of class schedules and textbook choices discussed in strategic plans. These sources also provided information about the level of middle grade reform that may or may not have been implemented by the schools and whether the label "traditional" was appropriate. (p. 64)

However, Rathunde and Csikszentmihalyi's central hypothesis, "that students in Montessori middle schools would report more positive perceptions of their school environment and their teachers, more often perceive their classmates as friends, and spend more time in collaborative and/or individual work rather than didactic educational formats such as listening to a lecture" (p. 68), was tested by using quantitative methods:

> The main analyses used two-way multivariate analysis of covariance (MANCOVA) with school type (Montessori vs. traditional) and grade level (sixth vs. eighth) as the two factors. Gender, ethnicity, and parental education were covariates in all of the analyses. Overall multivariate F tests (Wilks's lambda) were performed first on related sets of dependent variables. If an overall F test was significant, we performed univariate ANOVAs as follow-up tests to the MANCOVAs. If necessary, post hoc analyses were done using Bonferroni corrections to control for Type I errors. Only students with at least 15 ESM signals were included in the multivariate analyses, and follow-up ANOVAs used students who had valid scores on all of the dependent variables. (p. 68)

● **Addressing Bias**   Because social scientists study people and organizations, their research is considered more valuable when conducted within a framework that minimizes the influence of personal or researcher bias on the study's outcome(s). When possible, social scientists strive for objectivity (in quantitative research) or neutrality (in qualitative research) in their research. This means that researchers undertake all possible measures to reduce the influence of biases on their research. Bias is sometimes inevitable, however, so social science research places a high value on honesty and transparency in the reporting of data. Each of the methods outlined above requires social scientists to engage in rigorous procedures and checks (e.g., ensuring appropriate sample sizes and/or using multiple forms of qualitative data) to ensure that the influence of any biases is as limited as possible.

The IRB Process and Use of Human Subjects

All research, whether student or faculty initiated and directed, must treat its subjects, or participants, with the greatest of care and consider the ethical implications of all its procedures. Although institutions establish their own systems and procedures for verifying the ethical treatment of subjects, most of these include an **institutional review board (IRB)**, or a committee of individuals whose job is to review research proposals in light of ethical concerns for subjects and applicable laws. Such proposals typically include specific forms of documentation that identify a study's purpose; rigorously detail the research procedures to be followed; evaluate potential risks and rewards of a study, especially for study participants; and ensure (whenever possible) that participants are fully informed about a study and the implications of their participation in it.

We encourage you to learn more about the IRB process at your own institution and, when appropriate, to consider your own research in light of the IRB policies and procedures established for your institution. Many schools maintain informational, educational, and interactive websites. You'll notice similarities in the mission statements of institutional review boards from a number of colleges and universities, as the following examples illustrate:

> **Duke University:** To ensure the protection of human research subjects by conducting scientific and ethical review of research studies while providing leadership and education for the research community

> **George Washington University:** To support [the] research community in the conduct of innovative and ethical research by providing guidance, education, and oversight for the protection of human subjects

> **Maricopa County Community College District:** [T]o review all proposed research involving human subjects to ensure that subjects are treated ethically and that their rights and welfare are adequately protected

Structural Conventions in the Social Sciences

In light of the variety of research methods used by social scientists, it is not surprising that there are also a number of ways social scientists report their research findings. In this section, we turn to strategies of rhetorical analysis that help us examine how scholars in the social sciences communicate their research to one another. Understanding how certain writing conventions support the work of social scientists, we believe, can help foster your understanding of this academic domain more broadly. Recall that in Chapter 6 we introduced a three-part method for analyzing texts by examining the conventions of structure, language, and reference. This section will focus on structural conventions, and the sections that follow will address language and reference. Rather than trying to master the conventions of every type of writing in the social sciences, your goal is to understand the general principles underlying social science writing conventions and to practice applying an analytical framework to any writing assignment you encounter.

Aya Matsuda is a linguist and social science researcher at Arizona State University, where she studies the use of English as an international language, the integration of a "World Englishes" perspective into U.S. education, and the ways bilingual writers negotiate identity. In her Insider's View, Matsuda explains that she learned the conventions of writing as a social scientist, and more particularly as a linguist, "mostly through writing, getting feedback, and revising."

As Matsuda also suggests, reading can be an important part of understanding the writing of a discipline. Furthermore, reading academic writing with a particular focus on the rhetorical elements used is a powerful way to acquire insight into the academic discipline itself, as well as a way to learn the literacy practices that professional writers commonly follow in whatever academic domain you happen to be studying.

IMRaD Format

Structural conventions within the fields of the social sciences can vary quite dramatically, but the structure of a social science report should follow logically from the type of study conducted or the methodological framework (quantitative, qualitative, or mixed methods) it employs. The more quantitative a study is, the more likely its reporting will reflect the conventions for scientific research, using IMRaD (Introduction, Methods, Results, and Discussion) format.

● **Introduction** The introduction of a social science report establishes the context for a study, providing appropriate background on the issue or topic under scrutiny. The introduction is also where you're likely to find evidence of researchers' review of previous scholarship on a topic. As part of these reviews, researchers typically report what's already known about a phenomenon or what's relevant in the current scholarship for their own research. They may also situate their research goals within some gap in the scholarship—that is, they explain how their research contributes to the growing body of scholarship on the phenomenon under investigation. If a theoretical perspective drives a study, as often occurs in more qualitative studies, then the introduction may also contain an explanation of the central tenets or the parameters of the researchers' theoretical lens. Regardless, an introduction in the social sciences generally builds to a statement of specific purpose for the study. This may take the form of a hypothesis or thesis, or it may appear explicitly as a general statement of the researchers' purpose, perhaps including a presentation of research questions. The introduction to Rathunde and Csikszentmihalyi's study provides an example:

> The difficulties that many young adolescents encounter in middle school have been well documented (Carnegie Council on Adolescent Development 1989, 1995; Eccles et al. 1993; U.S. Department of Education 1991). During this precarious transition from the elementary school years, young adolescents may begin to doubt the value of their academic work and their abilities to succeed (Simmons and Blyth 1987; Wigfield et al. 1991). A central concern of many studies is motivation (Anderman and Maehr 1994); a disturbingly consistent finding associated with middle school is a drop in students' intrinsic motivation to learn (Anderman et al. 1999; Gottfried 1985; Harter et al. 1992).
>
> Such downward trends in motivation are not inevitable. Over the past decade, several researchers have concluded that the typical learning environment in middle school is often mismatched with adolescents' developmental needs (Eccles et al. 1993). Several large-scale research programs have focused on the qualities of classrooms and school cultures that may enhance student achievement and motivation (Ames 1992; Lipsitz et al. 1997; Maehr and Midgley 1991). School environments that provide a more appropriate developmental fit (e.g., more relevant tasks, student-directed learning, less of an emphasis on grades and competition, more collaboration, etc.) have been shown to enhance students' intrinsic, task motivation (Anderman et al. 1999).
>
> The present study explores the issues of developmental fit and young adolescents' quality of experience and motivation by comparing five Montessori middle schools to six "traditional" public middle schools. Although the Montessori educational philosophy is primarily associated with early childhood education, a number of schools have extended its core principles to early adolescent education. These principles are in general agreement with the reform proposals associated with various motivation theories (Anderman et al. 1999; Maehr and Midgley 1991), developmental fit theories (Eccles et al. 1993), as well as insights from various recommendations for middle school reform (e.g., the Carnegie Foundation's "Turning Points" recommendations; see Lipsitz et al. 1997). In addition, the Montessori philosophy is consistent with the theoretical and practical implications of optimal experience (flow) theory (Csikszentmihalyi and Rathunde 1998). The present study places a special emphasis on students' quality of experience in middle school. More specifically, it uses the Experience Sampling Method (ESM) (Csikszentmihalyi and Larson 1987) to compare the school experiences of Montessori middle school students with a comparable sample of public school students in traditional classrooms. (pp. 341–42)

Provides an introduction to the topic at hand: the problem of motivation for adolescents in middle school. The problem is situated in the scholarship of others.

Reviews relevant scholarship: the researchers review previous studies that have bearing on their own aims—addressing the decline in motivation among students.

Identifies researchers' particular areas of interest

Although the introductory elements of Rathunde and Csikszentmihalyi's study actually continue for a number of pages, these opening paragraphs reveal common rhetorical moves in social science research reporting: establishing a topic of interest, reviewing the scholarship on that topic, and connecting the current study to the ongoing scholarly conversation on the topic.

● **Methods** Social science researchers are very particular about the precise reporting of their methods of research. No matter what the type of study (quantitative, qualitative, or mixed methods), researchers are very careful not only to identify the methods used in their research but also to explain why they chose certain ones in light of the goals of their study. Because researchers want to reduce the influence of researcher bias and to provide enough context so others might replicate or confirm their findings, social scientists make sure that their reports thoroughly explain the kinds of data they have collected and the precise procedures they used to collect that data (interviews, document analysis, surveys, etc.). Also, there is often much discussion of the ways the data were interpreted or analyzed (using case studies, narrative analysis, statistical procedures, etc.).

An excerpt from W. Cassidy, K. Brown, and M. Jackson's study on educators and cyberbullying provides an example of the level of detail at which scholars typically report their methods:

Provides highly specific details about data collection methods, and emphasizes researchers' neutral stance

> Each participant chose a pseudonym and was asked a series of 16 in-depth, semi-structured, open-ended questions (Lancy, 2001) and three closed-category questions in a private setting, allowing their views to be voiced in confidence (Cook-Sather, 2002). Each 45- to 60-minute audiotaped interview was conducted by one of the authors, while maintaining a neutral, nonjudgmental stance in regards to the responses (Merriam, 1988).

Provides detailed explanation of procedures used to support the reliability of the study's findings

> Once the interviews were transcribed, each participant was given the opportunity to review the transcript and make changes. The transcripts were then reviewed and re-reviewed in a backward and forward motion (Glaser & Strauss, 1967; McMillan & Schumacher, 1997) separately by two of the three researchers to determine commonalities and differences among responses as well as any salient themes that surfaced due to the frequency or the strength of the response (Miles & Huberman, 1994). Each researcher's analysis was then compared with the other's to jointly determine emergent themes and perceptions.

Connects the research to the development of theory

> The dominant themes were then reviewed in relation to the existing literature on educators' perceptions and responses to cyberbullying. The approach taken was "bottom-up," to inductively uncover themes and contribute to theory, rather than apply existing theory as a predetermined frame for analysis (Miles & Huberman, 1994). (p. 523)

You'll notice that the researchers do not simply indicate that the data were collected via interviews. Rather, they go to some lengths to describe the kinds of interviews they conducted and how they were conducted, as well as how those interviews were analyzed. This level of detail supports the writers' ethos, and it further highlights their commitment to reducing bias in their research. Similar studies might also report the interview questions at the end of the report in an appendix. Seeing the actual questions helps readers interpret the results on their own and also provides enough detail for readers to replicate the study or test the hypothesis with a different population, should they desire to do so. Readers of the study need to understand as precisely as possible the methods for data collection and analysis.

● **Results**   There can be much variety in the ways social science reports present the results, or findings, of a study. You may encounter a section identified by the title "Results," especially if the study follows IMRaD format, but you may not find that heading at all. Instead, researchers often present their results by using headings and subheadings that reflect their actual findings. As examples, we provide here excerpts from two studies: (1) Rathunde and Csikszentmihalyi's 2005 study on middle school student motivation, and (2) Cassidy, Brown, and Jackson's 2012 study on educators and cyberbullying.

In the Results section of their report, Rathunde and Csikszentmihalyi provide findings from their study under the subheading "Motivation and Quality-of-Experience Differences: Nonacademic Activities at School." Those results read in part:

> Follow-up ANCOVAs were done on each of the five ESM variables. Table 3 summarizes the means, standard errors, and significance levels for each of the variables.

Table 3

Univariate F-Tests for Quality of Experience in Nonacademic Activities at School by School Context

ESM Measure	School Context		F-test	p
	Montessori ($N = 131$)	Traditional ($N = 150$)		
Flow (%)	11.0 (1.7)	17.3 (1.6)	7.19	.008
Affect	.32 (.05)	.14 (.05)	6.87	.009
Potency	.22 (.05)	.16 (.05)	1.90	NS
Motivation	−.03 (.05)	−.12 (.05)	1.70	NS
Salience	−.38 (.04)	−.19 (.04)	11.14	.001

Means are z-scores (i.e., zero is average experience for the entire week) and are adjusted for the covariates gender, parental education, and ethnicity. Standard errors appear in parentheses. Flow percent indicates the amount of time students indicated above-average challenge and skill while doing nonacademic activities.

Result

Result

Result

Result

Consistent with the relaxed nature of the activities, students in both school contexts reported higher levels of affect, potency, and intrinsic motivation in nonacademic activities, as well as lower levels of salience and flow (see table 2). In contrast to the findings for academic work, students in both groups reported similar levels of intrinsic motivation and potency. In addition, students in the traditional group reported significantly more flow in nonacademic activities, although the overall percentage of flow was low. Similar to the findings for academic activities, the Montessori students reported better overall affect, and despite the fact that levels of salience were below average for both student groups, the traditional students reported that their activities were more important. (pp. 360–61)

You'll notice that in this section, the researchers remain focused on reporting their findings. They do not, at this point, go into great detail about what those findings mean or what the implications are.

Cassidy, Brown, and Jackson also report their findings in a Results section, and they subdivide their findings into a number of areas of inquiry (identified in the subheadings) examined as part of their larger study. Only the results are presented at this point in the article; they are not yet interpreted:

RESULTS

Familiarity with technology

Results

Despite the district's emphasis on technology, the educators (except for two younger teachers and one vice-principal) indicated that they were not very familiar with chat rooms and blogs, were moderately familiar with YouTube and Facebook and were most familiar with the older forms of communication—email and cellular phones.

Cyberbullying policies

Result

We asked respondents about specific cyberbullying policies in place at their school and their perceived effectiveness. Despite the district's priorities around technology, neither the school district nor either school had a specific cyberbullying policy; instead educators were supposed to follow the district's bullying policy. When VP17-A was asked if the district's bullying handbook effectively addressed the problem of cyberbullying, he replied: "It effectively addresses the people that are identified as bullying others [but] it doesn't address the educational side of it . . . about what is proper use of the Internet as a tool."

Result

P14-B wanted to see a new policy put in place that was flexible enough to deal with the different situations as they arose. VP19-B thought that a cyberbullying policy should be separate from a face-to-face bullying policy since the impact on students is different. He also felt that there should be a concerted district policy regarding "risk assessment in which you have a team that's trained at determining the level of threat and it should be taken very seriously whether it's a phone threat, a verbal threat, or a cyber threat." Participants indicated that they had not considered the idea of a separate cyberbullying policy before the interview, with several commenting that they now saw it as important. (pp. 524, 526–27)

Visual Representations of Data   The Results section of a report may also provide data sets in the form of tables and/or figures. Figures may appear as photos, images, charts, or graphs. When you find visual representations of data in texts, it's important that you pause to consider these elements carefully. Researchers typically use *tables* when they want to make data sets, or raw data, available for comparisons. These tables, such as the one Rathunde and Csikszentmihalyi include in their study of middle school students' motivation, present variables in columns and rows.

In this instance, the "background variable[s]" used to describe the student populations are listed in the column, and the rows compare values from two "school context[s]," Montessori and traditional schools. The table's title reveals its overall purpose: to compare "Montessori and Traditional Middle School Samples on Various Background Variables." Rathunde and Csikszentmihalyi describe the contents of their table this way:

> Table 1 summarizes this comparison. The ethnic diversity of the samples was almost identical. Both shared similar advantages in terms of high parental

Table 1

Comparison of Montessori and Traditional Middle School Samples on Various Background Variables

Background Variable	School Context	
	Montessori	Traditional
Ethnicity (%):		
European American	72.6	74.9
Asian American	10.2	7.8
Latino	1.9	3.4
African American	12.7	12.6
Other	2.6	1.2
Parental education	5.5	5.4
Home resources	29.6	29.5
School-related:		
Parental discussion	2.41	2.49
Parental involvement	2.11	2.10
Parental monitoring	1.69	1.66
Number of siblings	1.8	2.0
Mother employment (%)	71.6	74.1
Father employment (%)	83.7	88.1
Intact (two-parent) family (%)	81.0	84.0
Grade point average	1.97	1.93

Note. None of the differences reported in the table were statistically significant.

education (baccalaureate degree or higher), high rates of two-parent families, high family resources, and other indicators of strong parental involvement in their children's education. Although only one-third of the Montessori students received grades, *t*-tests indicated that both samples were comprised of good students (i.e., they received about half As and half Bs). (p. 356)

Researchers use *figures* when they want to highlight the results of research or the derived relationships between data sets or variables. *Graphs*, a type of figure, contain two axes—the horizontal x-axis and the vertical y-axis. The relationship between variables on these axes is indicated by the cells of overlap between the two axes in the body of the figure. Conventionally, the *x-axis* identifies an independent variable, or a variable that can be controlled; by contrast, the *y-axis* identifies the dependent variable, which is dependent on the variable identified in the x-axis. Here's a figure from Rathunde and Csikszentmihalyi's study:

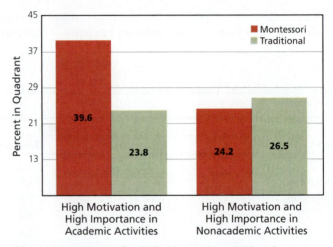

Figure 8.1 Percentage of undivided interest in academic and nonacademic activities

As with tables, the titles of figures reveal their overall purpose. In this case, the researchers demonstrate the "[p]ercentage of undivided interest in academic and nonacademic activities." Reading the figure, in this instance, comes down to identifying the percentage of "undivided interest" that students in Montessori and traditional middle schools (revealed in different colors, as the legend indicates) expressed in the quadrants "High Motivation and High Importance in Academic Activities" and "High Motivation and High Importance in Nonacademic Activities." Colored cells in the body of the graph reveal the percentages. Rathunde and Csikszentmihalyi note about this figure: "[O]n the key variable undivided interest, students in the traditional group reported a slightly higher percent of high-motivation and high-importance activities; this noteworthy change from academic activities is illustrated in figure 2" (p. 361).

Whenever you see charts or figures in social science reports, you should take time to do the following:

- Study the titles carefully.
- Look for legends, which provide keys to understanding elements in the chart or figure.
- Identify the factors or variables represented, and understand how those factors or variables are related, as well as how they are measured.
- Look closely for possible patterns.

● **Discussion**   The Discussion section of a social science report explains the significance of the findings in light of the study's aims. This is also where researchers reflect on the study more generally, highlight ways their study could be improved (often called "limitations"), and/or identify areas of further research that the study has brought to light. Researchers sometimes lay out the groundwork for continued research, based on their contribution, as part of the ongoing scholarly conversation on the topic or issue at hand. A few excerpts from the Discussion section of Rathunde and Csikszentmihalyi's study reveal their adherence to these conventional expectations:

DISCUSSION

Given the well-documented decline in students' motivation and engagement in middle school, and the ongoing emphasis on middle school reform (Cross 1990; Eccles et al. 1993; Lipsitz et al. 1997), an increasing number of studies have explored how to change classroom practices and school cultures in ways that provide a healthier fit for young adolescents (Ames 1992; Eccles et al. 1993; Felner et al. 1997; Maehr and Midgley 1991). The present study adds to this area of research by comparing the motivation and quality of experience of students from five Montessori middle schools and six traditional middle schools. (p. 362)

> Reveals why their study is important to the ongoing conversation on this topic

. . .

Results from the study showed that while engaged in academic work at school, Montessori students reported higher affect, potency (i.e., feeling alert and energetic), intrinsic motivation (i.e., enjoyment, interest), and flow experience than students from traditional middle schools. (p. 363)

> Discusses important findings

. . .

The present study did not look at whether such experiential differences translated into positive achievement and behavioral outcomes for the students. This is an important topic for future research. (p. 363)

> Identifies limitations in the study and an area for possible future research

Following are some additional structural conventions to consider when you are reading or writing in the fields of the social sciences.

Abstracts and Other Structural Conventions

● **Abstracts** Another structural feature of reports in the social sciences is the abstract. Abstracts typically follow the title of the report and the identification of the researchers. They provide a brief overview of the study, explaining the topic or issue under study, the specific purpose of the study and its methods, and offering a concise statement of the results. These elements are usually summarized in a few sentences. Abstracts can be useful to other researchers who want to determine if a study might prove helpful for their own work or if the methods might inform their own research purposes. Abstracts thus serve to promote collaboration among researchers. Though abstracts appear at the beginning of research reports, they're typically written after both the study and the research report are otherwise completed. Abstracts reduce the most important parts of a study into a compact space.

The following example from Rathunde and Csikszentmihalyi illustrates a number of the conventions of abstracts:

The study's purpose is identified.

Methods are briefly outlined.

Results are provided.

Implications of the research findings are noted.

This study compared the motivation and quality of experience of demographically matched students from Montessori and traditional middle school programs. Approximately 290 students responded to the Experience Sampling Method (ESM) and filled out questionnaires. Multivariate analyses showed that the Montessori students reported greater affect, potency (i.e., feeling energetic), intrinsic motivation, flow experience, and undivided interest (i.e., the combination of high intrinsic motivation and high salience or importance) while engaged in academic activities at school. The traditional middle school students reported higher salience while doing academic work; however, such responses were often accompanied by low intrinsic motivation. When engaged in informal, nonacademic activities, the students in both school contexts reported similar experiences. These results are discussed in terms of current thought on motivation in education and middle school reform.

● **Conclusion** On occasion, researchers separate out coverage of the implications of their findings (as part of a Discussion section) from other elements in the Discussion. When this occurs, these researchers typically construct a separate Conclusion section in which they address conventional content coverage of their study's limitations, as well as their findings' implications for future research.

● **Acknowledgments** Acknowledgment sections sometimes appear at the end of social science reports. Usually very brief, they offer a quick word of thanks to organizations and/or individuals who have helped to fund a study, collect data, review the study, or provide another form of assistance during the production of the study. This section can be particularly telling if you're interested in the source of a researcher's funding.

● **Appendices**   Social science research reports sometimes end with one or more appendices. Items here are often referenced within the body of the report itself, as appropriate. These items may include additional data sets, calculations, interview questions, diagrams, and images. The materials typically offer context or support for discussions that occur in the body of a research report.

● **Titles**   Research reports in the social sciences, as in the natural sciences, tend to have rather straightforward titles that are concise and that contain key words highlighting important components of the study. Titles in the social sciences tend not to be creative or rhetorical, although there is a greater tendency toward creativity in titles in qualitative studies, which are more typically language driven than numerically driven. The title of Barbara Allen's study reported in the academic journal *Technology in Society*, for instance, identifies the central issues her study examined as well as the study location: "Environmental Justice, Local Knowledge, and After-Disaster Planning in New Orleans." Similarly, the title of Rathunde and Csikszentmihalyi's article is concise in its identification of the study's purpose: "Middle School Students' Motivation and Quality of Experience: A Comparison of Montessori and Traditional School Environments."

Connect 8.4   **Observing Structural Features in the Social Sciences**

Although we've discussed a number of structural expectations for reports in the social sciences, we'd like to stress again that these expectations are conventional. As such, you'll likely encounter studies in the social sciences that rely on only a few of these structural features or that alter the conventional expectations in light of the researchers' particular aims. Find a scholarly article from the social sciences, either from Part Three or your own research, and examine it in terms of these structural features. If the article deviates from the conventions we've described, what might be the writers' reasons for any deviations?

- **IMRaD Format**   Does the report have a section labeled "Introduction" that establishes the context for the study and offers a review of the literature? Is there a "Methods" section that thoroughly explains the kinds of data the researchers have collected and the precise procedures they used? Are "Results" discussed and data presented? Is there a "Discussion" section that explains the significance of the researchers' findings?

- **Abstract**   Does the report begin with a brief summary of the study?

- **Title**   Does the title contain key words that highlight important components of the study?

Language Conventions in the Social Sciences

As with structural conventions, the way social scientists use language can vary widely with respect to differing audiences and/or genres. Nevertheless, we can explore several language-level conventional expectations for writing in the social sciences. In the following sections, we consider the use of both active and passive voice, as well as the use of hedging (or hedge words) to limit the scope and applicability of assertions.

Active and Passive Voice

Many students have had the experience of receiving a graded paper back from an English teacher in high school and discovering that a sentence or two was marked for awkward or inappropriate use of the passive voice. This does not mean that the passive voice is always to be avoided. As we discussed in Chapter 7, writers in English and other fields of the humanities often prefer the active voice, but writers in the social sciences and natural sciences often prefer the passive voice, and with good purpose.

To review, in the **active voice**, the subject of the sentence is the agent—the person or thing doing the action. By contrast, in the **passive voice**, the subject of the sentence has something done to them by an agent. The agent is either omitted or downplayed.

You may wonder why anyone would want to remove altogether the actor/agent from a sentence. The passive voice is often preferable in writing in the social sciences and natural sciences because it can foster a sense that researchers are acting objectively or with neutrality. This does not mean that natural or social scientists are averse to the active voice. However, in particular instances, the passive voice can go a long way toward supporting an ethos of objectivity, and its use appears most commonly in the Methods section of social science reports. Consider these two sentences that might appear in the Methods section of a hypothetical social science report:

Active Voice	We asked participants to identify the factors that most influenced their decision.
Passive Voice	Participants were asked to identify the factors that most influenced their decision.

In the example above, the action is "asking" and the agents are the researchers, "we." The passive voice construction deemphasizes the researchers conducting the study. In this way, the researchers maintain more of a sense of objectivity or neutrality and keep the focus on the study's subjects.

Hedging

Another language feature common to writing in the social sciences is **hedging**—limiting a claim by conditions or exceptions rather than making a definitive statement. Hedging typically occurs when researchers want to make a claim or propose an explanation but also want to be extremely careful not to overstep the scope of their findings based on their actual data set. Consider the following sentences:

> Participants <u>seemed to be</u> anxious about sharing their feelings on the topic.

> Participants <u>were</u> anxious about sharing their feelings on the topic.

When you compare the two, you'll notice that the first sentence "hedges" against making a broad or sweeping claim about the participants. The use of *seemed to be* is a hedge against overstepping, or saying something that may or may not be absolutely true in every case. Other words or phrases that are often used to hedge include the following, just to name a few:

apparently	perhaps
it appears that	possibly
likely	probably
might	some
partially	sometimes

Considering that social scientists make claims about human behavior, and that participants in a study may or may not agree with the conclusions, it's perhaps not surprising that writers in these fields often make use of hedging.

Connect 8.5   **Observing Language Features in the Social Sciences**

Continue your examination of the article you selected for Connect 8.4 using the questions below as a guide. If the article deviates from the conventions we've described, what might be the writers' reasons?

- **Voice**   Is the voice of the text primarily active or passive?

- **Hedging**   Is there evidence of hedging? That is, do the researchers limit claims about human behavior by conditions or exceptions rather than making definitive statements?

Reference Conventions in the Social Sciences

Scholars in the social sciences cite the work of others when establishing a context for their own research. Their use of sources establishes that they are aware of the latest research and thinking in the area of their own research, and it indicates that they are advancing the conversation around this research area. Most scholars in the social sciences follow the documentation style of the American

Psychological Association (APA) when crediting their sources. The values of the social sciences are reflected in this citation system, as we will explain.

Scholars use the APA method for documenting sources that are paraphrased, summarized, or cited as part of their reports. In APA style, in-text citations not only include the author's last name but also provide the year of publication. Page numbers are included for direct quotations, but more often social science writers paraphrase information, so the use of page numbers is infrequent. Full publication data for the sources is provided in the References section at the end of the paper, in a list alphabetically organized by author.

We can compare APA in-text citations to the MLA documentation system described in Chapter 6 through the following examples:

MLA   A recent study of slave narratives and contemporary events "links the current use of visual technologies and biometrics in racial profiling to the surveillance of enslaved people in the nineteenth century" (Ross 300).

        Through an examination of slave narratives and contemporary events, Ross argues that the "persistence of racial hypervisibility links the current use of visual technologies and biometrics in racial profiling to the surveillance of enslaved people in the nineteenth century" (300).

APA   The study reports that individuals who engage in perspective taking are more likely to benefit from feedback than those who do not (Sherf and Morrison, 2020).

        Sherf and Morrison (2020) report that individuals who engage in perspective taking are more likely to benefit from feedback than those who do not.

Although these examples by no means illustrate all the differences between MLA and APA styles of documentation, they do highlight the elevated importance that social science fields place on the year of a source's publication. Why? Imagine that you're reading a sociological study conducted in 2020 that examines the use of tobacco products among teenagers. The study references the finding of a similar study from 1990. By seeing the date of the referenced study in the in-text citation, readers can quickly consider the usefulness of the 1990 study for the one being reported on. Social scientists value recency, or the most current data possible, and their documentation requirements reflect this preference.

Another distinction that we've noted is that social scientists quote researchers in other fields far less frequently than scholars in the humanities do. Why is this so? For humanist scholars, language is of the utmost importance, and how someone conveys an idea can seem almost inseparable from the idea being conveyed. Additionally, for humanists, language is often the "unit of measure"—that is, *how* someone says something (like a novelist or a poet) is actually *what* is being studied. Typically, this is not the case for social science researchers (with the exception of fields such as linguistics and communication, although they primarily address how study participants say something and not how prior research reported its findings). Instead, social scientists tend to be much more interested in other researchers' methodology and findings than they are in the language through which those methods or finding are conveyed. As a result, social scientists are more likely to summarize or paraphrase source materials than to quote them directly.

For an example of papers in APA format, see Insider Example: Student Literature Review (pp. 190–98) and Insider Example: Student Theory Response Paper (pp. 201–9). For a discussion of the elements of citations and References lists, see "American Psychological Association (APA) Style" in the Appendix.

Connect 8.6   **Observing Reference Features in the Social Sciences**

Conclude your examination of the article you selected for Connect 8.4, using the questions below as a guide:

- **Engagement with Other Scholars**   Does the writer refer to other scholars' words or ideas? If so, in what ways? Are other scholars' words or ideas used to support the writer's argument, or do they serve to contrast with what the writer has to say? Does the writer quote directly from other writers?

- **Documentation**   Look closely at examples of how the writer cites the work of other scholars. What form of documentation applies? What type of information is valued?

Genres: Literature Review

Scholars in the social sciences share the results of their research in various ways. They might, for instance, compose a talk for a conference or publish a research report in a journal or a book. In the sections that follow, you'll have the opportunity to analyze and practice several common genres that you're likely to encounter in social sciences courses, beginning with the literature review.

A *literature review* (also referred to as a *review of scholarship*) is an analysis of published resources related to a specific topic. It is not a "review" in the sense of a critique (as in a movie review) but rather as an assessment of the current state of scholarship. The literature review is one of the most common genres you will encounter in academic writing. Though the genre occurs quite frequently in the social sciences, you can find evidence of reviews of scholarly literature in virtually every academic field—including the humanities, the natural sciences, and applied fields. It is so common because all scholars build on the work of others.

What Is the Rhetorical Context for This Genre?

Students and researchers may conduct a review of scholarship simply to establish what research has already been conducted on a topic, or the review may make a case for how new research can fill in gaps or advance knowledge about a topic. In the former situation, the resulting literature review may appear as a freestanding piece of writing; in the latter, a briefer review of scholarship may be embedded at the start (usually in the introduction) of a research study. In fact, most published scholarly articles include a review of literature in the introduction. For an example, see the Introduction to Mihaly Csikszentmihalyi and Kevin Rathunde's report within the discussion of IMRaD format on page 173.

Besides serving as a means to identify a gap in the scholarship or a place for new scholarship, a literature review helps to establish researchers' credibility by demonstrating their awareness of what has been discovered about a particular topic or issue. It further respectfully acknowledges the hard work of others within the community of scholarship. Equally important, the literature review illustrates how previous studies interrelate. A good literature review may examine how prior research is similar and different, or it may suggest how a group of researchers' work developed over several years and how scholars have advanced the work of others.

Strategies for Writing a Literature Review

● **Narrow the focus of your topic and determine the scope of your research.**   The scope of a freestanding literature review can vary greatly, depending on the knowledge and level of interest of the investigator conducting the review. For instance, you may have very little knowledge about autism, so your review of the scholarship might be aimed at learning about various aspects of the condition and issues related to it. If this is the case, your research would cast a pretty wide net. However, let's say you're quite familiar with certain critical aspects of issues related to autism and are interested in one aspect in particular—for example, the best therapies for addressing autism in young children. If this is the case, then you could conduct a review of scholarship with a more focused purpose, narrowing your net to only the studies that address your specific interest.

Regardless of the scope of your research interest, literature reviews should begin with a clear sense of your topic. One way to narrow the focus of your topic is by proposing one or more research questions about it (*What are researchers studying with regard to autism?*) or a narrower one (*What are the best therapies for addressing autism in young children?*). (See Chapter 5 for more support for crafting such research questions.)

● **Conduct your search for relevant studies.** Once you've clearly established your topic, the next step is to conduct your research. The research you discover and choose to read, which may be quite substantial for a literature review, is chosen according to the scope of your research interest. (For help in narrowing a search based on key terms in your research question, see Chapter 5.) As you search for and review possible sources, pay particular attention to the *abstracts* of studies, as they may help you quickly decide if a study is right for your purposes. And unless your review of scholarship targets the tracing of a particular thread of research across a range of years, you should probably focus on the most current research available.

● **Organize your sources.** After you've examined and gathered a range of source materials, determine the best way to keep track of the ideas you discover. Many students find this is a good time to produce an annotated bibliography as a first step in creating a literature review. (See Chapter 5 for more help on constructing annotated bibliographies.)

Another useful strategy for organizing your sources is a source synthesis chart. We recommend this as a way to visualize the areas of overlap in your research, whether for a broad focus (*What are researchers studying with regard to autism?*) or a more narrow one (*What are the best therapies for addressing autism in young children?*). Here's an abbreviated example of a source synthesis chart for a broad review of scholarship on autism:

	Topics We Expect to Emerge in Scholarship			
Authors of Study	*Issues of Diagnosis*	*Treatments*	*Debate over Causes*	*Wider Familial Effects*
Solomon et al. (2012)	pp. 252–55 Notes: emphasizes problems families face with diagnosis	pp. 257–60 Notes: examines and proposes strategies for family therapists	p. 253 Notes: acknowledges a series of possible contributing factors	
Vanderborght et al. (2012)		pp. 359–67 (results) Notes: examines use of robot for storytelling		
Grindle et al. (2012)		pp. 208–313 (results) Notes: school-based behavioral intervention program (ABA)		p. 229 Notes: home-based therapy programs
Lilley (2011)	pp. 135–37 Notes: explores the roles of mothers in diagnosis processes	pp. 143–51 Notes: explores rationales and lived experiences of ABA and non-ABA supporters		

In this case, the studies that we read are named in the column under "Authors of Study." The topics or issues that we anticipated would emerge from our review of the sources are shown in the top row. Based on our reading of a limited number of studies, four at this point, we can already discern a couple of areas of overlap in the scholarship: the diagnosis of autism in children and intervention programs for children with autism. We can tell which researchers talked about what issues at any given time because we've noted the areas (by page number, along with some detail) where they addressed these issues. The empty cells in the synthesis chart reveal that our review of the sources, thus far at least, suggests there is less concern for those topics. We should note, however, that our review of sources is far from exhaustive. If you're able to create a visual representation of your research such as this one, then you're well on your way to creating a successful literature review. Keep in mind that the more detailed you can make your synthesis chart, the easier your process may be moving forward.

● **Synthesize your sources.**   Synthesizing sources is the process of identifying and describing the relationships between and among researchers' ideas or approaches. What trends emerge? Does the Grindle et al. study say something similar to the Lilley study about behavioral interventions? Something different? Do they share methods? Do they approach the issue of behavioral interventions similarly or differently? Defining the relationships between the studies and making these relationships explicit is critically important to your success. As you read the sources, you'll likely engage in an internal process of comparing and contrasting the researchers' ideas. You might even recognize similarities and differences in the researchers' approaches to the topic. Many of these ideas will probably be reflected in your synthesis chart, and you might consider color-coding (or highlighting in different colors) various cells to indicate types of relationships among the researchers you note.

A quick review of the abstract to "The Experience of Infertility: A Review of Recent Literature," a freestanding literature review published in the academic journal *Sociology of Health and Illness*, demonstrates the areas of synthesis that emerged from the professionals' examination of recent research on infertility:

> About 10 years ago Greil published a review and critique of the literature on the socio-psychological impact of infertility. He found at the time that most scholars treated infertility as a medical condition with psychological consequences rather than as a socially constructed reality. This article examines research published since the last review. More studies now place infertility within larger social contexts and social scientific frameworks, although clinical emphases persist. Methodological problems remain, but important improvements are also evident. We identify two vigorous research traditions in the social scientific study of infertility. One tradition uses primarily quantitative techniques to study clinic patients in order to improve service delivery and to

Four synthesis points: (1) more recent studies approach the topic of infertility differently; (2) there remains a focus on examining infertility from a clinical viewpoint; (3) there are still questions about research methods, but there have also been "important improvements" in methods; (4) two trends emerged from these scholars' review of the current research.

assess the need for psychological counseling. The other tradition uses primarily qualitative research to capture the experiences of infertile people in a sociocultural context. We conclude that more attention is now being paid to the ways in which the experience of infertility is shaped by social context. We call for continued progress in the development of a distinctly sociological approach to infertility and for the continued integration of the two research traditions identified here.

Presents conclusions reached as a result of the literature review project

Another example, this one a brief excerpt from the introduction to Csikszentmihalyi and Hunter's "Happiness in Everyday Life: The Uses of Experience Sampling," demonstrates the kind of synthesis that typically appears in reviews of scholarship when they're embedded as part of a larger study:

> Cross-national comparisons suggest that macro-social conditions such as extreme poverty, war, and social injustice are all obstacles to happiness (Inglehart & Klingemann, 2000; Veenhoven, 1995). Chance events like personal tragedies, illness, or sudden strokes of good fortune may drastically affect the level of happiness, but apparently these effects do not last long (Brickman et al., 1978; Diener, 2000).

The writers indicate that there is agreement between researchers: both Inglehart & Klingemann (2000) and Veenhoven (1995) have confirmed the finding in "cross-national comparisons."

Again, the writers indicate there is agreement between researchers: both Brickman et al. (1978) and Diener (2000) have confirmed this finding.

● **Remember SLR as you draft and revise.**   The Writing Project that follows suggests a structure for your literature review. Apply what you've learned in this chapter about writing conventions in the social sciences as you draft each section of your literature review. Focus on developing your ideas and supporting your points in the first draft, and then use the revision to further clarify your points and work on style. When you proofread, be sure to check for typos in the source names and dates.

Writing Project   **Literature Review**

Your goal in this writing project, a freestanding literature review, is to provide an overview of the research that has been conducted on a topic of interest to you.

THE INTRODUCTION

The opening of your literature review should introduce the topic you're exploring and assess the state of the available scholarship on it: What are the current areas of interest? What are the issues or elements related to a particular topic being discussed? Is there general agreement? Are there other clear trends in the scholarship? Are there areas of convergence and divergence?

THE BODY

Paragraphs within the body of your literature review should be organized according to the issues or synthesized areas you're exploring. For example, based on the synthesis chart shown earlier, we might suggest that one of the body sections of a broadly focused review of scholarship on autism should concern issues of diagnosis. We might further reveal, in our topic sentence to that section of the literature review, that we've synthesized the available research in this area and that it seems uniformly to suggest that although many factors have been studied, no credible studies establish a direct link between any contributing factor and the occurrence of autism in children. The rest of that section of our paper would explore the factors that have been examined in the research to support the claim in our topic sentence.

Keep in mind that the body paragraphs should be organized according to a claim about the topic or ideas being explored. They should not be organized merely as successive summaries of the sources. Such an organization does not promote effective synthesis.

THE CONCLUSION

Your conclusion should reiterate your overall assessment of the scholarship. Notify your readers of any gaps you've determined in the scholarship, and consider suggesting areas where future scholarship can make more contributions.

TECHNICAL CONSIDERATIONS

Keep in mind the conventions of writing in the social sciences that you've learned about throughout this chapter. Use APA documentation procedures for in-text documentation of summarized, paraphrased, and cited materials, as well as for the References page at the end of your literature review.

....

Insider Example
Student Literature Review

William O'Brien, a first-year writing student who had a particular interest in understanding the effects of sleep deprivation, composed the following literature review. As you read, notice how William's text indicates evidence of synthesis both between and among the sources he used to build his project. Notice also that he follows APA style conventions in his review. ▶

Effects of Sleep Deprivation: A Literature Review

William O'Brien

Department of English, North Carolina State University

Comp II: Writing in the Disciplines

Prof. Roy Stamper

October 29, 2015

Effects of Sleep Deprivation: A Literature Review

Everybody knows the feeling of having to struggle through a long day after a night of poor sleep, or sometimes even none at all. You may feel groggy, cloudy, clumsy, or unable to think of simple things. Sometimes you may even feel completely fine but then get angry or frustrated easily. These effects are amplified when poor sleep continues for a long period of time. In a society with an ever-increasing number of distractions, it is becoming harder for many people to get the recommended amount of sleep. Sleep issues plague the majority of the U.S. population in one way or another. The Centers for Disease Control recognizes insufficient sleep as a public health epidemic.

A lot of research is being conducted relating to sleep and sleep deprivation, and for good reason. Most researchers seem to agree that short-term sleep deprivation has purely negative effects on mental functioning in general. However, the particular types of effects caused by poor sleep are still being debated, as are the long-term implications of sleep deprivation. The questions for researchers, then, are under what circumstances do these negative effects begin to show, to what extent do they show, and most significant, what exactly are these negative effects?

Short-Term Effects of Sleep Deprivation

In order to examine the direct and immediate effects of sleep deprivation, numerous researchers rely on experimentation, which allows them to control for variables. Minkel et al. (2012) identified a gap in the research relating to how sleep deprivation affects the stress response (p. 1015). To investigate this connection, the researchers divided healthy adults into two groups. Participants in the first group acted as the control and were allowed a 9-hour sleeping opportunity during the night. The second group was not allowed to

---

The writer establishes the general topic, sleep deprivation, in the opening paragraph.

SYNTHESIS POINT: scholars agree on the negative effects of short-term sleep deprivation.

SYNTHESIS POINT: questions remain about the effects of long-term sleep deprivation.

Focuses on scholarship that uses experimental studies to examine the effects of short-term sleep deprivation.

sleep at all during that night. The next day, the participants completed stressful mental tasks (primarily math) and were asked to report their stress levels and mood via visual scales (Minkel et al., 2012, pp. 1016–1017). The researchers hypothesized that the participants who did not sleep would have higher stress responses than the rested group, and that sleep loss would increase the stress response in proportion to the severity of the stressor (p. 1016). Their findings, however, showed that while the negative response to stressors was more profound for the sleep-deprived group, the differences in stress response between groups were not significant for the high-stressor condition. Still, the research clearly showed that sleep-deprived people have "significantly greater subjective stress, anger, and anxiety" in response to low-level stressors (p. 1019).

Research by Jugovac and Cavallero (2012) focused on the immediate effects of sleep deprivation on attention through three attentional networks: phasic alerting, covert orienting, and executive control (Jugovac & Cavallero, 2012, p. 115). The study tested 30 young adults using the Attention Network Test (ANT), the Stanford Sleepiness Scale (SSS), and the Global Vigor-Affect Scale (GVA) before and after a 24-hour sleep deprivation period (p. 116). (All participants were subjected to sleep deprivation, because the tests before the sleep deprivation served as the control.) The findings built upon the idea that sleep deprivation decreases vigilance and that it impairs the "executive control" attentional network, while appearing to leave the other components (alerting and orienting) relatively unchanged (pp. 121–122). These findings help explain how one night of missed sleep negatively affects a person's attention, by distinguishing the effects on each of the three particular attentional networks.

> Links the two studies reviewed according to their similar focus on short-term effects of sleep deprivation

Research by Giesbrecht et al. (2013) focused on the effects that short-term sleep deprivation has on dissociation. This research connects sleep deprivation to mental illness rather than just temporarily reduced mental functioning. The researchers used 25 healthy undergraduate students and kept all participants awake throughout one night. Four different scales were used to record their feelings and dissociative reactions while being subjected to two different cognitive tasks (Giesbrecht et al., 2013, pp. 150–152). The cognitive tasks completed before the night of sleep deprivation were used to compare the results of the cognitive tasks completed after the night of sleep deprivation. Although the study was small and the implications are still somewhat unclear, the study showed a clear link between sleep deprivation and dissociative symptoms (pp. 156–158).

It is clear that sleep deprivation negatively affects people in many different ways. These researchers each considered a different type of specific effect, and together they form a wide knowledge base supporting the idea that even a very short-term (24-hour) loss of sleep for a healthy adult may have multiple negative impacts on mental and emotional well-being. These effects include increased anxiety, anger, and stress in response to small stressors (Minkel et al., 2012), inhibited attention—the executive control attentional network more specifically (Jugovac & Cavallero, 2012)—and increased dissociative symptoms (Giesbrecht et al., 2013).

Long-Term Effects of Sleep Deprivation

Although the research on short-term effects of sleep deprivation reveals numerous negative consequences, there may be other, less obvious, implications that studies on short-term effect cannot illuminate. In order to better understand these other implications, we must examine research

---

The writer links this study to the continuing discussion of short-term effects of sleep deprivation but also notes a difference.

This paragraph provides a summative synthesis, or an overview of the findings among the sources reviewed.

The writer shifts to an examination of the long-term effects of sleep deprivation and acknowledges a shift in the methods for these studies.

relating to the possible long-term effects of limited sleep. Unfortunately, long-term sleep deprivation experiments do not seem to have been done and are probably not possible (due to ethical reasons and safety reasons, among other factors). A study by Duggan, Reynolds, Kern, and Friedman (2014) pointed out the general lack of previous research into the long-term effects of sleep deprivation, but it examined whether there was a link between average sleep duration during childhood and life-long mortality risk (p. 1195). The researchers analyzed data from 1,145 participants in the Terman Life Cycle Study from the early 1900s, which measured bedtime and wake time along with year of death. The amount of sleep was adjusted by age in order to find the deviations from average sleep time for each age group. The data were also separated by sex (Duggan et al., 2014, pp. 1196–1197). The results showed that, for males, sleeping either more or less than the regular amount of time for each age group correlated with an increased life-long mortality risk (p. 1199). Strangely, this connection was not present for females. For males, however, this is a very important finding. Since we can surmise that the childhood sleep patterns are independent of and unrelated to any underlying health issues that ultimately cause the deaths later on in life, it is more reasonable to assume causation rather than simply correlation. Thus, the pattern that emerged may demonstrate that too little, or too much, sleep during childhood can cause physiological issues, leading to death earlier in life, reaffirming the importance of sleep for well-being.

> Establishes one of the study's central findings related to long-term effects of sleep deprivation.

While this study examined the relationship between sleep duration and death, a study by Kelly and El-Sheikh (2014) examined the relationship between sleep and a slightly less serious, but still very important, subject: the adjustment and development of children in school over a period of time. The study followed 176 third grade children (this number dropped to 113 by the end of the study) as they progressed through school for five years, recording sleep patterns and characteristics of adjustment (Kelly & El-Sheikh, 2014, pp. 1137–1139). Sleep was recorded both subjectively through self-reporting and objectively though "actigraphy" in order to assess a large variety of sleep parameters (p. 1137). The study results indicated that reduced sleep time and poorer-quality sleep are risk factors for problems adjusting over time to new situations. The results also indicate that the opposite effect is true, but to a lesser extent (p. 1146).

The negative impact of poor sleep on a person's ability to adjust to new situations is likely due to the generally accepted idea that sleep deprivation negatively affects cognitive performance and emotional regulation, as described in the Kelly and El-Sheikh article (2014, pp. 1144–1145). If cognitive performance and emotional regulation are negatively affected by a lack of sleep, then it makes sense that the sleep-deprived child would struggle to adjust over time as compared to a well-rested child. This hypothesis has important implications. It once again affirms the idea that receiving the appropriate amount of quality sleep is very important for developing children. This basic idea does not go against the research by Duggan et al. (2014) in any way; rather, it complements it. The main difference between each study is that the research by Duggan et al. shows that too much sleep can also be related to a greater risk of death earlier in life. Together, both articles provide evidence that deviation from the appropriate amount of sleep causes very negative long-term effects, including, but certainly not limited to, worse adjustment over time (Kelly & El-Sheikh, 2014) and increased mortality rates (Duggan et al., 2014).

> Provides a summative synthesis that examines relationships between the sources and considers implications of findings

Conclusion

This research provides great insight into the short-term and long-term effects of sleep deprivation. Duggan et al. (2014) showed increased mortality rates among people who slept too much as well as too little. This result could use some additional research. Through the analysis of each article, we see just how damaging sleep deprivation can be, even after a short period of time, and thus it is important to seriously consider preventative measures. While sleep issues can manifest themselves in many different ways, especially in legitimate sleep disorders such as insomnia, just the simple act of not allowing oneself to get enough sleep every night can have significant negative effects. Building on this, there seems to be a general lack of discussion on *why* people (who do not have sleep disorders) do not get enough time to sleep. One possible reason is the ever-increasing number of distractions, especially in the form of electronics, that may lead to overstimulation. Another answer may be that high demands placed on students and adults through school and work, respectively, do not give them time to sleep enough. The most probable, yet most generalized, answer, however, is that people simply do not appropriately manage their time in order to get enough sleep. People seem to prioritize everything else ahead of sleeping, thus causing the damaging effects of sleep deprivation to emerge. Regardless, this research is valuable for anyone who wants to live a healthy lifestyle and function at full mental capacity. Sleep deprivation seems to have solely negative consequences; thus, it is in every person's best interests to get a full night of quality sleep.

Conclusion acknowledges what appears as a gap in the scholarship reviewed.

References

Duggan, K., Reynolds, C., Kern, M., & Friedman, H. (2014). Childhood sleep duration and lifelong mortality risk. *Health Psychology, 33*(10), 1195–1203. https://doi.org/10.1037/hea0000078

Giesbrecht, T., Smeets, T., Leppink, J., Jelicic, M., & Merckelbach, H. (2013). Acute dissociation after one night of sleep loss. *Psychology of Consciousness: Theory, Research, and Practice, 1*(S), 150–159. https://doi.org/10.1037/2326-5523.1.S.150

Jugovac, D., & Cavallero, C. (2012). Twenty-four hours of total sleep deprivation selectively impairs attentional networks. *Experimental Psychology, 59*(3), 115–123. https://doi.org/10.1027/1618-3169/a000133

Kelly, R., & El-Sheikh, M. (2014). Reciprocal relations between children's sleep and their adjustment over time. *Developmental Psychology, 50*(4), 1137–1147. https://doi.org/10.1037/a0034501

Minkel, J., Banks, S., Htaik, O., Moreta, M., Jones, C., McGlinchey, E., Simpson, N., & Dinges, D. (2012). Sleep deprivation and stressors: Evidence for elevated negative affect in response to mild stressors when sleep deprived. *Emotion, 12*(5), 1015–1020. https://doi.org/10.1037/a0026871

Genres: Theory Response Essay

In a theory response essay, students apply a social science theory to personal experiences. They may use a psychological, sociological, or communication theory as a lens through which to explain their own or others' behaviors. Whether they are using elements of Freud's dream theories to help understand their own dreams or using an interpersonal communication theory to understand why people so easily engage with them, the theory they're working with provides the frame for their analysis of some event or action. The theory is the core of any theory response.

What Is the Rhetorical Context for This Genre?

A theory response essay is an academic assignment that helps students learn to think like social scientists. The audience for this assignment is the instructor, and sometimes the audience is peers as well. The assignment has several purposes: (1) it allows students to engage with the fundamental elements of social sciences (theories), (2) it allows students to attend to the basic processes of data collection that are common in the social sciences, and (3) it often is quite engaging for faculty to read and interesting for students to write.

Strategies for Writing a Theory Response Essay

● **Identify a workable theory.**   Precisely because a theory is the core of a theory response essay project, it's crucial that in the beginning stage of such a project, you work with a theory that is actually applicable to the event, action, or phenomenon you want to understand better. You also want to choose a theory that genuinely interests you. Luckily, theories of human behavior and human system interactions abound. If you are not assigned a theory for the project, then consider the places where you might go about locating a workable theory. Textbooks in the social sciences frequently make reference to theories, and numerous academic websites maintain lists and explanations of social science theories. Here are a few categories of theories that students often find interesting:

addiction theories	parenting style theories
birth order theories	stages of grieving theories
friendship theories	

If you're unable to locate a workable theory that's "ready-made" for application to some experience(s), then consider building a theory based on your reading of a social science study. Though this certainly makes completing the assignment challenging, it is not without rewards.

● **Recall and describe events that you could view through the theory's lens.**
Regardless of whether you're working with a particular theory or constructing a theory of behavior based on one or more studies, consider making a list of the "moments" or events in your life that the theory might help you understand further. Your next step might be to write out detailed descriptions of those events as you see or remember them. Capture as much detail as you can, especially if you're writing from memory.

● **Conduct research if necessary.**   Some instructors might ask you to collect and analyze the experiences of others. If you're assigned to do this, then you'll need to consider a data-collection method very carefully and ask your instructor if there are specific procedures at your institution that you should follow when collecting data from other people. We recommend, for now, that you think about the methods most commonly associated with qualitative research: observations, interviews, and open-ended surveys. These rich data-producing methods are most likely to provide the level of detail about others' experiences needed to evaluate the elements of your theory.

● **Apply and analyze the theory.**   Whether you are working with your own experiences or others', apply the theory (all of its component parts) to the experiences you've collected to see what it can illuminate: Where does it really help you understand something? Where does it fail to help? How might the theory need to change to account for your or others' experiences?

Writing Project   Theory Response Essay

The goal of this writing project is to apply a theoretical framework from an area of the social sciences to your own experiences, to the experiences of others, or to both. The first step is to choose a theoretical framework that has some relevance to you, providing ample opportunity to reflect on and write about your own experiences in relation to the theory.

THE INTRODUCTION

The introduction to your study should introduce readers to the theory and explain all of its essential elements. You should also be clear about whether you're applying the theory to your own experiences, to the experiences of others, or to both. In light of the work you did applying the theory, formulate a thesis that assesses the value of the theory for helping to understand the "moments," events, or phenomena you studied.

THE BODY

The body can be organized in a number of ways. If your theory has clear stages or elements, then you can explain each one and apply it to relevant parts of your experiences or those of others. If the theory operates in such a way that it's difficult to break into parts or stages or elements, then consider whether or not it's better to have subheadings that identify either (1) the themes that emerged from your application or (2) your research subjects (by pseudonym). In this case, your body sections would be more like case studies. Ultimately, the organization strategy you choose will depend on the nature of the theory you're applying and the kinds of events you apply it to. The body of your project should establish connections among the theory's component elements.

THE CONCLUSION

The conclusion of your study should assert your overall assessment of the theory's usefulness. Reiterate how the theory was useful and how it wasn't. Make recommendations for how it might need to be changed in order to account for the experiences you examined in light of the theory.

TECHNICAL CONSIDERATIONS

Keep in mind the conventions of writing in the social sciences that you've learned about throughout this chapter. Use APA documentation procedures for in-text documentation of summarized, paraphrased, and cited materials, as well as for the References page at the end of your study.

....

Insider Example

Student Theory Response Paper

Matt Kapadia, a first-year writing student, was interested in understanding the ways people rationalize their own successes and failures. In the following paper, he analyzes and evaluates a theory about the social science phenomenon of attribution (as described at changingminds.org) through the lenses of both his own and others' experiences. As you read Matt's paper, pay close attention to the moments when he offers evaluation of the theory. Ask yourself if his evaluation in each instance makes sense to you, based on the evidence he provides. Notice also that he follows APA style conventions in his paper. ▶

Evaluation of the Attribution Theory

Matt Kapadia

Department of English, North Carolina State University

Comp II: Writing in the Disciplines

Dr. Caroline Ruiz

October 29, 2016

Evaluation of the Attribution Theory

In an attempt to get a better sense of control, human beings are constantly attributing cause to the events that happen around them (Straker, 2008). Of all the things people attribute causes to, behavior is among the most common. The attribution theory aims to explain how people attribute the causes of their own behaviors compared to the behaviors of those around them. Behaviors can be attributed to both internal and external causes. Internal causes are things that people can control or are part of their personality, whereas external causes are purely circumstantial and people have no control over the resulting events (Straker, 2008). The attribution theory uses these internal and external causes to explain its two major components: the self-serving bias and the fundamental attribution error. The self-serving bias evaluates how we attribute our own behaviors, whereas the fundamental attribution error evaluates how we attribute the behaviors of those around us (Straker, 2008). This paper evaluates how applicable the attribution theory and its components are, using examples from personal experience as well as data collected from others. Based on the findings of this evaluation, I believe the attribution theory holds true on nearly all accounts; however, the category of the self-serving bias might need revision in the specific area dealing with professionals in any field of study or in the case of professional athletes.

> The writer establishes a thesis that includes an evaluation of the theory's usefulness in various contexts.

Attribution Theory: An Explanation

The foundation of the attribution theory is based in the nature of the causes people attribute behaviors to, whether it be internal or external. A person has no control over an external cause (Straker, 2008). An example would be a student failing a math test because the instructor used the wrong answer key. In this case, the student had no control

> In this paragraph and the next two, the writer reviews and exemplifies the component parts of the theory. That is, the writer offers an explanation of the theory, with examples to illustrate points, as appropriate.

over the grade he received, and it did not matter how much he had studied. A bad grade was inevitable. A person can also attribute behavioral causes to internal causes. Internal causes are in complete control of the person distributing the behavior and are typically attributed to part of the individual's personality (Straker, 2008). An example would be a student getting a poor grade on his math test because he is generally lazy and does not study. In this case, the student had complete control of his grade and chose not to study, which resulted in the poor grade. These two causes build up to the two major categories within the attribution theory.

The first major category of the attribution theory is that of self-serving bias. This category explores how people attribute causes to their own behaviors. It essentially states that people are more likely to give themselves the benefit of the doubt. People tend to attribute their poor behaviors to external causes and their good behaviors to internal causes (Straker, 2008). An example would be a student saying he received a poor grade on a test because his instructor does not like him. In this case, the student is attributing his poor behavior, making a poor grade on the test, to the external cause of his instructor not liking him. However, following the logic of the theory, if the student had made a good grade on the test, then he would attribute that behavior to an internal cause such as his own good study habits.

The second category of the attribution theory, the fundamental attribution error, states the opposite of the self-serving bias. The fundamental attribution error talks about how people attribute cause to the behaviors of those around them. It states that people are more likely to attribute others' poor behaviors to internal causes and their good behaviors to external causes (Straker, 2008). An example would be a student saying his friend got a better grade on the math test than him because the instructor likes his friend more. The student jumps to the conclusion that his friend's good grade was due to the external cause of the instructor liking the friend more. Moreover, if his friend had done poorly on the test, the student would most likely attribute the poor grade to an internal factor, such as his friend not studying for tests.

Personal Experiences

A situation from my personal experiences that exemplifies the ideas of the attribution theory is my high school golfing career. For my first two years of high school, I performed relatively poorly on the golf course. My team consistently placed last in tournaments, and I ranked nowhere near the top golfers from neighboring high schools. I blamed my performance on factors such as the wind and flat-out bad luck. At the same time, I attributed my teammates' poor performances to factors such as not practicing hard enough to compete in tournament play. In doing this, I became no better a golfer because I was denying that the true cause of my poor scores was the fact that I was making bad swings and not putting in the hours of work needed to perform at a higher level. I finally recognized this during my junior year of high school. I started to realize that blaming everything but myself was getting me nowhere and that the only way to improve was to take responsibility for my own play. I started practicing in areas where my game needed improvement and putting in hours at the driving range to improve my swing memory. In doing this, I became a much better player; by the time my senior season came around, I was ranked one of the top golfers in my conference and one of the best amateur players in the state of North Carolina. However, my team still did not perform well due to my teammates' performance, which I continued to attribute to their poor practice habits.

This experience reflects the attribution theory in several ways. I displayed self-serving bias in my early years of high

The writer details a particular personal experience that he'll later analyze through the lens of the theory.

In this section, the writer analyzes his experiences through the lens of the theory.

school golf. I attributed all of my poor performances to external causes, such as the wind, that I could not control. At the same time, I was displaying the fundamental attribution error in attributing my teammates' poor performances to internal causes such as not practicing hard enough. Throughout my high school golf career, I displayed the ideas of the attribution theory's category of the fundamental attribution error. However, during my junior and senior seasons my attributions moved away from the attribution theory's category of the self-serving bias. I began to attribute my poor performance to internal causes instead of the external causes I had previously blamed for my mishaps.

I believe that this is generally true for any athlete or professional seeking improvement in his or her prospective field. If a person continues to follow the ideas discussed in the category of the self-serving bias, he is not likely to improve at what he is trying to do. If Tiger Woods had constantly attributed his bad play to external causes and not taken responsibility for his actions as internal causes, he would have never become the best golfer in the world. Without attributing his poor behaviors to internal causes, he would have never gained the motivation to put in the hours of work necessary to make him the best. This observation can be applied to any other professional field, not only athletics. Personal improvement is only likely to take place when a person begins to attribute his or her poor behaviors to internal causes. I believe athletes and professionals represent problem areas for the theory of self-serving bias. However, the ideas of the fundamental attribution error generally hold true.

Experiences of Others

To evaluate the attribution theory, I conducted an experiment to test both the fundamental attribution error and the self-serving bias. The test subjects were three friends in the same class at North Carolina State University: MEA101,

The writer provides some insight into his methods for collecting data on the experiences of others.

Introduction to Geology. The students were asked to write down if their grades were good or bad on the first test of the semester ("good" meant they received an 80 or higher on the test, and "bad" meant they received below an 80). After the three students had done this for themselves, they were asked to attribute the grades of the others to a cause. This activity provided a clear sample of data that could test the validity of the self-serving bias and the fundamental attribution error. The reason I chose a group of friends versus a group of random strangers was that when people know each other they are more likely to attribute behavioral causes truthfully, without worrying about hurting anyone's feelings.

For the purposes of this experiment, the test subjects will be addressed as Students X, Y, and Z to keep their names confidential. The results of the experiment were as follows. The first student, Student X, received a "bad" grade on the test and attributed this to the instructor not adequately explaining the information in class and not telling the students everything the test would ultimately cover. However, Students Y and Z seemed to conclude that the reason Student X got a "bad" grade was because he did not study enough and is generally lazy when it comes to college test taking. Student Y received a "good" grade on the test and attributed this to studying hard the night before and to the fact that the test was relatively easy if one studied the notes. Students X and Z seemed to conclude that Student Y is a naturally smart student who usually receives good grades on tests regardless of how much he or she studies. Finally, Student Z received a "bad" grade on the test and attributed this to the instructor not covering the material on the test well enough for students to do well, a similar response to Student X. However, Students X and Y attributed Student Z's poor grade to bad study habits and not taking the class seriously.

In this section, the writer provides the results of his data collection.

These results tend to prove the ideas of both of the attribution theory's categories. Student X attributed his poor grade to the external cause of the instructor not covering the material well enough, demonstrating the self-serving bias. Students Y and Z attributed Student X's poor grade to the internal cause of Student X not studying hard enough and being a generally lazy college student, exemplifying the ideas of the fundamental attribution error. Student Y attributed her good grade to the internal cause of good study habits, also exemplifying the self-serving bias. However, Students X and Z felt that the reason for Student Y's success was the external cause of being a naturally good student who does well with or without studying, reflecting the ideas of the fundamental attribution error. Student Z's results also hold true to the theory. Student Z attributed his poor grade to the external cause of the instructor not covering the material adequately, a belief shared by Student X. Also holding true to the fundamental attribution error, both Students X and Y attributed Student Z's failure to the internal cause of poor study habits. Based on the findings of this experiment, I can say that both the fundamental attribution error and the self-serving bias hold true on all accounts.

Conclusion

Overall, I believe the attribution theory's categories of the self-serving bias and the fundamental attribution error are very applicable to everyday life. Based on the data gathered through personal experiences and the experiences of others through the experiment described in this analysis, I believe the theory holds true in the vast majority of situations where people attribute causes to behaviors and/or actions. The only area needing revisions is the self-serving bias when applied to the specific situations of professionals in a field of study or in the case of professional athletes. In both situations,

---

In this section, the writer discusses the implications of his findings for his overall evaluation of the theory.

The writer concludes his response paper by reviewing his overall evaluation of the theory in light of his own and others' experiences he analyzed.

improvement must occur in order to become a professional, and the only way this is likely to happen is by accepting internal fault for poor behaviors. By accepting internal fault, a person gains the motivation to put in the hours of work necessary to learn and improve at what he or she is trying to do. Without this improvement and learning, the ability to reach the professional level is slim to none. This displays the exact opposite of the attribution ideas that are described in the self-serving bias. With the exception of this small niche of situations that falsify the self-serving bias, the validity of the attribution theory is confirmed on all accounts.

Reference

Straker, D. (2008). *Attribution theory*. Retrieved from
   changingminds.org: http://changingminds.org/
   explanations/theories/attribution_theory.htm

Genres: Poster Presentation

A poster presentation is a visual representation of the findings of a research study, and it is a common written genre in the social sciences and natural sciences. Social scientists often organize their posters using IMRaD as an organizing strategy, and they make the poster visually appealing to highlight the findings that might be most interesting to the audience.

What Is the Rhetorical Context for This Genre?

Poster presentations are often designed for professional and academic conferences where multiple people will be presenting the results of research at the same time. The audience is typically other researchers in the same field, although that might differ depending on the type of event at which the poster is being displayed. Often the researcher or research team stand with their poster and answer questions from audience members as they walk around to view the posters. The poster, therefore, is intended as a starting point for conversation, but it also should stand on its own by highlighting important findings.

Strategies for Designing a Poster Presentation

● **Identify important elements of the study.**   A poster has limited space, so the first task of the author is to determine what is most important to highlight on the poster. Many researchers will use IMRaD as an organizing frame, so they might include a brief description of the study (Introduction); the research methods used; the results of the study; and the discussion, application, or interpretation of the results. Of these four parts of the IMRaD format, the most attention is usually given to the results in a poster presentation, and they are often presented in a visually appealing way—perhaps through a graph or chart to visually demonstrate the most important findings or a table to compare and contrast more than one group. The most effective poster presentations consider the interests and needs of the specific audience who will be viewing the poster, and the researcher focuses on highlighting those elements.

● **Develop an organizational strategy that is visually appealing.**   Successful poster presentations are visually appealing. Specifically, they pay attention to white space, they don't use too many words, they use large font sizes so that the audience can understand the results, and they use visual images and graphics to help the reader quickly interpret what they are reading on the poster. They also consider the layout of the information, keeping in mind that readers tend to start at the top and left-hand side of a poster to find information, working their way down and to the right. Some poster presentations even provide visual cues for readers so they know where to go next in their viewing of the poster (with the use of headings, numbers, or arrows, for example).

● **Consider any requirements from event organizers.**   When a poster is being presented at an event, the event organizers typically provide specifications about the size of the poster and how it will be presented. Some questions you might consider are the following:

- Do you need to print the poster on a certain type of material? For example, should it be on posterboard, or on paper? Or will it be displayed digitally?
- What size/dimensions do the event organizers request for your poster?
- Do you need to bring a stand or other materials to display the poster, or will that be provided?
- Will you have a table to provide materials or handouts to those viewing your poster?

In addition to these questions, you will also need to consider how to transport your poster to the event. Make sure you have a plan and give yourself plenty of time to get your poster printed and packed for transportation, should that be applicable.

Writing Project   **Poster Presentation**

The goal of this writing project is to design a poster that presents the results of research that you have conducted. The poster might present data that you have collected, or it might present findings from a review of literature you have conducted.

THE CONTENT

The content of your poster should include the title of your study, your name, a basic introduction to the study, and major findings. If there are sources that you cite in the content of your poster, you will also want to consider how and where to include references.

VISUAL DESIGN

As you present your findings, consider how to place elements in a visually logical and appealing way. Consider the use of white space on your poster so that your audience is not overwhelmed by the content. What information could be presented visually to help your audience quickly interpret the importance of your findings?

TECHNICAL CONSIDERATIONS

As you design your poster, work in a software program that will allow you to move visual elements around with ease. Many students have found PowerPoint, Google Slides, Keynote, and other slide presentation programs to be the best way to design a poster.

Insider Example

Professional Poster Presentation

Researchers Dana Gierdowski and Susan Miller-Cochran created this poster titled "Diversifying Design: Understanding Multilingual Perceptions of Learning in a Flexible Classroom" for the annual conference of the International Society for the Scholarship of Teaching and Learning. The poster was designed to engage conference attendees in a discussion with the authors about their work on the kinds of writing classroom designs that multilingual students preferred to support their learning.

Diversifying Design: Understanding Multilingual Perceptions of Learning in a Flexible Classroom

Researchers: Dana Gierdowski & Susan Miller-Cochran

The "Flexible" Classroom

- Situated in NCSU's First-Year Writing (FYW) Program
- Designed to engage students more in the writing process
- Designed to give instructors more pedagogical variety
- Outfitted with mobile furnishings, mobile whiteboards, & multiple fixed LCDs
- Student-owned laptop computers used in the space
- Collected data from ESL students in a FYW course

To begin to understand how ESL students responded to the flex room, data were collected that focused on student preferences for room layout and perceptions of their ideal writing classroom.

Methods

Data were collected from nine students in a first-year writing class for ESL writers. The student participants shared their perspectives by completing:

- Interviews about their perceptions of learning in the flex room
- Maps of their "ideal" writing classrooms
- Charrette-style placement of the furnishings in the room

Data were coded for consistency of patterns and themes. Inter-rater reliability was tested with Cohen's Kappa, with a Kappa strength of .805 (very good) for the ideal classroom design and a Kappa strength of .625 (good) for the charrette.

Student	Gender	Age	Native Language
1	F	23	Korean
2	F	19	Mandarin Chinese
3	F	19	Indonesian
4	M	20	Arabic/English
5	M	20	Arabic
6	M	21	French
7	F	21	German
8	M	18	Telugu
9	F	20	Mandarin Chinese

Sample Patterns of Arrangement

Students were given maps of their current classroom and were asked to layout the existing furniture in their preferred arrangement.

"I put them next to each other because I felt that if they were alone in one space they would be too isolated. I didn't feel comfortable when I was sitting alone at one of these tables. I like to be a part of a group and work together." –Student 7

"It's more organized instead of just having a lot of furniture thrown around the room." –Student 4

"The desks would be nearby the LCDs so you can connect to them...maybe we could have something that can connect to the iPad so we don't have to bring a computer. For a 50-minute class, I would rather bring my iPad than a heavy laptop." –Student 3

Sample Conceptual Maps

Students were asked to design an ideal writing classroom if given an unlimited budget.

"I'm not sure I like the set-up groups that you always have to sit with and work with. I kind of liked the other class I was in before (with) big tables." –Student 4

"The furniture should be easy to move...I think that if you have a group of three or four, you should have tables that when you put them together they become organized...into a triangle or something." –Student 3

"I would like to have a big screen (in the front of the room) for the whole class because everybody's looking at the teacher." –Student 7

Preliminary Results

Placement of the Instructor

- 5 students placed the teacher at the front of the class
- 2 students placed the instructor in the center of the class
- **7 students out of 9 (77%) designed an ideal classroom that remained instructor-centered**

Placement of the Students

- Overall, students placed the fewest furnishings in the quarter of the room with the teacher's computer
- Overall, students placed the highest number of furnishings in the quarter of the room opposite the teacher's computer
- **7 students (77%) placed students in groups in their ideal classrooms**

Student Technology

- 6 students included LCDs in their ideal classrooms
- 3 students indicated that student computers would be provided by the institution
- **6 students included writing technology for students in their ideal classrooms (laptops or desktops)**

Questions for Discussion

- What influence does experience in *prior learning* environments have on student preferences?
- What influence does experience in *current learning* environments have on student preferences?
- How might this type of research impact your own teaching?
- What constraints do you have to work with/around in your own instructional environment?
- If given an unlimited budget, what is the one feature you would like to have in your classroom that you don't currently have?

Relevant Resources

Beichner, R., Bernold, L., Burniston, E. Dail, P. Felder, R. Gastineau, J. et al. (1999). Case study of the physics component of an integrated curriculum. American Journal of Physics, 67(S1), S16-S24.

Bennett, A.M., Moeller, M. & Ball, E. (2006). Designing collaborative learning spaces: Where material culture meets mobile writing processes. Programmatic Perspectives, 1(2), 139-166.

Boys, J. (2011). Towards creative learning spaces: London: Routledge.

Matsuda, P. (2006). The myth of linguistic homogeneity in U.S. college composition. College English, 68 (6), 637-651.

Mitz, R. M. (2004). The inertia of classroom furniture: Unituating the classroom. In E. Nagelhout & C. Rutz (Eds.), Classroom spacial writing instruction (pp. 13-26). Creskill, NJ.

Taylor, S. S. (2008). Effects of studio space on teaching and learning: Preliminary findings from two case studies. Innovative Higher Education, 33(4), 217-228.

- **Observation plays a critical role in the social sciences.** The academic fields of the social sciences, including sociology, psychology, anthropology, communication studies, and political science, among others, make observations about human behavior and interactions, as well as the systems and social structures we create to organize the world around us.

- **Social science research rests on theories of human behavior and human systems,** propositions that are used to explain specific phenomena. Social science research contributes to the continual process of refining these theories.

- **Researchers in the social sciences typically establish a hypothesis,** or a testable proposition that provides an answer or predicts an outcome in response to the research question(s) at hand, at the beginning of a research project.

- **Social science researchers must make choices about the types of methods they use** in any research situation, based on the nature of their line of inquiry and the kind of research question(s) they seek to answer. They may use a quantitative, qualitative, or mixed-methods research design to collect data for analysis.

- **Social scientists must guard against bias in their research.** They rely on rigorous procedures and checks (e.g., ensuring appropriate sample sizes and/or using multiple forms of qualitative data) to ensure that the influence of any biases is as limited as possible.

- **IMRaD format—Introduction, Methods, Results, and Discussion—is a common structure used for the organization of research reports in the social sciences.** Although research reports in the social sciences may appear in any number of forms, much of the scholarship published in these fields appears in the IMRaD format.

- **The passive voice and hedging are uses of *language*** that characterize, for good reason, social scientific writing.

- **APA style is the most common documentation style used for *reference*** in the fields of the social sciences.

- **The genres of the literature review, the theory response paper, and the poster presentation are often produced in the fields of the social sciences.**

Reading and Writing in the Natural Sciences

Each of us has likely observed something peculiar in the natural world and asked, "Why does it do that?" or "Why does that happen?" Perhaps you've observed twinkling stars in the night sky and wanted to know why such distant light seems to move and pulse. Or perhaps you've wondered why, as you drive, trees closer to your car appear to rush by much faster than trees in the distance. Maybe you can recall the first time you looked at a living cell under a microscope in a biology course and wondered about the world revealed on the slide.

Scholars who work in the **natural sciences** study observable phenomena in the natural world and search for answers to the questions that spark their interests about these phenomena. Their work contributes to solutions to problems facing individuals and societies, from improving crop yields to the search for a coronavirus vaccine. The disciplines of the natural sciences include a wide array of fields of academic research, from agricultural and life sciences to physical sciences. Examples of disciplines within these fields include biology, botany, zoology, astronomy, physics, chemistry, and geology.

Interdisciplinary research is quite common in the natural sciences. An **interdisciplinary field** is an area of study in which different disciplinary perspectives or methods are combined into one. In such instances, methods for data collection often associated with one field may be used within another field of study. Consider biochemistry—a combination of biology and chemistry. In biochemistry, methods often associated with chemistry research are useful in answering questions about living organisms and biological systems. A biochemist may study aspects of a living organism such as blood alkalinity and its impact on liver function.

No matter the specific fields in which scientists work, they all collect, analyze, and explain data. Scientists tend to embrace a shared set of values, and as a result they typically share similar desires about how best to conduct research. The importance of any scientific study and its power to explain a natural phenomenon, then, are largely based on how well a researcher or research team

ANDREA TSURUMI

designs and carries out a study in light of the shared values and desires of the community's members.

In this chapter, we describe a process of writing activities involved in scientific research. We present a four-step scientific writing process that maps onto the elements of the scientific method. The process begins with careful observation of natural phenomena and leads to the development of research questions. This step is followed by an investigation that culminates in the reporting or publication of the research. You'll have the opportunity to examine several academic genres and learn the principles underlying genre conventions in the natural sciences.

Research in the Natural Sciences

For most social scientists, observation of natural phenomena is the first step in the process of conducting research. Something in the natural world captures their attention and compels them to pose questions. Some moments of scientific observation are iconic—such as Newton's observation of an apple falling from a tree as inspiration for his theory of gravity.

The search for understanding of natural phenomena can take scientists to many different places, and there is much variety in the ways they engage in research. One aspect that holds this diverse group of disciplines together, though, is a set of common values and procedures used in conducting research.

You're probably already familiar with or at least have heard about the scientific method, a protocol for conducting research in the sciences. The following table illustrates how the elements of the scientific method map onto a scientific writing process:

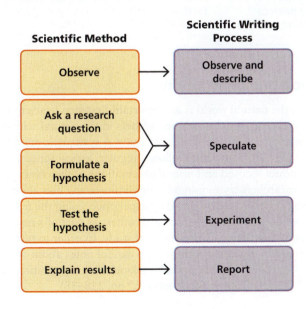

Completing the steps of a research project in a logical order and reporting the results accurately are keys to mastering research and writing in the natural sciences. You must observe and describe an object of study before you can speculate as to what it is or why it does what it does. Once you've described and speculated about a particular phenomenon and posed a research question and a hypothesis about it, then you're positioned well to construct an experiment (if appropriate) and collect data to test whether your hypothesis holds true. When you report the results of your research, you must describe these steps and the data collected accurately and clearly. These research and writing steps build on one another, and we explore each step in more detail moving forward.

Observation and Description

Observation in the natural world is an important first step in scientific inquiry. Beyond simple observation, though, researchers in the natural sciences conduct systematic observations of their objects of study. A systematic approach to observation requires researchers to follow a regular, logical schedule of observation and to conduct focused and *neutral* observations of the object of study. In other words, researchers try to minimize or eliminate any bias about the subject matter and simply record everything they experience, using the five senses. These observations, when written up to share with others as part of a research report, form the basis of description of the object of study. In order to move from observation to description, researchers must keep careful notes about their systematic observations. We discuss one method of tracking those observations later in the chapter (see "Genres: Observation Logbook," pp. 228–38).

Connect 9.1   **Thinking about Systematic Observation in the Sciences**

Read student Kedric Lemon's logbook account of his observations of various batteries (see Insider Example: Student Observation Logbook, pp. 230–38). Then answer the following questions:

- What type of data was Lemon collecting every day? How was he able to quantify his observations?
- Which of his senses was he relying on?
- Was he able to remain neutral, or do you detect any biases? Explain.

From Description to Speculation

The distinction between description and speculation is a subtle but important one to understand as it relates to scientific inquiry. While descriptive writing gives a *who*, *what*, *where*, and/or *when* account of an observable phenomenon, speculative writing seeks to explain *how* or *why* something behaves the way that it does. Speculative writing is most commonly associated with asking a research question and formulating a hypothesis—the second and third steps of the scientific method.

The process of articulating an explanation for an observed phenomenon and speculating about its meaning is an integral part of scientific discovery. By collecting data on your own and then interpreting that data, you're engaging in the production of knowledge even before you begin testing a proposed hypothesis. In this respect, scientific discovery is similar to writing in the humanities and the social sciences. Scientists interpret data gained through observation, modeling, or experimentation much in the same way that humanists interpret data collected through observation of texts. The ability to *observe systematically* and *make meaning* is the common thread that runs through all academic research.

Descriptive writing seeks to define an object of study, and it functions like a photograph. Speculative writing engages by asking *how* or *why* something behaves the way that it does, and in this sense it triggers a kind of knowledge production that is essential to scientific discovery. Following a writing process that moves a researcher from describing a phenomenon to considering *how* or *why* something does what it does is a great strategy for supporting scientific inquiry.

To this end, we encourage you to collect original data as modeled in the Insider Examples presented at the end of this chapter—the observation logbook, the research proposal, and the lab report. Your view on the natural world is your own, and the data you collect and how you interpret that data are yours to decide. The arguments you form based on your data and your interpretation of that data can impact your world in small or very large ways.

Go outdoors and locate any type of animal (a squirrel, bird, butterfly, frog, etc.) as an object of study. Decide beforehand the amount of time you'll spend observing your subject (five minutes may be enough), and write down in a notebook as many observable facts as possible about your subject and its behavior. Consider elements of size, color, weight, distance traveled, and interaction with other animals or physical objects. If you're able to make a video or take a picture (e.g., with a cell phone camera), please do so. Then write a paragraph under each of these two headings:

- **Description**   Write all the observable facts about your subject, as if you were reporting it to someone who had never seen this animal before.

- **Speculation**   Offer your theory about why the animal appears or behaves the way you observed it.

From Speculation to Research Questions and Hypothesis

You can move on to formalize your speculation by writing research questions, formulating a hypothesis, and designing a research study. In all these stages, writing helps you clarify your thinking and solidify your plans. Writing research questions and hypotheses in the natural sciences is a process similar to those activities in the social sciences (see Chapter 8). Devoting time to several days of focused observation, collecting data, and writing and reflecting on your object of study should trigger questions about what you're observing.

● **Open-Ended and Closed-Ended Questions**   As you write research questions, you might consider the difference between open-ended and closed-ended research questions. A **closed-ended question** can be answered by *yes* or *no*. By contrast, an **open-ended question** provokes a fuller response. Here are two examples:

Closed-Ended Question	Is acid rain killing off the Fraser fir population near Mount Mitchell in North Carolina?
Open-Ended Question	What factors contribute to killing off the Fraser fir population near Mount Mitchell in North Carolina?

Scientists use both open-ended and closed-ended questions. Open-ended questions usually begin with *What*, *How*, or *Why*. Closed-ended questions can be appropriate in certain instances, but they can also be quite polarizing. They often begin with *Is* or *Does*. Consider the following two questions:

Closed-Ended Question	Is global warming real?
Open-Ended Question	What factors contribute to global warming?

Rhetorically, the closed-ended question divides responses into *yes* or *no* answers, whereas the open-ended question provokes a more thoughtful response. Neither form of question is better per se, but the forms do function differently. If you're engaging in a controversial subject, a closed-ended research question might serve your purpose. If you're looking for a more complete answer to a complex issue, an open-ended question might serve you better.

● **Hypotheses**   Once you've established a focused research question, informed by or derived on the basis of your observation and speculation about a natural science phenomenon, then you're ready to formulate a **hypothesis**. This will be a testable proposition that provides an answer or that predicts an outcome in response to the research question(s) at hand.

Research Question	Do female house finches remove eggs from their own nests?
Hypothesis	Our hypothesis is that female house finches remove eggs from their own nests.

Connect 9.3   **Developing Research Questions and a Hypothesis**

Review the observation notes and the descriptions and explanations you produced in Connect 9.2. What potential research questions emerged? Write down at least two research questions that emerged from your observations, and then attempt to answer each question in the form of a hypothesis. You also have the option of writing research questions and hypotheses about another phenomenon that you've observed and are more interested in.

Research Study Design

Natural scientists collect evidence through systematic observation and experimentation, and they value methods that are quantifiable and replicable. In some instances, the natural sciences are described as "hard" sciences and the social sciences as "soft." This distinction stems from the tendency for natural scientists to value quantitative methods over qualitative methods, whereas social scientists often engage in both forms of data collection and sometimes combine quantitative and qualitative methods in a single study. (See "Methods" in Chapter 8 for more on quantitative and qualitative methods.) Natural scientists value experiments and data collection processes that can be repeated to achieve the same or similar results, often for the purposes of generalizing their findings. Social scientists acknowledge the fluidity and variability of social systems and therefore also highly value qualitative data, which helps them to understand more contextual experiences.

● **Testing Hypotheses**   In the previous two sections, we discussed how to conduct systematic observation that leads to the description of a phenomenon, and then we explored processes for speculating about what you observed in order to construct a research question and a hypothesis. One way to test a hypothesis is to engage in a systematic observation of the target of your research phenomenon. Imagine that you're interested in discovering factors that affect the migration patterns of bluefin tuna, and you've hypothesized that water temperature has some effect on those patterns. You could then conduct a focused observation to test your hypothesis. You might, for instance, observe bluefin tuna in their migration patterns and measure water temperatures along the routes.

Another way to test a hypothesis, of course, is to design an experiment. Experiments come in all shapes and sizes, and one way to learn about the experimental methods common to your discipline is by reading the "Methods" sections of peer-reviewed scholarly articles in your field. Every discipline has slightly different approaches to experimental design. Some disciplines, such as astronomy, rely almost exclusively on non-experimental systematic observation, while others rely on highly controlled experiments. Chemistry is a good example of the latter.

● **Comparative Experiments**   One of the most common forms of experimental design is the *comparative experiment*, in which a researcher tests two or more types of objects and assesses the results. For example, an engineering student may want to test different types of skateboard ball bearings. She may design an experiment that compares a skateboard's distance rolled when using steel versus ceramic bearings. She could measure distances rolled, speed, or the time it takes to cover a preset distance when the skateboard has steel bearings and when it has ceramic bearings.

In some disciplines of the natural sciences, it is common practice to test different objects against a control group. A *control group* is used in a comparative experimental design to act as a baseline with which to compare other objects. For example, a student researcher might compare how subjects score on a memorization test after having consumed (a) no coffee, (b) two cups of decaf coffee, or (c) two cups of caffeinated coffee. In this example, the group of subjects consuming no coffee would function as a control group.

The IRB Process and Use of Human Subjects

Regardless of a study's design, it is important to realize that academic institutions have very clear policies regarding experimental designs that involve human subjects, whether that research is being conducted by individuals in the humanities, the social sciences, or the natural sciences. Both professional and student researchers are required to submit proposals through an *institutional review board*, or IRB. In the United States, institutional review boards operate under federal law to ensure that any experiment involving humans is ethical. This is often something entirely new to undergraduate students, and it should be taken seriously. No matter how harmless a test involving human subjects may seem, you should determine if you must submit your research plans through an IRB. This can often be done online. Depending on the nature and scope of your research, though, the processes of outlining the parameters of your research for review may be quite labor-intensive and time-consuming. You should familiarize yourself with the protocol for your particular academic institution. An online search for "institutional review board" and the name of your school should get you started. (For more information, see "The IRB Process and Use of Human Subjects" in Chapter 8.)

Insider's View
Physiologist Paige Geiger on the Integrity of Scientific Writing

COURTESY OF PAIGE GEIGER

"A biomedical scientist performs basic research on questions that have relevance to human health and disease, biological processes, and systems. We design scientific studies to answer a particular research question and then report our results in the form of a manuscript for publication. Good science is only as good as the research study design itself. We value innovation, ideas, accurate interpretation of data, and scientific integrity. There is an honor system to science that the results are accurate and true as reported. Manuscripts are peer-reviewed, and there is inherent trust and belief in this system."

Connect 9.4   Freewriting about an Experiment

Building on your research question and hypothesis from Connect 9.3, imagine how you might learn more about your subject as a natural scientist. Freewrite for five minutes about how you could collect data that would test your hypothesis. As you write, consider feasible methods that you could follow soon, as well as methods that might extend beyond the current semester but that you could develop into a larger project for later use in your undergraduate studies. Consider whether an experiment or a systematic observation would be more useful. Most important, use your imagination and have fun.

Values Underlying Writing in the Natural Sciences

After observing and describing, speculating and hypothesizing, and conducting an experimental study or systematic observation, scientists move toward publishing the results of their research. This is the final step of the scientific method and the final stage of the scientific writing process that we introduced at the beginning of the chapter: scientists explain their results by reporting their data and discussing their implications. There are multiple forms through which scientists report their findings, and these often depend on the target audience. For instance, scientists presenting their research results at an academic conference for the consideration of their peers might report results in the form of a poster presentation. Research results can also be presented in the form of an academic journal article. Scientists who want to present their results to a more general audience, though, might issue a press release.

No matter the differences in genre and disciplinary focus, a set of core values connects writing in the natural sciences. These values shared among members of the scientific community have an impact on the communication practices and writing conventions of natural science fields. We'll discuss these values first and then, in the pages that follow, point out how they are reflected in Structure, Language, and Reference (SLR).

Objectivity

As we noted earlier, *objectivity* (or neutrality) in observation and experimentation is essential to the research that scientists do. Most researchers in the natural sciences believe that bias undermines the reliability of research results. When scientists report their results, therefore, they often use rhetorical strategies to bolster the appearance of objectivity in their work. Examples include the use of scientific jargon and an IMRaD organization that mirrors the scientific method process.

Replicability

Like objectivity, the replicability of research methods and findings is important to the production and continuation of scientific inquiry. Imagine that a scientific report reveals the discovery that eating an orange every day could help prevent the onset of Alzheimer's disease. This sounds great, right? But how would the larger scientific community go about verifying such a finding? Multiple studies would likely be undertaken in an attempt to replicate the original study's finding. If the finding couldn't be replicated by carefully following the research procedures outlined in the original study, then that discovery wouldn't contribute much, if anything at all, to ongoing research on Alzheimer's disease precisely because the finding's veracity couldn't be confirmed. Examples of rhetorical strategies linked to replicability include meticulous detail and precision with language.

Recency

Scientific research is an ongoing process wherein individual studies or research projects contribute bits of information that help fill in a larger picture or research question. As research builds, earlier studies and projects become the bases for additional questioning and research. As in other fields, like the social sciences, it's important that scientific researchers remain current on the developments in research in their respective fields of study. To ensure that their work demonstrates recency—that is, it is current and draws on knowledge of other recent work—researchers in the sciences select references and use documentation styles that highlight recent publication dates.

Cooperation and Collaboration

Unlike the clichéd image of the solitary scientist spending hours alone in a laboratory, most scientists would probably tell you that research in their fields takes place in a highly cooperative and collaborative manner. In fact, large networks of researchers in any particular area often comprise smaller networks of scholars who are similarly focused on certain aspects of a larger research question. These networks may work together to refine their research goals in light of the work of others in the network, and researchers are constantly sharing—through publication of reports, team researching, and scholarly conferences—the results of their work. In the humanities, where ideas are a reflection of the individuals who present them, researchers and writers often direct commentary toward individuals for their ideas when there's cause for disagreement or dissatisfaction with other researchers' ideas. Conventionally, however, science researchers treat others in their field more indirectly when objections to their research or findings come up. Instead of linking research problems to individuals, scientists generally direct their dissatisfaction with others' work at problems in the research process or design. This approach highlights the importance of cooperation and collaboration as shared values of members of the scientific community.

Structural Conventions in the Natural Sciences

As we examine structural conventions—that is, conventions governing how writing is organized—keep in mind that your goal is not to master every type of writing in the natural sciences. Instead, your goal should be to understand how scientific values inform scientific writing conventions.

IMRaD Format

Research studies in the natural sciences typically follow the IMRaD (Introduction, Methods, Results, and Discussion) format. The structure of IMRaD parallels the ordered processes of the scientific writing process: observe and describe, speculate, experiment, and report. This reporting structure underscores the importance of objectivity because it reflects the prescribed steps of the scientific method, which is itself a research process that scientists follow to reduce or eliminate bias.

- The *Introduction* is where researchers describe what they have observed and how it relates to their speculations and hypotheses, and it is also where they report what is already known about a phenomenon or what is relevant in the current scholarship for their own research. Hypothesis statements predict the outcome of a research study, but the very nature of a prediction leaves open the possibility of other outcomes. By opening this "space" of possibility, scientists acknowledge that other researchers could potentially find results that differ from their own. In this way, scientists confirm the importance of replicability to their inquiry process.

- In the *Methods* section, researchers thoroughly explain the precise procedures they used to collect data and why they chose those methods. They may discuss how the data were interpreted or analyzed.

- The *Results* and *Discussion* sections report new information about the data the researchers gathered and their explanations and interpretations of what those results might mean. The Discussion section might also include suggestions for future research, demonstrating how research in the sciences is always building upon prior research.

For an example of a science paper in IMRaD format, see Insider Example: Student Lab Report, which begins on page 248. Also see Chapter 8, "IMRaD Format," for an extended discussion with examples.

Other Structural Conventions

● **Titles**   Scientists tend to give their reports very clear titles, reflecting the value of objectivity. Rarely will you find a "creative" or rhetorical title in science writing. Instead, scientists prefer descriptive titles or titles that say exactly what the reports are about rather than titles that play with language (as in the humanities).

● **Presentation of Researchers' Names**   As you examine published research reports, you will find that very often they provide a list, prominently, of the names of individuals who contributed to the research and to the reporting of that research. This information usually appears at the top of reports just after the title, and it may also identify the researchers' institutional and/or organizational affiliations. Names typically appear in an order that identifies principal researchers first. Naming all the members of a research team acknowledges the highly cooperative nature of the researching processes that many scientists undertake.

Observing Structural Features in the Natural Sciences

Although we've discussed a number of structural expectations for writing in the natural sciences, we'd like to stress again that these expectations are conventional. As such, you'll likely encounter studies in the natural sciences that rely on only a few of these structural features or that alter the conventional expectations in light of the researchers' particular aims. Find a scholarly article from the natural sciences, either from Part Three or your own research, and examine it in terms of these structural features. If the article deviates from the conventions we've described, what might be the writer's reasons?

- **IMRaD Format**   Does the report have a section labeled "Introduction" where the researchers describe what they have observed and how it relates to their speculations and hypotheses? Is there a "Methods" section that thoroughly explains the precise procedures they used to collect data? Are "Results" discussed and data presented? Is there a "Discussion" section that explains the significance of the researchers' findings and that includes suggestions for future research?

- **Title**   Does the title contain key words that highlight important components of the study?

- **Authors' Names**   Does the article list a team of people as study authors? Are there institutions included with their names? Does it appear that there are principal researchers who are listed first?

Language Conventions in the Natural Sciences

The way natural scientists use language reflects their emphasis on objectivity, replicability, cooperation, and collaboration.

Jargon

The word *jargon* often has negative connotations, but **jargon** is simply the specialized vocabulary used by a particular community of scholars. For example, a scientific researcher might refer to a particular rose as *Rosa spinosissima* rather than by a common name that could vary from region to region. By using the Latin name, the writer also positions the plant in terms of its genus (*Rosa*) and species (*spinosissima*), which indicates how the plant is both similar to and distinct from other plants. The use of jargon in this instance is actually clarifying for the intended audience of other botanists. Using jargon is a means of communicating with precision, and precision in language is fundamental to objective expression.

Numbers and Other Details

Scientific reports are often filled with charts and figures, and these are often filled with numbers. Scientists prefer to communicate in numbers because unlike words, which can inadvertently convey the wrong meaning, numbers are more fixed in terms of their ability to communicate specific meaning. Consider the difference between describing a tree as "tall" and giving a tree's height in feet and inches. This represents the difference between communicating somewhat qualitatively and entirely quantitatively. The preference for communicating in numbers, or quantitatively, enables members of the scientific community to reduce, as much as possible, the use of words. As writers use fewer words and more numbers in scientific reports, the reports appear to be more objective. One of the conventional expectations for scientific writing involves the level of detail and specificity, particularly in certain areas of research reporting (e.g., Methods sections). Scientists report their research methods in meticulous detail to ensure that others can replicate their results. This is how scientific knowledge builds. Verification through repeated testing and retesting of results establishes the relative value of particular research findings. It's not surprising, then, that the Methods sections of scientific research reports are typically highly detailed and specific.

Active and Passive Voice

As we discussed in Chapter 8, writers in the social sciences and natural sciences often prefer the **passive voice** because it can foster a sense that researchers are acting objectively or with neutrality. With the passive voice, the focus is on the study's subjects; the researchers are not visible as the subjects of sentences. This does not mean that scientists never use *we* or *I* in their writing; sometimes it is helpful for clarity. Consider these two sentences from an article in the journal *NeuroImage*:

Active Voice	In the present study, we extended a previous study (Shah et al., 2013) and investigated the cerebral representation maps of expert writers, comparing them to inexperienced writers.
Passive Voice	All of the participants were asked about their experience and practice of creative writing.

Connect 9.6 **Observing Language Features in the Natural Sciences**

Continue your examination of the article you selected for Connect 9.5, using the questions below as a guide. If the article deviates from the conventions we've described, what might be the writer's reasons?

- **Jargon** Does the writer use specialized vocabulary to communicate with precision?

- **Numbers and Other Details** Approximately what percent of the data is communicated quantitatively, rather than through words? Is there a high level of detail and specificity so that others could replicate the results?

- **Active and Passive Voice** How often do the authors use *we* or *I*? Is there a section of the paper where they use the passive voice exclusively?

Reference Conventions in the Natural Sciences

Scientists often cite the work of others when establishing a context for their own research. Their use of recent sources reflects the value of recency, and it indicates that they are advancing the conversation around this research area. Most scholars in the natural sciences follow the documentation style of the American Psychological Association (APA) or the Council of Science Editors (CSE) when crediting their sources. These documentation styles highlight the publication year by including it as part of the in-text citation, as in the following citation in APA style:

> A team working in Guangxi, China, discovered a new species of Gesneriacaeae, *Primulina titan*, that resembles *P. hunanensis* but can be distinguished by a combination of morphological characteristics of leaf, bract, corolla, stamen and pistil (Xin et al., 2020).

This citation would be the same in CSE style, except that the comma after the authors names would not be used. For a discussion of the elements of citations and References lists, see "American Psychological Association (APA) Style" and "Council of Science Editors (CSE) Style" in the Appendix.

Insider's View
Conservation Biologist Michelle LaRue on Learning Science Writing Conventions

COURTESY OF MICHELLE LARUE

"I learned the conventions of science writing through literature review, imitation, and a lot of practice: this often included pages and pages of feedback from advisors and colleagues. Further, reading wildlife and modeling articles helped me focus on the tone, writing style, and format expected for each journal. After that, it was all about practicing my writing skills.

"I also learned the KISS principle during my undergraduate career: Keep It Simple, Stupid. This mantra reminds me to revise my writing so it's clear, concise, and informative. It is my opinion that science writing can be inherently difficult to understand, so it's important to keep the message clear and straightforward.

"I find that as I progress and hone my writing and research skills, sitting down to write gets easier, and I have been able to move up in the caliber of journal in which I publish papers. Writing is a skill that is never perfected; striving for the next best journal keeps me focused on improvement."

Connect 9.7 **Observing Reference Features in the Natural Sciences**

Conclude your examination of the article you selected for Connect 9.5. Can you identify the documentation style? If you are having difficulty, go back to the original journal and see if you can find the reference style required for the publication. What type of information is valued?

Genres: Observation Logbook

An observation logbook is a place for researchers to keep systematic notes on their object of study. It provides an organized space to focus, record, and reflect on observations made over a series of hours, days, or weeks. Students may be asked to provide their logbooks as part of an assignment in a natural sciences course. Often the logbook is accompanied by a narrative that describes and speculates on the observation as a whole.

What Is the Rhetorical Context for This Genre?

Systematic and carefully recorded observations can lay a solid foundation for further exploration of a subject. These observations might take place as an initial step in the scientific writing process, or they might be part of the data collection that occurs when testing a hypothesis. The observation logbook is a foundational part of the research process that precedes the construction of a formal lab report. As a student, your audience is your instructor. As a researcher, typically your audience would be people who are collaborating with you in some way on the project. Observation logbooks are usually not published.

Sometimes observation logbooks include speculation in addition to description, but the two types of writing should be clearly distinguished by headings to ensure that the more objective observations are not confused with any speculation. Speculation, you'll remember, occurs at the stage of formulating research questions and a hypothesis.

Strategies for Working with an Observation Logbook

● **Determine your subject, purpose, and method.** Even if your subject is determined by your instructor, you may be able to find a focus for your study that aligns with your own interests and curiosity. Decide what kind of changes or behaviors you wish to observe and what you hope to learn through your observations. This information will not only inform your methods of observation and how often you will observe, but it will also provide the basis for the introduction section of your final logbook.

● **Decide how to record and organize your observations.** Because the logbook is meant to help you collect evidence through systematic observation, consider creating a series of questions or a list of data points that you will focus on in each session. Put this in a format and medium that will be easy for you to fill out. Consider whether a multimodal data collection process that includes digital photos and video-recorded evidence would be right for your project. Decide how many entries you will need based on how frequently you plan to observe, and be sure to have a place to record the date (and time, if applicable).

● **Observe and describe.** Keep accurate and detailed notes of your subject and methods. Write your notes in a form that can be shared with others either after each session or at the end of your entire observation period. This might also include converting data into charts or graphs, as in the Insider Example that begins on page 230. At the end of the entire period of observation, review your notes and draw conclusions:

- What did you learn about your object of study?
- What claims can you now make regarding your object of study?
- What evidence could you use from your observational logbook to support those claims?

● **Speculate.** Keep track of the questions that occur to you during your observations. What is surprising or puzzling? Are you observing changes that point to a hypothesis?

● **Remember SLR as you prepare your logbook for an audience.** The Writing Project that follows suggests a structure for sharing your completed observation logbook with others. Apply what you've learned in this chapter about the values of objectivity and replicability as you draft each section of your logbook. Focus on clearly describing and summarizing your observations in the first draft and creating the types of visuals (tables, graphs, diagrams, etc.) that show change over time. Use the revision stage to further clarify your points. When you proofread, be sure to check that you have not introduced any errors when transferring the data from your notes to your visuals.

> **Writing Project**   **Observation Logbook**

Your goal in this writing project is to share your observation logbook with an audience. You'll describe the purpose of your study, detail your observations for each session, summarize your overall observations, speculate about the meaning or significance of what you observed, and propose a hypothesis for further research.

THE INTRODUCTION

The opening of your observation should introduce what you are studying, how you plan to conduct your study, and what you hope to learn. It can be written in the future tense, assuming that you've written the introduction before beginning your observations.

THE LOG

Provide an entry for each session, describing your observations in accurate detail for a reader. Include visuals such as photographs, tables, and charts if such visuals would clearly communicate your observations.

THE NARRATIVE

In the narrative that follows the log, include two sections: a description of your object of study and speculation about your observations. In the Description section, refrain from explaining or speculating about behavior; simply write the observations that are most important to give a clear picture of what you studied and how you studied it. Make use of time measurements and physical measurements such as weight, size, and distance. In the Speculation section, theorize about why certain behaviors emerged in your object of study. You might begin by deciding which behaviors most surprised you or seem most interesting to you. You might also use the Speculation section as a place to begin thinking about future questions that could be explored as a follow-up to your observations.

....

Insider Example
Student Observation Logbook

In the following observation logbook, written using APA style conventions, student Kedric Lemon catalogs his observations concerning the efficiency of several types of batteries over a five-day period. His observations form the basis for his experimental study, which appears later in the chapter (see Insider Example: Student Lab Report, pp. 248–57). You'll notice that he carefully separates his observations and description from any speculation about why he observed what he did. ▶

**Comparing the Efficiency of Various Batteries
Being Used over Time**

Kedric Lemon
North Carolina State University
Professor Matthew Chu
November 4, 2020

Comparing the Efficiency of Various Batteries Being Used over Time

Logbook

Introduction

The purpose of this study is to see if some batteries can hold their charge for longer periods of time than others. Also, this observational study will determine if there is an overwhelming difference between generic brand and the top name-brand batteries, or if people are really just paying for the name. I will perform this study by first recording all of the batteries' initial voltages, and then each day I will allow each of the batteries to go on for an hour and a half and then again check the voltage. It is important that I test the voltage immediately after the batteries come out of the flashlight. Otherwise, results could vary. Before putting in the second set of batteries, I will allow the flashlight to cool down for an hour because after being in use for an hour and a half they are likely hot, and I am unsure if this can affect how fast the other batteries will be consumed. I will look first at how much charge was lost over the duration that they were used in the flashlight. Then I will compare them to one another to determine which one has lost the most over a day, and second, which of the batteries still holds the highest voltage. I hypothesize that the Duracell battery will decrease at the slowest rate and that it will have the highest initial voltage.

Friday, October 11, 2020

The initial voltages of all three types of batteries (with the two batteries in each flashlight averaged) are as follows:

Side annotations:

Establishes the purpose of the study and outlines an observational protocol

Outlines methods

Establishes a hypothesis

Begins a report on systematic observation of the phenomenon

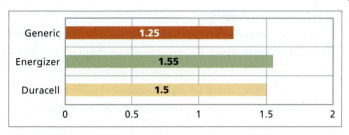

So from these initial observations the Energizer battery has the highest initial voltage.

After running all of the batteries for an hour and a half, the batteries had the following voltages:

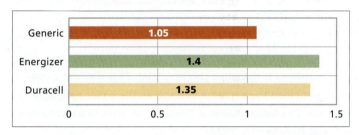

Energizer and Duracell both appear to be decreasing at approximately the same rates thus far in the observation, whereas the generic brand has already dropped much faster than the other two types of batteries. This observation raises the question: What is the composition of the Duracell and Energizer batteries that allows them to hold a better initial charge than the generic brand of batteries?

Observations leading to questions

Sunday, October 13, 2020

The three sets of batteries were placed into the flashlight, in the same order as the trial prior, to allow them all to have close to the same time between usages, again to try and avoid any variables. Today the data show similar results after all of the batteries ran in the flashlight for an hour and a half:

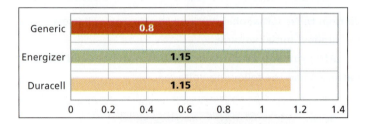

The generic brand of batteries did not decrease as significantly as it did after the first trial. This day the generic brand lost close to the same voltage as the other two types of batteries. The Energizer and Duracell had the same voltages.

Tuesday, October 15, 2020

On this day of observation the batteries were again placed into the flashlights for the trial time. The data for this day are as follows:

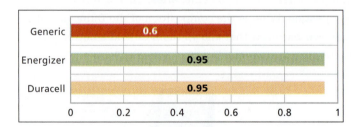

As in the preceding trial, the generic brand decreased by an amount similar to the other two batteries. Also, the generic brand's intensity has begun to decrease. However, both the other two batteries still give off a strong light intensity. This observation raises the question: At what voltage does the light

Provides evidence of the researcher's attempt to remain systematic in his observations

Student's observations continue to raise questions.

intensity begin to waver? Another question is: Will the other two batteries begin to have lower light intensity at approximately the same voltage as the generic, or will they continue to have a stronger light intensity for longer? The figures below show the change of light intensity of the generic brand of batteries from the beginning until this day's observation.

Figure 1. Before   *Figure 2.* After

Thursday, October 17, 2020

    The voltage readings for the batteries on this fourth day of observation are as follows:

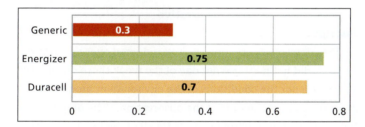

The generic brand is losing even more intensity when it is in the flashlight. It is obvious that it is getting near the end of its battery charge. Today was also the biggest decrease in charge for the generic brand of batteries. This is interesting because it is actually producing less light than before, so why does it lose more voltage toward the end of its life? Another observation is that again the Energizer brand holds more voltages than the Duracell. There is still no change in light intensity for the two name brands.

Saturday, October 19, 2020

The voltage readings for the batteries on the final day of observation are as follows:

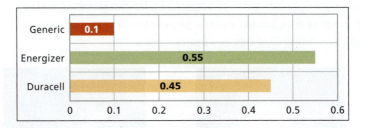

Today the generic battery hardly produced any light out of the flashlight by the end of the time period, although it still didn't drop to 0 voltage, so there are clearly still some electrons flowing in the current throughout the battery. Also, the Duracell battery has clearly dropped well below the Energizer now. The Duracell has shown a slight decrease in the light intensity compared to when the observational study first started. So what is the composition of the Energizer battery that makes it outlast the Duracell battery?

Narrative Description

Five days of observations were conducted over an eight-day period. It did not matter what day of the week these observations were made nor the conditions of the environment around the object of study at the time of the observations. The only thing that was constant environmentally for all of the batteries in the study was the temperature because more heat results in higher kinetic energy, which causes electrons to move faster. From the battery types available in this area, the following were chosen for the study: Duracell, Energizer, and a generic brand from Walmart. Before the first observation, each battery was tested with the voltmeter to determine its initial charge. This established which battery was the most powerful and provided a baseline from which to measure change over time.

The narrative description provides a summary of the student's systematic observation.

Each of these battery types was tested for the same amount of time for each day that they were observed. Because the flashlight took two batteries to operate, the voltages of each set of batteries were averaged, but the voltage of these batteries was determined to be very similar over the course of the observation. This similarity is a result of the entire circuit acting at the same time, causing equal electron transfer between the two batteries to occur, thus causing them to have equal voltages.

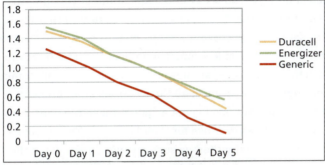

Final Graph from Five Days of Observations

The graph above shows the change in voltage over five days of observation. Duracell and Energizer were very similar to each other, with Energizer performing slightly higher than the Duracell brand. The generic had a lower initial voltage than the other two batteries and continued to decrease at a faster rate than the other two batteries. The graph also illustrates how quickly the generic brand lost its voltage toward the end of its life, whereas the other two batteries seemed to continue to decrease at approximately the same rate throughout.

Speculation

My initial hypothesis that the Duracell battery would decrease at the slowest rate was not supported by the data. An explanation for the strong performance of the Energizer battery is that the manufacturer combines lithium with the copper tip

Evaluates initial hypothesis (speculation) in light of the data on the cathode; this allows for a longer battery life than with a copper tip alone, as in the Duracell battery. The generic brand has a carbon and copper tip, which is not as effective as copper and lithium or copper alone. Also, the cathodes and anodes of the generic batteries may not be as professionally manufactured as the other two types of batteries. All of these differences could explain why there is a higher voltage density in the Energizer battery than in the other two batteries.

The data do not support my other hypothesis, that the Duracell battery would have the highest initial voltage. An explanation for the Energizer's stronger results is that the Energizer batteries contain alkaline metals, while the Duracell batteries do not. The low initial voltage of the generic brand of batteries may be because they are not packed as well. It takes special equipment to make all the electrons store properly, and the equipment used is not as powerful as the ones that Duracell and Energizer use for their batteries. These factors may account for why there is such a major difference in the rates at which the batteries lose their charge.

For further research into this topic I would recommend using a larger sample, because I used only two batteries for each type of battery. Also, I would recommend gathering data on the new rechargeable batteries, which are a popular option for consumers. A future experiment might also extend the time that the flashlight is left on, because others have observed that Duracell does better than Energizer over continuous usage.

Another interesting question to explore is which battery is the most cost-effective. Does the consumer still save money by buying the generic brand if it needs to be replaced sooner? A future experiment could attempt to quantify the answer to this question.

Further speculates about factors that contributed to rejection of the hypothesis

Provides suggestions for future research on the subject

Genres: Research Proposal

The research proposal is one of the most common genres of academic writing in the natural sciences. It provides a description and rationale for a research project before the work of executing the research begins.

What Is the Rhetorical Context for This Genre?

Professional scholars use the research proposal to plan out complex studies, to formulate their thoughts, and to submit their research designs to institutional review boards or to grant-funding agencies. The ability to secure grant funding (i.e., to write an effective research proposal and connect it to a realistic, clear budget) is a highly sought-after skill in a job candidate for many academic, government, and private industry positions. Because the research proposal is such an important vehicle for securing the funding and materials necessary to conduct research, much of the work of science could not get done without it.

Strategies for Writing a Research Proposal

A research proposal is an advanced genre of academic writing that requires practice and knowledge of the conventions expected by the institution you are writing for. As an undergraduate student, you can begin the process of developing familiarity with this genre.

● **Review the scholarly literature on your topic.**   Using the research techniques discussed in Chapter 5, investigate what work has already been done on your topic and make sure that your proposed research project fills a gap in the scholarship. You will use your findings in the introduction of your proposal to make an argument for the need for your research. This literature review also serves to demonstrate your knowledge of other scholars' research and to build your credibility as a researcher. See Chapter 8 for more on writing a literature review.

● **Think about your audience as you explain your proposed methods.**
You will likely collaborate with other students or your teacher as you develop a plan for testing your hypothesis. When it is time to put your plan in writing, describe your process in enough detail so that readers will be able to replicate your methods on their own. Make it clear what kind of data you will be collecting at each stage of the process. Check that you have covered when, where, and why as well as how you will be proceeding.

● **Remember SLR as you draft.**   The Writing Project that follows suggests a structure for your research proposal. Apply what you've learned in this chapter about the values of objectivity, replicability, and recency as you draft each section. Use the revision stage to further clarify your points. When you proofread, be sure to check that you have not introduced any inaccuracies.

Research Proposal

Your goal in this project is to share your plans for a research project with an audience. You will describe the purpose of your proposed research and situate it in the context of other research and then explain your hypothesis and how you plan to test it.

THE TITLE PAGE

The title page should include (1) the title of your proposal, (2) your name and the names of any co-authors/researchers, and (3) the name of your academic institution. Your instructor may require additional information such as a running header, date, or author's note. Be sure to ask your instructor what documentation and formatting style to use and what information is required in any specific writing context.

THE INTRODUCTION AND LITERATURE REVIEW

Use the Introduction section to explain the topic and purpose of the proposed research. Be sure to include your research question and/or your proposed hypothesis. Additionally, your Introduction should contextualize your research by reviewing scholarly articles related to your topic and showing how your proposed research fills a gap in what is already known about the topic. Specifically, the Introduction should explain how other researchers have approached your topic (or a closely related one) in the past, with attention to the major overlapping findings in that research.

METHODS

The Methods section of your research proposal should explain exactly what you will do to test your hypothesis (or answer your research question) and how you will do it. It differs from the Methods section of a lab report in several ways: (1) it should be written in the future tense, and (2) it should include more detail about your plans. Further, the Methods section should address how long your study will take and should specify how you will collect data (in a step-by-step descriptive manner).

DOCUMENTATION

The References list for a research proposal is essentially the same as the References list for a lab report or any other academic project. You will need to include the full citation information for any work you used in your literature review or in planning or researching your topic.

....

Insider Example
Professional Research Proposal

In the following example of a professional research proposal by Gary Ritchison, a biologist at Eastern Kentucky University, note how the Introduction section begins with a brief introduction to the topic (par. 1) and then proceeds to review the relevant literature on the topic (pars. 1 and 2). As you read, consider how a potential funding entity would likely view both the content and the form in which that content is presented. Also note that the References list is titled "Literature Cited." Minor variations like this are common from discipline to discipline and in various contexts. Here, Ritchison has followed CSE style conventions in his proposal. ▶

Hunting Behavior, Territory Quality, and Individual
Quality of American Kestrels (*Falco sparverius*)

Gary Ritchison

Department of Biological Sciences
Eastern Kentucky University

Introduction

American Kestrels (*Falco sparverius*) are widely distributed throughout North America. In Kentucky, these falcons are permanent residents and are most abundant in rural farmland, where they hunt over fields and pastures (Palmer-Ball 1996). Although primarily sit-and-wait predators, hunting from elevated perches and scanning the surrounding areas for prey, kestrels also hunt while hovering (Balgooyen 1976). Kellner (1985) reported that nearly 20% of all attacks observed in central Kentucky were made while kestrels were hovering. Habitats used by hunting kestrels in central Kentucky include mowed and unmowed fields, cropland, pastures, and plowed fields (Kellner 1985).

Several investigators have suggested that male and female American Kestrels may exhibit differences in habitat use during the non-breeding period, with males typically found in areas with greater numbers of trees, such as wooded pastures, and females in open fields and pastures (Stinson et al. 1981; Bohall-Wood and Collopy 1986). However, Smallwood (1988) suggested that, when available, male and female kestrels in south-central Florida established winter territories in the same type of habitat. Differential habitat use occurred only because migratory female kestrels usually arrived on wintering areas before males and, therefore, were more likely to establish territories in the better-quality, more open habitats before males arrived (Smallwood 1988).

In central Kentucky, many American Kestrels are residents. As a result, male and female kestrels would likely have equal opportunity to establish winter territories in the higher-quality, open habitats. If so, habitat segregation should be less apparent in central Kentucky than in areas further south, where wintering populations of kestrels are

Establishes the topic and provides background information on American Kestrels

Reveals evidence of a review of previous scholarship

Establishes a local context for research

largely migratory. In addition, territory quality should be correlated with individual quality because higher-quality resident kestrels should be able to defend higher-quality territories.

The objectives of my proposed study of American Kestrels will be to examine possible relationships among and between hunting behavior, territory quality, and individual quality in male and female American Kestrels. The results of this study will provide important information about habitat and perch selection by American Kestrels in central Kentucky in addition to the possible role of individual quality on hunting behavior and habitat use.

Reveals research purposes and identifies significance of the proposed research

Methods

Field work will take place from 15 October 2000 through 15 May 2001 at the Blue Grass Army Depot, Madison Co., Kentucky. During the study period, I will search for American Kestrels throughout accessible portions of the depot. Searches will be conducted on foot as well by automobile.

An attempt will be made to capture all kestrels observed using bal-chatri traps baited with mice. Once captured, kestrels will be banded with a numbered aluminum band plus a unique combination of colored plastic bands to permit individual identification. For each captured individual, I will take standard morphological measurements (wing chord, tarsus length, tail length, and mass). In addition, 8 to 10 feathers will be plucked from the head, breast, back, and wing, respectively. Plumage in these areas is either reddish or bluish, and the quality of such colors is known to be correlated with individual quality (Hill 1991, 1992; Keyser 1998). Variation in the color and intensity of plumage will be determined using a reflectance spectrometer (Ocean Optics S2000 fiber optic spectrometer, Dunedin, FL), and

This section provides a highly detailed description of proposed research procedures, or methods.

these values will be used as a measure of individual quality. To confirm that plumage color and intensity are dependent on condition, we will use tail feather growth rates as a measure of nutritional condition during molt. At the time of capture, the outermost tail feathers will be removed and the mean width of daily growth bars, which is correlated with nutritional condition (Hill and Montgomerie 1994), will be determined.

Each focal American Kestrel (N = at least 14;7 males and 7 females) will be observed at least once a week. Observations will be made at various times during the day, with observation periods typically 1 to 3 hours in duration. During focal bird observations, individuals will be monitored using binoculars and spotting scopes. Information will be recorded on a portable tape recorder for later transcription. During each observation, I will record all attacks and whether attacks were initiated from a perch or while hovering. For perches, I will note the time a kestrel lands on a perch and the time until the kestrel either initiates an attack or leaves for another perch (giving up time). If an attack is made, I will note attack distances (the distance from a perch to the point where a prey item was attacked) and outcome (successful or not). If successful, an attempt will be made to identify the prey (to the lowest taxonomic category possible).

The activity budgets of kestrels will also be determined by observing the frequency and duration of kestrel behaviors during randomly selected 20-min observation periods (i.e., a randomly selected period during the 1- to 3-hour observation period). During these 20-minute periods, the frequency of occurrence of each of the following behaviors will be recorded: capturing prey, preening, engaging in nonpreening comfort movements (including

References established methods, or those used by other researchers, to support his own method design scratching, stretching wing or tail, shaking body plumage, cleaning foot with bill, and yawning), vocalizing, and flying. The context in which flight occurs, including pounces on prey, and the duration of flights and of preening bouts will also be recorded.

Territories will be delineated by noting the locations of focal kestrels, and the vegetation in each kestrel's winter territory will be characterized following the methods of Smallwood (1987). Possible relationships among hunting behavior (mode of attack, perch time, attack distance and outcome [successful or unsuccessful], and type of prey attacked), territory vegetation, time budgets, sex, and individual quality will be examined. All analyses will be conducted using the Statistical Analysis System (SAS Institute 1989).

Literature Cited

Balgooyen TG. 1976. Behavior and ecology of the American Kestrel in the Sierra Nevada of California. Univ Calif Publ Zool 103:1–83.

Bohall-Wood P, Collopy MW. 1986. Abundance and habitat selection of two American Kestrel subspecies in north-central Florida. Auk 103:557–563.

Craighead JJ, Craighead FC Jr. 1956. Hawks, owls, and wildlife. Harrisburg (PA): Stackpole.

Hill GE. 1991. Plumage coloration is a sexually selected indicator of male quality. Nature 350:337–339.

Hill GE. 1992. Proximate basis of variation in carotenoid pigmentation in male House Finches. Auk 109:1–12.

Hill GE, Montgomerie R. 1994. Plumage colour signals nutritional condition in the House Finch. Proc R Soc Lond B Biol Sci 258:47–52.

Kellner CJ. 1985. A comparative analysis of the foraging behavior of male and female American Kestrels in central Kentucky [master's thesis]. [Richmond (KY)]: Eastern Kentucky University.

Keyser AJ. 1998. Is structural color a reliable signal of quality in Blue Grosbeaks? [master's thesis]. [Auburn (AL)]: Auburn University.

Mengel RM. 1965. The birds of Kentucky. Lawrence (KS): Allen Press. (American Ornithologists' Union monograph; 3).

Palmer-Ball B. 1996. The Kentucky breeding bird atlas. Lexington (KY): Univ. Press of Kentucky.

SAS Institute. 1989. SAS user's guide: statistics. Cary (NC): SAS Institute.

Smallwood JA. 1987. Sexual segregation by habitat in American Kestrels wintering in southcentral Florida: vegetative structure and responses of differential prey availability. Condor 89:842–849.

Smallwood JA. 1988. The relationship of vegetative cover to daily rhythms of prey consumption by American Kestrels wintering in southcentral Florida. J Raptor Res 22:77–80.

Stinson CH, Crawford DL, Lauthner J. 1981. Sex differences in winter habitat of American Kestrels in Georgia. J. Field Ornithol 52:29–35.

Genres: Lab Reports

Lab reports offer a written account of the purpose, methods, results, and meaning of an experiment or systematic observation.

What Is the Rhetorical Context for This Genre?

Lab reports are the formal reporting mechanism for research in the sciences. When scientists publish an article that reports the results of a research study, it is generally in the form of a lab report. The audience for the report is usually other scientists, who would be reading to see what the report's findings contribute to their understanding of the research topic.

If a group of researchers writes a research proposal before writing a lab report, they've already completed the first two sections of the lab report and only need to revise the report to reflect what they actually accomplished in the study (instead of what they planned to do). The Results and Discussion sections report new information about the data they gathered and what they offer as explanations and interpretations of what those results might mean. The Discussion section might also include suggestions for future research, demonstrating how research in the sciences is always building upon prior research.

Strategies for Composing a Lab Report

Like the research proposal, the lab report is a professional genre that you learn through studying the work of others and practicing in your courses. Lab reports usually follow the IMRaD format.

● **Revise your research proposal.**   If you wrote a research proposal prior to conducting your lab work, you already have the basis for the Introduction and Methods sections of your lab report. You'd only need to revise the report to reflect what you actually accomplished in the study (instead of what you planned to do). If you did not do a research proposal, review the strategies provided in "Genres: Research Proposal" on page 239.

● **Consider visuals that will communicate your findings.**   Do you have a large quantity of data that you can organize into types and categories? If so, consider using a table. Are you showing a change over time that would be more clearly illustrated with a graph? Would a photograph or short video support your description of a process or a phenomenon? Does the subject of your inquiry have parts that could be labeled in an illustration? Think of visuals as a powerful way to communicate information, rather than decorative additions.

● **Remember SLR as you draft.**   The Writing Project that follows suggests a structure for your research proposal. Apply what you've learned in this chapter about the values of objectivity, replicability, and recency as you draft each section. Use the revision stage to further clarify your points. When you proofread, be sure to check that you have not introduced any inaccuracies.

Writing Project   ## Lab Report

For this writing project, you will report results from either experimentation or systematic observation. Your research could take place in an actual laboratory setting, or it could just as easily take place in the wider environment around you. Regardless, be sure to check with your instructor about whether your lab report should be based on formal observation or experimentation. Since lab reports use IMRaD organizational format, your report should include the following sections: Introduction, Methods, Results, and Discussion.

THE INTRODUCTION

In the Introduction, establish the topic and purpose of your project. Be sure to include your research question and/or your proposed hypothesis. Additionally, your Introduction should contextualize your research by reviewing scholarly articles related to your topic and showing how your proposed research fills a gap in what is already known about the topic. Specifically, the Introduction should explain how other researchers have approached your topic (or a closely related one) in the past, with attention to the major overlapping findings in that research.

METHODS

The Methods section should explain how you tested your hypothesis (or answered your research question). It should specify the details of your process in a step-by-step descriptive manner that could be replicated by another scientist.

RESULTS AND DISCUSSION

The Results and Discussion sections report new information about the data you gathered and your explanations and interpretations of what those results might mean. The Discussion section might also include suggestions for future research, demonstrating how research in the sciences is always building upon prior research.

....

Insider Example

Student Lab Report

In the following sample lab report, Kedric Lemon revisits the question of which battery type is most effective. He draws on the information gathered in his observation logbook (pp. 230–38) to design a research study that allows him to conduct further investigation to answer his research question. ▶

Which Type of Battery Is the Most Effective When Energy Is Drawn Rapidly?

Kedric Lemon

North Carolina State University

Professor Matthew Chu

November 4, 2020

The researcher provides a descriptive, non-rhetorical title.

Which Type of Battery Is the Most Effective When Energy Is Drawn Rapidly?

Introduction

Batteries power many of the products that we use every day, from the TV remote to the car we drive to work. AA batteries are one of the most widely used battery types, but which of these AA batteries is the most effective? Almeida, Xará, Delgado, and Costa (2006) tested five different types of batteries in a study similar to mine. They allowed each of the batteries to run the product for an hour. The product they were powering alternated from open to closed circuit, so the batteries went from not giving off energy to giving off energy very quickly. The researchers then measured the pulse of the battery to determine the charge. The pulse test is a very effective way of reading the battery because it is closed circuit, meaning it doesn't run the battery to find the voltage, and it is highly accurate. They found that the Energizer battery had the largest amount of pulses after the experiment. The Energizer had on average 20 more pulses than the Duracell battery, giving the Energizer battery approximately a half hour longer in battery life when being used rapidly. Booth (1999) also performed a battery experiment using the pulse test. Unlike the experiment performed by Almeida et al., Booth's experiment involved allowing the batteries to constantly give off energy for two hours, and then measuring the pulse. My observational study is closer to Booth's because the product I used, a flashlight, was constantly drawing energy from the battery. Booth found that the Duracell battery had over 40 more pulses per minute than the Energizer battery, which means that the battery could last for an hour longer than the Energizer battery and was therefore more effective.

In today's market, rechargeable batteries are becoming increasing popular. Zucker (2005) compared 16 different types

The report follows the conventional IMRaD format.

The researcher establishes a focus for his research by positing a research question.

Reviews previous research, and connects that research to the current research project of rechargeable batteries. Most of these batteries were Nickel Metal Hydride, but some were the more traditional rechargeable AA battery, the Nickel Cadmium. Zucker looked at how these batteries fared on their second charge after being discharged as closely as possible to empty; rechargeable batteries are not allowed to go to 0 volts because then they cannot be recharged. Zucker found that all but four of the batteries came back up to at least 70% of their initial charge, two of which did not even recharge at all. The two most effective rechargeable batteries were Duracell and Energizer, which both came back to 86% of the first charge. However, the Energizer rechargeable battery had the higher initial charge, so Zucker concluded that the Energizer battery was the most effective rechargeable battery. Yu, Lai, Yan, and Wu (1999) looked at the capacity of three different Nickel Metal Hydride (NiMH) rechargeable batteries. They first took three different types of NiMH batteries and found the electrical capacity through a voltmeter. After, they measured the volume of each of the batteries to discover where it fell in the AA battery range of 600 to 660 mAh/cm3. They used this to test the efficiency of the NiMH batteries, as there are slightly different chemical compositions inside the batteries. In the end they concluded that the NiMH battery from the Duracell brand was the most efficient.

Continues review of previous scholarship on this topic

Li, Daniel, and Wood (2011) looked at the improvements being made to lithium ion AA batteries. Lithium ion AA batteries are extremely powerful and have been studied by many researchers. Li et al. tested the voltage of the lithium ion AA rechargeable battery and found that the starting voltage was on average 3.2 volts. That is more than the average onetime-use AA battery. They further found that what makes modern lithium ion batteries so much more powerful are the cathodes, which are composed of materials that significantly increase the rate of reactions.

The objective of this study is to determine which brand of regular AA batteries is the most efficient and to compare a generic rechargeable battery to these regular AA batteries. While my initial research question concerned the effectiveness of batteries over extended usage, for my final study I wanted to look at how batteries reacted when they were being used very quickly. Two research questions drove this study: Which type of battery is the most effective for rapid uses? How do regular AA batteries compare to a generic AA rechargeable battery? My hypothesis for this experiment is that the Energizer battery will be the most effective battery when energy is being taken from the battery rapidly.

Method

Observation Logbook

In my observation logbook I looked at how different types of batteries compared when they were being tested through a flashlight. The batteries I observed were Duracell, Energizer, and a generic brand. Each set of batteries was placed in a flashlight that ran for one continuous hour. After the hour was up, the voltage was tested with a voltmeter. This process was repeated four times, for a total of five days of observations. The batteries were stored at a consistent temperature over the course of the study because temperature affects kinetic energy. The flashlight remained off for one hour between each test so it could cool down.

Margin notes:

Establishes specific research questions on the basis of previous observations

Hypothesis

Reports on research previously conducted

For the follow-up study, I looked at another aspect of battery performance—how batteries compare when they are being used in quick bursts, rapidly changing from using no energy to using a lot of energy. In addition, I added a rechargeable battery to the study. A strobe light was used instead of a flashlight because a strobe light quickly turns on and off automatically. The batteries were attached to a voltmeter immediately after they were taken out of the strobe light. Each set of batteries was in the strobe light for 20 minutes.

Variables that remained constant for this experiment were the temperature of the room as well as the temperature of the strobe light. For this reason I allowed the strobe light a 30-minute cooldown before I put the next set of batteries into it.

Limitations

Because of budget constraints, the sample size was small. A larger sample size would correct for variations among individual batteries within a brand; data from many batteries would have been averaged. Another limitation of the study was imprecise data, due to a low-quality voltmeter and lack of access to a thermocouple to verify the data. Because the voltmeter was not finely calibrated, the data might not have been completely accurate. With a thermocouple, the temperature of the battery could have been measured and the voltage located on a graph provided by a secondary source. Lack of access to a pulse test reader was another limitation; such an instrument can estimate battery life with high precision.

Results

My results from my logbook provided me with primarily quantitative data. For each of the types of batteries I found these results:

Provides a detailed account of research procedures

The researcher uses technical language, or jargon.

Outlines the major findings of the study. A number of results are also presented visually, in the form of graphs and figures.

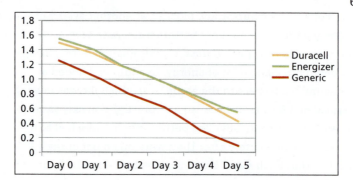

The researcher frequently presents results in tables and charts.

The Energizer battery started off with the largest initial charge of 1.55 volts. On average the Energizer battery lost .16 volts for every hour. The Duracell battery had an initial charge of 1.5 volts and lost an average of .18 volts per hour. Last, the generic brand of battery had an initial voltage of 1.25 volts and lost on average .23 volts every hour.

In this experiment the Energizer battery again had the highest starting charge and highest ending charge. The Duracell AA battery was close behind the Energizer. The generic brand of batteries came next, followed by the rechargeable battery.

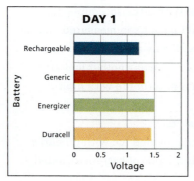

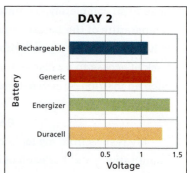

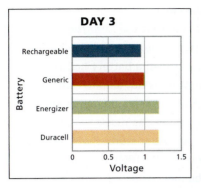

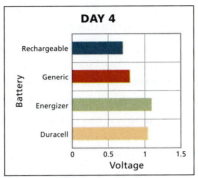

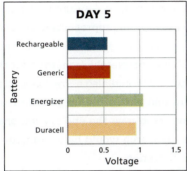

This experiment showed similar results to what I had found in my logbook. The Duracell and Energizer batteries were both very similar, while the generic brand lagged behind.

Battery	Initial voltage (volts)	Final voltage (volts)	Average volts lost (volts/20 min)
Energizer	1.60	1.10	0.10
Duracell	1.55	0.95	0.12
Generic	1.40	0.60	0.16
Rechargeable	1.20	0.55	0.13

The table shows that the Energizer battery had the best results in all categories.

Discussion

Provides an overview of the implications of major findings in light of previous scholarship

Through this experiment I found that the Energizer battery is the most effective battery when used in rapid bursts. Also, I found that the rechargeable battery had very bad ratings. The rechargeable battery is not able to commit as many of its chemicals to solely providing the maximum amount of energy; it has to provide some of the chemicals to the battery's capabilities of recharging. Other studies with similar methods (Booth 1999; Yu, Lai, Yan, & Wu 1999) determined that the Duracell battery was the most effective.

If I had had more days to conduct this experiment, I could have more accurately represented the usefulness of the rechargeable battery, because after it exhausted its first charge it came back completely recharged for the next day. A longer testing period would also allow the batteries to drain more completely, and data could be gathered on how the regular batteries acted near the end of their charge. An area of study for further research would be to compare different types of rechargeable batteries.

If the experiment had a longer overall duration or if the strobe light had been left on for a longer time, it is likely that the rechargeable battery would be ahead of the generic battery in terms of the average voltage lost. It is also likely that the gap would have been larger between the Duracell battery and the Energizer battery because looking at my results from the observation logbook shows that the Energizer battery does a lot better than the Duracell battery toward the end of its life. It appears the Duracell battery does not handle the rapid uses as well as the extended uses.

These results show that the Energizer battery is the most effective battery for rapid use and, from my observation logbook, the most effective for extended use. The value of the rechargeable battery is inconclusive because the data on the rechargeable battery do not take into account its sole advantage, recharging. It would also be interesting to see how the Duracell and Energizer rechargeable batteries compare to their regular batteries.

References

Almeida, M. F., Xará, S. M., Delgado, J., & Costa, C. A. (2006). Characterization of spent AA household alkaline batteries. *Waste Management, 26*(5), 466–476. https://doi.org/10.1016/j.wasman.2005.04.005

Booth, S. A. (1999). High-drain alkaline AA-batteries. *Popular Electronics, 16*(1), 5.

Li, J., Daniel, C., & Wood, D. (2011). Materials processing for lithium-ion batteries. *Journal of Power Sources, 196*(5), 2452–2460. https://doi.org/10.1016/j.jpowsour.2010.11.001

Yu, C. Z., Lai, W. H., Yan, G. J., & Wu, J. Y. (1999). Study of preparation technology for high performance AA size Ni–MH batteries. *Journal of Alloys and Compounds, 293*(1–2), 784–787. https://doi.org/10.1016/S0925-8388(99)00463-6

Zucker, P. (2005). AA batteries tested: Rechargeable batteries. *Australian PC User, 17*(6), 51.

Provides a list of sources used in the construction of the lab report

tip sheet

Reading and Writing in the Natural Sciences

- **Systematic observation plays a critical role in the natural sciences.** The disciplines of the natural sciences rely on methods of observation to generate and answer research questions about how and why natural phenomena act as they do.

- **Many natural scientists work in interdisciplinary fields of study.** These fields, such as biochemistry and biophysics, combine subject matter and methods from more than one field to address research questions.

- **Scientists typically conduct research according to the steps of the scientific method:** observe, ask a research question, formulate a hypothesis, test the hypothesis through experimentation, and explain results.

- **The scientific writing process follows logically from the steps of the scientific method:** observe and describe, speculate, experiment, and report.

- **To test their hypotheses, or their proposed answers to research questions, natural scientists may use multiple methods.** Two common methods are systematic observation and experimentation.

- **Scientific research proposals are typically vetted by institutional review boards (IRB).** Committees that review research proposals are charged with the task of examining all elements of a scientific study to ensure that it treats subjects equitably and ethically.

- **Conventional rhetorical features of the scientific community reflect the shared values of the community's members.** Some of these values are objectivity, replicability, recency, and cooperation and collaboration.

- **Members of the scientific community frequently produce a number of genres.** These include the observation logbook, the research proposal, and the lab report.

Reading and Writing in the Applied Fields

This chapter offers a basic introduction to a handful of the many applied fields that students often encounter or choose to study as part of their college experience. In some cases, one or more of these applied fields may correspond to your intended major(s) or to selected areas of focus for your intended career. Throughout the chapter, we explore some of the kinds of writing that commonly occur in these fields and that are regularly produced by both students and professionals working in these fields. Because the applied fields vary so much, and since it would be impossible to generalize conventional expectations for communication across these diverse fields, our aim here is not to teach you to become an expert researcher or communicator in these fields. Instead, our purpose is to highlight a rhetorical approach to these fields that would be helpful for any student attempting to acclimate to one or more of the diverse communities of the applied fields and their expectations.

Applied fields are areas of academic study that focus on the production of practical knowledge and that share a core mission of preparing students for specific careers. Often, such preparation includes hands-on training. The applied fields that we will look at in this chapter are nursing, teaching, business, law, engineering, and information technology. A list of some additional applied fields appears below.

ANDREA TSURUMI

Some Applied Fields

Accounting	Journalism
Architecture	Manufacturing technology
Aviation technology	Physical education
Counseling	Social work
Cybersecurity	Software development
Forensics	Sports psychology
Hospitality management	Statistics

As you might expect, research that occurs in the applied fields is quite varied. These variations among the fields are often reflected in the kinds of questions each field asks and attempts to answer, the forms of evidence it relies on, the data-collection methods it employs, and the ways it reports findings from research to differing audiences. Nevertheless, research in the applied fields typically attempts to solve problems. An automotive engineering team, for example, might start with a problem like consumers' reluctance to buy an all-electric vehicle. To address the issue, the engineering team would first attempt to define the scope of the problem. Why does the problem exist? What are the factors contributing to consumers' reluctance to buy an all-electric vehicle? Once the problem has been identified and clearly defined, the team of researchers can then begin to explore possible solutions.

Examples of large-scale problems that require practical applications of research include issues such as racial inequality in the American criminal justice system, the lack of clean drinking water in some nonindustrialized nations and U.S. cities, obesity and heart disease, and ways to provide outstanding public education to children with special needs. These are all real-world problems scholars and practitioners in the applied fields are working to solve this very moment.

Professionals in applied fields often work in collaboration with one another, or in teams, to complete research and other projects, and professors who teach in these areas frequently assign tasks that require interaction and cooperation among a group of students to create a product or to solve a problem. In the field of business management, for example, teams of professionals often must work together to market a new product. Solid communication and interpersonal skills are necessary for a team to manage a budget, design a marketing or advertising campaign, and engage with a client successfully all at the same time. As such, the ability to work cooperatively—to demonstrate effective interpersonal and team communication skills—is highly valued among professionals in the applied fields. You shouldn't be surprised, then, if you're one day applying for a job in an applied field and an interviewer asks you to share a little about your previous experiences working in teams to successfully complete a project. As you learn more about the applied fields examined in this chapter, take care to note those writing tasks completed by teams, or those moments when cooperation among professionals working in a particular field is highlighted by the content of the genres we explore.

Connect 10.1   **Considering Additional Applied Fields**

Visit your college or university's website, and locate a listing of the majors or concentrations offered in any academic department. In light of the definition of an *applied field* proposed above, consider whether any of the majors or ➔

concentrations identified for that particular discipline could be described as applied fields. Additionally, spend some time considering your own major or potential area of concentration: Are you studying an applied field? Are there areas of study within your major or concentration that could be considered applied fields? If so, what are they, and why would you consider them applied fields?

Rhetoric and the Applied Fields

Because applied fields are centrally focused on preparing professionals who will work in those fields, students are often asked to engage audiences associated with the work they'll do in those fields after graduation. Imagine that you've just graduated from college with a degree in business management and have secured a job as a marketing director for a business. What kinds of writing do you expect to encounter in this new position? What audiences do you expect to be writing for? You may well be asked to prepare business analyses or market reports. You may be asked to involve yourself in new product management or even the advertising campaign for a product. All these activities, which call for different kinds of writing, will require you to manage information and to shape your communication of that information into texts that are designed specifically for other professionals in your field—such as boards of directors, financial officers, or advertising executives. As a student in the applied field of business management, you therefore need to become familiar with the audiences, genres, conventions, and other expectations for writing specific to your career path that extend beyond academic audiences. Being mindful of the rhetorical situation in which you must communicate with other professionals is essential to your potential success as a writer in an applied field.

As with more traditional academic writing, we recommend that you analyze carefully any writing situation you encounter in an applied field. You might begin by responding to the following questions:

1. **Who is my audience?**   Unlike the audience for a lab report for a chemistry class or the audience for an interpretation of a poem in a literature class, your audience for writing in an applied field is just as likely to be non-academic as academic. Certainly, the writing most students will do in their actual careers will be aimed at other professionals in their field, not researchers or professors in a university. In addition to understanding exactly who your audience is, you'll want to be sure to consider the specific needs of your target audience.

2. **In light of my purpose and my audience's needs, is there an appropriate genre I should rely on to communicate my information?**   As in the more traditional academic disciplines, there are many genres through which professionals in applied fields communicate. Based on an analysis of your rhetorical

situation, and keeping your purpose for writing in mind, you'll want to consider whether the information you have to share should be reported in a specific genre: Should you write a memorandum, a marketing proposal, or an executive summary, for instance? Answering this question can help you determine if there is an appropriate form, or genre, through which to communicate your information.

3. **Are there additional conventional expectations I should consider for the kind of writing task I need to complete?**   Beyond simply identifying an appropriate genre, answering this question can help you determine how to shape the information you need to communicate to your target audience. If the writing task requires a particular genre, then you're likely to rely on features that conventionally appear as part of that genre. Of course, there are many good reasons to communicate information in other ways. In these situations, we recommend that you carefully consider the appropriateness of the structural, language, and reference features you employ.

In the sections that follow, we offer brief introductions to some applied fields of study and provide examples of genres that students and professionals working in these fields often produce. We explore expectations for these genres by highlighting conventional structure, language, and reference features that writers in these fields frequently employ.

Health Fields

One of the fastest-growing segments of the U.S. economy is related to health services. As the population of the country ages, and as science and medicine come together to lengthen average life spans, it's not surprising that health professionals of all sorts, including those with various levels of training and expertise in providing emotional, mental, and physical health services, are in high demand.

Along with this increased demand and the continued development of the medical arts as a result of scientific discoveries and technological advances, it's also not surprising that the allied health fields are constantly expanding and evolving to meet the needs of patients. The Association of Schools of Allied Health Professionals defines *allied health* as "those health professions that are distinct from medicine and nursing." Allied health professionals typically work in a highly cooperative manner with other professionals, including medical doctors and nurses, to provide various forms of direct and indirect care to patients. In fact, allied health professionals regularly have a role to play in the prevention, diagnosis, treatment, and recovery from illness for most patients. A small sampling of the many diverse allied health fields includes the following:

- Medical assistant
- Nutritionist
- Occupational therapist

- Phlebotomist
- Physical therapist
- Physician assistant
- Radiographer
- Respiratory therapist
- Speech pathologist

Most of us have had experiences with nurses, who, along with physicians and other health professionals, serve on the front lines of preventing and treating illness in our society. In addition to their hands-on engagement with individuals in clinical and community settings, nurses spend a good deal of their time writing—whether documenting their observations about patients in medical charts, preparing orders for medical procedures, designing care plans, or communicating with patients. A student of nursing might encounter any number of additional forms of writing tasks, including nursing care plans for individuals, reviews of literature, and community or public health assessment papers, just to name a few. Each of these forms of communication requires that nurses be especially attuned to the needs of various audiences. A nurse communicating with a patient, for example, might have to translate medical jargon so that the individual can fully understand his or her treatment. Alternatively, a nurse who is producing a care plan for a patient would likely need to craft the document such that other nurses and medical professionals could follow methodically the assessments and recommendations for care. Some nurses, especially those who undertake advanced study or who

Insider's View
Janna Dieckmann on Research in Nursing

COURTESY OF JANNA DIECKMANN

"Research in nursing is varied, including quantitative research into health and illness patterns, as well as intervention to maximize health and reduce illness. Qualitative research varies widely, including research in the history of nursing, which is my focus. There is a wide variety of types of writing demanded in a nursing program. It is so varied that many connections are possible. Cross-discipline collaborations among faculty of various professional schools are valued at many academic institutions today. One of my colleagues conducted research on rats. Another looked at sleep patterns in older adults as a basis for understanding dementia onset. One public health nursing colleague conducts research on out-of-work women, and another examines cross-cultural competence. These interests speak to our reasons for becoming nurses—our seeking out of real life, of direct experience, of being right there with people, and of understanding others and their worlds."

prepare others to become nurses, often design, implement, or participate in research studies.

● **Discharge Instructions**   If you've ever been hospitalized, then you probably remember the experience quite vividly. It's likely that you interacted with a nurse, who perhaps assessed your health upon arrival. You were also likely cared for by a nurse, or a particular group of nurses, during your stay. Nurses also often play an integral role in a patient's discharge from a hospital. Typically, before a patient is released from a hospital, a nurse explains to the patient (and perhaps a family member or two, or another intended primary caregiver) and provides in written form a set of instructions for aftercare. This constitutes the discharge instructions.

This document, or series of documents, includes instructions for how to care for oneself at home. The instructions may focus on managing diet and medications, as well as caring for other needs, such as post-operative bandaging procedures. They may also include exercise or diet management plans recommended for long-term recovery and health maintenance. These plans may include seeing an allied health professional such as a physical or occupational therapist. Often presented in a series of bulleted items or statements, these lists are usually highly generic; that is, the same instructions frequently apply for patients with the same or similar health conditions. For this reason, discharge instruction forms may include spaces for nurses or other healthcare professionals to write in more specific information relating to a patient's individual circumstances. As well, discharge instructions frequently include information about a patient's follow-up care with his or her doctor or primary caregiver. This could take the form of a future appointment time or directions to call for a follow-up appointment or to consult with another physician. An additional conventional element of discharge instructions is a list of signs of a medical emergency and directions concerning when and how to seek medical attention immediately, should certain signs or symptoms appear in the patient. Finally, discharge instructions are typically signed and dated by a physician or nurse, and they are sometimes signed by the patient as well.

Many patients are in unclear states of mind or are extremely vulnerable at the time of release from a hospital, so nurses who provide and explain discharge instructions to patients are highly skilled at assessing patients' understanding of these instructions.

....

Insider Example

Discharge Instructions

The following text is an example of a typical set of discharge instructions. As you read the document, consider areas in the instructions that you think a nurse would be more likely to stress to a patient in a discharge meeting: What would a nurse cover quickly? What would a nurse want to communicate most clearly to a patient? ▶

FIRST HOSPITAL
Where Care Comes First

Patient's Name:	John Q. Patient
Healthcare Provider's Name:	First Hospital
Department:	Cardiology
Phone:	617-555-1212
Date:	Thursday, May 8, 2021
Notes:	**Nurses can write personalized notes to the patient here.**

Discharge Instructions for Heart Attack

A heart attack occurs when blood flow to the heart muscle is interrupted. This deprives the heart muscle of oxygen, causing tissue damage or tissue death. Common treatments include lifestyle changes, oxygen, medicines, and surgery.

Steps to Take

Home Care

- Rest until your doctor says it is okay to return to work or other activities.
- Take all medicines as prescribed by your doctor. Beta-blockers, ACE inhibitors, and antiplatelet therapy are often recommended.
- Attend a cardiac rehabilitation program if recommended by your doctor.

Diet

Eat a heart-healthy diet:

- Limit your intake of fat, cholesterol, and sodium. Foods such as ice cream, cheese, baked goods, and red meat are not the best choices.
- Increase your intake of whole grains, fish, fruits, vegetables, and nuts.
- Discuss supplements with your doctor.

Your doctor may refer you to a dietician to advise you on meal planning.

Physical Activity

The American Heart Association recommends at least 30 minutes of exercise daily, or at least 3–4 times per week, for

---

Provides identifying information about the patient, as well as name and contact information of healthcare provider

Much of the information provided in discharge instructions is generic, so nurses can provide "personalized notes" here.

Provides a brief overview of the patient's medical issue treated by the healthcare provider

Provides specific instructions for the patient to follow upon release from the medical facility

Note that each of these directions begins with a verb, stressing the importance of taking the action indicated.

patients who have had a heart attack. Your doctor will let you know when you are ready to begin regular exercise.

- Ask your doctor when you will be able to return to work.
- Ask your doctor when you may resume sexual activity.
- Do not drive unless your doctor has given you permission to do so.

Medications

The following medicines may be prescribed to prevent you from having another heart attack:

- Aspirin, which has been shown to decrease the risk of heart attacks
  ○ Certain painkillers, such as ibuprofen, when taken together with aspirin, may put you at high risk for gastrointestinal bleeding and also reduce the effectiveness of aspirin.
- Clopidogrel or prasugrel
  ○ Avoid omeprazole or esomeprazole if you take clopidogrel. They may make clopidogrel not work. Ask your doctor for other drug choices.
- ACE inhibitors
- Nitroglycerin
- Beta-blockers or calcium channel blockers
- Cholesterol-lowering medicines
- Blood pressure medicines
- Pain medicines
- Anti-anxiety or antidepressant medicines

If you are taking medicines, follow these general guidelines:

- Take your medicine as directed. Do not change the amount or the schedule.
- Do not stop taking them without talking to your doctor.
- Do not share them.
- Ask what the results and side effects are. Report them to your doctor.
- Some drugs can be dangerous when mixed. Talk to a doctor or pharmacist if you are taking more than one drug. This includes over-the-counter medicine and herbal or dietary supplements.
- Plan ahead for refills so you do not run out.

Lifestyle Changes and Prevention

Together, you and your doctor will plan proper lifestyle changes that will aid in your recovery. Some things to keep in mind to recover and prevent another heart attack include:

Note that specific directions are listed in a series of bulleted sections. Bulleted lists make the information easier to read and follow.

Directions are provided in as few words as possible.

- If you smoke, talk to your doctor about ways to help you quit. There are many options to choose from, like using nicotine replacement products, taking prescription medicines to ease cravings and withdrawal symptoms, participating in smoking cessation classes, or doing an online self-help program.
- Have your cholesterol checked regularly.
- Get regular medical check-ups.
- Control your blood pressure.
- Eat a healthful diet, one that is low in saturated fat and rich in whole grains, fruits, and vegetables.
- Have a regular, low-impact exercise program.
- Maintain a healthy weight.
- Manage stress through activities such as yoga, meditation, and counseling.
- If you have diabetes, maintain good control of your condition.

Follow-Up

Since your recovery needs to be monitored, be sure to keep all appointments and have exams done regularly as directed by your doctor. In addition, some people have feelings of depression or anxiety after a heart attack. To get the help you need, be sure to discuss these feelings with your doctor.

Schedule a follow-up appointment as directed by your doctor.

Provides directions for how to "follow up" with medical provider(s)

Call for Medical Help Right Away If Any of the Following Occurs

Call for medical help right away if you have symptoms of another heart attack, including:

- Chest pain, which may feel like a crushing weight on your chest
- A sense of fullness, squeezing, or pressure in the chest
- Anxiety, especially feeling a sense of doom or panic without apparent reason
- Rapid, irregular heartbeat
- Pain, tingling, or numbness in the left shoulder and arm, the neck or jaw, or the right arm
- Sweating
- Nausea or vomiting
- Indigestion or heartburn
- Lightheadedness, weakness, or fainting
- Shortness of breath
- Abdominal pain

Identifies emergency indicators

If you think you have an emergency, call for medical help right away.

Education

When your teachers tell you that writing is important, they're probably conveying a belief based on their own experiences. Professional educators do a lot of writing. As students, you're aware of many contexts in which teachers

Insider's View
Vice Chancellor Bruce Moses on Writing as an Administrator

COURTESY OF BRUCE MOSES

"In my college administrative role, I typically engage in two types of writing, expository and persuasive (argumentative) writing. College administrators spend a significant amount of time investigating ideas, collecting and evaluating evidence that supports these ideas, and presenting innovations to their colleagues through expository writing. The exploration of these ideas requires an extensive amount of research to build a strong case based on logic, facts, peer-based examples, and expert opinions. Typically, innovative ideas are met with scrutiny, which requires presenting multiple arguments to convince the audience that your idea is a logical option. The culture of higher education institutions necessitates that the narrative presents appropriate contextualized evidence, consideration of alternative views, and incorporates inclusive voices from across the college.

"My experience with persuasive writing often involves responding to outside agencies that have standards, regulations, and laws the college has an external accountability to meet. It is similar to writing a law brief. In most cases, the content contains issues that the reader can dispute if the facts of the matter and argument do not significantly meet the minimum threshold of the standard, regulation, and law. My goals are to be short in content, concise, and to provide data or evidence that supports my argument or synopsis."

write on a daily basis. They have project assignment sheets to design, papers to comment on and grade, websites to design, and e-mails to answer, just to name a few. However, educators also spend a great deal of time planning classes and designing lesson plans. Though students rarely see these written products, they are essential, if challenging and time-consuming, endeavors for teachers.

● **Lesson Plan**   When designing a lesson plan, teachers must consider many factors, including their goals and objectives for student learning, the materials needed to execute a lesson, the activities students will participate in as part of a lesson, and the methods they'll use to assess student learning. Among other considerations, teachers must also make sure their lesson plans help them meet prescribed curricular mandates.

....

Insider Example
Student Lesson Plan

The following lesson plan for a tenth-grade English class was designed by Myra Moses, who at the time of writing the plan was a doctoral candidate in education. In this plan, Moses begins by identifying the state-mandated curricular standards the lesson addresses. She then identifies the broader goals of her lesson plan before establishing the more specific objectives, or exactly what students will do to reach the broader learning goals. As you read, notice that all the plan's statements of objectives begin with a verb, as they identify actions students will take to demonstrate their learning. The plan ends by explaining the classroom activities the teacher will use to facilitate learning and by identifying the methods the instructor will use to assess student learning. These structural moves are conventional for the genre of a lesson plan.

Educational Standard ➤ Goals ➤ Objectives ➤ Materials ➤ Classroom Activities ➤ Assessment

▶

Lesson Plan

Overview and Purpose

This lesson is part of a unit on Homer's *Odyssey*. Prior to this lesson students will have had a lesson on Greek cultural and social values during the time of Homer, and they will have read the *Odyssey*. In the lesson, students will analyze passages from the *Odyssey* to examine the author's and characters' points of view. Students will participate in whole class discussion, work in small groups, and work individually to identify and evaluate point of view.

Education Standards Addressed

This lesson addresses the following objectives from the NC Standard Course of Study for Language Arts: English II:

1.02 Respond reflectively (through small group discussion, class discussion, journal entry, essay, letter, dialogue) to written and visual texts by:
- relating personal knowledge to textual information or class discussion.
- showing an awareness of one's own culture as well as the cultures of others.
- exhibiting an awareness of culture in which text is set or in which text was written.

1.03 Demonstrate the ability to read, listen to, and view a variety of increasingly complex print and non-print expressive texts appropriate to grade level and course literary focus, by:
- identifying and analyzing text components (such as organizational structures, story elements, organizational features) and evaluating their impact on the text.
- providing textual evidence to support understanding of and reader's response to text.
- making inferences, predicting, and drawing conclusions based on text.
- identifying and analyzing personal, social, historical, or cultural influences, contexts, or biases.

5.01 Read and analyze selected works of world literature by:
- understanding the importance of cultural and historical impact on literary texts.

Identifies the state-mandated curricular elements, or the educational objectives, the lesson addresses. Notice that these are quite broad in scope.

Goals

1. To teach students how to identify and evaluate an author's point of view and purpose by examining the characters' point of view
2. To teach students to critically examine alternate points of view

Teacher identifies specific goals for the lesson. These goals fit well within the broader state-mandated curricular standards.

Objectives

Students will:

1. Identify point of view in a story by examining the text and evaluating how the main character views his/her world at different points in the story.
2. Demonstrate that they understand point of view by using examples and evidence from the text to support what they state is the character's point of view.
3. Apply their knowledge and understanding of point of view by taking a passage from the text and rewriting it from a supporting character's point of view.
4. Evaluate the rationality of a character's point of view by measuring it against additional information gathered from the text, or their own life experience.

Objectives identify what students will do as part of the lesson. Notice that the statements of objectives begin with verbs.

Materials, Resources

- Copies of *The Odyssey*
- DVD with video clips from television and/or movies
- Flip chart paper
- Markers
- Directions and rubric for individual assignment

Identifies materials needed for the lesson

Activities

Session 1

1. Review information from previous lesson about popular cultural and social views held during Homer's time (e.g., Greek law of hospitality). This would be a combination of a quiz and whole class discussion.
2. Teacher-led class discussion defining and examining point of view by viewing clips from popular television shows and movies.
3. Teacher-led discussion of 1 example from *The Odyssey*. E.g., examine Odysseus's point of view when he violates Greek law of hospitality during his encounter with the Cyclops, Polyphemus. Examine this encounter through

Outlines classroom procedures for the two-day lesson plan

the lens of what Homer might be saying about the value
Greeks placed on hospitality.
4. In small groups the students will choose 3 places in the
epic and evaluate Odysseus's point of view. Students
will then determine what Odysseus's point of view might
reflect about Homer's point of view and purpose for that
part of the epic.
5. Groups will begin to create a visual using flip chart
paper and markers to represent their interpretations of
Odysseus's point of view to reflect about Homer's point of
view and purpose.

Session 2
1. Groups will complete visual.
2. Groups will present their work to the rest of the class.
3. The class will discuss possible alternate interpretations of
Homer's point of view and purpose.
4. Class will review aspects of point of view based on
information teacher provided at the beginning of the class.
5. Beginning during class and finishing for homework,
students will individually take one passage from the
epic that was not discussed by their groups and do the
following:
   • write a brief description of a main character's point of
     view
   • write a response to prompts that guide students in
     evaluating the rationality of the main character's point
     of view based on information gathered from the text, or
     the students' own life experience
   • rewrite the passage from a supporting character's point
     of view

Assessment
• Evaluate students' understanding of Greek cultural/social
  values from Homer's time through the quiz.
• Evaluate group's understanding of point of view by
  examining the visual product—this artifact will not be
  graded, but oral feedback will be provided that should
  help the students in completing the independent
  assignment.
• Evaluate the written, individual assignment.

Identifies how the
teacher will assess
students' mastery
of the concepts and
material covered in
the lesson

Business

Communication in businesses takes many forms, and professionals writing in business settings may spend substantial amounts of time drafting e-mails and memos, or writing letters and proposals. In some instances, businesses may hire individuals solely for their expertise in business communication practices. Such individuals are highly skilled in the analysis and practice of business communication, and their education and training are often aimed at these purposes. Still, if your experiences lead you to employment in a business setting, you're likely to face the task of communicating in one or more of the genres frequently used in those settings. It's no surprise, then, that schools of business, which prepare students to work in companies and corporations, often require their students to take classes that foster an understanding of the vehicles of communication common to the business setting. In the following section, we provide some introductory context and an annotated example of a business memorandum, a common genre of communication in the business community.

● **Memorandum**   The memorandum, or memo, is a specialized form of communication used within businesses to make announcements and to share information among colleagues and employees. Although memos serve a range of purposes, like sharing information, providing directives, or even arguing a particular position, they are not generally used to communicate with outside parties, like other companies or clients. While they may range in length from a couple of paragraphs to multiple pages, they're typically highly structured according to conventional expectations. In fact, you'd be hard-pressed to find an example of a professional memo that didn't follow the conventional format for identifying the writer, the audience, the central subject matter, and the date of production in the header. Also, information in memos typically appears in a block format, and the content is often developed from a clear, centralized purpose that is revealed early on in the memo itself.

....

Insider Example

Student Memorandum

The following is an example of a memo produced by a student in a professional writing class. His purpose for writing was to share his assessment of the advantages and drawbacks of a particular company he's interested in working for in the future. As you read, notice how the information in the opening paragraphs forecasts the memo's content and how the memo summarizes its contents in the concluding passages. We've highlighted a number of the other conventional expectations for the memo that you'll want to notice. ▶

MEMO

To: Jamie Larsen
          Professor, North Carolina State University
From: James Blackwell
          Biological Engineering, North Carolina State University
Date: September 2, 2014
Subject: Investigative Report on Hazen and Sawyer

I plan on one day using my knowledge gained in biological engineering to help alleviate the growing environmental problems that our society faces. Hazen and Sawyer is a well-known environmental engineering firm. However, I need to research the firm's background in order to decide if it would be a suitable place for me to work. Consequently, I decided to research the following areas of Hazen and Sawyer engineering firm:

- Current and Past Projects
- Opportunities for Employment and Advancement
- Work Environment

The purpose of this report is to present you with my findings on Hazen and Sawyer, so that you may assist me in writing an application letter that proves my skills and knowledge are worthy of an employment opportunity.

Current and Past Projects

Founded in 1951, Hazen and Sawyer has had a long history of providing clean drinking water and minimizing the effects of water pollution. The company has undertaken many projects in the United States as well as internationally. One of its first projects was improving the infrastructure of Monrovia, Liberia, in 1952. I am interested in using my knowledge of environmental problems to promote sustainability. Designing sustainable solutions for its clients is one of the firm's main goals. Hazen and Sawyer is currently engaged in a project to provide water infrastructure to over one million people in Jordan. Supplying clean drinking water is a problem that is continuously growing, and I hope to work on a similar project someday.

Opportunities for Employment and Advancement

Hazen and Sawyer has over forty offices worldwide, with regional offices in Raleigh, NC, Cincinnati, OH, Dallas, TX, Hollywood, FL, Los Angeles, CA, and its headquarters in New York City. The company currently has over thirty job openings at offices across the United States. I would like to live in the

The writer uses conventional formatting in the To, From, Date, and Subject lines.

Paragraphs are blocked and single-spaced.

Reasons for the student's interest in this company are bulleted and become the developed sections in the remainder of the memo. Important information is often bulleted in memos.

The memo announces its purpose clearly, forecasting the content to follow.

Headers are used to break up the content in memos. In this instance, the student uses headers that correspond to the areas of interest in the company he is exploring for potential employment.

The writer relies on formal language, evidenced here by avoiding contractions.

Raleigh area following graduation, so having a regional office here in Raleigh greatly helps my chances of finding a local job with the company. Hazen and Sawyer also has offices in Greensboro and Charlotte, which also helps my chances of finding a job in North Carolina. I am interested in finding a job dealing with stream restoration, and the Raleigh office currently has an opening for a Stream Restoration Designer. The position requires experience with AutoCAD and GIS, and I have used both of these programs in my Biological Engineering courses.

In addition to numerous job openings, Hazen and Sawyer also offers opportunities for professional development within the company. The Pathway Program for Professional Development is designed to keep employees up-to-date on topics in their fields and also stay educated to meet license requirements in different states. Even if I found a job at the Raleigh office, I would most likely have to travel out of state to work on projects, so this program could be very beneficial. I am seeking to work with a company that promotes continuous professional growth, so this program makes me very interested in Hazen and Sawyer.

Work Environment
Hazen and Sawyer supports innovation and creativity, and at the same time tries to limit bureaucracy. I am seeking a company that will allow me to be creative and assist with projects while not being in charge initially. As I gain experience and learn on the job, I hope to move into positions with greater responsibility. The firm offers a mentoring program that places newly hired engineers with someone more experienced. This program would help me adapt to the company and provide guidance as I gain professional experience. I hope to eventually receive my Professional Engineering license, so working under a professional engineer with years of experience would be a great opportunity for me. Hazen and Sawyer supports positive relationships among its employees, by engaging them in social outings such as sporting events, parties, picnics, and other activities.

References
Hazen and Sawyer—Environmental Engineers and Scientists. Web. 2 Sept. 2014. <http://www.hazenandsawyer.com/home/>.

Notice the organizational pattern employed in the body paragraphs. The writer begins by describing potential employer and then relates that information to his particular needs, desires, or circumstances.

References are usually indicated in an attachment.

Connect 10.4   **Considering Audience Values for a Business Memo**

Business memos are typically addressed to a specific audience, most often made up of business professionals. Study the sample student memo on pages 274–76 carefully and write a one-paragraph description of its intended audience. As part of your response, answer the following questions about the audience:

- Who is the intended audience for the memo? How do you know who the intended audience is?

- What does the audience need to learn from the memo? How do you know what the intended audience needs to learn?

- What does the memo's intended audience value, based on their position or role? How does the memo address or connect to those values?

Criminal Justice and Law

Millions of people are employed in the areas of law and criminal justice in the United States. When we encounter the terms *law* and *criminal justice*, the image of a lawyer, or attorney, often comes to mind first. No doubt, attorneys make vital contributions to almost every aspect of our lives; their work helps us to understand, to enforce, and even to change our policies, procedures, and laws, whether they are civil or criminal in nature. Though attorneys make a significant contribution to our system of governance, they actually represent only a fraction of the vast number of professionals who work in the U.S. criminal justice system.

If you've ever watched a crime show on television, then you've likely been exposed to some of the many areas of training and expertise that make up the U.S. criminal justice system. Professionals who work in the fields of criminal justice are responsible for enforcing our laws and ensuring the safety of our communities. They are also responsible for such jobs as investigating crime scenes, staffing our jails and prisons, and providing essential services to victims of crimes and to those charged with or convicted of a crime. Careers in the fields of criminal justice range from forensic technician to parole officer to corrections counselor. While each of these career paths requires a different level of training and expertise, and many colleges and universities offer specific plans of study that culminate in certification or licensure in these diverse areas, they are unified by a commitment to the just treatment of all individuals under the law.

As criminologist Michelle Richter notes in her "Insider's View," there are various reasons that might compel an individual to choose a career in criminal justice, and there are various constituencies to whom differing careers in the fields of criminal justice must deliver support and services. Here's a small sampling of the many career paths available to those interested in the field of criminal justice:

- Bailiff
- Correctional officer
- Corrections counselor
- Court reporter
- Emergency management director
- Fire inspector
- Forensic science technician
- Legal secretary
- Paralegal
- Police detective
- Sheriff and deputy sheriff

Insider's View
Criminologist Michelle Richter on Choosing a Career in Criminal Justice

"Motivation can be really critical. . . . If you want to work with people, it gets really complex. Do you want to work with law-abiding citizens or folks who have not been convicted of anything? Or do you want to work with the offender population? Do you want to work with the victim population? If you're looking at offenders, do you want to work with adults? Juveniles? Men, women, the elderly, the disabled, the mentally disabled? Most of the time students go into criminal justice, criminology, and forensics to understand a particular type of behavior, or to make the world a better place, or to make it safer, or something has happened to them in the past, and they want to make sure nobody ever has to go through that again. So there's a wide variety of reasons for being here."

Most of us probably have clichéd understandings of the law at work. Many of these likely originated from television shows and movies. In these scenarios, there's almost always lots of drama as the lawyers battle in court, parse witnesses' words, and attempt to sway a judge or jury to their side of a case.

In real life, the practice of law may not always be quite as dramatic or enthralling as it appears on the screen. In fact, many lawyers rarely, or maybe never, appear in court. A criminal defense attorney may regularly appear before a judge or jury in a courtroom setting, but a corporate lawyer may spend the majority of her time drafting and analyzing business contracts. This difference is directly related to the field of law an individual specializes in, be it criminal law, family law, tax law, or environmental law, just to name a few.

Regardless of an attorney's chosen specialization, though, the study of law remains fundamentally concerned with debates over the interpretation of language. This is because the various rules that govern our lives—statutes, ordinances, regulations, and laws, for example—are all constructed in language. As you surely recognize, language can be quite slippery, and rules can often be interpreted in many different ways. We need only briefly to consider current debates over free speech issues or the "right to bear arms" or marriage equality to understand how complicated the business of interpreting laws can become. In the United States, the U.S. Supreme Court holds the authority to provide the final interpretation on the meaning of disputed laws. However, there are lots of legal interpretations and arguments that lower courts must make on a daily basis, and only a tiny portion of cases are ever heard by the U.S. Supreme Court.

As in the other applied fields, there are many common forms of communication in the various fields of law, as lawyers must regularly communicate with different kinds of stakeholders, including clients, other lawyers, judges, and law enforcement officials. For this reason, individuals working in the legal professions are generally expert at composing e-mail messages, memos, letters to clients, and legal briefs, among other genres. The following example of an e-mail communication from an attorney provides a glimpse into one type of writing through which lawyers frequently communicate.

● **E-Mail Correspondence**   As you might expect, technological advances can have a profound impact on the communication practices of professionals. There may always be a place for hard copies of documents, but e-mail communication has no doubt replaced many of the letters that used to pass between parties via the U.S. Postal Service. Like most professionals these days, those employed in the legal fields often spend a lot of time communicating with stakeholders via e-mail. These professionals carefully assess each rhetorical situation for which an e-mail communication is necessary, both (1) to make sure the ideas they share with stakeholders (the explanations of legal procedures, or legal options, or applicable precedents, etc.) are accurate, and (2) to make sure they communicate those ideas in an appropriate fashion (with the appropriate tone, clarity, precision, etc.).

Insider Example

E-Mail Correspondence from Attorney

The following example is an e-mail sent from a practicing lawyer to a client. In this instance, the lawyer offers legal advice concerning a possible donation from a party to a foundation. As you read the lawyer's description of the documents attached to his e-mail correspondence with the client, pay attention to the ways the attorney demonstrates an acute awareness of his audience, both in terms of the actual legal advice he provides and in terms of the structure and language of his message. ▶

Establishes the level of familiarity and tone

Provides transactional advice, explaining what procedure needs to occur between the two parties involved: a donor and a receiving foundation

Provides additional advice to protect the interests of the parties in the event that either party decides to back out of the transaction

Explains more specific details included in the attached legal documents to protect the interests of the Foundation

Communicates a willingness to continue the relationship with the client

Provides standard identification and contact information for communication between and among professionals

Dear _____

As promised, here are two documents related to the proposed gift of the ABC property to the XYZ Foundation (the "Foundation"). The first document summarizes the recommended due diligence steps (including the creation of a limited liability company) that should take place prior to the acceptance of the property, accompanied by estimated costs associated with each such step. The second document contains a draft "pre-acceptance" agreement that the Foundation could use to recover its documented costs in the event that either the donor or the Foundation backs out of a gift agreement following the due diligence process.

You will note that we have limited the Foundation's ability to recover costs in the event that the Foundation is the party that "pulls the plug." In such a scenario, the Foundation could recover costs only if it reasonably determines that either (i) the property would create a risk of material exposure to environmentally related liabilities or (ii) the remediation of environmental issues would impose material costs on the Foundation. We realize that even in light of this limiting language, the agreement represents a fairly aggressive approach with the donor, and we will be glad to work with you if you wish to take a softer stance.

Please don't hesitate to call me with any questions, concerns, or critiques. As always, we appreciate the opportunity to serve you in furthering the Foundation's good work.

Best regards,

Joe

Joseph E. Miller, Jr.
Partner

joe.miller@FaegreBD.com
Direct: +1 317 237 1415
FaegreBD.com Download vCard
FAEGRE BAKER DANIELS LLP
300 N. Meridian Street
Suite 2700
Indianapolis, IN 46204, USA

Connect 10.5   **Considering Rhetorical Context for a Lawyer's E-mail**

Study the Insider Example of an e-mail correspondence from an attorney. Analyze the rhetorical context for the e-mail by describing the following elements:

- **Author.**   Who is the author and what do you know about him?

- **Audience.**   Who is the intended audience? What do you know about their desires, beliefs, or values?

- **Topic.**   What is the e-mail about? What is the author's relationship to the topic? What is the audience's relationship to the topic?

- **Purpose.**   Why is the author writing about this topic? What does the author hope to achieve?

Conclude your description with a brief comment on the likely effectiveness of the e-mail for its intended audience. Explain how you reached that conclusion.

Engineering

Engineers shape our daily lives in countless ways. Nearly everything we might purchase at a store has been shaped by one or more engineers, who design, develop, and deliver products that make our lives better. Their influence is evident in the roads we drive on, in the design and construction of the buildings in which we learn and work, and in the technologies we employ on a daily basis. *Engineering* is a broad term used to describe various applied fields of study that rely on mathematical and scientific concepts to analyze, design, model, and/or develop structures for practical purposes. Some fields of engineering include:

- Chemical engineering
- Civil engineering
- Computer engineering
- Electrical engineering
- Mechanical engineering
- Nuclear engineering

In addition to being skilled in science and mathematics, engineers typically are highly adept at teamwork: they work with others to identify problems, propose solutions, and develop tools or systems to respond to those problems. For example, it would likely take a rather large team of engineers with varying backgrounds and expertise to diagnose a flaw in the design of an airplane, to offer a new design in response, and to test the new design for safety and reliability. The work of engineers also requires a substantial amount of writing.

● **PowerPoint Training Slides**   One form of communication engineers often engage in involves the training of others. Imagine, for instance, that you're a lead engineer at a nuclear power plant, and you are tasked with the job of training a group of newly hired engineers in the technical operations of the plant. Likely as not, you would have to produce a substantial amount of training material. In the Insider Example below, we offer a look at such training materials, which often take the form of PowerPoint slides. As you study the slides, pay attention to evidence that points to an audience of trainees.

Insider Example

PowerPoint Slides

The slides and accompanying script in this Insider Example illustrate one of the many types of texts that engineers produce.

Notice when the slides rely on images to convey information in a concise form.

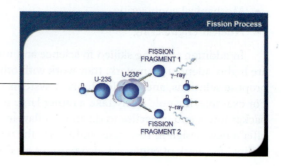

- A U-235 nucleus absorbs a neutron, resulting in U-236* in the "excited state," indicated by the asterisk.
- A fraction of a second later, the nucleus splits into 2 new nuclei, or fission fragments, emitting 2 or 3 neutrons and gamma rays.
- A self-sustaining chain reaction occurs when enough neutrons produced from fission events go on to produce more fissions.
- Once the chain reaction is self-sustaining, the reactor is critical.

Notice that each slide has a title that indicates its topic.

Notice the use of bulleted lists in a number of slides. These lists indicate important ideas or concepts to be discussed during the presenter's remarks.

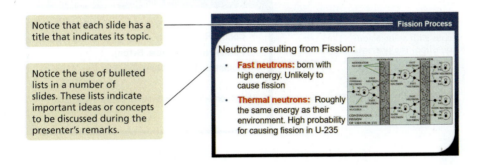

Fission Process

Neutrons resulting from Fission:

- **Fast neutrons:** born with high energy. Unlikely to cause fission
- **Thermal neutrons:** Roughly the same energy as their environment. High probability for causing fission in U-235

- These 2 terms are related to the amount of energy a neutron has:
  - **Fast neutrons** are born with a large amount of energy and are unlikely to cause fission. As they travel through the moderator (water), they slow down, or thermalize.
  - **Thermal neutrons** are at roughly the same energy as their environment.
- The majority of fission-induced neutrons are born fast.
- Reactor coolant acts as a moderator to "thermalize" fast neutrons.
- As the fast neutrons collide with hydrogen atoms in H_2O, they transfer energy to the water molecules, which thermalizes the neutrons.

Notice that each slide contains a relatively small amount of information. Most of the content of the presentation appears in the notes, which are discussion points for the presenter to raise.

Reactivity

$$\rho = 1 - \frac{1}{K_{eff}}$$

- For a critical reactor $\rho = 0$
- For a supercritical reactor $\rho > 0$
- For a subcritical reactor $\rho < 0$

- Recall the definitions of reactivity.
- The relationship between ρ and $K_{eff} \rightarrow \rho = 1 - 1/K_{eff}$
- For a critical reactor $\rho = 0$
- For a supercritical reactor $\rho > 0$
- For a subcritical reactor $\rho < 0$

Notice that the final slide ends with a discussion question. The presentation is designed to end with a discussion between the presenter and those attending the presentation.

Factors Affecting Reactivity

- Fuel
- Control Rods
- Poisons (FP, Burnable, Boron)
- Moderator Temperature (T_{AVG})

Which ones can Maintenance personnel affect?

- All of these factors affect the overall "net" core reactivity.
- The fuel represents positive reactivity because more fuel means more fissions, and more neutrons. This reactivity decreases over core life as fuel is "burned" up.
- Control rods add negative reactivity because they absorb neutrons, preventing them from being absorbed by the fuel. Neutrons absorbed by the control rods are considered leakage in the 6-factor formula. This reactivity decreases (gets less negative) slightly over the life of the control rod.
- Poisons built into the fuel, FPs (fission products) and boron dissolved in the moderator also absorb neutrons and add negative reactivity. These are accounted for in the thermal utilization factor.
- Because the moderator is what thermalizes the neutrons, it adds positive reactivity. Because of what's physically happening in the moderator, its density affects reactivity. As temperature decreases, the density increases, which results in more collisions. This results in less leakage out of the core and an increase in thermal neutrons, which adds positive reactivity.

Information Technology

Professionals in information technology (IT) are interested in how to store, retrieve, manipulate, and transmit data through technology. Usually IT professionals are working with computer technology, but they might also work with other kinds of technology used to share information. People who work in IT can be found in all kinds of businesses and other establishments because information is shared via technology in nearly every possible occupation and profession. IT professionals work at the school that you attend, and they also work at companies and organizations all over the world.

The broad field of IT contains many different areas of specialization, including the following:

- Cyber- and network security
- Data management
- Data analytics
- Systems technology and administration
- Entrepreneurship
- Software development
- Web design and application development

Understanding how to communicate detailed information to a broad range of audiences is a foundation of successful communication in IT. An IT professional might have to communicate the same information both to people who understand and have specialized knowledge of a system and also to people who do not have that specialized knowledge but need to understand the broader implications of what the IT professional is recommending or building. Sometimes an IT professional's writing is almost like a translation. It is essential that the IT professional have both a high level of expertise in his or her area of specialization as well as effective communication strategies to explain that work to clients, colleagues, and management. In the following Insider's View, Tom Tolleson explains why it is important to communicate effectively to avoid misunderstandings that lead to wasted energy and effort.

TOM TOLLESON

"I communicate to groups with a fairly wide range of technical skill. I have to provide the context in which complex behaviors occur and explain the impact. Sometimes I need to provide options for a strategy based on the situation. The feedback that computer technicians often receive is 'What are the details?'—usually followed by 'That's too many details.' My solution for this is to provide a sort of inverted-pyramid style of writing where I give a non-technical summary of the issue in the first paragraph followed by an increasing level of details in subsequent paragraphs (usually preceded by a warning that a dive into data is imminent).

"The only thing that matters is if the audience can understand what I'm communicating. Misunderstandings can result in lot of time and effort being wasted, not to mention frustration. Because electronic media is so integral to my work, I find that succinct writing based on a thoughtful understanding of another person's role, context, and technical understanding is much more helpful than robust and properly formatted writing. I save that for presentations, papers, and documentation."

Insider Example
Student Summary of Shift Operations

In the following Insider Example, student Chrischale Panditharathne explains and analyzes a programming process in the computer language C. She uses technical language to explain the process and provides step-by-step instructions for how to conduct a shift operation. Pay attention to the structure, language, and referencing conventions that she uses in her analysis. ▶

Chrischale Panditharathne

Professor Thomas

November 18, 2017

Shift Operations in C

Among the other bitwise operations available in C, such as AND, OR, XOR, and NOT, there is also one called the shift operation. The bitwise shift allows you to shift a binary value to the right or left by a desired number of bits. However, because each bit pattern is required to have a certain size (for instance, 32 bit or 64 bit), the shift operation also adds bits to either end of the existing bit pattern when the excess bits after the shift are dropped off. Think of this as a pipe, closed loosely at either end, filled with water. If someone wanted to have new water in the pipe, one would open the bottom end and the water near the bottom would empty. You close the pipe when you've emptied enough. However, as a rule the pipe must always be full, so you add more water in from the top to ensure it remains full. Another, albeit less practical way to do it would be to pump in water from the bottom and have the excess spill out from the top. The type of water one would pump in to replace the water lost changes according to which side it was emptied from in the first place.

This is how bit shifting works. Bits are pushed from the right or left and replaced with either 1s or zeros depending on the type of shift and the Most Significant Bit in the bit pattern.

The ability to perform shifts ensures you can keep your code portable between compilers, and therefore between machines, since compilation format depends on the compiler itself, and not the particular machine the code is running on.

C allows programmers to perform three kinds of shifts on binary bit patterns. The type of shift only differs by the direction in which it is shifted and which bit, 0 or 1, is used to fill in the gaps once the existing bit pattern is pushed left or right.

C is a computing language. Like English and other spoken languages, computing languages have their own rules and syntax.

Chrischale uses an analogy to help clarify a complex technical topic.

1. **Logical Left Shift** ($<<$).

   The most straightforward of shifts, the left shift is always logical and simply shifts bits to the left and fills in the rest of the space with 0s.

   For example, let's say bit pattern x = 01100010

0	1	1	0	0	0	1	0

   x $<<$ 3

   0   1   1

0	0	0	1	0	0	0	0

   Zeros are pushed in to replace the three bits that were pushed out the left end. The logical left shift is basically equivalent to multiplying a number by 2.

2. **Logical Right Shift** ($>>$).

   The logical right shift is similar to the logical left shift, and it shifts bits to the right, filling the gaps with 0s.

   For example, let's say bit pattern x = 01100010

0	1	1	0	0	0	1	0

   x $>>$ 3

0	0	0	0	1	1	0	0

   0   1   0

   Zeros are pushed in to replace the three bits that were pushed out the right end.

3. **Arithmetic Right Shift** ($>>$).

   The arithmetic right shift is a little more complicated but is the most commonly used. It too shifts the bit pattern to the right, but instead of always filling the gaps with 0s, it will fill them with the most significant bit. This is useful when we want to preserve the sign of the bit pattern we are dealing with.

Binary code is a computer language that sends commands to the machine using combinations of 1s and 0s.

For example, let's say bit pattern x = 11100010

1	1	1	0	0	0	1	0

x >> 3

1	1	1	1	1	1	0	0	0	1	0

Most Significant Bit is pushed in to replace the three bits that were pushed out the right end.

The issue with having two kinds of right shifts is that you could use either arithmetic or logical right shift, and the code would still work. This is problematic because if one compiler assumes right shifts to be logical and the other assumes right shifts to be arithmetic, then there could be grave consequences in bit manipulation and calculations. Little mistakes like this are what cause losses of millions in real-world projects, so it is crucial to understand the difference.

Therefore, the convention in C is to use the arithmetic right shift if the integer is signed, that is, the integer value represents only positive numbers, or logical shift if the integer is unsigned, that is, the integer could be both positive and negative. This only applies to C, however. In other programming languages the convention is similar but with additional rules as to how and when each shift is applied.

Writing Project **Genre Analysis of Writing in an Applied Field**

In this chapter, you've read about some of the conventions of writing in the applied fields. You might be interested in a field that's not represented in this chapter, though. For this assignment, you will conduct research to discover more about the kinds of writing that are common within a particular applied field—ideally, one you're interested in. You might conduct either primary or secondary research to respond to this assignment. However, you should focus on collecting examples of the kinds of writing done in the field. Consider the following steps to complete this assignment:

1. Collect examples of the kinds of writing done in the field.
2. Describe the different genres and how they relate to the work of that applied field.
3. Look for comparisons and contrasts across those genres. Do any commonalities point to conventions shared across genres? Are there differences that are important to notice? What do the patterns across the genres tell you about the work and values of that applied field?

Variation: Imagine that your audience is a group of incoming students interested in the same field of study you've researched for this project. Your task is to write a guide for those students about the conventions of writing expected in this applied field. Depending on what you have found, you may need to identify what conventions are appropriate for specific genres of writing.

....

Insider Example

Student Genre Analysis of Electrical and Computer Engineering Standards

In this Insider Example, Reece Neff, a first-year writing student, responds to an assignment that asked him to describe some of the conventional rhetorical features of a genre of writing specific to his intended field of study, computer engineering. In his response, Reece identifies some of the structural, reference, and language features characteristic of the Institute of Electrical and Electronics Engineers (IEEE) Standards and suggests that professionals' use of these features highlights some of the values shared by members of the computer engineering community. ▶

Reece Neff

English 101 – 051

Prof. Roy Stamper

May 4, 2017

Project Five

Electrical and Computer Engineering Standards:

A Rhetorical Analysis

Electrical and Computer Engineering (ECE) is a field that deals with improving circuits, transistors, and computer hardware/software to make life easier for those using those devices. Professionals in this field typically research and design innovative ways to use electronic components. In this field, ECE professionals typically write standards for their company or organization. Standards are crucial for product manufacturing in that company or organization because this provides continuity across all the designs, and this allows for the designs to work together easier for anyone designing a new method/process/product. "IEEE Standard for Floating-Point Arithmetic" by Institute of Electrical and Electronics Engineers Computer Society (IEEE) is an example of a standard widely used by ECE professionals who follow the IEEE standards. This standard contains instructions for how ECE professionals should write and process bits in low-level programming. This standard also contains similar conventional features across other standards written by ECE professionals. "Introducing Students to Disciplinary Genres: The Role of the General Composition Course" by P. Linton et al. asserts that these conventional features can be classified into three distinct categories: structure, which controls the argument's progression; reference, which is the way that the writer uses outside work; and language, which covers basic sentence structure. This standard utilizes many conventional features of structure, reference, and language, and analysis of

Reece provides a brief introduction to the field of study.

Reece describes the specific genre, along with the specific example of this genre, on which his analysis focuses.

Reece asserts a thesis that identifies the categories of rhetorical features he'll describe. He also points to a larger purpose in his analysis, which is to demonstrate that the rhetorical features he'll describe reflect values held by members of this professional community.

these features reveals the values of ECE professionals: easily referenceable material and collaboration.

One category of conventional features that Linton et al. define is structure. They state that these conventions "control the flow of the argument and, more importantly, determine the kinds of cues available to readers" (66). One convention of structure found in IEEE's standard is headings and subheadings that promote the value of easily referenceable information within the ECE community. For example, IEEE includes "Floating-point formats" (6) with multiple subheadings such as "Binary interchange format encodings" (9) and "Decimal interchange format encodings" (10). IEEE then goes on to explain each of the subheadings. Another example of this is IEEE's heading "Operations" (17), going into more detail with the subheadings "Quiet-computational operations" (23) and "Signaling-computational operations" (24), and finally explaining what each of those subheadings is. This detailed organization allows the ECE professionals that are designing something to quickly and easily reference the material that they are trying to find. Their time is valuable, so they cannot waste it trying to find information buried deep within a text—they need a reliable way to easily and quickly find that information. This adds to the value of easily referenceable information that ECE professionals need when viewing standards as they try to design new methods or products.

Another convention of structure that IEEE uses in its standard is the inclusion of a definitions section, which improves readability, thus promoting the value of collaboration. IEEE inserts a "Definitions, abbreviations, and acronyms" (3) section and provides definitions such as ". . . **applicable attribute:** The value of an attribute governing a particular . . ." (3) and ". . . **arithmetic format:** A floating-point format that

---

Reece introduces a category of conventions he'll address first, structural conventions.

One structural feature he'll look at is the use of headings and subheadings.

Provides examples from the genre

Explains what the use of headings and subheadings might suggest about the values of this community

can be used to represent . . ." (3). These definitions provide the reader interpretations of each word the writer(s) agreed with. This way, everyone is on the same page in terms of understanding what each word means, leaving less room for misinterpretation among the ECE community. IEEE's improvement of readability by including a definitions section promotes collaboration between ECE professionals because they will be able to interpret the standard more effectively.

The second category of conventional features, reference, aims to "establish standard ways of addressing the work of other scholars; they encode the formal or public relationships among members of the discourse community" (Linton et al., 66). A convention of reference that IEEE uses in its standard is the inclusion of an informative bibliography which promotes the value of collaboration between ECE professionals. IEEE adds a bibliography at the end, stating "(informative)" (53), meaning they did not reference this material in the text. This bibliography is purely meant to expand the reader's knowledge on this topic by looking at other sources that use this standard. In the bibliography, IEEE states at the beginning "The following documents might be helpful to the reader" and then includes a myriad of documents related to this standard. The inclusion of an informative bibliography such as this one allows the reader to expand his/her knowledge on the usage of this standard and to show other works by ECE professionals. Because of this, IEEE's inclusion of an informative bibliography promotes the value of collaboration between ECE professionals.

Another convention of reference that IEEE utilizes is the inclusion of revisions, which also promotes the value of collaboration between ECE professionals. IEEE includes a parenthetical if their standard is a revision of an older standard. In this standard, this is located in the top right

Reece introduces a second category of conventional features he'll examine, reference.

Describes how references appear in the genre

Provides a rationale for the use of these reference features that is grounded in the community's shared belief or goals hand of the title page stating "**IEEE Std 754™-2008** (Revision of IEEE Std 654-1985)" (IEEE i). This revision parenthetical shows that this standard was revised from the previous 1984 standard of floating-point arithmetic. The parenthetical allows readers to go back to the original document and review changes between the two. IEEE's inclusion of a revision parenthetical promotes the value of collaboration between ECE professionals because this shows (subjective) improvement on a previous document.

The final category of conventional features that Linton et al. define is language, which "guide[s] phrasing at the sentence level" (66) and "reflect[s] characteristic choices of syntax and diction" (66). A convention of language that IEEE uses in its standard is the inclusion of bullet points, which increases readability, promoting the value of easily referenceable information within the ECE community. Going more in detail from the headings and subheadings, IEEE includes bullet points to help explain each topic in the subheadings. An example of this includes an example in the "Formats" overview of "Floating-point formats" where IEEE states "Five basic formats are defined in this clause:

- Three binary formats, with encodings in lengths of 32, 64, and 128 bits.
- Two decimal formats, with encodings in lengths of 64 and 128 bits" (6).

Another example of IEEE's use of bullet points can be seen in the "Infinity arithmetic" subheading where IEEE defines "The exceptions that do pertain to infinities are signaled only when

- ∞ is an invalid operand (see Figure E-7: IEEE 7, Level 2)
- ∞ is created from finite operands by overflow (see Figure E-7: IEEE 7, Level 4) or division by zero (see Figure E-7: IEEE 7, Level 3)
- remainder (subnormal, ∞) signals underflow" (34).

Reece identifies a third category of conventions he'll examine, language.

In this paragraph, Reece focuses on the use of bullet points in the genre.

Provides examples

The use of these bullet points allows IEEE to condense their information into smaller and concise chunks. This makes it easier for ECE professionals to reference and use the information found within the standard. Because of this, IEEE's use of bullet points promotes the value of easily referenceable information.

Another convention of language that IEEE uses is the inclusion of diagrams and tables, making them easier to read, promoting the value of collaboration between ECE professionals. IEEE includes tables and diagrams such as:

Level 1	$\{-\infty \ ... \ 0 \ ... \ +\infty\}$	Extended real numbers.
many-to-one ↓	*rounding*	↑ projection (except for NaN)
Level 2	$\{-\infty \ ... \ -0\} \cup \{+0 \ ... \ +\infty\} \cup NaN$	Floating-point data—an algebraically closed system.
one-to-many ↓	*representation specification*	↑ many-to-one
Level 3	**(sign, exponent, significand)** $\cup \{-\infty, +\infty\} \cup$ qNaN $\cup$ sNaN	Representations of floating-point data.
one-to-many ↓	*encoding for representations of floating-point data*	↑ many-to-one
Level 4	0111000...	Bit strings.

Figure E-7. IEEE 7, Levels 1-4.

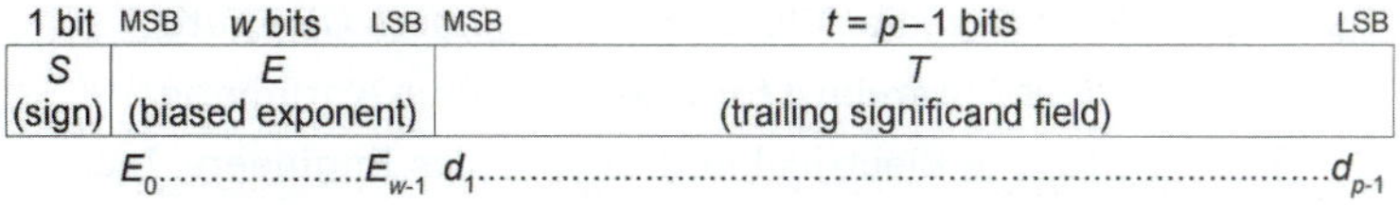

1 bit	MSB	w bits	LSB	MSB	$t = p-1$ bits		LSB
S (sign)		E (biased exponent)			T (trailing significand field)		

$E_0 .... E_{w-1} \ d_1 .... d_{p-1}$

Figure E-8. IEEE 9

The inclusion of tables and diagrams makes interpretation easier with some of the concepts that the standards are trying to describe. Without trying to explain something in hundreds of words, IEEE inserts a table or diagram to describe a topic easier and reduce misinterpretation of it. Increased proper interpretation of the standard makes it easier for ECE professionals to collaborate with each other without any conflicts with the interpretation of this standard. Thus, IEEE's

> Provides a rationale for the use of bullet points that is grounded in the community's values or beliefs

In this conclusion to his analysis, Reece reiterates his position that the rhetorical features identified highlight values shared among members of this applied field community.

inclusion of tables and diagrams promotes the value of collaboration between ECE professionals.

The analysis of IEEE's standard shows many kinds of conventional features as illustrated by Linton et al.—structure, reference, and language. The analysis of this standard shows that the use of these conventions reflects the values of ECE professionals in being easily referenceable, and collaborative. One feature that could not be explored were normative references because as they were present in many other standards published by ECE professionals, they were not present in this standard. This analysis hopes to help students further increase their understanding of ECE standards in the applied field and to spur further analysis of different genres of writing in the applied fields.

Identifies another conventional feature of the genre that was not present in the text he analyzed

Works Cited

Institute of Electrical and Electronics Engineers Computer
Society. "IEEE Standard for Floating-Point Arithmetic."
The Institute of Electrical and Electronics Engineers, Inc.,
2008. doi: 10.1109/IEEESTD.2008.4610935

Linton, Patricia, et al. "Introducing Students to Disciplinary
Discourse: The Role of the General Composition Course."
Language and Learning across the Disciplines, vol. 1, no. 2,
1994, pp. 63–78.

tip sheet

Reading and Writing in the Applied Fields

- **The applied fields focus on the practical application of knowledge and career preparation.** Many applied fields also focus on problem-solving as part of the practical application of knowledge.

- **When beginning a writing task in applied fields, carefully analyze the rhetorical situation.** Consider your purpose and your audience carefully, and assess the appropriateness of responding in a particular genre.

- **Much of the writing in applied fields follows conventional expectations for structure, language, and reference appropriate to the fields.** Regardless of your writing task, you should be aware of these conventional expectations.

- **Students and professionals in applied fields often communicate information through field-specific genres.** Nurses, for example, often construct discharge directions, just as students and professionals in the fields of law often compose legal briefs.

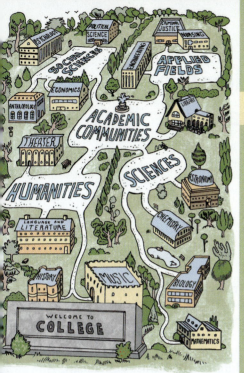

ANDREA TSURUMI

PART THREE

Entering Academic Conversations

Readings and Case Studies

The four chapters in Part Three allow you to practice reading the kinds of popular and scholarly arguments you'll encounter in your courses. The popular sources show how the principles of rhetoric operate in public persuasion. The academic articles are grouped into casebooks that let you see how different disciplines view similar topics through different lenses.

Constructing Identity: Writing, Language, and the Self

T he readings in this chapter explore what writing means to us as people and highlight how important writing is to scholars in every discipline. The chapter opens with selections from several popular sources that address the topic of writing. Jimmy Baca's "Coming into Language" exemplifies a poet's use of the literacy narrative genre, sharing how writing can be a form of freedom. Jia Tolentino's "The I in Internet" addresses the themes of writing, visibility, and agency in digital spaces. Robin Dembroff and Daniel Wodak's "If Someone Wants to Be Called 'They' and Not 'He' or 'She,' Why Say No?" explores the themes of writing, language use, and identities through the example of how we use language to reference gender, either intentionally or not. Finally, the four selections in the academic case study explore the role of writing in different disciplines from the perspectives of scholars in those fields of study.

Our purpose in providing these articles is to offer a context for engaging in discussion about what writing is, what it means to us as individuals and as scholars, and how writing and reading both contribute to shaping our identity and our sense of community and provide a means through which we can critically examine our lives. Questions to consider as you read the three popular articles may include the following:

- How does writing contribute to your understanding of who you are?

- What is knowledge? How do writing and language use contribute to our knowledge?

- How does language use impact freedom and access to freedom for all members of society?

- What roles do writing, reading, and education play in contributing to social and economic equality or inequality?

In the academic case study section of this chapter, we feature scholarship on writing from a variety of academic disciplines to reveal the impact and value of writing:

- **Humanities** How do students understand the importance of learning to write effectively in their majors?
- **Social Sciences** How can writing affect well-being? Specifically, how can writing letters of gratitude affect happiness, life-satisfaction, and depression?
- **Natural Sciences** What happens in our brains to create meaning as we process words on a page?
- **Applied Fields** How might the use of storytelling impact the efficacy of nursing research?

Coming into Language

JIMMY SANTIAGO BACA

Jimmy Santiago Baca is an American poet of Apache and Chicano descent. Orphaned as a child, Baca eventually became homeless and spent five years in a maximum-security prison on drug possession charges. While in prison, Baca taught himself to read and write. There, he also began to write poetry. Baca has since published numerous books of poetry, including, most recently, *When I Walk through That Door, I Am: An Immigrant Mother's Quest* (2019). His memoir, *A Place to Stand*, was published in 2001. In the essay below, published in 1991 in *Working in the Dark: Reflections of a Poet of the Barrio*, Baca recounts his experience of prison and traces his transformational journey toward literacy and self-empowerment.

On weekend graveyard shifts at St. Joseph's Hospital I worked the emergency room, mopping up pools of blood and carting plastic bags stuffed with arms, legs, and hands to the outdoor incinerator. I enjoyed the quiet, away from the screams of shotgunned, knifed, and mangled kids writhing on gurneys outside the operating rooms. Ambulance sirens shrieked and squad car lights reddened the cool nights, flashing against the hospital walls: gray—red, gray—red. On slow nights I would lock the door of the administration office, search the reference library for a book on female anatomy and, with my feet propped on the desk, leaf through the illustrations, smoking my cigarette. I was seventeen.

One night my eye was caught by a familiar-looking word on the spine of a book. The title was *450 Years of Chicano History in Pictures*. On the cover were black-and-white photos: Padre Hidalgo exhorting Mexican peasants to revolt against the Spanish dictators; Anglo vigilantes hanging two Mexicans from a tree; a young Mexican woman with rifle and ammunition belts crisscrossing her breast; César Chávez and field workers marching for fair wages; Chicano railroad workers laying creosote ties; Chicanas laboring at machines in textile factories; Chicanas picketing and hoisting boycott signs.

From the time I was seven, teachers had been punishing me for not knowing my lessons by making me stick my nose in a circle chalked on the blackboard. Ashamed of not understanding and fearful of asking questions, I dropped out of school in the ninth grade. At seventeen I still didn't know how to read, but those pictures confirmed my identity. I stole the book that night, stashing it for safety under the slop sink until I got off work. Back at my boardinghouse, I showed the book to friends. All of us were amazed; this book told us we were alive. We, too, had defended ourselves with our fists against hostile Anglos, gasping for breath in fights with the policemen who outnumbered us. The book reflected back to us our struggle in a way that made us proud.

Most of my life I felt like a target in the cross-hairs of a hunter's rifle. When strangers and outsiders questioned me I felt the hang-rope tighten around my neck and the trapdoor creak beneath my feet. There was nothing so humiliating as being unable to express myself, and my inarticulateness increased my sense of jeopardy. Behind a mask of humility, I seethed with mute rebellion.

Before I was eighteen, I was arrested on suspicion 5 of murder after refusing to explain a deep cut on my forearm. With shocking speed I found myself hand-cuffed to a chain gang of inmates and bused to a hold-ing facility to await trial. There I met men, prisoners, who read aloud to each other the works of Neruda, Paz, Sabines, Nemerov, and Hemingway. Never had I felt such freedom as in that dormitory. Listening to the words of these writers, I felt that invisible threat from without lessen—my sense of teetering on a rotting plank over swamp water where famished alligators clapped their horny snouts for my blood. While I listened to the words of the poets, the alliga-tors slumbered powerless in their lairs. The language of poetry was the magic that could liberate me from myself, transform me into another person, transport me to places far away.

And when they closed the books, these Chicanos, and went into their own Chicano language, they made barrio life come alive for me in the fullness of its vital-ity. I began to learn my own language, the bilingual words and phrases explaining to me my place in the universe.

Months later I was released, as I had suspected I would be. I had been guilty of nothing but shat-tering the windshield of my girlfriend's car in a fit of rage.

Two years passed. I was twenty now, and behind bars again. The federal marshals had failed to provide convincing evidence to extradite me to Arizona on a drug charge, but still I was being held. They had ninety days to prove I was guilty. The only evidence against me was that my girlfriend had been at the scene of the crime with my driver's license in her purse. They had to come up with something else. But there was nothing else. Eventually they negotiated a deal with the actual drug dealer, who took the stand against me. When the judge hit me with a million-dollar bail, I emptied my pockets on his booking desk: twenty-six cents.

One night in my third month in the county jail, I was mopping the floor in front of the booking desk. Some detectives had kneed an old drunk and handcuffed him to the booking bars. His shrill screams raked my nerves like a hacksaw on bone, the desperate protest of his dignity against their inhu-manity. But the detectives just laughed as he tried to rise and kicked him to his knees. When they went to the bathroom to pee and the desk attendant walked to the file cabinet to pull the arrest record, I shot my arm through the bars, grabbed one of the attendant's university textbooks, and tucked it in my overalls. It was the only way I had of protesting.

It was late when I returned to my cell. Under 10 my blanket I switched on a pen flashlight and opened the thick book at random, scanning the pages. I could hear the jailer making his rounds on the other tiers. The jangle of his keys and the sharp click of his boot heels intensified my solitude. Slowly I enunciated the words . . . p-o-n-d, ri-pple. It scared me that I had been reduced to this to find comfort. I always had thought reading a waste of time, that nothing could be gained by it. Only by action, by moving out into the world and confront-ing and challenging the obstacles, could one learn anything worth knowing.

Even as I tried to convince myself that I was merely curious, I became so absorbed in how the sounds created music in me and happiness, I for-got where I was. Memories began to quiver in me, glowing with a strange but familiar intimacy in which I found refuge. For a while, a deep sadness overcame me, as if I had chanced on a long-lost friend and mourned the years of separation. But soon the heartache of having missed so much of life, that had numbed me since I was a child, gave way, as if a grave illness lifted itself from me and I was cured, innocently believing in the beauty of life again. I stumblingly repeated the author's name as I fell asleep, saying it over and over in the dark: Words-worth, Words-worth.

Before long my sister came to visit me, and I joked about taking her to a place called Xanadu and getting her a blind date with this *vato*[1] named Coleridge who lived on the seacoast and was *malias*[2] on morphine. When I asked her to make a trip into enemy territory to buy me a grammar book, she said she couldn't. Bookstores intimidated her, because she, too, could neither read nor write.

Days later, with a stub pencil I whittled sharp with my teeth, I propped a Red Chief notebook on my knees and wrote my first words. From that moment, a hunger for poetry possessed me.

Until then, I had felt as if I had been born into a raging ocean where I swam relentlessly, flailing my arms in hope of rescue, of reaching a shoreline I never sighted. Never solid ground beneath me, never a resting place. I had lived with only the desperate hope to stay afloat; that and nothing more.

But when at last I wrote my first words on the page, I felt an island rising beneath my feet like the back of a whale. As more and more words emerged, I could finally rest: I had a place to stand for the first time in my life. The island grew, with each page, into a continent inhabited by people I knew and mapped with the life I lived.

I wrote about it all—about people I had loved or hated, about the brutalities and ecstasies of my life. And, for the first time, the child in me who had witnessed and endured unspeakable terrors cried out not just in impotent despair, but with the power of language. Suddenly, through language, through writing, my grief and my joy could be shared with anyone who

[1]In Chicano dialect: dude. (JSB)
[2]In Chicano dialect: strung out. (JSB)

would listen. And I could do this all alone; I could do it anywhere. I was no longer a captive of demons eating away at me, no longer a victim of other people's mockery and loathing, that had made me clench my fist white with rage and grit my teeth to silence. Words now pleaded back with the bleak lucidity of hurt. They were wrong, those others, and now I could say it.

Through language I was free. I could respond, escape, indulge; embrace or reject earth or the cosmos. I was launched on an endless journey without boundaries or rules, in which I could salvage the floating fragments of my past, or be born anew in the spontaneous ignition of understanding some heretofore concealed aspect of myself. Each word steamed with the hot lava juices of my primordial making, and I crawled out of stanzas dripping with birth-blood, reborn and freed from the chaos of my life. The child in the dark room of my heart, who had never been able to find or reach the light switch, flicked it on now; and I found in the room a stranger, myself, who had waited so many years to speak again. My words struck in me lightning crackles of elation and thunderhead storms of grief.

When I had been in the county jail longer than anyone else, I was made a trustee. One morning, after a fistfight, I went to the unlocked and unoccupied office used for lawyer-client meetings, to think. The bare white room with its fluorescent tube lighting seemed to expose and illuminate my dark and worthless life. When I had fought before, I never gave it a thought. Now, for the first time, I had something to lose—my chance to read, to write; a way to live with dignity and meaning, that had opened for me when I stole that scuffed, second-hand book about the Romantic poets.

"I will never do any work in this prison system as long as I am not allowed to get my G.E.D." That's what I told the reclassification panel. The captain flicked off the tape recorder. He looked at me hard and said, "You'll never walk outta here alive. Oh, you'll work, put a copper penny on that, you'll work."

15

After that interview I was confined to deadlock 20 maximum security in a subterranean dungeon, with ground-level chicken-wired windows painted gray. Twenty-three hours a day I was in that cell. Then, just before Christmas, I received a letter from Harry, a charity house Samaritan who doled out hot soup to the homeless in Phoenix. He had picked my name from a list of cons who had no one write to them. I wrote back asking for a grammar book, and a week later received one of Mary Baker Eddy's treatises on salvation and redemption, with Spanish and English on opposing pages. Pacing my cell all day and most of each night, I grappled with grammar until I was able to write a long true-romance confession for a con to send to his pen pal. He paid me with a pack of smokes. Soon I had a thriving barter business, exchanging my poems and letters for novels, commissary pencils, and writing tablets.

One day I tore two flaps from the cardboard box that held all my belongings and punctured holes along the edge of each flap and along the border of a ream of state-issue paper. After I had aligned them to form a spine, I threaded the holes with a shoestring, and sketched on the cover a hummingbird fluttering above a rose. This was my first journal.

Whole afternoons I wrote, unconscious of passing time or whether it was day or night. Sunbursts exploded from the lead tip of my pencil, words that grafted me into awareness of who I was; peeled back to a burning core of bleak terror, an embryo floating in the image of water, I cracked out of the shell wide-eyed and insane. Trees grew out of the palms of my hands, the threatening otherness of life dissolved, and I became one with the air and sky, the dirt and the iron and concrete. There was no longer any distinction between the other and I. Language made bridges of fire between me and everything I saw. I entered into the blade of grass, the basketball, the con's eye and child's soul.

At night I flew. I conversed with floating heads in my cell, and visited strange houses where lonely women brewed tea and rocked in wicker rocking chairs listening to sad Joni Mitchell songs.

Before long I was frayed like rope carrying too much weight, that suddenly snaps. I quit talking. Bars, walls, steel bunk and floor bristled with millions of poem-making sparks. My face was no longer familiar to me. The only reality was the swirling cornucopia of images in my mind, the voices in the air. Midair a cactus blossom would appear, a snake-flame in blinding dance around it, stunning me like a guard's fist striking my neck from behind. The prison administrators tried several tactics to get me to work. For six months, after the next monthly prison board review, they sent cons to my cell to hassle me. When the guard would open my cell door to let one of them in, I'd leap out and fight him — and get sent to thirty-day isolation. I did a lot of isolation time. But I honed my image-making talents in that sensory-deprived solitude. Finally they moved me to death row, and after that to "nut-run," the tier that housed the mentally disturbed.

As the months passed, I became more and more 25 sluggish. My eyelids were heavy, I could no longer write or read. I slept all the time.

One day a guard took me out to the exercise field. For the first time in years I felt grass and earth under my feet. It was spring. The sun warmed my face as I sat on the bleachers watching the cons box and run, hit the handball, lift weights. Some of them stopped to ask how I was, but I found it impossible to utter a syllable. My tongue would not move, saliva drooled from the corners of my mouth. I had been so heavily medicated I could not summon the slightest gestures. Yet inside me a small voice cried out, I am fine! I am hurt now but I will come back! I'm fine!

Back in my cell, for weeks I refused to eat. Styrofoam cups of urine and hot water were hurled at me. Other things happened. There were beatings, shock therapy, intimidation.

Later, I regained some clarity of mind. But there was a place in my heart where I had died. My life had compressed itself into an unbearable dread of being. The strain had been too much. I had stepped over that line where a human being has lost more than he can bear, where the pain is too intense, and he knows he is changed forever. I was now capable of killing, coldly and without feeling. I was empty, as I have never, before or since, known emptiness. I had no connection to this life.

But then, the encroaching darkness that began to envelop me forced me to re-form and give birth to myself again in the chaos. I withdrew even deeper into the world of language, cleaving the diamonds of verbs and nouns, plunging into the brilliant light of poetry's regenerative mystery. Words gave off rings of white energy, radar signals from powers beyond me that infused me with truth. I believed what I wrote, because I wrote what was true. My words did not come from books or textual formulas, but from a deep faith in the voice of my heart.

I had been steeped in self-loathing and rejected by everyone and everything—society, family, cons, God, and demons. But now I had become as the burning ember floating in darkness that descends on a dry leaf and sets flame to forests. The word was the ember and the forest was my life . . .

Writing bridged my divided life of prisoner and free man. I wrote of the emotional butchery of prisons, and my acute gratitude for poetry. Where my blind doubt and spontaneous trust in life met, I discovered empathy and compassion. The power to express myself was a welcome storm rasping at tendril roots, flooding my soul's cracked dirt. Writing was water that cleansed the wound and fed the parched root of my heart.

I wrote to sublimate my rage, from a place where all hope is gone, from a madness of having been damaged too much, from a silence of killing rage. I wrote to avenge the betrayals of a lifetime, to purge the bitterness of injustice. I wrote with a deep groan of doom in my blood, bewildered and dumbstruck; from an indestructible love of life, to affirm breath and laughter and the abiding innocence of things. I wrote the way I wept, and danced, and made love.

Reading Questions

1. In what ways was Jimmy Baca's writing a source of freedom in his life?

2. How did Baca's Chicano history play a role in how he perceived his identity, and how does he indicate that his identity has shaped his writing?

Rhetoric Questions

3. What imagery from Baca's essay evokes the most emotion in you and why?

4. Consider Baca's audience and purpose. Who does he see as his audience, and what does he want them to do?

Response Question

5. Baca writes: "I always had thought reading a waste of time, that nothing could be gained by it. Only by action, by moving out into the world and confronting and challenging the obstacles, could one learn anything worth knowing" (par. 10). To what degree do you agree with this perspective? What experiences of "moving out into the world and confronting and challenging the obstacles" have you learned from the most in your lifetime?

The I in Internet

JIA TOLENTINO

Jia Tolentino has been a staff writer at the *New Yorker* since 2016. She studied English at the University of Virginia and the University of Michigan, and she writes short fiction in addition to essays on music, race, marriage, and popular culture. The essay below appears in her 2019 book *Trick Mirror: Reflections on Self-Delusion*, which spent several weeks on the *New York Times* Bestseller List. In the essay, Tolentino explores how we present ourselves in online spaces, creating identities to ever-increasing public audiences.

In the beginning the internet seemed good. "I was in love with the internet the first time I used it at my dad's office and thought it was the ULTIMATE COOL," I wrote, when I was ten, on an Angelfire subpage titled "The Story of How Jia Got Her Web Addiction." In a text box superimposed on a hideous violet background, I continued:

> But that was in third grade and all I was doing was going to Beanie Baby sites. Having an old, icky bicky computer at home, we didn't have the Internet. Even AOL seemed like a far-off dream. Then we got a new top-o'-the-line computer in spring break '99, and of course it came with all that demo stuff. So I finally had AOL and I was completely amazed at the marvel of having a profile and chatting and IMS!!

Then, I wrote, I discovered personal webpages. ("I was astonished!") I learned HTML and "little Javascript trickies." I built my own site on the beginner-hosting site Expage, choosing pastel colors and then switching to a "starry night theme." Then I ran out of space, so I "decided to move to Angelfire. Wow." I learned how to make my own graphics. "This was all in the course of four months," I wrote, marveling at how quickly my ten-year-old internet citizenry was evolving. I had recently revisited the sites that had once inspired me, and realized "how much of an idiot I was to be wowed by *that*."

I have no memory of inadvertently starting this essay two decades ago, or of making this Angelfire subpage, which I found while hunting for early traces of myself on the internet. It's now eroded to its skeleton: its landing page, titled "THE VERY BEST," features a sepia-toned photo of Andie from *Dawson's Creek* and a dead link to a new site called "THE FROSTED FIELD," which is "BETTER!" There's a page dedicated to a blinking mouse GIF named Susie, and a "Cool Lyrics Page" with a scrolling banner and the lyrics to Smash Mouth's "All Star," Shania Twain's "Man! I Feel Like a Woman!" and the TLC diss track "No Pigeons," by Sporty Thievz. On an FAQ page—there was an FAQ page—I write that I had to close down my customizable cartoon-doll section, as "the response has been enormous."

It appears that I built and used this Angelfire site over just a few months in 1999, immediately after my parents got a computer. My insane FAQ page specifies that the site was started in June, and a page titled "Journal"—which proclaims, "I am going to be completely honest about my life, although I won't go too deeply into personal thoughts, though"—features entries only from October. One entry begins: "It's so HOT outside and I can't count the times acorns have fallen on my head, maybe from exhaustion." Later on, I write, rather prophetically: "I'm going insane! I literally am addicted to the web!"

In 1999, it felt different to spend all day on the 5 internet. This was true for everyone, not just for ten-year-olds: this was the *You've Got Mail* era, when it seemed that the very worst thing that could happen online was that you might fall in love with your business rival. Throughout the eighties and nineties, people had been gathering on the internet in open forums, drawn, like butterflies, to the puddles and blossoms of other people's curiosity and expertise. Self-regulated newsgroups like Usenet cultivated lively and relatively civil discussion about space exploration, meteorology, recipes, rare albums. Users gave advice, answered questions, made friendships, and wondered what this new internet would become.

Because there were so few search engines and no centralized social platforms, discovery on the early internet took place mainly in private, and pleasure existed as its own solitary reward. A 1995 book called *You Can Surf the Net!* listed sites where you could read movie reviews or learn about martial arts. It urged readers to follow basic etiquette (don't use all caps; don't waste other people's expensive bandwidth with overly long posts) and encouraged them to feel comfortable in this new world ("Don't worry," the author advised. "You have to *really* mess up to get flamed."). Around this time, GeoCities began offering personal website hosting for dads who wanted to put up their own golfing sites or kids who built glittery, blinking shrines to Tolkien or Ricky Martin or unicorns, most capped off with a primitive guest book and a green-and-black visitor counter. GeoCities, like the internet itself, was clumsy, ugly, only half functional, and organized into neighborhoods: /area51/ was for sci-fi, /westhollywood/ for LGBTQ life, /enchanted-forest/ for children, /petsburgh/ for pets. If you left GeoCities, you could walk around other streets in this ever-expanding village of curiosities. You could stroll through Expage or Angelfire, as I did, and pause on the thoroughfare where the tiny cartoon hamsters danced. There was an emergent aesthetic—blinking text, crude animation. If you found something you liked, if you wanted to spend more time in any of these neighborhoods, you could build your own house from HTML frames and start decorating.

This period of the internet has been labeled Web 1.0—a name that works backward from the term Web 2.0, which was coined by the writer and user experience designer Darcy DiNucci in an article called "Fragmented Future," published in 1999. "The Web we know now," she wrote, "which loads into a browser window in essentially static screen-fuls, is only an embryo of the Web to come. The first glimmerings of Web 2.0 are beginning to appear. . . . The Web will be understood not as screenfuls of texts and graphics but as a transport mechanism, the ether through which interactivity happens." On Web 2.0,

the structures would be dynamic, she predicted: instead of houses, websites would be portals, through which an ever-changing stream of activity—status updates, photos—could be displayed. What you did on the internet would become intertwined with what everyone else did, and the things other people liked would become the things that you would see. Web 2.0 platforms like Blogger and Myspace made it possible for people who had merely been taking in the sights to start generating their own personalized and constantly changing scenery. As more people began to register their existence digitally, a pastime turned into an imperative: you had to register yourself digitally to exist.

In a *New Yorker* piece from November 2000, Rebecca Mead profiled Meg Hourihan, an early blogger who went by Megnut. In just the prior eighteen months, Mead observed, the number of "weblogs" had gone from fifty to several thousand, and blogs like Megnut were drawing thousands of visitors per day. This new internet was social ("a blog consists primarily of links to other Web sites and commentary about those links") in a way that centered on individual identity (Megnut's readers knew that she wished there were better fish tacos in San Francisco, and that she was a feminist, and that she was close with her mom). The blogosphere was also full of mutual transactions, which tended to echo and escalate. The "main audience for blogs is other bloggers," Mead wrote. Etiquette required that, "if someone blogs your blog, you blog his blog back."

Through the emergence of blogging, personal lives were becoming public domain, and social incentives—to be liked, to be seen—were becoming economic ones. The mechanisms of internet exposure began to seem like a viable foundation for a career. Hourihan cofounded Blogger with Evan Williams, who later cofounded Twitter. JenniCam, founded in 1996 when the college student Jennifer Ringley started broadcasting webcam photos from her dorm room, attracted at one point up to four million daily visitors, some of whom paid a subscription fee for quicker loading images. The internet, in promising a potentially unlimited audience, began to seem like the natural home of self-expression. In one blog post, Megnut's boyfriend, the blogger Jason Kottke, asked himself why he didn't just write his thoughts down in private. "Somehow, that seems strange to me though," he wrote. "The Web is the place for you to express your thoughts and feelings and such. To put those things elsewhere seems absurd."

Every day, more people agreed with him. The call of self-expression turned the village of the internet into a city, which expanded at time-lapse speed, social connections bristling like neurons in every direction. At ten, I was clicking around a web ring to check out other Angelfire sites full of animal GIFs and Smash Mouth trivia. At twelve, I was writing five hundred words a day on a public LiveJournal. At fifteen, I was uploading photos of myself in a miniskirt on Myspace. By twenty-five, my job was to write things that would attract, ideally, a hundred thousand strangers per post. Now I'm thirty, and most of my life is inextricable from the internet, and its mazes of incessant forced connection—this feverish, electric, unlivable hell.

As with the transition between Web 1.0 and Web 2.0, the curdling of the social internet happened slowly and then all at once. The tipping point, I'd guess, was around 2012. People were losing excitement about the internet, starting to articulate a set of new truisms. Facebook had become tedious, trivial, exhausting. Instagram seemed better, but would soon reveal its underlying function as a three-ring circus of happiness and popularity and success. Twitter, for all its discursive promise, was where everyone tweeted complaints at airlines and bitched about articles that had been commissioned to make people bitch. The dream of a better, truer self on the internet was slipping away. Where we had once been free to be ourselves online, we were now *chained* to ourselves online, and this made us self-conscious. Platforms that promised connection began inducing mass alienation. The freedom promised by the internet started to seem like something whose greatest potential lay in the realm of misuse.

Even as we became increasingly sad and ugly on the internet, the mirage of the better online self continued to glimmer. As a medium, the internet is defined by a built-in performance incentive. In real life, you can walk around living life and be visible to other people. But you can't just walk around and be visible on the internet—for anyone to see you, you have to *act*. You have to communicate in order to maintain an internet presence. And, because the internet's central platforms are built around personal profiles, it can seem—first at a mechanical level, and later on as an encoded instinct—like the main purpose of this communication is to make yourself look good. Online reward mechanisms beg to substitute for offline ones, and then overtake them. This is why everyone tries to look so hot and well-traveled on Instagram; this is why everyone seems so smug and triumphant on Facebook; this is why, on Twitter, making a righteous political statement has come to seem, for many people, like a political good in itself.

Reading Questions

1. In the essay, Tolentino describes how she first started using the Internet. What is one of the websites that she describes frequently using when she was younger, and how does she describe it as being different from today's social media sites?

2. Choose one of the examples that Tolentino gives of a negative use of social media. Why does she characterize it as negative?

Rhetoric Questions

3. Tolentino explains Goffman's research and how people constantly engage in "performances" to create identities. How does this idea align with the rhetorical concept of audience?

4. In the first paragraph of the essay, Tolentino describes writing online in a textbox "on a hideous violet background." How do the visual design choices made online contribute to the rhetorical effectiveness of a website? How is that similar to or different from writing in print?

Response Questions

5. Tolentino describes an old website that she created that is still accessible on the Internet, even though the information on the website isn't an accurate description of who she is now. Do you ever think about how things you post online might be interpreted in the future? If so, how and why? If not, why not?

6. Tolentino provides many examples of the different ways that people use the Internet to create and project their identities. What is one use of the Internet that she describes that you could relate to? What was your experience?

If Someone Wants to Be Called "They" and Not "He" or "She," Why Say No?

ROBIN DEMBROFF AND DANIEL WODAK

Robin Dembroff is an assistant professor of philosophy at Yale University, and Daniel Wodak is an assistant professor of philosophy at the University of Pennsylvania. This article appeared in the *Guardian*, a British daily newspaper available online that also covers international news and publishes editions for different countries. Dembroff and Wodak both study issues of gender from the perspective of philosophy and have published widely.

Most people prefer to be called "he" or "she." But others, like Kelsey, do not: they want to be referred to by gender-neutral pronouns like "they." Should you defer to Kelsey's preferences? Many people think no. Some, like University of Toronto professor Jordan Peterson, have recently garnered celebrity status by taking a stand against gender-neutral pronouns: "I don't recognize another person's right to determine what pronouns I use to address them," Peterson has said. His view is common among social conservatives.

We think people should not use gender-specific pronouns for genderqueer people—people that do not identify as men or as women. We can start here: why should we use some words, rather than others, to refer to people?

A common answer among the left is because we should respect people's preferences. If you're talking about Kelsey, you should use whatever pronouns Kelsey prefers, and Kelsey prefers "they."

Many on the right believe this is dogmatic. After all, many people prefer not to use "they" for Kelsey. Whose preferences matter more? From conservatives' perspective, liberals just assume that Kelsey's preferences matter more than theirs, and do so in the service of a political agenda.

Is that assumption misguided? Consider an anal- 5 ogy. As a Muslim civil rights leader, Muhammad Ali rejected the name he was given at birth (Cassius Clay) because it represented a Christian identity that he rejected. He instead chose the name Ali.

But others preferred to use Clay. Whose preferences matter more? We think the answer is clear. Ali's identity is what's at issue, so his preferences matter more.

But maybe you think there is more to say about why conservatives' preferences matter. Many on the far right rally around the mantra "There are only two genders!" They apparently believe that calling Kelsey "they" would affirm that Kelsey is not a man or a woman—an idea they flatly reject. Peterson makes this point in exaggerated fashion, refusing to be an "ideological puppet," or a "mouthpiece of some murderous ideology."

Here the debate typically turns to whether it is right that there are only two genders. But even if we granted this point, the argument fails. Perhaps people should not be "bullied" into affirming identities that they reject. But this does not give anyone the right to deny those identities.

This point is important because of something the usual rhetoric around pronouns obscures: gender-neutral pronouns are gender-neutral. "They" does not communicate that Kelsey is genderqueer in the way that "he" would communicate that Kelsey is a man or "she" would communicate that Kelsey is a woman. "They" refrains from ascribing a particular gender to Kelsey. This is why "they" is often used in colloquial English as a singular gender-neutral pronoun for people who probably aren't genderqueer. ("Who is at the door?" "Dunno—go see what they want.") "They" is often used this way, and has been used this way since the Shakespearean era. It's nothing new. (Note that even Peterson uses singular "they" in an earlier quote.)

Conservatives think they should not be forced to affirm that Kelsey is non-binary. But "they" does not affirm that Kelsey is any particular gender; it just avoids saying anything about Kelsey's gender. As long as Kelsey should not be ascribed a gender they reject,

we should not use "he" or "she" for Kelsey. We can all respect Kelsey without anyone being "bullied" into being a mouthpiece for any ideology.

To our mind, everything else in this debate is a distraction. The far right defends their devotion to "he" and "she" by appealing to freedom of speech. But freedom of speech at most gives us "a right to do wrong." Arguably, freedom of speech may give you a legal right to use racial slurs. But it doesn't make it right to use racial slurs. Exercising a right to do wrong is still a way of doing something wrong. The same goes for using "he" or "she" for those who prefer otherwise: even if freedom of speech gives you a legal right to do so, it is still wrong.

Appeals to grammaticality are similar. Many opposed to gender-neutral pronouns claim that singular use of "they" is "non-standard" English; the *National Review* decries "stupid people" engaged in an "asinine effort" to "de-pluralize 'they.'" The sentence "They are my good friend" may strike you as ungrammatical. But notice that we say things like "You are my good friend" with ease. Using "they" as a singular or plural third-person pronoun is no different from how we already use "you" as a singular or plural second-person pronoun.

More importantly, just as we recognize the distinction between morality and law, we should recognize a distinction between morality and grammar. Doing what is morally right sometimes requires challenging legal rules. Why should grammatical rules be different?

We should focus on what matters: whether and why we should (not) use particular pronouns. It is wrong to use pronouns that deny someone's identity. This is enough to see why we should use gender-neutral pronouns for non-binary people. In fact, once we see the virtues of using a gender-neutral pronoun like "they" for some people, maybe we should just use "they" for everyone.

Reading Questions

1. What historical example do Dembroff and Wodak give as an analogy to using someone's preferred gender pronouns?

2. According to Dembroff and Wodak, what makes *they* a gender-neutral pronoun?

Rhetoric Questions

3. The *Guardian* is generally regarded as a fairly liberal-leaning publication. What audience do you think Dembroff and Wodak are trying to reach in this essay, given the publication venue and how they developed their argument? Point to two or three examples from the essay that support your conclusion.

4. Dembroff and Wodak use several different rhetorical appeals (ethos, logos, pathos) in their essay. Choose one example of an appeal and describe why it is an example of ethos, logos, or pathos.

Response Questions

5. Can you recall a time that someone assumed something about your identity that was incorrect? What was the circumstance, and how did you respond?

6. In the last sentence of the essay, Dembroff and Wodak present the possibility that perhaps *they* should be used for everyone. Why do you think they end the essay with this suggestion?

Academic Case Study: The Scholarship of Writing

ACADEMIC CASE STUDY • THE SCHOLARSHIP OF WRITING   HUMANITIES

Teaching Writing in the Disciplines: Student Perspectives on Learning Genre

MARY GOLDSCHMIDT

Mary Goldschmidt works in the Center for Teaching and Learning Excellence at the University of Scranton. Prior to that, she directed the writing program at the College of New Jersey, where she introduced a focus on writing in the disciplines. The following article first appeared in the journal *Teaching and Learning Inquiry* and reports on the results of a study Goldschmidt conducted where she learned from students how they developed expertise in the kinds of writing they needed to master in their field of study.

ABSTRACT

Writing in the Disciplines curricula can both challenge and reinforce assumptions that writing is a general skill that students will already have learned prior to doing the specialized writing in their chosen field of study. Rhetorical genre studies, however, tends to emphasize the situated nature of writing expertise, and thus supports the exploration of more sustained and varied forms of writing instruction in higher education. This article reports on a qualitative study that gave priority to a rich source of pedagogical insight: student writers themselves. In-depth interviews and surveys were used to examine the pedagogical practices and curricular experiences identified by students as being most helpful in developing undergraduate expertise in their discipline's research genre. These student-centered descriptions of successful genre learning point the way toward curricular and instructional models that emphasize the intellectual, affective, and relational nature of writing.

Keywords: genre, writing in the disciplines, academic literacy, psychology, computer science

INTRODUCTION

Although it is a commonplace in writing research that written communication is a social competency as much as it is a cognitive skill, many faculty members continue to ask why their students haven't "learned to write" prior to entering their classes. They see neither their courses nor disciplines as places where students might do that learning. As the blame is passed down the line, underlying assumptions about language and writing remain unnoticed and uninterrogated: that academic writing is always situated, and that it is not merely a tool but a complex social action central to how a disciplinary community produces knowledge (Kaufer and Young, 1993; Russell, 2002; Bazerman et al., 2005; Carter, 2007; Elton, 2010). To the extent that these concepts don't inform the curricular and pedagogical decisions in higher education, our students don't experience "writing" as a form of engaged participation.[1]

Yet, as scholarship in rhetorical genre studies has made clear (Miller, 1984; Cooper, 1989; Hunt, 1994; Russell, 1995; Prior, 1998; Artemeva, 2008; Bazerman, 2009b; Bawarshi and Reiff, 2010), writing is best learned when there is intention:

> what is necessary is an occasion and a need to mean: some kind of rhetorical exigency which will elicit performance. Current theoretical reconceptualizations of genre as [a] recurring response to a rhetorical context highlight precisely these dimensions of social motive, rhetorical responsiveness and context. (Freedman, 1994, p. 201)

Genre mastery, therefore, can be seen not only as a primary measure of student writing proficiency—"the writer loses control of the writing when he or she does not understand the genre" (Bazerman, 2009a, p. 504)—but also as an important pedagogical vehicle. As Beaufort and Williams have argued, "genre theory forces us to ask ourselves if we aren't creating artificial barriers in our minds when we say, in subject areas outside writing and rhetoric, that we don't or can't teach writing" (2005, p. 63). Our students' writing reflects the degree to which they are capable of "doing the analytical work of the discipline," and thus teaching a discipline's genre is teaching the discipline (p. 64). Indeed, most Writing in the Disciplines (WID) programs foreground genre in ways that first-year writing curricula cannot.[2]

Beginning in 2005, I had the opportunity to help implement a WID curriculum, providing support for departments as they identified and redesigned their designated writing intensive (WI) courses. Two majors in particular, psychology and computer science, developed second-year (sophomore) courses that focused on early exposure to the scientific research article as intentional preparation for fourth-year (senior) research writing in the capstone course. These departments provided an opportunity to examine how students move from seeing genre merely as a template to seeing it as a complex rhetorical construct for participating in their field.

I conducted in-depth, text-based, qualitative interviews with two groups of students: seniors whose records indicate that they had mastered their discipline's primary research genre, and sophomores who were in the early stages of learning those genres. Grounded theory, a qualitative methodology in which the coding is derived inductively from the data through a constant comparative data collection and analysis process, was used to better understand students' tacit knowledge of their own literate activity (Bryant and Charmaz 2010). The interviews were supplemented by surveys with sophomore and senior cohorts in each major. My study extends the work of Thaiss and Zawacki's influential *Engaged Writers and Dynamic Disciplines: Research on the Academic Writing Life* (2006) which set out to clarify the elusive nature of "academic writing" across the range of disciplines in the academy by asking those who are best informed and most directly involved: their own colleagues and students. As a systematic analysis of students' experience learning genre, my study is also a form of inquiry within the Scholarship of Teaching and Learning that seeks to examine the constituent features of an experience, or what Hutchings calls a "What is" type of question, offering a thick description of what learning genre looks like (Hutchings, 2000, p. 4).

In selecting participants, I used the framework provided by Thaiss and Zawacki's three stages of undergraduate disciplinary writing development.

Table 1

Sequenced Writing Intensive Courses in Psychology and Computer Science

Required Writing Intensive Courses	Psychology	Computer Science
First-year seminar	Any discipline	Any discipline
Pre-requisites	Methods and Tools Design and Statistical Analysis	Computational Problem-Solving Data Structures and Algorithms
Mid-level WI course in the major	Research Seminar	Programming in the Large
Senior-level WI capstone course in the major	Internship, Special Topics, or Independent Research/Thesis	Internships or Mentored Research

In this model, stage one writers assume there is a universal set of rules for college-level writing, and they try to understand these expectations based on a limited number of courses. Stage two writers, having experienced a far more diverse set of courses, adopt a "radically relativistic view" (p. 139) in which differing expectations are seen merely as the idiosyncrasies of faculty members and not as differences that align with disciplinary standards. Stage three writers, however, have moved toward "building a complex but organic sense of the structure of the discipline," are able to perceive "coherence-within-diversity," and, most importantly, achieve a sense of their own "place within the disciplinary enterprise" (p. 139).

I purposely chose to work with seniors who had, in fact, arrived at stage three, and I intentionally selected departments whose faculty members view their courses as places of "learning to write."[3] Specifically, I wanted to expand the portion of Thaiss and Zawacki's study that looked at what students "say about how they learn to write in their disciplines" (p. 96). While Thaiss and Zawacki used student surveys, focus groups, and proficiency exams, a more situated study of these writers using in-depth interviews has much to teach us about how we can best facilitate students' writing expertise. In what follows I review my study's institutional context and methodology, describe my findings, and offer concluding reflections for pedagogical practice.

INSTITUTIONAL CONTEXT AND METHODOLOGY

This study was conducted at a mid-sized, four-year state college in the mid-Atlantic region of the United States, where majors are offered in one of seven different liberal arts or professional schools. Throughout the 2005 to 2008 academic years, the college implemented a WID curriculum, wherein two already-required courses in the major were redesigned to meet writing intensive guidelines. Thus throughout their college years, students take three WI courses: a first-year seminar in any discipline, a mid-level WI course in the sophomore or junior year, and a WI capstone course in the senior year. Table 1 above outlines the progression of courses taken by students majoring in psychology and computer science.

The mid-level WI course for psychology is a research seminar involving a full empirical study conducted by students in small groups; they spend the entire semester writing all four sections (Introduction, Methods, Results, and Discussion) using APA format. Data is derived from an internal collection of empirical research studies conducted at the college by psychology faculty and undergraduate students. In the comparable mid-level WI course for computer science majors (on software engineering), students write papers in which they justify software application recommendations; here, the faculty member provides a template which uses many of the conventions of ACM papers (Association for Computing Machinery), even though students are not conducting research.

Over the course of the 2012 spring semester, I conducted ten in-depth, text-based interviews with students enrolled in the mid-level and senior-level writing intensive courses in each of the two participating majors.[4] Participants included three psychology seniors and three computer science seniors, as well as three psychology sophomores and one computer science sophomore. GPAs ranged from 3.324 to 3.913. All had taken a WI first year seminar on topics as diverse as the Beatles, Irish Cinema, and the Mind-Body Connection.

Among seniors, I intentionally limited requests to those doing independent research to ensure that they would be writing the discipline's major genre. All but one intended to go on to graduate school. The senior participants, in other words, have made it to Thaiss and Zawacki's stage three, possessing a "nuanced idea of the discipline" (2006, p. 110). They are, therefore, "excellent informants" (Morse, 2007, p. 231) for examining students' perceptions of the most helpful experiences in developing disciplinary writing expertise.

In January of that same semester, I also administered a survey to the sophomore and senior cohorts in each major. The response rate in computer science was 63% among seniors and 38% among sophomores, and in psychology it was 40% among seniors and 56% among sophomores.

Repositioned grounded theory (RGT) was used for its privileging of the language of participants, its acknowledgment of disciplinary assumptions ("sensitizing concepts"), and its iterative process of coding and analysis to derive interpretive categories (Charmaz 2002, 2006; Bryant and Charmaz 2010). The central disciplinary sensitizing concept informing my analysis is that disciplines are not "separate divisions of declarative knowledge," but rather, "ways of doing and thus ways of knowing and writing, modes of inquiry rather than static territories of knowledge" (Carter, 2007, p. 410). I was interested in discovering the activities that students perceive to have been most helpful in learning the scientific research article genre—a genre

that is radically different from humanities-based writing preparation dominant in both high school and general education curricula.

Questions included open-ended inquiries about their development as writers over the course of their college career, perceived changes in their writing over time, awareness of different kinds of writing expected in different college courses, the most important lessons learned about how to write for courses in the major, experiences that have affected their development as a writer in the major, the most challenging aspect of writing in the major, and advice they would give to a first year student. In addition, text-based questions were used to have students re-examine their papers from mid-and senior-level WI courses. Students were asked to point to places where they felt most/least competent and confident about their writing ability, to passages which they learned to do in either the prerequisite or the mid-level WI course, to passages where they encountered a new challenge, and to passages which reflect their growth as a writer.

Results suggest that students gain the greatest rhetorical sophistication through a variety of forms of dialogue with more experienced members of their discourse community, through using genre templates early on in their curricular experience—especially when courses are intentionally sequenced—and through purposeful forms of reading and emulating scholarship in the field.

TALKING GENRE: EXTENDING STUDENTS' AUDIENCE AWARENESS TO THE DISCIPLINARY COMMUNITY

The first significant category that emerged from the 15 action codes was dialogue. The various kinds of "talk" that participants described all involve an informed professional who has discipline-specific expectations for successful writing. These scenarios included everything from thesis committee meetings in which faculty advisors provide oral feedback on drafts, to informal talk that, over time, has come to function as a form of mentoring. The passages underscore Prior's argument that textual production includes "talking and listening, reading and writing, thinking and feeling, observing and acting" (1998, p. 137). These heterogeneous actions stress the holistic nature of "enculturation," with the social action achieved through the dialogues reflecting both an intellectual and affective component to genre learning.

Cecelia, a psychology senior, emphasized how in her meetings with her thesis advisor the dynamics involved a back-and-forth between equals, not a one-directional critique more reminiscent of a traditional teacher-student relationship. For example, when her advisor would point to something that she felt wasn't clear, she would prompt Cecelia to explain her rationale:

> If I said something like—I remember this too—I would say a word that like I thought had a lot of meaning but really didn't. So like, I don't know like, "Emotion regulation is suppressing or expressing emotion" and she would be like well "No it's not" and "if you think it is, why is it?"[5]

This faculty member invites Cecelia to interact in a way that reflects respect for her knowledge, a process only feasible between co-members in the discipline. This relationship is illustrated again when Cecelia described a thesis committee meeting as one of the most important moments that influenced her development as a writer: "All of them were like 'Wow, this is a really good paper. It's a really interesting study, like I want to know what happens.' And that kind of validates that like oh, I'm doing something right." Her committee's validation of her as someone whose work they want to read has significant instructional ramifications.

Similar instances of this form of "talk" include Danny's discussion of what he called a breakthrough moment as a psychology writer. He referred not to specific papers or achievements, but to how faculty members actually speak to him. His desire for future dialogue is one of the primary motivations for his writing:

> Well, I think that, and this is going to sound really nerdy, but I think that I, cause like I'm applying to graduate school, I just have such a respect for faculty . . . I really want to, in the way that I write and the way that I speak, I want to be respected by them. So when I talk to these people, I want to speak in the most sophisticated

way because that's how they speak to me. And, you know I want them to . . . I want to one day be, I don't know, their peers, does that make sense? [I suggested the term "colleague."] Yeah, their colleagues. So then I think that also sort of drives me to try to improve.

The desire to be treated as a colleague becomes a major motivation for Danny to be more effective in his writing.

In a similar way, senior psychology major Michelle revealed how talk with faculty members has shaped her rhetorical development:

> I knew that one of my audience members was a social psychology professor, so when I was writing I always had him in the back of my head, making sure that this was all accurate information, making sure he wouldn't stop and say, "no that's not accurate."

In this case, anticipating the conversation with her committee functioned to expand her knowledge of differences among sub-fields within the discipline.

Michelle also cited having a real audience beyond her professors as a key factor in her increasing effectiveness as a writer: "I'm going to be presenting this paper and hopefully one day get it published. So those people, if they don't know what I'm saying they're going to question it and that'll just kind of, um, limit the validity of it, especially in terms of how other people view it." Seeing her writing manifested in a social context (a conference) allows her to understand its validity as a function of her audience's understanding of her ideas, a strong motivating factor for her writing.

Michelle and her peers are describing a new motivation, a new *socially* constituted exigence for their writing. While in their general education classes they were primarily concerned with getting good grades or fulfilling requirements, they now consistently describe their concern with trying to meet the expectations of the discourse community. This change can be seen in how Justin, a senior computer science major, compared his writing for general education courses to his current research. He knows that one of his ongoing challenges as a writer is trying to cover too much material, and his descriptions of earlier writing often sound like what Bean has called the "all about" or "data-dump" paper—characteristic of many novice college writers who are "overwhelmed with information and uncertain what to do with it" (1995, p. 23). In a course on the Vietnam War and Gender, for example, Justin explained that there was so much material to write about that he felt he'd be "penalized" if he "didn't include everything." The focus on a penalty indicates a primary concern with a grade.

His description of his senior-level disciplinary writing, however, has shifted to a more specific concern about meeting the expectations of readers in the computer science field. He still has to make decisions about what to include, but it is now framed in terms of what will gain him the acceptance and respect of community members. Here, for example, he talks about his realization of a very human, embodied audience for whom he needs to write his methodology section:

> If I was trying to get into, say, just a minor conference or something, and I want to present this, and I wanna say here, "you know this is the problem and we wanted to make this scalable database system that people can use," I don't want to stand up there and talk about "then I did this, and then I used this tool."

If he were to do that, he feels he would likely get the following reaction: "'Yeah we know that's how you do that, you're wasting our time.'" Aware of his readers' knowledge base, he knows that he cannot "re-explain" to them what they already know. Through these imagined harsh critics, Justin reminds himself that he cannot assume a general, non-disciplinary audience.

Justin's genre learning is particularly instructive because he double majored in economics but has gained a level of mastery only in computer science writing. He explained how much of his growth has come from the way the computer science department has "cared for me, nurtured me, more than the other." In response to what advice he would give a first year student, he said "number one" was getting involved with faculty since they provide the guidance and support without which it is very difficult to succeed. Indeed, as Justin pointed out, although he is "more prone to be involved with a project in computer science" than in economics due to his primary career interest in that field, that difference in engagement

with each department perpetuates the problem, "because I don't know how I would go about being involved with a project in economics, because it just seems like all theory to me." This lack of understanding, fueled in part by a lack of relationships, has had profound effects on Justin's genre learning. He acknowledged that he has a "good grasp on the computer science way of doing things," but when it comes to his economics thesis, he has "no idea what to do." In short, Justin doesn't know what "social action" would look like in economics; he doesn't know what its genres *do*.

"LESS SUPERVISION AND MORE OWNERSHIP": MOVING FROM TEMPLATE TO DISCIPLINARITY

Another experience identified by participants as supportive of their genre learning was using the template provided by the faculty member from the mid-level writing intensive course. Most sophomores were still at a stage where "filling in the blanks" was essential to being able to complete their papers. Although the technical language required in the sciences—so different from what's acceptable in the humanities—was also mentioned as a stumbling block, it was the structure of the genre itself that seemed quite alien, as psychology senior Michelle explained:

> the first time I encountered writing like this was in [the Methods and Tools course], where even then I was like "what's a methods section, why would you put that into a formal paper?" It seems more of something that would be an appendix, or just like something separate, because it breaks the flow of the paper, cause, I thought, because it was another title, why would you, you know? That was the first time I ever encountered having to write like that, and at first it was very bizarre. Now when I look at every other class, I think "why aren't they like psych papers, it would make so much more sense."

By her final year, Michelle has internalized the scientific research article to such an extent that it now seems the norm to her. But her initial sense of confusion is not atypical. It harkens back to a question posed twenty years ago by Dias when he asked how his students can "close the gap between their writing and writing as it is modeled in the texts they continually meet in the disciplinary journals they read?" (1994, p. 194). Both this section and the next address how the students in my study answer that question.

The sophomore computer science majors who completed the survey all mentioned the "professional article style" of papers in their major as something significantly "different" from any writing they do elsewhere in college. As one student put it:

> One of the more difficult aspects is the layout of computer science papers. Unlike other papers, computer science papers follow an "outline." Each section is numbered (e.g. Section 1: Introduction, Section 1.1: More Information, etc.). This somewhat alien organization can be intimidating at first.

The computer science sophomore participant, Rick, indicated a comparable concern with structure when he identified his biggest challenge as simply understanding the difference between the abstract and the introduction. Senior computer science major, John, also mentioned that in the mid-level WI course "the whole format of [the paper] was new . . . the abstract, introduction, like having all those." Following a model, however, proved crucial: "She gave us a document that had kind of what you should have in each section, which helped a lot, because there's a standard, and you kind of have to keep to the standard otherwise it's not good. So that definitely helped."

The following description of writing her first empirical research paper from psychology sophomore Nicole similarly reflects how important consulting a template is for genre learning (in the psychology curriculum, students receive an outline of the research article in the prerequisite methods course, usually taken a semester prior to the mid-level writing intensive course):

> I think kind of the whole structure is what I learned from [the previous course]. And when I was writing it and . . . hitting that road block . . . is when I took out, um, one of the packets that he gave us, and looked at how he told us how to lay this out. So it was kind of just like: put an idea here and then give me some articles

that support it. And put your next idea here and give me some articles that support it. And then after all that tell me how that leads up to what you're going to do.

Nicole is still following directions, in part because her professor realizes that at this stage, only rudimentary attention can be given to the complex rhetorical moves of the introduction, but she is gaining an introductory sense of the *purpose* of the structure.

Melissa, a psychology sophomore who had completed the mid-level writing intensive course by the time the interview was conducted, also referred to the helpfulness of the template from the prerequisite course, despite realizing its limitations:

> [The Methods and Tools course] was more about the format: what goes into what section. We did that one paper at the end but it wasn't very in-depth, it was more kind of like surface level, following a format. But I feel that looking back now, it was, we didn't, I didn't really understand a lot of it. We kind of, I mean we followed by example, but I feel like more of the writing, understanding and being able to replicate was in [the WI course].

Melissa's answer draws a distinction between surface copying or imitating and *writing*, an action that is far more complex because it involves a depth of understanding of the genre's disciplinarity.[6]

The explicit instructional component within the sequence of courses in this department's curriculum indicates a successful attempt by the faculty to articulate tacit genre knowledge in a way that is accessible to undergraduates early in the major. Nowhere is this more visible than in the survey responses to the prompt, "List some characteristics of a good paper written for a psychology course." Half of the sophomores identified adhering to APA guidelines as "the most difficult aspect of writing for your psychology courses," yet their ability to articulate the genre's structure and other requirements is fairly comprehensive. The following two answers are representative of many of the 36 responses:

> A good paper has a short abstract that still summarizes the paper clearly with all of its main points, an introduction that gives a great background to your topic, a methods section that describes exactly what you did

and how you did it, a results section that delivers your results, and a discussion section that describes what the results mean.

A good paper written in psychology has a clearly funneled introduction. The introduction and literature review are divided by topic, not by prior studies. The methods and research sections are written clearly, concisely, and in proper APA format. The discussion session is a backwards funnel, is not redundant, and offers insight to statistical results. A psychology paper should be informative, but easy to understand as well.

On the one hand, these descriptions would likely please any faculty member teaching the mid-level WI course. On the other hand, the ability to describe does not necessarily translate into performance. Perhaps more importantly, these and other responses are more like the checklists one might see on an assignment sheet. They don't necessarily reflect an understanding of the disciplinarity of the genre: its rhetorical complexity, its audience, or its purpose—beyond that of earning a grade.

In contrast, nearly half of the senior respondents say that a good paper must be well-informed and reflect the author's knowledge of the material, that it must "successfully utiliz[e] the research of others to support your own investigation," and that it should present the "theoretical background and basis for topic/study." These concerns are not focused on structure, but rather, on function in relation to an audience—in other words, with the socio-rhetorical actions that genres perform.

Senior interview participants were likewise able to talk with ease about their understanding that genre is not a format "that must be slavishly followed," but a set of "rhetorical choices" that must be carefully negotiated throughout the text (Bazerman, 2009a, p. 504). Danny, for example, noted that although the other sections of the research article follow "strict guidelines," the introduction "has the most leeway in how you construct it" because "the challenging thing is to talk about why your research will be different and why it will be important." To do this, he explained that

you have to find things that, things in existing research that are not talked about enough, not talked about at all, that are confusing or contradictory. It translates into the writing because then how do you piece that together

coherently, so that your audience understands what you're talking about, and they can follow your logic in your mind, how you connected everything.

Danny is concerned with the logic that his introduction has to perform: it must contextualize and justify the questions at the heart of his study, and it must do so in a way that leads the reader to see the gap, absence, or contradiction being addressed. To use the terminology developed by Swales in his linguistic analysis of the scientific research article, Danny sees that his text must establish a territory, establish a niche, and then occupy that niche (1990, p. 141).

Several seniors highlighted the difference between knowing the structure of the genre and actually "doing" it, but the most striking account comes from Cecelia. Her senior thesis deals with three variables, two of which are well-known and accepted concepts. Her contribution is positing the third concept's relationship with the other two, a task made harder because she can find only one paper on the concept, and it's from a different subfield in psychology: "So I had to kinda turn something that was largely psycho-linguistic and make it into like a clinical construct." Highly aware of her role in relation to other discourse community members, Cecelia admitted that developing a rationale for a meditational hypothesis was "close to impossible" because "not only was it a mediational hypothesis but it was something with mitigation which just doesn't exist in the literature. All this makes sense in my head but if no one can see that it's regulation then there's really no point to it." Cecelia's challenge as described here is not merely the difficulty of working with multiple causal variables. Rhetorically, she is aware that she must set up her hypotheses using the terms that the discourse community will recognize. As a student so highly sensitive to the rhetorical demands of the introduction, Cecelia illustrates how her genre performance has moved well beyond following a template.

READING AND EMULATING

During her interview, sophomore psychology major Nicole described several strategies she used to address the challenges she was facing in her research seminar paper (the mid-level WI course). To help her more effectively transition "between the different articles in a way that made it all flow and lead up to my research," she said that she frequently went back to her notes and handouts from the previous class. Like others, she relied on the template for guidance. But in addition, Nicole mentioned another activity that was cited universally by the seniors as one of the most important ways they learned to write: "just all the reading that I've had to do from my different psych classes, like article reading, without even really realizing it kind of showed me what that writing was supposed to do." She doesn't say that reading the scholarship showed her what the writing was supposed to look like, but instead, *what it was supposed to do*.

All six seniors identify reading as either the top piece of advice they would give to a first year student ("Be a good reader, number one. Read everything, especially scientific articles. If you can't understand one, you can't really be expected to write your own"), or as the thing that contributed the most to their own development as a writer ("The most influential way that I learned how to write is reading other psych articles and following by example"). Participants spoke about the importance of reading most often in the context of learning how to emulate, a process involving an awareness of how articles are structured and how authors use the structure effectively to achieve their desired ends — a process similar to what Greene calls "mining the text" or reading with a sense of authorship (1992, pp. 156–61).

Computer science senior, John, for example, noted that the abstract in his current paper is "more thoughtful" than the abstract in one of his papers from the mid-level course thanks to the intentional two-step method he used: "I looked at people's abstracts in the ACM library" and then compared them to what he'd done in his own previous papers. John's is an active process that goes beyond rote imitation. In fact, John referred to active reading as a "turning point" in his sense of himself as a writer. The first time he wrote a full research article was the fall prior to the interview, in a Mentored Research course. It was going to be

submitted for a conference, and therefore would be peer reviewed. That semester, he explained,

> I had to do mostly just reading to prepare for that. So by the time I had read 20–30 papers, I had gotten an idea of like what has been published and what it takes to be published. I was a lot more critical of myself then than I would have been if I didn't read all those papers because I didn't know what it took to be published. That was probably the turning point.

Reading enabled an active, self-evaluative process of applying the standards and norms of the field to his own writing.

John also remarked that he wished he'd been exposed to published scholarship earlier than he was: "And I wish we did have more reading before that. I think it would have helped us understand what we have to emulate." He is not alone. Danny said that although "it's unpopular" to assign 20-page research articles to "college freshmen," even just the exposure helps: "It gets you accustomed to the style, it gets you accustomed to how people speak, how they write." His first "foray" into reading published scholarship enabled him to "see how things were written" so that he "could emulate that or begin to incorporate that into mine." Finally, Justin also expresses the need for earlier exposure to scholarship, even calling this a "short-coming of the department" that they "haven't really been pushing students to analyze" academic papers. He sees now that his growth "has come through emulating, just emulating what I see."

This emphasis on reading was echoed in the survey 35 in ways that provide instructive insights about the sequence of courses in this WID curriculum. Students were asked, "What experiences in your undergraduate career have best prepared you for the writing you've done so far as a psychology/computer science major? (Check all that apply)." Choices included the first year seminar, a first year composition class, the mid-level WI class, other courses in the major, general education classes, a specific paper you wrote, working with a particular professor, a faculty member's feedback on papers, the experience of reading published scholarship, and "Other." Students were then asked to rank their selections.

Among computer science sophomores, 86% of respondents selected the mid-level WI course, with 50% of those indicating this as their top choice. The remaining top rankings were split (17% each) among reading published scholarship, working with a particular professor, and other (high school writing). Among seniors, the mid-level WI course and reading published scholarship were the top selections (60% each); of these, 44% of respondents ranked the mid-level WI course as their top choice, and 22% ranked reading published scholarship at the top. That both sophomores and seniors valued the mid-level WI class so highly might well be a function of the fact that there are very few writing assignments in other courses in the curriculum (aside from writing code and commentary on the code).

Among psychology majors, the trends are similar, with two important differences. First, the sophomores identified the prerequisite courses (69%) more frequently than the mid-level WI course (56%) as that which best prepared them for their writing in the major. Second, the prerequisite course in which students first received the template for the scientific research article was identified as the first choice by 28% of respondents, and the mid-level WI course was ranked as the top choice among 26%. The selections by senior psychology majors echo those made by the computer science students, with 81% of respondents selecting the mid-level WI course and reading published scholarship. Of these, 52% ranked the mid-level WI course first, and 15% ranked reading published scholarship as first.

The survey results in conjunction with the interviews suggest that the specific curriculum design for these two departments in this WID program worked in tandem with pedagogical practices (especially in psychology) that emphasized reading scholarly articles.

CONCLUSION

Concern with student writing in higher education is obviously not limited to the United States. Lillis and Turner articulated the growing sense of the "problem" of student writing in higher education in the UK fifteen years ago (2001). Their specific focus was on the difficulties created when students are "welcomed into the academy by the rhetoric of widening participation, but at the same time denied an adequate participation by taken-for-granted assumptions about academic conventions" (p. 66). Once again, assumptions about language are at the center: when students can replicate the "institutionally embedded socio-rhetorical norms of scientific rationality, language remains invisible" (p. 65). Lillis and Turner's call for putting language (and not student "deficits") at the center of pedagogical reforms (see also Haggis, 2006), is another reason for paying close attention to how students experience their own academic literacy development.

The in-depth interviews in my study indicated that what was most valued by students is having "strong and growing access to disciplinary discourses, practices, and relationships" (Prior, 1998, p. 133). Their dialogue with faculty members helped foster relationships that provided a strong sense of disciplinary understanding and identity. These relationships both stemmed from and resulted in additional faculty-student projects, including summer research grants, conference proposals and presentations, and other paraprofessional experiences such as online technology forums and institutional research pools. Participants' disciplinary genre learning and their emerging sense of membership within the discipline echo the findings of other WID studies as summarized by Russell, particularly Jolliffe and Brier's study of political science and nursing students, where "acquisition, use, and awareness" of the discipline's knowledge was directly related to the extent of students' self-image as "soon-to-be-professionals" and their active involvement in professional work (2001, p. 10).

More direct instructional practices were also essential in supporting their disciplinary writing. The use of templates, while not sufficient in and of itself, provided a foundation for later "deep participation" so necessary for disciplinary enculturation (Prior, 1998, p. 103). By the time they were seniors, students in both majors found "texts reasonably transparent and appropriable" (Prior, 1998, p. 133). The reading and emulating promoted by the faculty members in their departments is an example of "modeling," a pedagogical practice identified by multiple other studies as essential for genre learning in WID (Russell, 2001, p. 17).

The reading activities noted by these participants are similar to practices developed in a comprehensive pedagogical study in chemistry, where a "read-analyze-write approach to genre-based instruction" was used with undergraduates at Northern Arizona University (Stoller and Robinson, 2012, p. 46). Their method of explicit identification of the rhetorical moves used in chemistry articles has since been developed into a textbook and companion website (Stoller and Robinson, 2012).

My study, although limited in scope, nevertheless offers support for other calls that stress the importance of "teaching writing" in the disciplines. As Carter has argued, such movements do not ask faculty in the disciplines to become "writing teachers," but rather, to "see that their responsibility for teaching the ways of knowing and doing in their disciplines also extends to writing, which is not separate from but essential to their disciplines" (2007, p. 408). Such commitments can work in concert with WAC and newer composition initiatives such as "Writing about Writing" (Downs and Wardle 2007; Wardle 2009) to create curricula where writing can be experienced as a purposeful activity "within a rich, multi-dimensional communicative environment" (Bazerman and Prior, 2005, p. 164).

Equally important is the question not examined in my study: what does it look like when students do not learn genre, or do not make it to Thaiss and Zawacki's stage three of undergraduate disciplinary writing development? What is their learning experience of genre like when they remain mired in navigating what they see only as the expectations of individual faculty members? Future studies in this area, again from the student perspective, would shed important light on why some things are hard for students to learn, and thereby enhance our understanding not only of the learning process more broadly, but also of methodologies for the Scholarship of Teaching and Learning.

NOTES

1. My research was made possible in part by the 2011–2013 Elon University Research Seminar on Critical Transitions: Writing and the Question of Transfer. Special thanks to Jessie Moore, Associate Director of the Center for Engaged Learning at Elon University and associate professor of Professional Writing & Rhetoric in the Department of English, for her feedback on earlier versions of this manuscript.

2. The field of Composition and Rhetoric in the U.S. has raised serious questions about the genres that dominate traditional curricular models, whether that be through broad calls to do away with first year writing courses altogether (Connors 1995; Petraglia 1995; Smits 2004), activity system theory and a critique of first-year composition's ability to teach disciplinary genres out of context (Russell 1995; Bawarshi 2003; Downs & Wardle 2007; Wardle 2009), or empirical studies showing that for a variety of reasons transfer from one genre to another either seldom happens or students don't expect that it will (Beaufort 2007; Nelms & Dively 2007; Bergman & Zepernick 2007; Wardle 2007; Clarke & Hernandez 2001; Driscoll 2011).

3. The scholarship on genre learning involves decades-long, international debates about the efficacy of explicit instruction in teaching genre, with some studies contending that explicit teaching is neither necessary nor helpful, and others providing evidence that explicit instruction can be effective (for authoritative summaries, see Freedman 1994, and Bawarshi & Reiff, 2010, pp. 110–126). This curriculum, where there was "explicit" teaching of the scientific research article genre, thus offered a window into these dynamics.

4. This study was IRB approved in 2011. All student names have been changed.

5. I chose a naturalized transcription method, without editing repetitions or the frequent use of "like" etc., in order to capture both the conversational nature of the interviews and students' often difficult articulation of their understanding of their own literacy development.

6. If Melissa means "replicate" in its scientific sense, as I believe she does, then her comment suggests the mid-level WI course can entail a step beyond simply copying a template. Instead, there is the potential for an experience of replicating an experimental study to test for reliability, a skill which requires an independent ability to conduct research.

REFERENCES

Artemeva, N. (2008). Toward a unified theory of genre learning. *Journal of Business and Technical Communication*, 22, 160–185.

Bawarshi, A. (2003). *Genre and the invention of the writer.* Logan, UT: Utah State University Press.

Bawarshi, A., and M. Reiff. (2010). *Genre: An introduction to history, theory, research and pedagogy.* West Lafayette, IN: The WAC Clearinghouse and Parlor Press. Retrieved from http://wac.colostate.edu/books/bawarshi_reiff/

Bazerman, C. (2009a). The problem of writing knowledge. In S. Miller (Ed.), *The Norton book of composition studies* (pp. 502–514). New York: W. W. Norton and Company

Bazerman, C. (2009b). Genre and cognitive development: Beyond writing to learn. In C. Bazerman, A. Bonini, and D. Figueiredo (Eds.), *Genre in a changing world* (pp. 279–294). Fort Collins, CO: The WAC Clearinghouse and Parlor Press. Retrieved from http://wac.colostate.edu/books/genre.

Bazerman, C., and P. Prior. (2005). Participating in emergent socio-literate worlds: Genre, disciplinarity, interdisciplinarity. In R. Beach, J. Green, M. Kamil, and T. Shanahan (Eds.), *Multidisciplinary perspectives on literacy research* (2nd ed.) (pp. 133–178). Cresskill, NJ: Hampton Press.

Bazerman, C., et al. (2005). *Reference guide to writing across the curriculum.* West Lafayette, IN: The WAC Clearinghouse and Parlor Press. Retrieved from http://wac.colostate.edu/books/bazerman_wac/

Bean, J. (1995). *Engaging ideas* (1st ed.). San Francisco, CA: Jossey-Bass Publishers.

Beaufort, A. (2007). *College writing and beyond: A new framework for university writing instruction.* Logan, UT: Utah University Press.

Beaufort, A., and J. Williams. (2005). Writing history: Informed or not by genre theory. In A. Herrington and C. Moran (Eds.), *Genre across the curriculum* (pp. 44–64). Logan, UT: Utah State University Press.

Bergman, L., and J. Zepernick. (2007). Disciplinarity and transference: Students' perceptions of learning to write. *WPA: Writing Program Administration 31*(1/2), 124–149.

Bryant, A., and K. Charmaz. (2010). Grounded theory in historical perspective: An epistemological account. In A. Bryant and K. Charmaz (Eds), *The Sage handbook of grounded theory* (pp. 31–57). Los Angeles, CA: Sage.

Carter, M. (2007). Ways of knowing, doing and writing in the disciplines. *College Composition and Communication 58*(3), 385–418.

Charmaz, K. (2002). Qualitative interviewing and grounded theory analysis. In J. Gubrium and J. Holstein (Eds.), *Handbook of interview research: Context and method* (pp. 675–694). London: Sage.

Charmaz, K. (2006). *Constructing grounded theory: A practical guide through qualitative analysis.* Thousand Oaks, CA: Sage.

Clark, I., and A. Hernandez. (2011). Genre awareness, academic argument, and transferability. *The WAC Journal, 22.* Retrieved from http://wac.colostate.edu/journal/vol22/clark.pdf

Connors, R. (1995). The new abolitionism: Toward a historical background. In J. Petraglia (Ed.), *Reconceiving writing, rethinking writing instruction* (pp. 3–26). Mahwah, NJ: Lawrence Earlbaum.

Cooper, M. (1989). The ecology of writing. In M. Cooper and M. Holzman (Eds.), *Writing as social action* (pp. 1–13). Portsmouth, NH: Boynton/Cook.

Dias, P. (1994). Initiating students into genres of discipline-based reading and writing. In A. Freedman and P. Medway (Eds.), *Learning and teaching genre* (pp. 193–206). Portsmouth, NH: Boynton/Cook.

Downs, D., and E. Wardle. (2007). Teaching about writing, righting misconceptions: (Re)envisioning "first-year composition" as "introduction to writing studies." *College Composition and Communication 58*(4), 552–584.

Driscoll, D. (2011). Connected, disconnected, or uncertain: Student attitudes about future writing contexts and perceptions of transfer from first-year writing to the disciplines. *Across the Disciplines 8.2.* Retrieved from http://wac.colostate.edu/atd/articles/driscoll2011/index.cfm

Elton, L. (2010). Academic writing and tacit knowledge. *Teaching in Higher Education 15*(2), 151–160.

Freedman, A. (1994). "Do as I say": The relationship between teaching and learning new genres. In A. Freedman and P. Medway (Eds.), *Genre and the new rhetoric* (pp. 191–210). Bristol, PA: Taylor and Francis, Inc.

Greene, S. (1992). Mining texts in reading to write. *Journal of Advanced Composition 12*, 151–170.

Haggis, T. (2006). Pedagogies for diversity: Retaining critical challenge amidst fears of "dumbing down." *Studies in Higher Education 31*(5), 521–535.

Hunt, R. (1994). Traffic in genres, in classrooms and out. In A. Freedman and P. Medway (Eds.), *Genre and the new rhetoric* (pp. 211–230). Bristol, PA: Taylor and Francis, Inc.

Hutchings, P. (2000). *Opening lines: Approaches to the scholarship of teaching and learning.* Menlo Park, CA: The Carnegie Foundation for the Advancement of Learning. Retrieved from http://www.carnegiefoundation.org/elibrary/approaching-scholarship-teaching-and-learning

Kaufer, D., and R. Young. (1993). Writing in the content areas. In L. Odell (Ed.), *Theory and practice in the teaching of writing: Rethinking the disciplines* (pp. 71–104). Carbondale, IL: Southern Illinois University Press.

Lillis, T., and J. Turner. (2001). Student writing in higher education: Contemporary confusion, traditional concerns. *Teaching in Higher Education 6*(1), 57–68.

Miller, C. (1984). Genre as social action. *Quarterly Journal of Speech* 70, 151–167.

Morse, J. (2007). Sampling in grounded theory. In A. Bryant and K. Charmaz (Eds.), *The Sage handbook of grounded theory* (pp. 229–244). Los Angeles: Sage.

Nelms, G., and R. Leathers Dively (2007). Perceived roadblocks to transferring knowledge from first-year composition to writing-intensive major courses: A pilot study. *WPA: Writing Program Administration*, *31*(1/2), 214–245.

Petraglia, J. (1995). Writing as an unnatural act. In J. Petraglia (Ed.), *Reconceiving writing, rethinking writing instruction* (pp. 79–100). Mahwah, NJ: Lawrence Earlbaum.

Prior, P. (1998). *Writing/Disciplinarity: A sociohistoric account of literate activity in the academy.* Mahwah, NJ: Lawrence Erlbaum Associates.

Russell, D. (1995). Activity theory and its implications for writing instruction." In J. Petraglia (Ed.), *Reconceiving writing, rethinking writing instruction* (pp. 51–77). Mahwah, NJ: Lawrence Earlbaum.

Russell, D. (2001). Where do the naturalistic studies of WAC/WID point? A research review. In S. McLeod, et al. (Eds.), *WAC for the new millennium: Strategies for continuing writing-across-the-curriculum programs* (pp. 259–288).

Urbana, IL: NCTE. Retrieved from http://wac.colostate.edu/books/millennium/chapter11.pdf

Russell, D. (2002). *Writing in the academic disciplines: A curricular history* (2nd ed.). Carbondale, IL: Southern Illinois University Press.

Smits, D. W. (2004). *The end of composition studies.* Carbondale, IL: Southern Illinois University Press.

Stoller, F., and M. Robinson. (2012). Chemistry journal articles: An interdisciplinary approach to move analysis with pedagogical aims. *English for Specific Purposes* 32, 45–57.

Swales, J. (1990). *Genre analysis: English in academic and research settings.* Cambridge: Cambridge University Press.

Thaiss, C., and T. Meyers Zawacki. (2006). *Engaged writers and dynamic disciplines: Research on the academic writing life.* Portsmouth, NH: Boynton/Cook.

Wardle, E. (2007). Understanding "transfer" from FYC: Preliminary results of a longitudinal study. *WPA: Writing Program Administration*, *31*(1/2), 65–85.

Wardle, E. (2009). "Mutt genres" and the goal of FYC: Can we help students write the genres of the university? *College Composition and Communication*, 60:4, 765–789.

Reading Questions

1. In the introduction to her study, Goldschmidt describes Thaiss and Zawacki's three stages of undergraduate disciplinary writing development. Based on her descriptions of the three stages, where would you place yourself? Why?

2. Using your own words and interpretation of Goldschmidt's results, how would you describe the three patterns that she found helped support students as they develop disciplinary writing expertise?

Rhetoric Questions

3. Goldschmidt's article appeared in a journal that is written for faculty interested in teaching and learning, and those faculty come from all different disciplines across higher education. Take a look at Goldschmidt's opening paragraph. Why do you think she began her article the way that she did, by repeating the common assumptions that faculty members have about college writing?

4. Take a look at the different sections of Goldschmidt's article. Where does she cite the majority of her external sources? Why do you think she cites sources more in that section?

Response Questions

5. Of the three strategies that Goldschmidt describes as being most helpful to students in developing their writing expertise, which one resonates the most with you? Why?

6. In the section titled "Reading and Emulating," Goldschmidt writes that "Danny said that although 'it's unpopular' to assign 20-page research articles to 'college freshmen,' even just the exposure helps." Do you agree with Danny? Why or why not?

ACADEMIC CASE STUDY • THE SCHOLARSHIP OF WRITING   SOCIAL SCIENCES

Letters of Gratitude: Further Evidence for Author Benefits

STEVEN M. TOEPFER, KELLY CICHY, AND PATTI PETERS

The authors—Steven M. Toepfer, Kelly Cichy, and Patti Peters—all worked at Kent State University when this article was published. Toepfer and Cichy are both associate professors in the Human Development and Family Studies Program, and Peters worked in the Office of Research where she assisted faculty with statistics in their research. The article below describes data they collected and analyzed in a research study on how writing letters of gratitude affect happiness, life-satisfaction, and depression. The article originally appeared in the *Journal of Happiness Studies*.

ABSTRACT

This study examined the effects of writing letters of gratitude on three primary qualities of well-being; happiness (positive affect), life-satisfaction (cognitive evaluation), and depression (negative affect). Gratitude was also assessed. Participants included 219 men and women who wrote three letters of gratitude over a 3 week period. A two-way mixed method ANOVA with a between factor (writers vs. non-writers) and within subject factor (time of testing) analysis was conducted. Results indicated that writing letters of gratitude increased participants' happiness and life satisfaction, while decreasing depressive symptoms. The implications of this approach for intervention are discussed.

Keywords: well-being, happiness, life satisfaction, gratitude, writing, letters, intentional activity

1. INTRODUCTION

The scholarly spotlight has long shined on writing-oriented gratitude inductions as a means for improving well-being. However, within this body of research there is little data regarding a sustained "*letters of gratitude*" writing campaign. The purpose of this investigation was to focus on the cumulative effect of writing over time as it relates to components of subjective well-being: gratitude, happiness, life-satisfaction, and depressive symptoms. The impetus for the current investigation was derived from a pilot study by Toepfer and Walker (2009).

The Toepfer and Walker (2009) study employed a three-letter method which examined changes over time in happiness, life-satisfaction, and gratitude compared to controls. Results showed significant gains in happiness and gratitude as writing progressed. The 2009 study was encouraging but hampered by a small sample size ($n = 84$) and a failure to address negative affect, an important feature of well-being. The current investigation sought to replicate the initial study with a more powerful sample size and extend its scope by assessing change in depressive symptoms. Goals were to reexamine the extent to which well-being, as measured by happiness, life-satisfaction, gratitude, and depressive symptoms, would change in response to writing letters of gratitude over time.

2. SUBJECTIVE WELL-BEING AND ITS COMPONENTS

For the purposes of this investigation the concept of subjective well-being (SWB) is used as an overarching term which includes components of positive affect (e.g., gratitude, happiness, life-satisfaction), and unpleasant affect (e.g., depressive symptoms) according to its general use in the literature (Howell et al. 2007). Subjective well-being, often referred to as "well-being," is conceptualized as including both emotional (high positive and low negative affect) and cognitive (life-satisfaction) components (Diener and Diswas-Diener 2008). Accordingly, SWB is employed here as an umbrella term that addresses the heterogeneous but highly related construct of well-being which encompasses emotional and cognitive components (Howell et al. 2007).

Gratitude has been conceptualized in numerous ways, most commonly as either a moral trait or an emotional state (Froh et al. 2008). Both constructs have clearly been linked to subjective well-being, demonstrating that happy people tend to be grateful people (Watkins 2004). This study focused on the emotional state of gratitude as a means to elicit change in well-being. As an emotional state gratitude is commonly defined as an amalgam of appreciation, thankfulness, and a sense of wonder (Emmons and Sheldon 2002). It is comprised of various qualities which result in a more favorable appraisal of overall well-being (Buss 2000; Diener 2000; Diener and Larse 1993; Strack et al. 1991; Suh et al. 1998). These favorable qualities are typically emotional expressions directed toward an external agency or entity following perceived aid from that source which is interpreted as costly, valuable, and altruistically intended (Lane and Anderson 1976; Tesser et al. 1968; Wood et al. 2008a; b). Those who express gratitude more frequently have been shown to improve on measures of well-being (Fredrickson and Joiner 2002) and generate more positive affect (Emmons 2008; Emmons and McCullough 2003) by provoking participants to extract more satisfaction and enjoyment from life events as a result of positive experiences (Sheldon and Lyubomirsky 2006). Watkins (2008) described gratitude as follows; "It is as if our enjoyment is incomplete unless some praise or gratitude is expressed to the source of our enjoyment" (Watkins, p. 167). McCullough et al. (2004) showed that such gratitude based moods can be created from the "bottom-up"

to influence well-being in a positive way. The current study examines the psychological benefit of expressing gratitude as a bottom-up effect to examine change in well-being.

It should be noted that in some cases gratitude 5 has been defined as "a sense of thankfulness and joy in response to receiving a gift, whether the gift be a tangible benefit from a specific other or a moment of peaceful bliss evoked by natural beauty" (Peterson and Seligman 2004, p. 554). This investigation limited the expression of gratitude to less tangible factors by excluding "thank you notes" in order to isolate interpersonal qualities of support and corresponding feelings of gratitude.

Many definitions of happiness have been used in the literature, from overall life satisfaction to fleeting feelings of pleasure, but this study employs the term happiness to denote the frequent experience of positive emotion (Lyubomirsky et al. 2005a). This narrower use of the term is accepted as a means to address the influence of frequently experienced positive emotion, a cornerstone of the happiest people (Diener et al. 1991). Researchers have found that positive emotion may include feelings of gladness, joy, and contentment (Griffin 2006; Lyubomirsky 2001). The present investigation hypothesized that by working with gratitude, a highly related quality that requires re-experiencing past interpersonal events which contained positive affect, happiness would increase. Such improvements have been previously shown due to the influence of gratitude by those who practice it (Emmons and McCullough 2003).

Life-satisfaction is referred to as the cognitive and personal assessment of one's overall quality of life and is based on unique or personalized criteria, which shows variance between individuals (Shin and Johnson 1978; Goldbeck et al. 2007). Research indicates it is a cognitive comparison or evaluation of personal criteria that a person uses to assess general satisfaction with life (Diener et al. 1985; Pavot and Diener 1993; Moller and Saris 2001; Van Praag et al. 2003) and has been used as an overall measurement of life satisfaction (Diener et al. 1985; Headey and

Wearing 1989). Tatarkiewicz (1976) drew a connection between life-satisfaction and happiness stating that "life as a whole" (p. 8) is an important indication of one's affective state as one important index of happiness. However, Sheldon and Lyubomirsky (2007) have shown these correlations to be modest, indicating that one is not always an indicator of the other, especially as context varies. For the purposes of this investigation life satisfaction is therefore considered distinct from happiness as it may be influenced separately from happiness over the course of the letter writing campaign.

3. DEPRESSIVE SYMPTOMS

Depressive symptoms assess negative affect and its contribution to well-being. Depression can be defined not only by high levels of negative affect but relative levels compared to positive affect (Watson and Clark 1995). The influence on well-being depends on the frequency of those positive and negative emotions one experiences (Diener et al. 1991). Negative affect (NA) and positive affect (PA) have shown moderate inverse relations across individuals (Lyubomirsky et al. 2005a, b). Numerous studies have linked the effect of negative emotions (ill-being) to compromised health functioning and increased illness (Booth-Kewley and Friedman 1987; Herbert and Cohen 1993; Segerstorm and Miller 2004). It is the interrelated coexistence of NA and PA that warrants the inclusion of depressive symptoms as an indicator of well-being.

The depression literature on writing is broad and varied. Generally, a robust literature exists regarding writing as a vehicle for managing depression (L'Abate et al. 1992; Esterling et al. 1999; Koopman et al. 2005; Sloan et al. 2008), but previous investigations have not measured depressive symptoms under the conditions proposed by this study. Research related to depressive symptoms has shown that writing about past trauma has decreased depressive symptomotology over time (Dominguez et al. 1995; Greenberg and Stone 1992; Murray and Segal 1994). Longitudinal research on writing points to the antithesis of depression, happiness, as a factor which can fend off depression related issues (Cohen et al. 2006). Long-term

documentation of the effectiveness of cognitive and behavioral interventions to combat negative affect and depression has encouraging implications for the possibility of elevating long-term happiness (Gloaguen et al. 1998). This warrants further examination of the Toepfer and Walker (2009) results which, in addition to showing significant change for happiness, found a non-significant trend in life-satisfaction, suggesting this approach may have implications as a behavioral intervention.

4. INTENTIONAL ACTIVITY

An intentional activity is described as a willful and self-directed act (Sheldon and Lyubomirsky 2007) and is the vehicle for change in this study, but it has not always been accepted as a springboard to well-being. In fact it has been suggested that changing one's happiness is "futile" (Lykken and Tellegen 1996, p. 189). The "hedonic treadmill" is commonly cited to show that people adapt to positive change, quelling the impact of self-directed behavior (Brickman et al. 1978). Yet, a rapidly growing body of research has tabled contradictory evidence. The model of sustainable happiness (Lyubomirsky et al. 2005b; Sheldon and Lyubomirsky 2006) suggests that people can do something about their own happiness—intentionally. Recent literature suggests that self-directed activity can improve well-being (Sheldon 2008; Seligman et al. 2005; Charles et al. 2001; Gloaguen et al. 1998). In one three-part study it was demonstrated that intentional activity had a significant impact on sustained happiness when compared to circumstantial events, suggesting that intentional activity is a powerful mediating variable (Sheldon and Lyubomirsky 2006). Kashdan (2007) reviewed converging evidence from different psychological fields to conclude, "self-regulatory strategies can promote resilience, create and sustain positive moods and intrinsic motivation, and aid in the repair of different negative emotion" (p. 303). It is that sentiment, backed by the sustainable happiness model, which motivated this re-investigation of gratitude letters.

5. THE POWER OF WRITING

A robust literature concerning the value of expressive writing indicates numerous psychological and health benefits for writers (King 2001; Sheldon and Lyubomirsky 2006; Seligman et al. 2005) while the marriage of gratitude and writing has long been a metric for assessing well-being (King 2001; Sheldon and Lyubomirsky 2006; Seligman et al. 2005; Watkins et al. 2003). Pennebaker and Seagal (1999) showed that writers experienced positive effects when their writing included higher levels of positive emotion words, a moderate level of negative emotions words, and increased insight words (Pennebaker and Seagal 1999). Increased positive mood has been shown to be the result of various gratitude inductions, the most notable of which was a gratitude letter writing condition (Watkins et al. 2003). The highly structured nature of both writing and talking create a narrative that generates understanding and meaning (Singer 2004; Smyth et al. 2001), provides definition and a sense of control of emotion and experience (Pennebaker and Graybeal 2001), and integrates memories with self-understanding (Blagov and Singer 2004). This suggests that reflecting on memories of gratitude in an organized format and taking ownership of a preexisting cache of gratitude influences well-being because writing shapes these experiences. Specifically, positive and insightful writing that is a hallmark of the gratitude letter is associated with many outcomes including health improvements (Esterling et al. 1999; Pennebaker et al. 1997). Pennebaker's (1997) writing paradigm supports the use of increased insight and positive emotion words as a vehicle for change and has elicited positive outcomes in a multitude of studies (Lyubomirsky et al. 2006; Emmons and McCullough 2003).

Writing inductions for non-letter formats have received abundant attention. These studies have typically employed methods such as counting your blessings and weekly journals (Emmons and McCullough 2003). The use of letters has primarily been restricted to a single document or act of kindness rather than a continued effort (VandeCreek et al. 2002). The current study extended the gratitude-writing literature by introducing multiple letters over time.

6. METHODS

6.1. Participants

Participants were 219 adults, 31 men and 188 women randomly selected from a research pool across three campuses at a large Midwestern university. Participant age ranged from 18 to 65 with a mean of 25.7 (SD = 11). The total sample was composed of 89% ($n = 195$) Caucasian, 7% ($n = 16$) African-American, 1% ($n = 3$) Hispanic, 1% ($n = 3$) multicultural, and 1% ($n = 2$) who self-identified as "other." The participants were largely traditional in terms of being young adults, 61% ($n = 134$) being single and never married. Those who completed all stages of the project were compensated with research extra credit.

Beyond asking new questions, the present investigation addressed limitations of the pilot; sample size, randomization, and more controlled handling of the letters. The current project increased the sample size from 84 to 219 participants. The 2009 study assessed participants directly from the primary investigator's classes for the experimental group, whereas the current study canvassed a wide variety of students from different classes, majors, and campuses for both the control and experimental groups outside of the primary investigator's courses. Finally, more rigorous control of the letters was maintained. The original study found that a fraction of participants received positive feedback from earlier letter recipients before they finished writing the third, creating a potential confound. To prevent recipient feedback, letters were held until the entire data collection process was completed.

6.2. Procedure

Participants in the experimental group (letter writers) were instructed to complete the battery of questionnaires four times at 1-week intervals. During weeks two, three, and four they composed a letter of gratitude, resulting in four measurement periods.

The control group completed the same inventories at time one and four without the writing component. Participants were not privy to the upcoming letters. Instead, they were told only that an additional assignment was forthcoming. The instructions for composing the letters were identical each week, with the condition that there could be no repeat recipients. Both groups had filled out the questionnaires at the same time electronically from a computer lab. The experimental group was given a 24-h window between the writing assignment and the surveys but most participants completed both within a 1-h period. Sixty-two percent of participants wrote between half a page to one full page and 79% of writers took 15–30 min to do so.

Participants in the experimental group ($n = 1,141$) composed letters either by hand or word processor. Research supports either method as it has been shown to make no significant difference when used for similar expressive writing studies (Harlyey et al. 2003). The element that makes a difference is a focus on meaningful content. Participants were therefore instructed to write non-trivial letters of gratitude to an individual to express appreciation for them. Participants were asked to be reflective, write expressively, and compose letters from a positive orientation while avoiding "thank you notes" for material gifts. Writing was restricted to three letters to avoid "over-practicing" or a plateau effect of diminishing returns (Brickman and Campbell 1971; Lyubomirsky et al. 2005a, b).

Letters were individually examined by the primary investigator to insure the basic guidelines (e.g., non-triviality, expression of gratefulness, return address, a stamped envelope, etc.) were followed. The primary investigator mailed the physical letters after the final composition in order to prevent recipient feedback. Participants were aware that letters would be mailed to the intended recipients, therefore increasing the psychological realism and ownership of the exercise.

6.3. Measures

Questionnaires took approximately 15 min to complete and included a demographic form (completed once at T1), a series of items assessing gratitude, life satisfaction, happiness, depressive symptoms, and an exit survey (completed at T4), which included questions regarding participant experiences, such as time spent writing, method, and general perceptions of the process.

6.3.1. GRATITUDE

Gratitude was assessed using the Gratitude Questionnaire—6 (GQ6), a brief self-report measure of the disposition toward experiencing gratitude (McCullough et al. 2002). Participants answered 6 items on a scale of 1 (*strongly disagree*) to 7 (*strongly agree*). Example questions include, "I have so much in my life to be thankful for," and "Long amounts of time can go by before I feel grateful to something or someone." The GQ-6 demonstrates good internal reliability across multiple studies, with alphas between .82 and .87 (McCullough et al.).

6.3.2. LIFE SATISFACTION

Life satisfaction was assessed by The Satisfaction [20] with Life Scale (SLS), a 5-item measure that assesses life satisfaction as a whole (Diener et al. 1985). Example questions include, "In most ways my life is close to my ideal," and "I am satisfied with life." The scale does not assess satisfaction with specific life domains, such as health or finances, but allows subjects to personally integrate and weigh these domains (Diener, et al.; Pavot et al. 1991). Strong internal reliability and moderate temporal stability are illustrated by a coefficient alpha of .87 (Diener et al. 1985).

6.3.3. HAPPINESS

We used The Subjective Happiness Scale (SHS), a short 4-item questionnaire to assess subjective happiness with regard to absolute ratings and ratings relative to peers (Lyubomirsky and Lepper 1999). Scores range from 1 to 7 per question, a score of "1" indicating low levels of happiness and "7" a high score. Example questions include, "Compared to most of my peers, I consider myself:" with options for "not a very happy person" to "a very happy person" and "Some people are generally very happy. They enjoy life regardless of what is going on, getting the most out of everything. To what extent does this characterization describe you?" Internal consistency for the SHS has been found to be stable across seven different studies ($N = 2,732$) with a range between good-to-excellent with regard to validity and reliability, demonstrating alphas that ranged 0.85–0.95 (Lyubomirsky and Lepper 1999). High test–retest stability (Pearson's $r = 0.90$ for 4 weeks and 0.71 for 3 months) scores have also been reported.

6.3.4. DEPRESSIVE SYMPTOMS

The 10-item Center for Epidemiological Studies Depression Scale (CES-D10) was used to assess depressive symptoms (Lorig et al. 2001; Radloff 1977). Its primary use is to identify current depressive symptoms in community or non-clinical samples during the previous week (Radloff 1977). Participants were asked how often they felt the following ways in the past week on a 4-point scale from 1 (*rarely or none at all*) to 4 (*most of the time*). Higher CES-D scores indicate more frequent depressive symptoms. Representative questions include, "I was bothered by things that usually don't bother me," and "My sleep was restless." Higher total scores indicate more frequent and severe depression. The CES-D has been shown to be a reliable measure for assessing the frequency, types, and duration of depressive symptoms across racial, gender, and age categories (Knight et al. 1997; Radloff 1977; Roberts et al. 1989). The CES-D demonstrates high internal consistency ($\alpha = .85 - .90$) across studies (Radloff 1977).

7. RESULTS

Results are presented in two parts: findings for the well-being variables (i.e., gratitude, happiness, and life satisfaction) followed by the ill-being variable (depressive symptoms). The test–retest correlations revealed significant positive associations between pretest and posttest scores for gratitude ($r = 0.42$, $P < .001$), happiness ($r = 0.78$, $P < .001$), life satisfaction ($r = 0.81$, $P < .001$), and depressive symptoms ($r = 0.71$, $P < .001$).

7.1. Between and Within Group Differences in Components of Subjective Well-Being

To test the effects of writing letters of gratitude on individuals' subjective well-being, we conducted a series of 2 (Time) × 2 (Group) mixed method ANOVAs, separately for each well-being variable (i.e., gratitude, happiness, and life satisfaction) and depressive symptoms. We used mixed method ANOVAs because this study includes both between and within subject effects. In this study, time is a within subject effect, whereas group is a between subject effect. Time refers to within person differences from pretest to posttest. Group refers to differences between the experimental group (i.e., writers) and the control group (i.e., non-writers). Table 1 presents the means for the experimental and control groups on the well-being variables and depressive symptoms for the four measurement periods.

7.1.1. GRATITUDE

Contrary to our expectations, there was no significant main effect of time for gratitude (Table 2). Reports of gratitude did not significantly differ between the pretest and the posttest. We also did not find a significant time × group interaction, suggesting there was no significant effect on gratitude from writing the letters of gratitude.[1]

7.1.2. HAPPINESS

Results for happiness revealed a significant main effect of time that was qualified by a significant time × group interaction (Table 2). Happiness was significantly higher at posttest than at pretest; however, follow-up analyses separated by group revealed that this difference was only significant for the experimental group ($F(1,104) = 7.04$, $P < .01$). As expected, the experimental group reported higher levels of happiness at posttest ($M = 20.62$, SD = 3.88) than

[1]We explored whether the effects of letter writing varied by initial levels of gratitude by conducting a series of regression analyses for each of the dependent variables that included the interaction between pretest gratitude and group (i.e., experimental vs. control). Our results did not provide support for gratitude as a moderator of the treatment effect.

Table 1

Means on well-being scales over time

	Time	
	Pre-test	**Post-test**
Happiness (SHS)		
Letter-writers	19.72 ($n = 105$, SD = 3.9)	20.62 ($n = 105$, SD = 3.8)
Non-writers	19.68 ($n = 78$, SD = 4.28)	19.58 ($n = 78$, SD = 4.16)
Life satisfaction (SLS)		
Letter-writers	23.49 ($n = 105$, SD = 5.95)	26.24 ($n = 105$, SD = 6.59)
Non-writers	23.42 ($n = 78$, SD = 6.8)	23.06 ($n = 78$, SD = 6.52)
Gratitude (GQ6)		
Letter-writers	29.35 ($n = 105$, SD = 3.38)	29.67 ($n = 105$, SD = 3.81)
Non-writers	29.45 ($n = 78$, SD = 2.99)	28.77 ($n = 78$, SD = 3.68)
Depression (CES-D)		
Letter-writers	12.88 ($n = 105$, SD = 4.69)	11.56 ($n = 105$, SD = 5)
Non-writers	11.35 ($n = 78$, SD = 4.46)	11.40 ($n = 78$, SD = 4.42)

they did at pretest ($M = 19.72$, SD = 3.92), whereas there was no significant difference between pretest ($M = 19.68$, SD = 4.28) and posttest ($M = 19.58$, SD = 4.16) for the control group.

7.1.3. LIFE SATISFACTION

Similarly, results for life satisfaction revealed a significant main effect of time that was qualified by a significant time × group interaction (Table 2). Life satisfaction was significantly higher at posttest than at pretest for both the experimental, $F(1,104) = 33.53$, $P < .001$ and the control group, $F(1,104) = 6.35$, $P < .01$. The experimental group's life satisfaction improved from pretest ($M = 23.49$, SD = 5.95) to posttest ($M = 26.24$, SD = 6.59), whereas the control group's life satisfaction slightly declined from pretest ($M = 23.42$, SD = 6.81) to posttest ($M = 23.06$, SD = 6.52).

7.1.4. DEPRESSIVE SYMPTOMS

Results also revealed a significant main effect of time for depressive symptoms that was qualified by a significant time × group interaction (Table 2). Participants reported significantly fewer depressive symptoms at posttest compared to at pretest;

however, follow-up analyses separated by group indicated that this difference was only significant for the experimental group, $F(1, 104) = 8.58$, $P < .01$, not for the control group, $F(1, 77) = 0.26$, $P > .05$. Consistent with our expectations, the experimental group reported significantly fewer depressive symptoms at posttest ($M = 11.56$, SD = 5.03) compared to at pretest ($M = 12.88$, SD = 4.69).

Finally, we conducted a series of analyses intended to test whether the benefits of the writing campaign accumulated over time. We could not assess whether there was a treatment effect at T2 or T3 because the control groups only reported on the dependent variables at T1 and T4. In an effort to still explore the issue of dosage and consider whether our results were more than mood manipulation, we assessed how the well-being variables changed from T2 to T3 in the experimental group and found there were no significant changes in gratitude, happiness, or depressive symptoms from T2 to T3. These analyses suggest that the changes observed in happiness and depressive symptoms accumulated across the study period and represent more than a brief mood manipulation.

Table 2

Results of Repeated Measures ANOVA's on the well-being scales

	df	MS	F
Happiness (SHS)			
Within-subjects			
Time	1	14.06	3.96*
Time × Group	1	22.28	6.27**
Error	181	3.55	
Between-subjects			
Group	1	26.41	0.91
Error	181	29.10	
Life satisfaction (SLS)			
Within-subjects			
Time	1	128.19	17.92***
Time × Group	1	216.62	30.28***
Error	181	7.153	
Between-subjects			
Group	1	234.42	3.09
Error	181	75.98	
Gratitude (GQ6)			
Within-subjects			
Time	1	2.98	0.42
Time × Group	1	22.10	3.10
Error	181	7.14	
Between-subjects			
Group	1	14.36	0.83
Error	181	17.30	
Depressive symptoms (CES-D)			
Within-subjects			
Time	1	35.70	5.72*
Time × Group	1	41.73	6.68**
Error	181	6.24	
Between-subjects			
Group	1	64.25	1.70
Error	181	37.70	

*$P < .05$, **$P < .01$, ***$P < .001$

In summary, our findings provide partial support [30] for our hypotheses. Contrary to our expectations, gratitude did not change in response to writing the letters of gratitude. As anticipated, writing letters of gratitude seemed to increase participants' happiness and life satisfaction, while decreasing participants' depressive symptoms.

8. DISCUSSION

The present investigation sought to replicate a previous study by Toepfer and Walker (2009) which examined the effects of a letters of gratitude writing campaign as a means for improving important qualities of well-being. The goals of the current study were twofold: (1) to examine the durability of the original study with a more appropriate sample in terms of size and selection, and (2) to extend the scope of the original investigation by assessing depressive symptoms as an outcome.

Significant findings from the current study supported much of the previous research and showed new evidence that depression is influenced by letters of gratitude. The previous investigation showed significant findings regarding happiness and gratitude. Happiness demonstrated a cumulative effect after each letter and compared to non-writers or controls. Gratitude showed significant improvements for writers compared to non-writers (Toepfer and Walker 2009). The current study supported the Toepfer and Walker (2009) findings on happiness over time and compared to non-letter writers. Both studies were consistent in showing that the writing campaign of three letters improved affective states of happiness which includes feelings of gladness, satisfaction, fulfillment (Griffin 2006; Myers 1992). Regarding life-satisfaction, the present study found significant improvement over time and compared to non-writers, whereas the original study did not. The Toepfer and Walker (2009) pilot investigation showed no significant results for life-satisfaction but demonstrated a trend over time. Replicating the original study yielded significant findings over time and compared to non-writers. These differing findings suggest that cognitive evaluations of one's life are improved by engaging in an expressive writing campaign which uses gratitude as a vehicle for change. This is encouraging because it indicates the intentional activity has a broader impact than initially reported by Toepfer and Walker (2009), influencing both the affective and cognitive domains.

Gratitude yielded no significant change in the current study, unlike the previous investigation. Toepfer and Walker (2009) reported a significant interaction between groups for letter writers and non-writers. The current investigation did not show significant improvement either between or within groups. Therefore, the claim that working with gratitude can bolster gratitude cannot be supported in the current investigation. Based on the design and methodology of the current study we can only speculate as to the reasons for gratitude's lack of responsiveness. First, it is possible the small sample size of the first study yielded an unrepresentative sample. The larger, randomized sample of the current investigation may represent a broader range of participants and reflect a more accurate picture of gratitude. Second, gratitude may be less subject to change because it is a fixed quality. The GQ-6 and the design of the study may not possess the sensitivity to distinguish the difference between state and trait qualities of gratitude. It is possible that the conceptual nature of gratitude we used (McCullough et al. 2002) hinges on trait qualities (e.g., optimism, life satisfaction, hope, spirituality and religiousness, empathy, and pro-social behavior) that are less likely to be influenced by such a gratitude induction. Participants were grateful due to a preexisting understanding of a relationship with a person which might also be stable. As a result, gratitude may not change due to treatment.

Depression was a new consideration in the current investigation. It was examined to assess whether or not letters of gratitude would decrease depressive symptoms. Results indicated that the writing campaign showed significant decreases in symptomatology over time and compared to non-writers. The findings present interesting implications for letters of gratitude as a way to reduce depressive symptoms as well as an intervention for those suffering from depressive symptoms. It is important to note that the CES-D is not a measure of major depression, but instead a metric for depressive symptoms, and is often used to screen for pre-clinical signs of depression in the normal population (Radloff 1977). As a measure of the level of depressive symptoms the CES-D may not be a strong tool for screening for clinical depression or major depression (Roberts et al. 1989) regardless of high correlates with clinician rating measures of depression such as the Hamilton, the Beck Depression Inventory, and the SCL-90 (Weissman et al. 1977). Nonetheless, writing letters of gratitude may have potential for alleviating depressive symptoms prior to more severe clinical depression. Further investigation is required before such claims can be made but the results are promising.

8.1. Limitations and Future Directions

This study showed numerous improvements in well-being as a result of writing letters of gratitude, yet it is not without its limitations. The present investigation consisted of a sample that was largely limited to Caucasian females. A more heterogeneous sample would improve generalizability.

It is also important to acknowledge that the time frame between the writing intervention and the final measurement assessment was relatively brief. Due to this brief time frame, it is difficult to know for certain if the intervention produced lasting changes in subjective well-being or a short-term boost in participants' mood. Although, we cannot claim with certainty that the intervention produced lasting effects in well-being, the accumulated effect of time is promising as it suggests more than mood manipulation. Future research should attempt to further address the issue of dosage by including longer-term follow-up assessments to determine how long the intervention effects last.

Future research would benefit from one important component—parceling out the difference between writing versus the benevolent act. As a means for manipulating gratitude the letters of gratitude required both expressive writing and, through the writing process, the intentional act of kindness which was to thank others. The investigation hinged on the intentional use of expressing gratitude in written form to till the soil of well-being, so to speak, and produce a fertile context for the related qualities (happiness, life-satisfaction, and gratitude itself) to grow. Participants expressed written gratitude to real people, essentially, a benevolent act. Part of the process, beyond formulating and reflecting on gratitude, is the act of reaching out to others as a meaningful way to spark gratitude and ignite well-being. However, further investigation is warranted in order to parcel out the differences between acts of kindness and the gratitude letter. In addition, it would be beneficial to better understand the differences between writing letters of gratitude versus other methods of writing (e.g., thank you notes). Also, future investigations may benefit from a second look at gratitude and the measurement of it. No significant improvement in gratitude was found using the GQ6 but this may be explained by the instrument's tendency to measure trait rather than state qualities of gratitude. Finally, future research should address questions about the interpersonal factors, including relationship style, emotional bonds, or attachment style. This study did something unique. It introduced psychological accountability and ownership for the sentiments contained within the letters. In so doing, interpersonal factors were introduced. Letters were not sent until the third and final letter was composed, in order to prevent feedback prior to completing the entire process, but interpersonal influences may remain. Does this accountability matter? Were long-term writer-recipient effects introduced? Did participants talk with recipients? These are important questions beyond the scope of the current study to be explored by future research.

9. CONCLUSIONS

The current investigation presented evidence that supported the Toepfer and Walker (2009) letters of gratitude study, particularly in the domains of happiness and life-satisfaction, suggesting the short writing campaign improves important qualities of well-being. It fortified the initial study with a new finding regarding significantly decreased levels of depressive symptoms as a result of the writing activity. In addition to supporting the 2009 pilot study the present investigation contributes to the literature by further clarifying that writing letters of gratitude has a cumulative effect that benefits the author. The implications are that this type of expressive writing can benefit those who suffer from depressive symptoms. Further research is necessary, but gratitude letters may be a simple intervention for those who struggle with such symptomatology.

Gratitude appears to be a powerful and preexisting resource that when utilized can produce positive effects upon well-being. As a tool for mining that resource letters of gratitude have produced positive outcomes related to important qualities of well-being: happiness, life-satisfaction, and depressive symptoms. The current investigation provided further evidence of these benefits.

REFERENCES

Blagov, P. S., & Singer, J. A. (2004). Four dimensions of self-defining memories (Specificity, meaning, content, and affect) and their relationships to self-restraint, distress, and repressive defensiveness. *Journal of Personality, 72*(3), 481–512.

Booth-Kewley, S., & Friedman, H. S. (1987). Psychological predictors of heart disease: A quantitative review. *Psychological Bulletin, 101*(3), 343–362.

Brickman, P., & Campbell, D. T. (1971). Hedonic relativism and the good society. In M. H. Appley (Ed.), *Adaptation-level theory: A symposium*. London: Academic Press.

Brickman, P., Coates, D., & Janoff-Bulman, R. (1978). Lottery winners and accident victims: Is happiness relative? *Journal of Personality and Social Psychology, 36*, 917–927.

Buss, D. (2000). The evolution of happiness. *American Psychologist, 55*(1), 15–23.

Charles, S. T., Reynolds, C. A., & Gatz, M. (2001). Age-related differences and change in positive and negative affect over 23 years. *Journal of Personality and Social Psychology, 80*, 136–151.

Cohen, S., Doyle, W. J., & Baum, A. (2006). Socioeconomic status is associated with stress hormones. *Psychosomatic Medicine, 68*, 414–420.

Diener, E. (2000). *Is happiness a virtue? The personal and societal benefits of positive emotions.* Paper presented at the Positive Psychology Summit. Washington, DC.

Diener, E., & Diswas-Diener, R. (2008). *Happiness: Unlocking the mysteries of psychological wealth.* Malden, MA: Blackwell Publishing.

Diener, E., & Larsen, R. J. (1993). The experience of emotional well-being. In M. Lewis & J. Haviland (Eds.), *Handbook of emotions.* New York: Guilford Press.

Diener, E., Emmons, R. A., Larsen, R. J., & Griffin, S. (1985). The satisfaction with life scale. *Journal of Personality Assessment, 49,* 71–75.

Diener, E., Sandvik, E., & Pavot, W. (1991). Happiness is the frequency, not the intensity, of positive versus negative affect. In F. Strack, M. Argyle, & N. Schwarz (Eds.), *Subjective well-being: An interdisciplinary perspective* (pp. 119–139). Oxford, England: Pergamon Press.

Dominguez, B., Valderrama, P., Meza, M. A., Perea, S. L., Silva, A., Martinez, G., et al. (1995). The roles of emotional reversal and disclosure in clinical practice. In J. W. Pennebaker (Ed.), *Emotion, disclosure, and health* (pp. 255–270). Washington, DC: American Psychological Association.

Emmons, R. A. (2008). Gratitude, subjective well-being, and the brain. In M. Eid & R. J. Larsen (Eds.), *The science of subjective well-being.* New York: Guilford Press.

Emmons, R. A., & McCullough, M. E. (2003). Counting blessings versus burdens: An experimental investigation of gratitude and subjective well-being in daily life. *Journal of Personality and Social Psychology, 84,* 377–389.

Emmons, R. A., & Sheldon, C. S. (2002). Gratitude and the science of positive psychology. In C. R. Snyder & S. J. Lopez (Eds.), *Handbook of positive psychology.* New York: Oxford University Press.

Esterling, B. A., L'Abate, L., Murray, E. J., & Pennebaker, J. W. (1999). Empirical foundations for writing in prevention and psychotherapy: Mental and physical health outcomes. *Clinical Psychology Review, 19*(1), 79–96.

Fredrickson, B. L., & Joiner, T. (2002). Positive emotions trigger upward spirals toward emotional well-being. *Psychological Science, 13*(2), 172–175.

Froh, J. J., Sefick, W. J., & Emmons, R. A. (2008). Counting blessings in early adolescents: An experimental study of gratitude and subjective well-being. *Journal of School Psychology, 46,* 213–233.

Gloaguen, V., Cottraux, J., Cucherat, M., & Blackburn, I. (1998). A meta-analysis of the effects of cognitive therapy in depressed patients. *Journal of Affective Disorders, 49,* 59–72.

Goldbeck, L., Schmitz, T. G., Besier, T., Herschback, P., & Henrich, G. (2007). Life satisfaction decreases during adolescence. *Quality of Life Research, 16*(6), 969–979.

Greenberg, M. A., & Stone, A. A. (1992). Emotional disclosure about traumas and its relation to health: Effects of previous disclosure and trauma severity. *Journal of Personality and Social Psychology, 63,* 75–84.

Griffin, J. (2006). What do happiness studies study? *Journal of Happiness Studies, 8*(1), 139–148.

Harlyey, J., Sotto, R., & Pennebaker, J. (2003). Speaking versus typing: A case study of the effects of using voice-recognition software on academic correspondence. *British Journal of Educational Technology, 34*(1), 5–16.

Headey, B., & Wearing, A. (1989). Personality, life events, and subjective well-being: Toward a dynamic equilibrium model. *Journal of Personality and Social Psychology, 57*(4), 731–739.

Herbert, T. B., & Cohen, S. (1993). Depression and Immunity: A meta-analytic review. *Psychological Bulletin, 113*(3), 472–486.

Howell, R. T., Kern, M. L., & Lyubomirsky, S. (2007). Health benefits: Meta-analytically determining the impact of well-being on objective health outcomes. *Health Psychology Review, 1*(1), 83–136.

Kashdan, T. B. (2007). New developments in emotion regulation with an emphasis on the positive spectrum of human functioning. *Journal of Happiness Studies, 8,* 303–310.

King, L. A. (2001). The health benefits of writing about life goals. *Personality and Social Psychology Bulletin, 27,* 798–807.

Knight, R. G., Williams, S., McGee, R., & Olaman, S. (1997). Psychometric properties of the Center for Epidemiologic Studies Depression Scale (CES-D) in a sample of women in middle life. *Behavior Research & Therapy, 35*(4), 373–380.

Koopman, C., Tasneem, I., Holmes, D., Classen, C. C., Palesh, O., & Talor, W. (2005). The effects of expressive writing on pain, depression, and posttraumatic stress disorder symptoms in survivors of intimate partner violence. *Journal of Health Psychology, 10*(2), 211–221.

L'Abate, L., Boyce, J., Fraizer, R., & Russ, D. (1992). Programmed writing: Research in progress. *Comprehensive Mental Health Care, 2,* 45–62.

Lane, J., & Anderson, N. H. (1976). *Integration of intention and outcome in moral judgment, 1–5.* New York: Springer Publishing Company.

Lorig, K. R., Sobel, D. S., Ritter, P. L., Laurent, D., & Hobbs, M. (2001). Effects of a self-management program for patients with chronic disease. *Effective Clinical Practice, 4,* 256–262.

Lykken, D., & Tellegen, A. (1996). Happiness is a stochastic phenomenon. *Psychological Science, 7,* 186–189.

Lyubomirsky, S. (2001). Why are some people happier than others? The role of cognitive and motivational processes in well-being. *American Psychologist, 65*(3), 239–249.

Lyubomirsky, S., & Lepper, H. (1999). A measure of subjective happiness: Preliminary reliability and construct validation. *Social Indicators Research, 46,* 137–155.

Lyubomirsky, S., King, L., & Diener, E. (2005a). The benefits of frequent positive affect: Does happiness lead to success? *Psychological Bulletin, 131*(6), 803–855.

Lyubomirsky, S., Sheldon, K. M., & Schkade, D. (2005b). Pursuing happiness: The architecture of sustainable change. *Review of General Psychology, 9,* 111–131.

Lyubomirsky, S., Sousa, L., & Dickerhoof, R. (2006). The cost and benefits of writing, talking, and thinking about triumphs and defeats. *Journal of Personality and Social Psychology, 90*(4), 692–708.

McCullough, M. E., Emmons, R. A., & Tsang, J. (2002). The grateful disposition: A conceptual and empirical topography. *Journal of Personality and Social Psychology, 82,* 112–127.

McCullough, M. E., Tsang, J., & Emmons, R. A. (2004). Gratitude in intermediate affective terrain: Links of grateful moods to individual differences and daily emotional experience. *Journal of Personality and Social Psychology, 86,* 295–309.

Moller, V., & Saris, W. E. (2001). The relationship between subjective well-being and domain satisfactions in South Africa. *Social Indicators Research, 55*(1), 97–114.

Murray, E. J., & Segal, D. L. (1994). Emotional processing in vocal and written expression of feelings about traumatic experiences. *Journal of Traumatic Stress, 7,* 391–405.

Myers, D. G. (1992). *The pursuit of happiness: Discovering the pathway to fulfillment, well-being, and enduring personal joy.* New York: Avon.

Pavot, W., & Diener, E. (1993). Review of the satisfaction with life scale. *Psychological Assessment, 5*(2), 164–172.

Pavot, W., Diener, E., Colvin, C. R., & Sandvik, E. (1991). Further validation of the satisfaction with life scale: Evidence for the cross-method convergence of well-being measures. *Journal of Personality Assessment, 57,* 149–161.

Pennebaker, J. W. (1997). *Opening up: The healing power of expressive emotion.* New York: Guilford.

Pennebaker, J. W., & Graybeal, A. (2001). Patterns of natural language use: Disclosure, personality, and social integration. *Current Directions in Psychological Science, 10*(3), 90–93.

Pennebaker, J. W., & Seagal, J. D. (1999). Forming a story: The health benefits of narrative. *Journal of Clinical Psychology, 55*(10), 1243–1254.

Pennebaker, J. W., Mayne, T. J., & Francis, M. E. (1997). Linguistic predictors of adaptive bereavement. *Journal of Personality and Social Psychology, 72*(4), 863–871.

Peterson, C., & Seligman, M. E. P. (2004). *Character strengths and virtues: A handbook and classification.* New York: Oxford University Press.

Radloff, L. S. (1977). The CES-D scale: A self-report depression scale for research in the general population. *Applied Psychological Measurement, 1,* 385–401.

Roberts, R., Vernon, S. W., & Rhoades, H. M. (1989). Effects of language and ethnic status on reliability and validity of the CES-D with psychiatric patients. *Journal of Nervous and Mental Disease, 177,* 581–592.

Segerstorm, S. C., & Miller, G. E. (2004). Psychological stress and the human immune system: A meta-analytic study of 30 years of inquiry. *Psychological Bulletin, 130*(4), 601–630.

Seligman, M. E. P., Steen, T. A., Park, N., & Peterson, C. (2005). Positive psychology progress: Empirical validation of interventions. *American Psychologist, 60,* 410–421.

Sheldon, K. M. (2008). Assessing the sustainability of goal-based changes in adjustment over a four-year period. *Journal of Research in Personality, 42*(1), 223–229.

Sheldon, K. M., & Lyubomirsky, S. (2006). How to increase and sustain positive emotion: The effects of expressing gratitude and visualizing best possible selves. *The Journal of Positive Psychology, 1*(2), 73–82.

Sheldon, K. M., & Lyubomirsky, S. (2007). Achieving sustainable gains in happiness: Change your actions, not your circumstances. *Journal of Happiness Studies, 7*(1), 55–86.

Shin, D. C., & Johnson, D. M. (1978). Avowed happiness as an overall assessment of the quality of life. *Social Indicators Research, 5,* 475–492.

Singer, J. A. (2004). Narrative identity and meaning making across the adult lifespan: An introduction. *Journal of Personality, 72*(3), 437–460.

Sloan, D. M., Marx, B. P., Epstein, E. M., & Dobbs, J. L. (2008). Expressive writing buffers against maladaptive rumination. *Emotion, 8*(2), 302–306.

Smyth, J., True, N., & Souto, J. (2001). Effects of writing about traumatic experiences: The necessity for narrative structuring. *Journal of Social & Clinical Psychology, 20,* 161–172.

Strack, F., Argyle, M., & Schwarz, N. (1991). In F. Strack (Ed.), *Subjective well-being: An interdisciplinary perspective, Questions on happiness: Classical topics, modern answers, blind spots.* Oxford UA: Pergamon Press. (VIII, 291 S Graph. Darst. ISBN: 0-08-037264-3).

Suh, E., Diener, E., Oishi, S., & Triandis, H. C. (1998). The shifting basis of life satisfaction judgments across cultures: Emotions versus norms. *Journal of Personality and Social Psychology, 74*(2), 482–493.

Tatarkiewicz, W. (1976). *Analysis of happiness. Melbourne international philosophy series.* Warszawa: Polish Scientific Publishers.

Tesser, A., Gatewood, R., & Driver, M. (1968). Some determinants of gratitude. *Journal of Personality and Social Psychology, 9,* 233–236.

Toepfer, S. M., & Walker, K. (2009). Letters of gratitude: Improving well-being through expressive writing. *Journal of Writing Research, 1*(3), 181–198.

Van Praag, B. M. S., Frijters, P., & Ferrer-i-Carbonell, A. (2003). The anatomy of subjective well-being. *Journal of Economic Behavior & Organization, 51*(1), 29–49.

VandeCreek, L., Janus, M. D., Pennebaker, J. W., & Binau, B. (2002). Praying about difficult experiences as self-disclosure to God. *The International Journal for the Psychology of Religion, 12*(1), 29–39.

Watkins, P. C. (2004). Gratitude and subjective well-being. In R. A. Emmons & M. E. McCullough (Eds.), *The psychology of gratitude* (pp. 167–192). New York: Oxford University Press.

Watkins, P. C. (2008). *The psychology of gratitude.* New York: Oxford University Press.

Watkins, P. C., Woodward, K., Stone, T., & Kolts, R. L. (2003). Gratitude and happiness: Development of a measure of gratitude, and relationships with subjective well-being. *Social Behavior and Personality, 31*, 431–452.

Watson, D., & Clark, L. A. (1995). Depression and the melancholic temperament. *European Journal of Personality, 9*, 351–366.

Weissman, M., Sholomskas, D., Pottenger, M., Prusoff, B., & Locke, B. Z. (1977). Assessing depressive symptoms in five psychiatric populations: A validation study. *American Journal of Epidemiology, 106*, 203–214.

Wood, A. M., Joseph, S., & Maltby, J. (2008a). Gratitude uniquely predicts satisfaction with life: Incremental validity above the domains and facets of the five factor model. *Personality and Individual Differences, 45*, 49–54.

Wood, A. M., Maltby, J., Stewart, N., & Joseph, S. (2008b). Conceptualizing gratitude and appreciation as a unitary personality trait. *Personality and individual differences, 44*, 619–630.

Reading Questions

1. The authors describe a prior study from 2009 that two of the authors conducted. What do they describe as the weaknesses of the study that they wanted to improve upon in this study?

2. Some of the results in this study were similar to the 2009 study, and some of the results were different. Choose one result that was similar and one that was different, and describe what the two studies found.

Rhetoric Questions

3. The article includes a section titled "Limitations and Future Directions." Why do you think the authors include that section? What purpose does it serve in the article?

4. "Section 6.2: Procedure" describes what the researchers and participants did in detail. Why would the authors include such a detailed description? What questions did you still have about the procedure after reading that section?

Response Questions

5. Have you written a letter of gratitude before? If you were going to write a letter of gratitude to someone, who would you write to and what would you say?

6. Were the results of the study surprising to you in any way? Why or why not?

Mapping Visual Symbols onto Spoken Language along the Ventral Visual Stream

J. S. H. TAYLOR, MATTHEW H. DAVIS, AND KATHLEEN RASTLE

This article was written by a team of three scientists from different universities in the United Kingdom. In their article, which appeared in *Proceedings for the National Academy of Sciences* (*PNAS*), the research team shares the results of a study that examined readers' brain activity through the use of fMRIs (functional magnetic resonance imaging) as they constructed meaning from written texts. The researchers' findings "advance our understanding of how the brain comprehends language from arbitrary visual symbols."

ABSTRACT

Reading involves transforming arbitrary visual symbols into sounds and meanings. This study interrogated the neural representations in ventral occipitotemporal cortex (vOT) that support this transformation process. Twenty-four adults learned to read 2 sets of 24 novel words that shared phonemes and semantic categories but were written in different artificial orthographies. Following 2 wk of training, participants read the trained words while neural activity was measured with functional MRI. Representational similarity analysis on item pairs from the same orthography revealed that right vOT and posterior regions of left vOT were sensitive to basic visual similarity. Left vOT encoded letter identity and representations became more invariant to position along a posterior-to-anterior hierarchy. Item pairs that shared sounds or meanings, but were written in different orthographies with no letters in common, evoked similar neural patterns in anterior left vOT. These results reveal a hierarchical, posterior-to-anterior gradient in vOT, in which representations of letters become increasingly invariant to position and are transformed to convey spoken language information.

Keywords: orthography, fMRI, representation, learning, reading

Reading acquisition requires the brain to abstract away from the visual forms of written words to access spoken language information. This abstraction

Author contributions: J.S.H.T., M.H.D., and K.R. designed research; J.S.H.T. performed research; J.S.H.T. analyzed data; and J.S.H.T., M.H.D., and K.R. wrote the paper.

The authors declare no conflict of interest.

requires encoding distinctive information about each visual symbol (e.g., "d" has a circle to the left, and "b" has a circle to the right), but in a way that permits recognition irrespective of variations in case, font, size (1, 2), or position in a word (e.g., the b in Cab is the same as the B in Bad) (3). For skilled readers, this process culminates in an inextricable link between the perception of a word's visual form and the stored linguistic knowledge it represents (4). The current study delineates how representations along the ventral visual stream support this transformation.

Neuroimaging research suggests that abstraction away from veridical visual form in reading is achieved by left ventral occipitotemporal cortex (vOT). Neural priming effects are observed in this region for cross-case (e.g., rage–RAGE) and location-shifted (e.g., #RAGE–RAGE#) written word pairs (5, 6). Patterns of activity across voxels in left vOT are also more similar for pairs of letters with the same abstract identity (e.g., R and r) than for letter pairs sharing visual, phonological, or motoric features (7). Dehaene et al. (8) proposed that, from posterior-to-anterior left vOT, neural representations become increasingly invariant to retinal location and encode increasingly complex orthographic information. Supporting this, along this axis, left vOT shows a gradient of selectivity for the word likeness of written forms (9). Representations in middle-to-anterior left vOT also appear to be sensitive to higher-level language information (10–12). For example, this region shows masked neural priming effects for word–picture pairs that have the same spoken form and represent the same concept (e.g., a picture of a lion primed the word LION, and vice versa; ref. 13). However, while existing research implicates the left vOT in encoding important information during reading, the nature of the representations that support this process are not well specified.

The current study used representational similarity analysis (RSA) of brain responses measured with functional MRI (fMRI) to delineate how the vOT processing stream encodes information about written words to support computation of higher-level language information. In particular, we sought to uncover how vOT represents letter identity and position, and the extent to which representations along this pathway come to capture word sounds and meanings. To do so, we trained participants for 2 wk to read 2 sets of pseudowords constructed from 2 different artificial orthographies. Each item had a distinct meaning and comprised 4 symbols, 3 representing the pseudoword phonemes and a final silent symbol. Phonemes and semantic categories were shared between the 2 orthographies and, for each participant, one orthography had a systematic mapping between the final symbol of each word and the word's semantic category (see *SI Appendix*, *SI Methods* for details). This allowed us to manipulate word form, sound, and meaning (Fig. 1) in a manner that would be hard to achieve in natural languages (however, see refs. 12 and 14). Following training, we examined the multivoxel patterns of fMRI responses (for an illustration of this method, see ref. 7) evoked when participants covertly retrieved the meanings of

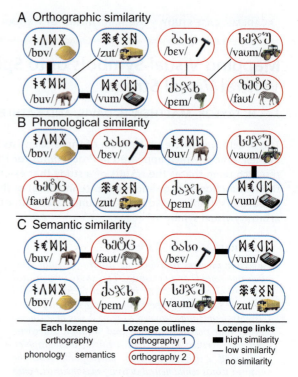

Figure 1. Schematic of 3 possible similarity structures between a subset of the trained words. Each lozenge contains the orthographic, phonological, and semantic form of an item, with items from one orthography in blue lozenges, and those from the other in red lozenges. A thicker line between pairs indicates greater similarity. (A) Orthographic similarity reflects the number of symbols (out of 4) shared in the same position, although analyses also examined symbols shared across positions. (B) Phonological similarity reflects the number of phonemes (out of 3) shared in the same position. (C) Semantic similarity reflects shared semantic category. Note that phonological and semantic similarity analyses excluded within-orthography pairs, and so were not confounded by orthographic similarity.

Significance

Learning to read is the most important milestone in a child's education. However, controversies remain regarding how readers' brains transform written words into sounds and meanings. We address these by combining artificial language learning with neuroimaging to reveal how the brain represents written words. Participants learned to read new words written in 2 different alphabets. Following 2 wk of training, we found a hierarchy of brain areas that support reading. Letter position is represented more flexibly from lower to higher visual regions. Furthermore, higher visual regions encode information about word sounds and meanings. These findings advance our understanding of how the brain comprehends language from arbitrary visual symbols.

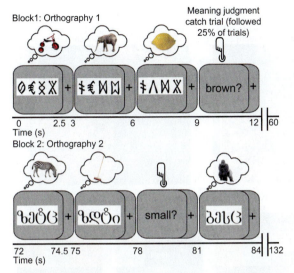

Block1: Orthography 1

Meaning judgment catch trial (followed 25% of trials)

Block 2: Orthography 2

Figure 2. The fMRI scanning procedures. Participants viewed and covertly retrieved the meanings of the trained words while neural activity was measured with fMRI (acquisition/repetition time 2 s). The 2 orthographies were presented in alternating 60-s blocks, and each item (*n* = 24 per orthography) was presented 16 times across four 15-min runs.

the newly learned written words (see Fig. 2 for scanning paradigm). Our analyses (see Fig. 3 for predicted models of similarity) sought to determine whether and how representations in vOT capture the separate orthographic, phonological, and semantic similarity across newly learned words.

RESULTS

Reading Artificial Orthographies Evokes Extensive Activity in vOT (Fig. 4). Following 9 d of training on the new words written in the 2 orthographies, 24 native English-speaking adults gave correct meanings for 92% (SD = 16%) of items and correct pronunciations for 86% (SD = 22%) of items (all results collapsed across the 2 orthographies; no significant differences between them). They also pronounced 79% (SD = 33%) of untrained items correctly, indicating extraction of individual symbol–sound mappings (see also ref. 15). Furthermore, trained items (mean response time 1,731 ms, SD = 592 ms) were read faster than untrained items (2,716 ms,

SD = 988 ms, $t[22] = 6.05, P < 0.001$), mirroring reading speeds for words versus pseudowords in familiar orthographies such as English, and replicating previous work using artificial orthographies (16, 17).

Fig. 4A (*SI Appendix*, Table S1) shows significant activation of bilateral occipitotemporal cortices, bilateral inferior and superior parietal cortices, left inferior frontal and precentral gyri, and the supplementary motor area, when participants covertly read the learned words. Activation was assessed relative to the unmodeled resting baseline, excluding meaning judgment catch trials, during scanning runs that took place after the last day of training. As in previous work with artificial orthographies (17), these regions closely correspond to those activated when adults read words written in natural alphabetic languages (18). Subsequent analyses focus on six 4-mm-radius spherical regions of interest (ROIs) in bilateral vOT (Fig. 4B). From posterior to anterior, the ROIs were located in inferior occipital cortex/lingual gyrus (ROI 1), fusiform gyrus/inferior occipital cortex (ROI 2), inferior occipital cortex (ROI 3), and inferior temporal gyrus (ROIs 4 to 6) (anatomical labels were generated by MRICron; ref. 19, based on ref. 20). These ROIs were selected a priori from published literature showing increasingly selective responses to word-like stimuli from posterior-to-anterior vOT (9).

Posterior and Right vOT Neural Response Patterns Are Sensitive to Basic Visual Similarity (Fig. 5). We first determined whether vOT representations of newly learned words are sensitive to their low-level visual similarity. We constructed a visual dissimilarity matrix (predicted DSM) using the simple cell representations (s1 layer) from the Hierarchical Model and X (HMAX) model of visual object recognition, which comprises Gabor filters of varying orientation and size (ref. 21; see also ref. 22). This visual DSM was computed as 1 minus the Pearson correlation between the s1 layer representations for all word pairs from within the same orthography (Fig. 3A). We computed a neural DSM, the voxel-wise dissimilarity (1 minus the Pearson correlation) between responses to all within-orthography word pairs in searchlights across the whole brain. We

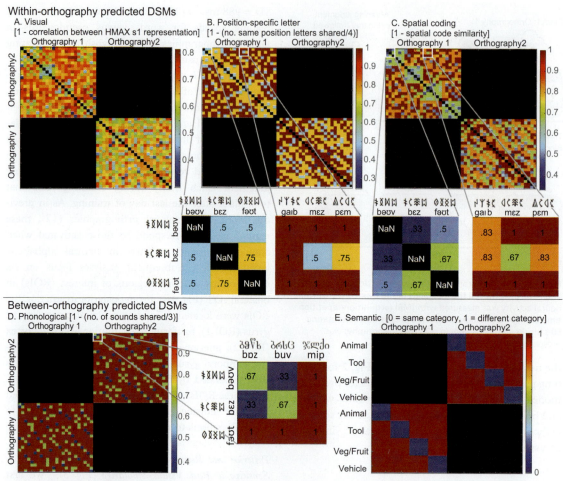

Figure 3. Predicted dissimilarity matrices for the learned words based on (*A*) 1 minus correlation between s1 layer representations from the HMAX model, (*B*) 1 minus proportion of shared same-position letters, (*C*) 1 minus spatial coding similarity, in which the similarity between item pairs is graded according to the distance in position between shared letters, (*D*) 1 minus proportion of shared same-position phonemes, and (*E*) shared (0) or not shared (1) semantic category. *A–C* included only within-orthography pairs, since items written in different orthographies share no letters. *D* and *E* included only between-orthography pairs to ensure that effects were specific to shared sounds or meanings, not shared letters. Note that the assignment of orthography to phonological forms and meanings was counterbalanced across participants; therefore, the visual and semantic predicted DSMs shown are those used for half of the participants (*SI Appendix, SI Methods*). The Spearman correlations among the within-orthography DSMs are visual and position-specific letter DSMs (*r* = 0.53, *r* = 0.51, for each half of the participants), visual and spatial coding DSMs (*r* = 0.48, *r* = 0.43), and position-specific letter and spatial coding DSMs (*r* = 0.86).

then conducted a Spearman correlation between the predicted DSM and neural DSM (see *SI Appendix*, Fig. S1 and Table S2 for whole-brain results). The mean correlations for each participant were extracted from vOT ROIs using MarsBaR (see also ref. 23) and

submitted to second-level one-sample *t* tests to identify ROIs in which the correlation was greater than zero. The visual DSM was positively correlated with the neural response patterns in all right-hemisphere vOT ROIs except the most anterior, but only in the 2 most posterior

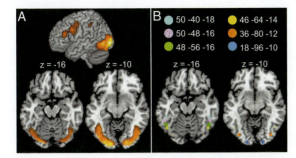

Figure 4. (*A*) Univariate activation during reading of trained words, *P* < 0.001 uncorrected, *P* < 0.05 familywise error cluster extent corrected. (*B*) Location of 4-mm-radius spherical vOT ROIs taken from ref. 9.

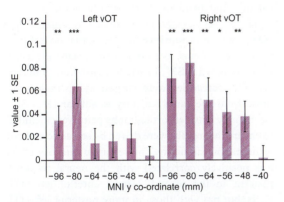

Figure 5. Correlations between the neural and visual DSM in left- and right-hemisphere ROIs, from posterior to anterior vOT along the *x* axis. MNI *y* coordinates express the distance in millimeters from the anterior commissure to the center of each ROI in Fig. 4*B*. Asterisks denote whether second-level one-sample *t* tests in each ROI indicated a significantly greater than zero correlation (one-tailed *t* test, ***P < 0.001, **P < 0.01, *P < 0.05). SE bars are appropriate for these one-sample *t* tests.

left-hemisphere vOT ROIs. Fig. 5 and *SI Appendix*, Table S5 show this posterior and right-hemisphere distribution of sensitivity to basic visual form, which was confirmed with an ANOVA that obtained main effects of hemisphere, $F(1, 23) = 5.12$, $P = 0.03$, $\eta^2 = 0.02$, and region, $F(3.50, 80.54) = 8.17$, $P < 0.001$, $\eta^2 = 0.09$, with no interaction between them, $F(3.17, 72.84) < 1$ (Greenhouse Geisser correction applied where Mauchly's test indicated that the assumption of sphericity was violated).

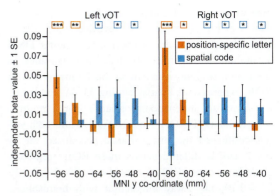

Figure 6. Results of a simultaneous multiple regression analysis examining the independent variance in the neural DSM accounted for by the position-specific letter and spatial coding DSMs. Left- and right-hemisphere ROIs go from posterior to anterior vOT along the *x* axis. Red and blue bars show the mean independent beta value for the position-specific letter and spatial coding DSMs. Asterisks denote whether second-level one-sample *t* tests on the resulting beta values for each predicted DSM in each ROI were significantly greater than zero (one-tailed *t* test, ***P < 0.001, **P < 0.01, *P < 0.05). SE bars are appropriate for these one-sample *t* tests.

Letter Representations Are More Invariant across Position in Anterior than Posterior vOT (Fig. 6). We computed a position-specific letter DSM (Fig. 3*B*) as 1 minus the proportion of same-position letters shared between all within-orthography word pairs, and a more position-invariant letter DSM (Fig. 3*C*), in which the similarity between items pairs is graded according to the distance in position between shared letters (spatial coding model; ref. 3). These were both correlated with the neural response patterns in all 6 ROIs in left and right vOT (*SI Appendix*, Fig. S1 and Tables S3–S5). While results from the visual DSM suggest that representations in right and posterior left vOT reflect aspects of visual form, these analyses suggest that left midanterior vOT represents a word's component letters.

We next investigated whether letter representations become more invariant to position along the vOT processing hierarchy. We conducted a multiple regression analysis (see *SI Appendix*, *SI Results* for justification) in searchlights across the whole brain, including both the position-specific and spatial coding DSMs as predictors, and extracted the independent beta values for each model from the vOT ROIs. As shown in Fig. 6, this analysis revealed that, in both left and right vOT, the position-specific letter DSM accounted for significant independent variance in the neural response patterns in the 2 most posterior ROIs, whereas the spatial coding DSM accounted for significant independent variance in the middle-to-anterior vOT ROIs. An ANOVA on the beta values confirmed that the variance accounted for by the 2 DSMs differed across these ROIs (region × DSM interaction, $F[2.80, 64.40] = 13.60, P < 0.001, \eta^2 = 0.13$; no 3-way interaction with hemisphere, $F[2.74, 63.07] = 2.26, P = 0.096$). These results suggest that the representation of letter identity is tied to information about letter position in bilateral posterior vOT but not in bilateral midanterior vOT, and that spatial coding provides one candidate model for characterizing how the position of letters within words is represented in these more anterior vOT regions (see *SI Appendix, SI Results* for an alternative open-bigram coding model).

Middle-to-Anterior vOT Response Patterns Capture Phonological and Semantic Similarity (Fig. 7). Our final analyses examined whether the vOT processing hierarchy encodes the phonological and semantic

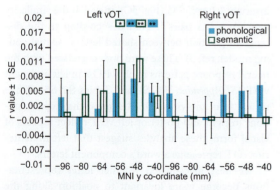

Figure 7. Correlations between the neural and phonological (cyan) and semantic (white) DSMs in left- and right-hemisphere ROIs, from posterior to anterior vOT along the *x* axis. Asterisks denote whether second-level one-sample *t* tests in each ROI indicated a significantly greater than zero correlation (one-tailed *t* test, **$P < 0.01$, *$P < 0.05$). SE bars are appropriate for these one-sample *t* tests.

properties of written words. We used a phonological predicted DSM, computed as 1 minus the proportion of same-position phonemes shared between item pairs (Fig. 3*D*). Crucially, this included only between-orthography pairs, such that similarity was based on shared phonemes for items that shared no letters. Second-level one-sample *t* tests demonstrated a significant correlation between the phonological DSM and neural response patterns in the 2 most anterior left vOT ROIs, but not with those in more posterior left vOT ROIs or right-hemisphere ROIs (Fig. 7, whole-brain searchlight results in *SI Appendix*, Fig. S3 and Table S7). Thus, neural representations in left inferior temporal gyrus reflect information about phonological form, independent of orthographic form.

Neural representations in middle-to-anterior left vOT were also sensitive to the semantic similarity between items. We computed a semantic category predicted DSM, in which items from different semantic categories were classed as dissimilar and those from the same category as similar (Fig. 3*E*). Again, only between-orthography pairs were included to ensure that results were driven by semantic and not orthographic similarity. The semantic category DSM was positively correlated with the neural response patterns in the second 2 most anterior left vOT ROIs, but not with those in more posterior left vOT ROIs or right-hemisphere ROIs (Fig. 7, whole-brain searchlight results in *SI Appendix*, Fig. S3 and Table S8). Thus, left inferior temporal gyrus also encoded semantic information about the newly learned words.

DISCUSSION

Reading requires the brain to map visual information onto language information. Research suggests that the ventral visual stream plays a key role in this process, but the nature of the representations that underpin this transformation remain unspecified. Using RSA, we demonstrated that, whereas right vOT and left posterior inferior occipital cortex represent written words in terms of their low-level visual form, left middle-to-anterior vOT represents words in terms of their letters. Furthermore, these orthographic representations become progressively more abstract along the posterior-to-anterior processing hierarchy. The response patterns indicated that information about letter identity is more invariant across position in anterior inferior occipital cortex and inferior temporal gyrus than in posterior inferior occipital cortex. Transformation away from veridical visual form was even greater in midanterior left inferior temporal gyrus, where representations were sensitive to shared sounds and semantic categories of words written in different orthographies. Our research thus demonstrates how the ventral stream transforms visual inputs to meaningful linguistic information, and reveals the representations that make this possible.

Substantial research in cognitive psychology has sought to specify the nature of the orthographic codes that support visual word recognition (24). Various computational models consider the challenge of mapping retinotopically organized visual information onto location-invariant orthographic representations that specify within-word letter position, for example using spatial (3) or open bigram (24, 25) coding. Our results provide support for these cognitive models. Neural patterns in middle-to-anterior vOT were better characterized by spatial coding than by position-specific letter coding, and a supplementary analysis also showed this to be true for open-bigram relative to position-specific coding. However, while position-specific letter coding characterized response patterns in posterior vOT better than spatial (or open-bigram) coding, neural responses in these regions could also be accounted for by a visual model (21). These data therefore support cognitive models in suggesting that location specificity gives way to more location-invariant representations at hierarchically higher levels of the ventral processing stream (*SI Appendix*, *SI Discussion*). However, further work is necessary to determine exactly how this location invariance is achieved (whether by multiletter representations or something more akin to spatial coding) and, more broadly, to examine whether and where vOT representations of written words are better characterized by these visual word recognition models than by generic models of visual processing, such as HMAX (21, 26).

Location-invariant letter coding (a hallmark of skilled reading; ref. 25) is critical for establishing the mapping between written and spoken language because it allows each experience of a letter to converge on the same spoken language representation. The observation that neural response patterns were similar for words that shared sounds, despite sharing no letters, indicates that phonological information shapes representations in mid-anterior regions of the left vOT hierarchy. One interpretation of this result is that representations in this part of the left vOT processing pathway are phonological. However, an intriguing alternative is that this result reflects the emergence of abstract letter identities (ALIs) for symbols from the 2 orthographies that correspond to the same sound. The existence of such ALIs is supported by studies of cross-case (e.g., rage–RAGE) and cross-script (e.g., Japanese Kanji–Kana) similarity using behavioral (1, 2, 27) and neural (5–7, 28) measures (although the orthographic nature of cross-script effects is still debated; refs. 29). By this account, phonology is not represented in left vOT, but nonetheless plays a crucial role in shaping the abstract orthographic representations in this region, since it is shared sounds that bind together these cross-script visual forms.

An overlapping region of left midanterior vOT encoded information about the meanings of the words, showing similar neural response patterns for item pairs that were from the same semantic category, but shared no letters. This finding is in line with previous neuroimaging studies (11, 12) and with the view that the ventral reading pathway maps from word form to meaning (18). By examining the full vOT hierarchy and disentangling orthographic, phonological, and semantic similarity, we have shown that, even with relatively little experience of a writing system, left midanterior vOT representations capture the spoken language associations of written words. Further research should establish whether phonological and semantic information is intrinsically represented in this region, or whether these aspects of spoken language shape organization of orthographic representations through interactions with other brain areas (30). It will also be important to specify how linguistic influences on vOT change over time; both in the short term while reading a word (10, 13) and during the long process of reading development (31).

In summary, our study provides strong empirical support for a hierarchical, posterior-to-anterior gradient in vOT that represents increasingly abstract information about written words. In line with Dehaene et al.'s (8) proposal, we found that representations in posterior visual regions are tied to location and may encode low-level visual information, whereas letter identity was represented in left midanterior vOT with a degree of location invariance. These location-invariant letter representations are then further transformed in left midanterior vOT to encode aspects of a word's pronunciation and meaning. These results contribute to our understanding of how the brain maps from arbitrary visual symbols to rich linguistic representations, ultimately enabling the experience of language through the visual modality.

METHODS

Materials and datasets are available at refs. 32 and 33.

Participants. Twenty-four native English-speaking students (19 females) aged 18 to 30 y from Royal Holloway University of London (RHUL) participated. Participants were right-handed with no history of learning disabilities or hearing or vision impairments. RHUL Ethics Committee approved the research. Participants signed an informed consent form, and were paid for participation.

Stimuli and Behavioral Training. Over 9 sessions, participants learned to read 2 sets of 24 consonant–vowel–consonant pseudowords written in 2 different unfamiliar alphabets and assigned an English common noun meaning. Each item comprised 4 symbols; 3 corresponding to the pseudoword phonemes, and a final silent symbol. Training tasks required mapping between written form and sound or meaning (see *SI Appendix, SI Methods* for details).

MRI Scanning Procedure. After behavioral training, participants completed eight 15-min fMRI scanning runs over 2 d. Runs alternated between visual (orthographic forms) and auditory (phonological forms) presentation of the words. Only visual runs are reported here (paradigm shown in Fig. 2). Visual stimuli were projected onto a screen at the rear end of the scanner bore and viewed via a mirror mounted on the head coil. Each stimulus was 320×112 pixels presented at a distance of 77 cm giving an image of $6.30 \times 2.20°$ visual angle. In each visual run, the orthographic form of each trained item was presented 4 times, with the order of item presentation and repetition randomized within run. On each trial, participants were instructed to think about the item's meaning. Catch trials followed 25% of trials (one per item) and presented a single word question on the screen (small?, dangerous?, heavy?, long?, Britain?). Participants used a button box to respond YES or NO with respect to the previous item. Performance was 84% correct (SD = 13%). Trials were 2,500 ms, with a 500-ms intertrial interval. Runs were split into 20 trial blocks (16 standard, 4 catch), alternating between the 2 orthographies. Blocks were separated by a 12-s rest period (blank screen). After the first 5 participants, we decided to monitor attention during scanning. Therefore, for participant 6 onward, after blocks 1, 4, 7, and 10, participants saw a feedback screen that read "100% – well done!", or "25/50/75% – oops try and concentrate!," indicating the percentage of catch trials on which they had responded. Functional imaging acquisition parameters and preprocessing details are given in *SI Appendix, SI Methods*.

fMRI Analyses. Smoothed, normalized functional images were used for univariate analyses, whereas, for multivariate analyses, we used unsmoothed native-space images. For both analyses, regressors were included to model the 6 movement parameters and the mean for each run, with rest blocks providing an implicit baseline. For univariate analyses, additional regressors were included for standard and catch trials, as well as feedback trials for participants 6 to 24. Contrast images from the first-level model (average of all standard trials) were entered into a second-level one-sample t test, using participants as a random effect. For multivariate analyses, for each run, separate regressors were included for each trained item

($n = 48$), plus a regressor of no interest that included catch trials, as well as feedback trials for participants 6 to 24. T-statistic maps were generated for the contrast of each item in each run relative to the unmodeled rest period, creating 192 statistical maps. As T maps combine the effect size weighted by error variance for a modeled response, they provide high-classification accuracy in multivariate analyses, since results are not unduly influenced by large, but highly variable, response estimates (34).

Searchlight RSA was conducted on these T maps using the CoSMoMVPA toolbox (35). First, a mean T map was generated for each item, collapsed across run. Using spherical searchlights with a radius of 3 voxels (minimum 2 voxels per searchlight), data were extracted from gray-matter masked (voxels with >0.01 gray matter probability) native-space T maps. A neural DSM was then constructed for each searchlight, in which each cell represents 1 minus the Pearson product moment correlation between the voxel-wise T statistic for each pair of items. For each searchlight, the Spearman rank correlation between the neural DSM and a set of predicted DSMs was calculated. The correlation between the predicted and neural DSM for each searchlight was converted to a z value using a Fisher transform, to conform to statistical assumptions (normality) required for second-level parametric tests. This Fisher-transformed correlation coefficient was then returned to the searchlight's central voxel. Whole-brain Fisher-transformed correlation maps were normalized to Montreal Neurological Institute (MNI) space using parameters estimated during the segmentation stage of preprocessing. Using these maps, second-level one-sample t tests identified voxels in which the correlation across participants between the predicted and neural DSM was greater than zero.

We also used multiple regression to assess the relative contribution of predicted DSMs to explaining variance in the neural DSM. This yields beta values at each searchlight location that express the independent variance in the neural DSM accounted for by each predicted DSM, independent of other predicted DSMs. Whole-brain beta-statistic maps were normalized to MNI space, and maps of beta values were submitted to second-level one-sample t tests to identify voxels in which the independent variance in the neural DSM accounted for by each predicted DSM was greater than zero.

ROI analyses were conducted in six 4-mm-radius spherical ROIs in left and right vOT based on ref. 9 (Fig. 4B). Mean correlation/beta values in these ROIs were extracted from whole-brain searchlight maps using MarsBaR (36). Second-level one-sample t tests were used to identify ROIs in which the correlation/ independent beta value was greater than zero.

We used 3 predicted DSMs to test models of visual word form representation. Each included only within-orthography pairs, since no letters are shared between the 2 orthographies. The visual DSM used HMAX simple-cell representations (s1 layer; ref. 21, see also ref. 22), which were generated for the greyscale image of each item (source code at http:// maxlab.neuro.georgetown.edu/hmax.html#updated). These are simulated by Gabor filters of 4 orientations (0°, 90°, –45°, 45°) and 16 sizes (7 to 37 pixels), yielding 64 simple cell maps, which were vectorized and concatenated to form a representational vector for each item. Dissimilarity was computed as 1 minus the Pearson correlation between the vectors for each item pair. The position- specific letter DSM was computed as 1 minus the proportion of letters shared in the same position for each item pair. For example, ⵟⵛⵯⵏ /bɛz/ and ⵟⵊⵯⵏ /bəʊv/ share 2/4 letters, whereas ⵟⵛⵯⵏ /bɛz/ and ⵀⵊⵊⵏ /fəʊt/ share 1/4 letters. In the spatial coding DSM, the similarity between item pairs was graded according to the distance in position between shared letters, with additional weighting for shared beginning and/or end letters, with similarity values generated using Match Calculator (http://www.pc.rhul.ac.uk/staff/c .davis/utilities/matchcalc/index.htm). For example, ⵟⵊⵯⵏ /bəʊv/ and ⵍⵛⵟⵏ /pɛb/ have a similarity of 0.38, whereas ⵟⵊⵯⵏ /bəʊv/ and ⵟⵛⵯⵏ /bɛz/ have a similarity of 0.67, since /b/ is in a different position in the first pair but in the same position in the second. Dissimilarity was expressed as 1 minus these similarity values.

We also tested models of phonological and seman- 25 tic similarity. Only between-orthography item pairs were included, to ensure results were independent of orthographic similarity. The phonological DSM was computed as 1 minus the proportion of same-position phonemes shared. For example, ⵣⵣⵍⵍ /bəʊv/ and ষ৩৬ /buv/ share 2/3 phonemes. The semantic DSM had values of zero for item pairs from the same semantic category, and 1 for pairs from different categories.

ACKNOWLEDGMENTS

Funding for this work was provided by the Economic and Social Research Council (ES/L002264/1) and the Medical Research Council (SUAG/008 RG91365).

REFERENCES

[1] J. S. Bowers, Different perceptual codes support priming for words and pseudowords: Was Morton right all along? *J. Exp. Psychol. Learn. Mem. Cogn.* **22**, 1336–1353 (1996).

[2] J. S. Bowers, In defense of abstractionist theories of repetition priming and word identification. *Psychon. Bull. Rev.* **7**, 83–99 (2000).

[3] C. J. Davis, The spatial coding model of visual word identification. *Psychol. Rev.* **117**, 713–758 (2010).

[4] M. S. Seidenberg, Language at the Speed of Sight: *How We Read, Why So Many Can't, and What Can Be Done about It* (Basic Books, 2017).

[5] S. Dehaene *et al.*, Cerebral mechanisms of word masking and unconscious repetition priming. *Nat. Neurosci.* **4**, 752–758 (2001).

[6] S. Dehaene et al., Letter binding and invariant recognition of masked words: Behavioral and neuroimaging evidence. *Psychol. Sci.* **15**, 307–313 (2004).

[7] D. Rothlein, B. Rapp, The similarity structure of distributed neural responses reveals the multiple representations of letters. *Neuroimage* **89**, 331–344 (2014).

[8] S. Dehaene, L. Cohen, M. Sigman, F. Vinckier, The neural code for written words: A proposal. *Trends Cogn. Sci.* **9**, 335–341 (2005).

[9] F. Vinckier et al., Hierarchical coding of letter strings in the ventral stream: Dissecting the inner organization of the visual word-form system. *Neuron* **55**, 143–156 (2007).

[10] C. J. Price, J. T. Devlin, The interactive account of ventral occipitotemporal contributions to reading. *Trends Cogn. Sci.* **15**, 246–253 (2011).

[11] M. M. Rundle, D. Coch, A. C. Connolly, R. H. Granger, Dissociating frequency and animacy effects in visual word processing: An fMRI study. *Brain Lang.* **183**, 54–63 (2018).

[12] S. Fischer-Baum, D. Bruggemann, I. F. Gallego, D. S. P. Li, E. R. Tamez, Decoding levels of representation in reading: A representational similarity approach. *Cortex* **90**, 88–102 (2017).

[13] F. Kherif, G. Josse, C. J. Price, Automatic top-down processing explains common left occipito-temporal responses to visual words and objects. Cereb. *Cortex* **21**, 103–114 (2011).

[14] L. Zhao et al., Orthographic and phonological representations in the fusiform cortex. *Cereb. Cortex* **27**, 5197–5210 (2017).

[15] J. S. H. Taylor, K. Plunkett, K. Nation, The influence of consistency, frequency, and semantics on learning to read: An artificial orthography paradigm. *J. Exp. Psychol. Learn. Mem. Cogn.* **37**, 60–76 (2011).

[16] J. S. H. Taylor, K. Rastle, M. H. Davis, Distinct neural specializations for learning to read words and name objects. *J. Cogn. Neurosci.* **26**, 2128–2154 (2014).

[17] J. S. H. Taylor, M. H. Davis, K. Rastle, Comparing and validating methods of reading instruction using behavioural and neural findings in an artificial orthography. *J. Exp. Psychol. Gen.* **146**, 826–858 (2017).

[18] J. S. H. Taylor, K. Rastle, M. H. Davis, Can cognitive models explain brain activation during word and pseudoword reading? A meta-analysis of 36 neuroimaging studies. *Psychol. Bull.* **139**, 766–791 (2013).

[19] C. Rorden, H.-O. Karnath, L. Bonilha, Improving lesion-symptom mapping. *J. Cogn. Neurosci.* **19**, 1081–1088 (2007).

[20] N. Tzourio-Mazoyer et al., Automated anatomical labeling of activations in SPM using a macroscopic anatomical parcellation of the MNI MRI single-subject brain. *Neuroimage* **15**, 273–289 (2002).

[21] T. Serre, L. Wolf, S. Bileschi, M. Riesenhuber, T. Poggio, Robust object recognition with cortex-like mechanisms. *IEEE Trans. Pattern Anal. Mach. Intell.* **29**, 411–426 (2007).

[22] N. Kriegeskorte, M. Mur, P. Bandettini, Representational similarity analysis–Connecting the branches of systems neuroscience. *Front. Syst. Neurosci.* **2**, 4 (2008).

[23] H. Blank, M. H. Davis, Prediction errors but not sharpened signals simulate multivoxel fMRI patterns during speech perception. *PLoS Biol.* **14**, e1002577 (2016).

[24] J. Grainger, W. van Heuven, "Modeling letter position coding in printed word perception" in *The Mental Lexicon*, P. Bonin, Ed. (Nova Science Publishers, New York, NY, 2003), pp. 1–24.

[25] J. Grainger, Orthographic processing: A 'mid-level' vision of reading: The 44th Sir Frederic Bartlett Lecture. *Q. J. Exp. Psychol. (Hove)* **71**, 335–359 (2018).

[26] M. Riesenhuber, T. Poggio, Hierarchical models of object recognition in cortex. *Nat. Neurosci.* **2**, 1019–1025 (1999).

[27] J. S. Bowers, Y. Michita, An investigation into the structure and acquisition of orthographic knowledge: Evidence from cross-script Kanji-Hiragana priming. *Psychon. Bull. Rev.* **5**, 259–264 (1998).

[28] L. Pylkkänen, K. Okano, The nature of abstract orthographic codes: Evidence from masked priming and magnetoencephalography. *PLoS One* **5**, e10793 (2010).

[29] K. Nakamura, S. Dehaene, A. Jobert, D. Le Bihan, S. Kouider, Subliminal convergence of Kanji and Kana words: Further evidence for functional parcellation of the posterior temporal cortex in visual word perception. *J. Cogn. Neurosci.* **17**, 954–968 (2005).

[30] F. Bouhali et al., Anatomical connections of the visual word form area. J. Neurosci. **34**, 15402–15414 (2014).

[31] T. Hannagan, A. Amedi, L. Cohen, G. Dehaene-Lambertz, S. Dehaene, Origins of the specialization for letters and numbers in ventral occipitotemporal cortex. *Trends Cogn. Sci.* **19**, 374–382 (2015).

[32] J. Taylor, M. H. Davis, K. Rastle, Mapping visual symbols onto spoken language along the ventral visual stream. Open Science Framework. https://osf.io/fxy7j/. Deposited 15 March 2019.

[33] J. Taylor, M. H. Davis, K. Rastle. Mapping visual symbols onto spoken language along the ventral visual stream.NeuroVault.https://neurovault.org/collections/4882/. Deposited 15 March 2019.

[34] M. Misaki, Y. Kim, P. A. Bandettini, N. Kriegeskorte, Comparison of multivariate classifiers and response normalizations for pattern-information fMRI. Neuroimage **53**, 103–118 (2010).

[35] N. N. Oosterhof, A. C. Connolly, J. V. Haxby, CoSMoMVPA: Multi-modal multivariate pattern analysis of neuroimaging data in Matlab/GNU Octave. *Front. Neuroinform.* **10**, 27 (2016).

[36] M. Brett, J.-L. Anton, R. Valabregue, J.-B. Poline, Region of interest analysis using an SPM toolbox. *NeuroImage* **16**, 1140 (2002).

Reading Questions

1. The article's introductory sections establish the context for the researchers' study. According to the researchers, what is the gap in the current scholarship on the topic that their study addresses?

2. Briefly describe the design of the researchers' experiment. As part of your description, comment on both the study's participants and the experimental methods the researchers employed.

3. What are the study's central findings? How are you able to determine this, based on your reading of the researchers' article?

4. According to the researchers, how do their study's findings support current cognitive models, and what recommendations do they offer for further research in this area?

Rhetoric Questions

5. Take a close look at the title of the article. What does the language use in the title tell you about who the authors imagine as their audience?

6. Briefly describe what you see as the researchers' strategy for reporting their findings. What organizational pattern do they use?

7. Choose one of the images included in the article and explain how it functions to provide clarity to the researchers' report.

Response Questions

8. The researchers rely on a lot of jargon in their research report. Although they often provide definitions for some of the specialized language they use, describe your

experience reading the article. How difficult was it for you to read, and what do you believe accounts for this difficulty?

9. For someone who is not a neuroscientist, what might be most interesting about this study? Imagine you are writing a short description (perhaps for Twitter) of what someone might find interesting about this study. What would you highlight?

Writing about Nursing Research: A Storytelling Approach

GAVIN FAIRBAIRN AND ALEX CARSON

Gavin Fairbairn is Professor of Health and Social Sciences at Leeds Metropolitan University, UK. He was previously Professor of Education at Liverpool Hope and Professor of Nursing and Midwifery at the University of Glamorgan. His research and publications focus on ethics and academic literacies. The article below, written with Alex Carson, a registered nurse and Senior Lecturer in Sociology and Ethics at North-East Wales Institute of Higher Education, argues in favor of using storytelling as a means of reporting research so that it can be read and understood by "the maximum possible number of people, whether they are nurses, policy makers, or colleagues in other healthcare professions." The article was published in 2002 in the journal *Nurse Researcher*.

> To learn more about nursing as an applied field of inquiry, see "Health Fields" in Chapter 10.

In this article, Gavin Fairbairn and Alex Carson argue that much of what is written by nurses is needlessly difficult, especially when it concerns research they have carried out. The authors make a positive contribution to the ways in which nurses think about what they write and how they write it, suggesting that one way in which things might become better would be for nurses to view their writing as a form of storytelling.

STORYTELLING AS RESEARCH METHODOLOGY

> To learn more about quantitative and qualitative research methods, see "Methods" in Chapter 8.

Stories sometimes feature in the methodology of nursing research, although many prefer to label them as "case studies" or "accounts" (Tilley 1995). However, narrative approaches are often sidelined. We all know why; it has to do with the ascendancy of methods drawn from, and sometimes caricaturing, the physical sciences. This is regrettable since stories have much to offer as a way of understanding. Even when storytelling methods are utilized, the boldness of researchers is often circumscribed by an acknowledgement that narratives can be seen as just another data-collection method (Crepeau 2000, McCance *et al* 2001). Different approaches have been adopted in the attempt to systematize the ways in which stories are gathered and analyzed. For example, Koch (1998) provides a conventional methodological structure for the use of storytelling, in the context of a discussion of whether storytelling is really research.

In our view it is regrettable that storytelling as a research method is often viewed merely as a way of gathering data to be manipulated in various ways, which probably involves cutting them up into little labelled specimens — themes and sub-themes — that can be sorted and counted and weighed. There is undoubtedly value, at times, in analyzing stories at the level of the concepts or words used. However, to treat stories in this way is to fail to respect the tellers of these stories. It is to fail to listen to their voices. It is to make the assumption that our interpretation of their experience is more valid than their telling of it. Our view of the place of storytelling in nursing research is that it should be viewed less as a method of collecting data, which requires systematic methods for analysis, and more as what it really is — a way of listening to and learning from each other. There are good reasons for this.

Fairbairn and Carson establish the topic of their report: the "problem" of storytelling as a research and reporting method.

Fairbairn and Carson establish their central claim. Read more about making claims in Chapter 4, "Making Claims."

Much of human life is conducted through story. Many of our social institutions are comprised almost entirely of opportunities for telling and retelling stories, for sharing the narratives that constitute our lives. Consider the questions: "How was work today?" and "How is the data collection going?" which invite stories in response, as do the questions: "How did you sleep last night?" "Have your bowels moved yet?" and "How are you feeling now?" Much of nursing involves telling and listening to stories of various kinds. Nurses listen to stories whenever patients tell them what is going on in their lives, and they also tell them every time they pass on information about patients.

Researchers in nursing undertake their work because they want to be able to tell more accurate and more helpful stories about how the world of nursing works. Indeed, there is a sense in which all research, regardless of the methods adopted, is concerned with telling stories about us and about the world. Of course, the stories nurse researchers tell are inhabited not by people, but by ideas, theories, questions, and suggestions about, for example, the ways in which patients can best be cared for and treated, which draw on research results. The plots for those stories develop through the research process — by formulating questions and methods for answering them, by gathering data and by attempting to make sense of it.

Fairbairn and Carson explore a number of reasons to reconsider the place of storytelling in nursing research. To more on this rhetorical strategy, see Chapter 4, "Supporting Reasons with Evidence."

In our view, the only real value of nursing research is the contribution it can 5 make to the development of nursing practice: in order that patients can be cared for and treated in more helpful, more beneficial ways. That is why we think that nursing researchers should try to write about their findings in such a way that the maximum possible number of people, whether they are nurses, policy makers or colleagues in other healthcare professions, are able to understand what they have to say.

WHY DO NURSING RESEARCHERS WRITE ABOUT THEIR WORK?

You may think that the answer to this question is obvious. For example, you may believe that their principal motivation is the wish to share their research

Fairbairn and Carson use headings to break their article into sections that focus on a main idea. This helps the reader see the shape of their argument in order to preview and review it.

findings and the ideas they have developed about theory and practice. These days, when emphasis is placed on the need to ensure that practice in health care is evidence-based as far as possible, you might even entertain the idea that most nurse researchers write about their findings in order to contribute to the body of available evidence, with the hope and expectation that their work can help to make the world a better place in which to be a patient. Of course, some of them probably do, at least some of the time. However, there are other, arguably less worthy agendas on the horizon. For example, the need to develop and maintain a research profile in order to gain promotion; the need to publish in the highly regarded (usually international, peer-reviewed) journals; and to be considered "Research active" in terms of the Research Assessment Exercise (RAE).

There are other less worthy reasons for academic writing, including the desire to give public displays of familiarity with accepted jargon, and with theories and research methods that are currently in vogue. This is likely to go hand-in-hand with the wish to demonstrate the ability to write in dense, difficult-to-decipher prose (Fairbairn 1996). You may find it hard to believe that there are any researchers in nursing who actually wish to be difficult in their writing. In that case we will have to agree to differ, because we entertain a significant degree of skepticism about whether much of what gets published in nursing journals is motivated primarily, or even at all, by the wish to communicate with others. Many researchers who in their everyday lives manage to talk in quite ordinary ways seem actively to cultivate a new and less understandable way of speaking, and to adopt a new language when they are writing. It is almost as if they believe that the academic enterprise is about confusing, rather than illuminating, and aimed at obfuscation, rather than clarity. This is just as true in nursing as it is in any other discipline.

SURROUNDING YOURSELF WITH AN AURA OF INTELLECTUAL PROWESS AND ERUDITION: SOME TIPS

Of course, obfuscation and a lack of clarity can be useful. For one thing, if you manage to achieve the right degree of tortured difficulty in the prose you adopt, you can prevent anyone really understanding what you are saying, and thus having the opportunity to criticize you. Not only that, but the more difficult your writing, the more chance you have of convincing your readers that what you have to say is worthwhile, and the more clever you will appear to at least some of them. And so, if you want to look really clever as an author, you may wish to take note of some of the ways in which you can surround yourself with an aura of intellectual prowess and erudition.

1. First, choose your words carefully. For example, it is worth developing the habit of using big words where small ones would do, and difficult words

Fairbairn and Carson identify writing practices of nursing researchers that they believe obfuscate meaning and detract from their ability to communicate effectively: use of jargon, overuse of citations, and unnecessary references, as well as a lack of structure in reporting.

where possible, rather than where necessary; words like *obfuscation and erudition* (which respectively mean, "confusion" or "muddle" and "scholarship" or "sophistication").

In general it is best always to introduce difficult words without any expla- 10
nation as to their meaning. That way, readers who do not understand what you are talking about will assume that they are at fault and not you. It is particularly helpful to use jargon where ordinary language would convey meaning better. Doing so can see off potential critics, who may think they can detect flaws in what you say or perhaps a lack of rigor in your thinking, but be afraid to say so, because they do not speak the same language as you and fear the dreadful consequences of looking ignorant.

Notice the rather dramatic shift in tone that occurs here. Fairbairn and Carson are mocking the kind of "erudite" writing that, from their perspective, "obfuscates" meaning.

Using jargon from your own area of specialty helps to convey a sense of embeddedness in the tradition and values of your discipline. But it can be even more helpful to use jargon from other fields, for example, sociology or philosophy, in relation to which you can realistically expect that many of those who will read your work will be a little unsure and thus less likely to challenge you.

2. Next, it is worth attending to your use of referencing and citation. Cultivate the habit of making liberal use of references with no real reason for doing so — the more obscure the better. Doing so can help to give the impression of scholarship, because it suggests familiarity, not only with work by others that has actually influenced the way in which you have pursued your own research, but with a wider range of sources. "Dropping" the names of significant nursing researchers and theorists into your writing is especially helpful, because it signals your right to belong to the academic club of which you are a member, or of which you wish to become a member, because you can utter the names of the great and the famous.

Within every academic discipline there are authors that it is worth citing if you want to be taken seriously, and nursing is just like other disciplines in this regard. It is always helpful to refer to at least one of the major nurse theorists in your work, whatever it is about. Curiously though, you may do even better by citing a range of famously difficult theorists in, for example, philosophy and sociology, including Heidegger, Hegel, and Husserl, Derrida, Foucault, and Habermas, even if you haven't read them in detail (or even at all) and therefore cannot make substantive use of what they say.

3. Finally, it can be a really good idea if, in reporting your research, you adopt a style that is as devoid of structure as possible, so that your reader never quite knows where she is or where she is going, as she wanders around looking for something to understand. Even better is to confuse things further by avoiding structure while liberally sprinkling your work with apparent structural signposts, which actually mean nothing. For example, you might claim to offer an argument in favor of a conclusion, without actually doing so, or you may refer back to something you said earlier, even though you did not in fact say it.

The liberal use of words and phrases that seem to imply an argument or a logical train of thought is especially helpful, like *therefore, however, in contrast, finally, and of course*. However, if you adopt this tactic, you must assiduously avoid arguing and you must avoid the temptation to allow logic to enter the picture.

Consider the effect of Fairbairn and Carson acknowledging the severity of their own reactions to "obfuscatory and opaque" writing.

Perhaps we are guilty of painting an over-gloomy picture. Nonetheless, countless 15 academics write in the obfuscatory and opaque style we have been criticizing and unfortunately nursing researchers are not totally blameless in this regard. If you find yourself wanting to argue against our view, a quick browse through a few academic nursing journals should persuade you otherwise, provided you browse with an open mind. Try doing so while bearing in mind questions such as these: Is this as clear and coherent as it might be? Is it well structured and easy to follow? Are all of these references strictly necessary? Do they all add something? Even worse, a quick browse through some of nursing's professional periodicals ought to convince anyone who is willing to be convinced that opaqueness, over-referencing, and stylistic complexity is now acceptable even at the level of professional publication.

Notice the familiar, conversational tone established here. Consider how it contributes to the substance of the author's argument about the use of storytelling as a response to opaqueness.

ACADEMIC WRITING AS STORYTELLING

How could things become better? Well, one thing that could happen is that nursing could accept that it has no need to emphasize its seriousness as an academic discipline by promoting a style of writing among its writers and researchers that emulates other disciplines. Editors of nursing journals and periodicals could ensure that those who are permitted the privilege of publishing in its professional and academic press are expected to lay aside tortuous, over-referenced prose in favor of a more direct style. Of course, we are not the first authors to attempt to promote a more direct style of writing. For example, Webb (1992) has argued that the first person — in which the author appears as "I" — is appropriate at times. This is to be commended, though we think that use of the first person can be helpful in more contexts than Webb seems to consider appropriate.

In light of the authors' earlier comments on excessive referencing, consider the relevance and appropriateness of this reference. For more on paraphrasing, see "Paraphrasing" in Chapter 5.

Another way in which nurses could improve the ways in which they write about their research is by viewing their task in terms of storytelling. Researchers in nursing have stories to tell. In telling them they share information about how they came to their conclusions, about their methods and hypotheses, about the genealogy into which their work slots, its parentage and forebears and the quarrels it might have with alternative views.

Nursing researchers and different sub-groups within nursing not only have different areas of interest but different ways of telling stories. Some will employ visual means such as graphs and tables to show what they have found. Others will approach their storytelling in ways that do not lend themselves to the use of such visual supports. The stories nursing researchers tell may thus be told in different languages, or in different dialects of the same language. However, thinking of academic writing as a genre of storytelling is helpful in facilitating academic writers in developing their writing, regardless of their level of experience or the research methods they have adopted (Fairbairn 2000).

> Consider the ways in which academic writing might be considered a genre of storytelling.

Certain features of successful storytelling are found in the best academic writing, but are notably missing from the worst. For example, a good narrative writer engages her audience and holds its attention by making her plot and the way she introduces it sufficiently interesting to seduce us into reading further. And she does it by ensuring that the characters that inhabit the world she is creating are sufficiently believable to motivate us to pursue the narrative to find out what happens to them. Good academic writers, including those who write well about nursing research, do similar things, though in general the characters with whom they populate their texts are not people, but hypotheses, methods, results and so on.

CONCLUSION

If nursing researchers want to change the clinical world and the quality of patient care, they must undertake research that is relevant to practice. They must also ensure that they tell their tales as well as they can, because it is only by doing this that they can ensure that those who might be in a position to make use of their findings can understand what they are saying.

If they are to be successful in telling stories, nurse researchers must weave 20 the various elements together in coherent, interesting, and easily understandable narratives, making clear their relationship to the intellectual landscape they inhabit. If they fail to do so they will greatly reduce the possibility that their work can contribute to the development of practice. In our view this will be to fail at the last and perhaps the most important hurdle in the research process.

> Fairbairn and Carson end with a call to action for nursing researchers. Consider what, specifically, they are calling upon their readers to do.

REFERENCES

Crepeau EB (2000) Reconstructing Gloria: a narrative analysis of team meetings. *Qualitative Health Research.* 10, 6, 766–787.

Fairbairn GJ (1996) Academic writing for publication and public performance: communication or display? *Curriculum.* 17, 3, 188–194.

Fairbairn G (2000) Developing academic storytelling. *Education Today.* 50, 2, 32–38.

Koch T (1998) Story telling: is it really research? *Journal of Advanced Nursing.* 28, 6, 1182–1190.

McCance TV *et al* (2001) Exploring caring using narrative methodology: an analysis of the approach. *Journal of Advanced Nursing.* 33, 3, 350–356.

Tilley S (1995) Accounts, accounting and accountability in psychiatric nursing. In Watson R (Ed) *Accountability in Nursing Practice.* London, Chapman Hall.

Webb C (1992) The use of the first person in academic writing: objectivity, language and gate-keeping. *Journal of Advanced Nursing.* 17, 747–752.

> Fairbairn and Carson use the documentation format specified by the journal *Nurse Researcher* in their guidelines to authors.

Reading Questions

1. In your own words, explain Fairbairn and Carson's objections to how storytelling is currently viewed as a research method.

2. Identify two reasons Fairbairn and Carson provide to support their contention that nursing research would be improved if researchers saw "their task in terms of storytelling" (par. 17).

Rhetoric Questions

3. Look closely at the headings Fairbairn and Carson use to guide their readers through their argument. Choose two and offer a brief analysis of their effectiveness as headings. Are they appropriate? Why or why not? Could they be improved? If so, how?

4. In what ways do Fairbairn and Carson practice what they preach? In other words, how does their article conform to or deviate from their recommendations for improving research reporting in nursing?

Response Questions

5. Fairbairn and Carson call for a reconsideration of the role of storytelling in nursing research. Are there other academic or professional fields of inquiry that you believe might benefit by emphasizing storytelling more? If so, what are they, and how would they benefit from more storytelling? If not, then why not?

6. The researchers suggest that their article may be "painting an over-gloomy picture" of the state of writing in nursing (15). Do you agree or disagree that they paint "an over-gloomy picture"? Why or why not?

Writing Project   Contribution to a Scholarly Conversation

For this assignment, compose an academic essay that contributes to the scholarly conversation surrounding a topic related to writing. For example, in "Writing in the Disciplines: Student Perspectives on Learning Genre," Mary Goldschmidt positions herself within the scholarly conversation in the field of Writing Studies regarding how to support students as they advance in their studies and write within their majors.

Using the readings in this chapter as a model, you might choose a topic related to how writing on social media platforms shapes our identity, or how language conventions such as pronoun rules can affect people who do not fit within the assumptions of Standard English. No matter what topic you choose, think about how particular disciplinary perspectives might ask questions about the topic and how those questions can inform your research.

One of your first steps will therefore be to explore others' ideas by conducting research into your topic. Using the research skills you developed in Chapter 4, remember to think about research not just as gathering supporting evidence for your own argument. Think about research also as tracing out a conversation among scholars:

- What are others saying about your topic?
- Is there room for change, refinements, or redefinition in what they are saying about your topic?
- How might you contribute to this conversation?

Depending on your instructor and the expectations of your disciplinary perspective, you may choose to conduct research by designing a study, collecting data, and analyzing your results. Follow appropriate disciplinary and genre expectations in structuring your argument, providing evidence for your claims, and citing your sources.

Love Matters: Examining Our Closest Bonds

The readings in this chapter provide a glimpse into various aspects of love, marriage, and family. Bringing together a wide variety of sources, the chapter presents multiple views on these topics, based on individuals' self-reporting and reflection on their own experiences, as well as on data derived from large surveys and interviews.

The chapter begins with a reading that reports on recent trends in the ever-changing construction of the American family and the ways those changes have impacted the strategies companies employ to market their products today. The text that follows examines the relationships between parents and children, focusing on the phenomenon of helicopter parents, or parents who are overly involved in their children's lives. The final popular reading in the chapter explores the cultural tradition of arranged marriages and ponders questions about its appropriateness and value in modern times.

As you read selections from the chapter, we hope you will consider the relationships between your own experiences and those presented in the popular and academic readings offered. We encourage you to consider critically the issues they raise and to pose your own questions about those issues. These might include the following:

- What constitutes a marriage?
- What constitutes a family?
- How have definitions of *family* changed over time?
- How are individuals included and excluded from social legitimacy as a family? How are those lines drawn in our society?
- How do individuals negotiate their own family identities in times of trial or change?
- How do your own family experiences align with those described in the readings?

The academic case study for this chapter focuses on love. It comprises readings that explore the topic from a range of scholarly perspectives:

- **Humanities** How have dominant notions of love and marriage been challenged historically?

- **Social Sciences** What do African American young adult women look for in a potential long-term partner?

- **Natural Sciences** How does our body chemistry change when we experience love?

- **Applied Fields** What trends characterize the use of dating apps specifically among lesbian, gay, and bisexual individuals, and how might knowledge of those trends be useful for companies' development of market strategies?

How the Definition of an American Family Has Changed

ELLEN BYRON

Since 2000, Ellen Byron has been a staff reporter at the *Wall Street Journal*, where she writes about consumer issues. She is the recipient of a New York Press Club award for best consumer reporting. In the article below, which was published in the Business section of the *Wall Street Journal* in December 2019, Byron explores ways the American family has changed over the past decade and how those changes have affected companies and their engagement with consumers.

The transformation of the American family deepened over the past decade, as an increasingly diverse array of arrangements replaced the married-with-children paradigm.

Marriage is playing a smaller role within families, as more people delay tying the knot, live together without marrying or divorce. One exception is same-sex couples, who are marrying at higher rates after winning the nationwide right in a 2015 Supreme Court ruling. Separately, multigenerational households are becoming more prevalent, with more children growing up in homes with multiple generations.

It all represents an increasing distance from the nuclear-family structure considered traditional for decades. The changes solidify shifts that have been mounting since then, erasing the notion of one dominant family type. In the early 1960s, two-thirds of children were raised in male-breadwinner, married-couple families. By contrast, today there is no one family-and-work arrangement that encompasses the majority of children, demographers say. "That dominant model declined, but it's not like it was replaced by one thing," says Philip Cohen, professor of sociology at the University of Maryland. "It was replaced by a peacock's tail, a plethora of different arrangements."

This fragmentation is causing businesses to overhaul their approach. Housing builders are designing homes with more flexibility, to accommodate a greater variety of family arrangements. And consumer-product makers are adjusting package sizes and increasingly reflecting more family types in advertising.

Here are some of the most important changes: 5

MARRIAGE PLAYS A SMALLER ROLE . . .

Fewer children are being raised by married parents. In 2017, one in four parents who lived with a child was unmarried, up from one in 10 in 1968, according to Gretchen Livingston, a former senior researcher with Pew Research Center.

"You'll see that marriage takes up a smaller slice than it used to: People get married later, they're more likely to get divorced than in the old days, and they're more likely to spend some amount of time in cohabitating relationships," says Dr. Cohen.

The financial crisis stalled—but didn't reverse—that trend. The percentage of families with children and two parents, either married or unmarried, fell from 87% in 1970 to 70% in 2008, and has plateaued since, according to Census Bureau data.

But even among two-parent households, more couples are cohabitating without getting married. About a third of unmarried parents were cohabitating couples in 2017, up from 20% in 1997, according to the Pew Research Center.

. . . BUT MORE SAME-SEX COUPLES ARE MARRYING

One group in which marriage rates are rising is gay 10 people, after the Supreme Court's 2015 nationwide legalization of same-sex marriage capped a rapid transformation in Americans' acceptance of same-sex unions. Today some 543,000 households are made up of same-sex, married couples, according to the Census Bureau. A further 469,000 households have same-sex unmarried partners living together. Currently, 191,000 children live with same-sex parents, according to the Census Bureau.

MULTIGENERATIONAL HOUSEHOLDS RISE . . .

More children are being raised in households with multiple generations under one roof. Twenty percent of the U.S. population lived in multigenerational households in 2016, up from 17% in 2009 and 12% in 1980, according to the Pew Research Center. (Pew defines the arrangement as a household with two or more adult generations, or including grandparents and grandchildren younger than 25.)

The causes are varied. Increasing ethnic and racial diversity means more families incorporate cultural traditions of multigenerational living. Separately, the opioid crisis has fueled a rise in grandparents serving as primary caretakers of their grandchildren. And an aging population means more midlife parents are taking in their own parents.

More sons are caring for aging parents. Marcus Waller, a Chicago postal worker, moved back in with his mother, Melida Butler, who had rheumatoid arthritis. She since passed away.

. . . AND ADULT CHILDREN MOVE BACK

Another big factor in multigenerational living: Many young adults returned home—or never left—in the aftermath of the financial crisis. In 2019, 32% of 18- to 34-year-olds are living in a parent's home, up from 28% in 2007. "That's millions of people who suddenly lived in the basement with their parents," says Deutsche Bank Chief Economist Torsten Slok. "Moving out, getting a loan and getting a job has turned out to create a number of complications and have had a significant impact on family arrangements of U.S. households."

COMPANIES CHANGE THEIR PLAYBOOKS

The demographic trends are already having a major 15 impact on business—from housing to consumer products. In the housing industry, widely varying family types mean homes must offer more flexibility, says KB Home Chief Executive Jeffrey Mezger. KB Home sells made-to-order new-home construction in eight states, allowing buyers to choose how many bedrooms and bathrooms their house will have, and the size of their gathering areas, especially the kitchen, living and eating spaces.

"We're seeing more extended families, and a lot of our two-story homes today have a bedroom on the first floor for the parent that may live with the family," says Mr. Mezger. "In the old days, you'd have a half-bath and possibly a den, but we've retooled our floor plans to include a bedroom downstairs and a full bath."

Consumer-product makers are deepening their household research and no longer catering mainly to one dominant family type. They have rolled out smaller packaging sizes for families with fewer members and advertising that depicts gay, straight and single-parent families with a range of races and ethnicities, all intended to reflect the widening diversity of American families, companies say.

"What picture comes to mind when we think of a traditional U.S. household—a mom and a dad of different sexes and then a boy and a girl, right?" says Kirti Singh, chief analytics and insights officer at Procter & Gamble Co., maker of Pampers diapers, Tide laundry detergent and Pantene shampoo. "That picture is indeed evolving dramatically."

Reading Questions

1. According to Byron, what are two specific trends that characterize the changing nature of the American family over the past decade?

2. Among what group of people has the marriage rate risen over the past decade, and what reasoning does Byron use to explain this trend?

3. Byron refers to the changes in the American family as "fragmentation" (par. 4). What does she mean by this?

Rhetoric Questions

4. Briefly describe the sources of evidence on which Byron relies. Comment on their appropriateness in light of her purpose and the needs of her audience.

5. How would you describe the organizational structure of Byron's article, and why might that organization be appropriate for her intended audience?

6. Choose one sentence from Byron's article that you feel represents her style. Then, in a brief paragraph, explain why you selected the sentence you did.

Response Questions

7. One of Byron's sources, Philip Cohen, a professor of sociology, describes the transformation of the American family in the past decade as a "peacock's tail" (3). Based on Byron's description of the changes the American family structure has undergone, propose another image that might visualize the current state of the American family. Explain your image selection.

8. Consider how changes in your own family situation might be reflected in Byron's descriptions of today's American family. Does Bryon's article reflect your family? If so, in what ways? If not, what do you believe she is missing?

Kids of Helicopter Parents Are Sputtering Out

JULIE LYTHCOTT-HAIMS

Julie Lythcott-Haims is a former dean of freshmen and undergraduate advising at Stanford University. She is the author of *Real American: A Memoir* (2017) and *Your Turn: How to Be an Adult* (2021) and is a regular contributor on issues related to parenting for the *CBS This Morning* show. In the article below, which was excerpted from her *New York Times* bestseller *How to Raise an Adult: Break Free of the Overparenting Trap and Prepare Your Kid for Success* (2015), Lythcott-Haims draws on her own experiences, the results of academic studies, and expert testimony to explore the negative effects of helicopter parenting on children.

Academically overbearing parents are doing great harm. So says Bill Deresiewicz in his groundbreaking 2014 manifesto *Excellent Sheep: The Miseducation of the American Elite and the Way to a Meaningful Life.* "[For students] haunted their whole lives by a fear of failure—often, in the first instance, by their parents' fear of failure," writes Deresiewicz, "the cost of falling short, even temporarily, becomes not merely practical, but existential."

Those whom Deresiewicz calls "excellent sheep" I call the "existentially impotent." From 2006 to 2008, I served on Stanford University's mental health task force, which examined the problem of student depression and proposed ways to teach faculty, staff, and students to better understand, notice, and respond to mental health issues. As dean, I saw a lack of intellectual and emotional freedom—this existential impotence—behind closed doors. The "excellent sheep" were in my office. Often brilliant, always accomplished, these students would sit on my couch holding their fragile, brittle parts together, resigned to the fact that these outwardly successful situations were their miserable lives.

In my years as dean, I heard plenty of stories from college students who believed they *had* to study science (or medicine, or engineering), just as they'd *had* to play piano, *and* do community service for Africa, *and, and, and.* I talked with kids completely uninterested in the items on their own résumés. Some shrugged off any right to be bothered by their own lack of interest in what they were working on, saying, "My parents know what's best for me."

One kid's father threatened to divorce her mother if the daughter didn't major in economics. It took this student seven years to finish instead of the usual four, and along the way the father micromanaged his daughter's every move, including requiring her to study off campus at her uncle's every weekend. At her father's insistence, the daughter went to see one of her econ professors during office hours one weekday. She forgot to call her father to report on how that went, and when she returned to her dorm later that evening her uncle was in the dorm lobby looking visibly uncomfortable about having to "force" her to call her dad to update him. Later this student told me, "I pretty much had a panic attack from the lack of control in my life." But an economics major she was indeed. And the parents got divorced anyway.

In 2013 the news was filled with worrisome statistics about the mental health crisis on college campuses, particularly the number of students medicated for depression. Charlie Gofen, the retired chairman of the board at the Latin School of Chicago, a private school serving about 1,100 students, emailed the statistics off to a colleague at another school and asked, "Do you think parents at your school would rather their kid be depressed at Yale or happy at University of Arizona?" The colleague quickly replied, "My guess is 75 percent of the parents would rather see their kids depressed at Yale. They figure that the kid can straighten the emotional stuff out in his/her 20's, but no one can go back and get the Yale undergrad degree."

Here are the statistics to which Charlie Gofen was likely alluding:

In a 2013 survey of college counseling center directors, 95 percent said the number of students with significant psychological problems is a growing concern on their campus, 70 percent said that the number of students on their campus with severe psychological problems has increased in the past year, and they reported that 24.5 percent of their student clients were taking psychotropic drugs.

In 2013 the American College Health Association surveyed close to 100,000 college students from 153 different campuses about their health. When asked about their experiences, at some point over the past 12 months:

• 84.3 percent felt overwhelmed by all they had to do

• 60.5 percent felt very sad

• 57.0 percent felt very lonely

• 51.3 percent felt overwhelming anxiety

• 8.0 percent seriously considered suicide

The 153 schools surveyed included campuses in all 50 states, small liberal arts colleges and large research universities, religious institutions and non-religious, from the small to medium-sized to the very large. The mental health crisis is not a Yale (or Stanford or Harvard) problem; these poor mental health outcomes are occurring in kids everywhere. The increase in mental health problems among college students may reflect the lengths to which we push kids toward academic achievement, but since they are happening to kids who end up at hundreds of schools in every tier, they appear to stem not from what it takes to get into the most elite schools but from some facet of American childhood itself.

As parents, our intentions are sound — more than 10 sound: We love our kids fiercely and want only the very best for them. Yet, having succumbed to a combination of safety fears, a college admissions arms race, and perhaps our own needy ego, our sense of what is "best" for our kids is completely out of whack. We don't want our kids to bonk their heads or have hurt feelings, but we're willing to take real chances with their mental health?

You're right to be thinking *Yes, but do we know whether overparenting causes this rise in mental health problems?* The answer is that we don't have studies proving causation, but a number of recent studies show *correlation*.

In 2010, psychology professor Neil Montgomery of Keene State College in New Hampshire surveyed 300 college freshmen nationwide and found that students with helicopter parents were less open to new ideas and actions and more vulnerable, anxious, and self-conscious. "[S]tudents who were given responsibility and not constantly monitored by their parents — so-called 'free rangers' — the effects were reversed," Montgomery's study found. A 2011 study by Terri LeMoyne and Tom Buchanan at the University of Tennessee at Chattanooga looking at more than 300 students found that students with "hovering" or "helicopter" parents [were] more likely to be medicated for anxiety and/or depression.

A 2012 study of 438 college students reported in the *Journal of Adolescence* found "initial evidence for this form of intrusive parenting being linked to problematic development in emerging adulthood . . . by limiting opportunities for emerging adults to practice and develop important skills needed for becoming self-reliant adults." A 2013 study of 297 college students reported in the *Journal of Child and Family Studies* found that college students with helicopter parents reported significantly higher levels of depression and less satisfaction in life and attributed this diminishment in well-being to a violation of the students' "basic psychological needs for autonomy and competence." And a 2014 study from researchers at the University of Colorado–Boulder is the first to correlate a highly structured childhood with less executive function capabilities. Executive function is our ability to determine which goal-directed actions to carry out and when and is a skill set lacking in many kids with attention deficit disorder or attention deficit hyperactivity disorder.

The data emerging about the mental health of our kids only confirms the harm done by asking so little of them when it comes to life skills yet so much of them when it comes to adhering to the academic plans we've made for them.

Karen Able is a staff psychologist at a large public university in the Midwest. (Her name has been changed here because of the sensitive nature of her work.) Based on her clinical experience, Able says, "Overinvolved parenting is taking a serious toll on the psychological well-being of college students who can't negotiate a balance between consulting with parents and independent decision-making."

When parents have tended to do the stuff of life for kids—the waking up, the transporting, the reminding about deadlines and obligations, the bill-paying, the question-asking, the decision-making, the responsibility-taking, the talking to strangers, and the confronting of authorities, kids may be in for quite a shock when parents turn them loose in the world of college or work. They will experience setbacks, which will feel to them like failure. Lurking beneath the problem of whatever thing needs to be handled is the student's inability to differentiate the self from the parent.

When seemingly perfectly healthy but overparented kids get to college and have trouble coping with the various new situations they might encounter—a roommate who has a different sense of "clean," a professor who wants a revision to the paper but won't say specifically what is "wrong," a friend who isn't being so friendly anymore, a choice between doing a summer seminar or service project but not both—they can have real difficulty knowing how to handle the disagreement, the uncertainty, the hurt feelings, or the decision-making process. This inability to cope—to sit with some discomfort, think about options, talk it through with someone, make a decision—can become a problem unto itself.

Madeline Levine, psychologist and author of *The Price of Privilege*, says that there are three ways we might be overparenting and unwittingly causing psychological harm:

1. When we do for our kids what they can *already* do for themselves;

2. When we do for our kids what they can *almost* do for themselves; and

3. When our parenting behavior is motivated by our own egos.

Levine said that when we parent this way we deprive our kids of the opportunity to be creative, to problem solve, to develop coping skills, to build resilience, to figure out what makes them happy, to figure out who they are. In short, it deprives them of the chance to be, well, human. Although we overinvolve ourselves to protect our kids and it may in fact lead to short-term gains, our behavior actually delivers the rather soul-crushing news: *Kid, you can't actually do any of this without me.*

As Able told me: 20

When children aren't given the space to struggle through things on their own, they don't learn to problem solve very well. They don't learn to be confident in their own abilities, and it can affect their self-esteem. The other problem with never having to struggle is that you never experience failure and can develop an overwhelming fear of failure and of disappointing others. Both the low self-confidence and the fear of failure can lead to depression or anxiety.

Neither Karen Able nor I is suggesting that grown kids should never call their parents. The devil is in the details of the conversation. If they call with a problem or a decision to be made, do we tell them what to do? Or do we listen thoughtfully, ask some questions based on our own sense of the situation, then say, "OK. So how do you think you're going to handle that?"

Knowing what could unfold for our kids when they're out of our sight can make us parents feel like we're in straitjackets. What else are we supposed to do? If we're not there for our kids when they are away from home and bewildered, confused, frightened, or hurting, then who will be?

Here's the point—and this is so much more important than I realized until rather recently when the data started coming in: The research shows that figuring out for themselves is a critical element to people's mental health. Your kids have to be there for *themselves*. That's a harder truth to swallow when your kid is in the midst of a problem or worse, a crisis, but taking the long view, it's the best medicine for them.

Reading Questions

1. Lythcott-Haims refers to those students who appear overwhelmed by the prospect of failure as "existentially impotent" (par. 2). What does she mean by this?

2. What evidence does Lythcott-Haims provide to suggest that the mental health crisis among students may be related to their experience of an American childhood?

3. What specific examples does Lythcott-Haims provide to illustrate overparenting?

Rhetoric Questions

4. Who do you believe is the primary audience for Lythcott-Haims's article? What elements of the article lead you to this conclusion?

5. Lythcott-Haims presents the results of several academic studies to support various claims in her argument. How effective is this strategy on you as a reader? Why?

6. What elements of Lythcott-Haims's argument support her ethos as a writer on the topic of helicopter parents?

Response Questions

7. Based on the content of Lythcott-Haims's argument, what two pieces of advice would you offer to parents for adjusting their children's experiences of childhood?

8. How would you describe your own experiences of being parented and the potential impacts of that parenting on your level of independence?

What "Indian Matchmaking" Tells Us about Love

VIKRAM ZUTSHI

Vikram Zutshi is a columnist and filmmaker who divides his time between the United States, Latin America, and South East India. His writings have appeared in numerous newspapers and magazines, including *Vice*, *Rolling Stone*, *LA Weekly*, and *Times of India*. His latest filmic productions include *Tijuana Dreams* (2018), a documentary about the U.S. immigration crisis, and *Darshan: The Living Art of India* (2018), an exploration of Indian and Nepalese traditional arts. In the opinion piece below, which was published on the digital media platform *Fair Observer* in August 2020, Zutshi writes about the practice of arranged marriages and ponders questions regarding its appropriateness and value in modern times.

When the show "Indian Matchmaking" dropped on Netflix, my initial reaction was one of revulsion. Matchmaker Sima Taparia and her clients represented everything I loathed about the culture I was born into. Of course, I was not blind to my personal triggers and biases, having grown up in a conservative and patriarchal family environment.

Despite my reservations, I clicked on the first episode. The characters depicted in the show were largely relatable and familiar. The show, however, turned out to be a lot more nuanced than I had initially thought. The matchmaker's call for "flexibility and compromise" in relationships had upset many Indian Netflix subscribers. Are these qualities really such a bad thing, I wondered? Isn't it necessary to make allowances for the shortcomings of others in any relationship, whether personal or professional, in order to make it work?

Can any relationship survive without the willingness to iron out kinks that will perforce appear from time to time? And are so-called "love marriages" really as egalitarian as they are made out to be? People usually partner up with those who possess qualities that they find desirable, such as their physical attributes, career prospects, ethnicity and social class.

In my opinion, the show does not condone regressive stereotypes, as some have suggested. It simply holds up a mirror to our ingrained preferences and prejudices, reflecting the good along with the bad and the ugly. Akshay, with his pathological mother fixation, and Aparna, with her hyper-ambitious, control freak of a mother, were two of the examples that stood out for me.

Volumes have been written about the trauma 5 inflicted on impressionable young minds by overbearing parents. Unrealistic life goals and a toxic home environment are known causes of depression among youth the world over and have been seen to cause mental health issues that could linger for a lifetime if not diagnosed and treated in time.

ARRANGED MARRIAGE

When I was in my late twenties, I agreed to give arranged marriage a try on the prodding of friends and family. I was not the typical candidate. I did not fit into the holy Indian trinity of doctor-lawyer-engineer, nor did I have any interest in cricket, Bollywood or the trappings of organized religion. But what I did have was a large network of well-connected relatives and family friends who were willing to vouch for my upstanding moral character and social pedigree. I was not aware that I possessed these qualities but decided to go along for the heck of it.

My first rendezvous was at the coffee shop of a hotel on Marine Drive, in what was then Bombay, now Mumbai. I was to meet a London-based lawyer, who like me had grown up in Mumbai. We started off by talking about our shared south Mumbai roots. Pretty mundane stuff. She noticed the iPod sticking out of my pocket and asked what type of music I liked. At this, I launched into an impassioned spiel about the Grateful Dead, Ozric Tentacles and Gong, "the greatest psychedelic rock bands in music history." "Do you need drugs to get into that stuff"? she asked innocuously. "Sure, certain substances can greatly enhance the experience," I replied.

"Have you taken any of these substances yourself?" she inquired in her clipped British accent. I could see where the conversation was going but decided to proceed anyway. "Yeah, I dropped some acid at a Grateful Dead concert in my freshman year at college. It was a life-changing experience."

After a few moments of silence, I asked what type of law she practiced. "I am a criminal defense attorney," she answered dryly. "Great. I've been looking for someone like you," I said with a chuckle. Soon after we parted ways, promising to stay in touch. It was the last I saw of her. Clearly, I was not her type. She did not think I was "husband material," and she was probably right.

My next meeting happened a few months later, in 10 Los Angeles. This time it was with an interior decorator, a "creative type" that my aunt promised I would gel with. We met at a Brazilian restaurant near Venice Beach. She was attractive, free-spirited and very intelligent. We had similar tastes in music and books, and we both loved Brazilian churrasco. Soon we were guzzling caipirinhas and cracking up about arranged marriages. The irony was not lost on either of us. She had agreed to the meeting for the same reason I had, out of sheer curiosity.

She told me about a guy she was set up with a few months ago, an IT professional deeply influenced by Bollywood tropes about the ideal NRI — non-resident Indian male. He had modeled himself after one of the characters in a popular Karan Johar film. Predictably, their rendezvous ended soon after she informed him about the string of men she had dated in the past.

As we talked, I could not help noticing other men in the restaurant staring at her. She could have had any one of them she wanted. It made me feel insecure, and I redoubled my efforts to woo her. Was it the Indian in me that made me react in that manner? I could not be sure. Certain aspects of the mating game, like the relationship between social capital and desirability, are universal and not limited to any particular ethnicity. In this case, she clearly had the upper hand. For some unfathomable reason, she took a liking to me and we ended up seeing each other for a couple of months before mutually deciding we were not the "marrying kind."

INADEQUACY OF MODERN RELATIONSHIPS

When the show dropped, I reached out to Selina Sheth, a Mumbai-based writer, for her opinion. "Arranged marriage is not the problem, the way it is treated in cultures like India is," she explained. "It is one thing to have preferences (all men and women do) but to ascribe value judgments to these preferences can be and has shown to be damaging. Traditionally, marriage was a social, family and economic construct, but in today's times, can a list of ticked boxes mean you are compatible in the deeper sense of the word?"

Indeed, Taparia had admitted the same with her observation that "nowadays, marriages are breaking like biscuits." The documentary series offers a counterpoint to the inadequacy of modern relationships by showing a series of charming elderly couples clearly happy and content with each other after several decades of living together. They had all been introduced to each other by well-meaning relatives. For contrast, we are also introduced to Rupam, a divorced single mother who bypasses the matchmaker route to find love on a dating site. Clearly, times are changing. Indian men and women are increasingly breaking free of the shackles of tradition and finding their own partners. Whether these alliances are any more successful than the arranged kind is debatable.

It has been shown that Indian-American couples who met through arranged marriage were as satisfied in their relationships as those that chose their own partners. Indeed, a 2012 NDTV-IPSOS survey indicated that three-quarters of Indians between the ages of 18 and 35 prefer to enter arranged marriages. The tradition, however, has not remained stagnant. Whereas in the past the bride and groom did not have much of a choice in the matter as the parents had the final say, today it has evolved into an Indian version of speed dating. You are set up with a series of meetings with prospective partners where both males and females are free to move on if their expectations are not met.

Of course, in many parts of rural India, young people are still coerced into marriage, or worse, killed for not adhering to caste laws. But can we really expect centuries of dogma to change overnight? For instance, there are still forest tribes that consume human flesh in some parts of the world. Perhaps the enlightened op-ed writers at *The New York Times* and *The Guardian* would like to take a shot at educating the cannibals?

"Progressing beyond conservative ideals is a sign of bravery, but also privilege. It usually means you have a support system and the social space to exist outside of the narrow confines of tradition," says Smriti Mundhra, the executive producer of "Indian Matchmaking." "Not everybody has that privilege, and not everybody has had a chance to deprogramme themselves from the ideas they've internalized over generations. Not everybody believes they need to be deprogrammed!"

On a personal note, I did end up getting married eventually. It was not an arranged alliance. We had met through mutual friends and in a euphoric moment decided to get hitched. It did not last very long. We separated after two years of living together, realizing we had very different life goals and aspirations. I was too much of a libertine to remain in a monogamous relationship, and she was completely immersed in her medical residency, making it impossible to spend enough time to get to know each other adequately. It was nobody's fault that the marriage fell apart—it was just the natural progression of things. All relationships must have a beginning and end, and ours ended sooner than expected.

"A great marriage is not when the 'perfect couple' comes together," writes Dave Meurer, the author of "Good Spousekeeping." "It is when an imperfect couple learns to enjoy their differences." I am currently in a relationship with someone as imperfect as me, and we are slowly learning to enjoy our differences, naturally with fistfuls of salt. So far, so good.

Reading Questions

1. Based on your close reading of the first four paragraphs of Zutshi's argument, what do you believe he hopes to achieve in his piece?

2. According to Zutshi, in what ways has the tradition of arranged marriages, for many Indians, evolved over time?

Rhetoric Questions

3. Zutshi relies on multiple sources of evidence to inform his exploration of arranged marriages. Which source provides the most effective evidence, in your opinion? Why?

4. Zutshi's article is organized into three sections. What do you see as his overall purpose of each of the three sections?

Response Questions

5. Do you believe an arranged marriage can be as successful as a "love marriage" today? Why or why not?

6. Zutshi's piece frequently poses questions to the reader. What are two questions you still have about arranged marriages or the impacts arranged marriages can have on those who might choose to participate in them?

Academic Case Study: Perspectives on Love

ACADEMIC CASE STUDY • PERSPECTIVES ON LOVE   HUMANITIES

The Strategies of Forbidden Love: Family across Racial Boundaries in Nineteenth-Century North Carolina

WARREN E. MILTEER JR.

Warren E. Milteer Jr. is currently an assistant professor of history at the University of South Carolina. In this article, which appeared in the Spring 2014 edition of the *Journal of Social History*, Milteer explores "forbidden love" and makes the case that "free women of mixed ancestry and white men developed relationships that mimicked legally sanctioned marriages" in nineteenth-century North Carolina. His argument, which relies heavily on primary document analysis, explores the wider implications for these seemingly impossible historical constructs. Readers are cautioned that the essay includes a racial epithet within a primary source quotation used as evidence. The document also contains other disturbing language and stories that reflect the racist social systems affecting the historical actors at the center of the analysis.

ABSTRACT

This article contends that although local beliefs and legal edicts attempted to discourage sexual and familial relationships between women of color and white men in North Carolina, free women of mixed ancestry and white men developed relationships that mimicked legally sanctioned marriages. These unions often produced children who maintained frequent interaction with both parents. In nineteenth-century Hertford County, North Carolina, free women of mixed ancestry and their white partners developed creative strategies to deal with the legal limitations inherent in their situation. Women and men in these relationships found ways to secure property rights for women and children and developed methods to prevent legal scrutiny of their living arrangements.

By the early to mid-nineteenth century, Hertford County, located in the tobacco- and cotton-growing intercoastal plain of North Carolina, had developed a reputation throughout the eastern seaboard as a place where free women of mixed ancestry lived outside of marriage with white men.[1] In 1853, William D. Valentine, a prominent organizer in the Hertford County Whig Party, wrote in reference to the practice: "So common has it long been that I apprehend it is tolerated by married men in this locality. They too indulge. The whites are more blamable than the low degraded colored."[2] Calvin Scott Brown heard similar tales of sexual encounters across racial boundaries as he traveled toward Hertford County to begin his work as an administrator of a new school for people of color during the 1880s: "I remember on my way here for the first time from Franklin, Virginia, a man on the boat asked me where I was going . . . I told him I was going to Winton." The man responded that the inhabitants of Hertford County "were the most degraded people upon the face of the earth." He said that mulatto women "lived with white men and that white men came from as far as Baltimore to have the mulatto girls."[3]

Historical records, including accounts from children produced from relationships between free women of mixed ancestry and white men, support these rumors of sexual exploitation in nineteenth-century Hertford County. Mollie Cherry Hall Catus remembered that her white father, Albert Vann,

> would come in at bed-time and even before his wife died he would come and stay with my mother [Sallie Ann Hall] all night and get up and go to his house the next morning. His children despised us and I despised them and all their folks, and I despised him. . . . He had plenty of property but didn't give mother one thing.[4]

Many non-white women, both enslaved and free, lived under similar conditions as Sallie Ann Hall, and many of their children had the same attitudes about their white fathers' actions. However, the historical record demonstrates that not all free women of mixed ancestry served their white partners as concubines.

Learn more about the use of **descriptive titles** in the humanities in Chapter 7, "Descriptive and Rhetorical Language."

Although abstracts are more common in the social and natural sciences, they do sometimes occur in the humanities. Learn more about **abstracts** in Chapter 8, "Abstracts and Other Structural Conventions."

Milteer uses the CMS documentation style, where superscript numbers refer to endnotes. Historians prefer this style, which allows for lengthier notes on sources.

Learn more about the use of **primary source evidence** in Chapter 5, "Choosing Your Sources."

In several instances, relationships between free women of mixed ancestry and white men took the form of long-term dedicated partnerships.[5]

Milteer identifies the subject of his study, "long-term monogamous relationships between free women of mixed ancestry and white men," but acknowledges a lack of available primary evidence to help us understand those relationships.

This study focuses on long-term monogamous relationships between free women of mixed ancestry and white men who probably would have married if legal and social circumstances had been different. North Carolina law banned marriage between whites and non-whites for most of the nineteenth century, yet many free women of mixed ancestry and white men still built lifetime partnerships. Legal restrictions alone could not dissuade these men and women from sharing their lives together. Although historical sources reveal relatively few relationships of this type in contrast with the often-cited situations of concubinage, scholars must acknowledge that some whites and non-whites in the nineteenth century, just as people today, desired to share their lives together regardless of the lack of legal recognition and social approval. Because the law did not permit these unions, evidence of their existence is at best hidden and sometimes does not appear at all in surviving documents. These unions' lack of legal recognition coupled with destruction of the majority of Hertford County's pre–Civil War court records preclude an exact count of how many of these relationships existed at any particular time. Yet the surviving evidence still allows scholars to understand how free women of mixed ancestry and white men navigated through a society that refused to publicly approve their relationships.[6]

Milteer establishes the focus of his argument as exploring how these couples "navigated through a society that refused to publicly approve their relationships."

Learn more about thesis statements in the humanities in Chapter 7, "Structural Conventions in the Humanities."

This article contends that although local beliefs and legal edicts discouraged sexual and familial relationships between women of color and white men, some free women of mixed ancestry actively developed relationships with white men that often resembled legally sanctioned marriages. These illegal unions often produced children who maintained frequent interaction with both parents. Free women of mixed ancestry and their white partners developed creative strategies to deal with the legal limitations inherent in any unrecognized union. Even as state lawmakers banned and illegitimated their relationships, women and men in these relationships found ways to secure property rights for women. They developed creative strategies to pass on wealth to their children, who by law were illegitimate and therefore not entitled to their fathers' estates. These couples even found ways to obscure the illegality of their living arrangements in an era when an unmarried couple living in the same house constituted fornication and adultery, which courts treated as a single crime in North Carolina.

Although contemporary observers suggested that Hertford County had an 5 unusual propensity for unions between non-white women and white men, a closer examination of family histories and surviving documents from other areas would likely reveal that couples across the United States sought solutions for similar domestic issues. Through much of the nineteenth century, the majority of states prohibited marriages between whites and non-whites.[7] Free non-white women and white men in these parts of the nation undoubtedly used many of the same strategies employed by couples in Hertford County to overcome legal obstacles and social stigmas. They along with couples composed of white women and non-white men, both without the legal protections of marriage, would have needed to seek out special arrangements to protect and pass down family assets, provide care to children, and shield themselves from public scrutiny and legal prosecution.

Since 1715, North Carolina law had either discouraged or banned marriage between whites and non-whites. The first law to address marriage fined any white man or woman who intermarried with "any Negro, Mulatto or Indyan Man or Woman" fifty pounds. The General Assembly updated this law in 1741 by levying the same fine on any white man or woman who married "an Indian, negro, mustee, or mulatto man or woman, or any person of mixed blood to the third generation, bond or free."[8] Neither of these laws actually prohibited intermarriage between whites and non-whites but simply discouraged marriages by imposing heavy fines. Both laws also fined clergy and other officials who married whites to non-whites. These laws appear to have discouraged the issuances of legal marriage bonds to mixed couples in Hertford County and many other parts of the state. Nevertheless, in 1830 the General Assembly passed an act banning "any free negro or free person of color" from marrying "a white person."[9] In 1875, a state convention added a similar intermarriage ban to the North Carolina Constitution.[10]

For the past generation, historians have endeavored to understand relationships between non-white women and white men in the United States through the laws governing marriage in the colonial and national periods. Historians have reviewed court cases at the municipal, state, and federal levels in order to understand how different localities treated people living in unlawful mixed unions. Past scholars have focused on the exploitative nature of many of these relationships, in which white men extracted sexual favors from women of color, most of whom had no form of recourse in a society that ignored the sexual indiscretions of offending white men. However, more than a generation of new scholarship has clearly demonstrated that white planters, politicians, and plebeians* also took part in liaisons with women of color that were more mutually beneficial and often long-term.[11]

Yet only the most recent scholarship has begun to uncover the intricacies of daily life for women of color, white men, and their families. Scholars

*plebeians: members of lower social classes.

Milteer reviews
the work of
other scholars
on this topic and
identifies a gap
in the scholarship
to which his study
responds.

have shown that familial relationships between whites and non-whites existed despite legal prohibitions, but much work still needs to be completed in order to understand how women of color and white men managed family life in communities that refused to give legal recognition to their unions. Even less is understood about the unique position of free women of color involved in illicit unions with white men. Slave status placed limitations on women that caused relationships between enslaved women and white men to be inherently skewed in the favor of white men, whether those white men intended to treat those women as long-term partners or brief subjects of their sexual aggression. However, freedom offered women of color a greater variety of possible relationships with white men, which scholars have yet to fully explore. Free women of color had choices far beyond those available to enslaved women. These women, like white women, had the option to marry free men of their own race, engage in contracts, and own and sell property. When they chose to engage in relationships with white men, free women of color had greater freedom than enslaved women to determine and shape their familial relations and could reap greater benefits from those interactions. Most importantly, these couples helped to develop the rationale for such relationships and the guidelines for how free women of color and white men carried out their relationships in public and private spaces.

The free women of mixed ancestry who chose to develop life-long relationships with white men in nineteenth-century Hertford County came from a variety of family backgrounds, but most were not wealthy. Louisiana Weaver's father, Charles Weaver, was a poor and sickly man of color who struggled to provide for his family and often depended on the labor of his wife, Delilah, and their children in order to make ends meet. Celia Garnes, the daughter of Daniel and Betsey Garnes, grew up in a household in which her parents had trouble supporting their children and were almost forced by the courts to bind out** several of their sons. Sallie Yeates Bizzell was the daughter of Velia Bizzell, a free-born woman of mixed ancestry, who toiled in local fisheries as a fish cleaner, making only half what her male counterparts made for the same day's work. Whoever Sallie's father was, he did not provide for the family. Mary Jane and Susan Chavis also grew up under tough circumstances. Both girls were the daughters of Emmaline Chavis, a free woman of color; however, they had different fathers. Mary Jane was the daughter of Samuel Powell, a white man, who left her mother alone with six children after he was shot and killed in a brawl. Susan was reportedly the daughter of Nathaniel Turner, a free man of color, who was between marriages at the time of Susan's birth. Strong tensions appear to have existed between Susan's parents, as Turner brought larceny charges against Emmaline Chavis for stealing bacon from his storehouse. These women who chose to build

---

**bind out: to apprentice, or place someone in service to another.

relationships with white men sought better adult lives than those they experienced as children and did not find legal husbands who could help them reach that goal.[12]

Financial mobility likely played a significant role in the choices of free women of mixed ancestry. In an era in which women in general had limited opportunities for work and faced significant wage discrimination, free women of mixed ancestry had to consider the financial security and social standing of potential mates. For a poor woman looking to move up financially, a relationship with a well-established white man who was willing to build a long-term relation was a promising opportunity. A white man could not directly pass on the benefits of whiteness to a woman of color and her children as he could for a white woman and her children. White enforcement of racial boundaries limited free people of color's access to certain exclusively white networks, therefore limiting a white man's ability to extend his social connections. However, a white man could convey property obtained through connections to these networks and, as long as he lived, he could pass on some of the intangible benefits of being part of middle- and upper-class white social circles.

The second-class social and political position of non-white men in North Carolina's social hierarchy may have influenced women's companion choices. During much of the nineteenth century, the law and social customs granted white men privileges, which men of color, especially slaves, could not enjoy. White superiority, in effect, was not simply an ideology, but in many instances a social reality. Free women of mixed ancestry may have taken this reality into consideration and used it to rationalize their mate selections. Calvin Scott Brown recalled, "When I first came here [to Hertford County] I often heard mulatto women say that they would rather be a white man's concubine than a nigger's wife."[13] Brown's statement suggests that at least some women of mixed ancestry in Hertford County viewed certain non-whites as the inferiors of white men. Historians have found non-white women in other societies including much of Latin America and the Caribbean who used similar logic to support their choices to embrace illicit arrangements with white men over legally sanctioned marriages to non-whites.[14] As in other slave or former slave societies, Hertford County residents drew significant distinctions between different groups of non-white people. Free people of color were politically and legally distinct from enslaved people, who had no civil rights in American slave societies. After emancipation, people continued to draw meaningful distinctions between the old free people of color and newly emancipated slaves and their descendants. In Hertford County, social divisions between "mulattoes," which included almost all of the old free population of color, and "blacks" reinforced these lines of distinction. Women of mixed ancestry in Hertford County may have taken these distinctions into consideration when choosing marriage partners. A woman's choice of a partner

10

Milteer identifies a number of factors that likely influenced "women's companion choices," including financial stability, as well as their social and political positioning.

had long-term implications for both her and any children that she might have. Associations with a man of lower social status would have ultimately diminished the social standing of a woman of higher social position.

Basic feelings of love, admiration, and affection versus purely economic and social motivations may have driven relationships between free women of mixed ancestry and white men. Examples exist from all time periods and areas of the world where people with different social statuses, ancestral origins, economic positions, and belief systems have crossed socially constructed boundaries in order to build loving relationships. At least some free women of mixed ancestry and white men likely moved beyond the social constructions that attempted to order their world to fulfill their desires for love and acceptance from another human being whom they found attractive and desirable. The racial categories used to divide people with different ancestries, appearances, and community positions could not always overcome natural attraction. Laws against marriage between whites and non-whites attempted to curb the influences of attraction and affection and make unions across racial boundaries socially unacceptable. The people who engineered marriage laws attempted to impose their beliefs about appropriate behavior through granting or denying the privilege of marriage. However, their attempts could not convince every couple to deny their own feelings in order to conform to the societal norm.

Although love and attraction likely played an important part in the development of relationships between free women of mixed ancestry and white men, the social and economic realities still carried considerable weight in the rationale of relationships. Social and economic status of the participants in these relationships could determine the feasibility of living in a socially unacceptable manner. Free women of mixed ancestry who chose white mates usually selected men of high standing in the community. Christian Wiggins partnered with Noah Cotton, a planter and descendant of a long-established Hertford County family. Louisiana Weaver established a family with James Kiff, the county tax collector and a businessman. Sallie Yeates Bizzell developed a long-term relationship with Richard Henry Shield, a well-respected doctor. Mary Jane Chavis's partner was James Norfleet Holloman, a successful merchant and active participant in local Democratic Party politics.[15] Most free women of mixed ancestry who had white partners chose men of wealth and prestige. Free women of mixed ancestry made their mate selections just as carefully as women who contracted in legal marriage with the hope of securing economic stability.

For non-white women, associations with men of high social position were imperative to social mobility as well as immunity from legal prosecution for fornication and adultery. Hertford County's courts never brought white men of high status into court for committing fornication and adultery with women of color. The elite white power structure that controlled the local judiciary was

> Milteer opens this paragraph with a transition statement that signals a shift in his argument.

generally unwilling to shame publicly members of its own group by placing well-to-do white male fornicators on trial. Social respectability resulting from birth into well-established families, economic success, or connections to important white-only social networks protected these men from legal prosecution. Only the relationships of white men who lacked these attributes faced prosecution.

The backgrounds of two white men prosecuted for fornication and adultery 15 with women of color during the March 1854 term of Hertford County Court illustrate this class-based legal double standard. The court charged two couples, William Futrell and Frusa Reid and Wiley Ezell and Celia Garnes, with fornication and adultery. William Futrell appears to have come from a poor farming family. The 1850 Census lists the Futrell family as owners of real estate worth only $48. Wiley Ezell owned a modest amount of real property, but the circumstances of his birth as the son of an unwed mother likely stained his reputation in the community. At their trials, both couples pled not guilty, and in the end the jury found only Futrell and Reid guilty of fornication and adultery. The jury acquitted Ezell and Garnes of all charges, although their cohabitation and children should have served as enough evidence to find the couple in the wrong. The Hertford County court records do not explain how Ezell and Garnes won their case; however, the list of jurors contains a possible clue. Starkey Sharpe Harrell, one of the jurors in the Ezell and Garnes case, carried on a relationship with Emma Butler, a free woman of color, and may have sympathized with Ezell. Records from a later period suggest that Harrell and Ezell maintained a close relationship, and Ezell named Harrell the executor of his estate. Ezell came from a lower-class background, but at the time of trial may have begun to surround himself with people of wealth and good reputation. Cases like the *State v. Futrell and Reid* and the *State v. Ezell and Garnes* were a rarity in Hertford County, appearing on the court docket usually no more than once every five or ten years. The second of these cases shows that of those white men and women of color brought into court, only a few actually ended with a guilty verdict and punishment for the couples.[16]

Even though relations between free women of mixed ancestry and white men usually went unprosecuted, couples took precautions to limit the public visibility of their unlawful arrangements. In the antebellum period, some free women of mixed ancestry openly lived with their white partners, but most white men, attempting to maintain a façade to protect their respectability, kept two separate houses. One house, usually the main family quarters, served as the primary residence of the woman and her children. Another house, sometimes larger and sometimes smaller, was the permanent residence of the white father. This was the arrangement that Sallie Yeates Bizzell and Richard Henry Shield set up for their family. In the 1850s, Shield purchased a piece of property to maintain as his own residence. Then Bizzell purchased a small five-acre tract beside Shield,

> Notice the use of **hedging**, or qualifying language, in this paragraph. Learn more in Chapter 7, "Hedging."

which served as her regular residence.[17] Jesse Rob Weaver remembered that his mother, Louisiana Weaver, and father, James Kiff, set up a similar situation for their family in the 1870s and 1880s. Weaver stated, "My father provided a good large farm. One part was [my mother's] through his efforts. . . . He had one farm and house joining our field and he with our help worked both farms."[18]

When mothers and fathers maintained separate residences, children and both parents still often came together in one or the other of these physical spaces for family time. Jesse Rob Weaver recalled going back and forth between his mother's and father's houses as a youngster. A Hertford County teacher recollected that one of the daughters of Mary Jane Chavis and James Norfleet Holloman, who grew up at the turn of the century, told this teacher that "her father used to come see her mother every day and every night. He would sit around the fire with the whole family and talk just like any other father."[19] Although many free women of mixed ancestry and white men attempted to create an illusion of physical separation, their families experienced a life more similar to those headed by two parents than those headed by only a single parent. These families' façades were formalities, not realistic attempts to hide illicit relationships. As shown in the example of the teacher, people in the neighborhood knew the reality of their neighbors' situations.

Inside these households, free women of mixed ancestry and their white partners negotiated the operations of daily life for their families. Women engaged in long-term relationships with white partners could maintain significant power in family decision making. They ruled the domestic realm of their households and worked side by side with their white partners to make decisions about other family matters such as finances. Clarence Chavis, son of Mary Jane Chavis and James Norfleet Holloman, remembered that his father was "very attentive" to his mother and stated, "What was produced on the farm he and she agreed mutually as to how best to dispose of it. He always consulted her about how was best to spend the money."[20] Jesse Rob Weaver recalled that his mother "handled" the money that his father brought home.[21] Cooperation between women and men in these mixed-status relationships was imperative to their survival. Neither the woman nor man was bound by law to maintain their partnership. Unlike the relationships of married couples, the state had not sanctioned their relationship, so the law could not require court or legislative approval if the woman and man chose to dissolve their union. Of course the woman was less likely than the man to walk away from a relationship that provided financial security, but unlike some enslaved women, a free woman of color did have a choice. A long-term relationship with a white man was not her only option.

Like most legally recognized couples, free women of mixed ancestry and white men living in long-term relationships produced children, who often became the focus of these couples' energies and affections. Although the law did not acknowledge the relationship between white fathers and their mixed children, fathers in long-term partnerships with those children's mothers typically played an important role in their children's support and development. An acquaintance of the Chavis family recalled that one of James Norfleet Holloman's daughters

> said that her father was a merchant and would often go to Baltimore and Norfolk and buy things and would never come home without bringing all of them something, from dolls to suits of clothes. She said she felt proud that he was her father. She said that although in public they called him Mr. H[olloman], at home they called him daddy, and he was as sweet and loving to them as any father. . . . I have known this family all my life and know most of these things were true.

Holloman's daughter Bessie added that her father would allow his children to borrow his horses and buggies. Clarence Chavis remembered that his father "paid the children's school bills."[22]

Wiley Ezell recognized his children by Celia Garnes in a similar manner by providing for their needs. Even when they were adults, Ezell helped his children financially. Ezell ran an account with the merchants Knight and Barham on behalf of his son Joseph Garnes. Purchases on the account included essential items such as shoes and clothing. Ezell also aided his son Albert Garnes and son-in-law Henry T. Lassiter, husband of his daughter Delia Ann, by purchasing corn on their behalves through his own credit account.[23]

James Kiff supported his children as many of his contemporaries in the same situation did. His son Jesse Rob Weaver recalled that Kiff

> would come to our house every morning and every night. He would eat there sometimes. He would tell us what to do each day. . . . He arranged for us to have gifts and things as any father would do. I stayed with him mostly till he died. I would stay at nights and sleep with him.

Kiff also provided his children with many other essential needs, including sending them to school and helping them to maintain their mother's farm.[24] Although the law denied recognition to families like the Kiff-Weaver family, they still found ways to carve out spaces where members could live like the legally recognized families around them. White fathers' contributions to their non-white families reveal their desires to create the kind of family experience for themselves and their children that their married neighbors had. By failing to grant white men and non-white women the right to marry, the law placed a handicap on attempts to create a legitimate household. However, the dedication of white fathers who bypassed legally and socially imposed obstacles in order to care for their loved ones elucidates the complicated nature of respectability in nineteenth-century Southern society. Social norms and North Carolina law required fathers to take care of their children if both parties were free. However,

20

Milteer identifies a number of strategies that white men and non-white women used to "create the kind of family experience for themselves and their children that their married neighbors had."

those same social norms and laws created obstacles for white fathers to provide for non-white children.

Deep ties to extended family across the color line further highlight the determination of couples to enjoy an unbounded family life. Wiley Ezell went beyond simply helping his children. In 1851, he extended a loan to his partner's brother, Noah Garnes, for $18.68, which Ezell never collected.[25] James Kiff's sister, Penny Hedgepath, played an important role in the lives of his children. Jesse Rob Weaver retained very fond memories of his aunt, whom he helped to take care of after the death of his father. He remembered, "I thought she could cook the best food I ever ate. She was good to all of us and would give us some of anything she had to eat."[26] These examples demonstrate that racial divisions and lack of legal recognition sometimes failed to overcome the social significance given to common ancestry and extended kinship. Lawmakers sought to define the family as a racially uniform unit by prohibiting marriage across the color line, but people on the ground, at least occasionally, rejected this notion.[27]

Women of mixed ancestry, when they spent many years in close unions with white men, worked with their partners to set up some form of financial security for themselves and their children. White men used a number of legally enforceable options in order to provide for their families at the time of their deaths. Wills, promissory notes, and property transfers before death were all methods to provide financial security to partners and children with no legally recognized familial relationship. During the nineteenth century, several white men left wills in the hands of trusted friends who promised to take care of children and partners. Before his death in 1815, Noah Cotton dictated a will leaving all his property to his nine children and partner, Christian Wiggins, whom some people in the community recognized as "Christian Cotton." John Vann, the executor of the will, made a conscious effort to obtain shelter, food, and education for Noah's and Christian's children. Using funds from Noah's estate sale and receipts from the rental of his plantation and two slaves, Vann paid the monthly bills for the children's upkeep.[28]

Many years later, Richard W. Knight followed the example of men like Noah Cotton and used a will to protect the future interests of his family. Sometime in the late nineteenth century, Knight had begun a long-term relationship with Susan Chavis, which produced three daughters. Desiring to pass on his wealth to them, Knight wrote his will in 1908 leaving all of his property, "real, personal, and mixed," to Susan Chavis. He requested that at Susan's death, all of his property be divided among the couple's three daughters, Mary S. Roberts, Mattie J. Chavis, and Hattie F. Graves. Knight appointed James Norfleet Holloman, the partner of Mary Jane Chavis, Susan's half-sister, as the executor of his estate. In 1913, two witnesses supported the authenticity of the will at the probate court after Knight's death. There is no evidence to suggest that Susan and her children did not ultimately receive the property left to them.

Milteer explores instances where white men used wills, promissory notes, and property transfers through deed changes to "protect the future interests" of their families.

Wiley Ezell attempted to create a similar situation for his partner Celia 25
Garnes and their children. In his will, Ezell left his home place to his children with
the prerequisite that they care for their mother for the rest of her life. Ezell made
Starkey Sharpe Harrell, the juror from the 1854 fornication and adultery case, his
executor.[29] Unlike the cases of Noah Cotton and Richard Knight, however, several people challenged Ezell's last wishes. Soon after Ezell's death in 1879, Harrell
sent notice to the court renouncing his right as executor of the Ezell estate. The
court then replaced Harrell with John F. Newsome. Newsome moved quickly
after his appointment and began the process of settling Ezell's numerous debts,
including several notes on behalf of Celia Garnes and her sons, Joseph, Daniel,
and Albert. While Newsome was in the process of settling the estate, Ezell's niece,
C. Elizabeth Futrell, and her husband Amos filed a suit against Celia Garnes
and her four children claiming that the will devising all of Ezell's property to the
Garneses was not Ezell's true last will and testament. Benjamin B. Winborne,
the lawyer for the Futrells, argued that Elizabeth, as the sole daughter of Ezell's
only sister, was her uncle's only heir at law. The probate judge ruled in favor
of the Futrells, but Newsome refused to surrender the assets of the estate to
them. Failing to gain Newsome's cooperation, the Futrells sued Newsome as the
administrator of the estate and in 1882 won a judgment in their favor.

Wills were imperfect means to transfer property to loved ones. When
legitimate heirs challenged the rights of children and partners with no
legally recognized connection to a man, the law could be swayed against the
wishes of the progenitor. Celia Garnes and her children never collected all
that Ezell intended for them to have from his estate. However, the Garneses
successfully procured some of Ezell's assets through other means. Daniel,
Albert, and Celia Garnes collected debts from the estate for various sorts
of work. Whether the Garneses actually performed this work or Ezell simply
gave them notes to collect against his estate for fear that someone might
challenge his will is not clear. The Garneses also took possession of much of
Ezell's personal property, including the contents of his house by purchasing
them at his estate sale. Celia Garnes and her children failed to gain all that
Ezell intended to leave to them, but under the circumstances, the outcome
could have been much worse.[30]

Some white men relied solely on promissory notes to convey wealth to their
partners and progeny. Before their deaths, men would issue these notes to their
partners and children. Upon their deaths, the women and children could use the
notes to make claims against the estates of the white progenitors. This was the
arrangement made between Sallie Yeates Bizzell and Richard Henry Shield. In
1867, Shield gave Bizzell a promissory note for $1,500 with interest. In the note,
he specifically stated that he, his heirs, and executors guaranteed this debt to
Bizzell. After Shield's death in 1870, Sallie collected the value of the note from

the executor of his estate.[31] Surviving sources do not explain Shield's reasoning for leaving Bizzell a promissory note versus leaving a will with instructions. Shield probably understood that while wills could be contested, promissory notes were collectible no matter who was the bearer.

Although promissory notes were a safer method for white men to pass on wealth to their partners and children, legal heirs still challenged the exchange of notes. James Kiff left his children "notes or mortgages amounting to $18,000," as his son Jesse Rob Weaver remembered. Just days before his death in 1882, Kiff gave the notes to his son Samuel Weaver. James may have suspected that his brother, William Kiff, would try to block his wishes. Indeed, William qualified as administrator of his brother's estate and then attempted to claim all of his brother's property, including the notes. William sued James's children for the notes, taking the case all the way to the North Carolina Supreme Court. Jesse Rob explained that his uncle "tried to get everything from us but he failed. My father had things so fixed that he couldn't get it."[32] After each of William Kiff's appeals, the courts sided with the defendants and secured the Weavers' rights to their father's property.[33]

Promissory notes were the most effective means of passing property posthumously on to illegitimate children whose inheritance rights could be challenged by legal heirs, such as siblings or nieces and nephews. The Kiff and Weaver case demonstrates that many participants in mixed relationships were well aware of the dissatisfaction of close family members in regards to their relationships. They knew that if they set up the executions of their estates carefully, the legal system was bound to back their actions. Into the 1880s, at least some courts were unwilling to challenge the exchange of notes, even when people of color were involved. A ruling against the Weaver children would have represented a ruling for chicanery. In the Weaver case, the courts were unwilling to create a precedent with such disastrous potential.

While promissory notes were more reliable than wills, making real estate property transfers through deeds during the man's lifetime was the most secure way to transfer property to his family. Unlike with wills and promissory notes, men could personally prevent challenges to their wishes by guaranteeing that the register of deeds recorded the deeds in the county records. In 1870, James Kiff made his first land transfer to his partner, Louisiana Weaver. The deed states that Kiff sold Weaver several tracts of land for $498.33. Two subsequent deeds also state that Weaver paid Kiff for real estate. The facts that Kiff and Weaver were engaged in an intimate relationship and that single women in nineteenth-century Hertford County had little ability to accrue large sums of money suggest that an actual exchange of money between Kiff and Weaver was very unlikely. But Kiff knew that a deed of sale was much stronger than a deed of gift, the method often chosen to exchange property through relatives. He likely chose a deed of sale because creditors and other parties could challenge deeds of gift.[34]

Other partners and fathers used deeds of sale to transfer land to their families. Soon after the birth of his last child, James Norfleet Holloman deeded his partner, Mary Jane Chavis, a tract of land adjoining his other properties. The deed of sale states that Mary Jane Chavis paid Holloman $200. Almost twenty years later, Holloman transferred the cemetery lot where the family had recently buried Mary Jane Chavis to his son, Clarence Chavis. The deed for this land transfer implied that Clarence Chavis paid his father for the small cemetery plot. Richard W. Knight used similar tactics to grant land to his daughter, Mattie J. Chavis. In 1906, shortly before his death, Knight transferred a lot in the town of Union to his daughter under the supposition that Mattie J. Chavis paid him $130 for the property.[35] None of these men used the more contestable deeds of gift to transfer property to their families. As long-time buyers and sellers of land, they were cognizant of the possible implications of one type of land transfer over another. In the cases of Kiff, Holloman, and Knight, the historical record clearly demonstrates that all of these men knew one another and operated within some of the same social circles. Similarities in the methods used by white men to convey real estate to their non-white families suggest that these men may have shared strategies for the secure transfer of property.

Free women of mixed ancestry and their white partners worked with ingenuity to create environments for their families to thrive despite living in a state that denied their partnerships and children legal recognition. The material circumstances of the women of mixed ancestry involved in long-term partnerships with white men improved drastically over their lives. All of the women in this article grew up poor, but by the time of their deaths most owned their own homes and sometimes additional properties. At her death in 1914, Louisiana Weaver was one of the wealthiest women of color in her locality. Weaver owned several tracts of land and in her will bequeathed $100 in gold to each of her five sons. The children of these women enjoyed much more comfortable lives than their mothers experienced in their early years. Most of the children of these couples married, established families, owned property, and generally enjoyed financial success. Some of the children and grandchildren of these couples intermarried and others married the children of other successful families.[36] Although the law discouraged or prevented women of mixed ancestry from marrying their white partners, these women clearly demonstrated that inconsistencies in the law could be exploited to their benefit and that of their children.

These conclusions should not imply that free women of mixed ancestry built long-term partnerships with white men only for financial gain. While the historical record has a difficult time revealing love between human beings, the

Milteer is careful to explain that the role of "love" is difficult to assess from the available historical records.

examples cited in this paper reveal that at least in some situations, relationships between free women of mixed ancestry and white men were bound together by mutual respect. Furthermore, some neighbors and friends recognized the bonds between free women of mixed ancestry, white men, and their children, and went to great lengths to respect those bonds even when the law granted those bonds no such respect.

Peggy Pascoe's work has shown that communities continued to debate the extent to which these laws should be enforced against white men even as lawmakers and judges attempted to strengthen white supremacy through tougher enforcement of laws banning relationships between whites and non-whites. Scholars have demonstrated that stronger enforcement of marriage restrictions and the proliferation of extralegal activities to punish and discourage sex between whites and non-whites came about during and after the Civil War. However, Pascoe noted that lawmakers and judges sought to target with increased persecution a particular type of relationship, those between white women and non-white men. She argues that not until the 1890s did the desire to uphold white supremacy make officials, judges, and juries more likely to subject white men "to the full range of the disabilities of miscegenation law." Even past this period up to the *Loving v. Virginia* decision, which found state miscegenation laws unconstitutional, the rights of white men continued to threaten the full enforcement of marriage and cohabitation restrictions.[37] The examples in this article show that even into the first decade of the twentieth century, the white power structure in Hertford County, at least in some cases, decided to uphold the rights of white men to choose their partners over widespread demands to prosecute white-non-white relationships.

The relationships discussed in this article reveal the limitations of race as a method to stratify society. Many people in the nineteenth century argued that the separation of races was a product of nature or even divine provenance. However, long-term partnerships between free women of mixed ancestry and white men demonstrate that such arguments were more political in nature than grounded in biological science or biblical scripture. The relationships in this study suggest that had such faulty argumentation not dominated nineteenth-century law and society, many mixed couples would have sought legal recognition. Their determination to build strong families, secure property rights, and uphold a public image of respectability supports the supposition that given the choice, they would have selected marriage. Free women of mixed ancestry and their white partners did not want to live on the edge of society; they simply hoped—and strived—to define their own relationships and build their own families.

In the conclusion, Milteer summarizes the major findings of his study and indicates their overall significance.

ENDNOTES

I completed the research for this article with support from the Center for the Study of the American South and North Caroliniana Society. I would like to thank Kathleen DuVal, Susannah Loumiet, and the two anonymous reviewers for the *Journal of Social History* for their thoughtful comments and suggestions. Participants at the Thinking Gender Conference at UCLA and Virginia Tech's Bertoti Conference also provided valuable feedback on earlier versions of this article. I would also like to acknowledge the staffs of the State Archives of North Carolina, the Moorland-Spingarn Center, and the Southern Historical Collection for helping me procure primary source materials. Finally, I would like to express my gratitude to the descendants of the families discussed in this article for their friendship and support. Address correspondence via email: wemilteer@ hotmail.com.

"Endnotes" or "Notes" are a feature of the CMS (Chicago Manual of Style) documentation system.

1. "Women of mixed ancestry" in this context refers to women with various combinations of European, Native American, and African ancestry. Throughout the nineteenth century, Hertford County residents drew important distinctions between slaves and their descendants, who locals generally categorized as black, and free people of color, most who usually fell under the mulatto category. In nineteenth-century North Carolina, the term *mulatto* was not used exclusively to refer to people of African descent. People descended from native peoples and Europeans also fell under the mulatto category. "Women of mixed ancestry" reinforces this ambiguity. See William D. Valentine Diary, Volume 12, 164–65, Southern Historical Collection (hereafter SHC); *State v. William Chavers* (Dec. 1857), Supreme Court Cases, State Archives of North Carolina (hereafter SANC).

2. William D. Valentine Diary, Volume 13, 85, SHC.

3. E. Franklin Frazier Papers Box 131–92, Folder 7; Manuscript Division, Moorland-Spingarn Research Center, Howard University (hereafter EFFP Box 131–92, Folder 7, MDMSRCHU).

4. EFFP Box 131–92, Folder 7, MDMSRCHU.

5. For further discussion of the contrast between concubinage and long-term relationships between free women of color and white men, see Kenneth Aslakson, "The 'Quadroon-Plaçage' Myth of Antebellum New Orleans: Anglo-American (Mis)interpretations of a French-Caribbean Phenomenon," *Journal of Social History* 3 (2012): 709–34.

6. *Guide to Research Materials in the North Carolina State Archives: County Records* (Raleigh, 2002), 177. For further discussion of marriage as a public institution, see Nancy Cott, *Public Vows: A History of Marriage and the Nation* (Cambridge, 2000).

7. Peggy Pascoe, *What Comes Naturally: Miscegenation Law and the Making of Race in America* (New York, 2009), 42–43.

8. Walter Clark, ed., *The State Records of North Carolina*, vol. 23 (Goldsboro, 1904), 65, 160. For further discussion of the impacts of these laws in colonial North Carolina, see Kirsten Fischer, *Suspect Relations: Sex, Race, and Resistance in Colonial North Carolina* (Ithaca, 2002).

9. *Acts Passed By the General Assembly of the State of North Carolina at the Session of 1830–1831* (Raleigh, 1831), 9–10.

10. *Amendments to the Constitution of North Carolina, Proposed by the Constitutional Convention of 1875 and the Constitution As It Will Read As Proposed to Be Amended* (Raleigh, 1875), 65.

11. For general studies of mixed marriages in the United States, see Gary B. Nash, *Forbidden Love: The Secret History of Mixed-Race America* (New York, 1999); Peter Wallenstein, *Tell the Court I Love My Wife: Race, Marriage, and Law—An American History* (New York, 2002). For further

discussion of relations between enslaved women and white men see Deborah Gray White, *Ar'n't I a Woman: Female Slaves in the Plantation South* (New York, 1985); Kent Anderson Leslie, *Woman of Color, Daughter of Privilege: Amanda America Dickson 1849–1893* (Athens, 1995); Jean Fagan Yellin, *Harriet Jacobs: A Life* (New York, 2004); Annette Gordon-Reed, *The Hemingses of Monticello: An American Family* (New York, 2008). For further discussion of relations between free women of color and white men, see Adele Logan Alexander, *Ambiguous Lives: Free Women of Color in Rural Georgia, 1789–1879* (Fayetteville, 1991); Victoria E. Bynum, *Unruly Women: The Politics of Social and Sexual Control in the Old South* (Chapel Hill, 1992); Joan Martin, "Plaçage and the Louisiana Gens de Couleur Libre: How Race and Sex Defined the Lifestyles of Free Women of Color" in *Creole: The History and Legacy of Louisiana's Free People of Color*, ed. Sybil Kein (Baton Rouge, 2000); Joshua D. Rothman, *Notorious in the Neighborhood: Sex and Families across the Color Line in Virginia, 1787–1861* (Chapel Hill, 2003); Amrita Chakrabarti Myers, *Forging Freedom: Black Women and the Pursuit of Liberty in Antebellum Charleston* (Chapel Hill, 2011).

12. Richard R. Weaver Pension File, National Archives and Records Administration; Hertford County County Court Minutes, Volume 1, May 1832, SANC; Letter J. A. Anderson to Chesson and Armstead, John B. Chesson Papers, Box 1, Chesson Papers Miscellaneous, SANC; William D. Valentine Diary, Volume 13, 188, SHC; State v. Emmy Chavers, Hertford County Civil and Criminal Action Papers, Box 1, Civil and Criminal Cases 1864, SANC; Death Certificate of Susan Chavis, SANC.

13. EFFP Box 131–92, Folder 7, MDMSRCHU. The context of Calvin Scott Brown's statement appears to suggest that the term "nigger" may have referred specifically to people recognized in the community as "black" and would not have included "mulattoes" or people recognized as being of mixed ancestry.

14. Mavis Christine Campbell, *The Dynamics of Change in a Slave Society: A Sociopolitical History of the Free Coloreds of Jamaica, 1800–1865* (London, 1976), 51; David Brion Davis, *Inhuman Bondage: The Rise and Fall of Slavery in the New World* (New York, 2006), 180.

15. Benjamin B. Winborne, *The Colonial and State Political History of Hertford County* (Raleigh, 1906), 235, 333.

16. Hertford County County Court Minutes, Volume 3, March 1854, SANC; 1850 United States Federal Census, Hertford County, North Carolina, Northern District, 291a, 309a; EFFP Box 131–92, Folder 7, MDMSRCHU. The 1850 Census lists two men named William Futrell living in the same Hertford County household. Which of these men was involved in the case with Frusa Reid is unclear.

17. Hertford County Record of Deeds, Volume A, 653, SANC.

18. EFFP Box 131–92, Folder 7, MDMSRCHU. The 1870 Census confirms the proximity between Louisiana Weaver's house and James Kiff's place as described by Jesse Rob Weaver. See 1870 United States Federal Census, Hertford County, North Carolina, Winton Township, 54.

19. EFFP Box 131–92, Folder 7, MDMSRCHU.

20. EFFP Box 131–92, Folder 7, MDMSRCHU.

21. EFFP Box 131–92, Folder 7, MDMSRCHU.

22. EFFP Box 131–92, Folder 7, MDMSRCHU.

23. Hertford County Estates Records, Box 13, Ezell, Wiley, SANC.

24. EFFP Box 131–92, Folder 7, MDMSRCHU.

25. Hertford County Estates Records, Box 13, Ezell, Wiley, SANC.

26. EFFP Box 131–92, Folder 7, MDMSRCHU.

27. For further discussion of the way lawmakers attempted to define family through marriage laws, see Cott, *Public Vows*, 24–55.

28. Will of Noah Cotton 1815, John Vann Papers, Box 4, SANC; Estate of Noah Cotton, John Vann Papers, Box 3, SANC.

29. Hertford County Record of Wills, Volume C, 222, SANC.

30. Hertford County Estates Records, Box 13, Ezell, Wiley, SANC.

31. Hertford County Estates Records, Box 40, Shields, Richard H., SANC.

32. EFFP Box 131–92, Folder 7, MDMSRCHU.

33. North Carolina Supreme Court ruled that Samuel Weaver was entitled to his father's notes after the settlement of all of James Kiff's debts. See *William Kiff Admr. v. Samuel Weaver et al.* 94 NC 274 (Feb 1886), Supreme Court Cases, SANC.

34. Hertford County Record of Deeds, Volume B, 50–51, SANC; Hertford County Record of Deeds, Volume F, 548–49, SANC; Hertford County Record of Deeds, Volume H, 196–97, SANC.

35. Hertford County Record of Deeds, Volume V, 172–73, SANC; Hertford County Record of Deeds, Volume 50, 172, SANC; Hertford County Record of Deeds, Volume 32, 88, SANC.

36. Hertford County Record of Wills, Volume D, 324–26, SANC. Examples of intermarriages between families include the marriage of Louisiana Weaver and James Kiff's son to Sallie Yeates Bizzell and R. H. Shield's daughter and the marriage between Mary Jane Chavis and J. N. Holloman's son, to Sallie Yeates Bizzell and R. H. Shield's granddaughter. See Hertford County Marriage Register and Hertford County Marriage Licenses in the State Archives of North Carolina for further examples.

37. Pascoe, *What Comes Naturally*, 10–11. For further discussion of changes in the regulation of relationships between whites and non-whites after the Civil War, see Martha Hodes, *White Women, Black Men: Illicit Sex in the Nineteenth-Century South* (New Haven, 1997).

Reading Questions

1. Milteer acknowledges a number of difficulties that attend the kind of historical research presented in the article. What are they?

2. According to Milteer, what is a likely financial justification for mixed free women choosing to develop long-term relationships with white men? What evidence does he provide for this?

3. What, according to Milteer, seems to be the role of love in mate selection for the mixed free women he discusses in the article?

Rhetoric Questions

4. What is the primary form of evidence that Milteer uses to support his conclusions?

5. The article's introduction includes testimony from a number of individuals. What is the effect of the use of personal testimony on you as a reader?

Response Questions

6. Milteer writes, "Lawmakers sought to define the family as a racially uniform unit by prohibiting marriage across the color line, but people on the ground, at least occasionally, rejected this notion" (par. 22). Do you see evidence of individuals rejecting lawmakers' definitions of marriage or family in society today? Explain.

7. What does Milteer mean when he writes, "The relationships discussed in this article reveal the limitations of race as a method to stratify society" (par. 35)? In what ways does Milteer's article reveal these limitations?

African American Young Adult Women's Stories about Love: What I Want in a Long-Term Partner

JADA E. BROOKS AND DARREN D. MOORE

Jada Brooks is an associate professor and coordinator of family, child, and community services in the department of Family and Consumer Sciences at Virginia State University. Darren Moore is an associate professor and director of the Marriage and Family Therapy Program at Tuoro University Worldwide. He is also a licensed marriage and family therapist. In their article, which was published in 2020 in the *Journal of Black Studies*, Brooks and Moore report the results of a qualitative study designed to assess the attitudes and desires of young adult African American women toward marriage and long-term partner selection.

ABSTRACT

African American marriage rates have declined over the years. This qualitative study examines the ways in which African American young adult women describe their desires in potential long-term (possibly marriage) partners. The following research questions guided the study: (a) What are young adult African American women's perceptions as it relates to long-term relationships and marriage? and (b) What qualities do African American young adult women desire in a long-term partner? A total of 35 African American young adults participated in the study. Findings for the study indicated that childhood observations of family members' relationships, personality traits, and values had great influence in the type of partner desired. The study offers several recommendations for future research and strategies for marriage and family practices in the African American community.

Keywords: African American women, young adults, emerging adulthood, relationships, marriage, mate selection

MARRIAGE IN THE AFRICAN AMERICAN COMMUNITY

For African Americans, family is one of the most important institutions in the community (Franklin, 2007) with the institution and history of marriage being studied by many researchers (Dixon, 2009; King, 1999; King & Allen, 2009). In past generations, the majority of African American households consisted of married couples (Belgrave & Allison, 2019). In more recent decades, there has been a steady decline in marriage among African Americans (Belgrave & Allison, 2019), with African Americans having the lowest marriage rate of all racial groups (Chambers & Kravitz, 2011). Furthermore, when African Americans engage in marriage, they do so much later in life when compared with Caucasians (Dixon, 2009).

Previous research has indicated both positive and negative feelings about marriage in African American women (King, 1999; King & Allen, 2009). A quantitative study was conducted by King and Allen (2009) examining characteristics of ideal marriage partners for a total of 344 Black men and women. Participants were primarily single and in their 30s. Findings from the study indicated that female respondents were more likely than male respondents to emphasize the importance of education and financial status in potential marriage partners (King & Allen, 2009). Furthermore, the majority of participants preferred African American partners; however, about 45% indicated that race would not matter when choosing a partner (King & Allen, 2009). This finding suggests that income and socioeconomic status is important to some African Americans as it relates to the establishment of and stability of the family system.

Researchers have also suggested that differences in income between African American men and women may contribute to difficulties in finding a mate.

A study conducted by Chaney and Marsh (2008) found that African American men may struggle with finding marital partners due to their feelings of inadequacy and low self-esteem related to making less money than their female counterparts. Chaney and Marsh (2008) suggested that this perspective regarding finances also contributes to men's desire to cohabitate rather than committing to marriage. The authors noted this is due to the low level of confidence based on one's perceived inability to provide for one's family, making African American men less likely to marry. Marks and colleagues (2008) interviewed 30 African American couples regarding marriage and have found that finances and work-related stress can serve as a source of stress for couples. However, couples in the research study also reported that financial stress can serve as a mechanism that supports couple cohesion and reinforces commitment to the family system. In this example, couples may find refuge in one another as they work together as team to combat financial issues and obtain financial goals. Other researchers have suggested that financial strain reduces marital satisfaction for African Americans (Bryant et al., 2008, 2010; Lincoln & Chae, 2010).

Although there has been a significant amount of research that has been conducted regarding problems within African American marital couples and a decline in marriage rates among African Americans, there has been less discussion about protective factors and successful African American marriages (Phillips et al., 2012). Research is needed to explore the experience of African American couples who have successful relationships. Learning about successful African American marriages may inform how individual male and females go about the process of mate selection. The way in which individual African Americans are currently thinking about relationships may contribute to the outcome. However, this would need to be examined in future research. Nevertheless, the current research adds another dimension to what could potentially help to inform what is known about the relationship dynamics of African American college females. In addition, studies are needed to explore the experiences of African American young adults' desire to marry and characteristics of potential long-term partners.

DATING RELATIONSHIPS AND MARRIAGE IN YOUNG ADULTS

Empirical findings have suggested that millennials [5] have different views toward dating relationships and marriage, when compared with older adult populations. In particular, some of the discussion has focused on young adults deciding to delay dating and marriage (Martin et al., 2014). Likewise, other discussions have centered on topics related to technology use within the context of dating relationships (LeFebvre, 2018) and millennials in the workplace (Queiri et al., 2014). However, there has been less discussion that includes a focus on contextual factors such as race/ethnicity and gender among young adults as it pertains to dating relationships.

Although there have been several researchers that have examined the attitudes and beliefs of dating relationships among African Americans over time, there has been less of a focus on the dating preferences and mate selection among young African American adult females. Ross (1997) conducted a study regarding attitudes toward dating among 236 female and 149 male African American college students and found that skin complexion, wealth, and level of attractiveness were significant factors. In particular, Ross (1997) found that

> females were more likely than males: (a) to prefer to marry someone with more material wealth than themselves and (b) agree that having a good time and getting along with their mates are more important than the person being attractive. (p. 561)

Interestingly enough, males were more likely than females: (a) to prefer dating light-skinned persons, (b) to prefer marrying a person with light skin, and (c) to be more willing to marry a person from a lower social class than their own (p. 561). Additional research has suggested that familial background has a direct impact on dating attitudes and preferences for African Americans (Murty & Roebuck, 2015). For example, Murty and Roebuck (2015) conducted a study where they explored parental approval rates of interracial dating among African American college students (38% males and 62% females) that attended Historically Black Colleges and Universities (HBCU). In particular, the researchers found that African American college students from more urban areas receive higher rates of parental approval of interracial dating when compared with counterparts who are from more rural areas. Likewise, there has been some discussion about the correlation of family instability during early childhood with cynical attitudes regarding marriage among young African Americans (Simons et al., 2012).

Scholars have suggested that there is an imbalance among African American women when compared with African American men on college campuses which has implications on racial identity and mate selection (Henry, 2008, 2013; Watt, 2006). One study regarding mate selection among African American male and female college students found that both genders seek financial stability, education, and someone that has a spiritual foundation (King & Allen, 2009). Other researchers have focused on the historical reasons for lower marriage rates in African Americans when compared with their White counterparts (Besharov & West, 2001). Additional research is needed to explore the contemporary attitudes and perceptions of young adult African American women. Furthermore, research regarding motivational factors, mate selection, and barriers to dating and marital relationships among African American young adult women is warranted.

Although previous studies have addressed the declining marriage rates, feelings about marriage, differences in income, delays in marriage, and changes in dating patterns in the African American community, few studies have specifically examined what African American young adult women look for in a partner. Having some insight regarding what African American young adult women look for may contribute to the scholarly literature and may inform what we know about the dating attitudes and behaviors among this population. The purpose of this study was to address the gap in the literature by examining African American young adult women's desires in potential long-term (possibly marriage) partners. The following research questions guided the study: (a) What are young adult African American women's perceptions as it relates to long-term relationships and marriage? and (b) What qualities do African American young adult women desire in a long-term partner?

METHOD

Procedures

Permission to conduct the study was granted by the Institutional Review Board at the participating university, an HBCU located in the mid-Atlantic region of the United States. An HBCU was selected to collect data specifically because of the high enrollment of African American women. Participants for the study were recruited through behavioral and social science courses on campus with minimal extra credit being offered as incentive to participate (five points added to the lowest test score; tests were 150 points each).

Data for the study were collected in narrative 10 format. Narrative research allows participants to tell the story about their experience (Miller, 2018). The narrative prompt included questions about the qualities participants desired in a partner and the decision-making process on transitioning from dating to pursuing a committed relationship with a potential partner. All students enrolled in the courses used for recruitment were allowed to complete a narrative assignment. Students not identifying as African American women were omitted from the data for the study. In addition, all participants were able to opt out of the study, however all students identifying as African American women between the ages of 18 and 35 years agreed to participate and allow their narrative to be included in the data. Upon receiving written narratives, identifying information was removed and pseudonyms were created for each participant.

Sample

A total of 35 participants were included in the current study (see Table 1). Participants for the study were between the ages of 19 and 32 years of age.

Table 1

Participants

Name	Age (years)	Name	Age (years)
Annika	23	Lauren	23
Arianna	22	London	23
Brenda	21	Mia	22
Brooklyn	19	Michelle	25
Cadence	20	Nadia	20
Charity	20	Nicole	19
Dana	32	Portia	22
Elizabeth	21	Rachelle	23
Ella	20	Robin	20
Fatima	23	Sasha	19
Felicia	22	Sierra	21
Gabrielle	19	Sonia	22
Imani	22	Sydney	19
Layla	22	Tamera	21
Jaclyn	20	Tracy	19
Jennifer	20	Yvonne	19
Kayla	19	Zoe	22
Kiera	22		

All participants were college students attending an HBCU majoring in a variety of areas including fashion and merchandising, business, and child development. Participants were enrolled in courses related to human development and multicultural issues at the time of the study. Course material included such topics as relationships, marriage, cohabitation, parenting, and divorce as well as other areas related to marriage and families. The courses were a part of the general education sequence allowing enrollment for students from a variety of academic, family, and economic backgrounds.

Analysis

Analysis of the data began with the authors for the study independently examining the narratives multiple times. Themes and categories were identified through open coding. Rossman and Rallis (2003) describe themes and categories as "overlapping"; however, categories describe a segment of your data whereas a theme describes more subtle processes (p. 282). Emerging themes and categories were identified and organized into broad topics based on the frequency of responses by participants. The number of codes were reduced using fast mapping (Rossman & Rallis, 2003), a technique used to connect themes and categories to one another. Similar categories and themes were merged to form a final list of codes. Emerging codes from participant perceptions included family experience, personality traits, values, and physical attraction related to mate selection. The final coding scheme was applied for another round of analysis of the narratives. The following section provides a summary of the themes identified in the study.

FINDINGS

The reasons we fall in love may be a mystery, but the reasons we stay in love are far less elusive. There may be no such thing as the perfect partner, but an ideal partner can be found in someone who has developed themselves in certain ways that go beyond the surface (Imani, 20).

Selecting a Partner

When describing what was important in selecting a long-term mate, participants at times found it challenging to describe in words what they desired. Although many expressed that they wanted to eventually settle down in a long-term relationship, it was often difficult to determine what would be the right fit as it relates to a long-term potential marriage partner. As Zoe, age 22, indicated "When it comes to picking out a "mate" who you want to call your own can be very difficult. Sometimes you just don't know what someone's intentions are." Gabrielle had similar thoughts:

It is very difficult to pinpoint exactly what you are looking for in a mate. You learn upon going on your first date that there are so many aspects of one's character that you learn that you are attracted to or repelled by.

In contrast, Lauren, age 23, indicated instinct in selecting a partner, "I believe sometimes you have that gut feeling that the person is the one for you. It's like at times you just know if that's where you want to be." Nevertheless, participants shared their personal stories about characteristics and qualities that were important in selecting a long-term partner. Family experience, personality traits, and values were noted most often by participants. Furthermore, physical attraction was not deemed as important by the majority of the participants in the current study.

Family Experience

Although childhood experiences and family members were not directly asked about in the study, the first finding that was evident related to the role of family members' relationships. Several participants noted the romantic relationships of their mothers and grandmothers and the influence it had over their desires in a long-term marital partner. Others noted the absence of their biological father or strong male figure impacting their perceptions of a romantic relationship. Zoe provided a good example of the importance of family and parental relationships as it relates to seeking romantic relationships and how one views relationships, "I believe in relationships. I'm not just talking about boyfriend and girlfriend relationships; I am referring to relationships such as mother-daughter, father-son, and so on. Relationships are very important to me." The impact of forming relationships throughout childhood was evident as children generally obtain values about relationships through their experiences.

Brooklyn, the only participant who openly identified as heterosexual (this was not a part of any question or demographics), described her experiences growing up in a traditional heterosexual two-parent household and the implications family structure had on her expectations for a mate. She also explained what she does not want in a long-term mate based on observations of her grandfather's value system as it pertains for relationships:

> I am a heterosexual African American female and I grew up in a heterosexual household where my father was the head of house and he fit all of the stereotypes

of a husband and my mother mostly fit the stereotypes of a wife and mother. The environment where you grow up in has a great influence on your mindset because what you grow up with is all you know until you come in contact with something that contradicts those principles. In my case, when it comes to a partner, I unintentionally look for the same qualities that I have found in the father figure who happens to be my father. However, I resent men who resemble my grandfather because he is still stuck in his ways where women belong in the kitchen and have to cater to the man.

Arianna, age 22, shared her childhood experience and the connection to her desires in a spouse or long-term partner. Arianna's story suggests a strong connection in the role of family members and the example they provide for healthy or unhealthy relationships. Furthermore, because of the absence of her parents she also took on the role as caregiver for siblings at an early age:

> My grandmother raised me, my mother was absent, and I have no clue who my father is, so the feeling of neglect was high for me. I was raised to be a caretaker early because I was the oldest . . . I personally don't like the feeling of neglect because my biggest downfall is looking to my spouse to protect and love me more because I never had a father, or father figure to teach me aspects, and what not to deal with in a male. Not having a father figure left me with jumping into relations with males not knowing if one cares about me as much as I do him.

In contrast Jacklyn, age 20, had a strong father throughout her life. Her father's character directly influenced her desires in a relationship,

> I would seek a person that has the same ethics as my father. He would be employed, independent, family oriented, grounded spiritually, own a car and must be a good provider. Most importantly he must possess the desire to achieve.

The role of fathers or strong male role models was present in many participants, stressing the importance of childhood experiences in mate selection.

Mothers and female role models were also noted by participants as influencing their choices in relationships. London expressed how her childhood experiences with the women in her family influenced what she looks for in a long-term marriage partner.

Rather than stating what she desired in a partner, she addressed the qualities she did not want based on what she experienced as a child within her family:

> Most of the women in my family have chosen mates that were the exact opposite of them. Where the women in my family were strong minded and full of pride, the men were not. While their partners were selfish and disrespectful, I am going to have the opposite. What I did not realize at the time was their relationships were a generational thing . . . I was accustomed to seeing the man be a dependent and the woman carrying everything on her own. I cannot remember it being any other way in my family. I came from a long line of women that catered to men. I do not know how long it has been that way, but it is what I came to understand as "normal."

Family implications were noted with potential [20] partners parental relationships, specifically with their mothers. Several participants noted that the influence of a long-term partner's relationship with his or her mother was a defining point in establishing a romantic connection. Cadence, age 20, said it in this way: "Most males who have a good relationship with their mothers are usually more affectionate and loyal to you because they treat you how they would like someone to treat their mothers, or any female in their family."

Personality Traits

Participants for the study defined several areas related to personality as desirable in a potential long-term or marriage partner. Specifically, participants identified having a sense of humor, being "outgoing," being responsible and mature, and honesty, trust, and faithfulness as the most desirable personality characteristics. Imani described it in this way:

> As we get to know the people we date, these are invaluable traits to both look for in them and to strive for in ourselves. These ideal attributes include: maturity, openness, honesty and integrity, empathy, respect, affection, a sense of humor, and an education. You do not have to be perfect but as long as you have most of these things it is possible, we can grow old together.

The majority of participants indicated that trust was a major factor in determining if someone was a good potential long-term partner. Dana, the oldest participant in the study, connected trust to various characteristics desired in a partner:

> The power of trust is inclusive of being reliable, good, and honest. If I cannot trust you as my mate it makes no sense being in a relationship with you. In addition, my mate should be spiritual, loves to cook, flexible, successful, independent, fun, funny, playful, family oriented and should portray similar values and goals as mine.

London had similar thoughts while addressing the need for a partner who is a provider. She addressed not wanting to struggle, specifically addressing her desires even in her childhood of her expectations for a relationship. In her written narrative, she also noted previous relationships with men who were unable to hold long-term and consistent employment:

> For me, my partner was going to show me respect and love me unconditionally. He also needed to be strong and more importantly be a provider. If it was one thing that I learned early on, it would be a real man would not stand by and watch a woman struggle. I have always been a believer in the 'if I got you then you got me' system. I had planned from about age ten that our household was going to be strong and it was going to happen that way with the both of us doing it together.

Some participants were not as selective in personality traits, but valued happiness as it related to a potential long-term partner. Furthermore, many had created a "timeline" for marriage, even as young adults. Considering current statistics of African American women marriage rates, it is not surprising that some of the participants had the goal of getting married within years of their current age. Rachelle, age 23, spoke extensively on what factors are important in mate selection and wanting to be married by a certain age:

> I'm not really a female who has a certain type when it comes to males, I just want to be with someone who makes me happy and respects me for the person I am . . . I'm 23 now I think that at this age I should be with someone I consider spending some years with as I would love to be married by the time I'm 30.

One factor that appears to be unique to this sam- [25] ple of African American young adult women was the specific desire for a partner who had a "sense of pride" in their identity. This was addressed through references to language, clothing, and professional behavior. For some participants, this was important as they were on track to become professionals in various fields of study. Several participants described wanting a partner who dressed in clothing that fit them appropriately, spoke proper English, and overall knew how to conduct themselves in a professional manner.

Annika explained the "professional" characteristics she wanted in a partner in a way that addressed behavior, education, and wanting a nice life, "I do not date guys that have the street mentality because they are constantly looking over their shoulders and think that the cops are after them. He has to have education and want the finer things in life." Layla had a similar description of wanting a potential partner who could "conduct themselves" in public, have an "intelligent conversation," and be themselves in all settings, "I do not like when a person feels they have to act a certain way around certain people. I like a person who can be themselves around any group of people and is still comfortable." She added, that if a person was missing even one of those qualities she would "lose interest quickly" and not view them as someone with "long-term potential."

Robin, an aspiring attorney, had an experience with a former partner who used "Ebonics," also referred to as Black English, which is often associated with slang terms (Belgrave & Allison, 2019). Robin went on to describe the value of acquiring a college education and how that directly influences her choice in a partner:

> In the future, I will be an attorney who will be surrounded by professionals on a daily basis, so my partner must be able to act professionally. I have dated a guy that was completely unprofessional. At restaurants, he would order his food using only Ebonics, which was very embarrassing to me. I have had a partner who was bothered by how much I spoke about and valued my college education. He would rather talk about Ralph Lauren, Gucci, and Louis Vuitton, which did not interest me at all. Whenever I mention school, he would change the subject or blatantly tune me out. This was

upsetting to me because right now, attending college is the greatest achievement I have made.

Personality traits were overall the most cited factor for a potential mate by the participants in this study. Wanting a partner who would be a "good fit" in personality and lifestyle was extremely important. Further, it is worth noting that humor and trust were cited most often among participants as determining factors for a long-term partner.

Values

Education, finances, desires for a family, religion, and goals were addressed in the value system of participants in the study. The vast majority of participants desired a partner who had a similar values system. This included homeownership and educational goals as well as respect for himself, his partner, and their families and community. Felicia, a 22-year-old participant, indicated how respect was an important value for her in a partner, "respect for himself, as well as for me is a requirement of any partner of mine. If the man doesn't care about his own well-being, future, or life, there is no way I will be with him." Likewise, Michelle focused on finding a partner who would be like a teammate and supporter. Her description centered around dreams and motivation:

> I want someone who I can be comfortable around to share my dreams to. I want someone who motivates me when I just feel like giving in and I do the same for them in return. There's nothing like having someone on your team that is as passionate and has that "go for it" type of attitude.

Having a partner that shared similar religious convictions was cited by many of the participants. Religion varied in description, however most included the importance of similar religious values. Jennifer shared her thoughts on the connection between religion with courtship and marriage:

> I am a Christian, so the qualities that I look for in a partner are to see whether or not the guy is saved and is a true man of God . . . When I court or date a man, the main goal within the relationship is to get married one day if the Lord allows. Prior to getting in a relationship we have to agree and ask each other if we both want

to get married, why we want to get married, how does God view a courtship, and how we will stay pure until we get married.

Gabrielle, age 19, also noted faith and a relationship with God as an important factor in selecting a long-term partner. She connected other character traits as part of her ideal partner:

> In a partner, the first quality I look for is faith and relationship with God. I value one with goals, has a good spirit, kind hearted, humorous, free-spirited, athletic, wits, quick thinker, adaptable in all aspects, and attractive. I love individuals that love spending time with their family, music, dancing, shopping, and traveling. I have encountered so many individuals that have some or a few of these qualities.

Sasha had a similar experience, providing a detailed description of a previous relationship that was not ideal. She describes her growth and maturity at a faster pace than her partner and the implications that experience had on her desires in a partner:

> I was in a three year relationship with someone I thought I would be with forever. I thought we were growing together but I seem to be moving a little faster. I told myself that I could wait for him to grow up and mature but each day it became harder and harder. I told him how I was feeling and he said he would change but I believe in not changing anyone everyone moves at his or her own pace. I stayed with him for another 3 months and nothing changed. If I feel as though someone is holding me back then I cannot be with them.

Ultimately, participants had ideas for what values were most important in selecting long-term partners. In addition, several participants noted what they would not find as acceptable for a long-term partner. Infidelity, dishonesty, unemployment, and lack of pride were identified by many of the participants as characteristics that were not desired.

Physical Attraction

It is worth noting that while physical attraction did appear in the data, most participants had no specific desires in physical characteristics. Brenda was one of the few exceptions that noted what was ideal physically in a partner, "I want an athlete. I like a guy who is physically fit and takes good care of themselves."

Brenda did not indicate why physical appearance was an important factor in selecting a long-term mate. Sierra explained the importance of attractiveness, defined as presentable, in a long-term partner:

> Primarily I look for someone who is attractive. I am often attracted by nice smiles and good looks. I like my partner to be well groomed, with a presentable dress style. Although looks aren't everything, presentation is a major impression and reflection of one's self.

In contrast, 20-year-old Nadia was representative 35 of most of the women in the study. Physical appearance was not as important as other characteristics such as personality and values:

> The qualities that I look for in a partner are internal, meaning that I appreciate what's in the inside more than what is on the outside. I appreciate a man's personality, sense of humor, and religious beliefs. A personality of a man is most important because although they are handsome, they could be the complete opposite in the inside.

Regarding physical attraction, though often viewed as important in longterm relationships, participants in this study did not report valuing this characteristic as much as personality traits and values. This may be related to the population in which the study occurred. This finding could have implications for further research on mate selection in African American women.

DISCUSSION

The purpose of this study was to examine African American young adult women's desires in potential long-term partners. Deciding what characteristics are most important during the search for love and commitment is a personal choice. For African Americans, the task can be challenging as researchers continue to report a decline in the overall marriage rate of African Americans (Belgrave & Allison, 2019) in recent decades. In addition, African Americans have the lowest marriage rate of any racial group (Chambers & Kravitz, 2011) and there continues to be a decline in marriage within the African American community as compared with African Americans in previous generations (Belgrave & Allison, 2019). Although research has focused on the historical reasons of lower marriage rates of African Americans when compared with their White counterparts (Besharov & West, 2001), the current study focused on African American young adult women and their desires in long-term partners as previous research has indicated both positive and negative feelings about marriage in African American women (King, 1999; King & Allen, 2009).

Research has suggested that familial background has a direct impact on dating attitudes and preferences, including geographic location for African Americans (Murty & Roebuck, 2015). Furthermore, there has been discussion regarding the correlation of family instability in early childhood and cynical attitudes regarding marriage among young African Americans (Simons et al., 2012). The current study sheds new light on the value of early experiences with family relationships and the influence of those experiences on characteristics desired in a long-term partner among this population.

Many participants recalled observing the relationships of their mothers, grandmothers, and other significant female relatives and role models throughout their childhood. The experiences of female relatives were often described as negative, with participants noting that women were "responsible" in maintaining the relationship. Furthermore, the male partner was described by several participants as not carrying their "weight" in household duties, financial responsibilities, and parenting practices. It is also worth noting that participants cited absentee fathers as influencing their mate selection process. Generally, the mention of an absentee father was associated with unpleasant and unwanted characteristics in a long-term partner.

In a study by King and Allen (2009) examining 40 characteristics of ideal marriage partners in African American men and women, female respondents were more likely than male respondents to emphasize the importance of education and financial status in potential marriage partners. Furthermore, Chaney and Marsh (2008) suggested that differences in income between African American men and women may contribute to difficulties in finding a mate, with men indicating a struggle with selecting potential marital partners due to their feelings of inadequacy and low self-esteem related to making less money than females. The current study had similar findings with participants indicating the importance of education and financial status in potential long-term partners. These values were cited by the majority of the participants with many wanting someone who was similar to them in educational level. It is worth noting that the sample for the current study were young adult women who were enrolled in college, while the King and Allen study had a blended sample with varying educational backgrounds. King and Allen (2009) also found that the majority of participants in their study preferred African American partners, with about 40% not having a preference. The current study did not find any racial preferences in selecting long-term partners.

Finally, previous research (Ross, 1997) found that skin complexion and level of attractiveness were significant factors in potential partners in an African American sample. In contrast, findings from the current study suggest that the majority of participants did not cite physical appearance and attraction as an important trait in a long-term partner. Personality traits and values were described as most important overshadowing physical attractiveness. Participants indicated characteristics such as humor, trust, religious practices, honesty, and ambition as more important than physical attributes. Furthermore, pride in one's identity and professionalism were also desired in potential long-term partners.

The findings from this study suggests that the period of emerging adulthood is a pivotal time during the development of African American women, specifically when considering decisions regarding dating and long-term committed relationships. In particular, the research has relevance when considering how family scholars, educators, and consultants can best serve African American women, who may be looking to shift from casual dating to long-term coupling or perhaps marriage. The data may be used to assist African American women in learning more about themselves, and their unique experiences on college campuses. Furthermore, the findings could be used to develop programming that could be offered on campus through student counseling centers or through relevant student organizations. A relationships expert may be able to use the information to develop resources on college campuses that specifically target African American women, that focus on African American female empowerment, that also validate one's experiences. One of the benefits of working with a relationships expert may be in the expert's ability to facilitate in-depth discussions about wants, needs, and desires that may be difficult for African American women to voice alone.

Although the current study suggests relevance for African American women, the research also has implications for African American men and other men who may consider developing dating relationships with this population. Black men in particular may find the data useful as they approach dating relationships. Although some African American men may have assumptions about dating African American women, the results can be used to further inform dating. One might argue that if African American men want to date African American women, they need to have a better sense to how African American women view relationships. Furthermore, a relationship coach or marriage and family therapist may be able to work with couples who may be struggling to maintain their relationships, by incorporating data found in the study to enhance relationships. The authors recommend that the data be used to help further the conversation about dating relationships among African American women, men, and families, as well as emerging adults across all race and ethnic backgrounds.

This study is helpful in understanding African American young adult women's perceptions of long-term partners, however several limitations should be noted. First, the study took place in an HBCU setting. Although this was helpful in recruiting African American young adult women, the sample was limited to those who were pursuing a college degree. Including young adult women who are not pursing higher education, who are college bound, or who

are single mothers may have influenced the findings from the study. Furthermore, because of the narrative format of data collection, clarification on responses could not be addressed. For example, several participants noted the importance and value of education, however we were unable to seek clarity on their definitions of education and what was included such as trade school, higher education, or other options. In addition, demographic information regarding family household composition was not included in data collection. That information may have been helpful with the findings associated with family experiences. Another limitation of the study would be in the lack of generalizability of the research findings. Qualitative research is not focused on generalizability, but including a quantitative dimension to the study could have provided some additional data that could be used to better understand the phenomenon of mate selection for college African American women.

FUTURE RESEARCH

The results from the study provide a great foundation for future research. When considering the limitations, there are a variety of ways to expand the current scholarship. One way to expand upon the research is to consider the development of future qualitative, quantitative, and mixed methodological examinations. For example, the themes that emerged from the current study could be used to develop a follow-up study that would include collecting quantitative data among African American women in college. In particular, this might include collecting data on African American women at various HBCUs to see if the quantitative data confirms the results of the current study. In addition, it might be interesting to consider ways to compare African American female college students at HBCUs to African American female college students at Predominately White Institutions (PWIs). Students may have different experiences, and it may be interesting to compare and contrast across types of academic institutions to include public and private schools. Further expanding beyond African

American female college students and expanding to African American males may enhance the findings of future studies. Such a quantitative study could show differences and/or similarities that may be important as one considers mate selection and the formation of couple relationships.

Furthermore, through quantitative research methods, future studies should consider other areas such as how themes may influence or even predict dissatisfaction, dissolution, or general conflict within relationships.

It is important to continue to explore experiences, attitudes, and perspectives of African American women. Furthermore, consideration should be given to a more inclusive sample of African American women related to education, income, and family household composition. Although the current study focused on developmental years of emerging adult females, consideration should be given to exploring how other African American women approach dating and relationships. Obtaining similar data from older adults may provide a larger context by which to examine relationships over time. It is equally important to explore dating relationship experiences among same sex, interracial, and other diverse populations of couples. Given that a significant number of attitudes and beliefs about dating are formulated during childhood socialization and rearing, it would be interesting to learn about what African American women are taught as children specifically related to dating (including what they are told to look for in a mate).

In addition, while this study was focused on African American women's attitudes and perceptions of dating and long-term relationships, in a future study it would also be interesting to gain insight regarding what characteristics and personality traits the sample deem to be important when considering procreation. One might assume that the characteristics that African American women look for in a dating or long-term committed relationship are the same when considering the selection of a partner to have children with. However, this is something that would need to be further examined. In addition, how African American

women define fatherhood and successful fatherhood among African American men (Moore et al., 2018) and other men in general may have implications on relationships, parenting, and family dynamics over time.

To provide a more comprehensive analysis of the phenomenon, it would be interesting to explore gender differences by duplicating the study utilizing a sample of African American men. Likewise, it would be interesting to see if the results to the study are similar or different as one considers clinical and educational implications for men when compared with women. Other contextual factors that might be important to include in future research are race/ethnicity, religion, and geographic location. In the existing study, the sample was selected from a Historically Black College. Conducting a study of African American young adult women who are beyond the college years may be worth examining. Expanding this research may also include exploring this topic among African American women in various geographic locations and exploring the lived experiences of other women of color beyond African Americans, among other topics.

REFERENCES

Belgrave, F. Z., & Allison, K. W. (2019). *African American psychology: From Africa to America*. SAGE.

Besharov, D. J., & West, A. (2001). African American marriage patterns. In A. Thernstrom & S. Thernstrom (Eds.), *Beyond the color line* (pp. 95–113). Hoover Institution Press.

Bryant, C. M., Taylor, R. J., Lincoln, K. D., Chatters, L. M., & Jackson, J. S. (2008). Marital satisfaction among African Americans and Black Caribbeans: Findings from the national survey of American life. *Family Relations, 57*, 239–253.

Bryant, C. M., Wickrama, K. A. S., Bolland, J., Bryant, B. M., Cutrona, C. E., & Stanik, C. E. (2010). Race matters, even in marriage: Identifying factors linked to marital outcomes for African Americans. *Journal of Family Theory & Review, 2*(3), 157–174.

Chambers, A. L., & Kravitz, A. (2011). Understanding the disproportionately low marriage rate among African Americans: An amalgam of sociological and psychological constraints. *Family Relations, 60*, 648–660.

Chaney, C., & Marsh, K. (2008). Factors that facilitate relationship entry among married and cohabiting African Americans. *Marriage & Family Review, 45*, 26–51.

Dixon, P. (2009). Marriage among African Americans: What does the research reveal? *Journal of African American Studies, 13*, 29–46.

Franklin, J. H. (2007). African American families. In H. P. McAdoo (Ed.), *Black families* (4th ed., pp. 3–6). SAGE.

Henry, W. J. (2008). Black female millennial college students: Dating dilemmas and identity development. *Multicultural Education, 16*, 17–21.

Henry, W. J. (2013). The Black gender gap: A commentary on intimacy and identity issues of Black college women. *The Professional Counselor, 3*, 185.

King, A. (1999). African American females' attitudes toward marriage: An exploratory study. *Journal of Black Studies, 29*, 416–437.

King, A., & Allen, T. T. (2009). Personal characteristics of the ideal African American marriage partner: A survey of adult Black men and women. *Journal of Black Studies, 39*, 570–588.

LeFebvre, L. E. (2018). Swiping me off my feet: Explicating relationship initiation on Tinder. *Journal of Social and Personal Relationships, 35*(9), 1205–1229.

Lincoln, K. D., & Chae, D. H. (2010). Stress, marital satisfaction, and psychological distress among African Americans. *Journal of Family Issues, 31*, 1081–1105.

Marks, L. D., Hopkins, K., Chaney, C., Monroe, P. A., Nesteruk, O., & Sasser, D. D. (2008). "Together, we are strong": A qualitative study of happy, enduring African American marriages. *Family Relations, 57*, 172–185.

Martin, S. P., Astone, N. M., & Peters, H. E. (2014). *Fewer marriages, more divergence: Marriage projections for millennials to age 40*. Urban Institute.

Miller, S. A. (2018). *Developmental research methods* (5th ed.). SAGE.

Moore, D., Jefferson, B., & Armstrong, J. (2018). Barriers to successful fatherhood among African American men. *The Griot: The Journal of African American Studies, 37*, 54–82.

Murty, K. S., & Roebuck, J. B. (2015). African American HBCU students' attitudes and actions toward interracial dating & marriage: A survey analysis. *Race, Gender & Class, 22*, 136–153.

Phillips, T. M., Wilmoth, J. D., & Marks, L. D. (2012). Challenges and conflicts . . . strengths and supports: A study of enduring African American marriages. *Journal of Black Studies, 43*, 936–952.

Queiri, A. R., Dwaikat, N. K., & Yusoff, W. F. W. (2014, May 14–15). *Motivational methods for millennials: Balancing between workplace reality and millennials' expectations* [Conference session]. International Conference on Economics, Social Sciences and Languages (ICESL'14), Singapore.

Ross, L. E. (1997). Mate selection preferences among African American college students. *Journal of Black Studies, 27*(4), 554–569.

Rossman, G. B., & Rallis, S. F. (2003). *Learning in the field: An introduction to qualitative research* (2nd ed.). SAGE.

Simons, R. L., Simons, L. G., Lei, M. K., & Landor, A. M. (2012). Relational schemas, hostile romantic relationships, and beliefs about marriage among young African American adults. *Journal of Social and Personal Relationships, 29*(1), 77–101.

Watt, S. K. (2006). Racial identity attitudes, womanist identity attitudes, and self-esteem in African American college women attending historically Black single-sex and coeducational institutions. *Journal of College Student Development, 47*(3), 319–334.

Reading Questions

1. Brooks and Moore review the findings of numerous other studies that have examined mate-selection patterns and partner preferences among African Americans. Based on their review of this research, what are some of the factors that may account for the declining marriage rates among African Americans?

2. According to Brooks and Moore's results, what three considerations (or themes) emerged from their data as the most significant influences on young adult African American women's attitudes toward partner selection?

3. What did Brooks and Moore find were the two most important personality traits young adult African American women desire in their potential partners?

Rhetoric Questions

4. Brooks and Moore employ a structural pattern for reporting their findings. How would you describe this pattern, and why might that pattern be appropriate in light of their study's larger design?

5. How would you describe the difference in the ways Brooks and Moore use and cite the work of other researchers (secondary sources) and how they use and cite the primary data they collected in their study?

Response Questions

6. What qualities do you look for in a potential long-term partner? What are the most important and least important among these qualities?

7. Do you find any of the study's central findings surprising? Why or why not? What might your answers reveal about your own beliefs and attitudes regarding partner selection?

ACADEMIC CASE STUDY • PERSPECTIVES ON LOVE   NATURAL SCIENCES

Hormonal Changes When Falling in Love

DONATELLA MARAZZITI AND DOMENICO CANALE

Donatella Marazziti is a professor of psychiatry and the director of the laboratory of psychopharmacology at the University of Pisa, Italy. She has researched and published widely on the subjects of love and biochemistry, and she is author of the best-seller *The Nature of Love* (2002), among other scholarly texts. In this study, co-written with Domenico Canale, the researchers examine hormonal changes in individuals who have recently fallen in love. They conclude that the hormonal changes identified are "reversible, state-dependent, and probably related to some physical and/or psychological features typically associated with falling in love." The study was published in the journal *Psychoneuroendocrinology* in 2004.

SUMMARY

To fall in love is the first step in pair formation in humans and is a complex process which only recently has become the object of neuroscientific investigation. The little information available in this field prompted us to measure the levels of some pituitary, adrenal, and gonadal hormones in a group of 24 subjects of both sexes who had recently (within the previous six months) fallen in love, and to compare them with those of 24 subjects who were single or were part of a long-lasting relationship. The following hormones were evaluated by means of standard techniques: FSH, LH, estradiol, progesterone, dehydroepi-androsterone sulphate (DHEAS), cortisol, testosterone, and androstenedione.

The results showed that estradiol, progesterone, DHEAS, and androstenedione levels did not differ between the groups and were within the normal ranges. Cortisol levels were significantly higher amongst those subjects who had recently fallen in love, as compared with those who had not. FSH and testosterone levels were lower in men in love, while women of the same group presented higher testosterone levels. All hormonal differences were eliminated when the subjects were retested from 12 to 24 months later. The increased cortisol and low FSH levels are suggestive of the "stressful" and arousing conditions associated with the initiation of a social contact. The changes of testosterone concentrations, which varied in opposite directions in the two sexes, may reflect changes in behavioral and/ or temperamental traits which have yet to be clarified. In conclusion, the findings of the present study would indicate that to fall in love provokes transient hormonal changes, some of which seem to be specific to each sex.

1. INTRODUCTION

The formation of pair bonding is relevant in several animal species, and particularly in mammals since, in some cases, it ensures not only that a new couple is formed which can thus generate offspring, but also that a safe and stable environment is set up wherein the newborn can receive sufficient care to enable them to mature and become capable of surviving alone (Bowlby, 1969; Kleiman, 1977; Carter et al., 1997a, 1997b).

The process of pair bonding in humans begins with the subjective experience of falling in love, which sometimes leads to the establishment of long-lasting relationships: for this reason, its function exceeds that of reproduction alone and, given its relevance to the survival of the species, it would not be surprising if it were regulated by precise and long-standing neural mechanisms (Uvnäs-Moberg, 1997, 1998; Carter, 1998). Indirect evidence of the biological process involved in falling in love is provided by cross-cultural studies which suggest that it is present in virtually all societies and is, perhaps, genetically determined (Jankoviak and Fischer, 1992). Furthermore, common features of this process can be identified in studies from all over the world and include: perception of an altered mental state, intrusive thoughts and images of the other, sets of behavioral patterns aimed at eliciting a reciprocal response, and a definite course and predictable outcome (Leckman and Mayes, 1999).

One of the first biological hypotheses with regard to falling in love associates this state to increased levels of phenylethylamine, on the basis of the similarities between the chemical structure of this neurotransmitter and that of amphetamines which provoke mood changes resembling those typical of the initial stage of a romance; however, no empirical data have been gathered to support this theory (Liebowitz, 1983). The strong suggestion is that different mechanisms

may be involved (Panksepp, 1982; Jankoviak, 1986; Hazan and Shaver, 1987; Fisher, 1992; Porges, 1998; Insel and Young, 1997), and it has been recently demonstrated that the intrusive thoughts of the early, romantic phase of falling in love are underlaid by a decreased functionality of the serotonin transporter (Marazziti et al., 1999).

The complexity of the process would seem, therefore, to be understood better when we consider falling in love as a basic emotion, such as anxiety or fear, due to the activation of the amygdala and related circuits and neurotransmitters (Bartels and Zeki, 2000; LeDoux, 2000). Consistent with this hypothesis is the observation that stress and threatening situations may facilitate the onset of new social bonds and intimate ties (Bowlby, 1973; Reite, 1985; Kraemer, 1992; Panksepp et al., 1994). The review of animal data is beyond the scope of this paper; however, it should perhaps be noted also that stress and corticosterone have been demonstrated to promote pair bonding formation in different species (DeVries et al., 1995, 1996; Hennessy, 1997; Levine et al., 1997; Mendoza and Mason, 1997). Furthermore, these elements induce the synthesis and release of neuropeptides, such as oxytocin, which are involved in the subsequent processes, including sexual and maternal behaviors and, more in general, positive social contacts, which reduce anxiety (McCarthy et al., 1992; Numan, 1994; Carter, 1998). The literature relevant to humans in this regard is meager, albeit in agreement with animal findings, and suggests that the activation of the hypothalamic-pituitary-adrenal (HPA) axis due to stressful experiences or, more in general, to arousal, may trigger the development of different kinds of social attachment, possibly also that which begins with falling in love (Milgram, 1986; Chiodera et al., 1991; Simpson and Rhole, 1994).

Given the paucity of data in this field and the unexplored questions regarding the possible role of gonadal hormones, our study aimed at evaluating the levels of some pituitary, adrenal, and gonadal hormones in a homogenous group of subjects of both sexes who were in the early, romantic phase of a loving relationship, and to compare them with those of subjects who were single or were already in a long-lasting relationship.

2. SUBJECTS AND METHODS

2.1. Subjects

Twenty-four subjects (12 male and 12 female, mean age ± SD: 27 ± 4 years) who declared that they had recently fallen in love were recruited from amongst residents (17) and medical students (7), by means of advertisement. They were selected according to the criteria already applied in a previous study (Marazziti et al., 1999), in particular: the relationship was required to have begun within the previous 6 months (mean ± SD: 3 ± 1 months) and at least four hours a day spent in thinking about the partner (mean ± SD: 9 ± 3 hours), as recorded by a specifically designed questionnaire.

Twenty-four subjects (12 female and 12 male, mean age ± SD: 29 ± 3), belonging to the same environment and with similar educational levels, with either a long-lasting (mean ± SD: 67 ± 28 months) or no relationship, served as the control group.

No subject had a family or personal history of any major psychiatric disorder or even subthreshold symptoms, or had ever taken psychotropic drugs, except for three who occasionally took benzodiazepines because of difficulties in sleeping at night, as assessed by a detailed psychiatric interview conducted by one of the authors (DM). In addition, all subjects had undergone the following rating scales: the Hamilton Rating Scale for Depression (Hamilton, 1960), the Hamilton Rating Scale for Anxiety (Hamilton, 1959), and the Yale-Brown Obsessive-Compulsive Rating Scale (Goodman et al., 1986), with the results that all total scores fell within the normal range.

All subjects, except for four singles (three women and one man), were indulging in normal and regular sexual activity, as assessed by self-report questionnaires and, during the psychiatric interview, no differences were noted between the romantic lovers and the control subjects.

The women had regular menstrual cycles and were 10 not taking contraceptive pills. Their blood samples were drawn in the early follicular phase (between the third and the fifth day of the menses); the men had no history of genital disease or hypogonadism. All subjects were free of physical illness, were neither heavy cigarette smokers nor belonged to high-risk HIV individuals, and all underwent a general and detailed check-up, carried out by one of the authors (DC).

All gave their informed written consent to their inclusion in the study.

2.2. Hormonal Measurements

Venous blood (10 ml) was collected between 8 and 9 a.m. from fasting subjects and centrifuged at low-speed centrifugation (200 × g, for 20 min, at 22°C) to obtain serum which was stored at −20°C until the assays, which were performed within a few days.

The following hormones were evaluated by means of standard techniques in duplicate for each point, by biologists who were blind to each subject's conditions: FSH, LH, estradiol, progesterone (chemiluminescent immuno-assay, CMIA, Architect, Abbott, Abbott Park, USA), dehydroepiandrosterone sulphate (DHEAS) (Spectria, Orion Diagnostic, Essoo, Finland), cortisol (CMIA, DPC, Immulite, Los Angeles, USA), testosterone, and androstenedione (RIA, Testo-CTK, Diasorin Biomedica, Saluggia, Italy).

2.3. Statistics

The differences in hormone levels between subjects of the two sexes who recently had or had not fallen in love were measured by means of the Student t-test (unpaired, two-tailed). The possible effects of the length of the relationship or of the time devoted to thinking about the partner on the hormonal levels were assessed according to Pearson's analysis. All analyses were carried out using the SSPS version 4.0, by means of personal computer programs (StatView V) (Nie et al., 1998).

3. RESULTS

Table 1 shows that cortisol levels (ng/ml) were sig- 15 nificantly higher in the subjects who had recently fallen in love, as compared with control subjects

Table 1

Hormonal Levels in Subjects in the Early Stage of Falling in Love and in Control Subjects

	Subjects in love		Control subjects	
	M	F	M	F
FSH	3.2 ± 1.1 ^	8.1 ± 4.2	9.3 ± 3.8	9.1 ± 3.1
LH	6.9 ± 2.3	12.3 ± 3.4	7.1 ± 2.8	10 ± 4.3
Estradiol	< 50	170 ± 23	< 50	145 ± 32
Progesterone	< 0.2	0.57 ± 0.3	< 0.2	0.55 ± 0.3
Testosterone	4.1 ± 1.0 *	1.2 ± 0.4 **	6.8 ± 2.1	0.6 ± 0.2
DHEAS	2736 ± 1122	2232 ± 986	2450 ± 1000	2315 ± 980
Cortisol	224 ± 21 °	243 ± 41 °°	165 ± 21	172 ± 44
Androstenedione	2.0 ± 1.0	2.1 ± 0.7	2.1 ± 0.7	1.9 ± 0.7

M, male; F, female.

^Significant: $p < 0.0001$; *Significant: $p < 0.003$; **Significant: $p < 0.001$; °Significant: $p < 0.001$; °°Significant: $p < 0.0001$.

$(239 \pm 39$ vs 168 ± 31, $p < 0.001)$, with no difference between women and men.

The levels of LH, estradiol, progesterone, DHEAS, and androstenedione did not differ between the groups and were within normal ranges according to the sex and the follicular phase of the women.

On the other hand, testosterone levels (ng/ml) in men who had recently fallen in love were significantly lower than in singles or individuals with a long-lasting relationship $(4.1 \pm 1.0$ vs 6.8 ± 2.1, $p > 0.003)$; the results in women were the opposite, that is, higher levels in the women from the first group, as compared with those from the second $(1.2 \pm 0.4$ vs 0.6 ± 0.2, $p < 0.001)$.

FSH levels were significantly lower in men who had fallen in love than in those from the control group $(p < 0.0001)$.

When the cortisol, testosterone, and FSH levels were re-tested in 16 out of the total of 24 subjects in love, from 12 to 28 months later, no differences from control subject levels were detected. Hormonal measurements were also repeated in 15 out of the total of 24 control subjects after the same time interval, but no significant differences from those of the first assessment were noted (data not shown).

The length of the relationship and the time spent in thinking about the partner did not affect hormonal levels.

Singles or subjects with a long-lasting relationship did not differ in any of the parameters evaluated.

4. DISCUSSION

The main bias of this study is probably represented by the criteria used for selecting the subjects who had fallen in love since, despite our best efforts, no definite indication was available. Since the altered mental state associated with falling in love seems to have a precise time course, with an average duration of between 18 months and 3 years (Tennov, 1979; Marazziti et al., 1999), we chose the length of the relationship as one criterion which, furthermore, can easily be recorded. The other main criterion adopted was the time spent in thinking about the partner which, according to various authors, represents a core feature of this phase (Tesser and Paulhus, 1976; Tennov, 1979; Shea and Adams, 1984). One might perhaps infer that the subjects who are in love suffer from a moderate form of OCD, or have an obsessive-compulsive personality, a positive family history of OCD or even obsessive-compulsive subthreshold symptoms; however, we excluded all these possibilities by means of the psychiatric interview and specific questionnaires. It might also be judged questionable that our hormonal evaluation was performed on a single sample; however, this could represent a bias for LH measurement only, for which a pulsatile pattern is well recognized.

However, in spite of this limitation, our study led to some intriguing and innovative findings, in particular that healthy subjects of both sexes who had recently fallen in love did show some hormonal changes.

The first finding was that the cortisol levels were higher in subjects in love, as compared with those from the control group. This condition of "hypercortisolemia" is probably a non-specific indicator of some changes which occur during the early phase of a relationship, reflecting the stressful conditions or arousal associated with the initiation of a social contact which helps to overcome neophobia.* Such conditions appear to be fundamental, as a moderate level of stress has been demonstrated to promote attachment and social contacts in both animals and humans (DeVries et al., 1995, 1996; Hennessy, 1997; Levine et al., 1997; Mendoza and Mason, 1997). In addition, different data indicate an association between HPA activation following stressful experiences and the development of social attachment which, in turn, promotes physiological states which reduce anxiety and related negative sensations (Hinde, 1974; Milgram, 1986; Simpson and Rhole, 1994; Legros, 2001). We observed no difference in cortisol levels between women and men, but this is perhaps not surprising, given indications that they represent rather an unspecific reaction to different triggers.

*neophobia: fear of new things.

On the other hand, while LH, estradiol, progesterone, DHEAS, and androstenedione levels did not differ between men and women, the testosterone concentrations showed some sex-related peculiarities: in both men and women who were at the early stage of a relationship, they were lower and higher, respectively, than those in men and women from the control group. Although none reached pathological levels, all subjects presented this finding, as if falling in love tended temporarily to eliminate some differences between the sexes, or to soften some male features in men and, in parallel, to increase them in women. It is tempting to link the changes in testosterone levels to changes in behaviors, sexual attitudes, or, perhaps, aggressive traits which move in different directions in the two sexes (Zitzmann and Nieschlag, 2001); however, apart from some anecdotal evidence, we have no data substantiating this which would justify further research. Similarly, we have no explanation for the decreased level of FSH in male subjects who were in love, apart from the suggestions that it may represent another marker of hypothalamic involvement in the process of falling in love.

It is noteworthy that when we measured the cortisol, testosterone, and FSH levels for a second time, 12–18 months later, in those 16 (out of the total of 24) subjects who had maintained the same relationship but were no longer in the same mental state to which they had referred during the first assessment and now reported feeling calmer and no longer "obsessed" with the partner, the hormone levels were no different from those of the control group. This finding would suggest that the hormonal changes which we observed are reversible, state-dependent, and probably related to some physical and/or psychological features typically associated with falling in love.

In conclusion, our study would suggest that falling in love represents a "physiological" and transient condition which is characterized (or underlaid) by peculiar hormonal patterns, one of which, involving testosterone, seems to show a sex-related specificity.

Studies are now in progress to establish whether the noted hormonal changes may be related to the modifications of specific behaviors, such as aggression or sexual or attachment attitudes.

ACKNOWLEDGMENTS

We thank Prof. Lucia Grasso and the technical staff of the hormone laboratory of the "Dipartimento di Endocrinologia" of the University of Pisa for performing the hormone assay. We express our gratitude to Prof. Aldo Pinchera and Prof. Enio Martino of the same department for the fruitful discussion during the preparation of the manuscript, and to Dr. Elena Di Nasso from the "Dipartimento di Psichiatria, Neurobiologia, Farmacologia e Biotecnologie," who was helpful in selecting the subjects included in the study.

REFERENCES

Bartels, A., Zeki, S., 2000. The neural basis of romantic love. Neuroreport 11, 3829–3838.

Bowlby, J., 1969. Attachment and Loss. Attachment. vol. 1. Basic Books, New York.

Bowlby, J., 1973. Attachment and Loss. Separation: anxiety and anger. vol. 2. Basic Books, New York.

Carter, C.S., 1998. Neuroendocrine perspectives on social attachment and love. Psychoneuroendocrinol 23, 779–818.

Carter, C.S., DeVries, A.C., Taymans, S.E., 1997a. Peptides, steroids and pair bonding. Ann NY Acad Sci 807, 260–268.

Carter, C.S., Lederhendler, I.I., Kilpatrick, B. (eds.), 1997b. The integrative neurobiology of affiliation. Ann NY Acad Sci 807.

Chiodera, P., Salvarani, C., Bacchi-Modena, A., Spallanzani, R., Cigarini, C., Alboni, A., Gardini, E., Coiro, V., 1991. Relationship between plasma profiles of oxytocin and adrenocorticotropic hormone during suckling or breast stimulation in women. Horm & Res 35, 119–123.

DeVries, A.C., DeVries, M.B., Taymans, S.E., Carter, S.C., 1995. The modulation of pair bonding by corticosteroids in female prairie voles. Proc Natl Acad Sci USA 92, 7744–7748.

DeVries, A.C., DeVries, M.B., Taymans, S.E., Carter, S.C., 1996. The effects of stress on social preferences are sexually dimorphic in prairie voles. Proc Natl Acad Sci USA 93, 11980–11990.

Fisher, H., 1992. Anatomy of Love. Fawcett Columbine, New York.

Goodman, W.K., Price, L.H., Rasmussen, S.A., 1986. The Yale Brown Obsessive-Compulsive Scale I: Development, use and reliability. Arch Gen Psychiatry 46, 1006–1011.

Hamilton, M., 1959. The assessment of anxiety state by rating. Br J Med Psychol 32, 50–55.

Hamilton, M., 1960. A rating scale for depression. J Neurol Neurosurg Psychiatry 23, 56–62.

Hazan, C., Shaver, P., 1987. Romantic love conceptualized as an attachment process. J Personal Soc Psychol 52, 511–524.

Hennessy, M.B., 1997. Hypothalamic-pituitary-adrenal responses to brief social separation. Neur Biobehav Rev 21, 11–29.

Hinde, R.A., 1974. Biological Bases of Human Social Behavior. McGraw-Hill, New York.

Insel, T.R., Young, L.J., 1997. The neurobiology of attachment. Nature Rev 2, 129–136.

Jankoviak, W.R., 1986. A psychobiological theory of love. Psychol Rev 93, 119–130.

Jankoviak, W.R., Fischer, E.F., 1992. A cross-cultural perspective on romantic love. Ethol 31, 149–155.

Kleiman, D., 1977. Monogamy in mammals. Quart Rev Biol 52, 39–69.

Kraemer, G.W., 1992. A psychobiological theory of attachment. Behav Brain Sci 15, 493–520.

Leckman, J.F., Mayes, L.C., 1999. Preoccupations and behaviors associated with romantic and parental love. Perspectives on the origin of obsessive-compulsive disorder. Child & Adol Psychiatry Clin North Am 1, 635–665.

LeDoux, J.E., 2000. Emotion circuits in the brain. Ann Rev Neurosci 2, 155–184.

Legros, J.J., 2001. Inhibitory effects of oxytocin on corticotrope function in humans: are vasopressin and oxytocin ying-yang neurohormones? Psychoneuroendocrinol 26, 649–655.

Levine, S., Lyons, D.M., Schatzberg, A.F., 1997. Psychobiological consequences of social relationships. Ann NY Acad Sci 807, 210–218.

Liebowitz, M.R., 1983. The Chemistry of Love. Little, Brown and Company, Boston.

Marazziti, D., Akiskal, H.S., Rossi, A., Cassano, G.B., 1999. Alteration of the platelet serotonin transporter in romantic love. Psychol Med 29, 741–745.

McCarthy, M.M., Kow, L.M., Pfaff, D.W., 1992. Speculations concerning the physiological significance of central oxytocin in maternal behavior. Ann NY Acad Sci 652, 70–82.

Mendoza, S.P., Mason, W.A., 1997. Attachment relationships in New World primates. Ann NY Acad Sci 807, 203–209.

Milgram, N.A., 1986. Stress and Coping in Time of War: Generalizations from the Israeli Experiences. Brunner Mazel, New York.

Nie, N.H., Hull, C.H., Steinbrenner, K., Bent, D.H., 1998. Statistical Package for the Social Science (SPSS), 4th ed. McGraw-Hill, New York.

Numan, M., 1994. Maternal behavior. In: Knobil, E., Neill, I. (eds.), The Physiology of Reproduction. Raven Press, New York, pp. 221–302.

Panksepp, J., 1982. Toward a psychobiological theory of emotions. Behav Brain Res 5, 407–467.

Panksepp, J., Nelson, E., Silvy, S., 1994. Brain opioids and mother-infant social motivation. Acta Pediatr Suppl 397, 40–46.

Porges, S.W., 1998. Love and emotions. Psychoneuroendocrinol 23, 837–861.

Reite, M., 1985. The Psychobiology of Attachment and Separation. Academic Press, New York.

Shea, J.A., Adams, G.R., 1984. Correlates of romantic attachment: a path analysis study. J Youth Adol 13, 27–31.

Simpson, J.A., Rhole, W.A., 1994. Stress and secure base relationships in adulthood. Adv Pers Relat 5, 181–204.

Tennov, D., 1979. Love and Limerence. The Experience of Being in Love. Stein and Day, New York.

Tesser, A., Paulhus, D.L., 1976. Toward a causal model of love. J Pers & Soc Psychol 34, 1095–1103.

Uvnäs-Moberg, K., 1997. Physiological and endocrine effects of social contact. Ann NY Acad Sci 807, 146–163.

Uvnäs-Moberg, K., 1998. Oxytocin may mediate the benefit of positive social interaction and emotions. Psychoneuroendocrinol 23, 819–835.

Zitzmann, M., Nieschlag, E., 2001. Testosterone levels in healthy men and the relation to behavioural and physical characteristics: facts and constructs. Eur J Endocrinol 144, 183–197.

Reading Questions

1. The study's introduction explicitly establishes the researchers' goals for their study. What are those goals?

2. Based on what criteria do the researchers select study participants for their experimental group—those who had recently fallen in love?

Rhetoric Questions

3. How does the introduction establish the significance or importance of the researchers' work for their audience?

4. Closely analyze the structure of the study's Discussion section. Based on your analysis, what do you see as the section's organizational logic? In other words, what do you believe the researchers set out to achieve in this section of the study?

5. Identify areas in the study where the researchers first acknowledge and then offer response to the effects of possible limitations to their study's methods or findings. Do these areas strengthen or weaken their report? Explain your response.

Response Questions

6. The researchers write that falling in love "tended temporarily to eliminate some differences between the sexes, or to soften some male features in men and, in parallel, to increase them in women" (par. 25). Consider a time when you've fallen in love or when you've witnessed what you thought was someone falling in love. Do your experiences support the researchers' conclusion in this instance?

7. Do you have any anecdotal evidence, based on personal experiences, that might support or challenge any of the researchers' central findings? If so, what are they? Explain your answers.

Use of Online Dating Websites and Dating Apps: Findings and Implications for LGB Populations

KRISTINE JOHNSON, M. OLGUTA VILCEANU, AND MANUEL C. PONTES

Kristine Johnson, lead author of the following study, is an associate professor of advertising at Rowan University. She has written extensively about consumer attitudes and market strategies, and her studies have been published in a number of academic journals. This study, conducted with her colleagues M. Olguta Vilceanu and Manuel C. Pontes, also of Rowan University, examines the use of online dating websites and apps among members of the lesbian, gay, and bisexual communities. It appeared in the *Journal of Marketing Development and Competitiveness* in 2017.

Data and findings from the Pew Foundation's "Internet and American Life Project Tracking Survey" (2013) were adjusted through the use of sampling weights to estimate for general US population parameters. Univariate and multivariate analysis indicate that lesbian, gay, and bisexual adults are significantly more likely to flirt online and to use online dating websites and dating apps than heterosexual adults. Findings enhance understanding of LGB consumer decision-making processes, promote creation of LGB lifestyle-focused technologies and promotional messages for non-heterosexual niche audiences, and contribute to a better understanding of LGB online dating habits and usage.

INTRODUCTION

The popularity of online dating has increased substantially since its inception. What was once viewed as a social stigma is now widely accepted to be a "good way to meet people" (Smith and Anderson, 2014, para. 3). In fact, research indicates 87 percent of single American males and 83 percent of single American females view online dating as socially acceptable (Statistics and Facts, 2015).

The growth in online dating is due in part on the advancement and adoption of new technologies, as well as the number of available options. For instance, the mobile-only application, Tinder—an app that provides search results based on location—continues to be immensely popular (Bilton, 2014), while longer-standing, more traditional online dating sites such as Match.com and eHarmony are still very well utilized (Match Group, 2015; Harwell, 2015). Today,

more than ever, there are a plethora of specialized digital dating resources: *Grinder for Her*, designed specifically for the lesbian population; *Gluten-free Singles*, a dating site for health-conscience people, and *Ashley Madison*, an outlet for those seeking extramarital affairs. The growing emphasis on specialization is clearly evident, as over 500 dating-related applications can be found on *iTunes* (Wells, 2015).

Given the availability of digital dating outlets, this research is designed specifically to further investigate the relationship between sexual orientation and the use of digital dating services, dating applications, or online dating websites (the terms used interchangeably for the purposes of this study). Although scholars have researched digital dating among the LGBT (lesbian, gay, bisexual, and transsexual) populations, there remains a lack in the literature regarding LGBT adult use of these technologies in comparison to use of these technologies among heterosexual adults. Therefore, the results of this research may serve as a powerful springboard for further exploration of LGBT digital dating use and its associated implications, also from the perspective of individuals, groups, and various industries serving them, as well as the relationship between race/ethnicity and use of digital dating services.

LITERATURE REVIEW

Previous research on online dating included both in-depth qualitative and extensive quantitative investigations for differences in attitudes, goals, and preferences of adults who engage in online dating (Alterovitz & Mendelsohn, 2009; Cali et al., 2013); the process of selecting and pursuing potential partners for romantic relationships (Blackhart et al., 2014; Finkel et al., 2012; Heino, Ellison & Gibbs, 2010); and the conceptualizing and analyzing self and others' presentation strategies (Couch & Liamputtong, 2008; Geser, 2007; Guadagno & Sagarin, 2010; Hall et al., 2010; Lo, Hsieh & Chu, 2013). These studies focused on comparing concepts and strategies associated with online vs. offline dating. Participants tended to be Caucasian, white, heterosexual, and younger females.

These studies relied on respondents' self-reported 5 ages and results often emphasized heteronormative concepts such as online dating women's preference for older male partners, and online dating men's preference for younger female partners. Even after accounting for deceptive self-presentation (declaring younger ages) and strategies to identify deceptive presentation in others' profile (looking for clues about "true" age), such generalizations raised the issue of applicability within non-heterosexual populations. After all, for a male-male match to work, at least half of the dating population must be interested in exploring potential relationships with partners same age or younger.

The cited research also compared online dating to "traditional" or "conventional" heterosexual dating, therefore falling on stereotypical gender roles in their exploration of participant values and attitudes. Unsurprisingly, female online daters appeared to be looking for male partners with "status" (healthy and financially stable) and who could accommodate an "active lifestyle," while male online daters appeared to favor thin (rather than large-size), younger (by up to 15 years), sexually attractive and "well maintained" female partners who could help shoulder household chores—a situation resembling the equity trade-off in the "marriage mart" metaphor (Heino, Ellison & Gibbs, 2010). It remained to be seen what degree would these preferences be influenced by study participants' education and income level, and, furthermore, would such findings be reflected in the overall older adult population.

LGBT DATING LITERATURE

The literature connecting LGBT populations and digital dating examined a variety of issues, such as the reasons male online daters start or stop using the smartphone app Grindr (Brubaker, Ananny, & Crawford, 2014). Identified as an app for gay men, Grindr enables users to find nearby men to chat, seek potential dates, or to pursue intimate encounters. The research suggests the app was viewed as time consuming and took time away from other activities, including work. It was viewed as a means for objectifying men—something some study participants found to be disconcerting. Along with this, respondents claimed to stop using the app because it was believed it would not lead to finding the type of mate users were interested in meeting. In other research, the same dating app was explored in terms of impression formation and self-presentation. Blackwell, Birnholtz, and Abbott (2014) found that cosituation—a combination of physical and virtual presence—impacts how we behave and feel. For example, one study respondent suggested the app can make "every space a potentially gay space" (p. 10), even as users form impressions and judge potential partners from every piece of information provided (such as pictures, key words, personal interests and preferences). Profiles without photos, on the one hand, indicate lack of self-confidence, whereas full-body photos are perceived to be genuine and honest. By posting flattering photos, therefore, individuals can manage self-presentation in order to appear "hot" and appealing to potential dating partners.

This idea of using body image use as a tool to manage and judge self-presentation is also present in heterosexual male's perception of gay males' online dating profiles (Penney, 2014). Reinforcement of gender ideals or clichés may result in dating ads where "straight men" are searching for other "straight men" (Reynolds 2015), as well as the culture of creating and sharing of naked or semi-naked pictures for sexting and sexualizing in LGBT populations (Albury & Byron, 2014).

Interest in LGBT and online dating research dates back to the early 2000s, if not earlier, when a variety of services and websites began to target niche populations (Ridinger, 2005). In an investigation of how gay and bisexual men meet their partners, Prestage and colleagues (2015) gathered data from over 4,000 Australian males who met their partners online and preferred online dating to other methods of seeking dates and romantic partners. In their study, older men also used the Internet to meet significant others, thus indicating online dating is not always primarily used by younger men, as many had assumed. Overall, digital outlets were found to be used for pursuing both long-term romantic partnerships and casual sexual encounters.

HYPOTHESES

While previous researchers have examined LGBT use [10] of online dating, there is not much information comparing the extent of use of online dating services among heterosexual vs. LGBT adults. One of the advantages of using online dating services is self-identification of sexual orientation, interests, and availability—something not easy to ask or identify when seeking casual or long-term sexual encounters. Studies selecting participants from the databases of online dating service users tend to include early adopters of online dating options who are confident and comfortable communicating with an individual without facing judgmental implications. Given the proliferation of LGBT dating websites and apps, it is arguably imperative to further examine the use of these sites in order to gain an understanding of LGBT consumer groups, from both a personal and marketing perspective. Given the limitation of the original dataset collected by the *Pew Foundation's "Internet and American Life Project Tracking Survey,"* this study will focus primarily on lesbian, gay, and bisexual populations (LGB).

This study proposed the following hypotheses:

H1: Online flirtation is significantly more likely among LGB adults than among heterosexual adults.

H2: The use of online dating services is significantly more likely among LGB adults than among heterosexual adults.

METHODS

Data Source and Subjects

For this research, we used data collected by the Pew Foundation's "Internet and American Life Project Tracking Survey" conducted in Spring 2013 (Smith & Duggan, 2013). The data were obtained from telephone interviews with a nationally representative sample of adults (ages 18 or older) living in the continental US (n = 2, 252). Interviews were conducted by landline (n = 1,125) and cellphone (n = 1,127). Sampling weights were provided in the dataset (Smith & Duggan, 2013), and were used for the estimation of population parameters (Lumley, 2014).

Variables

The two dependent variables that are the focus of this study are whether the respondent 1) Ever flirted online and 2) Ever used an online dating site or mobile dating app. The use of an online dating site or mobile dating app was measured by two questions, a) Ever used an online dating site, and, b) Ever used a mobile dating app. Respondents, who answered "yes" to either question, were coded as having ever used a dating website or app.

The two independent variables of primary interest for this study are 1) Sexual Orientation (Lesbian/Gay/Bisexual or Straight), 2) Race/Ethnicity (Non-Hispanic White, Non-Hispanic Black, Hispanic, Non- Hispanic Other). The other covariates used for multivariate logistic regression are, 1) Relationship Status, 2) Sex (Men, Women), 3) Education (At least some college education, No college education), and 4) Household Income (0–29K, 30–74K, and 75K or more). Respondents' relationship status was coded into 4 levels based upon a) the length in years of their current relationship (0–5 years, 6 years or more) and b) whether they were currently looking for a relationship (No, Yes) (Table 1).

Statistical Analyses

Since the Pew survey data have sampling weights, [15] specialized software are needed to incorporate the sampling weights for estimation of population parameters. The estimates in this paper were produced using R (R Core Team, 2014) and the survey package for R (Lumley, 2004, 2014). For this research we used both univariate and multivariate logistic regression.

Results

Relationship Status. Results displayed in Table 1 showed that respondents who were not in a current relationship but were actively looking for a relationship were most likely to have flirted online (46.5%) or to have used a dating website or app (37.6%). Relative to this group, the likelihood of online flirtation was significantly lower among persons who were not in a relationship and not currently looking for a relationship (18.1%, t = −6.07, p < 0.01) and among persons who were in a relationship for six or more years (8.7%, t = −9.43, p < 0.01) and non-significantly lower among persons who were in a relationship for five years or less (42.5%, t = −0.72, p > 0.40). Relative to respondents who were not in a current relationship but were actively looking for a relationship, the likelihood of using a dating website or app was significantly lower among persons who were in a relationship for five years or less (20.9%, t = −3.36, p < 0.01), among persons who were not in a relationship and not currently looking for a relationship (10.4%, t = −6.72, p < 0.01) and among persons who were in a relationship for six or more years (2.9%, t = −10.21, p < 0.01). See Table 1.

Sexual Orientation and Race/Ethnicity (Multivariate Analyses). Results showed that lesbian, gay, or bisexual adults were significantly more likely than heterosexual adults to have flirted online (56.2% versus 19.9%, t(U) = 5.86, t(M) = 4.24, p < 0.01), and to have used a dating website or app (29.8% versus 10.5%, t(U) = 3.33, t(M) = 2.61, p < 0.01) (See Table 2). Univariate analyses showed that online flirtation was significantly more likely among non-Hispanic blacks (27.2%) than among non-Hispanic whites (18.8%, t = 2.43, p < 0.05); multivariate analysis showed that this difference was marginally significant (t = 1.90, p < 0.10). All other effects of race/ethnicity were non-significant.

Discussion

The results confirm the two hypotheses: 1) online flirtation is significantly more likely among LGB adults than among heterosexual adults, and 2) the use of online dating services is significantly more likely among LGB adults than among heterosexual adults. While marketing and advertising efforts focus on more commonly known dating websites such as Match.com and eHarmony, the findings suggest there is an untapped market among LGBT persons who use online dating websites and apps. Knowledge of this may enable advertisers to focus on digital marketing tactics designed to attract specific non-heterosexual niche audiences. This is

Table 1

Percentage of Adults Who Have Ever Flirted Online or Ever Used a Dating Website or App by Relationship Status

In a Relationship	Looking for a Relationship	Length of Current Relationship	% (SE)	t	% (SE)	t
	Current Relationship Status		Ever Flirted Online		Ever Used Dating Website or App	
Yes	Not asked	6 or more years	8.7 (1.07)**	−9.43**	2.9 (0.62)	−10.21**
No	No	Not asked	18.1 (1.76)**	−6.07**	10.4 (1.36)**	−6.72
Yes	Not asked	0–5 years	42.5 (2.87)	−0.72	20.9 (2.40)**	−3.36**
No	Yes	Not asked	46.5 (4.77)**	Ref	37.6 (4.62)**	Ref

% = percentage of US adults within group who have ever flirted online or ever used a dating website or app, SE = Standard error of estimate, t = t statistic, Ref = Reference group, significance levels: * = p < 0.05, ** = p < 0.01.

Table 2

Percentage of US Adults Who Have Ever Flirted Online or Ever Used a Dating Website or App

Group	Univariate		Multivariate	
	% (SE)	t(U)	β(SE)	t(M)
Ever Flirted Online				
Sexual Orientation				
LGB	56.2 (6.10)	5.86**	1.31 (0.31)	4.24**
Heterosexual (Ref)	19.9 (1.05)			
Race/Ethnicity				
Non-Hispanic Other	20.6 (4.01)	0.43	0.19 (0.32)	0.59
Hispanic	21.9 (2.76)	1.03	0.33 (0.21)	1.53
Non-Hispanic Black	27.2 (3.25)	2.43*	0.43 (0.23)	1.90†
Non-Hispanic White (Ref)	18.8 (1.19)			
Ever Used Dating Website or App				
Sexual Orientation				
LGB	29.8 (5.74)**	3.33**	0.99 (0.38)	2.61**
Heterosexual (Ref)	10.5 (0.80)			
Race/Ethnicity				
Non-Hispanic Other	8.1 (2.65)	−1.17	−0.37 (0.47)	−0.80
Hispanic	8.0 (1.83)	−1.64	−0.47 (0.31)	−1.53
Non-Hispanic Black	12.3 (2.42)	0.35	0.09 (0.28)	0.33
Non-Hispanic White (Ref)	11.4 (0.97)			

% = percentage of US adults within group who have flirted online or used a dating website or app, SE = Standard error of estimate, t(U) = univariate t statistic, β = logistic regression coefficient, SE = Standard error, t(M) = multivariate t statistic, significance: † = $p < 0.10$, * = $p < 0.05$, ** = $p < 0.01$.

Note: The other variables included in the multivariate logistic regression model were relationship status (see Table 1), sex, income level, and education level.

especially powerful given the availability of lifestyle digital dating resources (such as Bumble, Her, and Hinge for lesbians and Grindr and Manhunt for gay men). Although sometimes debated, aspects of this market are known to be affluent. This can further appeal to researchers given the noted spending power of these individuals. The study findings can also serve as a stepping stone for exploring new ways to study LGBT consumer habits. In fact, one may argue there are a multitude of digital dating outlets inquiries that could be examined more in-depth. These could include but are certainly not limited to an examination of the benefits of LGBT dating sites; attitudes toward available resources; gratifications and purpose of use, and time spent using these technologies. Researchers may also want to examine LGBT user perceptions of dating websites versus dating applications. Studies concerning LGBT flirting habits (i.e., texting, social media, email, other) may also be beneficial.

Aside from this, research suggests Non-Hispanic blacks (race only, not identified as LGBT) are slightly more likely to flirt online than Non-Hispanic whites. This too, arguably, warrants deeper exploration. For instance, which online resources are most used by this particularly segment and why? Again, a variety of questions could be asked in order to dig deeper and learn more about this finding. The same can also be said for those looking for a relationship (not identified as LGBT), as the research suggests these individuals are more likely to flirt online and use online dating websites.

From a LGBT consumer perspective, a greater [20] understanding of how and why people use these digital dating resources can create a marketing environment where the messages are meaningful and useful. This in turn can be advantageous for users in order to assist with decision-making processes to help fuel the creation of other LGBT lifestyle-focused technologies.

LIMITATIONS

The data from this study does not include responses from transgender individuals. It may be possible there were not enough self-reported respondents from this particular group. If this was the case, it may be an indicator that other methodologies may be more suitable to further understand individual segments of the LGBT population.

CONCLUSION

Study findings indicate lesbian, gay, and bisexual adults are significantly more likely to flirt online and to use online dating websites and dating apps than heterosexual adults. Implications include opportunities to assist with LGBT consumer decision-making processes, the creation of meaningful and useful promotional messages, and an indication for further development of LGBT lifestyle-focused technologies.

ENDNOTES

1. The Pew data from which this study is based includes data provided by only lesbian, gay and bisexual adult participants.

2. Although study findings are based solely on LBG data, it is arguably advantageous to apply the implications to the LGBT population.

REFERENCES

Albury, K., & Byron, P. (2014). Queering sexting and sexualisation. *Media International Australia* (153), 138–147.

Alterovitz, S. S.-R. & Mendelsohn, G.A. (2009). Partner preferences across the life span: Online dating by older adults. *Psychology and Aging, 24*(2), 513–517.

Blackhart, G.C., Fitzpatrick, J., & Williamson, J. (2014). Dispositional factors predicting use of online dating sites and behaviors related to online dating. *Computers in Human Behavior 33*, 113–118.

Blackwell, C., Birnholtz, J., & Abbott, C. (2015). Seeing and being seen: Co-situation and impression formation using Grindr, a location-aware gay dating app. *New Media & Society, 17*(7), 1117–1136. Retrieved from http://doi.org/10.1177/1461444814521595

Brubaker, J.R., Ananny, M., & Crawford, K. (2016). Departing glances: A sociotechnical account of "leaving" Grindr. *New Media & Society, 18*(3), 373–390. Retrieved from http://doi.org/10.1177/1461444814542311

Cali, B.E., Coleman, J.M., & Campbell, C. (2013). Stranger danger? Women's self-protection intent and the continuing stigma of online dating. *Psychology, Behavior, and Social Networking, 16*(12), 853–857.

Couch, D. & Liamputtong, P. (2008). Online dating and mating: The use of the Internet to meet sexual partners. *Qualitative Health Research, 8*(2), 268–279.

Finkel, E.J., Eastwick, P.W., Karney, B.R., Reis, H.T., & Sprecher, S. (2012). Online dating: A critical analysis from the perspective of psychological science. *Psychological Science in the Public Interest, 12*(1), 3–66.

Geser, H. (2007). Online search for offline partners: Matching platforms as tools of empowerment and retraditionalization. *Sociology in Switzerland: Towards Cybersociety and Vireal Social Relations.* Retrieved from http://socio.ch/intcom/t_hgeser19.pdf

Guadagno, R.E. & Sagarin, B.J. (2010). Sex differences in jealousy: An evolutionary perspective on online infidelity. *Journal of Applied Social Psychology 40*(10), 2636–2656.

Hall, J.A., Park, N., Song., & Cody, M.J. (2010). Strategic misrepresentation in online dating: The effects of gender, self-monitoring, and personality traits. *Journal of Social and Personal Relationships 27*(1), 117–135.

Heino, R.D., Ellison, N.B., & Gibbs, J.L. (2010). Relationshopping: Investigating the market metaphor in online dating. *Journal of Social and Personal Relationships, 27*(4), 427–447.

Lenhart, A., & Duggan, M. (2014). Couples, the Internet, and Social Media. Retrieved from http://www.pewresearch.org/fact-tank/2016/02/29/5-facts-about-online-dating/

Lo, S.-H., Hsieh, A.Y., & Chiu, Y.P. (2013). Contradictory deceptive behavior in online dating. *Computers in Human Behavior*, 29, 1755–1762.

Lumley, T. (2004). Analysis of complex survey samples. *Journal of Statistical Software*, 9(1), 1–19.

Lumley, T. (2014). Survey: analysis of complex survey samples. R package version 3.30.

Penney, T. (2014). Bodies under glass: Gay Dating apps and the affect-image. *Media International Australia* (153), 107–117.

Prestage, G., Bavinton, B., Grierson, J., Down, I., Keen, P., Bradley, J., & Duncan, D. (2015). Online dating among Australian gay and bisexual men: Romance or hooking up? *AIDS and Behavior*, 19(10), 1905–1913. Retrieved from http://doi.org/http://dx.doi.org/10.1007/s10461 -015-1032-z

R Core Team. (2015). R: A language and environment for statistical computing. Vienna, Austria: R Foundation for Statistical Computing. Retrieved from http://www.R-project.org

Reynolds, C. (2015). I am super straight and I prefer you be too: Constructions of heterosexual masculinity in online personal ads for "straight" men seeking sex with men. *Journal of Communication Inquiry, 39*(3), 213–231.

Ridinger, R. B. (2005). Gay, lesbian, bisexual, and transgender resources on the Web. *Choice, 42*(8), 1343–1354.

Smith, A., & Duggan, M. (2013). Online dating & relationships. Retrieved from http://www.pewinternet .org/2013/10/21/online-dating-relationships/

Smith, A., & Anderson, M. (2016). 5 Facts about Online Dating. Retrieved from http://www.pewresearch.org /fact-tank/2016/02/29/5-facts-about-online-dating/

Reading Questions

1. According to the study's authors, what is one of the gaps in the current scholarship on this topic that gives rise to the need for their current study?

2. What two specific hypotheses do the researchers set out to investigate as part of their study, and what results do they find as answers to their hypotheses?

Rhetoric Questions

3. The study's authors report their results in two categories: "Relationship Status" and "Sexual Orientation and Race/Ethnicity." What do you believe to be the authors' rationale for using these categories to report their results?

4. Based on the study's (unlabeled) abstract and conclusion, who do you believe are the target audiences for this study? What evidence can you provide to support your answer?

Response Questions

5. In what ways might the results of this study be useful to businesses or advertisers who want to target their products to members of the lesbian, gay, or bisexual communities?

6. As part of their Discussion, the authors identify a number of possible topics for further research. Select one of these possible topics and briefly explain the kind(s) of data you would need, as well as what research methods you might employ, to investigate the topic further.

Comparative Analysis of Research Methodologies

In this chapter, the writers draw on a wide variety of research methodologies to explore their research questions. For example, Warren E. Milteer Jr. relies heavily on analysis of historical documents to explore racial boundaries in nineteenth-century North Carolina, whereas Jada E. Brooks and Darren D. Moore use data from narratives written by Black female college students to explore their study participants' desires regarding long-term partners.

Drawing on the readings in the Academic Case Study in this chapter, compose a descriptive analysis of the methods utilized in two different academic disciplines. You might begin by identifying the following for each research report:

- **Research Question(s)**   What phenomenon are the researchers studying, and what do they want to know about it?

- **Research Methods**   What research methods are used to find answers to the research question(s)?

As you describe the researchers' methods, be sure to engage in analysis as well. In other words, consider why the researchers use the methods they do and how those methods compare to others. Conclude your descriptive analysis by highlighting any similarities or differences in the two disciplines' methods.

Mindful Eating: Food as Culture and Commodity

The readings in this chapter offer a number of perspectives, both popular and academic, on the history and development of food as traditional practice and as a marker of identity in our society. They also consider the intersections of food, scientific progress, and health. The chapter begins with an article that extols the virtues of cooking for ourselves in response to the question, "Why cook?" The second selection explores Mexican food as a new metaphor for America, positioning it against the classic image of the melting pot. In so doing, the article broaches some of the complex economic, social, and political realities of American society. In the third selection, the author explores the practice of Sunday dinners as a historical ritual among African Americans and considers its importance as a continuing tradition today.

These readings offer a wide range of perspectives on food and its various functions and meanings. We hope they inspire you to pose your own critical questions about the role of food in our lives. Such questions might include:

- What do an individual's food choices say about that person, if anything at all?

- What role should issues of sustainability play in our food purchase decisions?

- How does the food we eat relate to our personal identity, or how does it affect the ways we engage with other people?

- How does scientific progress affect the food we eat and thus our overall health?

The academic case study for this chapter provides a number of disciplinary perspectives on the topic of genetically modified (GM) foods:

- **Humanities**   What are some of the ethical concerns regarding GM foods?

- **Social Sciences**   Will consumers pay a premium for GM food products?

- **Natural Sciences**   What are the exposure levels of pesticides associated with GM foods among pregnant and non-pregnant women in eastern Canada?

- **Applied Fields**   How does consumer exposure to industry and consumer-oriented information about GM food products affect their willingness to purchase such products?

Why Cook?

MICHAEL POLLAN

Michael Pollan is one of the leading voices on food politics in America today. He is the Knight Professor of Science and Environmental Journalism at the U.C. Berkeley Graduate School of Journalism and the author of numerous award-winning articles and books, including *The Omnivore's Dilemma: A Natural History of Four Meals* (2006) and *In Defense of Food: An Eater's Manifesto* (2008). In the essay below, an excerpt from *Cooked: A Natural History of Transformation* (2013), Pollan maintains that Americans are increasingly separated from the food they eat because of the industrialization and specialization of modern food production. Further, Pollan argues that we must reconnect with the act of cooking for ourselves. Then (and only then) will we reconnect with our health and happiness.

I.

At a certain point in the late middle of my life I made the unexpected but happy discovery that the answer to several of the questions that most occupied me was in fact one and the same.

Cook.

Some of these questions were personal. For example, what was the single most important thing we could do as a family to improve our health and general well-being? And what would be a good way to better connect to my teenage son? (As it turned out, this involved not only ordinary cooking but also the specialized form of it known as brewing.) Other questions were slightly more political in nature. For years I had been trying to determine (because I am often asked) what is the most important thing an ordinary person can do to help reform the American food system, to make it healthier and more sustainable? Another related question is, how can people living in a highly specialized consumer economy reduce their sense of dependence and achieve a greater degree of self-sufficiency? And then there were the more philosophical questions, the ones I've been chewing on since I first started writing books. How, in our everyday lives, can we acquire a deeper understanding of the natural world and our species' peculiar role in it? You can always go to the woods to confront such questions, but I discovered that even more interesting answers could be had simply by going to the kitchen.

I would not, as I said, ever have expected it. Cooking has always been a part of my life, but more like the furniture than an object of scrutiny, much less a passion. I counted myself lucky to have a parent—my mother—who loved to cook and almost every night made us a delicious meal. By the time I had a place of my own, I could find my way around a kitchen well enough, the results of nothing more purposeful than all those hours spent hanging around the kitchen while my mother fixed dinner. And though once I had my own place I cooked whenever I had the time, I seldom *made* time for cooking or gave it much consideration. My kitchen skills, such as they were, were pretty much frozen in place by the time I turned thirty. Truth be told, my most successful dishes leaned heavily on the cooking of others, as when I drizzled my incredible sage-butter sauce over store-bought ravioli. Every now and then I'd look at a cookbook or clip a recipe from the newspaper to add a new dish to my tiny repertoire, or I'd buy a new kitchen gadget, though most of these eventually ended up in a closet.

In retrospect, the mildness of my interest in cook- 5
ing surprises me, since my interest in every other link of the food chain had been so keen. I've been a gardener since I was eight, growing mostly vegetables, and I've always enjoyed being on farms and writing about agriculture. I've also written a fair amount about the opposite end of the food chain—the eating end, I mean, and the implications of our eating for our health. But to the middle links of the food chain, where the stuff of nature gets transformed into the things we eat and drink, I hadn't really given much thought.

Until, that is, I began trying to unpack a curious paradox I had noticed while watching television, which was simply this: How is it that at the precise historical moment when Americans were abandoning the kitchen, handing over the preparation of most of our meals to the food industry, we began spending so much of our time thinking about food and watching other people cook it on television? The less cooking we were doing in our own lives, it seemed, the more that food and its vicarious preparation fascinated us.

Our culture seems to be of at least two minds on this subject. Survey research confirms we're cooking less and buying more prepared meals every year. The amount of time spent preparing meals in American households has fallen by half since the mid-sixties when I was watching my mom fix dinner to a scant 27 minutes a day. (Americans spend less time cooking than people in any other nation, but the general downward trend is global.) And yet at the same time we're talking about cooking more—and watching cooking, and reading about cooking, and going to restaurants designed so that we can watch the work performed live. We live in an age when professional cooks are household names, some of them as famous as athletes or movie stars. The very same activity that many people regard as a form of drudgery has somehow been elevated to a popular spectator sport. When

you consider that 27 minutes is less time than it takes to watch a single episode of *Top Chef* or *The Next Food Network Star*, you realize that there are now millions of people who spend more time watching food being cooked on television than they spend actually cooking it themselves. I don't need to point out that the food you watch being cooked on television is not food you get to eat.

This is peculiar. After all, we're not watching shows or reading books about sewing or darning socks or changing the oil in our cars, three other domestic chores that we have been only too happy to outsource—and then promptly drop from conscious awareness. But cooking somehow feels different. The work, or the process, retains an emotional or psychological power we can't quite shake, or don't want to. And in fact it was after a long bout of watching cooking programs on television that I began to wonder if this activity I had always taken for granted might be worth taking a little more seriously.

I developed a few theories to explain what I came to think of as the Cooking Paradox. The first and most obvious is that watching other people cook is not exactly a new behavior for us humans. Even when "everyone" still cooked, there were plenty of us who mainly watched: men for the most part, and children. Most of us have happy memories of watching our mothers in the kitchen, performing feats that sometimes looked very much like sorcery and typically resulted in something tasty to eat. In ancient Greece, the word for "cook," "butcher," and "priest" was the same—*mageiros*—and the word shares an etymological root with "magic." I would watch, rapt, when my mother conjured her most magical dishes, like the tightly wrapped packages of fried chicken Kiev that, when cut open with a sharp knife, liberated a pool of melted butter and an aromatic gust of herbs. But watching an everyday pan of eggs get scrambled was nearly as riveting a spectacle, as the slimy yellow goop suddenly leapt into the form of savory gold nuggets. Even the most ordinary dish follows a satisfying arc of transformation, magically becoming something more than the sum of its ordinary parts. And in almost every dish, you can find, besides the culinary ingredients, the ingredients of a story: a beginning, a middle, and an end.

Then there are the cooks themselves, the heroes 10 who drive these little dramas of transformation. Even as it vanishes from our daily lives, we're drawn to the rhythms and textures of the work cooks do, which seems so much more direct and satisfying than the more abstract and formless tasks most of us perform in our jobs these days. Cooks get to put their hands on real stuff, not just keyboards and screens but fundamental things like plants and animals and fungi. They get to work with the primal elements, too, fire and water, earth and air, using them—mastering them!—to perform their tasty alchemies. How many of us still do the kind of work that engages us in a dialogue with the material world that concludes—assuming the chicken Kiev doesn't prematurely leak or the soufflé doesn't collapse—with such a gratifying and delicious sense of closure?

So maybe the reason we like to watch cooking on television and read about cooking in books is that there are things about cooking we really miss. We might not feel we have the time or energy (or the knowledge) to do it ourselves every day, but we're not prepared to see it disappear from our lives altogether. If cooking is, as the anthropologists tell us, a defining human activity—the act with which culture begins, according to Claude Lévi-Strauss—then maybe we shouldn't be surprised that watching its processes unfold would strike deep emotional chords.

The idea that cooking is a defining human activity is not a new one. In 1773, the Scottish writer James Boswell, noting that "no beast is a cook," called *Homo sapiens* "the cooking animal." (Though he might have reconsidered that definition had he been able to gaze upon the frozen-food cases at Walmart.) Fifty years later, in *The Physiology of Taste*, the French gastronome Jean Anthelme Brillat-Savarin claimed that cooking made us who we are; by teaching men to use fire, it had "done the most to advance the cause of civilization." More recently, Lévi-Strauss, writing in *The Raw and the Cooked* in 1964, reported that many of the world's cultures entertained a similar view, regarding cooking as the symbolic activity that "establishes the difference between animals and people."

For Lévi-Strauss, cooking was a metaphor for the human transformation of raw nature into cooked culture. But in the years since the publication of *The Raw and the Cooked*, other anthropologists have begun to take quite literally the idea that the invention of cooking might hold the evolutionary key to our humanness. A few years ago, a Harvard anthropologist and primatologist named Richard Wrangham published a fascinating book called *Catching Fire*, in which he argued that it was the discovery of cooking by our early ancestors—and not tool making or meat eating or language—that set us apart from the apes and made us human. According to the "cooking hypothesis," the advent of cooked food altered the course of human evolution. By providing our forebears with a more energy-dense and easy-to-digest diet, it allowed our brains to grow bigger (brains being notorious energy guzzlers) and our guts to shrink. It seems that raw food takes much more time and energy to chew and digest, which is why other primates our size carry around substantially larger digestive tracts and spend many more of their waking hours chewing—as much as six hours a day.

Cooking, in effect, took part of the work of chewing and digestion and performed it for us outside of the body, using outside sources of energy. Also, since cooking detoxifies many potential sources of food, the new technology cracked open a treasure trove of calories unavailable to other animals. Freed from the necessity of spending our days gathering large quantities of raw food and then chewing (and chewing) it, humans could now devote their time, and their metabolic resources, to other purposes, like creating a culture.

Cooking gave us not just the meal but also the 15 occasion: the practice of eating together at an appointed time and place. This was something new under the sun, for the forager of raw food would have likely fed himself on the go and alone, like all the other animals. (Or, come to think of it, like the industrial eaters we've more recently become, grazing at gas stations and eating by ourselves whenever and wherever.) But sitting down to common meals, making eye contact, sharing food, and exercising self-restraint all served to civilize us. "Around that fire," Wrangham writes, "we became tamer."

Cooking thus transformed us, and not only by making us more sociable and civil. Once cooking allowed us to expand our cognitive capacity at the expense of our digestive capacity, there was no going back: Our big brains and tiny guts now depended on a diet of cooked food. (Raw-foodists take note.) What this means is that cooking is now obligatory—it is, as it were, baked into our biology. What Winston Churchill once said of architecture—"First we shape our buildings, and then they shape us"—might also be said of cooking. First we cooked our food, and then our food cooked us.

If cooking is as central to human identity, biology, and culture as Wrangham suggests, it stands to reason that the decline of cooking in our time would have serious consequences for modern life, and so it has. Are they all bad? Not at all. The outsourcing of much of the work of cooking to corporations has relieved women of what has traditionally been their exclusive responsibility for feeding the family, making it easier for them to work outside the home and have careers. It has headed off many of the conflicts and domestic arguments that such a large shift in gender roles and family dynamics was bound to spark. It has relieved all sorts of other pressures in the household, including longer workdays and overscheduled children, and saved us time that we can now invest in other pursuits. It has also allowed us to diversify our diets substantially, making it possible even for people with no cooking skills and little money to enjoy a whole different cuisine every night of the week. All that's required is a microwave.

These are no small benefits. Yet they have come at a cost that we are just now beginning to reckon. Industrial cooking has taken a substantial toll on our health and well-being. Corporations cook very differently from how people do (which is why we usually call what they do "food processing" instead

of cooking). They tend to use much more sugar, fat, and salt than people cooking for people do; they also deploy novel chemical ingredients seldom found in pantries in order to make their food last longer and look fresher than it really is. So it will come as no surprise that the decline in home cooking closely tracks the rise in obesity and all the chronic diseases linked to diet.

The rise of fast food and the decline in home cooking have also undermined the institution of the shared meal, by encouraging us to eat different things and to eat them on the run and often alone. Survey researchers tell us we're spending more time engaged in "secondary eating," as this more or less constant grazing on packaged foods is now called, and less time engaged in "primary eating"—a rather depressing term for the once-venerable institution known as the meal.

The shared meal is no small thing. It is a founda- 20 tion of family life, the place where our children learn the art of conversation and acquire the habits of civilization: sharing, listening, taking turns, navigating differences, arguing without offending. What have been called the "cultural contradictions of capitalism"—its tendency to undermine the stabilizing social forms it depends on—are on vivid display today at the modern American dinner table, along with all the brightly colored packages that the food industry has managed to plant there.

These are, I know, large claims to make for the centrality of cooking (and not cooking) in our lives, and a caveat or two are in order. For most of us today, the choice is not nearly as blunt as I've framed it: that is, home cooking from scratch versus fast food prepared by corporations. Most of us occupy a place somewhere between those bright poles, a spot that is constantly shifting with the day of the week, the occasion, and our mood. Depending on the night, we might cook a meal from scratch, or we might go out or order in, or we might "sort of" cook. This last option involves availing ourselves of the various and very useful shortcuts that an industrial food economy offers: the package of spinach in the freezer, the can of wild salmon in the pantry, the box of store-bought ravioli from down the street or halfway around the world. What constitutes "cooking" takes place along a spectrum, as indeed it has for at least a century, when packaged foods first entered the kitchen and the definition of "scratch cooking" began to drift. (Thereby allowing me to regard my packaged ravioli with sage-butter sauce as a culinary achievement.) Most of us over the course of a week find ourselves all over that spectrum. What is new, however, is the great number of people now spending most nights at the far end of it, relying for the preponderance of their meals on an industry willing to do *every*thing for them save the heating and the eating. "We've had a hundred years of packaged foods," a food-marketing consultant told me, "and now we're going to have a hundred years of packaged meals."

This is a problem—for the health of our bodies, our families, our communities, and our land, but also for our sense of how our eating connects us to the world. Our growing distance from any direct, physical engagement with the processes by which the raw stuff of nature gets transformed into a cooked meal is changing our understanding of what food is. Indeed, the idea that food has *any* connection to nature or human work or imagination is hard to credit when it arrives in a neat package, fully formed. Food becomes just another commodity, an abstraction. And as soon as that happens we become easy prey for corporations selling synthetic versions of the real thing—what I call edible foodlike substances. We end up trying to nourish ourselves on images.

Now, for a man to criticize these developments will perhaps rankle some readers. To certain ears, whenever a man talks about the importance of cooking, it sounds like he wants to turn back the clock, and return women to the kitchen. But that's not at all what I have in mind. I've come to think cooking is too important to be left to any one gender or member of the family; men and children both need to be in the kitchen, too, and not just for reasons of fairness or equity but because they have so much to gain by being there. In fact, one of the biggest reasons corporations were able to insinuate themselves into this part of our lives is because home cooking had for so long been denigrated as "women's work" and therefore not important enough for men and boys to learn to do.

Though it's hard to say which came first: Was home cooking denigrated because the work was mostly done by women, or did women get stuck doing most of the cooking because our culture denigrated the work? The gender politics of cooking are nothing if not complicated, and probably always have been. Since ancient times, a few special types of cooking have enjoyed considerable prestige: Homer's warriors barbecued their own joints of meat at no cost to their heroic status or masculinity. And ever since, it has been socially acceptable for men to cook in public and professionally—for money. (Though it is only recently that professional chefs have enjoyed the status of artists.) But for most of history most of humanity's food has been cooked by women working out of public view and without public recognition. Except for the rare ceremonial occasions over which men presided—the religious sacrifice, the July 4 barbecue, the four-star restaurant—cooking has traditionally been women's work, part and parcel of homemaking and child care, and therefore undeserving of serious—i.e., male—attention.

But there may be another reason cooking has not 25 received its proper due. In a recent book called *The Taste for Civilization*, Janet A. Flammang, a feminist scholar and political scientist who has argued eloquently for the social and political importance of "food work," suggests the problem may have something to do with food itself, which by its very nature falls on the wrong side—the feminine side—of the mind-body dualism in Western culture.

"Food is apprehended through the senses of touch, smell, and taste," she points out, "which rank lower on the hierarchy of senses than sight and hearing, which are typically thought to give rise to knowledge. In most of philosophy, religion, and literature, food is associated with body, animal, female, and appetite—things civilized men have sought to overcome with knowledge and reason."

Very much to their loss.

Reading Questions

1. Why, according to Pollan, do so many people enjoy watching others cook or reading about cooking?

2. Explain the connections Pollan makes between "the 'cooking hypothesis'" (par. 13) and advances in human sociability and civility.

3. According to Pollan, what are the effects, both positive and negative, of losing our connection to cooking?

Rhetoric Questions

4. Pollan argues that cooking "transformed" (16) humans and is central to our identity. What does he mean by this? What type of evidence does he provide to support this argument? Do you find his argument effective?

5. In this excerpt, Pollan admits that some of his claims may seem very large. What caveats does he offer in an effort to hedge these claims? How might you use hedging in your own writing?

Response Question

6. Consider your own experiences with cooking. What motivates you to cook when you do? What do you get from it, besides nutrition? What keeps you from cooking (more often)?

Taco USA: How Mexican Food Became More American Than Apple Pie

GUSTAVO ARELLANO

Gustavo Arellano is the former publisher and editor of *OC Weekly*, an alternative newspaper in Orange County, California. He is the author of two books, *Orange County: A Personal History* (2008) and *Taco USA: How Mexican Food Conquered America* (2012), as well as the writer behind ¡Ask a Mexican!, a nationally syndicated newspaper column. In the article below, published in 2012 in *Reason* magazine online, Arellano challenges misconceptions about the appropriation of Mexican food in America. Citing concoctions such as tater tot burritos and frozen margarita machines, Arellano uses personal narrative and historical research to argue that Mexican food has, in fact, conquered North America.

MAY 14, 2012, 12:00 PM—Exit 132 off Interstate 29 in Brookings, South Dakota, offers two possibilities. A right turn will take drivers through miles of farms, flatland that stretches to the horizon, cut up into grids by country roads and picturesque barns—a scenic route to nowhere in heartland America. But take a left at the light, and you wind up coasting through a college town of 19,000 that's more than 95 percent white. The city's small Latino minority—less than 1 percent of the population—is mostly students or faculty members passing through South Dakota State University. It was here, in late 2009, that I experienced an epiphany about Mexican food in the United States.

I had been visiting the campus and found myself desperate for a taste of home. For us Southern Californians, that means burritos. Google Maps found me four Mexican restaurants in town. One, named Guadalajara, is a small South Dakota chain with outposts in Pierre and Spearfish. The food there was fine: a mishmash of tacos, burritos, and bean-and-rice pairings. But talk to the waiters in Spanish, and their faces brighten; they trot out the secret salsa they make for themselves but don't dare share with locals for fear of torching their tongues.

The most popular restaurant in town that day was Taco John's. I didn't know it then, but Taco John's is the third-largest taco chain in the United States, with nearly 500 locations. But what lured me that morning was a drive-through line snaking out from the faux-Spanish revival building (whitewashed adobe and all) and into the street. Once I inched my rental car next to the menu, I was offered an even more outrageous simulacrum* of the American Southwest: tater tots, that most midwestern of snacks, renamed "Potato Olés" and stuffed into a breakfast burrito, nacho cheese sauce slowly oozing out from the bottom of the flour tortilla.

There is nothing remotely Mexican about Potato Olés—not even the quasi-Spanish name, which has a distinctly Castilian accent. The burrito was more insulting to me and my heritage than casting Charlton Heston as the swarthy Mexican hero in *Touch of Evil*. But it was intriguing enough to take back to my hotel room for a taste. There, as I experienced all of the concoction's gooey, filling glory while chilly rain fell outside, it struck me: Mexican food has become a better culinary metaphor for America than the melting pot.

Back home, my friends did not believe that a tater 5 tot burrito could exist. When I showed them proof online, out came jeremiads about inauthenticity, about how I was a traitor for patronizing a Mexican chain that got its start in Wyoming, about how the

simulacrum: the likeness or representation of a thing.

avaricious *gabachos* had once again usurped our holy cuisine and corrupted it to fit their crude palates.

In defending that tortilla-swaddled abomination, I unknowingly joined a long, proud lineage of food heretics and lawbreakers who have been developing, adapting, and popularizing Mexican food in El Norte since before the Civil War. Tortillas and tamales have long left behind the moorings of immigrant culture and fully infiltrated every level of the American food pyramid, from state dinners at the White House to your local 7-Eleven. Decades' worth of attempted restrictions by governments, academics, and other self-appointed custodians of purity have only made the strain stronger and more resilient. The result is a market-driven mongrel cuisine every bit as delicious and all-American as the German classics we appropriated from Frankfurt and Hamburg.

IMPERIALISM AND ENCHILADAS

Food is a natural conduit of change, evolution, and innovation. Wishing for a foodstuff to remain static, uncorrupted by outside influence—especially in these United States—is as ludicrous an idea as barring new immigrants from entering the country. Yet for more than a century, both sides of the political spectrum have fought to keep Mexican food in a ghetto. From the right has come the canard that the cuisine is unhealthy and alien, a stereotype dating to the days of the Mexican-American War, when urban legend had it that animals wouldn't eat the corpses of fallen Mexican soldiers due to the high chile content in the decaying flesh. Noah Smithwick, an observer of the aftermath of the Battle of San Jacinto in 1836, claimed "the cattle got to chewing the bones [of Mexican soldiers], which so affected the milk that residents in the vicinity had to dig trenches and bury them."

Similar knocks against Mexican food can be heard to this day in the lurid tourist tales of "Montezuma's Revenge" and in the many food-based ethnic slurs still in circulation: *beaner, greaser, pepper belly, taco bender, roach coach*, and so many more. "Aside from diet," the acclaimed borderlands scholar Américo Paredes wrote in 1978, "no other aspect of Mexican culture seems to have caught the fancy of the Anglo coiner of derogatory terms for Mexicans."

Thankfully, the buying public has never paid much attention to those prandial *pendejos*. Instead, Americans have loved and consumed Mexican food in large quantities almost from the moment it was available—from canned chili and tamales in the early 20th century to fast-food tacos in the 1960s, sit-down eateries in the 1970s, and ultra-pricey hipster mescal bars today. Some staples of the Mexican diet have been thoroughly assimilated into American food culture. No one nowadays thinks of "chili" as Mexican, even though it long passed for Mexican food in this country; meanwhile, every Major League baseball and NFL stadium sells nachos, thanks to the invention of a fast-heated chips and "cheese" combination concocted by an Italian-American who was the cousin of Johnny Cash's first wife. Only in America!

In the course of this culinary blending, a multi-billion-dollar industry arose. And that's where leftist critics of Mexican food come in. For them, there's something inherently suspicious about a cuisine responsive to both the market and the *mercado*. Oh, academics and foodies may love the grub, but they harbor an atavistic view that the only "true" Mexican food is the just-off-the-grill carne asada found in the side lot of your local *abuelita* (never mind that it was the invading Spaniards who introduced beef to the New World). "Mexico's European-and-Indian soul," writes Rick Bayless, the high priest of the "authentic" Mexican food movement, in his creatively titled book, *Authentic Mexican*, "feels the intuitions of neither bare-bones Victorianism nor Anglo-Saxon productivity"—a line reminiscent of dispatches from the Raj. If it were up to these authentistas, we'd never have kimchi tacos or pastrami burritos. Salsa would not outsell ketchup in the United States. This food of the gods would be locked in Mexican households and barrios of cities, far away from Anglo hands.

That corn-fed Americans love and profit from Mexican food is viewed as an open wound in Chicano intellectual circles, a gastronomic update of America's imperial taking of the Southwest. *Yanqui* consumption and enjoyment of quesadillas and margaritas, in this view, somehow signifies a weakness in the Mexican character. "The dialectic between representation and production of Mexican cuisine offers a critical means of gauging Latino cultural power, or, more precisely, the relative lack of such power," write scholars Victor Valle and Rudy Torres in their 2000 book *Latino Metropolis*. (Another precious thought from Valle and Torres concerns Mary Sue Milliken and Susan Feniger, two midwestern girls who came to Los Angeles and learned to love Mexican food during the 1980s, parlaying that fondness into a series of television shows and books under the billing "Two Hot Tamales." The academics claim the Tamales' success arose from "neocolonial appropriations of world cuisine by reviving a gendered variant of the Hispanic fantasy discourse." Um, yeah . . .)

With due respect to my fellow lefty professors, they're full of beans. I'm not claiming equal worth for all American interpretations of Mexican food; Taco Bell has always made me retch, and Mexican food in central Kentucky tastes like . . . well, Mexican food in central Kentucky. But when culinary anthropologists like Bayless and Diana Kennedy make a big show out of protecting "authentic" Mexican food from the onslaught of commercialized glop, they are being both paternalistic and ahistorical.

That you have a nation (and increasingly a planet—you can find Mexican restaurants from Ulan Bator to Sydney to Prague) lusting after tequila, guacamole, and *tres leches* cake isn't an exercise in culinary neocolonialism but something closer to the opposite. By allowing itself to be endlessly adaptable to local tastes, Mexican food has become a primary vehicle for exporting the culture of a long-ridiculed country to the far corners of the globe. Forget Mexico's imaginary *Reconquista* of the American Southwest; the *real* conquest of North America is a peaceful and consensual affair, taking place one tortilla at a time.

I'll never forget the delight I felt a couple of years ago when I worked on a series of investigative stories on Orange County neo-Nazis. One of the photos I unearthed showed two would-be Aryans scarfing down food from Del Taco, a beloved California chain best known for its cheap and surprisingly tasty burritos. The neo-colonizers have become the colonized, and no one even fired a shot.

TAMALES AND TRUNCHEONS

As long as Mexican food has existed in this country, government has tried to legislate it out of existence. This is partly because of stereotypes but mostly because government is government. The resulting underground Mexican food economy, meanwhile, has birthed some of the cuisine's most innovative trends.

In 1880s San Antonio, so-called chili queens—Mexican women who brought the Alamo City national attention by setting up impromptu stalls in city squares to sell fiery bowls of what was then known as *chile con carne*—began a decades-long game of cat and mouse with local officials. The authorities would declare a certain neighborhood legally off-limits, and the chili queens would shrug and move their tents to the outdoor plaza across the street, bringing with them their legions of loyal customers. It took until the 1940s for San Antonio bureaucrats to formally legalize the street vendors, but only if they subjected themselves to rigorous health inspections and hawked their food from white tents with screens. The public scorned these bowdlerized* women, and the chili queens disappeared within years.

The same story arc has played out nearly everywhere in the United States where there has been a Mexican with food to sell. Wandering tamale men spread across the United States during the 1890s until competitors and not-in-my-backyard types convinced city councils to pass laws against them. A century later, *loncheras* peddling tacos and burritos—first to construction sites, then to anywhere workers take their lunches—have encountered the same protectionism and prejudice. As the public embraces the convenience, affordability, and taste of food trucks, restaurant owners and the city officials they lobby have repeatedly attempted to squash the competition.

---

bowdlerized: stripped of offensive content.

Any new businesses in town will always make city planners and councilmen wary and greedy, of course. But the sad, surprising reality is that most of the resistance to *loncheras* comes from brick-and-mortar businesses. Instead of refining and broadening their offerings to keep up with their new competitors, the incumbents fall back on an argument straight out of a Mafia protection racket: Since we pay more taxes and business fees than food trucks, government should squash our competition so we can continue business as usual.

It's a strategy that has long worked. In 1992 tiny Pasco, Washington, set rules limiting where taco trucks could park and requiring them to pay $45 each month per parking spot. Pasco's restaurants, by contrast, paid only $35 a year for a license. Five street vendors took Pasco all the way up to the U.S. Court of Appeals for the 9th Circuit, arguing that the double standard was unconstitutional, but they ultimately lost. Similar crackdowns have taken place in Fresno (1995), Chicago (1997), Phoenix (1999), and Dallas (1999), where Planning Commissioner James Lee Fantroy sneered during a public hearing on the subject, "The proper preparation of food is one of those things that we must carefully watch. I don't think I could bring my family to one of these [trucks] and feel comfortable."

Even in Los Angeles, the second-largest Mexican metropolis in the world, the majority-Democrat L.A. County Board of Supervisors tried to ban food trucks as recently as four years ago. The city has destroyed carts selling unauthorized bacon dogs and even hauled off some entrepreneurs to jail, despite acknowledging that no bacon-dog customer has ever registered a complaint.

L.A. has a long history of putting the squeeze on Mexican-food peddlers. From 1900 to about 1925, the city council passed resolution after resolution trying to ban tamale wagons from downtown Los Angeles. The *tamaleros*, knowing what they meant to their legions of customers, fought back. In 1903, when the council tried to outlaw them altogether, tamale wagons formed a mutual-aid society and presented a petition with the signatures of more than 500 customers that read in part, "We claim that the lunch wagons are catering to an appreciative public and to deprive the people of these convenient eating places would prove a great loss to the many local merchants who sell the wagon proprietors various supplies." When the city council finally kicked the vendors out as part of the effort to create the sanitized, whitewashed ethnic fantasyland now known as Olvera Street, the vendors just went underground, where they flourished for decades and eventually transformed into *loncheras*.

In 2008 the L.A. County Board of Supervisors passed a resolution making parking a truck for longer than one hour in unincorporated communities such as East L.A. a misdemeanor with a maximum penalty of a $1,000 fine and six months in jail. The plan sparked a furious backlash—not only among the *loncheros*, who created La Asociación de Loncheros L.A. Familia Unida de California (Association of Loncheros Los Angeles United Family of California) to defend themselves, but among young bloggers and hipsters who had grown up patronizing *loncheras* after clubbing or working late. Soon black T-shirts emblazoned with a white *lonchera* and the statement "Carne Asada Is Not a Crime" flowered across Southern California, and a group of foodies helped the *loncheras* sue the board of supervisors. A Los Angeles Superior Court judge eventually overturned the supes' diktat.*

But it was mostly the will of the *loncheros*—almost all immigrants who initially came to the United States with no knowledge of English, let alone an understanding of our legal system—that earned the victory. In my homeland of Orange County, Roberto Guzmán led a group of *loncheros* in 2006 to sue the city of Santa Ana to be able to park on city streets from 9 A.M. until 9 P.M., seven days a week. His Cadillac-pink truck "Alebrije's" sells food from Mexico City—buttery, crepe-like quesadillas, massive chili-soaked sandwiches called *pambazos*, and a concoction of six tortillas covered with sautéed onions, bell peppers, jalapeños, and grilled ham, bacon, and carne asada called *alambres*.

---

diktat: a mandate without consent from the populace.

When the city council (also majority Democrat, and all Latino, making Santa Ana the largest city in the United States with such leadership) sought to negotiate with the *loncheros* to install a lottery system giving rights to some food trucks but not all, they refused. "Please," Guzmán scoffs. "It would've been favoritism all the way. I felt as if they were going to take away the sustenance of so many families. It was going to be a huge economic loss. And it was too much a worry that, at any moment, [the city] could take away the parking spots from us." Today Santa Ana is a *lonchera* paradise—and Guzmán owns three of them, with plans for more.

MARGARITA MILLIONAIRES

The self-appointed guardians of Mexican food in this country are right on one point: The popularity of Mexican food has indeed allowed many non-Mexicans to build multimillion-dollar fortunes. German immigrant William Gebhardt created Eagle Brand Chili Powder from the basement of a bar in New Braunfels, Texas, in the early 1890s, parlaying that into a canned food empire that lasts to this day. Glen Bell, founder of Taco Bell, got his idea for hard-shelled tacos from Mitla Café, a San Bernardino Mexican restaurant that stood across the street from Bell's burger stand during the early 1950s. The Frito-Lay company developed its most iconic chips, Fritos and Doritos, by purchasing the rights to those crunchy treats from Mexican immigrants. And Steve Ells, founder of Chipotle, which has mainstreamed massive burritos during the last decade, openly admits he was "inspired" by the burritos sold in San Francisco's famously Latino Mission District.

The easy response to critics of appropriation is that it's the market that decides who gets rich, not ethnic politics. Besides, obsessing over the many *gabachos* who have become Mexican-food millionaires ignores the many success stories involving Mexicans who displayed the same guile as their pasty-skinned contemporaries.

Larry Cano, for example, started out as a dishwasher at a Polynesian-themed restaurant in the

Los Angeles enclave of Encino, worked his way up enough to eventually buy the place, then renamed it El Torito—the chain that pioneered sit-down Mexican dining in the United States. In Texas, the Martinez and Cuellar families created empires with their El Fenix and El Chico chains, respectively, formalizing Mexican restaurants for the rest of the country and essentially creating the genre of Tex-Mex. In Southern California during the 1990s, the Lopez family, immigrants from the southern Mexico state of Oaxaca, helped popularize regional Mexican food in this country, fighting the double challenge of introducing Oaxacan food to both Americans *and* Southern California Mexicans who looked down on the cuisine as the domain of backward Indians. Today Mexican immigrants are following the Lopez/Oaxacan lead and selling their regional specialties nationwide.

And then there's the story of Mariano Martinez, scion of the Cuellars, who in 1971 created the frozen margarita machine. At his Dallas restaurant Mariano's, which serves heroic enchilada platters, Martinez birthed an empire off the slushy tequila drink, inventing an instant mix that has powered many a house party since. Nowadays Martinez disavows the frozen margarita—he prefers his fresh, with Cointreau. But Mariano's pride in his creation and his cuisine—long dismissed by "serious" food critics as forgettable—remains.

"I've seen them all over the years," he says. "They come in and do this upscale food. . . . Some of those places aren't there anymore. My little old place I have? Forty years later, we're still pumping the same food. Same phone number. Here I am plugging away at this little Tex-Mex peasant food that no one wanted to play with, that all the ivory tower critics made fun of. And with a drink that no one can resist."

Mariano's original frozen margarita machine is 30 now in the Smithsonian. And Mexican food marches on, a combo plate of freedom giving indigestion to busybodies and authentistas everywhere.

Reading Questions

1. Describe Arellano's initial reaction to Taco John's Potato Olés.

2. According to Arellano, what "staples of the Mexican diet have been thoroughly assimilated into American food culture" (par. 9)?

3. How does Arellano respond to leftist academic critiques about the appropriation of Mexican food in America?

Rhetoric Questions

4. Arellano writes extensively about the history of local laws and ordinances that regulate Mexican food in America. Locate one of these laws or ordinances. How does the example work within his larger argument? What does the example illustrate?

5. How does Arellano use personal narrative in this essay? Are there genres in your discipline in which personal narrative would be appropriate? Why or why not?

6. Arellano's essay culminates in a description of the frozen margarita machine and its inventor. How does this example illustrate his main argument?

Response Questions

7. Arellano says that a taste of home for Southern Californians like himself means burritos. What food would you consider as your "taste of home"? Explain your choice.

8. Arellano writes, "Food is a natural conduit of change, evolution, and innovation" (par. 7). What other cultural products might be considered conduits of change? Provide and explain several examples.

Sunday Dinners Are Sacred for African Americans

NNEKA OKONA

Nneka Okona is a freelance writer and journalist based in Atlanta, Georgia. She writes often about food, travel, the African Diaspora, and the American South. Her articles have appeared in the *Wall Street Journal*, *Travel + Leisure*, *Food & Wine*, and *National Geographic*, among others. The article below appeared in *Zora*, an online publication for women of color, in October 2019. In it, Okona traces the history of Sunday dinners as a tradition in the African American community and explores its continuing significance as a modern ritual.

As a child growing up in the South, I knew that Sunday was a holy and reverent day set aside from all the rest. Each one began the same: stirring from a deep sleep early in the morning, when the faintest light from sunrise was starting to appear; showering and dressing with preapproved outfits per my mother; shuffling off to the family car and loading up with my three sisters, church bound.

Spending time in church was part of the fabric of what it meant to be a member of my family. Throughout my childhood, we flitted from churches and denominations, including Southern Baptist, African Methodist Episcopal, and Catholicism. Not spending the start of the week in the "house of the Lord" rarely happened, and when it did, it was as if life itself had been disrupted. But there was another vital part of Sunday other than the ritualistic churchgoing: Sunday dinner. No Sunday was complete without the ornate feast my mother planned and prepared, often with my help.

After we spent the earlier half of Sunday in church, fellowshipping among other Black believers while receiving the pastor's sermon and musical selections from the choir, a light breakfast and quick nap set the stage for what was to come. I'd sleep too long, always, because waking up early for anything was a pain. And when I shook off the grogginess, I'd slink off to the kitchen to chip in with the tasks that needed to be completed to execute supper.

Memories like these I hold near and dear, as churchgoing is no longer a part of my life and hasn't been for years. The religiosity that was once an integral core of my identity and how I rooted my life has given way to other forms of nurturing and grounding myself—meditating, doing yoga, pulling tarot cards, listening to my intuition. Sunday dinner, however, has not been something I've been able to let go of so easily.

More than a tradition that has transitioned into a steady ritual for many Black families, Sunday dinner has a storied history. Dating back to the days of chattel slavery, enslaved Africans saw food as more than sustenance, as it had always been before. Sunday arose as that sole day of the week where they could pretend they were free.

William C. Whit muses about this history in his essay "Soul Food as Cultural Creation," included in a collection of essays edited by Anne L. Bower entitled *African American Foodways: Explorations of Food and Culture*. Whit writes, "Saturday night was usually the time for distributing slave provisions. This made possible the tradition of a larger than normal Sunday dinner—a practice that has continued with minor modification in many African American households."

That tradition stuck as those same enslaved Africans were emancipated and lived on to rebuild what it meant to live unencumbered with the harsh realities of being held captive.

One derivative of Sunday dinner and Sunday eating removes one step from the formula altogether: eating at church. Rather than trudge your entire family from church after spending the bulk of the day there, you simply moved to another part of the building—maybe down some steps to a basement emanating aromas or a fellowship hall lined with long tables—to feast on food the church mothers lovingly prepared.

This practice originated in the rural South, where the church stood as a beacon and a source of more than religious edification—it was a place to connect with other like-minded souls in the name of social connection. Joyce White, a food writer and former editor at *Heart & Soul*, penned a cookbook on the subject called *Soul Food: Recipes and Reflections from African-American Churches*. In the book, she discusses how, after moving to New York, she searched for the sort of community that had grounded her back home in Alabama and found it in the African American churches of Brooklyn and Harlem.

"The church started out as the site of social activities in our communities. It is where we went to school, got married, and held our graduation exercises and community rallies," White said in a piece for the *Chicago Tribune* on the subject. "Being people of color, we always liked to eat and break bread and show the bounty of our labor. The churches were our restaurants. We didn't have to worry about segregation or not feeling welcome."

Though the tradition of Sunday dinner and the mean-[10]ing it holds carries on from generation to generation, some women, like me, have figured out a way to merge the past with the present, creating new traditions and ways of communing over meals.

Shaun Chavis, a writer and editor based in Atlanta, Georgia, was an army brat during her childhood. Because of that, most of her younger years were spent moving around a lot. Seeing her extended family in Rocky Mount, North Carolina, was a special treat—one that happened rarely—and so was Sunday dinner. Chavis' family was strong in the church: Her maternal grandfather was a pastor, and his wife, her grandmother, a first lady. Following church, there was always a family Sunday dinner with an assortment of aunts, uncles, and cousins. Chavis fondly recalls her grandmother's rolls, as well as the creamed corn and tomato casserole she made.

"My maternal grandmother lived in a small town, and she was famous for her Parker House rolls," she says. "She also did really great vegetables. I don't remember her meats as much."

Chavis has tried to replicate this family experience for herself in her adulthood. When her father died in 2011, Chavis, immersed in grief, started hosting weekly dinner parties on Sundays as a way to be around friends as she healed. At the time, she lived in Birmingham, Alabama. Her friends would come over and prep, cook, and laugh together in what she describes as a "tiny" apartment. It met a need going back to her childhood.

"I grew up with not only the tradition but seeing these really important women in my life being upheld as great cooks," she says. "I wanted to be that. I wanted to be the person who's cooking for everybody."

Leni Sorenson, PhD, a culinary historian and [15] teacher, grew up in Southern California with different experiences outside of the typical Southern Sunday dinner custom. She didn't grow up religious, though she often went to a family member's house on Sunday—Aunt Mary.

"We would go to Aunt Mary's because she always had lots of food and was always cooking," Sorenson says. "[She and her daughters] would make big pans of hamburger patties that we might call Salisbury steaks today with a bit of gravy."

Gravy was a big thing in her family, especially on Sundays. And so, when Sorenson didn't go to her Aunt Mary's house, her stepfather cooked his favorites from his native Algiers, Louisiana: pots of pinto beans, collard greens seasoned with ham hocks, chicken or pork chop fricassee. These days, however, Sunday has taken on a new meaning, though she fondly reflects on the memory of what it used to be. Now a widow, Sorenson has four children and gets her fill of community gathered around her table with farmstead history dinners that she hosts at her home.

"I spend a lot of time alone," she says. "For me now, a lot of Sundays are a down day, because I'm doing these history dinners on Saturday evenings. Often, there's food left over, and that becomes Sunday dinner."

Like Chavis and Sorenson, for me, Sunday is a much quieter affair now than it was in my childhood. As a single, childless woman, I have no family of my own waiting for a massive Sunday spread. There is no external pressure at all for me to uphold this culinary tradition. And yet, each week, days in advance, I start planning a Sunday feast—for myself. I pick a main entrée, some sides, and even a dessert. I spend no less than four hours corralling all these ingredients and getting lost in the fun that is cooking from the heart.

I feel like my mother, the conductor of each meal, 20 willing all the players to take their places and making all the components sing together in a harmonious tune. And in the end, when a meal emerges, I am filled with peace, deep satisfaction, and pleasure. Then I remember why I embarked on this journey without an audience in the first place.

Reading Questions

1. According to Okona, what practices, rooted in the history of slavery in America, help to account for the importance of the ritual Sunday dinner in the African American community today?

2. Based on her descriptions, how are Okona's Sundays today both similar to and different from the Sundays of her childhood?

Rhetoric Questions

3. What point does Okona illustrate by providing descriptions of the Sunday dinner routines of Shaun Chavis and Leni Sorenson?

4. Okona cites a number of sources as part of her article. What strategy does she regularly employ to bolster their ethos and underscore their authority?

Response Questions

5. Okona's article explores a tradition—Sunday dinners—that expresses what it means to be a member of her family. Describe a tradition of your family that you continue to participate in today. Has that tradition remained the same or altered over time?

6. Explain briefly what you believe Okona means to convey to her readers in the final sentence of her article: "Then I remember why I embarked on the journey without an audience in the first place" (par. 20).

Academic Case Study: Genetically Modified Food

Genetically Modified (GM) Foods and Ethical Eating

FRANCIS DIZON, SARAH COSTA, CHERYL ROCK, AMANDA HARRIS, CIERRA HUSK, AND JENNY MEI

Francis Dizon, lead author of the following study, is an assistant sports dietitian at Duke University, where he provides nutrition education and counseling to student-athletes. In the study below, which was published in 2015 in the *Journal of Food Science*, Dizon and his colleagues explore "the relationship between the various applications of GM foods and their corresponding ethical issues" and find "a need to stay vigilant about the many ethical implications of producing and consuming GM foods and GMOs."

ABSTRACT

The ability to manipulate and customize the genetic code of living organisms has brought forth the production of genetically modified organisms (GMOs) and consumption of genetically modified (GM) foods. The potential for GM foods to improve the efficiency of food production, increase customer satisfaction, and provide potential health benefits has contributed to the rapid incorporation of GM foods into the American diet. However, GM foods and GMOs are also a topic of ethical debate. The use of GM foods and GM technology is surrounded by ethical concerns and situational judgment, and should ideally adhere to the ethical standards placed upon food and nutrition professionals, such as: beneficence, nonmaleficence, justice and autonomy. The future of GM foods involves many aspects and trends, including enhanced nutritional value in foods, strict labeling laws, and potential beneficial economic conditions in developing nations. This paper briefly reviews the origin and background of GM foods, while delving thoroughly into 3 areas: (1) GMO labeling, (2) ethical concerns, and (3) health and industry applications. This paper also examines the relationship between the various applications of GM foods and their corresponding ethical issues. Ethical concerns were evaluated in the context of the code of ethics developed by the Academy of Nutrition and Dietetics (AND) that govern the work of food and nutrition professionals. Overall, there is a need to stay vigilant about the many ethical implications of producing and consuming GM foods and GMOs.

Keywords: autonomy, beneficence, genetically modified food, justice, nonmaleficence

INTRODUCTION

Genetically modified (GM) foods are those whose genetic makeup has been altered "in a way that does not occur spontaneously" (WHO 2015). Other names for GM-classified foods include the terms "genetically engineered (GE)" and "transgenic" (Bawa and Anilakumar 2013). In contrast, organisms (for example, *bacteria*) that are GM are referred to as genetically modified organisms (GMOs). The process of genome manipulation involves the translocation of genes from multiple genetic sources, in a process widely known as recombinant deoxyribonucleic acid (rDNA) technology (Bawa and Anilakumar 2013). Three basic rDNA techniques include transformation, phage introduction, and nonbacterial transformation (Kuure-Kinsey and McCooey 2000). According to Kuure-Kinsey and McCooey (2000), transformation involves enzymatically excising a desired fragment of DNA, inserting it into a vector vehicle, and implanting the vector into a host cell (for example, *Escherichia coli*) for DNA reproduction. Moreover, Kuure-Kinsey and McCooey (2000) also explained nonbacterial transformation, where the DNA vector is inserted directly into the nucleus of a cell, instead of a bacterial host cell. A third technique also described by Kuure-Kinsey and McCooey (2000) which was phage induction, incorporates a bacteriophage (that is, *virus*) in place of a bacterial cell, with the same principles as transformation. Using these techniques, rDNA can be used to directly incorporate extraneous genetic material into the food matrix. Furthermore, insertion of rDNA into plant cells for industrial genetic modification primarily includes 2 prominent methods, which are the (1) gene gun method and (2) *Agrobacterium* method. The gene gun method involves bombarding target plant cells using gene-coated particles of gold or tungsten (Hain and Don 2003). Desired rDNA strands are coated on the entire surface of either gold or tungsten micromolecules, which are then propelled towards a plant cell using a vacuum chamber for random insertion into cells. However, the more common of the 2 methods is the use of *Agrobacterium tumefaciens*, a bacterium that parasitizes plants by inserting its DNA plasmid into cells to initiate host colonization (Hain and Don 2003). This process removes the DNA sequence that controls metabolism and replaces it with the bacterial rDNA strand (Hain and Don 2003). Using these 2 methods, scientists are able to implement rDNA technology for a myriad of industrial applications.

Further exploration of the history of GM foods shows the advancement of the science in rDNA technology as it applies to food technology. The first food industrial application was the development of the Flavr Savr™ tomato. Introduced in 1994, the Flavr Savr™ exhibited longer shelf-life due to its ability to suppress the polygalacturonase (PG) gene, which initiates the upregulation of the enzyme PG, that ripens plant products (Krieger and others 2008). This modification allowed for tomatoes with delayed ripening after harvest (Bawa and Anilakumar 2013). Unfortunately, the Flavr Savr™ tomato received little economic stimulation and consequently its production by Calgene was discontinued (Martin 2013). Other applications developments in GM foods include herbicide tolerance and insect resistance (Stone 2010), micronutrient enrichment, and pathogen resistance to bacteria, fungi and viruses (Weale 2010). While GM foods offer numerous health and agricultural benefits (Verma and others 2011), the public outlook on the consequences of genetic pollution and the ethical notions of genetic modification have given well-known infamy to GM foods (Kwieciński 2009).

With the surge of GM foods, the notion of ethical eating has surfaced. Ethical eating focuses on the "moral consequences of food choices" and food product development (Unitarian Universalist Association 2014). Issues regarding the ethics and morality of genetic modification and its industrial uses have echoed through both public and expert opinions. Most prevalent are (1) concerns surrounding the safety of GM food consumption, (2) the interference of the natural evolution of organisms, and more recently, (3) the potential benefits of GM foods increasing food insecurity (Weale 2010). Another major ethical concern surrounding GM foods is the disruption of natural biodiversity (that is, *a result of cross-pollination of genes from GM crops to natural foods*), and the potential impact on ecosystems (Murnaghan 2012). These concerns are pitted against various codes of ethics (AND 2009), which mandate that nutrition and food professionals contemplate the health and safety of the public in their practice. Thus, food scientists and nutrition professionals should exercise total autonomy, an ethical standard that must be abided by, when providing advice to clients or patients about the incorporation of GM foods into products, meal plans and diet changes. A rising issue is weighing the disadvantages of GM foods against the benefits, especially since GM foods have the potential to help developing nations in need of economic stimulation and food security. If such benefits do exist, the responsible use of GM foods should be employed, as failing to do so would be "contrary to the principles of justice and solidarity" (Weale 2010). The ethical principle of justice, in regards to GM foods, is concerned with providing fair and equal access to foods. On top of this principle, solidarity in the context of GM foods is the notion of "collaborative action" (Food and Agricultural Organization [FAO] 2015), working towards the end of food insecurity in developing nations. Ethical eating focuses on the morality and consequences of consuming GM foods, and thus encompasses many controversial and perplexing issues. GM foods are perceived as a double-edged sword in the food science community, the food industry, and by the public for the following reasons: (1) the need for transparency of the food-labeling regulations and (2) the moral dilemmas affiliated with the concerns of tampering with "Mother Nature"; both of which are weighed against (3) the advantages of food biotechnology which are discussed in this paper.

LABELING OF GMOs

Since their conception, GM crops and GMO-containing food products have been the center of the public's attention and is continuing to grow as more of these products enter the market. Approximately, 85% of corn is GM followed by 88% of cotton and 91% of soybeans all of which are now present in 75% to 80% of conventional processed foods in the United States (Center for Food Safety 2014).

With many GMO-containing food products available 5 in the marketplace, mandatory labeling of these products is debated. It is a general notion that it is the consumer's right to know (that is, *autonomy*) what contains GM ingredients, the Food and Drug Administration (FDA), however, does not have evidence concluding that GM foods differ from other foods in any meaningful or uniform way, or that foods developed by rDNA techniques present any different or greater safety concern than foods developed by traditional plant breeding (FDA 2001). Consequently, in the United States, labeling of GM products is not required. U.S. law only requires GM food labeling when "there is a substantial difference in the nutritional or safety characteristics of a new food" (Byrne and others 2014). From an ethical point of view, this policy may contradict the principle of autonomy, which in this context is the ability to provide to those who want detailed information about genetic modifications made to their food products. As evidenced by an average of 91% in favorable responses in opinion polls since 1992, an overwhelming majority of the American public supports GM food labeling (Wohlers 2013). Therefore, those seeking more information about their food may believe that food labeling of GM products would respect their autonomy, giving them the opportunity to make their own informed decisions.

International requirements and regulations of labeling GMOs

In contrast to the U.S.'s flexible labeling protocol regarding GM foods, as of 2013, 64 countries require GM labeling; with more than a third of these under a single European Union (EU) ruling, such as: the United Kingdom (UK), Italy, Croatia, Finland, and Greece (Davison 2010). GM organisms as well as processed foods, and ingredients that are produced from GM plants or GMOs are required to all be labeled. Many of these countries require mandatory labeling of nearly all GM foods and a labeling threshold of 0.9% to 1% GM content by weight (Center for Food Safety 2014). The threshold may refer to content per ingredient in each food item or GM ingredients which total 1% in the entire product (Center for Food Safety 2014).

Although there are no mandatory labeling requirements in the United States as previously mentioned, voluntary labeling has been in effect in the United State for some time. In 2001, the FDA proposed voluntary guidelines for companies that chose to label foods as to whether they do or do not contain GM ingredients if they see sufficient market opportunities for doing so (FDA 2001). The Non-GMO Project is the only third-party verification nonprofit organization that exists in America, which facilitates the labeling of non-GM/GMO food and products. Their mission is to preserve and build sources of non-GM/GMO products, as well as to educate consumers about consumption of GM/GMO products (Non-GMO Project 2015). This project directly relates to the ethical principle of autonomy, as the organization seeks to provide the opportunity for consumers to make more informed decisions about their food choices. Other than these efforts of the Non-GMO project product verification, there is no known regulation in place that facilitates or mandates the labeling of GMO foods.

Standard for labeling GM food

In April 2014, the Safe and Accurate Food Labeling Act (SAFLA) of 2015 was proposed by Congressmen Pompeo and Butterfield in order to keep American-produced food safe, nutritious, and affordable. The SAFLA of 2015 is an amendment to the 1938 Federal Food, Drug, and Cosmetic Act (FDCA), which makes the following provisions for the FDA to regulate: (1) a more uniform labeling system for the premarketing of GM food in the U.S. to avoid labeling inconsistencies in interstate commerce, (2) all new GM crop varieties and products before being commercialized, (3) special labeling for GM products if necessary to ensure their health and safety, (4) the use of the labeling terms such as "natural" on GM food products, and (5) label claims on products to be certified "GMO-Free" through a USDA accredited program. This new act can facilitate a consistent legal framework that companies could use to guide them in regards to labeling thus making the integrity of the food supply more transparent.

ETHICAL IMPLICATIONS OF GM FOODS AND GMOs

Generally, ethics is defined as the well-founded standards of what is right and wrong that appeal to a person's beliefs and values. In the food industry, ethics is defined as "a set of standards that govern or influence the conduct of behavior of a food/nutrition professional or organization and can be influenced by food customs and societal customs." (Academy of Nutrition and Dietetics [AND] 2009). These standards have further influenced the development of the code of ethics established by AND and the Institute of Food Technologists (IFT) which are to be reinforced by all registered dietitians (RDs), diet technicians, registered (DTRs) as well as food scientists. Namely, the 4 ethical principles to be upheld by food professionals as mandated by the AND are the following: (1) autonomy, (2) justice, (3) nonmaleficence, and (4) beneficence (AND 2009). Ethics apply to the food industry, especially regarding food labeling, as it is the duty of the food industry to exercise total "autonomy"; the consumer has a right to know what they are purchasing to make informed decisions. According to AND (2009), "autonomy ensures that a patient or client, or professional has the capacity to engage in individual decision-making specific to personal health or practice." The FDA and the U.S. Department of Agriculture (USDA) have legal written

standards for labeling the composition and ingredients of foods, but they do not currently have any specific requirements to specify if a product contains a GM byproduct. Without mandatory labeling requirements, food companies are able to continue selling GM foods those consumers cannot identify, which seemingly goes against the ethical principle of autonomy. Consequently, several states have had ballot initiatives to mandate the labeling of foods that contain GM products, although most have been unsuccessful. Some states with a degree of success include Connecticut and Maine, where they have made some progress in labeling laws that will go into effect if a certain number of states agree to pass similar laws. Presently, Vermont has been the only state successful to pass a mandatory GM-labeling law (Costanigro and others 2014).

Ethical implications of GM foods and food security

Labeling foods that are GM or GMO becomes an issue of ethics also due to the fact the health effects of consuming GM foods remain a grey area. However, when GM food is examined from the perspective of meeting the food-security needs of an ever-growing population, it seems that the benefits may outweigh the possible health side effects. This is grounded by the ethical principle of beneficence, which is defined by AND (2009) as "taking positive steps to benefit others, which includes balancing benefit, risks and costs when determining a policy." Many countries import the majority of their food supply due to weather, climate and pests which may hinder the availability or production of food crops respectively. Therefore, recognizing the need to incorporate GM foods or GMOs in the food supply chain has relieved them from paying such high prices for foods as well as concerns of food security (Dibden and others 2011). Such initiatives could appeal to the ethical principle of justice, where a fair and equitable food supply is encouraged (AND 2009).

ADVANTAGES OF GM FOODS IN PRODUCTION

The advantages of GM foods are very widespread, encompassing a variety of aspects of (1) increased food production and (2) health benefits, and are becoming increasingly more prevalent. Ethically, the advantages of GM foods relate to the principles of beneficence and justice in the hope that GMO technology will be able to help others in improving food security and minimizing health disparities as the possibilities of creating food with higher nutritional content and overall quality, as seen with the golden rice discussed later in this paper (Verma and others 2011). GM crops were originally introduced into commercial production over 17 y ago and have been adopted faster than any other agricultural advancements (Alberts 2013). With the world's population increasing at an alarming rate, especially in developing countries, there is a major threat posed to food security (Amofah 2014). Therefore, the magnitude of the introduction of GM crops may have a huge positive impact as it pertains to the ethical guiding principle of justice where a fair, equitable food supply is maintained. Climate change is also another environmental factor threatening food security, which may lead to malnutrition and other health problems due to the lack of food (Amofah 2014). Both the increasing population and changing climate poses the ethical dilemma of maintaining stewardship and utilizing available natural resources in a conscientious manner to ensure that they are available for future generations. Food biotechnology can be used to genetically modify agricultural produce to become pest-and weather-resistant, produce higher yields, improve quality and nutrition (Verma and others 2011).

Decreasing the usage of pesticides

Pests, diseases, and weather are all natural phenomena that commonly affect farmers when growing produce, causing them to rely on the use of chemical pesticides. However, consumers are less inclined to eat food that has been treated with pesticides due to their potential health hazards. Also, the runoff of agricultural waste from excessive pesticide and fertilizer usage can also contaminate the water supply, causing additional harm to the environment (Verma and others 2011). To counteract the aforementioned concerns of using pesticides and herbicides, scientists

have been able to use the *Bacillus thuringiensis* (B.t), a naturally occurring soil bacterium that produces crystal proteins or delta endotoxins, that are lethal to insect larva (Verma and others 2011). These toxic crystals react with the cells in the lining of the gut and paralyze the digestive system of the insect, causing them to stop feeding within hours. As a consequence, the infected insects often die from starvation in a few days (Cranshaw 2014). The B.t gene is incorporated in the genome of corn and other crops such as cotton and potatoes enabling them to produce the toxin against the insects. This eliminates the need for excessive pesticide use. B.t. crops are currently cultivated in 23 countries and were originally commercialized in the U.S. in 1996 (Verma and others 2011).

The production of GM B.t. crops poses ethical dilemmas of both nonmaleficence and beneficence. In efforts to do no harm (that is, nonmaleficence) to the environment and the consumers, the benefits must outweigh the potential risks (that is, beneficence) of these new chemicals. The safety of B.t. has been well documented, as (1) community exposure within the last 6 decades has not resulted in any adverse effects, (2) the lack of homology to any allergenic protein makes B.t. toxins nonallergenic, and (3) the human digestive system lack receptors that bind to the toxins, resulting in their instant degradation and causing no toxicological effects (Verma and others 2011).

Increasing weather-tolerant crops

Weather-tolerant and the development of new crops that can withstand inhospitable environments have been another advantage developed through the use of GM technology. The needs for higher yields have become drastically more prevalent as the acreage available for agriculture is diminishing (Barnes 2008). Farmers are not only dealing with reduced amounts of land available for agriculture due to the expanding population's needs for housing, but also because of reduced amounts of land suitable for cultivation under their current conditions as a result of land being exhausted of nutrients or unsuitable terrain (Goldbas 2014). With the use of biotechnology, GM plants are being propagated for increased yields that can grow in useless geographical areas plagued with droughts (Goldbas 2014). Farmers will have crops that can survive through longer periods of drought, cold, or high salt content in soil and groundwater (Verma and others 2011). A clear example of increasing weather tolerance can be seen with an antifreeze gene from cold-water fish that has been introduced into plants like tobacco, potatoes and initially tomatoes (Verma and others 2011). These proteins were discovered by Dr. Arthur Devries from fish that he collected at McMurdo Station in the early 1960s and have several commercial applications (NSF 2015). These antifreeze compounds are also found to be about 300 times more effective in preventing freezing than conventional chemical antifreezes at the same concentration (NSF 2015). Currently, investigators funded by the NSF have successfully introduced 2 of the 4 fish antifreeze genes into yeast and bacteria through recombinant DNA technology (NSF 2015). Researchers compared the crop yields obtained from crops that expressed the antifreeze gene from the flounder fish as compared to the conventional tomatoes and found that they were able to survive in lower temperatures and consequently resulted in higher crop yields. Gene technology enables the increase of production in plants, as well as their increased resistance to pests, viruses, and frost (Verma and others 2011). The introduction of pest-resistant, herbicide-tolerant, cold-, and drought-tolerant crops create potential for increased crop yield each growing season and helps to increase the overall food supply and food security (Amofah 2014) which exemplifies the ethical principles of justice and nonmaleficence.

Increasing nutritional content and quality

The nutritional content and quality of food crops such as rice and cassava are one of the largest areas of emerging interest for GM foods. Malnutrition is a continuing problem in developing countries, where people rely on a single crop such as rice for the main staple of their diet (Verma and others 2011). Rice is a major staple for almost half of humanity, and unfortunately white rice grains are a poor source of vitamin A (Alberts 2013). Research scientists, Ingo

Potrykus and Peter Beyer, have developed a rice variety that has β-carotene in its grains, a precursor to vitamin A. It took them 25 y in collaboration with the International Rice Research Institute (IRRI) to develop and test varieties that have sufficient amounts of β-carotene to eliminate the morbidity and mortality of vitamin A deficiency (Alberts 2013). This strain of rice, called "Golden Rice," was hypothesized to potentially prevent blindness due to vitamin A deficiency (Verma and others 2011). Vitamin A deficiency is a preventable disease and is as a result of a poor diet and poverty, responsible for 1.9 to 2.8 million deaths annually, with most occurring in women and children under 5-y-old (Albert 2013). Not only does vitamin A deficiency cause blindness, but also a compromised immune system, exacerbating many kinds of illnesses (Verma and others 2011). Research is also being conducted to develop Golden Rice that also has an increased iron content (Verma and others 2011). The ethical standard that this relates to is beneficence, as researchers are using GM technology in the hopes of helping others who are lacking nutritional sufficiency. Also nonmaleficence applies here as well, as researchers must consider whether or not their product will cause harm to the consumers and if an increased vitamin A and iron content in foods may have a negative side effect. Moreover, it may be worth noting that Golden Rice has been stabilized, safety-proven and is ready-to-use, but misplaced fear and misinformation may have prevented its authorized release to combat vitamin A deficiency.

The cassava plant is an example of another crop that has been altered to improve nutritional content in an effort to prevent diseases and morbidity in developing countries. The cassava is a starchy root eaten by peoples in tropical Africa, with approximately 40% of the food calories in the diet coming from it (Goldbas 2014). The GM variety boasts increased minerals, vitamin A, and protein content, which can prevent childhood blindness, iron deficiency anemia, and infections due to damaged immune systems, while also being pest-resistant due to GM technology (Goldbas 2014). This modified crop have increased nutritional content, but also increased pest resistance making it a more reliable and stable food supply for the people of tropical Africa. With the use of agricultural biotechnology, the nutritional properties of crops such as golden rice and cassava can be improved to enhance health by the fortification of desired vitamins and minerals and potentially prevent countless deaths.

CONCLUSION

This paper reviewed GM foods as it relates to ethical eating in the recent literature. Throughout its history, GM foods have been widely debated as (1) a result of their industrial applications and (2) potential consequences of their use. While their advantages are conceivably numerous (that is, *ranging from herbicide, pest, and weather tolerance to increased nutritional value to edible vaccines*), GM foods are criticized because of their application. Such ethical concerns involve adverse effects on human health, regulation of GM foods, cross-pollination, and a decrease in overall biodiversity. These concerns can affect whether one feels morally tarnished when consuming GM products. Particularly, the issue of GM food labeling has garnered great debate in the U.S. which does not provide for strict regulation on labeling of GM products and ingredients (that is, *contrary to 64 other world nations*). Also of recent interest is the potential application of GM foods in developing countries, where their production may spur economic activity and alleviate food insecurity. Further studies should perform more case analyses of the application of GM foods in developing countries and their ethical implications, as well as examine the public opinion of GM foods in U.S. culture compared to other nations.

REFERENCES

Academy of Nutrition and Dietetics (AND). 2009. American Dietetics Association/Commission on Dietetic Registration Code of Ethics for the Profession of Dietetics and Process for Consideration of Ethics Issues. J Acad Nutr Diet 109:1461–7.

Alberts B. 2013. Standing up for GMOs. Sci Mag 341:1320.

Amofah G. 2014. Recommendations from a meeting on health implications of genetically modified organisms. Ghana Public Health Assoc 48(2):117–9.

Barnes B. 2008. To GMO, or Not to GMO? Cotton Intl Mag 6(6):14–5.

Bawa A, Anilakumar K. 2013. Genetically modified foods: safety, risks, and public concerns–a review. J Food Sci Technol 50(6):1035–46.

Byrne P, Pendell D, Graff G. 2014. Labeling of genetically engineered foods. Available from http://www.ext.colostate.edu/pubs/foodnut/09371.pdf. Accessed 2015 April 9.

Center for Food Safety. 2014. Genetically engineered food labeling laws. Available from http://www.centerforfoodsafety.org/ge-map/. Accessed 2015 April 28.

Costanigro M, Lusk JL. 2014. The signaling effect of mandatory labels on genetically engineered food. J Food Policy 49:259–67.

Cranshaw WS. 2014. *Bacillus thuringiensis*. Available from http://www.ext.colostate.edu/pubs/insect/05556.html. Accessed 2015 April 28.

Davison J. 2010. GM plants: science, politics and EC regulations. Sci Direct 178(2):94–8.

Dibden J, Gibbs D, Cocklin C. 2011. Framing GM crops as a food security solution. J Rural Studies 29:59–70.

Food and Agricultural Organization. 2015. The role of ethics. Available from http://www.fao.org/docrep/008/y6634e/y6634e03.htm#fnB1. Accessed 2015 April 26.

Food and Drug Administration (FDA). 2001. DRAFT guidance for industry: voluntary labeling indicating whether foods have or have not been developed using bioengineering; draft guidance. Available from http://www.fda.gov/Food/GuidanceRegulation/GuidanceDocuments RegulatoryInformation/LabelingNutrition/ucm059098.htm. Accessed 2015 April 9.

Food and Drug Administration (FDA): FSIS. 2014. Meat and poultry labeling terms. Available from: http://www.fsis.usda.gov/wps/portal/fsis/topics/food-safety-education/get-answers/food-safety-fact-sheets/food-labeling/meat-and-poultry-labeling-terms/meat-and-poultrylabeling-terms. Accessed 2015 April 30.

Food and Drug Administration (FDA). 2015. FDA's role in regulating safety of GE foods. Available from: http://www.fda.gov/forconsumers/consumerupdates/ucm352067.htm. Accessed 2015 April 30.

Goldbas A. 2014. GMOS: what are they?. Intl J Childbirth Educ 29(3):20.

Hain P, Don L. 2003. Transformation 2 – Transformation Methods. Available from http://passel.unl.edu/pages/printinformationmodule.php?idinformationmodule=958077244. Accessed 2015 July 28.

International Dairy Foods Association (IDFA) 2014. IDFA Commends Reps. Pompeo and Butterfield for Bill to Establish Federal Standard for Voluntary GMO Labeling. Available from http://www.idfa.org/news-views/news-releases/article/2014/04/09/idfa-commends-reps.pompeo-and-butterfield-for-bill-to-establish-federal-standard-for-voluntary-gmo-labeling. Accessed 2015 April 9.

Krieger EK, Edwards A, Gilbertson LA, Roberts JK, Hiatt W, Sanders RA. 2008. The Flavr Savr tomato, an early example of RNAi technology. Hort Science 43(3):962.

Kuure-Kinsey M, McCooey B. 2000. The Basics of Recombinant DNA. Available from http://www.rpi.edu/dept/chem-eng/Biotech-Environ/Projects00/rdna/rdna.html. Accessed 2015 April 7.

Kwieciński J. 2009. Genetically modified abominations? EMBO Reports 10(11):1187–90.

Maghari BM, Ardekani AM. 2011. Genetically modified foods and social concerns. J Med Biotechnol 3(3):109–17.

Martin, C. 2013. The psychology of GMO. Curr Biol 23(9):R356–9.

Murnaghan I. 2012. Ethical Concerns and GM Foods. Available from http://www.geneticallymodifiedfoods.co.uk/ethical-concerns-gm-foods.html. Accessed 2015 April 7.

National Science Foundation. 2015. Fish Antifreeze Proteins. Available at http://www.nsf.gov/pubs/1996/nstc96rp/sb3.htm. Accessed 2015 April 28.

Păcurar DI, Thordal-Christensen H, Păcurar ML, Pamfil D, Botez C, Bellini C. 2011. *Agrobacterium tumefaciens*: from crown gall tumors to genetic transformation. Physiol Mol Plant Pathol 76(2):76–81.

Santa Clara University. 2010. What is ethics. Available from http://www.scu.edu/ethics/practicing/decision/whatisethics.html. Accessed 2015 April 30.

Stone GD. 2010. The anthropology of genetically modified crops. Ann Rev Anthropol 39: 381–400.

Unitarian Universalist Association (UUA). 2014. Ethical eating: food and environmental justice. Available from http://www.uua.org/environment/eating/. Accessed 2015 April 7.

United States Center for Food Safety. 2015. International labeling laws. Available from http://www.centerforfoodsafety.org/issues/976/ge-food-labeling/international-labelinglaws#. Accessed 2015 April 9.

University of Minnesota: School of Public Health: Environmental Health Sciences. 2003. GMO: harmful effects. Available from http://enhs.umn.edu/current/5103/gm/harmful.html. Accessed 2015 April 30.

Verma C, Nanda S, Singh RK, Singh RB, Mishra, S. 2011. A review on impacts of genetically modified food on human health. Open Neutraceut J 4:3–11.

Weale A. 2010. Ethical arguments relevant to the use of GM crops. New Biotechnol 27(5):582–7.

Wohlers A. (2013). Labeling of genetically modified food. Polit Life Sci 32(1):73–84.

World Health Organization. 2015. Food, genetically modified. Available from http://www.who.int/topics/food_genetically_modified/en/. Accessed 2015 April 7.

Reading Questions

1. In their study's Introduction, the authors identify numerous ethical concerns related to the development and use of GM foods. What are three of these concerns?

2. What are the four ethical principles under which food professionals like dietitians must operate?

3. According to the authors, what ethical principles might be involved in the development of GM products for food-insecure nations?

Rhetoric Questions

4. How would you describe the authors' strategy for reporting their conclusions and results throughout the study? As part of your response, offer a rationale for the authors' use of heading and subheadings.

5. Look closely at the study's Conclusion. How would you describe the conclusions they reach and report in this section of their study?

Response Question

6. Do any of the ethical concerns identified by the authors as part of their study intersect with your own concerns about GM foods? If so, which ones, and why?

Consumers' Willingness to Pay for Genetically Modified Foods with Product-Enhancing Nutritional Attributes

GREGORY COLSON AND WALLACE E. HUFFMAN

Gregory Colson is an associate professor of agricultural and applied economics at the University of Georgia. Before his death in 2020, Wallace E. Huffman was the C. F. Curtis Distinguished Professor of Agriculture and Life Sciences and a professor of economics and agricultural economics at Iowa State University. In their study below, which was published in 2011 in the *American Journal of Agricultural Economics*, the researchers examine customers' willingness to pay a premium for genetically modified food products and explore the implications of their findings for businesses.

The commercial successes of genetic modification (GM) during the past decade in the United States and Canada have been in feed, fiber, and oil crops but not primarily in food crops, with the exception of refined vegetable oils.[1] Early GM traits (e.g., herbicide tolerance, insect resistance) were obtained by transferring genes across species, largely from soil bacteria. This transgenic nature of genetically modified organisms (GMOs) has been one dimension of consumer resistance to GM—raising biodiversity, environmental, ethical, and safety concerns—and has been a factor in the larger controversy surrounding GM (for reviews of the GM debate, see Herdt 2006, Van den Bergh and Holley 2002). The global debate over GM encompasses a diverse set of interested parties who have disseminated information into the public domain, spanning the spectrum from Greenpeace calling GMOs "Frankenfoods" to the biotechnology industry suggesting that GMOs are "foods to feed the world" (see e.g., Lewis 1992, Gates 2000). This conflicted information environment has a direct impact on consumers' perspectives and valuations for GM foods (Rousu et al. 2007) and has played a role in the implementation of diverging adoption, labeling, and trade policies internationally.

While to date commercially available GM crops have been transgenic in nature, recently bioengineering breakthroughs have occurred using *intragenics*, where genes are moved long distances within species and without antibiotic markers. For example, the potato is the fourth leading source of calories worldwide (UN Food and Agriculture Organization 2009) and has a diverse, but very difficult to manipulate, genome. However, it can be manipulated using intragenic methods to move traits from primitive to commercial varieties. That is, genomic and metabolic pathway discoveries can be rapidly introduced into established commercial varieties to fast-track the breeding processes for new potato varieties. An additional advantage of these methods is that they do not use antibiotic markers to identify the location of inserted genes.[2] These are all proffered as reasons for a low regulatory hurdle for intragenic foods.

A second neoteric development tied to intragenic breakthroughs is a renewed interest by some bioengineering companies to develop GM food crops with "product-enhancing consumer attributes," or traits that directly benefit consumers. With the exception of the shortlived marketing attempts in the mid-90s of the "Flavr-Savr tomato" and a "high solids tomato" produced by Zeneca, commercially successful GM

---

[1] When raw plant oils from crops such as soybean, corn, cotton, and canola are refined, the resulting product is a pure lipid or fat, and hence the chemical content is exactly the same in oils made from GM and non-GM crops.

[2] For a more technical overview of intragenic versus transgenic engineering, see Rommens et al. (2004).

crops in the United States have possessed input traits (traits that reduce either the cost of production or the variance in the cost of production to farmers) and hence have benefited consumers only to the extent that they have lowered food prices.[3] With new intragenic GM techniques, it is feasible to dramatically enhance product attributes such as antioxidant and vitamin content in horticultural crops, thus developing new foods with attributes of direct value to consumers.

New research has the potential to differentiate consumers' willingness to pay (WTP) for food products containing enhanced nutrients due to intragenic and transgenic GM methods. The objective of this article is to assess consumers' WTP for new intragenic fresh vegetables with product-enhanced antioxidant and vitamin C levels. Individuals from a random set of telephone numbers in two metropolitan areas were contacted by an independent survey group in 2007 to obtain their agreement to participate, and participants came to a central location—a laboratory or classroom. Their WTP was obtained in a unique series of multiple-round random nth-price experimental auctions with randomized label and information treatments.

The article is organized as follows. In the following section, an overview of the conducted experimental auction is provided. The next section presents a summary of the collected data and analysis. In the final section, some conclusions are presented.

DATA COLLECTION

Data on consumer attitudes toward GM food labels with and without enhanced nutritional attribute statements were obtained from a series of laboratory experiments conducted in the spring of 2007. Participants for the study were solicited from the general public by an independent marketing organization in two different cities (Des Moines, Iowa, and

Harrisburg, Pennsylvania) in order to obtain a representative sample. Each experimental session consisted of four primary steps. After completing a series of consent forms and receiving financial compensation in the amount of $45, the ninety-eight participants were trained in the experimental auction method to be utilized: the random nth-price auction (Shogren et al. 2001). Training consisted of instructions, examples, a two-round practice auction, and a postpractice quiz on the nth-price auction mechanism.

After gaining familiarity with the nth-price auction, participants were provided with one of four randomly assigned information treatments: (*a*) an agribusiness (pro-biotech) perspective on GM consisting primarily of positive statements about it, (*b*) an environmental (anti-biotech) perspective on GM consisting primarily of negative statements about it, (*c*) both the pro- and anti-biotech perspectives, and (*d*) the pro- and anti-biotech perspectives with verifiable factual information on GM from independent sources. Each perspective was limited to a single standard page size and organized in a common fashion. A key reference point in the experiments was a fifth information "treatment" that was empty or did not contain any information.

After participants took a few minutes to digest the information treatment assigned to them, the auction began. In each of the four rounds of bidding, three products were offered for sale: one pound of broccoli, one pound of beefsteak tomatoes, and five pounds of russet potatoes—each in plain packaging. Products in each round bore a label indicating the type of commodity and the product weight. We refer to a label treatment consisting of only these statements as a "plain label." Two additional labeling statements were injected into two of the rounds: "intragenic GM" and "transgenic GM," both with the additional statement: "Enhanced levels of antioxidants and vitamin C."[4] The ordering of food labels across sessions was randomized.

---

[3]This indirect value of GM to consumers has been estimated to be quite sizable by Falck-Zepeda, Traxler, and Nelson (2000) and Moschini, Lapan, and Sobolevsky (2000).

[4]A fourth labeling treatment considered a generic statement of GM and is not used in this study.

After completion of all bidding rounds, the binding round was drawn, bids were posted and ranked on a whiteboard in the front of the lab (no bids were posted prior to this point), the random n was drawn to determine the clearing price, and winners were identified. All participants were then asked to complete a short exit questionnaire. Nonwinners were told that they were free to leave, and winners were told to go to an adjacent room to complete their purchases, exchanging money for goods. Given the incomplete regulatory status of the intragenic foods, we were unable to obtain the product-enhanced GM fresh vegetables to deliver to winners. As an alternative, winners were given plain labeled food products, similar to procedures followed by others in similar circumstances, such as Alfnes and Rickertsen (2003), Tonsor et al. (2005), and Corrigan et al. (2009). Receptiveness to the experiments was positive, and no complaint from participants was received.

DATA SUMMARY AND ANALYSIS

Table 1 presents the percent difference in bid prices across information treatments, averaged over individuals and commodities (broccoli, tomato, and potato), and between intragenic and transgenic labels with enhanced nutritional attributes and a plain label conventional alternative. Several key

Table 1
Average Differences in Bid Prices

Information Treatment	Intragenic[EN] vs. Plain Label (%)	Transgenic[EN] vs. Plain Label (%)
All treatments	25	5
No information	31	26
Pro-biotech only	63	19
Anti-biotech only	−12	−18
Pro- and anti-biotech	19	3
Pro- and anti-biotech and verifiable	18	−8

Note: [EN] denotes a product label with an enhanced nutrition statement.

results emerge from the bid price data. Averaged over all information treatments, consumers are willing to pay a premium for both intragenic (25%) and transgenic (5%) labels with enhanced vitamin C and antioxidant content relative to a conventional plain label alternative. This indicates that despite consumers' well-documented perceptions of GM foods as being weakly inferior to non-GM foods (see Lusk et al. 2005 for a review and meta-analysis), the positive attribute of enhanced nutrition mitigates this negative valuation, resulting in a willingness to pay a premium for products with a GM label. This is the first evidence that U.S. consumers are willing to pay a premium for an intragenic GM labeled food product relative to a conventional alternative. Moreover, this result opens the door to the possibility that the food industry in the United States may have an incentive to voluntarily label an intragenic GM food product as intragenic GM.

While the bid price data in table 1 shows that GM foods with enhanced nutrition have the potential to capture a position in the food market, we can shed more light on bidding behavior. First, consistent with the findings of Lusk et al. (2004) and Rousu et al. (2007), information injected into the experiments affects bidding behavior. Second, consider the mean difference in bid prices for a product with an intragenic enhanced-nutrition GM label compared with the bid prices for a similar product with a plain food label. Participants who did not receive any GM information were willing to pay a premium of 31%. The premium jumped to 63% when participants received pro-biotech information. When they received anti-biotech information, the GM label was discounted 12%. When participants received pro and anti-biotech information or all three types of information, the premium was about 19%. Second, the bid prices for a product with a transgenic enhanced-nutrients GM label relative to those for a similar product with a plain food label were all somewhat lower than for the intragenic food label—premiums were lower and discounts larger.

To reveal additional information about participants' bidding behavior, we summarize outcomes

Table 2

Relative Preferences for Intragenic with Enhanced Nutrition Label vs. Plain Label

Information Treatment	Prefer Intragenic^{EN} (%)	Indifferent (%)	Prefer Plain Label (%)
All treatments	48	32	20
No information	52	38	10
Pro-biotech only	74	15	11
Anti-biotech only	22	41	37
Pro- and anti-biotech	42	42	17
Pro- and anti-biotech and verifiable	50	23	27

Note: ^{EN} denotes a product label with an enhanced nutrition statement.

on bid price rankings in tables 2 and 3. Table 2 displays the percentage of individuals who, based upon their bid prices, preferred the intragenic GM label with enhanced nutrition over the conventional plain labeled product (i.e., those for which $Bid^{Intra} > Bid^{Plain}$), those who preferred the plain labeled product ($Bid^{Intra} < Bid^{Plain}$), and those who were indifferent between the two ($Bid^{Intra} = Bid^{Plain}$). Table 3 presents similar results for the transgenic GM label with enhanced nutrition. Across all information treatments (the first line of table 2), approximately half (48%) of the sample preferred intragenic GM labeled commodities to plain label alternatives, 20% preferred the plain label alternative, and 32% were indifferent. This indicates that across the information treatments, approximately 80% of

the sample viewed the intragenic GM label with enhanced nutrition as weakly superior to a conventional label. When participants received the pro- and anti-biotech perspectives and third party information, half of the sample preferred the intragenic GM label, with the remaining half of the sample being fairly evenly divided between preferring the plain label (27%) and being indifferent between the two (23%). This contrasts significantly with the findings for relative preferences between the transgenic GM label with enhanced nutrition and the plain label (table 3), where only about a quarter (29%) preferred the transgenic GM label and 50% preferred the plain label.

Finally, we provide some information about how participants' attributes affected their preferences for

Table 3

Relative Preferences for Transgenic with Enhanced Nutrition Label vs. Plain Label

Information Treatment	Prefer Transgenic^{EN} (%)	Indifferent (%)	Prefer Plain Label (%)
All treatments	37	28	35
No information	43	33	23
Pro-biotech only	61	13	26
Anti-biotech only	24	35	41
Pro- and anti-biotech	28	38	33
Pro- and anti-biotech and verifiable	29	21	50

Note: ^{EN} denotes a product label with an enhanced nutrition statement.

Table 4

Marginal Effects and Predicted Probabilities for Ordered Probit Models of Consumer
Preference Relationships

Model	Intragenic[EN] vs. Plain Label			Transgenic[EN] vs. Plain Label		
Preferred Product	**Intra**	**Indifferent**	**Plain**	**Trans**	**Indifferent**	**Plain**
Pro-biotech**,*	0.263	−0.125	−0.014	0.018	−0.023	−0.159
Anti-biotech**,−	−0.269	0.052	0.022	−0.119	−0.008	0.126
Pro- and anti-biotech	−0.046	0.016	0.030	−0.026	0.000	0.026
Pro- and anti-biotech and verifiable	−0.050	0.017	0.033	−0.126	−0.007	0.133
Age**,−	−0.007	0.002	0.004	−0.002	0.000	0.002
Education	−0.008	0.003	0.005	0.013	−0.001	−0.011
Exercise**,**	0.231	−0.084	−0.015	0.157	−0.031	−0.153
Gender	0.827	−0.029	−0.054	0.098	0.001	−0.098
Healthiness of diet	0.260	−0.010	−0.017	0.011	−0.002	−0.011
Household size*,−	−0.050	0.018	0.032	−0.022	0.004	0.022
Income*,−	0.001	−0.000	−0.001	−0.002	0.000	0.002
Positive GM opinion −,*	−0.030	0.010	0.019	0.140	−0.152	−0.125
Read food labels*,*	−0.138	0.054	0.084	−0.099	0.005	0.095
Predicted probability	0.479	0.351	0.170	0.357	0.310	0.338
Log-likelihood	−275.89			−302.00		
Likelihood ratio statistic	62.24			38.32		
p-Value	0.00			0.00		

Note: * and ** denote variable significance at 5% and 1%, respectively. Asterisks before the comma refer to the intragenic
equation; asterisks after the comma refer to the transgenic equation.

No information treatment dummy variable is excluded.

GM versus a plain labeled product. Two ordered
probit models are estimated (one for intragenic GM
and one for transgenic GM). For each model, the
dependent variable was coded as counts denoting
which label was preferred or whether the individual was indifferent. For brevity, in lieu of presenting
coefficient estimates which are difficult to interpret
(Greene 2003), table 4 reports the marginal effects,
predicted probabilities, and significance levels from
the two models of consumers' preference relationships.[5] Individuals who indicated that they frequently
read food labels were less likely to prefer either the
intragenic (13.8%) or transgenic (9.9%) labels and
more likely to be indifferent or prefer the plain labeled
products. Conversely, individuals who engaged in regular physical exercise were more likely to prefer the
intragenic and transgenic labels (23.1% and 15.7%,
respectively) and less likely to be indifferent or prefer
the plain labeled product. Individuals who entered
the experiments with a positive opinion of GM were
less likely to prefer intragenic GM and more likely
to be indifferent or prefer the plain labeled product,
but were more likely to prefer transgenic GM and less
likely to be indifferent or to prefer the plain labeled
product.

[5] Coefficient and standard error estimates are available
from the authors.

CONCLUDING REMARKS

While the controversy over benefits, costs, and hazards of genetically modified foods continues to unfold in the arenas of global politics and public information campaigns, the advancements in intragenic bioengineering present a new piece to the puzzle. Overall, we find in our experiments that consumers do value enhanced nutrition (antioxidants and vitamin C) obtained through GM. But consumers are more accepting of foods with enhanced nutrition obtained through intragenics compared with transgenics. Most notably, we find that consumers are willing to pay more for intragenic labels with enhanced nutrition compared with conventional plain labels. This opens the door for voluntary private sector labeling of GM foods with enhanced nutrition.

These results pose a dilemma for individuals and groups that have historically taken a position of staunch opposition to GM. While intragenics may present a more palatable form of bioengineering compared with transgenics, our laboratory experiments indicate that there is the potential for an even greater crowding out of non-GM foods. Although our findings present a somewhat positive picture for the potential of intragenics to obtain a foothold in the food market, they also suggest that information injected into the public domain will continue to play an important role in determining consumer acceptance. Our findings reveal that the information available to consumers when making purchase decisions has a significant effect on relative valuations for GM and non-GM labels. While pro-biotechnology information disseminated by agribusiness in isolation has significant positive effects on consumer valuations for GM labels, this effect is reduced when anti-biotechnology information is simultaneously injected into the market.

REFERENCES

Alfnes, F., and K. Rickertsen. 2003. European Consumers' Willingness to Pay for U.S. Beef in Experimental Auction Markets. *American Journal of Agricultural Economics* 85: 396–405.

Corrigan, J. R., D. P. T. Depositario, R. M. Nayga Jr., X. Wu, and T. P. Laude. 2009. Comparing Open-Ended Choice Experiments and Experimental Auctions: An Application to Golden Rice. *American Journal of Agricultural Economics* 91:837–853.

Falck-Zepeda, J. B., G. Traxler, and R. G. Nelson. 2000. Surplus Distribution from the Introduction of a Biotechnology Innovation. *American Journal of Agricultural Economics* 82: 360–369.

Gates, B. 2000. Will Frankenfood Feed the World? *Time* (June 19).

Greene, W. H. 2003. *Econometric Analysis,* 5th ed. Upper Saddle River, NJ: Prentice Hall.

Herdt, R. W. 2006. Biotechnology in Agriculture. *Annual Review of Environment and Resources* 34: 265–295.

Lewis, P. 1992. Mutant Foods Create Risks We Can't Yet Guess; Since Mary Shelley [Letter to the editor]. *New York Times* (June 16).

Lusk, J. L., L. O. House, C. Valli, S. R. Jaeger, M. Moore, B. Morrow, and W. B. Traill. 2004. Effect of Information About Benefits of Biotechnology on Consumer Acceptance of Genetically Modified Food: Evidence from Experimental Auctions in the United States, England, and France. *European Review of Agricultural Economics* 31: 179–204.

Lusk, J. L., M. Jamal, L. Kurlander, M. Roucan, and L. Taulman. 2005. A Meta-analysis of Genetically Modified Food Valuation Studies. *Journal of Agricultural and Resource Economics* 30: 28–44.

Moschini, G., H. Lapan, and A. Sobolevsky. 2000. Roundup Ready Soybeans and Welfare Effects in the Soybean Complex. *Agribusiness* 16: 33–55.

Rommens, C., J. Humara, J. Ye, H. Yan, C. Richael, L. Zhang, R. Perry, and K. Swords. 2004. Crop Improvement Through Modification of the Plant's Own Genome. *Plant Physiology* 135: 421–431.

Rousu, M., W. Huffman, J. Shogren, and A. Tegene. 2007. Effects and Value of Verifiable Information in a Controversial Market: Evidence from Lab Auctions of Genetically Modified Food. *Economic Inquiry* 45: 409–432.

Shogren, J., M. Margolis, C. Koo, and J. List. 2001. A Random nth-Price Auction. *Journal of Economic Behavior and Organization* 46: 409–421.

Tonsor, G. T., T. C. Schroeder, J. A. Fox, and A. Biere. 2005. European Preferences for Beef Steak Attributes. *Journal of Agricultural and Resource Economics* 30: 367–380.

UN Food and Agriculture Organization. 2009. *International Year of the Potato, 2008: New Light on a Hidden Treasure.* Rome: Author.

Van den Bergh, J., and J. M. Holley. 2002. An Environmental-Economic Assessment of Genetic Modification of Agricultural Crops. *Futures* 34: 807–822.

Reading Questions

1. What do the authors identify as the objective of their study?

2. In your own words, briefly describe the authors' data-collection method, or the nth-price auction.

3. Based on the study's findings, did customers demonstrate a preference for GM foods with enhanced nutrition obtained through transgenic or intragenic modification? According to the researchers, what are the implications of this particular finding?

Rhetoric Questions

4. Look closely at the four paragraphs that make up the Data Collection section of the study and write a brief description of the authors' language. Do they rely primarily on first- or third-person point of view? Do they rely primarily on active or passive voice? Why are their choices appropriate in light of their aims and intended audience?

5. Describe the relationship between the various tables presented as part of the study's report and the organization of the Data Summary and Analysis section of the report.

Response Questions

6. Do you consider the GM content of a product when you are making a purchase? If so, how does the GM content affect your decision? If not, why?

7. Based on the study's findings, describe a product label for a GM food product that might convince a potential customer to purchase the GM product over a similar but cheaper non-GM product.

ACADEMIC CASE STUDY • GENETICALLY MODIFIED FOOD   NATURAL SCIENCES

This plain, clear, and nonrhetorical title reflects language conventions of the sciences.

Maternal and Fetal Exposure to Pesticides Associated to Genetically Modified Foods in Eastern Townships of Quebec, Canada

AZIZ ARIS AND SAMUEL LEBLANC

Research in the natural sciences is typically conducted and reported on by more than one person, reflecting the collaborative nature of scientific work.

Aziz Aris is an investigator for the Mother and Child Axis at the Clinical Research Center and associate professor of obstetrics and gynecology at the University of Sherbrooke Hospital in Quebec, Canada. With Samuel Leblanc, co-author of the study below, the researchers report on their investigation into the presence of pesticides associated with genetically modified foods in women (pregnant and non-pregnant) in eastern Canada. As the authors indicate, one of the goals of their research is to help "develop procedures to avoid environmentally induced disease in susceptible populations such as pregnant women and their fetuses." This article first appeared in the journal *Reproductive Toxicology* in 2011.

ABSTRACT

Pesticides associated to genetically modified foods (PAGMF) are engineered to tolerate herbicides such as glyphosate (GLYP) and gluphosinate (GLUF) or insecticides such as the bacterial toxin bacillus thuringiensis (Bt). The aim of this study was to evaluate the correlation between maternal and fetal exposure, and to determine exposure levels of GLYP and its metabolite aminomethyl phosphoric acid (AMPA), GLUF and its metabolite 3-methylphosphinicopropionic acid (3-MPPA), and Cry1Ab protein (a Bt toxin) in Eastern Townships of Quebec, Canada. Blood of thirty pregnant women (PW) and thirty-nine nonpregnant women (NPW) was studied. Serum GLYP and GLUF were detected in NPW and not detected in PW. Serum 3-MPPA and CryAb1 toxin were detected in PW, their fetuses, and NPW. This is the first study to reveal the presence of circulating PAGMF in women with and without pregnancy, paving the way for a new field in reproductive toxicology including nutrition and uteroplacental toxicities.

Learn more about the conventional expectations for abstracts in Chapter 8, "Abstracts and Other Structural Conventions."

1. INTRODUCTION

An optimal exchange across the maternal-fetal unit (MFU) is necessary for a successful pregnancy. The placenta plays a major role in the embryo's nutrition and growth, in the regulation of the endocrine functions, and in drug biotransformation [1–3]. Exchange involves not only physiological constituents, but also substances that represent a pathological risk for the fetus such as xenobiotics that include drugs, food additives, pesticides, and environmental pollutants [4]. The understanding of what xenobiotics do to the MFU and what the MFU does to the xenobiotics should provide the basis for the use of the placenta as a tool to investigate and predict some aspects of developmental toxicity [4]. Moreover, pathological conditions in the placenta are important causes of intrauterine or perinatal death, congenital anomalies, intrauterine growth retardation, maternal death, and a great deal of morbidity for both mother and child [5].

Genetically modified plants (GMP) were first approved for commercialization in Canada in 1996 then became distributed worldwide. Global areas of these GMP increased from 1.7 million hectares in 1996 to 134 million hectares in 2009, an 80-fold increase [6]. This growth rate makes GMP the fastest-adopted crop technology [6]. GMP are plants in which genetic material has been altered in a way that does not occur naturally. Genetic engineering allows gene transfer (transgenesis) from an organism into another in order to confer them new traits. Combining GMP with pesticides-associated GM foods (PAGMF) allows the protection of desirable crops and the elimination of unwanted plants by reducing the competition for nutrients or by providing insect resistance. There is a debate on the direct threat of genes used in the preparation of these new foods on human health, as they are not detectable in the body, but the real danger may come from PAGMF [6–10]. Among the innumerable PAGMF, two categories are largely used in our agriculture since their introduction in 1996: (1) residues

This research report follows IMRaD format, beginning with "Introduction," and followed by "Materials and Methods," "Results," and "Discussion."

Aris and Leblanc establish necessary background information for their study, including the identification of a specific problem: the possible threat of pesticides-associated GM foods to human health.

derived from herbicide-tolerant GM crops such as glyphosate (GLYP) and its metabolite aminomethyl phosphoric acid (AMPA) [11], and gluphosinate ammonium (GLUF) and its metabolite 3-methylphosphinicopropionic acid (MPPA) [12]; and (2) residues derived from insect-resistant GM crops such as Cry1Ab protein [13,14].

Among herbicide-tolerant GM crops, the first to be grown commercially were soybeans which were modified to tolerate glyphosate [11]. Glyphosate [N-(Phosphonomethyl) glycine] is a nonselective, post-emergence herbicide used for the control of a wide range of weeds [15]. It can be used on non-crop land as well as in a great variety of crops. GLYP is the active ingredient in the commercial herbicide Roundup®. Glyphosate is an acid, but usually used in a salt form, most commonly the isopropylamine salt. The target of glyphosate is 5-enolpyruvoylshikimate 3-phosphate synthase (EPSPS), an enzyme in the shikimate pathway that is required for the synthesis of many aromatic plant metabolites, including some amino acids. The gene that confers tolerance of the herbicide is from the soil bacterium *Agrobacterium tumefaciens* and makes an EPSPS that is not affected by glyphosate. Few studies have examined the kinetics of absorption, distribution, metabolism, and elimination (ADME) of glyphosate in humans [15,16]. Curwin et al. [17] reported detection of urinary GLYP concentrations among children, mothers, and fathers living in farm and nonfarm households in Iowa. The ranges of detection were 0.062–5.0 ng/ml and 0.10–11 ng/ml for nonfarm and farm mothers, respectively. There was no significant difference between farm and nonfarm mothers and no positive association between the mothers' urinary glyphosate levels and glyphosate dust concentrations. These findings suggest that other sources of exposure such as diet may be involved.

Gluphosinate (or glufosinate) [ammonium dl-homoalanin-4-(methyl) phosphinate] is a broad-spectrum, contact herbicide. Its major metabolite is 3-methylphosphinicopropionic acid (MPPA), with which it has similar biological and toxicological effects [18]. GLUF is used to control a wide range of weeds after the crop emerges or for total vegetation control on land not used for cultivation. Gluphosinate herbicides are also used to desiccate (dry out) crops before harvest. It is a phosphorus-containing amino acid. It inhibits the activity of an enzyme, glutamine synthetase, which is necessary for the production of the amino acid glutamine and for ammonia detoxification [12]. The application of GLUF leads to reduced glutamine and increased ammonia levels in the plant's tissues. This causes photosynthesis to stop and the plant dies within a few days. GLUF also inhibits the same enzyme in animals [19]. The gene used to make plants resistant to gluphosinate comes from the bacterium *Streptomyces hygroscopicus* and encodes an enzyme called phosphinothricine acetyl transferase (PAT). This enzyme detoxifies GLUF. Crop varieties carrying this trait include varieties of oilseed rape, maize, soybeans, sugar beet, fodder beet, cotton, and rice.

The intended audience for this report would understand this specialized language (jargon) and value its precision.

Aris and Leblanc review the current state of scholarship on residues from herbicide-tolerant (GLYP, GLUF) and insect-resistant GM crops (Cry1Ab) that are the focus of this study.

As for GLYP, its kinetics of absorption, distribution, metabolism, and elimination (ADME) is not well studied in humans, except for a few poisoned-case studies [16,20,21]. Hirose et al. reported the case of a 65-year-old male who ingested BASTA, which contains 20% (w/v) of GLUF ammonium, about 300 ml, more than the estimated human toxic dose [20]. The authors studied the serial change of serum GLUF concentration every 3–6 h and assessed the urinary excretion of GLUF every 24 h. The absorbed amount of GLUF was estimated from the cumulative urinary excretion. The changes in serum GLUF concentration exhibited $T_{1/2\alpha}$ of 1.84 and $T_{1/2\alpha}$ of 9.59 h. The apparent distribution volume at b-phase and the total body clearance were 1.44 l/kg and 86.6 ml/min, respectively. Renal clearance was estimated to be 77.9 ml/min.

The Cry1Ab toxin is an insecticidal protein produced by the naturally 5 occurring soil bacterium *Bacillus thuringiensis* [22,23]. The gene (truncated *cry1Ab* gene) encoding this insecticidal protein was genetically transformed into maize genome to produce a transgenic insect-resistant plant (Bt-maize; MON810) and, thereby, provide specific protection against Lepidoptera infestation [13,14]. For more than 10 years, GM crops have been commercialized and approved as an animal feed in several countries worldwide. The Cry toxins (protoxins) produced by GM crops are solubilized and activated to Cry toxins by gut proteases of susceptible insect larvae. Activated toxin binds to specific receptors localized in the midgut epithelial cells [24,25], invading the cell membrane and forming cation-selective ion channels that lead to the disruption of the epithelial barrier and larval death by osmotic cell lysis [26–28].

Since the basis of better health is prevention, one would hope that we can develop procedures to avoid environmentally induced disease in susceptible populations such as pregnant women and their fetuses. The fetus is considered to be highly susceptible to the adverse effects of xenobiotics. This is because environmental agents could disrupt the biological events that are required to ensure normal growth and development [29,30]. PAGMF are among the xenobiotics that have recently emerged and extensively entered the human food chain [9], paving the way for a new field of multidisciplinary research, combining human reproduction, toxicology, and nutrition, but not as yet explored. Generated data will help regulatory agencies responsible for the protection of human health to make better decisions. Thus, the aim of this study was to investigate whether pregnant women are exposed to PAGMF and whether these toxicants cross the placenta to reach the fetus.

Aris and Leblanc establish the focus for their study: "to investigate whether pregnant women are exposed to PAGMF and whether these toxicants cross the placenta to reach the fetus."

2. MATERIALS AND METHODS

2.1. Chemicals and reagents

For the analytical support (Section 2.3), GLYP, AMPA, GLUF, APPA, and *N*-methyl-*N*-(tert-butyldimethylsilyl) trifluoroacetamide (MTBSTFA) +1%

tertburyldimethyl-chlorosilane (TBDMCS) were purchased from Sigma (St. Louis, MO, USA). 3-MPPA was purchased from Wako Chemicals USA (Richmond, VA, USA), and Sep-Pak Plus PS-2 cartridges, from Waters Corporation (Milford, MA, USA). All other chemicals and reagents were of analytical grade (Sigma, MO, USA). The serum samples for validation were collected from volunteers.

2.2. Study subjects and blood sampling

At the Centre Hospitalier Universitaire de Sherbrooke (CHUS), we formed two groups of subjects: (1) a group of healthy pregnant women ($n = 30$), recruited at delivery; and (2) a group of healthy fertile nonpregnant women ($n = 39$), recruited during their tubal ligation of sterilization. As shown in Table 1 of clinical characteristics of subjects, eligible groups were matched for age and body mass index (BMI). Participants were not known for cigarette or illicit drug use or for medical condition (i.e., diabetes, hypertension, or metabolic disease). Pregnant women had vaginal delivery and did not have any adverse perinatal outcomes. All neonates were of appropriate size for gestational age ($3423 \pm 375g$).

Blood sampling was done before delivery for pregnant women or at tubal ligation for nonpregnant women and was most commonly obtained from the median cubital vein, on the anterior forearm. Umbilical cord blood sampling was done after birth using the syringe method. Since labor time can take several hours, the time between taking the last meal and blood sampling is often a matter of hours. Blood samples were collected in BD Vacutainer 10 ml glass serum tubes (Franklin Lakes, NJ, USA). To obtain serum, whole blood was centrifuged at 2000 rpm for 15 min within 1 h of collection. For maternal samples, about 10 ml of blood was collected, resulting in 5–6.5 ml of serum. For cord blood samples, about 10 ml of blood was also collected by syringe, giving 3–4.5 ml of serum. Serum was stored at $-20°C$ until assayed for PAGMF levels.

Table 1
Characteristics of subjects

	Pregnant women ($n = 30$)	Nonpregnant women ($n = 39$)	P value[a]
Age (year, mean ± SD)	32.4 ± 4.2	33.9 ± 4.0	NS
BMI (kg/m^2, mean ± SD)	24.9 ± 3.1	24.8 ± 3.4	NS
Gestational age (week, mean ± SD)	38.3 ± 2.5	N/A	N/A
Birth weight (g, mean ± SD)	3364 ± 335	N/A	N/A

BMI, body mass index; N/A, not applicable; data are expressed as mean ±SD; NS, not significant.

[a]P values were determined by Mann-Whitney test.

Subjects were pregnant and nonpregnant women living in Sherbrooke, an urban area of Eastern Townships of Quebec, Canada. No subject had worked or lived with a spouse working in contact with pesticides. The diet taken is typical of a middle-class population of Western industrialized countries. A food market-basket, representative for the general Sherbrooke population, contains various meats, margarine, canola oil, rice, corn, grain, peanuts, potatoes, fruits and vegetables, eggs, poultry, meat, and fish. Beverages include milk, juice, tea, coffee, bottled water, soft drinks, and beer. Most of these foods come mainly from the province of Quebec, then the rest of Canada and the United States of America. Our study did not quantify the exact levels of PAGMF in a market-basket study. However, given the widespread use of GM foods in the local daily diet (soybeans, corn, potatoes, . . .), it is conceivable that the majority of the population is exposed through their daily diet [31,32].

The study was approved by the CHUS Ethics Human Research Committee on Clinical Research. All participants gave written consent.

See Chapter 9, "The IRB Process and Use of Human Subjects," for more on this statement.

2.3. Herbicide and metabolite determination

Levels of GLYP, AMPA, GLUF, and 3-MPPA were measured using gas chromatography-mass spectrometry (GC–MS).

2.3.1. CALIBRATION CURVE

According to a method described by Motojyuku et al. [16], GLYP, AMPA, GLUF, and 3-MPPA (1 mg/ml) were prepared in 10% methanol, which is used for all standard dilutions. These solutions were further diluted to concentrations of 100 and $10 \mu g/ml$ and stored for a maximum of 3 months at 4°C. A $1 \mu g/ml$ solution from previous components was made prior to herbicide extraction. These solutions were used as calibrators. A stock solution of DL-2-amino-3-phosphonopropionic acid (APPA) (1 mg/ml) was prepared and used as an internal standard (IS). The IS stock solution was further diluted to a concentration of $100 \mu g/ml$. Blank serum samples (0.2 ml) were spiked with $5 \mu l$ of IS (100 $\mu g/ml$), $5 \mu l$ of each calibrator solution (100 $\mu g/ml$), or 10, $5 \mu l$ of 10 $\mu g/ml$ solution, or 10, $5 \mu l$ of 1 $\mu g/ml$ solution, resulting in calibration samples containing 0.5 μg of IS (2.5 $\mu g/ml$), with 0.5 μg (2.5 $\mu g/ml$), 0.1 μg (0.5 $\mu g/ml$), 0.05 μg (0.25 $\mu g/ml$), 0.01 μg (0.05 $\mu g/ml$), or 0.005 μg (0.025 $\mu g/ml$), of each compound (i.e., GLYP, AMPA, GLUF, and 3-MPPA). Concerning extraction development, spiked serum with 5 $\mu g/ml$ of each compound was used as a control sample.

2.3.2. EXTRACTION PROCEDURE

The calibration curves and serum samples were extracted by employing a solid phase extraction (SPE) technique, modified from manufacturers' recommendations and from Motojyuku et al. [16]. Spiked serum (0.2 ml), prepared as described above, and acetonitrile (0.2 ml) were added to centrifuge tubes. The tubes were then vortexed (15 s) and centrifuged (5 min, 1600 × g). The samples were purified by SPE using 100 mg Sep-Pak Plus PS-2 cartridges, which were conditioned by washing with 4 ml of acetonitrile followed by 4 ml of distilled water. The samples were loaded onto the SPE cartridges, dried (3 min, 5 psi), and eluted with 2 ml of acetonitrile. The solvent was evaporated to dryness under nitrogen. The samples were reconstituted in 50 μl each of MTBSTFA with 1% TBDMCS and acetonitrile. The mixture was vortexed for 30 s every 10 min, 6 times. Samples of solution containing the derivatives were used directly for GC–MS (Agilent Technologies 6890N GC and 5973 Invert MS).

2.3.3. GC–MS ANALYSIS

Chromatographic conditions for these analyses were as follows: a 30 m × 0.25 mm Zebron ZB-5MS fused-silica capillary column with a film thickness of 0.25 μm from Phenomenex (Torrance, CA, USA) was used. Helium was used as a carrier gas at 1.1ml/min. A 2 μl extract was injected in a split mode at an injection temperature of 250°C. The oven temperature was programmed to increase from an initial temperature of 100°C (held for 3 min) to 300°C (held for 5 min) at 5°C/min. The temperatures of the quadrupode, ion source, and mass-selective detector interface were respectively 150, 230, and 280°C. The MS was operated in the selected-ion monitoring (SIM) mode. The following ions were monitored (with quantitative ions in parentheses): GLYP (454), 352; AMPA (396), 367; GLUF (466); 3-MPPA (323); IS (568), 466.

The limit of detection (LOD) is defined as a signal of three times the noise. For 0.2 ml serum samples, LOD was 15, 10, 10, and 5 ng/ml for GLYP, GLUF, AMPA, and 3-MPPA, respectively.

2.4. Cry1Ab protein determination

Cry1Ab protein levels were determined in blood using a commercially available double antibody sandwich (DAS) enzyme-linked immunosorbent assay (Agdia, Elkhart, IN, USA), following manufacturer's instructions. A standard curve was prepared by successive dilutions (0.1–10 ng/ml) of purified Cry1Ab protein (Fitzgerald Industries International, North Acton, MA, USA) in PBST buffer. The mean absorbance (650 nm) was calculated and used to determine samples concentration. Positive and negative controls were prepared with the kit Cry1Ab positive control solution, diluted 1/2 in serum.

2.5. Statistical analysis

PAGMF exposure was expressed as number, range, and mean ± SD for each group. Characteristics of cases and controls and PAGMF exposure were compared using the Mann–Whitney U-test for continuous data and by Fisher's exact test for categorical data. Wilcoxon matched pairs test compared two dependent groups. Other statistical analyses were performed using Spearman correlations.

Throughout the report, the authors aim to communicate their findings quantitatively, as is typical of science writing.

Analyses were realized with the software SPSS version 17.0. A value of $P < 0.05$ was considered as significant for every statistical analysis.

3. RESULTS

As shown in Table 1, pregnant women and nonpregnant women were similar in terms of age and body mass index. Pregnant women had normal deliveries and birth-weight infants (Table 1).

GLYP and GLUF were non-detectable (nd) in maternal and fetal serum, [20] but detected in nonpregnant women (Table 2, Fig. 1). GLYP was [2/39 (5%), range (nd-93.6 ng/ml), and mean ± SD (73.6 ± 28.2 ng/ml)] and GLUF was [7/39 (18%), range (nd-53.6 ng/ml), and mean ± SD (28.7 ± 15.7 ng/ml)].

> Tables provide a clear way to present quantitative data so that patterns can be seen.

Table 2
Concentrations of GLYP, AMPA, GLUF, 3-MPPA, and Cry1Ab protein in maternal and fetal cord serum

	Maternal ($n = 30$)	Fetal cord ($n = 30$)	P value[a]
GLYP			
Number of detection	nd	nd	nc
Range of detection (ng/ml)			
Mean ± SD			
AMPA			
Number of detection	nd	nd	nc
Range of detection (ng/ml)			
Mean ± SD (ng/ml)			
GLUF			
Number of detection	nd	nd	nc
Range of detection (ng/ml)			
Mean ± SD (ng/ml)			
3-MPPA			
Number of detection	30/30 (100%)	30/30 (100%)	$P < 0.001$
Range of detection (ng/ml)	21.9-417	8.76-193	
Mean ± SD (ng/ml)	120 ± 87.0	57.2 ± 45.6	
Cry1Ab			
Number of detection	28/30 (93%)	24/30 (80%)	$P = 0.002$
Range of detection (ng/ml)	nd-1.50	nd-0.14	
Mean ± SD (ng/ml)	0.19 ± 0.30	0.04 ± 0.04	

GLYP, glyphosate; AMPA, aminomethyl phosphoric acid; GLUF, gluphosinate ammonium; 3-MPPA, 3-methylphosphinicopropionic acid; Cry1Ab, protein from *Bacillus thuringiensis*; nd, not detectable; nc, not calculable because not detectable. Data are expressed as number (n, %) of detection, range, and mean ± SD (ng/ml).

[a]P values were determined by Wilcoxon matched pairs test.

AMPA was not detected in maternal, fetal, and nonpregnant women samples. The metabolite 3-MPPA was detected in maternal serum [30/30 (100%), range (21.9-417 ng/ml), and mean $\pm$ SD (120 $\pm$ 87.0 ng/ml)], in fetal cord serum [30/30 (100%), range (8.76-193 ng/ml), and mean $\pm$ SD (57.2 $\pm$ 45.6 ng/ml)], and in nonpregnant women serum [26/39 (67%), range (nd-337 ng/ml), and mean $\pm$ SD (84.1 $\pm$ 70.3 ng/ml)]. A significant difference in 3-MPPA levels was evident between maternal and fetal serum ($P < 0.001$, Table 2, Fig. 1), but not between maternal and nonpregnant women serum ($P = 0.075$, Table 3, Fig. 1).

Serum insecticide Cry1Ab toxin was detected in: (1) pregnant women [28/30 (93%), range (nd-1.5 ng/ml), and mean $\pm$ SD (0.19 $\pm$ 0.30 ng/ml)];

> Aris and Leblanc present only the findings of their research in this section of their report, which reflects IMRaD format conventions.

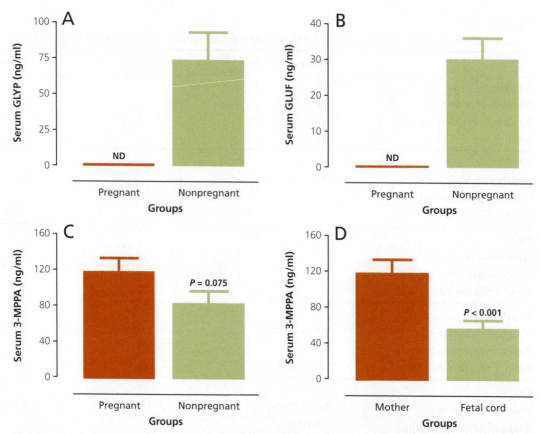

Figure 1. Circulating concentrations of glyphosate (GLYP: A), gluphosinate (GLUF: B), and 3-methylphosphinicopropionic acid (3-MPPA: C and D) in pregnant and nonpregnant women (A–C) and in maternal and fetal cord blood (D). Blood sampling was performed from 30 pregnant women and 39 nonpregnant women. Chemicals were assessed using GC-MS. *P* values were determined by Mann-Whitney test in the comparison of pregnant women to nonpregnant women (A–C). *P* values were determined by Wilcoxon matched pairs test in the comparison of maternal to fetal samples (D). A *P* value of 0.05 was considered as significant.

Table 3

Concentrations of GLYP, AMPA, GLUF, 3-MPPA, and Cry1Ab protein in serum of pregnant and nonpregnant women

	Pregnant women (*n* = 30)	Nonpregnant women (*n* = 39)	*P* value[a]
GLYP			
Number of detection	nd	2/39 (5%)	nc
Range of detection (ng/ml)		nd-93.6	
Mean ± SD		73.6 ± 28.2	
AMPA			
Number of detection	nd	nd	nc
Range of detection (ng/ml)			
Mean ± SD (ng/ml)			
GLUF			
Number of detection	nd	7/39 (18%)	nc
Range of detection (ng/ml)		nd-53.6	
Mean ± SD (ng/ml)		28.7 ± 15.7	
3-MPPA			
Number of detection	30/30 (100%)	26/39 (67%)	*P* = 0.075
Range of detection (ng/ml)	21.9-417	nd-337	
Mean ± SD (ng/ml)	120 ± 87.0	84.1 ± 70.3	
Cry1Ab			
Number of detection	28/30 (93%)	27/39 (69%)	*P* = 0.006
Range of detection (ng/ml)	nd-1.50	nd-2.28	
Mean ± SD (ng/ml)	0.19 ± 0.30	0.13 ± 0.37	

GLYP, glyphosate; AMPA, aminomethyl phosphoric acid; GLUF, gluphosinate ammonium; 3-MPPA, 3-methylphosphinicopropionic acid; Cry1Ab, protein from *Bacillus thuringiensis*; nd, not detectable; nc, not calculable because not detectable. Data are expressed as number (*n*, %) of detection, range, and mean ± SD (ng/ml).

[a]*P* values were determined by Mann-Whitney test.

(2) nonpregnant women [27/39 (69%), range (nd-2.28 ng/ml), and mean ± SD (0.13 ± 0.37 ng/ml)]; and (3) fetal cord [24/30 (80%), range (nd-0.14 ng/ml), and mean ± SD (0.04 ± 0.04 ng/ml)]. A significant difference in Cry1Ab levels was evident between pregnant and nonpregnant women's serum (*P* = 0.006, Table 3, Fig. 2) and between maternal and fetal serum (*P* = 0.002, Table 2, Fig. 2).

We also investigated a possible correlation between the different contaminants in the same woman. In pregnant women, GLYP, its metabolite AMPA, and GLUF were undetectable in maternal blood and therefore impossible to establish a correlation between them. In nonpregnant women, GLYP was detected in 5% of the subjects, its metabolite AMPA was not detected, and GLUF was detected in 18%; thus, no significant correlation emerged from these contaminants in the same subjects. Moreover, there was no correlation between 3-MPPA and Cry1AB in the same women, both pregnant and not pregnant.

4. DISCUSSION

Our results show that GLYP was not detected in maternal and fetal blood, but present in the blood of some nonpregnant women (5%), whereas its metabolite AMPA was not detected in all analyzed samples. This may be explained by the absence of exposure, the efficiency of elimination, or the limitation of the method of detection. Previous studies report that glyphosate and AMPA share similar toxicological profiles. Glyphosate toxicity has been shown to be involved in the induction of developmental retardation of fetal skeleton [33] and significant adverse effects on the reproductive system of male Wistar rats at puberty and during adulthood [34]. Also, glyphosate was harmful to human placental cells [35,36] and embryonic cells [36]. It is interesting to note that all of these animal and *in vitro* studies used very high concentrations of GLYP compared to the human levels found in our studies. In this regard, our results represent actual concentrations detected in humans and therefore they constitute a referential basis for future investigations in this field.

GLUF was detected in 18% of nonpregnant women's blood and not detected in maternal and fetal blood. As for GLYP, the non-detection of GLUF may be explained by the absence of exposure, the efficiency of elimination, or the limitation of the method of detection. Regarding the non-detection of certain chemicals in pregnant women compared with nonpregnant women, it is assumed that the hemodilution caused by pregnancy may explain, at least in part, such non-detection. On the other hand, 3-MPPA (the metabolite of GLUF) was detected in 100% of maternal and umbilical cord blood samples, and in 67% of the nonpregnant women's blood samples. This highlights that this metabolite is more detectable than

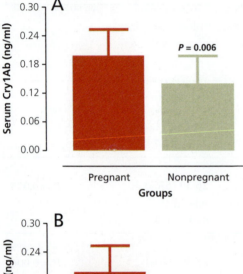

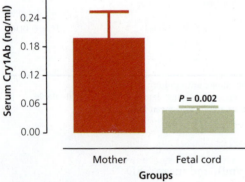

Figure 2. Circulating concentrations of Cry1Ab toxin in pregnant and nonpregnant women (A), and maternal and fetal cord (B). Blood sampling was performed from 30 pregnant women and 39 nonpregnant women. Levels of Cry1Ab toxin were assessed using an ELISA method. *P* values were determined by Mann-Whitney test in the comparison of pregnant women to nonpregnant women (A). *P* values were determined by Wilcoxon matched pairs test in the comparison of maternal to fetal samples (B). A *P* value of 0.05 was considered as significant.

its precursor and seems to easily cross the placenta to reach the fetus. Garcia et al. [37] investigated the potential teratogenic effects of GLUF in humans and found increased risk of congenital malformations with exposure to GLUF. GLUF has also been shown in mouse embryos to cause growth retardation, increased death, or hypoplasia [18]. As for GLYP, it is interesting to note that the GLUF concentrations used in these tests are very high (10 ug/ml) compared to the levels we found in this study (53.6 ng/ml). Hence, our data, which provide the actual and precise concentrations of these toxicants, will help in the design of more relevant studies in the future.

> Aris and Leblanc repeatedly note the need for additional research, laying the groundwork, based on their contribution, for additional studies.

On the other hand, Cry1Ab toxin was detected in 93% and 80% of mater- 25 nal and fetal blood samples, respectively, and in 69% of tested blood samples from nonpregnant women. There are no other studies for comparison with our results. However, trace amounts of the Cry1Ab toxin were detected in the gastrointestinal contents of livestock fed on GM corn [38–40], raising concerns about this toxin in insect-resistant GM crops: (1) that these toxins may not be effectively eliminated in humans and (2) there may be a high risk of exposure through consumption of contaminated meat.

5. CONCLUSIONS

> A Conclusion(s) section is sometimes used in an IMRaD format report to place the findings in the context of existing and future research.

To our knowledge, this is the first study to highlight the presence of pesticides-associated genetically modified foods in maternal, fetal, and nonpregnant women's blood. 3-MPPA and Cry1Ab toxin are clearly detectable and appear to cross the placenta to the fetus. Given the potential toxicity of these environmental pollutants and the fragility of the fetus, more studies are needed, particularly those using the placental transfer approach [41]. Thus, our present results will provide baseline data for future studies exploring a new area of research relating to nutrition, toxicology, and reproduction in women. Today, obstetric-gynecological disorders that are associated with environmental chemicals are not known. This may involve perinatal complications (i.e., abortion, prematurity, intrauterine growth restriction, and preeclampsia) and reproductive disorders (i.e., infertility, endometriosis, and gynecological cancer). Thus, knowing the actual PAGMF concentrations in humans constitutes a cornerstone in the advancement of research in this area.

CONFLICT OF INTEREST STATEMENT

The authors declare that they have no competing interests.

ACKNOWLEDGMENTS

This study was supported by funding provided by the Fonds de Recherche en Santé du Québec (FRSQ). The authors wish to thank Drs. Youssef AinMelk,

Marie-Thérèse Berthier, Krystel Paris, François Leclerc, and Denis Cyr for their material and technical assistance.

The use of brackets for reference numbers and the formatting of the citations reflect the "Vancouver" style used in biomedical, health, and other science publications.

REFERENCES

[1] Sastry BV. Techniques to study human placental transport. Adv Drug Deliv Rev 1999;38:17–39.

[2] Haggarty P, Allstaff S, Hoad G, Ashton J, Abramovich DR. Placental nutrient transfer capacity and fetal growth. Placenta 2002;23:86–92.

[3] Gude NM, Roberts CT, Kalionis B, King RG. Growth and function of the normal human placenta. Thromb Res 2004;114:397–407.

[4] Myllynen P, Pasanen M, Pelkonen O. Human placenta: a human organ for developmental toxicology research and biomonitoring. Placenta 2005;26:361–71.

[5] Guillette EA, Meza MM, Aquilar MG, Soto AD, Garcia IE. An anthropological approach to the evaluation of preschool children exposed to pesticides in Mexico. Environ Health Perspect 1998;106:347–53.

[6] Clive J. Global status of commercialized biotech/GM crops. In: ISAAA 2009. 2009.

[7] Pusztai A. Can science give us the tools for recognizing possible health risks of GM food? Nutr Health 2002;16:73–84.

[8] Pusztai A, Bardocz S, Ewen SW. Uses of plant lectins in bioscience and biomedicine. Front Biosci 2008;13:1130–40.

[9] Magana-Gomez JA, de la Barca AM. Risk assessment of genetically modified crops for nutrition and health. Nutr Rev 2009;67:1–16.

[10] Borchers A, Teuber SS, Keen CL, Gershwin ME. Food safety. Clin Rev Allergy Immunol 2010;39:95–141.

[11] Padgette SR, Taylor NB, Nida DL, Bailey MR, MacDonald J, Holden LR, et al. The composition of glyphosate-tolerant soybean seeds is equivalent to that of conventional soybeans. J Nutr 1996;126:702–16.

[12] Watanabe S. Rapid analysis of glufosinate by improving the bulletin method and its application to soybean and corn. Shokuhin Eiseigaku Zasshi 2002;43:169–72.

[13] Estruch JJ, Warren GW, Mullins MA, Nye GJ, Craig JA, Koziel MG. Vip3A, a novel *Bacillus thuringiensis* vegetative insecticidal protein with a wide spectrum of activities against lepidopteran insects. Proc Natl Acad Sci USA 1996;93:5389–94.

[14] de Maagd RA, Bosch D, Stiekema W. Toxin-mediated insect resistance in plants. Trends Plant Sci 1999;4:9–13.

[15] Hori Y, Fujisawa M, Shimada K, Hirose Y. Determination of the herbicide glyphosate and its metabolite in biological specimens by gas chromatography–mass spectrometry. A case of poisoning by Roundup herbicide. J Anal Toxicol 2003;27:162–6.

[16] Motojyuku M, Saito T, Akieda K, Otsuka H, Yamamoto I, Inokuchi S. Determination of glyphosate, glyphosate metabolites, and glufosinate in human serum by gas chromatography-mass spectrometry. J Chromatogr B: Anal Technol Biomed Life Sci 2008;875:509–14.

[17] Curwin BD, Hein MJ, Sanderson WT, Striley C, Heederik D, Kromhout H, et al. Urinary pesticide concentrations among children, mothers and fathers living in farm and non-farm households in Iowa. Ann Occup Hyg 2007;51:53–65.

[18] Watanabe T, Iwase T. Developmental and dysmorphogenic effects of glufosinate ammonium on mouse embryos in culture. Teratog Carcinog Mutagen 1996;16:287–99.

[19] Hoerlein G. Glufosinate (phosphinothricin), a natural amino acid with unexpected herbicidal properties. Rev Environ Contam Toxicol 1994;138:73–145.

[20] Hirose Y, Kobayashi M, Koyama K, Kohda Y, Tanaka T, Honda H, et al. A toxicokinetic analysis in a patient with acute glufosinate poisoning. Hum Exp Toxicol 1999;18:305–8.

[21] Hori Y, Fujisawa M, Shimada K, Hirose Y. Determination of glufosinate ammonium and its metabolite, 3-methylphosphinicopropionic acid, in human serum by gas

chromatography–mass spectrometry following mixed-mode solid-phase extraction and t-BDMS derivatization. J Anal Toxicol 2001;25:680–4.

[22] Hofte H, Whiteley HR. Insecticidal crystal proteins of *Bacillus thuringiensis*. Microbiol Rev 1989;53:242–55.

[23] Schnepf E, Crickmore N, Van Rie J, Lereclus D, Baum J, Feitelson J, et al. *Bacillus thuringiensis* and its pesticidal crystal proteins. Microbiol Mol Biol Rev 1998;62:775–806.

[24] Van Rie J, Jansens S, Hofte H, Degheele D, Van Mellaert H. Receptors on the brush border membrane of the insect midgut as determinants of the specificity of *Bacillus thuringiensis* delta-endotoxins. Appl Environ Microbiol 1990;56:1378–85.

[25] Aranda E, Sanchez J, Peferoen M, Guereca L, Bravo A. Interactions of *Bacillus thuringiensis* crystal proteins with the midgut epithelial cells of Spodoptera frugiperda (Lepidoptera: Noctuidae). J Invertebr Pathol 1996;68:203–12.

[26] Slatin SL, Abrams CK, English L. Delta-endotoxins form cation-selective channels in planar lipid bilayers. Biochem Biophys Res Commun 1990;169:765–72.

[27] Knowles BH, Blatt MR, Tester M, Horsnell JM, Carroll J, Menestrina G, et al. A cytolytic delta-endotoxin from *Bacillus thuringiensis* var. israelensis forms cation-selective channels in planar lipid bilayers. FEBS Lett 1989;244:259–62.

[28] Du J, Knowles BH, Li J, Ellar DJ. Biochemical characterization of *Bacillus thuringiensis* cytolytic toxins in association with a phospholipid bilayer. Biochem J 1999;338(Pt 1): 185–93.

[29] Dietert RR, Piepenbrink MS. The managed immune system: protecting the womb to delay the tomb. Hum Exp Toxicol 2008;27:129–34.

[30] Dietert RR. Developmental immunotoxicity (DIT), postnatal immune dysfunction and childhood leukemia. Blood Cells Mol Dis 2009;42:108–12.

[31] Chapotin SM, Wolt JD. Genetically modified crops for the bioeconomy: meeting public and regulatory expectations. Transgenic Res 2007;16:675–88.

[32] Rommens CM. Barriers and paths to market for genetically engineered crops. Plant Biotechnol J 2010;8:101–11.

[33] Dallegrave E, Mantese FD, Coelho RS, Pereira JD, Dalsenter PR, Langeloh A. The teratogenic potential of the herbicide glyphosate-Roundup in Wistar rats. Toxicol Lett 2003;142:45–52.

[34] Dallegrave E, Mantese FD, Oliveira RT, Andrade AJ, Dalsenter PR, Langeloh A. Pre- and postnatal toxicity of the commercial glyphosate formulation in Wistar rats. Arch Toxicol 2007;81:665–73.

[35] Richard S, Moslemi S, Sipahutar H, Benachour N, Seralini GE. Differential effects of glyphosate and Roundup on human placental cells and aromatase. Environ Health Perspect 2005;113:716–20.

[36] Benachour N, Seralini GE. Glyphosate formulations induce apoptosis and necrosis in human umbilical, embryonic, and placental cells. Chem Res Toxicol 2009;22:97–105.

[37] Garcia AM, Benavides FG, Fletcher T, Orts E. Paternal exposure to pesticides and congenital malformations. Scand J Work Environ Health 1998;24:473–80.

[38] Chowdhury EH, Shimada N, Murata H, Mikami O, Sultana P, Miyazaki S, et al. Detection of Cry1Ab protein in gastrointestinal contents but not visceral organs of genetically modified Bt11-fed calves. Vet Hum Toxicol 2003;45:72–5.

[39] Chowdhury EH, Kuribara H, Hino A, Sultana P, Mikami O, Shimada N, et al. Detection of corn intrinsic and recombinant DNA fragments and Cry1Ab protein in the gastrointestinal contents of pigs fed genetically modified corn Bt11. J Anim Sci 2003;81:2546–51.

[40] Lutz B, Wiedemann S, Einspanier R, Mayer J, Albrecht C. Degradation of Cry1Ab protein from genetically modified maize in the bovine gastrointestinal tract. J Agric Food Chem 2005;53:1453–6.

[41] Myren M, Mose T, Mathiesen L, Knudsen LE. The human placenta—an alternative for studying foetal exposure. Toxicol in Vitro 2007;21:1332–40.

1. The researchers establish early in the introduction that their focus is not concerned with the effects of genetically modified (GM) foods on humans; instead, their focus is on the effects of pesticides associated with GM foods (PAGMF): "There is a debate on the direct threat of genes used in the preparation of these new foods on human health, as they are not detectable in the body, but the real danger may come from PAGMF" (par. 2). What are the two categories of pesticides the researchers focus on?

2. According to the researchers, what are the potential benefits of their findings for the general public as well as for other academic researchers?

3. In light of their findings regarding the insecticide Cry1Ab toxin, what are two concerns that the researchers express?

Rhetoric Questions

4. The researchers frequently take caution not to overstate the implications of their findings. What strategies do the researchers use to hedge these implications?

5. The study's Introduction reviews previous research conducted on the pesticides under investigation. On average, how many previous studies are referenced in each paragraph of the introduction? What, if anything, might this number suggest about previous research in this area?

6. This research report includes a number of tables and figures. What are the main differences between the ways these visual elements are labeled? Do you find the tables or the figures easier to navigate and understand? Why?

Response Question

7. The researchers suggest that their work could "pav[e] the way for a new field of multidisciplinary research, combining human reproduction, toxicology, and nutrition" (par. 6). In your estimation, what could each of these fields likely contribute to the continued study of the potential toxicity of pesticides associated with GM foods?

ACADEMIC CASE STUDY • GENETICALLY MODIFIED FOOD   APPLIED FIELDS

The Marketing of Genetically Modified Food with Direct and Indirect Consumer Benefits: An Analysis of Willingness to Pay

GRANT ALEXANDER WILSON AND DAVID DI ZHANG

Grant Wilson, lead author of the following study, is a faculty member in the Department of Management and Marketing at the Edwards School of Business, University of Saskatchewan, Canada. In the following study, Wilson, along with his colleague David Di Zhang, also of the University of Saskatchewan, report the results of their investigation into consumers' acceptance of and willingness to pay for genetically modified (GM) food products. Their study, which provides advice for GM food marketers, was published in 2018 in the *Journal of Commercial Biotechnology*.

ABSTRACT

Genetically modified foods have traditionally been marketed as having direct industry benefits. Whereas, consumer benefits of genetically modified foods have been largely indirect, through price reduction. This study explores the marginal effects of differing value propositions on consumers' acceptance and willingness to pay for genetically modified foods among Canadians. Consumers' exposure to genetically modified food advertisements with industry-oriented benefits lowered both purchase intention and willingness to pay for genetically modified food. Consumers' exposure to non-genetically modified food advertisements with direct consumer benefits increased both purchase intention and willingness to pay. Most noteworthy, consumers' exposure to genetically modified food advertisements with both direct consumer benefits and industry-oriented benefits increased their willingness to pay. These findings provide insight into the future of successful genetically modified food marketing.

Keywords: genetically modified food; GM food marketing; marketing; willingness-to-pay; food biotechnology marketing

INTRODUCTION

Genetically modified (GM) food for human consumption has been a subject of intense public debate, as well as academic research. Despite the lack of scientific evidence to suggest GM foods are less safe than conventional foods, researchers have shown that consumers are reluctant of fully embracing the technology. For example, Lusk, Kurlander, Roucan, and Taulman[1] conducted a meta-analysis of 25 prior studies on GM food and reported that consumers placed a lower value on GM food relative to non-GM food. More recently, Hess, Lagerkvist, Redekop, and Pakseresht[2] conducted a meta-analysis of 214 relevant studies on the subject matter and concluded consumers responded negatively to GM foods with benefits such as increased food supply, price discounts, or extended shelf life.

Indeed, GM foods have typically been positioned to have direct industry benefits for producers, such as increased supply and prolonged shelf life. The benefits for consumers are mainly indirect, through price reduction.[3] Kaye-Blake, Saunders, and Cagatay[4] termed these industry-oriented GM products as

the first generation of GM food (GM1). Giannakas and Yiannaka[5] argue that GM1 food is facing much opposition and negative evaluation because it lacks direct benefits for consumers.

However, it appears that the biotechnology industry has been trying to communicate the direct consumer benefits for some time. For example, in the mid-1990s, Calgene's Flavr Savr™ tomato was approved in the United States and Canada.[6,7] While the original value proposition of the GM tomatoes was industry-oriented, designed to delay ripening, thereby extending its commercial shelf-life, the marketing of the product focused on its enhanced flavour.[6] The second generation of GM products (GM2) is poised to create direct benefits for consumers, such as increased nutrition, better taste, and environmental sustainability.[4,8-9] GM2 food has the potential of changing the consumer perception and acceptance of GM food for the better, as well as increase yield for the anticipated population growth.[5] Colson and Hoffman[3] conducted a choice experiment in the US and revealed that American consumers were willing to pay more for GM foods with enhanced nutrition, compared to conventional products. Ison and Kontoleon[10] conducted a survey in the UK and found significant market support for GM2 foods, as a large portion of the British consumers surveyed (33%) were willing to pay a premium for GM products that contained both direct and indirect benefits.

However, there are a number of issues that still require further investigation. First, there are very few actual GM2 food products currently on the market. The vast majority of the studies contained in Hess, Lagerkvist, Redekop, and Pakseresht's[2] meta-analysis have employed scenarios with fictional GM foods. As noted by the authors, consumers are sensitive to how questions are framed in such studies.[2] As a result, it is difficult to delineate true consumer intentions and what portion of the responses were the effects of manipulation treatments. In this study, we intend to measure the marginal effects of the manipulation treatments. Such marginal effects can provide insights into the potential value of future communication and marketing of GM2 foods.

Second, Hess, Lagerkvist, Redekop, and Pak-seresht[2] found that there are geographical disparities documented in the extant literature regarding the acceptance of GM1 food. For example, Canadian consumers were more likely to accept GM1 food than Japanese consumers. Dolgopolova and Teuber[11] found that Canadian consumers are likely to pay a lower price premium for health-enhanced foods. Accordingly, it is quite important to investigate the acceptance and willingness-to-pay (WTP) for GM2 food among Canadian consumers.

Third, while Hess, Lagerkvist, Redekop, and Pak-seresht[2] found that consumers are largely insensitive to the type of food products in prior studies (mostly GM1 food), Dolgopolova and Teuber[11] argue that consumer responses to health-enhanced foods are product-specific. In this study, we employed three types of fictitious GM2 foods. We chose to include food produced from wheat (bread), canola (canola oil), and soybeans (tofu) as they are prominent Canadian crops.[12] Moreover, all of the mentioned crops have GM varieties approved on the Canadian market.[13]

LITERATURE REVIEW

Factors That Influence Consumer WTP for GM Food

The perceived benefits of GM foods have been shown to be one of the most important factors to predict consumer acceptance.[14,15] The recent research on consumer attitudes toward GM foods has indicated that the types of benefits for GM1 food, such as increased supply and prolonged shelf life, are not appreciated by consumers and are unable to generate price premiums.[2] Several scholars have argued that only direct benefits to consumers can elicit positive consumer attitudes and product evaluations.[3,10]

The perceived risks of GM foods have been shown to negatively influence consumers' WTP.[14–18] Moon and Balasubramanian[16] found that if consumers perceived risks associated with GM foods, they were willing to pay premiums to purchase non-GM foods. Similarly, Chiang, Lin, Fu, and Chen[18] found that the higher the risk perception, the more likely consumers were willing to pay a premium to avoid GM foods.

Bukenya and Wright[17] found that consumers that had negative perceptions of GM food safety were willing to pay over 10% more for non-GM food.

Additionally, trust of the institutions involved in developing, regulating, and distributing GM food has also been shown to influence consumer attitudes.[15,19,20] The trust of the institution has been found to be important when assessing perceived risks and benefits.[20] For example, Li, Curtis, McCluskey, and Wahl[19] attributed Chinese consumers' WTP for GM food, in part, to their trust in the government as a food regulator.

A multitude of demographic factors, such as age, gender, and family income have been shown to have direct and indirect influences on consumers' acceptance of, and WTP for, GM food.[14–16]

Based on the findings reported in the extant literature, we present a base model of consumers' WTP for GM food that includes influencing factors such as perceived benefits, perceived risks, trust of institutions, and demographics. This model is similar to what Ison and Kontoleon[10] used in their study. The model can be expressed mathematically as follows:

$$\text{WTP} = \beta_1 * (\textbf{Perceived Benefits of GM Food})$$
$$+ \beta_2 * (\textbf{Perceived Risks of GM Food}) +$$
$$\beta_3 * (\textbf{Perceived Trust of Institutions}) + \beta_4 * (\textbf{Age})$$
$$+ \beta_5 * (\textbf{Gender}) + \beta_6 * (\textbf{Income}) + \beta_7 * (\textbf{Education})$$
$$+ \textit{error}$$

Of course, this paper is not intended to be a replication of Ison and Kontoleon's[10] UK study in the Canada context. We argue that, for better or worse, individual consumers have already accumulated some knowledge about GM food and formulated individual perceptions about GM food. Their attitude will influence their decisions. However, that is not to say that they would not respond to future marketing and communication attempts. Our intention is to detect the marginal effects of the communication treatments, controlling for participants' preexisting attitudes.

Consumer WTP for GM Food with Additional Communication without Direct Consumer Benefits

Numerous studies have explored consumers' WTP for GM versus non-GM food.[3,14,16–19,21–27] Findings from these studies have been mixed. Product attributes, particularly value propositions, have resulted in differing WTP premiums. For example, when direct consumer benefits of GM food are not presented, consumers often assign a premium to non-GM food or discount GM food.[16–18,22–25]

In Chern, Rickertsen, Tsuboi, and Fu's[22] study of US and Norwegian consumers, a large number of consumers were willing to pay a premium to avoid GM food when no direct consumer benefits were communicated. Specifically, Norwegian consumers were willing to pay a premium of 54% and 67% to avoid GM-fed salmon and GM salmon, respectively. Although slightly less than Norwegian consumers, US consumers were willing to pay a premium of 41% and 53% to avoid GM-fed salmon and GM salmon, respectively. However, when a clear consumer-oriented value proposition was communicated to consumers, the willingness to consume increased significantly.[22] Similarly, Chiang, Lin, Fu, and Chen[18] found Taiwanese consumers were willing to pay a premium of 7% to avoid GM-fed salmon.

Noussair, Robin, and Ruffieux[23] did not communicate a value proposition when they explored French consumers' WTP for food made with GM corn. Their results showed that when participants observed a GM label, WTP decreased by as much as 30%. A second study conducted by Noussair, Robin, and Ruffieux[24] showed that as much as 35% of participants refused to purchase GM biscuits. Moreover, roughly 40% were willing to purchase GM biscuits, but only if they were priced significantly less than the conventional alternative.

Assuming there would be a price premium for non-GM food, Moon and Balasubramanian[16] explored US and UK consumers' WTP for GM cereal with no value proposition. Moon and Balasubramanian[16] found that US consumers were willing to pay less than UK consumers for non-GM cereal. However, both US and UK consumers were willing to pay premiums for non-GM cereal over GM cereal, suggesting a desire to avoid GM food.

In other studies of US consumers, findings support the preference of non-GM food over the GM alternatives. Communicating only industry-oriented benefits but not direct consumer benefits, Huffman, Shogren, Rousu, and Tegene[21] found strong support for the preference of the non-GM potatoes, vegetable oil, and tortilla chips, as consumers were willing to pay a 14% premium for over the GM alternatives. In their second study, Rousu, Huffman, Shogren, and Tegene[25] found that US consumers discounted GM potatoes, vegetable oil, and tortilla chips by 7% to 13% as compared to non-GM food. Similarly, Bukenya and Wright[17] found that US consumers were willing to pay a premium of roughly 20% for non-GM tomatoes over GM tomatoes with industry-oriented value propositions.

There has been strong evidence to support that consumers generally assign a discount to GM food compared to the non-GM counterparts. When consumers have been presented GM foods with various industry-oriented benefits, but without clear direct consumer benefits, they have perceived GM foods as less desirable than non-GM foods. In other words, the marginal value of additional communication of indirect benefits is negative.

WTP = β_A *(Communicating Industry-Oriented Benefits of GM Food) + β_1*(Perceived Benefits of GM Foods) + β_2*(Perceived Risks of GM Foods) + β_3*(Trust of Institutions) + β_4*(Age) + β_5* (Gender) + β_6*(Income) + β_7*(Education) + error

Where βA is expected to be negative

Hypothesis 1: When only industry-oriented benefits are presented, consumers will perceive a negative marginal WTP for GM food compared to a conventional alternative.

Direct Consumer Benefits without Mentioning Genetic Modification

The labelling of GM foods is another controversial issue. Canada currently does not have mandatory GM labelling regulation.[28] As a result, communicating the direct consumer benefits of new and novel foods without mentioning the fact that they are made with GM ingredients is a real option. While the ethical issue of doing so is questionable, there is no legal requirement to clearly identify GM foods providing there are no safety concerns or nutritional changes.[28] Prior research has suggested that consumers are increasingly conscious about the link between health and diet.[29–31]

As functional foods, or nutrition-enhanced foods, are becoming more popular, scholars have extensively investigated consumers' attitudes, willingness to accept, and WTP for such foods. It has been revealed that health claims on food items positively influence consumers' purchase intentions and WTP for functional foods.[32,33] Consumers' WTP is often influenced by consumers' knowledge about the nutrition enhancements.[34] Moreover, consumers have reacted positively when information on health benefits has been provided.[35] Research has also indicated that consumers seem to prefer simple health statements[36] and well-known healthier options, such as whole grain over fortified white bread.[35] In addition, consumers that insist on organic foods may be less likely to purchase nutrition-enhanced foods.[33] Furthermore, because health attributes are often considered an attribute that is difficult to detect immediately, many scholars argue that effective government regulation and proper labelling would play an important role in helping consumers make informed choices.[37–42]

The body of literature on functional foods and consumer acceptance thereof seems to suggest that consumers are generally willing to pay a premium for direct consumer benefits, such as enhanced nutrition and other health-related benefits. It is highly likely that in the context of GM2 food, a possible strategic option is to solely focus on communicating the direct consumer benefits without mentioning the GM attribute. We would expect that the marginal value of communicating direct consumer benefits is positive.

WTP = β_B*(Communicating Direct Consumer Benefits of Non-GM Food) + β_1*(Perceived Benefits of GM Food) + β_2*(Perceived Risks of GM Food) + β_3*(Trust of Institutions) + β_4*(Age) + β_5*(Gender) + β_6*(Income) + β_7*(Education) + *error*

Where β_B is expected to be positive.

Hypothesis 2: When direct consumer benefits are presented without mentioning GM, consumers will perceive a positive marginal WTP for the product compared to a conventional alternative.

Clear Communication of GM Food with Both Direct and Indirect Consumer Benefits

Prior studies have found that when clear direct consumer benefits are communicated, results tend to differ. For example, Colson[26] explored US consumers' WTP for antioxidant- and vitamin-enhanced GM produce. The author's findings suggested that US consumers were willing to pay premiums for produce that was enhanced via genetic modification. The author concluded that consumers may be willing to pay a premium for GM-labelled food. Colson and Huffman[3] and Colson, Huffman, and Rousu[27] received similar results and concluded that there may be an incentive for GM labelling. Although these findings suggest that labelled GM food with direct consumer benefits elicit favourable consumer responses, the authors may have overemphasized the importance of the GM labelling at the expense of the direct consumer benefits. A few other studies support the notion that direct consumer benefits result in WTP premiums.[14,19]

Li, Curtis, McCluskey, and Wahl[19] explored Chinese consumers' WTP for vitamin-enhanced GM rice and soybean oil. Li, Curtis, McCluskey, and Wahl[19] found strong support for GM-enhanced food, as nearly 44% of consumers were willing to pay a premium for vitamin-enhanced GM rice and 73% of consumers were willing to pay a premium for vitamin-enhanced GM soybean oil. Unlike Colson's[26] conclusion, Li, Curtis, McCluskey, and Wahl[19] attribute the increased WTP effect as a result of the additional consumer health benefits, not its GM properties.

De Steur, Gellynck, Storozhenko, Liqun, Lambert, Van Der Straeten, and Viaene[14] explored consumer acceptance of GM food with health benefits related to neural-tube defects. Neural-tube defects are spinal cord and brain malformations in early human development.[43] Multivitamins with folic acid can reduce the risk of neural-tube defects. Neural-tube defects in the Shanxi Province are among the highest reported cases in the world. De Steur, Gellynck, Storozhenko, Liqun, Lambert, Van Der Straeten, and Viaene[14] explored the acceptance and WTP for GM rice with high folate content in Shanxi Province in China. De Steur, Gellynck, Storozhenko, Liqun, Lambert, Van Der Straeten, and Viaene[14] found that over 60% of consumers were willing to accept GM rice designed to contain folic acid. Moreover, nearly 80% of consumers were willing to pay a premium for GM rice designed to contain folic acid. Specifically, the average premium was 34% for the GM rice as compared to conventional rice. These results demonstrate strong consumer acceptance of and WTP for GM food aimed at reducing the risk of a severe illness.

These studies suggest that GM foods with clearly communicated and relevant consumer-oriented value propositions may have the potential to change the paradigm, receiving consumer acceptance and even price premiums in the marketplace.

> WTP = $\beta_A{}^\star$(**Communicating Industry-Oriented Benefits of GM Food**) + $\beta_B{}^\star$(**Communicating Direct Consumer Benefits of GM Food**) + $\beta_1{}^\star$ (**Perceived Benefits of GM Food**) + $\beta_2{}^\star$(**Perceived Risks of GM Food**) + $\beta_3{}^\star$(**Trust of Institutions**) + $\beta_4{}^\star$(**Age**) + $\beta_5{}^\star$(**Gender**) + $\beta_6{}^\star$(**Income**) + $\beta_7{}^\star$(**Education**) + *error*

Where $\beta_A{}^\star$ is expected to be negative and $\beta_B{}^\star$ is expected to be positive.

Hypothesis 3: When both industry-oriented and direct consumer benefits are presented, consumers will perceive a positive marginal WTP for GM food compared to a conventional alternative.

METHODOLOGY

We employed an online survey questionnaire method. Seven hundred and fifty (750) Canadian individuals over the age of 18 that lived in one of the western Canadian provinces (British Columbia, Alberta, Saskatchewan, and Manitoba) participated in the study.

The survey was experimental in nature. Participants were first asked a series of questions related to their general attitudes toward GM foods, including their perceived benefits of GM foods, perceived risks of GM foods, and trust of institutions in the context of GM foods. Participants were then randomly assigned to one of the three conditions (Table 1).

Each participant was shown three advertisements, one for bread, one for canola oil, and one for tofu. The advertisements in the first condition

Table 1
Marketing Messages

	Messages Included in Treatments		
	Industry-Oriented Benefits	**Direct Consumer Benefits**	**Note**
Condition 1	Yes	No	This condition is similar how GM1 food has been typically marketed.
Condition 2	No	Yes	This is similar to how Functional Foods are currently being marketed. Without a mandatory GM labelling regulation, this strategy can be a realistic option for the future marketing of GM2 food.
Condition 3	Yes	Yes	This would be a comprehensive marketing strategy of GM2 food, highlighting both direct and indirect benefits.
	No	No	Having neither direct nor indirect benefit is an unrealistic scenario. Hence, this condition is *not* used in the survey.

emphasized that foods were made with GM ingredients and that GM offers a number of industry-oriented value propositions that might indirectly benefit consumers. The benefits presented included higher yield, less pesticide usage, and increased global food supply. The messages contained in this condition were similar to typical messages in current GM food advertisements.

The advertisements in the second condition focused exclusively on the direct consumer benefits, such as better taste and enhanced nutrition. Advertisements in this condition did not mention genetic modification or any indirect benefits. This is similar to how functional foods are currently being marketed.

The advertisements in the third condition promoted both direct and indirect consumer benefits. These advertisements highlighted direct consumer benefits such as enhanced taste and nutrition derived through genetic modification.

After seeing these fictitious advertisements, participants were asked to indicate their intention to purchase (yes or no) and WTP for the products presented, relative to a conventional alternative.

Consumers' WTP for GM foods have been most commonly assessed via survey instruments.[14,16–18,19,22] or experimental auction markets.[3,21,23–27] Surveys have employed the contingent valuation (CV) method of measuring consumers' WTP. In these studies, the CV method allowed respondents to make valuations of foods by choosing pre-determined price premiums or discounts relative to baseline prices. For example, given the baseline price of a conventional product, survey respondents were asked to assign a predetermined premium or discount for a GM alternative.

In this study, we employed the CV method for assessing consumers' WTP for the delineated foods under the various conditions. The baseline price for a loaf of conventional bread was $3.00. The participants were asked to indicate how much of premium (or discount) they were willing to pay for the product shown in the advertisement. Similarly, the price for a one-liter bottle of conventional canola oil was set at $5.00 and the one pound package of tofu was set at $2.00. The participants were asked to indicate the

premium (or discount) they were willing to pay for the products shown in the advertisements.

All participants also provided demographic information pertaining their gender, age, education, and household income.

RESULTS

Demographics

Of the 750 responses, 377 (50.3%) were female, 367 (48.9%) were male, and three (0.4%) identified themselves as an alternative gender identity. According to Statistics Canada (2015a), there is roughly the same number of males as females in Canada. Therefore, the gender of respondents was fairly representative of the Canadian population. All participants were over 18 years of age. Seven (0.9%) were between the ages of 18 and 25, 98 (13.1%) were between the ages of 26 and 35, 144 (19.2) were between 36 and 45 years of age, 162 (21.6%) were between the ages of 46 and 55, 16 (21.3%) were between the ages of 56 and 65, and 173 (23.1%) were 65 or older. Based on Statistics Canada's[44] population, all age categories in this study were fairly representative of the Canadian population. Per Statistics Canada[45] data, the distribution of respondents was reflective of the population distribution in Western Canadian provinces. Respondents' median household income range was $5,001 to $6,000 per month, similar to the Canadian median household income of $6,379 per month.[46] Overall, the respondent demographics were representative of the Canadian population.

General Attitudes toward GM and WTP

The participants' general attitudes toward GM foods, including their perceived benefits of GM foods, perceived risks of GM foods, and trust of institutions were measured adopting the multi-dimensional scale used in Rodriguez-Entrena, Salazar-Ordonez, and Sayadi's[15] study. Because multiple items were used to measure the factors, we conducted a confirmatory factor analysis to test the dimensionality and loading. Using SPSS Amos, we specified a structural equation model with measurement items to load onto the intended factor and each of the factors to co-vary. The result suggested that the three-factor model fit the data well, with both the comparative fit index (CFI) and the root mean square error of approximation (RMSEA) in the acceptable range (CFI = 0.947; RMSEA = 0.078). All item-to-factor loadings were above 0.60. Hence, we were satisfied with the convergent validity of the measurement. The items that loaded onto the same factor were averaged to created composite indices for subsequent regression analysis.

As previously stated, our baseline model specifies, as commonly documented in the literature, that consumers' WTP for GM food is influenced by their perceived benefits, perceived risks, perceived trust, and a number of demographic characteristics.

In order to generate confidence in this baseline model, we used general linear regression model in SPSS. First, we ran a regression model with purchase intention as the dependent variable. The result shows that, as expected, consumers' general attitudes toward GM, which already exist in the minds of the

consumers prior to the marketing treatments, have significant influences on purchase intentions (Table 2). More specifically, in the bread condition, perceived benefits of GM food had a positive influence ($\beta_1 = 0.308$, p < 0.001), perceived risks of GM foods had a negative influence ($\beta_2 = -0.214$, p < 0.001), and the trust of institutions had a positive influence ($\beta_3 = 0.109$, p = 0.014) on purchase intention. Education, income, and age were not significant factors. However, gender influence was significant, as women tended to have lower purchase intentions ($\beta_5 = -0.075$, p = 0.021). Similar patterns are observed for the canola oil and tofu categories with minor variations (Table 2). For example, in the tofu condition, perceived trust of institutions was not a significant factor. However, age emerged as a significant predictor, where younger consumers exhibited a higher intention to purchase tofu ($\beta_4 = -0.083$, p = 0.021).

We also tested a model with WTP as the dependent variable. In this model, the dependent variable was actually the contingent, or marginal value of WTP, which was measured by the premium or

Table 2

Purchase Intentions Baseline Model

Product Category	Bread		Canola Oil		Tofu	
	Standardized Beta	Sig.	Standardized Beta	Sig.	Standardized Beta	Sig.
Perceived Benefits of GM Food	.380	.000	.427	.000	.207	.000
Perceived Risks of GM Food	−.214	.000	−.235	.000	−.125	.001
Trust of Institutions	.109	.014	.118	.006	.003	.959
Gender	−.075	.021	−.088	.005	−.064	.078
Age	−.020	.541	−.039	.199	−.083	.021
Education	.029	.373	.021	.489	.065	.070
Household Income	−.012	.708	−.019	.531	−.021	.559
Dependent Variable	Purchase Intention - Bread		Purchase Intention - Canola Oil		Purchase Intention - Tofu	
Model Statistics	Adjusted $R^2 = 0.256$		Adjusted $R^2 = 0.323$		Adjusted $R^2 = 0.070$	

Table 3

WTP Baseline Model

Product Category	Bread		Canola Oil		Tofu	
	Standardized Beta	Sig.	Standardized Beta	Sig.	Standardized Beta	Sig.
Perceived Benefits of GM Food	.092	.120	.030	.610	.114	.133
Perceived Risks of GM Food	−.169	.000	−.129	.005	−.100	.074
Trust of Institutions	.004	.950	.129	.029	.017	.822
Gender	.013	.764	−.006	.900	.092	.100
Education	−.014	.747	−.030	.504	−.084	.137
Household Income	.055	.216	.089	.046	.065	.246
Age	.041	.359	.044	.326	.008	.885
Dependent Variable	Marginal WTP for Bread		Marginal WTP for Canola Oil		Marginal WTP for Tofu	
Selection Criterion	Purchase Intention = 1		Purchase Intention = 1		Purchase Intention = 1	
Model Statistics	Adjusted R^2 = 0.024		Adjusted R^2 = 0.026		Adjusted R^2 = 0.016	

discounts assigned by participants. In this model, we only selected the cases where the participants had indicated that they were willing to purchase (positive purchase intention). The results indicated that in the bread category, only perceived risks had a significant negative influence on marginal WTP (β_2 = −0.169, p < 0.001) (Table 3). In the canola oil category, perceived risks (β_2 = −0.129, p = 0.005), the trust of institutions (β_3 = 0.129, p = 0.029), and household income (β_6 = 0.089, p = 0.046) were significant predictors, while in the tofu category, none of the independent variables had significant influence.

Our H1 predicted that, with consumers' general perceptions of GM foods their demographic characteristics, further promotion of genetic modification, and the associated indirect benefits would have a negative influence on consumers' WTP. In order to test this hypothesis, we took the same two-step approach as described above and added the variable of promoting the indirect benefits into the model.

The results indicate that the additional promotion of genetic modification and industry-oriented benefits of GM food (indirect consumer benefits) had a significant negative influence on purchase intentions in the bread (β_A = −0.149, p < 0.001), canola oil (β_A = −0.152, p < 0.001), and tofu (β_A = −0.141, p < 0.001) categories. Furthermore, promoting industry-oriented benefits had a significant negative influence on marginal WTP in the bread (β_A = −0.217, p < 0.001), canola oil (β_A = −0.209, p < 0.001), and tofu (β_A = −0.163, p < 0.001) categories. Hence, H1 was supported.

Our H2 predicted that the promotion of direct consumer benefits without mention of the presence of genetic modification would have a positive influence on consumers' WTP. In order to test this hypothesis, we added the variable of promoting direct consumer benefits into the baseline model. The results indicated that, the promotion of direct consumer benefits with no mention of genetic modification had significant positive influences on purchase intentions in the canola oil ($\beta_B = 0.107$, p < 0.001) and tofu ($\beta_B = 0.101$, p < 0.001) categories, but was not statistically significant in the bread category ($\beta_B = 0.061$, p = 0.056). Moreover, promoting direct consumer benefits had significant positive influence on marginal WTP in the bread ($\beta_B = 0.245$, p < 0.001), canola oil ($\beta_B = 0.200$, p < 0.001), and tofu ($\beta_B = 0.160$, p = 0.003) categories, supporting H2.

Our H3 predicted that when both industry-oriented and direct consumer benefits were promoted they would have unique and significant influences on consumers' WTP. In order to test this hypothesis, we added both variables promoting both the industry-oriented and direct consumer benefits into the baseline model. The results indicated that, the promotion of industry-oriented benefits had a significant negative influence on purchase intentions in the bread ($\beta_A = -0.156$, p < 0.001), canola oil ($\beta_A = -0.129$, p < 0.001), and tofu ($\beta_A = -0.114$, p = 0.005) categories, while the simultaneous promotion of direct consumer benefits had no significant influence on purchase intention in any of the categories. In terms of WTP, the results indicated that, as expected, the promotion of industry-oriented benefits had a negative influence on WTP. But these negative influences were only significant in the bread ($\beta_A = -0.117$, p < 0.001) and canola ($\beta_A = -0.141$, p < 0.001) categories, not in the tofu category ($\beta_A = -0.107$, p = 0.098). The simultaneous promotion of direct consumer benefits had a positive influence on WTP. The influences were significant only in the bread ($\beta_B = 0.183$, p < 0.001) and canola oil ($\beta_B = 0.129$, p < 0.001) categories, but not in the tofu category ($\beta_B = 0.101$, $p = 0.108$). Therefore, H3 was only partially supported.

Non-Purchasers

There were a substantial number of the participants that were not willing to purchase bread, canola oil, and tofu in all three treatment groups (Figure 1).

ANOVA was conducted in order to compare the percentage of participants not willing to purchase bread, canola oil, and tofu among the three treatment groups. Statistically significant differences were found among bread, canola oil, and tofu non-purchasers (Table 4).

Post-hoc Tukey tests revealed that the percentage of participants not willing to purchase GM food with industry-oriented (GM1) and direct consumer benefits (GM2) were significantly higher than non-GM with consumer benefits (enhanced) (Table 5).

Consumer purchase decisions are influenced by 45 many factors. It was not surprising that some consumers were not willing to purchase bread, canola oil, or tofu. However, it is telling to observe that there were significantly more participants not willing to purchase bread, canola oil, and tofu made with GM ingredients as compared to non-GM bread, canola oil, and tofu with consumer benefits. This suggests that some consumers are unwilling to purchase food based on the presence of GM ingredients. Moreover, the lack of statistical difference between the percentages of participants not willing to purchase GM food with industry-oriented (GM1) versus GM food with

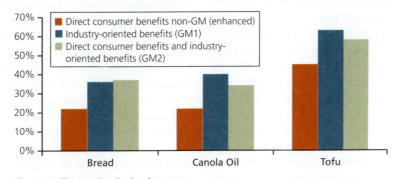

Figure 1. The Non-Purchasing Segment

Table 4

Non-Purchasers ANOVA

Product Category		Sum of Squares	df	Mean Square	F	Sig.
	Between Groups	3.678	2	1.839	8.671	.000
Bread	Within Groups	158.430	747	.212		
	Total	162.108	749			
	Between Groups	4.381	2	2.191	10.303	.000
Canola Oil	Within Groups	158.819	747	.213		
	Total	163.200	749			
	Between Groups	4.602	2	2.301	9.493	.000
Tofu	Within Groups	181.072	747	.242		
	Total	185.675	749			

direct consumer benefits (GM2) implies that some consumers are not willing to purchase food made with GM ingredients no matter how the advertisers describe the potential benefits.

GM2 Purchasers versus Non-Purchasers

ANOVAs were conducted in order to compare purchasers and non-purchasers of food items containing direct consumer benefits. The results indicate that purchasers versus non-purchasers did not differ significantly in terms of their income or education across all treatment groups. Moreover, there was no significant difference in terms of age among purchasers versus non-purchasers of bread and canola oil. However, the age of tofu purchasers and non-purchasers differed significantly. The results suggested that younger participants were more likely to purchase GM2 tofu. Across all treatment groups, there was a significant difference in terms of gender among purchasers and non-purchasers, with male participants being more willing to purchase GM2 food.

Additional ANOVAs were conducted to explore the differences between purchasers and non-purchasers with respect to their perception of benefits and risks as well as the trust of institutions. The results

indicated that, not surprisingly, the groups differ significantly on all three factors and among all treatment groups. The purchasers perceived the benefits as higher, the risks as lower, and information trust as higher than their non-purchasing counterparts.

DISCUSSION

Perceived benefits had a positive, and perceived risks had a negative, influence on consumers' purchase intention. Similarly, perceived benefits and risks had the same effect on consumers' WTP. This supports previous conclusions that perceived benefits in consumers' decisions to purchase GM food.[14,15] Moreover, the negative effect of perceived benefits on consumers' decisions to purchase GM food further supports extant literature.[14–18] The trust of institutions also proved to have a positive effect on purchase intentions and WTP. However, this relationship was only found in the bread and canola oil conditions. Although Yee, Traill, Lusk, Jaeger, House, Moore, Morrow, and Valli[20] found trust of institutions to be an important factor in Chinese consumers' WTP, we offer the thought that its magnitude of importance may not be universal across products or countries.

Table 5
Multiple Comparisons of Non-Purchasers

Product Category	(I) GROUP	(J) GROUP	Mean Difference (I-J)	Std. Error	Sig.	95% Confidence Interval Lower Bound	95% Confidence Interval Upper Bound
Bread	Enhanced	GM1	−.14562*	.04107	.001	−.2421	−.0492
		GM2	−.14967*	.04107	.001	−.2461	−.0532
	GM1	Enhanced	.14562*	.04107	.001	.0492	.2421
		GM2	−.00405	.04144	.995	−.1014	.0933
	GM2	Enhanced	.14967*	.04107	.001	.0532	.2461
		GM1	.00405	.04144	.995	−.0933	.1014
Canola Oil	Enhanced	GM1	−.18206*	.04113	.000	−.2786	−.0855
		GM2	−.12538*	.04113	.007	−.2220	−.0288
	GM1	Enhanced	.18206*	.04113	.000	.0855	.2786
		GM2	.05668	.04149	.359	−.0408	.1541
	GM2	Enhanced	.12538*	.04113	.007	.0288	.2220
		GM1	−.05668	.04149	.359	−.1541	.0408
Tofu	Enhanced	GM1	−.18627*	.04391	.000	−.2894	−.0831
		GM2	−.12959*	.04391	.009	−.2327	−.0265
	GM1	Enhanced	.18627*	.04391	.000	.0831	.2894
		GM2	.05668	.04430	.407	−.0474	.1607
	GM2	Enhanced	.12959*	.04391	.009	.0265	.2327
		GM1	−.05668	.04430	.407	−.1607	.0474

*The mean difference is significant at the 0.05 level.

Nonetheless, the combination of benefits, risks, and trust of institutions are considerations of consumers and impact their purchase intentions and value assigned to GM food.

Our first hypothesis was supported, as consumers' exposure to industry-oriented GM food advertisements lowered both the purchase intention and WTP. This supports previous findings, suggesting consumers generally assign a discount to GM food with indirect benefits. We offer two explanations for these relationships. First, consumers' purchase intentions and WTP may be lowered as they assign little value to the industry-oriented benefits. Secondly, in terms of WTP, consumers may view these industry-oriented benefits as efficiencies that lower costs and therefore demand discounts in the marketplace.

Hypothesis two was also supported, as consum- 50 ers' exposure to non-GM food advertisements with consumer benefits increased both their purchase intention and WTP. Intuitively this makes sense because direct benefits are presented to consumers in the absence of perceived risk from genetic modification. Logically, products are more appealing to consumers as more benefits are included in the offering.

Hypothesis three was partially supported, as consumers' exposure to GM food advertisements with direct consumer benefits and industry-oriented benefits increased their WTP in the bread and canola oil condition. However, this relationship was not found in the tofu condition. Nevertheless, it can be concluded that adding direct consumer benefits to GM food influences its perceived value. Of our findings, this is the most noteworthy. Our findings suggest that the value proposition, as opposed to solely how the food is made, is fundamental to consumers' WTP. Unlike previous studies that only explored consumers' WTP for GM food with industry-oriented benefits or direct consumer benefits in isolation, this study explores similar foods with differing value propositions. The implications of our study are great, both in terms of adding to the existing literature and GM food marketing.

IMPLICATIONS

Our study has several implications for academia. Our study adds to the growing body of consumer WTP for GM food research. Previous studies have separately explored consumers' WTP for GM food with industry-oriented benefits and direct consumers' benefits. However, our study is novel as it explores consumers' purchase intention and WTP for GM food with industry-oriented benefits (GM1), direct consumer benefits (GM2), and non-GM food with consumer benefits (functional food), providing evidence that value propositions play an essential role in consumer acceptance of food. Differing from the works

of Colson[26] and Colson, Huffman, and Rousu[27], our study finds that the consumer-oriented value proposition, as opposed to the GM-nature of the food, drives consumer willingness to pay. The findings highlight the importance of agricultural biotechnology embracing a market-orientated culture. A major component of a market orientation is to understand the needs of the consumers.[47] As Wilson, Perepelkin, Zhang, and Vachon[48] have revealed, market-oriented biotechnology companies generally outperform non-market oriented counterparts.

Our study's findings have the potential to create significant value for agriculture biotechnology companies. Particularly, our study finds that consumers are willing to accept and pay premiums for GM food that has personally relevant value. The findings offer some support for the notion that changing the value proposition from producer to consumer, may assist in changing the negative connotation associated with GM food. Knowing that feeding the world in 2050 will require leveraging agricultural biotechnology[49] and increased genetic modification in agriculture, it is necessary to gain widespread consumer support. Perhaps creating GM food with direct consumer benefits will play a critical role in gaining such support. Not only does the promotion of direct consumer benefits have the potential to change the paradigm, as shown by this study's data, it may also be a profitable endeavor.

LIMITATIONS

While our study provides significant insight into positioning GM food for consumer acceptance and WTP, several limitations must be delineated. First, although our study was representative of Canadian demographics, it was limited to Western Canada. Second, the range GM foods were limited to bread, canola oil, and tofu. Third, this study was conducted via survey research and not in an actual marketplace setting. Finally, as differences were found among bread, canola oil, and tofu, it may be of interest to explore other consumer acceptance and WTP for other foods at a national level.

REFERENCES

[1] Lusk, J. L., Jamal, M., Kurlander, L., Roucan, M. and Taulman, L. (2005) A Meta-Analysis of Genetically Modified Food Valuation Studies. *Journal of Agricultural and Resource Economics* 30(1): 28–44.

[2] Hess, S., Lagerkvist, C. J., Redekop, W. and Pakseresht, A. (2016) Consumers' Evaluation of Biotechnologically Modified Food Products: New Evidence from A Meta-Survey. *European Review of Agricultural Economics* 43(5): 703–736.

[3] Colson, G. J. and Huffman, W. E. (2011) Consumers' Willingness to Pay for Genetically Modified Foods With Producer-Enhancing Nutritional Attributes. *American Journal of Agricultural Economics* 93(2): 358–363.

[4] Kaye-Blake, W. H., Saunders, C. M. and Cagatay, S. (2008) Genetic Modification Technology and Producer Returns: The Impacts Of Productivity, Preferences, and Technology Uptake. *Review of Agricultural Economics* 30(4): 692–710.

[5] Giannakas, K. and Yiannaka, A. (2008) Market and Welfare Effects of Second-Generation, Consumer-Oriented GM Products. *American Journal of Agricultural Economics* 90(1): 152–171.

[6] Kramer, M. G. and Redenbaugh, K. (1994) Commercialization of A Tomato With An Antisense Polygalacturonase Gene: The FLAVR SAVR™ Tomato Story. *Euphytica* 79: 293–297.

[7] Health Canada. (1997) Safety Assessment of The Flavr Savr™ Tomato, https://www.canada.ca/en/health-canada/services/food-nutrition/geneticallymodified-foods-other-novel-foods/approved-products/information-safety-assessment-flavr-savr-tomato.html.

[8] Larue, B., West, G. E., Gendron, C. and Lambert, R. (2004) Consumer Response to Functional Foods Produced by Conventional, Organic, or Genetic Manipulation. *Agribusiness* 20(2): 155–166.

[9] Anderson, K., Jackson, L. A. and Nielsen, C. P. (2005) Genetically Modified Rice Adoption: Implications for Welfare and Poverty Alleviation. *Journal of Economic Integration* 20(4): 771–788.

[10] Ison, J. and Kontoleon, A. (2014) Consumer Preference for Functional GM Foods in The UK: A Choice Experiment. *AgBioForum* 17(1): 28–36.

[11] Dolgopolova, I. and Teuber, R. (2016) Consumers' Willingness-To-Pay for Healthy Attributes in Food Products: A Meta-Analysis. Paper Prepared For Presentation at the 2016 Agricultural & Applied Economics Association Annual Meeting, Boston, Massachusetts, July 31–August 2, 2016.

[12] Statistics Canada. (2017) Estimated Areas, Yield, Production, Average Farm Price and Total Farm Value of Principal Field Crops, http://www5.statcan.gc.ca/cansim/a26?lang=eng&id=10017.

[13] Government of Canada. (2018) Novel Food Decisions, https://www.canada.ca/en/health-canada/services/foodnutrition/genetically-modified-foods-other-novel-foods/approved-products.html.

[14] De Steur, H., Gellynck, X., Storozhenko, S., Liqun, G., Lambert, W., Van Der Straeten, D. and Viaene, J. (2010) Willingness-To-Accept and Purchase Genetically Modified Rice with High Folate Content in Shanxi Province, China. *Appetite* 54: 118–125.

[15] Rodriguez-Entrena, M., Salazar-Ordonez, M. and Sayadi, S. (2013) Applying Partial Least Squares to Model Genetically Modified Food Purchase Intentions in Southern Spain Consumers. *Food Policy* 40: 44–53.

[16] Moon, W. and Balasubramanian, S. K. (2003) Willingness to Pay for Non-Biotech Foods in the U.S. and U.K. *The Journal of Consumer Affairs* 37(2): 317–339.

[17] Bukenya, J. O. and Wright, N. R. (2007) Determinants of Consumer Attitudes and Purchase Intentions with Regard to Genetically Modified Tomatoes. *Agribusiness* 23(1): 117–130.

[18] Chiang, J., Lin, C., Fu, T. and Chen, C. (2012) Using Stated Preference and Prior Purchase Intention in the Estimation of Willingness to Pay A Premium For Genetically Modified Foods. *Agribusiness* 28(1): 103–117.

[19] Li, Q., Curtis, K. R., McCluskey, J. J. and Wahl, T. I. (2002) Consumer Attitudes Toward Genetically Modified Foods in Beijing, China. *Agbioforum* 5(4): 145–152.

[20] Yee, W., Traill, W. B., Lusk, J. L., Jaeger, S. R., House, L., Moore, M., Morrow, J. L. and Valli, C. (2008) Determinants of Consumers' Willingness to Accept GM Foods. *International Journal of Biotechnology* 10(2–3): 240–259.

[21] Huffman, W. E., Shogren, J. F., Rousu, M. and Tegene, A. (2001) The Value to Consumers of GM Food Labels in A Market With Asymmetric Information: Evidence From Experimental Auctions. *American Agricultural Economics Association*, August 5–8.

[22] Chern, W. S., Rickertsen, K., Tsuboi, N. and Fu, T. (2002) Consumer Acceptance and Willingness to Pay for Genetically Modified Vegetable Oil and Salmon: A Multiple-Country Assessment. *The Journal of Agrobiotechnology Management & Economics* 5(3): 105–112.

[23] Noussair, C., Robin, S. and Ruffieux, B. (2002) Do Consumers Not Care About Biotech Foods or Do They Just Not Read Labels? *Economics Letters* 75: 47–53.

[24] Noussair, C., Robin, S. and Ruffieux, B. (2004) Do Consumers Really Refuse to Buy Genetically Modified Foods? *The Economic Journal* 144(492): 102–120.

[25] Rousu, M., Huffman, W. E., Shogren, J. F. and Tegene, A. (2004) Are United States Consumers Tolerant of Genetically Modified Foods? *Review of Agricultural Economics* 26(1): 19–31.

[26] Colson, G. J. (2011) Improving Nutrient Content Through Genetic Modification: Evidence from Experimental Auctions on Consumer Acceptance and Willingness to Pay for Intragenic Foods. *American Journal of Agricultural Economics* 93(2): 654.

[27] Colson, G. J., Huffman, W. E. and Rousu, M. C. (2011) Improving the Nutrient Content of Food Through Genetic Modifications: Evidence from Experimental Auctions on Consumer Acceptance. *Journal of Agricultural and Resource Economics* 36(2): 343–364.

[28] Canadian Food Inspection Agency. (2017) Labelling of Genetically Engineered Foods in Canada Factsheet, http://www.inspection.gc.ca/food/labelling/foodlabelling -for-industry/method-of-production-claims/genetically -engineered-foods/eng/1333373177199/1333373638071.

[29] Anders, S. and Moser, A. (2010) Consumer Choice and Health: The Importance of Health Attributes for Retail Meat Demand in Canada. *Canadian Journal of Agricultural Economics* 58(2): 249–271.

[30] Malla, S., Hobbs, J. E. and Perger, O. (2007) Valuing Health Benefits of A Novel Functional Food. *Canadian Journal of Agricultural Economics* 55(1): 115–136.

[31] Cash, S. B., Goddard, E. W. and Lerohl, M. (2006) Canadian Health and Food: The Links Between Policy, Consumers, and Industry. *Canadian Journal of Agricultural Economics* 54(4): 605–629.

[32] Hirogaki, M. (2013) Estimating Consumers' Willingness to Pay for Health Food Claims: A Conjoint Analysis. *International Journal of Innovation, Management and Technology* 4(6): 541–546.

[33] Markosyan, A., McCluskey, J. and Wahl, T. (2009) Consumer Response to Information About A Functional Food Product: Apples Enriched with Antioxidants. *Canadian Journal of Agricultural Economics* 57(3): 325–341.

[34] La Barbera, F., Amato, M. and Sannino, G. (2016) Understanding Consumers' Intention and Behaviour Towards Functionalized Food: The Role of Knowledge And Food Technology Neophobia. *British Food Journal* 118(4): 885–895.

[35] Hellyer, N. E., Fraser, I. and Haddock-Fraser, J. (2012) Food Choice, Health Information and Functional Ingredients: An Experiment Auction Employing Bread. *Food Policy* 37(3): 232–245.

[36] Bitzios, M., Fraser, I. and Haddock-Fraser, J. (2011) Functional Ingredients and Food Choice: Results from A Dual-Mode Study Employing Means-End-Chain Analysis and Choice Experiment. *Food Policy* 36(5): 715–725.

[37] Roe, B., Levy, A. S. and Derby, B. M. (1999) The Impact of Health Claims On Consumer Search and Product Evaluation Outcomes: Results from FDA Experimental Data. *Journal of Public Policy & Marketing* 18(1): 89–105.

[38] Hailu, G., Boecker, A., Henson, S. and Cranfield, J. (2009) Consumer Valuation of Functional Foods and Nutraceuticals in Canada: A Conjoint Study Using Probiotics. *Appetite* 52(2): 257–265.

[39] Garretson, J. A. and Burton, S. (2000) Effects of Nutrition Facts Panel Values, Nutrition Claims, and Health Claims on Consumer Attitudes, Perceptions of Disease-Related Risks, and Trust. *Journal of Public Policy & Marketing* 19(2): 213–227.

[40] Wansink, B. (2003) How Do Front and Back Package Labels Influence Beliefs About Health Claims? *Journal of Consumer Affairs* 37: 305–316.

[41] Kozup, J. C., Creyer, E. H. and Burton, S. (2003) Making Healthful Food Choices: The Influence of Health Claims and Nutrition Information on Consumers' Evaluations of Packaged Food Products and Restaurant Menu Items. *Journal of Marketing* 67(2): 19–34.

[42] Zou, N. (2011) Canadian Consumers' Functional Food Choices: Labelling and Reference-Dependent Effects. Saskatoon. PhD thesis, University of Saskatchewan, Saskatoon, Saskatchewan.

[43] Botto, L. D., Moore, C. A., Khoury, M. J. and Erickson, D. (1999) Neural-Tube Defects. *New England Journal of Medicine* 341: 1509–1519.

[44] Statistics Canada. (2015) Population by Sex and Age Group, http://www.statcan.gc.ca/tables-tableaux /sumsom/l01/cst01/demo10a-eng.htm.

[45] Statistics Canada. (2015) Population by Year, by Province and Territory, http://www.statcan.gc.ca/tables-tableaux /sum-som/l01/cst01/demo02a-eng.htm.

[46] Statistics Canada. (2015) Median Total Income, by Family Type, by Province and Territory, http://www .statcan.gc.ca/tables-tableaux/sum-som/l01/cst01 /famil108a-eng.htm.

[47] Narver, J.C. and Slater, S.F. (1990) The Effect of a Market Orientation on Business Profitability. *Journal of Marketing* 54(4): 20–35.

[48] Wilson, G. A., Perepelkin, J., Zhang, D. D. and Vachon, M. A. (2014) Market Orientation, Alliance Orientation, And Business Performance in the Biotechnology Industry. *Journal of Commercial Biotechnology* 20(2): 32–40.

[49] Food and Agriculture Organization of the United Nations. (2009) How to Feed the World in 2050, http:// www.fao.org/fileadmin/templates/wsfs/docs/expert _paper/How_to_Feed_the_World_in_2050.pdf.

Reading Questions

1. According to the authors of the study, what are the traditional benefits of GM foods for producers? What are likely to be some of the benefits of second-generation GM foods (GM2) for consumers?

2. What reasoning do the study's authors provide for their selection of foods used as part of their study?

3. Briefly explain each of the researchers' three hypothesis. Then indicate whether the study's results confirm or challenge each of the hypotheses.

Rhetoric Questions

4. Look closely at the Methods and Results sections of the study and compare the language of the two sections in terms of the authors' use of active and passive voice. What do you find, and what may account for any differences you find?

5. Compare the information the researchers convey to their readers in the Results and Discussion sections of their report. What does the Discussion section add to the report?

Response Questions

6. The researchers found a significant difference in terms of how gender affected one of their study's result. Specifically, they concluded that men were more willing to purchase GM2 products. What do you believe could account for this gender difference?

7. Based on the study's findings, what advice would you give to a marketing firm preparing an advertisement campaign for a GM2 food product? What kinds of information would you advise the firm to include for consumers as part of its advertisements?

Writing Project   ## Persuasive Narrative

Some of the writers whose work for popular audiences is presented in this chapter offer compelling stories about their own or others' experiences as support for their larger claims about food, cultural identity, and class, among other concerns. Gustavo Arellano, in "Taco USA: How Mexican Food Became More American Than Apple Pie," for instance, explains how he came to experience an "epiphany about Mexican food in the United States." Nneka Okana, in "Sunday Dinners Are Sacred for African Americans," places her own experience of Sunday dinners within the larger context of Black history. In both cases, these personal narratives serve powerful persuasive purposes.

For this project, we invite you to craft a personal narrative that explores your own experience(s) with food in order to make a larger point or to support a claim about food, its sustainability, and/or its connections to larger concerns for American culture or society.

Consider first what you want to suggest to your readers, as you'll want to craft your text with that persuasive intent in mind: What is the overall point you want to emphasize in your narrative? For example, you might choose to make a case that we should eat organically as much as possible, or you might argue that we need to do more to support community gardens. You'll also need to decide if you want to state your position or argument outright or, instead, merely imply the position you're taking. Make the decision that best suits your needs.

Because your evidence for this argument is your personal experience(s), you'll want to consider carefully the structure of your narrative: Will you focus on a single event or experience? Will you focus on your engagement with food more broadly over a span of years? Regardless of the final organizational scheme you employ, remember that your experiences are meant to serve as evidence to support a claim.

Crime and Punishment: Investigating American Justice

This chapter includes a number of popular and academic texts that examine crime and justice in American society. The opening selections present perspectives from a number of popular sources. The first article by Inimai Chettiar examines trends in America's high incarceration rates to demonstrate how they have reached the point at which a continued rise in incarceration rates may be more harmful than helpful. Nicki Lisa Cole's essay, "Understanding the School-to-Prison Pipeline," contends that current disciplinary practices in schools push kids out of school and into the prison system. Finally, Ta-Nehisi Coates explores how the methods used by American police officers impact communities. These readings might spark your imagination as you consider questions about crime and justice in American society:

- Is our criminal justice system color-blind? Does it treat people equitably, regardless of race?

- What factors contribute to America's extraordinarily high incarceration rates, and what can be done about them?

- Does punishment in America need to change? If so, in what ways?

The academic case study in this chapter introduces a range of perspectives on the specific topic of capital punishment. Beyond the typical lines of inquiry about the death penalty in America (e.g., Does it act as a deterrent? Can it be fairly applied? Does it constitute "cruel or unusual" punishment?), the readings explore capital punishment from a number of perspectives:

- **Humanities** What does the final meal an inmate requests reveal about who he is and the relationship between different parties involved in carrying out the death penalty?

- **Social Sciences** How do movies affect viewers' moods about and attitudes toward the death penalty?

- **Natural Sciences**   Does the current execution drug cocktail work as intended? Is it constitutional?
- **Applied Fields**   How do perceptions of race and beliefs about the causes of human behavior affect whether or not people support the death penalty?

The Many Causes of America's Decline in Crime: A New Report Finds That Locking Up More Offenders Isn't Making People Any Safer—and May Even Be Counterproductive

INIMAI CHETTIAR

Inimai Chettiar is the federal legislative and policy director of the Justice Action Network in Washington, D.C. At the time she wrote this piece, she was the director of the Justice Program at the New York University School of Law's Brennan Center for Justice. She is coeditor of the book *Ending Mass Incarceration: Ideas from Today's Leaders* (2019). Chettiar's work on topics related to mass incarceration and criminal justice reform appears frequently in popular publications like the *New York Times, Washington Post, Bloomberg*, and the *Wall Street Journal*. In the article below, published in the *Atlantic* in February 2015, Chettiar presents research to suggest that increasing rates of incarceration do not necessarily make Americans safer.

The dramatic rise of incarceration and the precipitous fall in crime have shaped the landscape of American criminal justice over the last two decades. Both have been unprecedented. Many believe that the explosion in incarceration created the crime drop. In fact, the enormous growth in imprisonment only had a limited impact. And, for the past thirteen years, it has passed the point of diminishing returns, making no effective difference. We now know that we can reduce our prison populations and simultaneously reduce crime.

This has profound implications for criminal justice policy: We lock up millions of people in an effort to fight crime. But this is not working.

The link between rising incarceration and falling crime seems logical. Draconian penalties and a startling expansion in prison capacity were advertised as measures that would bring down crime. That's what happened, right?

Not so fast. There is wide agreement that we do not yet fully know what caused crime to drop.

Theories abound, from an aging population to growing police forces to reducing lead in the air. A jumble of data and theories makes it hard to sort out this big, if happy, mystery. And it has been especially difficult to pin down the role of growing incarceration.

So incarceration skyrocketed and crime was in free 5 fall. But conflating simple correlation with causation in this case is a costly mistake. A report from the Brennan Center for Justice at NYU School of Law, called *What Caused the Crime Decline?*, finds that increasing incarceration is not the answer. As Nobel laureate economist Joseph Stiglitz writes in the foreword, "This prodigious rate of incarceration is not only inhumane, it is economic folly."

Our team of economic and criminal justice researchers spent the last twenty months testing fourteen popular theories for the crime decline. We delved deep into over thirty years of data collected from all fifty states and the fifty largest cities. The results are sharply etched: We do not know with precision what

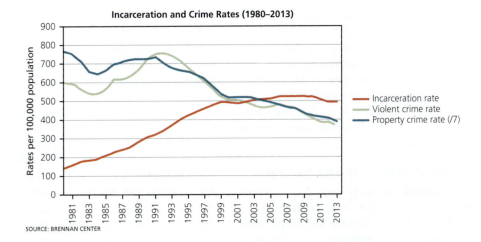

Incarceration and Crime Rates (1980–2013)

SOURCE: BRENNAN CENTER

caused the crime decline, but the growth in incarceration played only a minor role, and now has a negligible impact.

The drop in crime stands as one of the more fascinating and remarkable social phenomena of our time. For decades, crime soared. Cities were viewed as unlivable. Politicians competed to run the most lurid campaign ads and sponsor the most punitive laws. Racially tinged "wedge issues" marked American politics from Richard Nixon's "law and order" campaign of 1968 to the "Willie Horton" ads credited with helping George H. W. Bush win the 1988 election.

But over the past twenty-five years, the tide of crime and violence seemed to simply recede. Crime is about half of what it was at its peak in 1991. Violent crime plummeted 51 percent. Property crime fell 43 percent. Homicides are down 54 percent. In 1985, there were 1,384 murders in New York City. Last year there were 333. The country is an undeniably safer place. Growing urban populations are one positive consequence.

During that same period, we saw the birth of mass incarceration in the United States. Since 1990, incarceration nearly doubled, adding 1.1 million people behind bars. Today, our nation has 5 percent of the world's population and 25 percent of the world's prison population. The United States is the world's most prodigious incarcerator.

THE ROLE OF INCARCERATION

What do the numbers say? Did this explosion in 10 incarceration cause the crime decline?

It turns out that increased incarceration had a much more limited effect on crime than popularly thought. We find that this growth in incarceration was responsible for approximately 5 percent of the drop in crime in the 1990s. (This could vary from 0 to 10 percent.) Since then, however, increases in incarceration have had essentially *zero* effect on crime. The positive returns are gone. That means the colossal number of Americans cycling in and out of prisons and jails over the last thirteen years was not responsible for any meaningful fraction of the drop in crime.

The figure below shows our main result: increased incarceration's effectiveness since 1980. This is measured as the change in the crime rate expected to result from a 1 percent increase in imprisonment—what economists call an "elasticity." During the 1980s and 1990s, as incarceration climbed, its effectiveness waned. Its effectiveness currently dwells in the basement. Today, a 1 percent increase in incarceration would lead to a microscopic 0.02 percent decline in crime. This is statistically indistinguishable from having no effect at all.

Increased incarceration accounted for about 6 percent of the property crime decline in the 1990s, and 1 percent of that drop in the 2000s. The growth of incarceration had no observable effect on violent crime in the 1990s or 2000s. This last finding may initially seem surprising. But given that we are sending more and more low-level and non-violent offenders to prison (who may never have been prone to violent crime), the finding makes sense. Sending a non-violent offender to prison will not necessarily have an effect on *violent* crime.

How Rising Incarceration's Effect on Crime Waned

There is no question that some level of incarceration had some positive impact on bringing down crime. There are many habitual offenders and people committing serious, violent crimes who may need to be kept out of society. Criminologists call this the "incapacitation" effect: Removing someone from society prevents them from committing crimes.

But after a certain point, that positive impact ceases. The new people filling prisons do so without bringing down crime much. In other words, *rising* incarceration rates produce less of an effect on crime reduction. This is what economists call "diminishing returns." It turns out that the criminal justice system offers a near perfect picture of this phenomenon.

As incarceration doubled from 1990 to today, it became less effective. At its relatively low levels twenty years ago, incarceration may indeed have had some effect on crime. The positive returns may not have yet diminished.

Incarceration rates have now risen so high that further increases in incarceration are ineffective. Due to the war on drugs and the influx of harsher sentencing laws in the 1980s and 1990s, an increasing proportion of the 1.1 million prisoners added since 1990 were imprisoned for low-level or non-violent crimes. Today, almost half of state prisoners are convicted of non-violent crimes. More than half of federal prisoners are serving time for drug offenses. The system is no longer prioritizing arresting, prosecuting, and incarcerating the most dangerous or habitual offenders. In this case, each additional prisoner will, on average, yield less in terms of crime reduction. We have incarcerated those we should not have. This is where the "more incarceration equals less crime" theory busts.

Even those who have argued for the effectiveness of incarceration acknowledge this possibility. University of Chicago economist and *Freakonomics* co-author Steven Levitt found in his 2004 study that incarceration was responsible for over a third of the 1990s

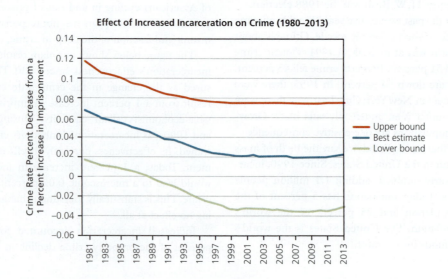

Effect of Increased Incarceration on Crime (1980–2013)

drop in violent crime. He noted that, "Given the wide divergence in the frequency and severity of offending across criminals, sharply declining marginal benefits of incarceration are a possibility," which, if present, could have affected his findings.

Decrease in Incarceration and Crime

Can the United States safely reduce its incarcerated population? After all, it would be too bad if reducing incarceration yielded a spike in crime.

Fortunately, there is a real-time experiment 20 underway. For many reasons, including straitened budgets and a desire to diminish prison populations, many states have started to cut back on imprisonment. What happened? Interestingly, and encouragingly, crime did not explode. In fact, it dropped. In the last decade, fourteen states saw declines in both incarceration and crime. New York reduced imprisonment by 26 percent, while seeing a 28 percent reduction in crime. Imprisonment and crime both decreased by more than 15 percent in California, Maryland, New Jersey, New York, and Texas. Eight states—Connecticut, Delaware, Massachusetts, Michigan, Nevada, North Carolina, South Carolina, and Utah—lowered their imprisonment rates by 2 to 15 percent while seeing more than a 15 percent decrease in crime.

This is all very significant. Incarceration is not just any government policy. Mass incarceration comes at an incredible cost. "A year in prison can cost more than a year at Harvard," Stiglitz points out. Taxpayers spend $260 billion a year on criminal justice. And there will continue to be less and less to show for it, as more people are incarcerated.

There are significant human costs as well—to individuals, families, communities, and the country. Spending a dollar on prisons is not the same as spending it on public television or the military. Prisons result in an enormous waste of human capital. Instead of so many low-level offenders languishing behind bars, they could be earning wages and contributing to the economy. Incarceration is so concentrated in certain communities that it has disrupted the gender balance and marriage rates.

The costs are intergenerational. There are 2.7 million minor children with a parent behind bars. More than one in nine black children have a parent incarcerated.

Research also shows that incarceration can actually *increase* future crime. Criminologists call this the "criminogenic effect" of prison. It is particularly powerful on low-level offenders. Once individuals enter prison, they are surrounded by other prisoners who have often committed more serious and violent offenses. Prison conditions also breed violent and antisocial behavior. Former prisoners often have trouble finding employment and reintegrating into society due to legal barriers, social stigma, and psychological scarring from prison. Approximately 600,000 prisoners reenter society each year. Those who can find employment earn 40 percent less than their peers, and 60 percent face long-term unemployment. Researchers estimate that the country's poverty rate would have been more than 20 percent lower between 1980 and 2004 without mass incarceration.

This lack of stability increases the odds that former prisoners will commit new crimes. The more people we put into prison who do not need to be there, the more this criminogenic effect increases. That is another plausible explanation for why our massive levels of incarceration are resulting in less crime control.

Our findings do not exist in a vacuum. A body of 25 empirical research is slowly coalescing around the ineffectiveness of increased incarceration. Last year, the Hamilton Project issued a report calling incarceration a "classic case of diminishing returns," based on findings from California and Italy. The National Research Council issued a hefty report last year, finding that crime was not the cause of mass incarceration. And, based on a summary of past research, the authors concluded that "the magnitude of the crime reduction [due to increased incarceration] remains highly uncertain and the evidence suggests it was unlikely to have been large."

We go a few steps further to fully reveal the complex relationship between crime and incarceration.

By using thirteen years of more recent data, gathered in the modern era of heavily elevated incarceration, combined with an empirical model that accounts for diminishing returns and controls for other variables, we are able to quantify the sharply declining benefits of overusing prison.

Other Factors Reducing Crime

But if it was not incarceration, then what did cause the crime decline?

There is no shortage of candidates. Every year, it seems, a new study advances a novel explanation. Levitt attributes about half the crime drop to the legalization of abortion. Amherst economist Jessica Reyes attributes about half the violent crime drop to the unleading of gasoline after the Clean Air Act. Berkeley law professor Franklin Zimring credits the police as the central cause. All three theories likely played some role.

Instead of a single, dominant cause, our research points to a vast web of factors, often complex, often interacting, and some unexpected. Of the theories we examined, we found the following factors had some effect on bringing down crime: a growth in income (5 to 10 percent), changes in alcohol consumption (5 to 10 percent), the aging population (0 to 5 percent),

and decreased unemployment (0 to 3 percent). Policing also played a role, with increased numbers of police in the 1990s reducing crime (0 to 10 percent) and the introduction of CompStat* having an even larger effect (5 to 15 percent).

But none is solely, or even largely, responsible for 30 the crime drop. Unfortunately, we could not fully test a few theories, as the data did not exist at the detailed level we needed for our analysis. For those, we analyzed past research, finding that inflation and consumer confidence (individuals' belief about the strength of the economy) probably had some effect on crime. The legalization of abortion and unleading of gasoline may also have played some role.

In aggregate, the fourteen factors we identified can explain some of the drop in crime in the 1990s. But even adding all of them together fails to explain the majority of the decrease.

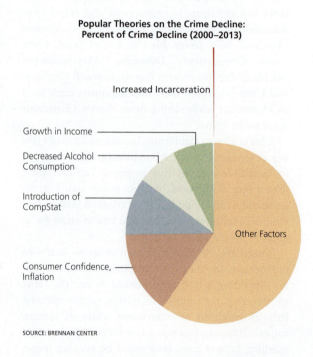

Popular Theories on the Crime Decline: Percent of Crime Decline (2000–2013)

Increased Incarceration

Growth in Income

Decreased Alcohol Consumption

Introduction of CompStat

Consumer Confidence, Inflation

Other Factors

SOURCE: BRENNAN CENTER

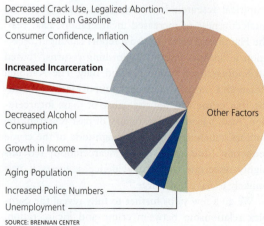

Popular Theories on the Crime Decline: Percent of Crime Decline (1990–1999)

Decreased Crack Use, Legalized Abortion, Decreased Lead in Gasoline

Consumer Confidence, Inflation

Increased Incarceration

Decreased Alcohol Consumption

Growth in Income

Aging Population

Increased Police Numbers

Unemployment

Other Factors

SOURCE: BRENNAN CENTER

CompStat: a crime-management system that identifies increases in crimes and assists in targeting resources to address those increases.

A Sensible Way Forward

No one factor brought down crime. Today, incarceration has become the default option in the fight against crime. But more incarceration is not a silver bullet. It has, in fact, ceased to be effective in reducing crime—and the country is slowly awakening to that reality. Incarceration can be reduced while crime continues to decline. The research shows this and many states are watching it unfold.

Where do we go from here? As President Obama said it in his State of the Union last month, "Surely we can agree that it's a good thing that for the first time in 40 years, crime and incarceration have come down together, and use that as a starting point for Democrats and Republicans, community leaders and law enforcement, to reform America's criminal justice system so that it protects and serves all of us."

And indeed, reforming our criminal justice system is emerging as a bipartisan cause. Everyone from Jeb Bush to Hillary Clinton to the Koch Brothers to George Soros has made similar calls.

We should listen to them. There are bold, practical policy solutions starting to gain bipartisan support. Incarceration can be removed as a punishment for many non-violent, non-serious crimes. Violations of technical conditions of parole and probation should not lead to a return trip to prison. Sentence maximum and minimum lengths can be downscaled across the board. There is little reason to jail low-risk defendants who are simply waiting for their trials to begin. And, government funding streams can change to reward reducing incarceration.

Crime is expensive. We do well to fight it. But 35 increasing incarceration is definitely not the answer.

Reading Questions

1. According to Chettiar, what are three possible theories that some use to account for the declining rates of crime in America over the past two decades?

2. What has happened to crime rates in states like New York, Texas, Massachusetts, and North Carolina, where imprisonment rates have been lowered in the past decade, according to Chettiar?

Rhetoric Questions

3. Chettiar references economic concepts, like "elasticity" and "diminishing returns," on a number of occasions. What is the effect of Chettiar couching her arguments in the language of economics on you as a reader? What does her use of those terms tell you about her perceived audience?

4. Chettiar's article includes four visual representations of data (charts and graphs). Look closely at each graph or chart and consider how the visual representation of data affects the effectiveness of the argument. Select one and describe your response.

Response Question

5. The final paragraph of Chettiar's argument is made up of three short sentences. Imagine that you've been tasked with writing a new conclusion for Chettiar's article that is made up of five sentences and maintains the short-sentence style. Write a new conclusion for Chettiar's article.

Understanding the School-to-Prison Pipeline

NICKI LISA COLE

Nicki Lisa Cole is a sociologist and freelance writer who researches and writes about issues related to social justice. Her article that appears below was originally published in the summer of 2020, in the midst of the COVID-19 pandemic and during a time of racial justice protests that followed the death of George Floyd. The piece was published on the website ThoughtCo.com, which describes itself as a reference website that publishes "expert-created education content."

The school-to-prison pipeline is a process through which students are pushed out of schools and into prisons. In other words, it is a process of criminalizing youth that is carried out by disciplinary policies and practices within schools that put students into contact with law enforcement. Once they are put into contact with law enforcement for disciplinary reasons, many are then pushed out of the educational environment and into the juvenile and criminal justice systems.

The key policies and practices that created and now maintain the school-to-prison pipeline include zero tolerance policies that mandate harsh punishments for both minor and major infractions, exclusion of students from schools through punitive suspensions and expulsions, and the presence of police on campus as School Resource Officers (SROs).

The school-to-prison pipeline is supported by budgetary decisions made by the U.S. government. From 1987–2007, funding for incarceration more than doubled while funding for higher education was raised by just 21 percent, according to PBS. In addition, evidence shows that the school-to-prison pipeline primarily captures and affects Black students, which mirrors the over-representation of this group in America's prisons and jails.

HOW IT WORKS

The two key forces that produced and now maintain the school-to-prison pipeline are the use of zero tolerance policies that mandate exclusionary punishments and the presence of SROs on campuses. These policies and practices became common following a deadly spate of school shootings across the U.S. in the 1990s. Lawmakers and educators believed they would help to ensure safety on school campuses.

Having a zero tolerance policy means that a school 5 has zero tolerance for any kind of misbehavior or violation of school rules, no matter how minor, unintentional, or subjectively defined it may be. In a school with a zero tolerance policy, suspensions and expulsions are normal and common ways of dealing with student misbehavior.

IMPACT OF ZERO TOLERANCE POLICIES

Research shows that the implementation of zero tolerance policies has led to significant increases in suspensions and expulsions. Citing a study by Michie, education scholar Henry Giroux observed that, over a four-year period, suspensions increased by 51 percent and expulsions by nearly 32 times after zero tolerance policies were implemented in Chicago schools. They jumped from just 21 expulsions in the 1994–95 school year to 668 in 1997–98. Similarly, Giroux cites a report from the *Denver Rocky Mountain News* that found that expulsions increased by more than 300 percent in the city's public schools between 1993 and 1997.

Once suspended or expelled, data show that students are less likely to complete high school, more than twice as likely to be arrested while on forced leave from school, and more likely to be in contact with the juvenile justice system during the year that follows the leave. In fact, sociologist David Ramey found, in a nationally representative study, that experiencing school punishment before the age of 15 is associated with contact with the criminal justice system for boys. Other research shows that students who do not complete high school are more likely to be incarcerated.

HOW SROs FACILITATE THE PIPELINE

In addition to adopting harsh zero tolerance policies, most schools across the country now have police present on campus on a daily basis and most states require educators to report student misbehavior to law enforcement. The presence of SROs on campus means that students have contact with law enforcement from a young age. Though their intended purpose is to protect students and ensure safety on school campuses, in many instances, the police handling of disciplinary issues escalates minor, non-violent infractions into violent, criminal incidents that have negative impacts on students.

By studying the distribution of federal funding for SROs and rates of school-related arrests, criminologist Emily G. Owens found that the presence of SROs on campus causes law enforcement agencies to learn of more crimes and increases the likelihood of arrest for those crimes among children under the age of 15.

Christopher A. Mallett, a legal scholar and expert [10] on the school-to-prison pipeline, reviewed evidence of the pipeline's existence and concluded that "the increased use of zero tolerance policies and police . . . in the schools has exponentially increased arrests and referrals to the juvenile courts." Once they have made contact with the criminal justice system, data show that students are unlikely to graduate high school.

Overall, what over a decade of empirical research on this topic proves is that zero tolerance policies, punitive disciplinary measures like suspensions and expulsions, and the presence of SROs on campus have led to more and more students being pushed out of schools and into the juvenile and criminal justice systems. In short, these policies and practices created the school-to-prison pipeline and sustain it today.

But why exactly do these policies and practices make students more likely to commit crimes and end up in prison? Sociological theories and research help answer this question.

INSTITUTIONS AND AUTHORITY FIGURES CRIMINALIZE STUDENTS

One key sociological theory of deviance, known as labeling theory, contends that people come to identify and behave in ways that reflect how others label them. Applying this theory to the school-to-prison pipeline suggests that being labeled as a "bad" kid by school authorities and/or SROs, and being treated in a way that reflects that label (punitively), ultimately leads kids to internalize the label and behave in ways that make it real through action. In other words, it is a self-fulfilling prophecy.

Sociologist Victor Rios found just that in his studies of the effects of policing on the lives of Black and Latino boys in the San Francisco Bay Area. In his first book, *Punished: Policing the Lives of Black and Latino Boys*, Rios revealed through in-depth interviews and ethnographic observation how increased surveillance and attempts at controlling "at-risk" or deviant youth ultimately foster the very criminal behavior they are intended to prevent. In a social context in which social institutions label deviant youth as bad or criminal, and in doing so, strip them of dignity, fail to acknowledge their struggles, and do not treat them with respect, rebellion and criminality are acts of resistance. According to Rios, then, it is social institutions and their authorities that do the work of criminalizing youth.

EXCLUSION FROM SCHOOL, SOCIALIZATION INTO CRIME

The sociological concept of socialization also helps [15] shed light on why the school-to-prison pipeline exists. After family, school is the second most important and formative site of socialization for children and adolescents where they learn social norms for behavior and interaction and receive moral guidance from authority figures. Removing students from schools as a form of discipline takes them out of this formative environment and important process, and it removes them from the safety and structure that the school provides. Many students who express behavioral issues at school are acting out in response to stressful or dangerous conditions in their homes or neighborhoods, so removing them from school and returning them to a problematic or unsupervised home environment hurts rather than helps their development.

While removed from school during a suspension or expulsion, youth are more likely to spend time with others removed for similar reasons, and with those who are already engaged in criminal activity. Rather than being socialized by education-focused peers and educators, students who have been suspended or expelled will be socialized more by peers in similar situations. Because of these factors, the punishment of removal from school creates the conditions for the development of criminal behavior.

HARSH PUNISHMENT

Further, treating students as criminals when they have done nothing more than act out in minor, non-violent ways weakens the authority of educators, police, and other members of the juvenile and criminal justice sectors. The punishment does not fit the crime and so it suggests that those in positions of authority are not trustworthy, fair, and are even immoral. Seeking to do the opposite, authority figures who behave this way can actually teach students that they and their authority are not to be respected or trusted, which fosters conflict between them and students. This conflict then often leads to further exclusionary and damaging punishment experienced by students.

THE STIGMA OF EXCLUSION

Finally, once excluded from school and labeled bad or criminal, students often find themselves stigmatized by their teachers, parents, friends, parents of friends, and other community members. They experience confusion, stress, depression, and anger as a result of being excluded from school and from being treated harshly and unfairly by those in charge. This makes it difficult to stay focused on school and hinders motivation to study and desire to return to school and to succeed academically.

Cumulatively, these social forces work to discourage academic studies, hinder academic achievement and even completion of high school, and push negatively labeled youth onto criminal paths and into the criminal justice system.

BLACK AND AMERICAN INDIAN STUDENTS FACE HARSHER PUNISHMENTS AND HIGHER RATES OF SUSPENSION AND EXPULSION

While Black people are just 13 percent of the total U.S. 20 population, they comprise the greatest percentage of people in prisons and jails—40 percent. Latinos are also over-represented in prisons and jails, but by far less. While they comprise 16 percent of the U.S. population they represent 19 percent of those in prisons and jails. In contrast, white people make up just 39 percent of the incarcerated population, despite the fact that they are the majority race in the U.S., comprising 64 percent of the national population.

Data from across the U.S. that illustrate punishment and school-related arrests show that the racial disparity in incarceration begins with the school-to-prison pipeline. Research shows that both schools with large Black populations and underfunded schools, many of which are majority-minority schools, are more likely to employ zero tolerance policies. Nationwide, Black and American Indian students face far greater rates of suspension and expulsion than do white students. In addition, data compiled by the National Center for Education Statistics show that while the percentage of white students suspended fell from 1999 to 2007, the percentage of Black and Hispanic students suspended rose.

A variety of studies and metrics show that Black and American Indian students are punished more frequently and more harshly for the same, mostly minor, offenses than are white students. Legal and educational scholar Daniel J. Losen points out that, though there is no evidence that these students misbehave more frequently or more severely than do white students, research from across the country shows that teachers and administrators punish them more—especially Black students. Losen cites one study that found that the disparity is greatest among non-serious offenses like cell phone use, violations of dress code, or subjectively defined offenses like being disruptive or displaying affection. Black first-time offenders in these categories are suspended at rates that are double or more than those for white first-time offenders.

According to the U.S. Department of Education's Office for Civil Rights, about 5 percent of white students have been suspended during their schooling experience, compared with 16 percent of Black students. This means Black students are more than three times as likely to be suspended than their white peers. Though they comprise just 16 percent of the total enrollment of public school students, Black students comprise 32 percent of in-school suspensions and 33 percent of out-of-school suspensions. Troublingly, this disparity begins as early as preschool. Nearly half of all preschool students suspended are Black, though they represent just 18 percent of total preschool enrollment. American Indians also face inflated suspension rates. They represent 2 percent of out-of-school suspensions, which is 4 times greater than the percentage of total enrolled students that they comprise.

Black students are also far more likely to experience multiple suspensions. Though they are just 16 percent of the public school enrollment, they are a full 42 percent of those suspended multiple times. This means that their presence in the population of students with multiple suspensions is more than 2.6 times greater than their presence in the total population of students. Meanwhile, white students are under-represented among those with multiple suspensions, at just 31 percent. These disparate rates play out not only within schools but also across districts on the basis of race. Data shows that in the Midlands area of South Carolina, suspension figures in a mostly-Black school district are double what they are in a mostly-white one.

There is also evidence that shows that the overly 25 harsh punishment of Black students is concentrated in the American south, where the legacy of human enslavement and Jim Crow exclusionary policies

and violence against Black people manifest in everyday life. Of the 1.2 million Black students who were suspended nationwide during the 2011–2012 school year, more than half were located in 13 southern states. At the same time, half of all Black students expelled were from these states. In many of the school districts located in these states, Black students comprised 100 percent of students suspended or expelled in a given school year.

Among this population, students with disabilities are even more likely to experience exclusionary discipline. With the exception of Asian and Latino students, research shows that "more than one out of four boys of color with disabilities . . . and nearly one in five girls of color with disabilities receives an out-of-school suspension." Meanwhile, research shows that white students who express behavioral issues in school are more likely to be treated with medicine, which reduces their chances of ending up in jail or prison after acting out in school.

BLACK STUDENTS FACE HIGHER RATES OF SCHOOL-RELATED ARRESTS AND REMOVAL FROM SCHOOL SYSTEM

Given that there is a connection between the experience of suspensions and engagement with the criminal justice system, and given that racial bias within education and among police is well-documented, it is no surprise that Black and Latino students comprise 70 percent of those who face referral to law enforcement or school-related arrests.

Once they are in contact with the criminal justice system, as the statistics on the school-to-prison pipeline cited above demonstrate, students are far less likely to complete high school. Those that do may do so in "alternative schools" for students labeled as "juvenile delinquents," many of which are unaccredited and offer lower quality education than they would receive in public schools. Others who are placed in juvenile detention centers or prison may receive no educational resources at all.

The racism embedded in the school-to-prison pipeline is a significant factor in producing the reality that Black and Latino students are far less likely than their white peers to complete high school and that Black, Latino, and American Indian people are much more likely than white people to end up in jail or prison.

What all of these data show us is that not only is the school-to-prison pipeline very real, but also, it is fueled by racial bias and produces racist outcomes that cause great harm to the lives, families, and communities of people of color across the United States.

Reading Questions

1. In the introduction, Cole names several factors that contribute to the school-to-prison pipeline. Name two of those factors and describe how Cole explains that those factors contribute to the trend.

2. In Cole's opening sentence, she writes, "The school-to-prison pipeline is a process through which students are pushed out of schools and into prisons" (par. 1). The sentence is written in the passive voice, meaning that the person or people doing the pushing are not identified in the sentence. Based on your reading of the article, who is Cole suggesting is doing the pushing?

Rhetoric Questions

3. Based on your reading of Cole's article, what would you identify as her purpose for writing? Point to a specific place in the article that helped you identify her purpose.

4. Cole shares several statistics in her article. What role do those numbers play in the article, and why do you think she includes them?

Response Questions

5. Which, if any, of the statistics that Cole shared surprised you the most? Why?

6. If Cole were to expand upon this article to elaborate on actions that should be taken to disrupt the school-to-prison pipeline, what do you anticipate she would emphasize? Why?

The Paranoid Style of American Policing

TA-NEHISI COATES

Ta-Nehisi Coates is a former national correspondent at the *Atlantic*, and his 2015 book, *Between the World and Me*, won the National Book Award for Nonfiction. He is well known for writing about cultural and political issues related to race, and he was a recipient of the MacArthur Foundation "Genius Grant." In the following article that appeared in the *Atlantic* in December 2015, Coates weaves together stories to develop the argument that the police should not be allowed to kill citizens without serious consequences and that to do otherwise threatens American democracy.

When I was around 10 years old, my father confronted a young man who was said to be "crazy." The young man was always too quick to want to fight. A foul in a game of 21 was an insult to his honor. A cross word was cause for a duel, and you never knew what that cross word might be. One day, the young man got into it with one of my older brother's friends. The young man pulled a metal stake out of the ground (there was some work being done nearby) and began swinging it wildly in a threatening manner. My father, my mother, or my older brother—I don't recall which—told the other boy to go inside of our house. My dad then came outside. I don't really remember what my father said to the young man. Perhaps he said something like "Go home," or maybe something like, "Son, it's over." I don't really recall. But what I do recall is that my dad did not shoot and kill the young man.

That wasn't the first time I'd seen my father confront the violence of young people without resorting to killing them. This was not remarkable. When you live in communities like ours—or perhaps any community—mediating violence between young people is part of being an adult. Sometimes the young people are involved in scary behavior—like threatening people with metal objects. And yet the notion that it is permissible, wise, moral, or advisable to kill such a person as a method of de-escalation, to kill because one was afraid, did not really exist among parents in my community.

The same could not be said for those who came from outside of the community.

This weekend, after a Chicago police officer killed her 19-year-old son Quintonio LeGrier, Janet Cooksey struggled to understand the mentality of the people she pays to keep her community safe:

> "What happened to Tasers? Seven times my son was shot," Cooksey said.
>
> "The police are supposed to serve and protect us and yet they take the lives," Cooksey said.
>
> "Where do we get our help?" she asked.

LeGrier had struggled with mental illness. When 5 LeGrier attempted to break down his father's door, his father called the police, who apparently arrived to find the 19-year-old wielding a bat. Interpreting this as a lethal threat, one of the officers shot and killed LeGrier and somehow managed to shoot and kill one of his neighbors, Bettie Jones. Cooksey did not merely have a problem with how the police acted, but with the fact that the police were even called in the first place. "He should have called me," Cooksey said of LeGrier's father.

Instead, the father called the Chicago Police Department. Likely he called them because he invested them with some measure of legitimacy. This is understandable. In America, police officers are agents of the state and thus bound by the social contract in a way that criminals, and even random citizens, are not. Criminals and random citizens are not paid to protect other citizens. Police officers are. By that logic, one might surmise that the police would be better able to mediate conflicts than community members. In Chicago, this appears, very often, not to be the case.

It will not do to note that 99 percent of the time the police mediate conflicts without killing people anymore than it will do for a restaurant to note that 99 percent of the time rats don't run through the dining room. Nor will it do to point out that most black citizens are killed by other black citizens, not police officers, anymore than it will do to point out that most American citizens are killed by other American citizens, not terrorists. If officers cannot be expected to act any better than ordinary citizens, why call them in the first place? Why invest them with any more power?

Legitimacy is what is ultimately at stake here. When Cooksey says that her son's father should not have called the police, when she says that they "are supposed to serve and protect us and yet they take the lives," she is saying that police in Chicago are police in name only. This opinion is widely shared. Asked about the possibility of an investigation, Melvin Jones, the brother of Bettie Jones, could muster no confidence. "I already know how that will turn out," he scoffed. "We all know how that will turn out."

Indeed, we probably do. Two days after Jones and LeGrier were killed, a district attorney in Ohio declined to prosecute the two officers who drove up, and within two seconds of arriving, killed the 12-year-old Tamir Rice. No one should be surprised by this. In America, we have decided that it is permissible, that it is wise, that it is moral for the police to de-escalate through killing. A standard which would not have held for my father in West Baltimore, which did not hold for me in Harlem, is reserved for those who have the maximum power—the right to kill on behalf of the state. When police can not adhere to the standards of the neighborhood, of citizens, or of parents, what are they beyond a bigger gun and a sharper sword? By what right do they enforce their will, save force itself?

When policing is delegitimized, when it becomes 10 an occupying force, the community suffers. The neighbor-on-neighbor violence in Chicago, and in black communities around the country, is not an optical illusion. Policing is (one) part of the solution to that violence. But if citizens don't trust officers, then policing can't actually work. And in Chicago, it is very hard to muster reasons for trust.

When Bettie Jones's brother displays zero confidence in an investigation into the killing of his sister, he is not being cynical. He is shrewdly observing a government that executed a young man and sought to hide that fact from citizens. He is intelligently assessing a local government which, for two decades, ran a torture ring. What we have made of our police departments [in] America, what we have ordered them to do, is a direct challenge to any usable definition of democracy. A state that allows its agents to kill, to beat, to tase, without any real sanction, has ceased to govern and has commenced to simply rule.

Reading Questions

1. In the opening story that Coates tells, what does he highlight about how his father responds to the young man who is threatening violence, and why does he indicate that it was not remarkable?

2. Coates clearly indicates that he does not see engaging in violence as part of the job of policing. Based on your reading of the article, what *does* he indicate as the role of the police?

Rhetoric Questions

3. Coates uses the word *paranoid* in the title of his essay, but interestingly, he does not use the word in the article at all. Why do you think he chose that word for his title? What does it signify, and what effect does it have to refrain from using the word in the essay itself?

4. Coates relies primarily on storytelling to build his argument. How would you classify the kind of rhetorical appeal that Coates develops in the article? What would the effect be if Coates relied on a different appeal to build the argument?

Response Questions

5. Recall a story that you heard in the news recently about a confrontation between the police and a private citizen. How did you respond when you read the article? What emotions did you feel, and why?

6. In the opening story of the article, Coates implies an analogy between the role of his father and the role of the police. How do you respond to that comparison? Do you see their roles as similar? Different? Why?

Academic Case Study: Capital Punishment

Final Meals: The Theatre of Capital Punishment

CHRISTOPHER COLLINS

Christopher Collins is an assistant professor of communication at Missouri State University. When he wrote this 2009 article, he was a doctoral candidate at Southern Illinois University. He teaches classes in communication theory, performance studies, and intercultural communication.

On August 5, 1981, Philip Workman shot and killed Lt. Ronald Oliver during a botched armed robbery. Oliver was shot through his torso and died behind a Wendy's restaurant in Memphis, Tennessee. As a result, Workman spent the last half of his life on death row before being executed by lethal injection on May 9, 2007. Before his death, the media became increasingly interested in Workman, not because of his crime, but because of the drama surrounding his last meal. Workman refused to accept his last meal of vegetarian pizza and instead asked that it be given to a homeless person. Workman was denied his last wish; however, activists across the country carried out his request. In Tennessee, 170 pizzas were delivered to The Nashville Union Rescue Mission. In Minnesota, a large order of pizzas was sent to an organization for troubled youth.[1] In Santa Fe, a man donated 26 pizzas to the St. Elizabeth Shelter.[2]

Such odd food requests are congruent with many of the choices made by death row inmates. Thomas Grasso, executed by Oklahoma in 1995, wanted spaghetti-O's. John Rook, executed by North Carolina in 1986, wanted a dozen hot dogs and two Cokes. Fast food is a highly prized last meal with the condemned dining on "takeout from McDonald's and Arby's. Pizza has been ordered more than steak."[3] As is evidenced by media reports about executions, there is a collective interest in final meals. Ty Treadwell and Michelle Vernon note, "Almost every newspaper article documenting an execution lists the condemned man's last meal."[4]

News stories informing the public about the final meal suggests that there is a desire to know the *Other* through food. Food is an important site for investigation since "the love of food is sort of a common denominator that connects everybody. When you read what they had for their final meal all of a sudden you might find something that you have in common with these people."[5] Final meals articulate the symbolic importance of food beyond its nutritive role and therefore is a site of entry into understanding the individuals incarcerated on death row. Food complicates the relationship between the condemned and the capital punishment system because "food exercises 'power' over people in terms of what it means to them."[6] The final meal forms a relationship between the condemned, the chef, the state, and the larger public. The final meal is an articulation of *who* and *what* inmates are through food. Barer-Stein explains that food:

> is much more than a tool of survival. Food is a source of pleasure, comfort, and security. Food is also a symbol of hospitality, social status, and religious significance. What we select to eat, how we prepare it, serve it, and even how we eat it are all factors profoundly touched by our individual cultural inheritance.[7]

The question about one's final meal is intriguing. If food functions as "a way of getting at some essential truth about each other,"[8] what truths are revealed in the final meals of inmates? This article analyzes the prisoner's final meal through three perspectives. Dwight Conquergood provides a framework for understanding execution as a theatrical performance. Terri Gordon complements Conquergood's work by explaining the final meal within the sacred, the spectacle, and the profane. Finally, Barbara Kirshenblatt-Gimblett provides a method for understanding food as a performance medium. This article aims to achieve an understanding of food as a performance object in order to understand the link between the condemned and the system of capital punishment.

In order to develop this analysis, the recipes of [5] Brian D. Price, a former head chef at the Huntsville penitentiary in Texas, are located throughout this article. Readers are encouraged to cook, eat, and co-perform food as a performance medium. In doing so, readers may place their bodies, both internally and externally, in a performance relationship with the condemned. Food as a performance medium asks readers to alter their relationship with the text. In performing final meals the lived body fosters a connection with the dead and produces a haunting within one's own body.

Hangman's Hamburger Steak

½ pound ground beef
1 large onion
1 teaspoon garlic powder
2 tablespoons Worcestershire sauce
½ teaspoon salt
½ teaspoon black pepper
1 egg
Flour (as needed)

Put ground beef into a large mixing bowl. Cut onion in half, mince ¼ of the onion and add it to the meat. Add garlic powder, Worcestershire sauce, salt, pepper and the egg. Mix well.

Add only enough flour to tighten mixture, forming meat into a large patty approximately one inch thick. Slice the remainder of the onion, separating into cut rings. Set greased grill at 325 degrees and cook patty for approximately 20 minutes or until golden brown on both sides, sautéing the sliced onions in the patty grease.

Remove patty when done and top with sautéed onions. Smother with Broadaxe Brown Gravy.[9]

CONQUERGOOD AND THE THEATER OF CAPITAL PUNISHMENT

The ritual of the final meal is central to the theater of capital punishment. Dwight Conquergood provides a theatrical framework for understanding execution as "a ritual of state killing."[10] The theater of the gallows engages an audience in a performance of salvation, rectifying their bodies to the power of the state.

Richard Schechner's definitions of "drama, script, theater, and performance"[11] complement Conquergood's research by providing a framework for analyzing the final meal. The final meal is defined as a site of "drama" in the "theater" of death row. "Scripts" are followed to sanction the production of capital punishment while various actors engage in the theatrical "performance" of judicial killing. During any singular act of choosing, ordering, and eating final meals, prisoners can use the ritual for their own dramatic purposes. The final meal is an important final performance.

Conquergood argues that the dramaturgy of contemporary executions functions to "differentiate between judicial killing and murder."[12] The practice of capital punishment distinguishes between civilian murder and a performance of execution committed by the state. Furthermore, last meals and judicial killing both serve as acts of selection. As the state engages in the act of judicial killing, it shows a discernment of taste through whom it executes.

Conquergood provides a performance approach to the death penalty that reveals how the system operates. A performance perspective produces a context in which final meals function as a site of dramatic action. The following section will now look specifically at the final meal and how it operates in a contemporary setting.

THE SACRED, THE SPECTACLE, AND THE LAST SUPPER

The sacred is prominent in contemporary last meals. [10] Death row chef Brain Price addresses the sacred in his work noting "I always thought of the last meals I prepared as a version of the Last Supper, when

Christ knew that he would die the next day."[13] Terri Gordon, in opposition to Price, argues that the sacred elements of the ritual have shifted in contemporary society. Gordon bases her argument in the commodification of the last meal in the public sphere. The media's proliferation of "last meal minutiae" altered perceptions of the final meal and has moved the act from the sacred to the profane.

Gordon points out how spectacle is still incorporated into capital punishment through three areas. First, spectacle is produced through various media outlets that often cover the final twenty-four hours of an inmate's life. Second, spectacle is carried out through the act of deathwatch (the last four days on death row). Finally, spectacle occurs through witnessing the execution. Gordon illustrates how the final meal conforms to Foucault's economies of power while arguing for the final meal as a form of surveillance. The final meal serves as "communal punishment, voyeuristic pleasure, and the production of knowledge."[14]

Gordon's analysis raises questions in regards to how the process of food operates in capital punishment. There is an "invisible control over the body that Foucault associates with disciplinary forms of power, a control that aims . . . to kill the spirit before it kills the body."[15] However, the question remains how does the final meal participate in such a protocol? How does the final meal kill the spirit before it kills the body? The next section of this article tries to answer this question through the work of Barbara Kirshenblatt-Gimblett's discussion of food as a performance medium.

FOOD AS A PERFORMANCE MEDIUM

The Bathers' Pavilion restaurant sits snuggly up against the Australian coast. French doors open to the ocean air as guests watch the sun sink into the water. The restaurant's web site even reminds visitors "as dusk falls you might forget momentarily that you're here for Serge Dansereau's equally seductive food."[16] One selection of the dining experience is the ability to tour the kitchen with Dansereau and "see the theatrical elements of a professional establishment in action."[17] Food as a performance medium is exquisite in Dansereau's restaurant. The food is a consumable art. The restaurant experience is a performance of food, staged on the plate, and unfolding in the mouth.

A similar food performance unfolds in the mouths of condemned inmates. The performance is different, the stage altered, but the poetics of food remain similar. The following section explains how food, viewed as a performance medium, gives insight into the ritualistic function of final meals. Barbra Kirshenblatt-Gimblett notes that food "is already performative and theatrical. An art of the concrete, food, like performance, is alive, fugitive, and sensory."[18] Food carries meaning; food creates meaning. Kirshenblatt-Gimblett conveys three ways to understand food as a performance medium: (1) "to perform is to do," (2) "to perform is to behave," and (3) "to perform is to show."[19] The three perspectives inform how the ritual of the last meal functions in the system of capital punishment.

The performance of food as a *doing* focuses upon the completion of the act. Kirshenblatt-Gimblett writes that food as *doing* is "to execute, to carry out to completion, to discharge a duty—in other words, all that governs the production, presentation, and disposal of food and their staging."[20] Food as *doing* is an act or a process. In reference to Schechner, *doing* is concerned with how food "scripts" are produced in the "theater"[21] of capital punishment. The final meal "script" illustrates the production, presentation, and disposal of the meal as a part of execution.

PRODUCTION

The final meal is one aspect of the larger inter-workings of *doing* food production in prison. Final meals are controlled by each state's Department of Corrections; therefore, the protocols surrounding food practices vary from state to state. Concerns for the precedent in the production of final meals arise since "the majority of the states indicate that this protocol is not required by statute. The majority of reporting states indicate that their written protocol is not public information."[22] The protocols of final meals outline production. Many states, such as Georgia, note that "specific data is not available to the public; however, general information regarding procedures has been shared with public entities through media representatives who witness executions."[23] Protocol information is a general account of the temporal happenings of production; however, Georgia's actions confirm Foucault's work on capital punishment as a concealed exercise of power.[24] The production of final meals, or the lack thereof, reveals the state's orientation toward power.

Alternatively, some states chose to reveal or terminate their execution protocols. Three states: California, Florida, and New Jersey, imposed a moratorium on the death penalty because of problems found in their execution procedures. On December 13, 2006 an:

> execution team punctured the veins in [Angel] Diaz's arms [while] putting in the intravenous catheters, forcing the drugs into the soft tissue instead. Diaz grimaced for as long as 26 minutes, suffering from 11-inch and 12-inch chemical burns on his left and right arms respectively, and took 34 minutes to die.[25]

In the midst of Diaz's botched execution, the Tennessee Department of Corrections decided to reinstate its capital punishment system. In order to comply with lethal injection procedures, the state of Tennessee released its *Report on Administration of Death Sentences.*[26] This report is informative, not just because it illuminates the procedures of lethal injection, but also for how it outlines the practice of *doing* food performance.

States control and manage the production of food. In doing so, states illustrate how they value the bodies of the condemned through production. Conflicting accounts of food rations inform the relationship between the condemned and the state. Food production in its temporal capacity exposes bodily values. The Tennessee Department of Corrections notes "Three (3) meals per day are fed to all condemned inmates, except holidays and weekends which will be two meals just as general population."[27] Typically holidays are socially defined times with increased food production for most citizens, however in prison the condemned are deprived of it.

Food production reveals the value assigned to prisoner's bodies. Don Reid, a former Texas Warden, writes, "The condemned are fed twice daily, at 9:30 a.m. and at 5:30 p.m. The state figures they don't burn up much energy."[28] Food production illustrates how states value *doing* in relationship to prisoners. The frequency with which inmates are fed highlights the time, energy, and monetary investment states are willing to make to sustain the bodies of capital offenders. Food production illustrates a hierarchy of bodily value.

The means of food production reveal *who* and *what* are valued by the state. Sidney W. Mintz argues that class and privilege reveal themselves through food *means.* Mintz illustrates four criterion for unveiling class and privilege: "(1) By what [the state] cooks and serves, (2) by supplying things out of season, (3) how [the state] cooks, (4) and by distinctive ingredients."[29] A discussion of *means* is important since prisons have a long history of deplorable food practices.

Aramark, a food company that provides service for several state penitentiaries, has been instrumental in cutting prisons' food costs. The average cost of food for an inmate is $2.20 a day.[30] This amount provides three meals for each inmate. Even at a low cost per meal, over time food in prison and death row is costly. Unfortunately, the reduction of such costs has come at the expense of food quality. In Florida, workers removed 700 pounds of turkey and beef for sloppy joes and diluted the rest of the meal's content with ketchup and tomato paste.[31] In Pennsylvania, Aramark was fined for improperly storing food in a prison bathroom.[32] In Portland, Oregon, the state Prison Food Administrator, Fred Monem, was under investigation for alleged kickbacks in relationship to food quality. Monem was named by several inmate lawsuits in "complaints about green bologna, moldy hamburger and food cartons reportedly marked 'fish bait only.'"[33] These accounts are by no means comprehensive; however, they do inform *what* type of conduct occasionally occurs with prison food practices.

Mintz's second tenet illustrates how class and privilege reveal themselves through supplying foods that are out of season.[34] Most states, due to the cost of prisoners' meals, only serve seasonal foods. In Texas and Virginia inmates must choose a final meal from

20

the assorted foods available in the prison kitchen. In North Carolina and Indiana the condemned may order a final meal from nearby restaurants. In Illinois, before the moratorium, condemned inmates were served anything they desired.[35] Each states' fulfillment of the final meal request informs the relationship between the state and the condemned. The protocols illustrate how states value the condemned. Final meals are as much an exhibition of state power as they are a meal choice.

I combine Mintz's third and fourth category to illustrate the process of cooking final meals. Each individual chef decides the process of how to cook the last supper.[36] Brian D. Price approaches the preparation of each final meal with care. Different meals have different preparation requirements. Price remembers one convict he cooked for "ordered butter beans which was difficult to prepare, but it was something his mum made him when he was a kid and I knew it would take him back to a time when it was peaceful. So I cooked them real slow."[37] Even though Price may take care in how these meals are cooked, his performance is still bound by the means of production.

Sister Helen Prejean, whose life was popularized in a portrayal by Susan Sarandon in *Dead Man Walking*, notes that preparation is located in states' cultural relationship to food. Prejean writes, "Southern hospitality is a real thing in Louisiana. Even the big deal made about the last meal is genuine in a state where food is given priority."[38] The preparation of a meal involves cultural context, recipe construction, and bodily process.

The knowledge of food making extends beyond the simple ability to follow instructions. Lisa Heldke points out that a recipe "is hardly a theory, where theory is defined in contradistinction to practice. An experienced baker can interpret a recipe as a set of practical guidelines which need to be adapted to local conditions. This knowledge is contextual and bodily [known]."[39] Cooking is a performance of bodily knowledge. Cooking as performance moves through cultural borders and into the bodies of others. A chef who cooks a final meal embodies a connection with the condemned through the production, presentation, and disposal of the meal.

PRESENTATION

Each state dictates the individual presentation of the last meal. The presentation of food, especially the final meal, goes beyond the simple act of "opening a package of Rhodes frozen bread dough."[40] There are very few records of how last meals are presented; however, Price notes:

> On the day of an execution the meal would have to be ready by 3:45pm and [I] would put the plates on a tray and cover it over with paper ('so no one could see it, as a matter of respect'). It would then be carried across the yard to the north-east corner of the prison which housed the death chamber. The inmate would eat at 4pm and two hours later would be killed by lethal injection.[41]

The presentation of the final meal illustrates connections between the condemned, the chef, and others involved in the system of capital punishment.

The presentation of food parallels the presentation of the prisoners' bodies. The protocol for preparing, presenting, and disposing of the condemned is highly figured, much like a recipe. The process of following the recipe produces bodily knowledge for all individuals involved in the meal and the execution.

DISPOSAL

Disposal connects the final meal, the condemned, and the system of capital punishment in a performance of consumption. Disposal "means we have foreknowledge that [food] will become us bodily, and that it will be expelled. Food stands in a special relationship to the self that is different from the merely edible."[42] The final meal becomes the body; however in the case of capital punishment, the food is rarely expelled. In contemporary executions disposal refers to the bodily remains. The body never produces waste; instead it symbolically functions as waste.

Preparation for the disposal of the body is performed after the inmate is placed on deathwatch. Deathwatch is the term for the four days prior to execution in which all of the inmate's actions are highly surveyed and dictated. The first two days are concerned with preparing the body of the condemned. During the first day, the "Chaplain requests instructions for release of the inmate's body in writing. If no recipient is designated, the Warden arranges for a pauper's burial."[43] On the second day, the same day the prisoner orders his/her final meal; the final disposal of the body is arranged as the "Chaplain confirms funeral arrangements with the family, if available."[44] On the third day the prisoner consumes their final meal. The disposal of waste is performed when the state disposes of the body and the interrupted bodily functions of the condemned. The state performs the final function of "food performance as a doing."[45] At midnight, on the fourth day, the execution occurs and the body is disposed. At the Huntsville penitentiary in Texas, if a condemned inmate has no family arrangements, his body is buried in the Joe Byrd Cemetery. The state marks the resting place of the body, not with a name, but with the prison identification number. An *X* is placed before the number to indicate execution. In Kirshenblatt-Gimblett's terms, the disposal and burial procedures further illustrate how the state reaffirms its authority through a performance of *doing* capital punishment.

Old Sparky's Sloppy Joes

2 pounds ground beef
1 teaspoon salt
½ teaspoon black pepper

1 teaspoon garlic powder
1 large chopped onion
1 large chopped bell pepper
2 16 ounce cans tomato sauce
2 ounce Worcestershire sauce
1 ounce liquid smoke
½ cup brown sugar
Hamburger buns

Season ground beef with salt, pepper and garlic powder. Cook over medium heat stirring often until meat is light brown. Add the onion, bell pepper, tomato sauce, Worcestershire sauce, liquid smoke and brown sugar. Reduce heat to low and simmer for approximately thirty minutes. Remove from stove and serve over split hamburger buns.[46]

EATING AND BEHAVING

The second position of food as a performance medium offered by Barbara Kirshenblatt-Gimblett is performance as *behavior*.[47] Behavior sets up a value relationship between performer and food. Kirshenblatt-Gimblett writes "to perform in this sense is to behave appropriately in relation to food at any point in its production or consumption or disposal, each of which may be subject to precise protocols or taboos."[48] The performance functions in two regards: the relationship between the condemned and their final meal request form, and the connection between the body and mind during the process of eating.

Meal request forms provide insight into how inmates behave in relationship to final meals. Before his execution, David Allen Castillo requested a huge feast of "twenty-four soft shell tacos, six enchiladas, six tostadas (chalupas), two whole onions, five jalapenos, two cheeseburgers, one chocolate milk shake, one quart of milk and one pack of Marlboro cigarettes."[49] Castillo's behavior complies with the established execution ritual. Castillo's over abundance illustrates the acceptance of his role in the ritual of execution.

In Oklahoma, Thomas Grasso requested steamed clams and a Cornish game hen glazed in sweet and sour sauce.[50] Both requests were denied, however, Grasso was most adamant about his request for SpaghettiOs. Instead Grasso received a can of Franco-American spaghetti. Grasso complained in his final statement "I did not get my SpaghettiO's. I got spaghetti. I want the press to know this!"[51] Grasso, in his last words, found it extremely important to communicate that the proper ritual of the final meal, and thus of the execution, was not followed. The final meal request form serves as a behavioral performance of food.

On the other end of the spectrum, some individuals use the request slip as a metaphorical performance. Alyda Faber, drawing on Catherine Bell's *Ritual Theory, Ritual Practice*, discusses the potential political weight of such food performances.[52] The ritual of final meals "orders the ambiguities and indeterminacies of experience into distinctions between good and evil, light and dark, spirit and flesh, above and below, inside and outside."[53] Faber notes that these dualisms frame "ultimate power and order in the world. The ritual agent learns this redemptive order through embodied practices."[54] The state uses the final meal ritual as an embodied practice that orders and illustrates its sovereignty.

The framework of the meal request forms allows individuals to interpret and read the actions beyond the space in which they are placed. Carlos Santana requested "justice, temperance, with mercy."[55] Santana's order is in direct relationship to the moralizing of violence and the distinctions drawn between good and evil. The final meal requests of both Danny Ray Harris and Jonathan Wayne Nobles further informs the distinction between good and evil. Harris ordered "God's saving grace, love, truth, peace and freedom,"[56] while Nobles ordered "Eucharist-sacrament."[57] The sacred elements of the final meal request forms parallel Faber's understanding of Saint Orlan's performance work. Saint Orlan is known for her themed cosmetic surgeries in which she uses her body as a site of ritualistic spectacle by "creating visceral and grotesque images that evoke sensations of awe and horror to elicit the sacred dimensions of the experience."[58] As with Orlan, Harris', Santana's, and Nobles' last meals "self designated saintliness through their attention to the creation of religious meanings and the significance of the body for religious ritual and imaginative acts."[59] In such cases the body of the condemned serves as a sacred site within the ritual of capital punishment. Final meals explicitly call upon a shift in purity. Food performances mark inmate behaviors as inviting or denying purity. An invitation of purity symbolizes a purging of the criminal or the unclean. Christian ideology frames the final meal as a "cosmic spiritual drama of sin and salvation."[60]

The Last Supper provides insight for understanding the final meal. Sister Helen Prejean writes about the final meals of Antonio James and John Brown.

Both men shared their last meal with the warden who executed them. Prejean writes:

> At these final meals they had all held hands and prayed and sung hymns and eaten and even laughed . . . there at the head of the table was Warden Cain, like a father figure, providing the abundance of the last meal—boiled crawfish—making everything as nice and friendly as he could, even though when the meal was done the inevitable protocol would have to be followed and, as warden, he would be obliged to do his job. In the chamber, he'd nod to the executioner to begin injecting the lethal fluids into the arm of the man whose hand he was holding and with whom he was praying.[61]

Prejean's account resonates with the story of Judas's betrayal of Jesus. During the Last Supper Judas dines with Jesus only to condemn his body to the Romans. The Last Supper places the final meal in a ritualistic framework. Rituals "draw their meaning, structure, style, and affective resonance from the traditions they reenact. They . . . reverberate within traditions they simultaneously reinvent and re-deploy for historically situated needs and purpose."[62] When the final meal is interpreted as a reenactment of the Last Supper, the body of the condemned is placed in Christian framework. The last meal functions as a movement toward purity and purification through execution.

Performing food as *behavior* is also apparent in the act of eating. Consumption as behavior is informed by the notion of body/mind. In *Phaedo*, Plato argues for a separation of the mind and body through food. Socrates instructs Simmias to ignore the body when he asks "Do you think that it is right for a philosopher to concern himself with the so-called pleasure connected with food and drink? Certainly not, Socrates, said Simmias."[63] In Platonic philosophy the death of the body is highly anticipated by the philosopher. Socrates sets up dueling ideologies of "mind/body, self/other, culture/nature, good/evil, reason/emotion."[64] The dualisms are located in the distinctions of "*ontological kind* and [those] of *value.*"[65] The last meal argues for a separation of mind and body.

Cartesian philosophy privileges the mind over the body arguing that the "living body is not fundamentally different from the lifeless; it is a kind of animated corpse, a functioning mechanism."[66] Food, in this regard, is not to be experienced by the prisoner as a bodily action and a union of body/mind. Rather, the final meal is a performance privileging the mind. The final meal serves to reinforce the dichotomy of body and mind through the supposed death of the body and continuation of the mind or soul. A similar idea can be found in Bordo's understanding of anorexia. Bordo notes that "starvation of the body is motivated by the dream to be 'without a body', to achieve 'absolute purity, hyperintellectuality and transcendence of the flesh."[67] The last meal is not a hunger for food as much as it is a gesture towards purity and transcendence of the flesh. The final meal often functions as an "evolution and expression of self."[68] Cherin provides an account of such a relationship to food when she notes, "I was hungering, it was true; but food apparently was not what I was hungering for."[69] As Curtin and Heldke put it, the final meal represents a "faulty construction of personhood which shows itself through food."[70] The final meal reinforces the Cartesian dualism in order to ease the process of execution for the state.

Posthumous Potato Salad

10 potatoes, quartered
1 cup mayonnaise
1 cup mustard
1 oz vinegar
2 cups chopped onions

1 cup chopped dill pickles or dill relish
1 cup sweet relish
8 boiled eggs, chopped
2 teaspoons salt
1 tablespoon sugar

½ teaspoon black pepper

Boil potatoes in a large (2 gal.) pot until potatoes are soft but still in quarter pieces. Cool potatoes in cold water, then drain water and put cooled potatoes in a large mixing bowl. Add mayonnaise, mustard and vinegar, mix at low speed until blended. Add onions, pickles, eggs, salt, sugar, and black pepper and mix well. Chill for one hour and serve cold.[71]

FOOD AS AN ACT OF SHOWING

The third and final position Barbara Kirshenblatt-Gimblett offers is "to perform food is to show."[72] *Showing* primarily occurs when "doing and behaving are displayed, when they are shown, when participants are invited to exercise discernment, evaluation, and appreciation, food events move towards the theatrical and, more specifically, towards the spectacular."[73] Food as showing is highly theatrical.

Food discernment *shows* an exercise of power. In her analysis of the historical production of sugar, Sidney W. Mintz highlights how food functions as *showing*. Mintz notes "sugar was a luxury food that gradually worked its way down the European class ladders, starting as a play thing of royalty and becoming a necessity of working people only much later."[74] The power of *showing* occurs through food production and what food comes to *mean*. She explains that sugar was:

> a rare and costly substance, its very consumption expressed a kind of power-much as our consumption of costly caviar or fresh abalone or fine wine does so, today. The king's ability to display and consume sugar was one of the ways for defining his power.[75]

A contemporary example of food as showing is illustrated on the Texas Department of Criminal Justice Web Site. The Web Site, at one time, posted final statements, crimes, and included all of the final meals of death row inmates in Texas. Conquergood writes "anyone who doubts that people sentenced to death in this country are overwhelmingly impoverished and working class should go to the website."[76] The Web Site highlights how final meals are a production and staging of class values. Brian D. Price points out "the most requested last meal is a cheeseburger and French fries."[77] American food such as hamburgers, fried chicken, ribs, hot dogs and pizza are all considered staples of the American diet; however, Mintz argues: "I don't think anyone wants to call that array a cuisine."[78] Mintz and Price illustrate how food selection functions as showing. The condemned are not choosing cuisine, but instead, are showing a discernment of taste and class value.

The state also regulates what foods can be used as a performance medium. Inmates may show discernment for specific food choices; however, their choices are provisional until the state recognizes and acknowledges their food selections. Carl E. Kelly, a Texas death row inmate, once requested wild game and lemonade; instead he was served a cheeseburger and French fries.[79] Harold Amos Barnard requested steak, French fries and wine but instead was served water and hamburger steak.[80] Often the quality of food is reduced due to cost. Food, by way of monetary investment, shows how each state values those inmates on death row.

CONCLUSION

Final meals are a performance site in the theater of capital punishment. Food becomes a powerful performance medium when framed within the context of capital theater. Furthermore, food extends beyond the prison walls and creates a site of empathic connection through the lived body. Leder points out that the body "is being in relationship to that which is other: other people, other things, an environment. Moreover, in a significant sense, the lived body helps to constitute this world-as-experienced."[81] Final meals produce a site that informs the public's relationship to the condemned.

In his last meal request, Robert Excell White ordered a "Mr. Hamberger -2x's, double order frie's, and onion rings-fried."[82] White's meal request is an intimate act of self. His misspelling, personification of food, and food choices suggest something of his person. The final meal ritual informs how power, production, and value function within the theater of capital punishment. Such is the case in the final meal request of Miguel A Richardson:

> Chocolate birthday cake with "2/23/90" written on top, seven pink candles, one coconut, kiwi fruit juice, one mango, grapes, lettuce, cottage cheese, peaches, one banana, one delicious apple, chef salad without meat and with thousand island dressing, fruit salad, cheese, and tomato slices. (He was only served chef salad with dressing, fruit salad, cheese, tomato slices, and a chocolate cake with 2/23/90 written on it.)[83]

Richardson's meal is a convergence of various temporal happenings that affect how the theater of capital punishment operates. The final meal provides an opportunity for limited agency before execution. In the theater of capital punishment, by accepting the ritual of the final meal, inmates are able to choose a representation of self through food before death.

NOTES

1. "Killer Gets Wish after Execution," *Los Angeles Times*, May 11, 2007, http://articles.latimes.com/2007/may/11/nation/na-briefs11.1 (accessed June 9, 2007), paragraph 2.

2. Ginger McGuire, "Condemned Man's Last Wish Helps Homeless," *Albuquerque Journal*, May 11, 2007, 3.

3. "Curious Follow Prisoners' Pick of Final Meals," *The News and Observer*, January 15, 2006, http://www.newsobserver.com/102/story/388886.html (accessed June 9, 2007), paragraph 3.

4. Ty Treadwell and Michelle Vernon, *Last Suppers: Famous Final Meals from Death Row* (Washington: Loompanics Unlimited, 2001), 6.

5. "Curious," paragraph 8.

6. Sidney Mintz, *Tasting Food, Tasting Freedom* (Boston: Beacon Press, 1996), 29.

7. Thelma Barer-Stein, *You Eat What You Are: People, Culture and Food Traditions* (Canada: Firefly Books, 1999), 14.

8. Barer-Stein, 14.

9. Brian D. Price, *Meals to Die For* (Texas: Dyna-Paige, 2004), 475.

10. Dwight Conquergood, "Lethal Theatre: Performance, Punishment, and the Death Penalty," *Theatre Journal* 54 (2002): 339–67.

11. Richard Schechner, *Performance Theory* (New York: Routledge, 1988), 71.

12. Conquergood, 360.

13. Terri J. Gordon, "Debt, Guilt, and Hungry Ghosts: A Foucauldian Perspective on Bigert's and Bergstrom's Last Supper," *Cabinet Magazine* (2006), www.cabinetmagazine.org/events/lastsuppergordon.php (accessed June 18, 2009), paragraph 17.

14. Gordon, paragraph 20.

15. Gordon, paragraph 22.

16. Welcome to the Bathers Pavilion, "Restaurant," batherspavilion.com.au (accessed May 16, 2009), paragraph 3.

17. Welcome to the Bathers Pavilion, "Chef's Table," paragraph 1.

18. Barbara Kirshenblatt-Gimblett, "Playing to the Senses: Food as a Performance Medium," *Performance Research* 4 (1999): 1–30.

19. Kirshenblatt-Gimblett, 1.

20. Kirshenblatt-Gimblett, 2.

21. Schechner, 71.

22. Florida Corrections Commission, *Supplemental Report: Execution Methods Used by States* (June 1997), http://www.fcc.state.fl.us/fcc/reports/methods/emcont.html (accessed June 9, 2007).

23. Florida Corrections Commission.

24. Michele Foucault, *Discipline and Punish: The Birth of the Prison*, trans. by Alan Sheridan (New York: Vintage, 1979).

25. Elizabeth Weil, "The Needle and the Damage Done," *New York Times Magazine*, February 11, 2007, 46–51.

26. Tennessee Department of Corrections, *Report on Administration of Death Sentences in Tennessee*, April 2007, http://tennessean.com/assets/pdf/DN71684430.PDF (accessed June 7, 2007).

27. Tennessee Department of Corrections, 47.

28. Don Reid, *Have A Seat, Please* (Huntsville: Texas Review Press, 2001), 6.

29. Mintz, 101.

30. Angel Riggs, "Prison Food: 'Big House' Horticulture: Prison Gardens Produce Tax Savings," *Tulsa World*, September 13, 2006.

31. Thomas Tobin, Editorial, "Prisons Need Better Food Service," *St. Petersburg Times*, July 2, 2002: B17.

32. Paul Muschick and Christopher Schnaars, "Pennsylvania Prison Kept Food Unsafely," *The Morning Call*, August 8, 2005.

33. "Oregon Prison Food Buyer Was Target of Lawsuit Over Food," Associated Press, January 29, 2007. Lexus-Nexus, http://web.lexis-nexis.com.proxy.lib.siu.edu/universe (accessed June 9, 2007).

34. Mintz, 101.

35. Treadwell and Vernon, 142–45.

36. Mintz, 101.

37. "Confessions of a Death Row Chef," *The Observer*, March 14, 2004, http://observer.guardian.co.uk/foodmonthly/story/0,1166253,00.html (accessed June 10, 2007), paragraph 19.

38. Sister Helen Prejean, *The Death of Innocents: An Eyewitness Account of Wrongful Executions* (New York: Vintage Books, 2005), 11.

39. Deane W. Curtin and Lisa M. Heldke, eds., *Cooking, Eating, Thinking: Transformative Philosophies of Food* (Bloomington: Indiana UP, 1992), 10.

40. Curtin and Heldke, 9.

41. "Confessions," paragraph 15.

42. Curtin and Heldke, 9.

43. Tennessee Department of Corrections, 61.

44. Tennessee Department of Corrections, 62.

45. Kirshenblatt-Gimblett, 1.

46. Price, 464.

47. Kirshenblatt-Gimblett, 1.

48. Kirshenblatt-Gimblett, 1.

49. Price, 295.

50. Treadwell and Vernon, 8.

51. Treadwell and Vernon, 8.

52. Alyda Faber, "Saint Orlan: Ritual as Violent Spectacle and Cultural Criticism," *The Drama Review* 46 (2002): 85–92.

53. Faber, 87.

54. Faber, 87.

55. Price, 170.

56. Price, 178.

57. Price, 298.

58. Faber, 87.

59. Faber, 87.

60. Conquergood, 346.

61. Prejean, 6.

62. Conquergood, 343.

63. Plato, "Phaedo," in *Cooking, Eating, Thinking: Transformative Philosophies of Food*, ed. by Deane W. Curtin and Lisa M. Heldke (Bloomington: Indiana UP, 1992), 24–27.

64. Curtin and Heldke, 5.

65. Curtin and Heldke, 5.

66. Drew Leder, "A Tale of Two Bodies: The Cartesian Corpse and the Lived Body," in *The Body and the Flesh: A Philosophical Reader*, ed. by Don Welton (Wiley-Blackwell, 1998): 117–30.

67. Curtin and Heldke, 7.

68. Kim Cherin, "Confessions of an Eater," in *Cooking, Eating, Thinking: Transformative Philosophies of Food*, ed. by Deane W. Curtin and Lisa M. Heldke (Bloomington: Indiana UP, 1992): 56–67.

69. Cherin, 61.

70. Curtin and Heldke, 7.

71. Price, 487.

72. Kirshenblatt-Gimblett, 1.

73. Kirshenblatt-Gimblett, 2.

74. Mintz, 12.

75. Mintz, 12.

76. Conquergood, 358.

77. "Confessions," paragraph 11.

78. Mintz, 114.

79. Price, 181.

80. Price, 190.

81. Leder, 123.

82. Price, 323.

83. Price, 448–49.

Reading Questions

1. What are some of the ways Collins explains that food production illustrates the value assigned to the bodies of the incarcerated?

2. Brian Price, a penitentiary chef, is quoted and referenced several times by Collins. How does Price view his role in the ritual of the final meal? Give one example of how he characterizes what he does.

Rhetoric Questions

3. Collins includes recipes in text boxes throughout the article from a penitentiary chef with such titles as "Hangman's Hamburger Steak." What purpose do these recipes serve in the article, and how do they contribute to the purpose of the article as a whole?

4. Collins uses subheadings throughout his article. What purpose do his subheadings serve for the reader?

Response Questions

5. Collins describes food as performance through the work of other scholars, including Barbara Kirshenblatt-Gimblett. He provides examples in the article, including a restaurant on the Australian coast where diners can tour the restaurant to experience the performance of food preparation. Where have you experienced food as performance? What was the context, and what was your experience and reaction?

6. Near the beginning of the article, Collins encourages readers "to cook, eat, and co-perform food as a performance medium" (par. 5). Were you tempted to do so? Did you try any of the recipes? Were you shocked that he would make such a suggestion? What was your response, and why did you respond the way you did?

ACADEMIC CASE STUDY • CAPITAL PUNISHMENT   SOCIAL SCIENCES

Capital Punishment in Films: The Impact of Death Penalty Portrayals on Viewers' Mood and Attitude toward Capital Punishment

BENEDIKT TILL AND PETER VITOUCH

Benedikt Till is a research associate at the Department of General Practice and Family Medicine, Center for Public Health, Medical University of Vienna and lecturer at the Medical University of Vienna. The following study was published in the *International Journal of Public Opinion Research* in 2012 with co-author Peter

Vitouch, a professor of media psychology in the Department of Communication and vice-dean of the Faculty of Social Science at the University of Vienna. The article examines the impact that filmic representations of capital punishments have on viewers' moods and attitudes.

INTRODUCTION

Since several decades there has been a lively debate on the legitimacy of the death penalty between those for and those against capital punishment (see e.g., Ellsworth & Gross, 1994; Fan, Keltner, & Wyatt, 2002; Niven, 2002). The entrance of capital punishment in the forefront of debate and consciousness at nearly all levels of society is due at least in part to the plethora of movies and books on this topic (Giles, 1995). But what is the effect of such media accounts on recipients?

The Impact of Fictional and Nonfictional Death Penalty Portrayals

In a laboratory experiment, Howells, Flanagan, and Hagan (1995) demonstrated that the screening of tapes of executions leads to reduced support for the death penalty. A study by Holbert, Shah, and Kwak (2004) suggests that viewing police reality shows, crime drama, and TV news is related to the endorsement of capital punishment. Furthermore, press coverage was found to be a driving force for opinion about capital punishment (Fan et al., 2002; Niven, 2002). An association between media use and support for the death penalty was also reported by Sotirovic (2001).

Evidence for fictional portrayals is rather heterogeneous. Slater, Rouner, and Long (2006) found increased support for the death penalty among viewers of a television drama that endorsed capital punishment. Mutz and Nir (2010) demonstrated that viewers who watched a fictional television program emphasizing flaws in the justice system exhibit a greater rejection of the death penalty than those who viewed a more positive portrayal of the criminal justice system. Other studies, however, found no change in attitude toward the death penalty among viewers of films focusing on capital punishment (e.g., Önder & Öner-Özkan, 2003; Peterson & Thurstone, 1970). Thus, the effects of fictional entertainment narratives dealing with capital punishment on viewers' attitudes toward the death penalty are still unclear and undetermined.

Emotional Audience Responses to Dramas

According to affective disposition theory (Zillmann, 1996), viewers enjoy a film the most when the protagonist benefits from the story's outcome. If the heroes fail, we feel bad for them—this might lead to negative emotions. Evidence from several studies suggests that individuals exposed to sad film endings experience significantly higher degrees of emotional stress and a deterioration of mood (e.g., Hesse, Spies, Hänze, & Gerrards-Hesse, 1992; Tannenbaum & Gaer, 1965).

Till and Vitouch lead with their research question. For insights into social science research, see Chapter 8, "Research Questions and Hypotheses."

The researchers review previous scholarship on the topic and establish a gap, or remaining question, that is unresolved by scholars.

On the other hand, Festinger's (1954) social comparison theory proposes that humans tend to evaluate their values, abilities, and living conditions by comparing them with those of other people. A comparison with the undesirable situation of a person sentenced to death might improve an individual's mood. Also, people may use sad films to cope with some negative experience in their lives (see e.g., Mares & Cantor, 1992; Nabi, Finnerty, Domschke, & Hull, 2006; Tan, 2008). Till, Niederkrotenthaler, Herberth, Vitouch, and Sonneck (2010) discovered a deterioration of mood and an increase of depression in viewers of films featuring the suicide of the protagonist. Concurrently, the viewers also reacted with a rise in life satisfaction and a drop in suicidality. However, studies focusing on emotional audience reactions to films dealing with capital punishment are rare.

> Till and Vitouch draw on theory as described in Chapter 8, "The Role of Theory in the Social Sciences."

> The researchers stress the originality of their study and thus indicate its potential to contribute to theory development.

DETERMINANTS OF FILM EFFECTS

Audience reactions to motion pictures and television programs are partly based on the characters who populate them and on the viewers' engagement in the process of impression formation in getting to know the respective persona (Hoffner & Cantor, 1991). Identification with media characters is defined as "an imaginative process through which an audience member assumes the identity, goals, and perspective of a character" (Cohen, 2001, p. 261). Several studies provided evidence that identification has the potential to amplify media-induced reactions in terms of emotions (e.g., Slater & Rouner, 2002; Tannenbaum & Gaer, 1965; Till et al., 2010), attitude changes (e.g., Basil, 1996; Gau, James, & Kim, 2009; Greenwood, 2004), and behavior modifications (e.g., Brown & Basil, 1995; Niederkrotenthaler et al., 2009; Perry & Perry, 1976).

The impact of a motion picture can also be determined by the way certain actions are portrayed in key scenes of the movie. Print media guidelines—for example, recommended restrictions for newspaper reports on suicide—are known to influence readers' imitation behavior (Etzersdorfer & Sonneck, 1998; Niederkrotenthaler & Sonneck, 2007; Sonneck, Etzersdorfer, & Nagel-Kuess, 1994). Accordingly, removing scenes from a film has been discussed as a means to mitigate possible negative effects of movies and television programs on their viewers and has been used by television stations to moderate their broadcasts and thereby avoid public criticism (Worringham & Buxton, 1997). The effectiveness of such editing, however, has been questioned in the past, since most studies on this topic have failed to demonstrate a significant influence on film effects (e.g., Ferracuti & Lazzari, 1970; Tannenbaum, 1978; Till et al., 2010; Till & Vitouch, 2008).

The present study investigates the impact of two films featuring the portrayal of the protagonist's death via capital punishment on their viewers' mood and attitude toward the death penalty and compares the effects of these two movies to those of edited versions—thus being the first study to examine emotional, as well as cognitive, audience responses to different versions of such films. The importance of using emotional, as well as cognitive, parameters to assess the impact of a drama was recently highlighted by Till et al. (2010). The following hypotheses were formulated:

> *H1:* The viewing of a film drama focusing on capital punishment has a negative influence on the viewers' mood.
>
> *H2:* The viewing of a film drama focusing on the negative aspects of capital punishment reduces the viewers' approval of the death penalty.
>
> *H3:* Excluding the protagonist's execution from a film that focuses on capital punishment reduces its impact on (a) the viewers' mood and (b) their attitudes toward the death penalty.
>
> *H4:* The more a viewer identifies with the dying protagonist of a film focusing on capital punishment, the greater is (a) the deterioration of his or her mood and (b) the reduction of his or her approval of the death penalty.

The researchers assert four hypotheses: H1, H2, H3 (a and b), H4 (a and b). Learn more about hypotheses in the social sciences by reading "Research Questions and Hypotheses" in Chapter 8.

METHODS

Design and Material

Group 1 viewed the movie *The Chamber* (United States, 1996), while group 2 watched *Dancer in the Dark* (Denmark/France, 2000). Both films portray the death penalty in a negative way and conclude with the explicit portrayal of (one of) the main character's execution. However, while *The Chamber* is a mainstream movie, in *Dancer in the Dark*, the plot and its depiction are rather unconventional due to the usage of different themes in the genres of the musical, the neo-realist film, and the melodrama. Furthermore, in *The Chamber* there is a certain amount of uncertainty regarding the convict's guilt, whereas in *Dancer in the Dark*, the crime—and thus the protagonist's innocence—is shown explicitly. Groups 3 and 4 saw an edited version of the respective film without the portrayal of the execution. However, it was still clear to the viewer that the protagonist was killed via death penalty. Only the execution itself was removed from the film, not the events immediately before and after the execution. The editing of the scenes was carried out in a manner one would expect from a television station to mitigate possible negative effects of its broadcasted program (see Worringham & Buxton, 1997).

Researchers explain their study's methods and design. Here, they discuss their four test groups of participants (movie viewers).

In *The Chamber*, a young attorney seeks to appeal the death sentence of his 10 grandfather, a Ku Klux Klan bomber, for the murder of a lawyer and his two small boys. Despite the attorney's efforts and the proof that his grandfather did not have the intention to kill his victims, the Ku Klux Klan bomber is executed in the gas chamber.

The researchers describe the movies viewed by respective test groups.

The film *Dancer in the Dark* involves a woman, Selma, who works day and night to save her son from the same disease she suffers from, a disease that inevitably will make her blind. When her neighbor and friend, a police officer, steals money from her to pay his debts, Selma confronts him and tries to get her money back. In the resulting turmoil, Selma shoots the police officer in self-defense. Despite her innocence, Selma gets sentenced to death. The film concludes with her execution by hanging.

Subjects

Participants were 121 individuals living in Austria ($n = 121$)—49 men (40.5%), with mean age of 34.20 years, and 72 women (59.5%), with mean age of 41.25 years.

Measures

Mood. Mood was measured by the subscales *Sorrow* and *Positive Mood* of a German short version of the *Profile of Mood States* by McNair, Lorr, and Doppleman (1971) using three items (adjectives such as "unhappy" or "sad") for sorrow and six items (adjectives such as "happy" or "merry") for positive mood on a 7-point scale ranging from 1—"not at all" to 7—"very strong" (sorrow: Cronbach's $\alpha = .89$; positive mood: Cronbach's $\alpha = .71$).

Attitude toward Capital Punishment. Attitudes toward capital punishment were measured by a questionnaire based on analogous scales developed by Önder and Öner-Özkan (2003), as well as Peterson and Thurstone (1970), using 11 items (statements such as "Life imprisonment is more effective than capital punishment") on a 5-point scale ranging from 1—"disagree" to 5—"agree." However, one item was excluded from the analysis to improve the scale's reliability (Cronbach's $\alpha = .91$).

Identification with the Protagonist. Identification was measured by a question- 15 naire based on an analogous scale developed by Cohen (2001) using 11 items (statements such as "I felt I knew exactly what character X was going through") on a 5-point scale ranging from 1—"disagree"—to 5—"agree." However, one item was excluded from the analysis to improve the scale's reliability (Cronbach's $\alpha = .85$).

In computing the parameters, scores on the negative items were reversed, so that high scores indicated a high level of the respective variable. The scores were then added together according to the instructions given in the respective manual.

Procedure

Participation in the study was voluntary and anonymous. The subjects' allocation to the experimental groups was randomized. It was ensured that the subjects

The researchers explain the measures used to evaluate participants' moods and attitudes before and after viewing one of the four movies (randomly assigned).

had not already seen the respective film in the past. Before the film, questionnaires on mood and attitudes toward capital punishment were completed by the participants. After the movie, these parameters were measured again, as well as the subjects' identification with the respective protagonist.

Learn more about quantitative methods and the use of statistical procedures in social science research by reading "Methods" in Chapter 8.

Data Analysis

Nonparametric tests were applied, since normal distribution could not be assumed within the given set of data. The subjects were disproportionately low on sorrow (skew ranging between 0.47 and 2.08, and kurtosis between −1.22 and 3.61) and approval of capital punishment (skew ranging between 0.48 and 2.18, and kurtosis between −0.78 and 5.23). An overview of the medians, percentiles, means, and standard deviations of the subjects' mood and attitudes toward capital punishment is shown in Table 1. Wilcoxon tests were performed to analyze the impact the films have on the subjects' mood and attitudes toward capital punishment. To examine to which extent identification influences the impact of the films, Spearman correlations were performed. An overview of the medians, percentiles, means, and standard deviations of the subjects' identification with the respective protagonist is shown in Table 2. For the Wilcoxon tests, the parameters' summarized scores before and after the movie screening were used to conduct the analysis. Change scores and the summarized score for identification were used for the correlations.

RESULTS

A summary of the results of the Wilcoxon tests can be found in Table 3. There was a significant deterioration of the subjects' positive mood in all four film groups (*The Chamber*: $Z = −4.06$, $n = 30$, $p < .001$; *The Chamber*, edited version: $Z = −4.27$, $n = 31$, $p < .001$; *Dancer in the Dark*: $Z = −4.61$, $n = 30$, $p < .001$; *Dancer in the Dark*, edited version: $Z = −3.57$, $n = 30$, $p < .001$). The screening of the movies also led to a significant increase of sorrow in all groups (*The Chamber*, edited version: $Z = −2.33$, $n = 31$, $p < .05$; *Dancer in the Dark*: $Z = −3.56$, $n = 30$, $p < .001$; *Dancer in the Dark*, edited version: $Z = −2.19$, $n = 30$, $p < .05$) except for the audience watching the original version of *The Chamber* ($Z = −0.70$, $n = 30$, $p = .47$).

Results confirm hypothesis 1.

Thus, Hypothesis 1 was confirmed. Furthermore, there was a significant swing toward unfavorable assessments of capital punishment in the groups watching the edited versions of the two films (*The Chamber*: $Z = −2.95$, $n = 31$, $p < .01$; *Dancer in the Dark*: $Z = −2.78$, $n = 30$, $p < .01$), but surprisingly, not among viewers of the original versions (*The Chamber*: $Z = −1.67$, $n = 30$, $p = .09$; *Dancer in the Dark*: $Z = −0.96$, $n = 30$, $p = .33$). Therefore, Hypothesis 2 was partly confirmed. Hypotheses 3a and 3b, on the other hand, were rejected—excluding the execution from the films did not reduce the impact on the viewers' mood and their attitudes toward the death penalty.

Hypothesis 2 is "partly confirmed," but hypothesis 3 (a and b) is rejected.

Table 1

Means (*M*), Standard Deviations (*SD*), Medians (*μ*), and Percentiles (P_{25}, P_{75}) for the Recipients' Mood and Attitudes toward Capital Punishment for Each Film before and after the Screening

		The Chamber (original)	Dancer in the Dark (original)	The Chamber (edited)	Dancer in the Dark (edited)
Positive mood					
Before	*M (SD)*	4.01 (1.24)	4.63 (1.35)	4.2 (1.26)	3.98 (1.29)
	P_{25}	3.25	3.45	3.5	2.95
	μ	4	4.66	4.33	4
	P_{75}	4.66	6	5.16	5.04
After	*M (SD)*	2.75 (1.41)	2.87 (1.59)	3.03 (1.37)	2.96 (1.42)
	P_{25}	1.62	1.33	1.83	1.5
	μ	2.58	2.58	3.16	3
	P_{75}	4	4.08	4	4.04
Sorrow					
Before	*M (SD)*	1.81 (1.38)	1.38 (0.69)	1.87 (1.3)	1.77 (1.17)
	P_{25}	1	1	1	1
	μ	1	1	1.33	1
	P_{75}	2.08	1.5	2.66	2.16
After	*M (SD)*	2 (1.25)	2.26 (1.37)	2.54 (1.37)	2.54 (1.68)
	P_{25}	1	1.25	1.33	1
	μ	1.5	2	2	2
	P_{75}	3	3.33	4	4
Attitudes toward capital punishment					
Before	*M (SD)*	2.41 (1.17)	2.12 (1.14)	2.18 (1.19)	1.98 (1.08)
	P_{25}	1.37	1.2	1.2	1.17
	μ	2.1	1.75	1.6	1.5
	P_{75}	3.32	2.92	3.3	2.85
After	*M (SD)*	2.28 (1.28)	2.06 (1.1)	1.96 (1.09)	1.67 (0.93)
	P_{25}	1	1	1	1
	μ	1.85	1.7	1.5	1.35
	P_{75}	3.07	2.7	2.5	2.05

Note. Values are means, standard deviations, medians, and percentiles of the parameters representing the subjects' positive mood, sorrow, and attitudes toward capital punishment based on the descriptive statistics analyzed via SPSS. The indices are based on means.

The authors use tables to organize their data so that readers can easily interpret it.

Table 2

Means (M), Standard Deviations (SD), Medians (μ), and Percentiles (P_{25}, P_{75}) for the Recipients' Identification with the Protagonist of the Respective Film

	The Chamber (original)	*Dancer in the Dark* (original)	*The Chamber* (edited)	*Dancer in the Dark* (edited)
M *(SD)*	2.59 (0.72)	3.00 (0.94)	2.83 (0.56)	3.40 (0.98)
P_{25}	2.07	2.30	2.50	2.57
μ	2.50	3.00	2.80	3.40
P_{75}	3.05	3.80	3.20	4.30

Note. Values are means, standard deviations, medians, and percentiles of the parameters representing the subjects' identification based on the descriptive statistics analyzed via SPSS. The indices are based on means.

For the correlations, the data across the four groups were collapsed and analyzed together, as only few differences were revealed between the respective films and film versions. Identification was significantly linked to the increase of sorrow (Spearman's $r = .39$, $r^2 = .15$, $n = 121$, $p < .001$) and the change of attitudes toward capital punishment (Spearman's $r = .21$, $r^2 = .04$, $n = 121$, $p < .05$), indicating that the more a viewer identified with the dying main character of the film, the more was the recipient's sadness increasing and the greater was his or her swing toward unfavorable assessments of the death penalty. Furthermore, there was a positive correlation between identification and the deterioration of positive mood close to statistical significance (Spearman's $r = .15$, $r^2 = .02$, $n = 121$, $p = .09$). Since identification was normally distributed, we performed regression analyses to further

Table 3

Findings from Wilcoxon Tests Performed on the Recipients' Mood and Attitudes toward Capital Punishment for Each Film

	The Chamber (original)	*Dancer in the Dark* (original)	*The Chamber* (edited)	*Dancer in the Dark* (edited)
Positive mood	−4.06***	−4.61***	−4.27***	−3.57***
Sorrow	−0.70	−3.56***	−2.33*	−2.19*
Attitudes toward capital punishment	−1.67	−0.96	−2.95**	−2.78**

*$p < .05$. **$p < .01$. ***$p < .001$. (two–tailed)

Note. Values are Z-values from Wilcoxon Tests representing the change of the subjects' positive mood, sorrow, and attitudes toward capital punishment.

examine the characteristics of the associations between the viewers' identification and the film effects. The influence of identification on the change of attitudes ($B = -3.01$, Standard error $= 1.46$, $p < .05$, $R^2 = .09$, adapted $R^2 = .08$, $F = 11.92$) and sorrow ($B = -4.27$, Standard error $= 1.18$, $p < .001$, $R^2 = .19$, $F = 29.36$) was significant—and close to statistical significance in terms of the reduction of positive mood ($B = 3.51$, Standard error $= 2.49$, $p = .16$, adapted $R^2 = .19$, $R^2 = .02$, adapted $R^2 = .01$, $F = 3.20$). In addition, Sobel-Tests with bootstrap estimates were conducted to verify mediation (see Preacher & Hayes, 2004). However, identification was not found to be a significant mediator variable for the film-induced attitude change ($Z = 1.17$, $n = 121$, $p = .23$, 95% CI $= -0.01$ to 0.04), the deterioration of positive mood ($Z = 1.21$, $n = 121$, $p = .22$, 95% CI $= -0.01$ to 0.08), and the increase of sorrow ($Z = -0.24$, $n = 121$, $p = .80$, 95% CI $= -0.09$ to 0.05). Thus, hypotheses 4a and b were rejected.

> After performing additional statistical analyses, the researchers reject hypothesis 4 (a and b).

DISCUSSION

The results of the present study show that recipients of films featuring the portrayal of the protagonist's execution are less happy and sadder after the screening than before. This effect is concordant with Zillmann's (1996) affective disposition theory proposing that an outcome victimizing the protagonist is deplored by the viewers and fits well with previous research demonstrating a deterioration of the viewers' mood after the screening of a drama (Hesse et al., 1992; Tannenbaum & Gaer, 1965; Till et al., 2010). It is interesting to note that this effect occurred in all groups showing no differences between the two motion pictures and the different film versions. The ineffectiveness of excluding scenes from a film to alter its emotional impact is consistent with findings of earlier research (see Ferracuti & Lazzari, 1970; Till et al., 2010; Till & Vitouch, 2008).

> The researchers discuss the meaning of their results and explore the implications of their findings for social science theory.

The negative portrayal of the death penalty in the two films also produced a diminished endorsement of capital punishment among the audience. This result is concordant with earlier research supporting the proposition that fictional television dramas can change people's opinion about the death penalty (Mutz & Nir, 2010; Slater et al., 2006). Given these results, it is plausible to assume that film dramas have the potential to affect viewers' political attitudes and influence their support not only for capital punishment, but also for other controversial public policies. However, a definite statement on this issue cannot be made based on our analyses.

> The researchers identify how their study's findings contribute to the body of research on the topic.

It is important to point out that the viewers' attitudes toward the death penalty changed only in the groups watching the edited versions of the movies. Usually, the removal of such film scenes is meant to mitigate film effects (see Worringham & Buxton, 1997), but in this case it increased the influence on the audience's attitudes. This finding is surprising and very puzzling because of its counterintuitive nature. A possible explanation for this result may be that recipients complement missing details in a film by using their imagination; this can lead to a more brutal or gruesome picture of an event in the viewer's imagination than actually displayed on screen, which might aggravate the impact of a movie (see Till & Vitouch, 2008). The human mind and its imaginativeness should not be neglected or underestimated. After all, the sheer imagination of an event can change attitudes and behavior (Anderson, 1983; Gregory, Burroughs, & Ainslie, 1985; Gregory, Cialdini, & Carpenter, 1982). This is in line with earlier findings that demonstrated a counterproductive impact of removing disturbing scenes from a film. Tannenbaum (1978), for example, reported higher physiological arousal when a violent scene of a film was deleted than without editing. He also found that some viewers believe to recall the deleted film scene, even though they never actually saw this particular scene. Therefore, simply removing a possibly disturbing scene from a film cannot be deemed to be an effective tool to mitigate potentially negative film effects.

Identification with the dying protagonist was not a significant mediator variable for the film-induced audience reactions. Various persuasion theories, such as the Elaboration Likelihood Model by Petty and Cacioppo (1986a, 1986b) or the Heuristic-Systematic Model by Chaiken (1980), suggest that absorption in a narrative and response to its characters enhance persuasive effects and suppress counter arguing, which is likely to be a necessary prerequisite for behavior change (Slater & Rouner, 2002). In this study, however, there is only limited evidence for identification to produce such effects. Maybe identification is not an adequate concept to comprehend the viewers' reception process, as suggested by Zillmann (1994, 1996). Other concepts, such as involvement (Krugman, 1965), transportation (Gerrig, 1993), modes of reception (Suckfüll & Scharkow, 2009), para-social interaction (Horton & Wohl, 1956), or empathy (Zillmann, 1991), might be more adequate to explore the psychological dynamics of how film messages may influence human emotions, attitudes, and behavior.

This study also has some limitations. First, most of our hypotheses were 25 tested in a before–after quasi-experimental design with repetition of the exact measures within a 2-hr period. This approach might have attenuated the films' effects. Furthermore, the distribution of several variables was too skewed to assume normal distribution of the data. Therefore, nonparametric tests were applied that are known to have less statistical power than parametric tests (Hodges & Lehmann, 1956). The fact that the data was not normally distributed is not uncommon (Altman & Bland, 1995), but is certainly noteworthy and needs to be considered at the interpretation of the results, including their generalization to the general public. A reason for the skewed distribution of the data might be the relatively small sample size (Altman & Bland, 1995). Finally, both movies in our study featured a critical or negative portrayal of the death penalty, so our results do not refer necessarily to all films focusing on capital punishment. However, most films in today's mainstream do not glorify capital punishment (see e.g., Giles, 1995).

Our results provide no reason to believe that people will suffer emotional distress due to watching motion pictures featuring the execution of the protagonist, but these films certainly deteriorate the viewers' mood and have the potential to influence their social values and beliefs. It also challenges Tyler and Boeckmann's (1997) proposition that support for capital punishment is strongly linked to values that reflect stable and long-standing political orientations, and it supports the notion that approval of the death penalty is based on emotion rather than factual information (Ellsworth & Gross, 1994). It seems that values and priorities communicated by television dramas have a nontrivial influence on public policies (Slater et al., 2006) by shaping people's political views through emotions (Mutz & Nir, 2010). Our study also clearly shows that the exclusion of death scenes is not an effective tool to mitigate the impact of a brutal or gruesome film. As we were able to demonstrate, that kind of editing may even lead to adverse effects. This finding highlights the need for new schemes to protect television viewers from harmful effects.

> *The researchers conclude by identifying the broader implications of their study for the effects of movies on viewers' ideas about capital punishment.*

> *The researchers note a possible area of interest for further investigation or future research.*

REFERENCES

> *The References follow APA style, which is the most commonly used documentation system in the social sciences. See the Appendix for details.*

Altman, D. G., & Bland, J. M. (1995). Statistics notes: The normal distribution. *British Medical Journal, 310,* 298.

Anderson, C. A. (1983). Imagination and expectation: The effect of imagining behavioral scripts on personal intentions. *Journal of Personality and Social Psychology, 45,* 293–305.

Basil, M. D. (1996). Identification as a mediator of celebrity effects. *Journal of Broadcasting & Electronic Media, 40,* 478–495.

Brown, W. J., & Basil, M. D. (1995). Media celebrities and public health: Responses to "Magic" Johnson's HIV disclosure and its impact on AIDS risk and high-risk behaviors. *Health Communication, 7*(4), 345–370.

Chaiken, S. (1980). Heuristic versus systematic processing and the use of source versus message cues in persuasion. *Journal of Personality and Social Psychology, 39,* 752–766.

Cohen, J. (2001). Defining identification: A theoretical look at the identification of audiences with media characters. *Mass Communication & Society, 4*(3), 245–264.

Ellsworth, P., & Gross, S. (1994). Hardening of the attitudes: Americans' views of the death penalty. *Journal of Social Issues, 50*(2), 19–52.

Etzersdorfer, E., & Sonneck, G. (1998). Preventing suicide by influencing mass-media reporting. The Viennese experience 1980–1996. *Archives of Suicide Research, 4,* 67–74.

Fan, D. P., Keltner, K. A., & Wyatt, R. O. (2002). A matter of guilt or innocence: How news reports affect support for the death penalty in the United States. *International Journal of Public Opinion Research, 14*(4), 439–452.

Ferracuti, F., & Lazzari, R. (1970). Indagine sperimentale sugli effetti immediati della presentazione di scene di violenza filmata [An experimental research on the immediate effects of the presentation of scenes of violence in motion pictures]. *Bollettino di Psicologia Applicata, 100–102,* 87–153.

Festinger, L. (1954). A theory of social comparison processes. *Human Relations, 7,* 117–140.

Gau, L.-S., James, J. D., & Kim, J.-C. (2009). Effects of team identification on motives, behavior outcomes, and perceived service quality. *Asian Journal of Management and Humanity Sciences, 4*(2–3), 76–90.

Gerrig, R. J. (1993). *Experiencing narrative worlds. On the psychological activities of reading.* New Haven, CT: Yale University Press.

Giles, J. E. (1995). Pop culture portrayals of capital punishment: A review of *Dead Man Walking* and *Among the Lowest of the Dead. American Journal of Criminal Justice, 20*(1), 137–146.

Greenwood, D. N. (2004). Transporting to TV-land: The impact of idealized character identification on self and body image. *Dissertation Abstracts International: Section B. Sciences and Engineering, 65*(6), 3222.

Gregory, W. L., Burroughs, W. J., & Ainslie, F. M. (1985). Self-relevant scenarios as an indirect means of attitude change. *Personality and Social Psychology Bulletin, 11*(4), 435–444.

Gregory, W. L., Cialdini, R. B., & Carpenter, K. M. (1982). Self-relevant scenarios as mediators of likelihood estimates and compliance: Does imagining make it so? *Journal of Personality and Social Psychology, 43*, 89–99.

Hesse, F. W., Spies, K., Hänze, M., & Gerrards-Hesse, A. (1992). Experimentelle Induktion emotionaler Zustände: Alternativen zur Velten-Methode [Experimental induction of mood states: Alternatives to the Velten method]. *Zeitschrift für Experimentelle und Angewandte Psychologie, 39*, 559–580.

Hodges, J., & Lehmann, E. L. (1956). The efficiency of some nonparametric competitors of the t test. *Annals of Mathematical Statistics, 27*, 324–335.

Hoffner, C., & Cantor, J. (1991). Perceiving and responding to mass media characters. In J. Bryant & D. Zillmann (Eds.), *Responding to the screen: Reception and reaction processes* (pp. 63–101). Hillsdale, NJ: Erlbaum.

Holbert, R. L., Shah, D. V., & Kwak, N. (2004). Fear, authority, and justice: Crime-related TV viewing and endorsements of capital punishment and gun ownership. *Journalism & Mass Communication Quarterly, 81*(2), 343–363.

Horton, D., & Wohl, R. R. (1956). Mass communication and para-social interaction. Observations on intimacy at a distance. *Psychiatry, 19*, 215–224.

Howells, G. N., Flanagan, K. A., & Hagan, V. (1995). Does viewing a televised execution affect attitudes toward capital punishment? *Criminal Justice and Behavior, 22*(4), 411–424.

Krugman, H. E. (1965). The impact of television advertising: Learning without involvement. *Public Opinion Quarterly, 29*, 349–356.

Mares, M. L., & Cantor, J. (1992). Elderly viewers' responses to televised portrayals of old age. Empathy and mood management versus social comparison. *Communication Research, 19*, 459–478. doi:10.1177/009365092019004004

McNair, D. M., Lorr, M., & Doppleman, L. F. (1971). *EITS manual for the profile of mood states.* San Diego, CA: Educational and Industrial Testing Service.

Mutz, D. C., & Nir, L. (2010). Not necessarily the news: Does fictional television influence real-world policy preferences? *Mass Communication and Society, 13*, 196–217.

Nabi, R. L., Finnerty, K., Domschke, T., & Hull, S. (2006). Does misery love company? Exploring the therapeutic effects of TV viewing on regretted experiences. *Journal of Communication, 56*, 689–706.

Niederkrotenthaler, T., & Sonneck, G. (2007). Assessing the impact of media guidelines for reporting on suicides in Austria: Interrupted times series analysis. *Australian and New Zealand Journal of Psychiatry, 41*, 419–428.

Niederkrotenthaler, T., Till, B., Kapusta, N. D., Voracek, M., Dervic, K., & Sonneck, G. (2009). Copycat effects after media reports on suicide: A population-based ecologic study. *Social Science & Medicine, 69*(7), 1085–1090.

Niven, D. (2002). Bolstering an illusory majority: The effects of the media's portrayal of death penalty support. *Social Science Quarterly, 83*(3), 671–689.

Önder, Ö. M., & Öner-Özkan, B. (2003). Visual perspective in causal attribution, empathy and attitude change. *Psychological Reports, 93*, 1035–1046.

Perry, D. G., & Perry, L. C. (1976). Identification with film characters, covert aggressive verbalization, and reactions to film violence. *Journal of Research in Personality, 10*(4), 399–409.

Peterson, R. C., & Thurstone, L. L. (1970). *Motion pictures and the social attitudes of children.* New York: Arno Press & *The New York Times.*

Petty, R. E., & Cacioppo, J. T. (1986a). *Communication and persuasion: Central and peripheral routes to attitude change.* New York: Springer.

Petty, R. E., & Cacioppo, J. T. (1986b). The elaboration likelihood model of persuasion. *Advances in Experimental Social Psychology, 19*, 123–205.

Preacher, K. J., & Hayes, A. F. (2004). SPSS and SAS procedures for estimating indirect effects in simple mediation models. *Behavior Research Methods, Instruments, and Computers, 36*, 717–731.

Slater, M. D., & Rouner, D. (2002). Entertainment-education and elaboration likelihood: Understanding the processing of narrative persuasion. *Communication Theory, 12*(2), 173–191.

Slater, M. D., Rouner, D., & Long, M. (2006). Television dramas and support for controversial public policies: Effects and mechanisms. *Journal of Communication, 56*, 235–252.

Sonneck, G., Etzersdorfer, E., & Nagel-Kuess, S. (1994). Imitative suicide on the Viennese subway. *Social Science & Medicine, 38*, 453–457.

Sotirovic, M. (2001). Effects of media use on complexity and extremity of attitudes toward the death penalty and prisoners' rehabilitation. *Media Psychology, 3*, 1–24.

Suckfüll, M., & Scharkow, M. (2009). Modes of reception for fictional films. *Communications, 34*, 361–384.

Tan, E. S. (2008). Entertainment is emotion: The functional architecture of the entertainment experience. *Media Psychology, 11*, 28–51.

Tannenbaum, P. H. (1978). Emotionale Erregung durch kommunikative Reize. Der Stand der Forschung [Emotional arousal via communicative stimuli. State of the art]. *Fernsehen und Bildung, 12*(3), 184–195.

Tannenbaum, P. H., & Gaer, E. P. (1965). Mood change as a function of stress of protagonist and degree of identification in a film viewing situation. *Journal of Personality and Social Psychology, 2*, 612–616.

Till, B., Niederkrotenthaler, T., Herberth, A., Vitouch, P., & Sonneck, G. (2010). Suicide in films: The impact of suicide portrayals on non-suicidal viewers' well-being and the effectiveness of censorship. *Suicide & Life-Threatening Behavior, 40*(4), 319–327.

Till, B., & Vitouch, P. (2008). On the impact of suicide portrayal in films: Preliminary results. In A. Herberth, T. Niederkotenthaler, & B. Till (Eds.), *Suizidalität in den Medien/Suicidality in the media: Interdisziplinäre Betrachtungen/Interdisciplinary contributions* (pp. 69–77). Münster, Germany: LIT.

Tyler, T. R., & Boeckmann, R. J. (1997). Three strikes and you are out, but why? The psychology of public support for punishing rule breakers. *Law & Society Review, 31*, 237–265.

Worringham, R., & Buxton, R. A. (1997). Censorship. In H. Newcomb (Ed.), *The encyclopedia of television* (Vol. 1, pp. 331–334). Chicago: Fitzroy Dearborn.

Zillmann, D. (1991). Empathy: Affect from bearing witness to the emotions of others. In J. Bryant & D. Zillmann (Eds.), *Responding to the screen: Reception and reaction processes* (pp. 135–167). Hillsdale, NJ: Erlbaum.

Zillmann, D. (1994). Mechanisms of emotional involvement with drama. *Poetics, 23*, 33–51.

Zillmann, D. (1996). The psychology of suspense in dramatic exposition. In P. Vorderer, H. J. Wulff, & M. Friedrichsen (Eds.), *Suspense: Conceptualizations, theoretical analyses, and empirical explorations* (pp. 199–231). Mahwah, NJ: Erlbaum.

Reading Questions

1. What do the authors present as their central research question? Where is this question located in their research report?

2. Based on their review of previous scholarship, are Till and Vitouch able to identify any areas of clear agreement among scholars? If so, what are they?

Rhetoric Questions

3. Take a look at the structure of the study's Discussion section paragraph-by-paragraph. How is it organized, and what is the logic guiding the organization? Is this organization likely to be helpful to the intended audience? Why or why not?

4. The researchers note a number of limitations affecting their study's results. For you as a reader, what is the effect of the authors' identifying these limitations?

Response Question

5. Identify a film that has directly influenced the way you feel about a particular social issue or topic. What was the social issue or topic? In what ways were you affected? Explain why you believe the film was able to affect your beliefs or attitudes.

ACADEMIC CASE STUDY • CAPITAL PUNISHMENT NATURAL SCIENCES

Lethal Injection for Execution: Chemical Asphyxiation?

TERESA A. ZIMMERS, JONATHAN SHELDON, DAVID A. LUBARSKY, FRANCISCO LÓPEZ-MUÑOZ, LINDA WATERMAN, RICHARD WEISMAN, AND LEONIDAS G. KONIARIS

Teresa A. Zimmers is the H. H. Gregg Professor of Cancer Research at Indiana University's School of Medicine. "Lethal Injection for Execution: Chemical Asphyxiation?," a study co-written with six of her colleagues at the University of Miami Miller School of Medicine and published in the online access journal *PLoS Medicine* in 2007, offers evidence to challenge "the conventional view of lethal injection [as] leading to an invariably peaceful and painless death." According to the editor of the journal that published the study, the researchers' findings call into question the constitutionality of the current lethal injection protocol.

ABSTRACT

Background

Lethal injection for execution was conceived as a comparatively humane alternative to electrocution or cyanide gas. The current protocols are based on one improvised by a medical examiner and an anesthesiologist in Oklahoma and are practiced on an ad hoc basis at the discretion of prison personnel. Each drug used, the ultrashort-acting barbiturate thiopental, the neuromuscular blocker pancuronium bromide, and the electrolyte potassium chloride, was expected to be lethal alone, while the combination was intended to produce anesthesia then death due to respiratory and cardiac arrest. We sought to determine whether the current drug regimen results in death in the manner intended.

Methods and Findings

We analyzed data from two US states that release information on executions, North Carolina and California, as well as the published clinical, laboratory, and veterinary animal experience. Execution outcomes from North Carolina and California together with interspecies dosage scaling of thiopental effects suggest that in the current practice of lethal injection, thiopental might not be fatal and might be insufficient to induce surgical anesthesia for the duration of the execution. Furthermore, evidence from North Carolina, California, and Virginia indicates that potassium chloride in lethal injection does not reliably induce cardiac arrest.

Conclusions

We were able to analyze only a limited number of executions. However, our findings suggest that current lethal injection protocols may not reliably effect death through the mechanisms intended, indicating a failure of design and implementation. If thiopental and potassium chloride fail to cause anesthesia and cardiac arrest, potentially aware inmates could die through pancuronium-induced asphyxiation. Thus the conventional view of lethal injection leading to an invariably peaceful and painless death is questionable.

EDITORS' SUMMARY

Background

Lethal injection is a common form of execution in a number of countries, most prominently the United States and China. The protocols currently used in the United States contain three drugs: an ultrashort-acting barbiturate, thiopental (which acts as an anesthetic, but does not have any analgesic effect); a neuromuscular blocker, pancuronium bromide (which causes muscle paralysis); and an electrolyte, potassium chloride (which stops the heart from beating). Each of these drugs on its own was apparently intended by those who derived the protocols to be sufficient to cause death; the combination was intended to produce anesthesia then death due to respiratory and cardiac arrest. Following a number of executions in the United States, however, it has recently become apparent that the regimen as currently administered does not work as efficiently as intended. Some prisoners take many minutes to die, and others become very distressed.

Why Was This Study Done?

It is possible that one cause of these difficulties with the injections is that the staff administering the drugs are not sufficiently competent; doctors and nurses in the United States are banned by their professional organizations from participating in executions and hence most personnel have little medical knowledge or skill. Alternatively, the drug regimens used might not be effective; it is not clear whether they were derived in any rational way. The researchers here wanted to investigate the scientific basis for the protocols used.

What Did the Researchers Do and Find?

They analyzed data from some of the few states (North Carolina and California) that release information on executions. They also assessed the regimens with respect to published data from clinical, laboratory, and veterinary animal studies. The authors concluded that in the current regimen thiopental might not be fatal and might be insufficient to induce surgical anesthesia for the duration of the execution, and that potassium chloride does not reliably induce cardiac arrest. They conclude therefore that potentially aware inmates could die through asphyxiation induced by the muscle paralysis caused by pancuronium.

What Do These Findings Mean?

The authors conclude that even if lethal injection is administered without technical error, those executed may experience suffocation, and therefore that "the conventional view of lethal injection as an invariably peaceful and painless death is questionable." The Eighth Amendment of the US Constitution prohibits cruel and unusual punishment. The results of this paper suggest that current protocols used for lethal injection in the United States probably violate this amendment.

Additional Information

Please access these Web sites via the online version of this summary at http://dx.doi.org/10.1371/journal.pmed.0040156.

- In a linked editorial the PLoS Medicine editors discuss this paper further and call for the abolition of the death penalty.

- The Death Penalty Information Center is a rich resource on the death penalty both in the United States and internationally.

- Information on challenges to lethal injection in various states, including California and North Carolina, is available from the University of California, Berkeley, School of Law.

- Human Rights Watch monitors executions in the United States.

- Amnesty International campaigns against the death penalty.

- A compendium of death-penalty-related links are available from a pro-death-penalty site, the Clark County Prosecuting Attorney.

INTRODUCTION

In the United States, lethal injection can be imposed in 37 states and by the federal government and military. The origin of the lethal injection protocol can be traced to legislators in Oklahoma searching for a less expensive and potentially more humane alternative to the electric chair [1]. Both the state medical examiner and a chairman of anesthesiology appear to have been consulted in the writing of the statute. The medical examiner has since indicated that no research went into his choice of drugs—thiopental, pancuronium bromide, and potassium chloride—but rather he was guided by his own experience as a patient [2]. His expectation was that the inmate would be adequately anesthetized, and that although each individual drug would be lethal in the dosage specified, the combination would provide redundancy. The anesthesiologist's input relating to thiopental was written into law as "the punishment of death must be inflicted by continuous, intravenous administration of a lethal quantity of an ultra-short-acting barbiturate in combination with a chemical paralytic agent" [3], although in practice Oklahoma uses bolus dosing of all three drugs [4,5]. Texas, the first state to execute a prisoner by lethal injection, and subsequently other jurisdictions copied Oklahoma's protocol without any additional medical consultation [1].

Although executioners invariably achieve death, the mechanisms of death and the adequacy of anesthesia are unclear. Used independently in sufficiently high doses, thiopental can induce death by respiratory arrest and/or circulatory depression, pancuronium bromide by muscle paralysis and respiratory arrest, and potassium chloride by cardiac arrest. When used together, death might be achieved by a combination of respiratory arrest and cardiac arrest due to one or more of the drugs used. Because thiopental has no analgesic effects (in fact, it can be antianalgesic) [6], and because pancuronium would prevent movement in response to the sensations of suffocation and potassium-induced burning, a continuous surgical plane of anesthesia is necessary to prevent extreme suffering in lethal injection.

Recently we reported that in most US executions, executioners have no anesthesia training, drugs are administered remotely with no monitoring for anesthesia, data are not recorded, and no peer review is done [7]. We suggested that such inherent procedural problems might lead to insufficient anesthesia in executions, an assertion supported by low postmortem blood thiopental levels and eyewitness accounts of problematic executions. Because of a current lack of data and reports of problems with lethal injection for executions, we sought to evaluate the three-drug protocol for its efficacy in producing a rapid death with minimal likelihood of pain and suffering.

METHODS

North Carolina lethal injection protocols were determined from Department of Corrections drug procurement records and testimony of prison personnel participating in the process. Times to death were determined from North Carolina Department of Corrections documents, including the Web site [8], official statements, and corroborating news and eyewitness reports. Start times were available for 33 executions, of which 19 could be independently confirmed. The North Carolina warden pronounces death after a flat line is displayed on the electrocardiogram (ECG) monitor for 5 min, thus time to death was calculated from start time to pronouncement of death less 5 min. Dosages were calculated from postmortem body weights taken from Reports of Investigation by the North Carolina Office of the Chief Medical Examiner. Information regarding the California protocol and execution logs and Florida and Virginia executions were obtained through available court documents [9,10,11]. Data are expressed as mean ± standard deviation. One-way ANOVA with Tukey's multiple comparison test was used for statistical analysis.

RESULTS

Data from North Carolina Executions

Three lethal injection protocols have been used in North Carolina from the first execution in 1984 to the most recent at the time of this writing in August 2006 (Figure 1A). The initial use of serial, intravenous (IV) injections of 3 g of thiopental and 40 mg of pancuronium bromide (referred to here as "Protocol A," $n = 8$, Figure 1A) was superseded by Protocol B in 1998. Protocol B consisted of serial injections of 1.5 g of thiopental, 80 mEq of potassium chloride, 40 mg of pancuronium bromide, 80 mEq of potassium chloride, and finally 1.5 g of thiopental ($n = 21$) [1,12]. After criticism from expert witnesses [13], in 2004 the injection order was changed to the current protocol of serial injections of 3 g of thiopental, 40 mg of pancuronium bromide, and 160 mEq of potassium chloride (Protocol C, $n = 11$) [14]. Each injection is performed in rapid succession with intermittent saline flushes to avoid drug precipitation. Until the last two executions in 2007, no assessment or monitoring of anesthesia was performed.

According to the North Carolina Department of Corrections, once the ECG monitor displays a flat line for 5 min, the warden declares death and a physician certifies that death has occurred [7,12]. Execution start times and declaration times were available for 33 of the 42 lethal injections conducted in North Carolina (Figure 1B). Mean times to death were 9.88 ± 3.87 min for Protocol A, 13.47 ± 4.88 min for Protocol B, and 9.00 ± 3.71 min for Protocol C. The mean time to death for Protocol B was significantly longer than for Protocol C ($p < 0.05$, Tukey-Kramer test after one-way ANOVA). No other differences were statistically significant. These data indicate that the five-dose regimen of Protocol B slightly prolonged time to death, but more importantly, they indicate that the addition of potassium chloride did not hasten death overall.

In contrast to clinical use of these same drugs, jurisdictions invariably specify mass quantities for injection rather than dosing by body weight. We sought to determine the actual doses used in executions using postmortem body weights recorded by the Office of the Medical Examiner. North Carolina injects 3 g of thiopental; however, in Protocol B inmates were given half the thiopental at the end, once all painful stimuli were administered and death should have

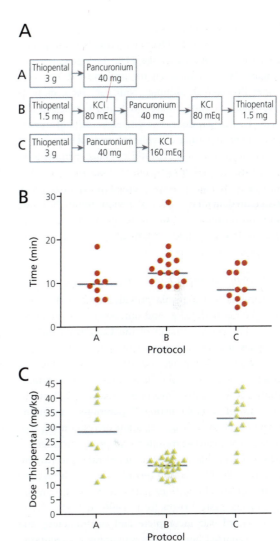

Figure 1 Lethal Injection Executions in North Carolina

(A) Schematic depicting quantity and order of drug administration in the three protocols.

(B) Time to death by protocol, calculated as the interval from execution start time to declaration of death, minus 5 min (see Methods).

(C) Actual dose of thiopental by body weight (not available for all inmates). In Protocol B, 1.5 g of thiopental was given after the pancuronium bromide and potassium chloride, once painful stimuli had been administered and death should have occurred; accordingly, only the first 1.5 g dose is plotted.

DOI:10.1371/JOURNAL.PMED.0040156.G001

been achieved. Thus we considered only the first 1.5 g for Protocol B. Overall the median thiopental dose was 20.3 mg/kg (range 11.2–44 mg/kg, $n = 40$) (Figure 1C). Virtually all of the lowest doses were under Protocol B, although four very large individuals executed under Protocols A and C received less than the median dose. Eyewitness reports of inmate movement including convulsions and attempts to sit up in four executions [15] did not cluster in the lowest doses, but rather occurred at doses of 17.1, 18.9, 19.6, and 21 mg/kg, all performed under Protocol B. Calculated median doses of pancuronium bromide and potassium chloride were 0.46 mg/kg (range 0.28–0.46 mg/kg) and 1.83 mEq/kg (range 1.11–2.35 mEq/kg), respectively.

Data from California Executions

Executions in California provided a second insight into the methodologies and outcomes in lethal injections. The public version of the California protocol specifies injection of 5 g of thiopental, 100 mg of pancuronium bromide, and 100 mEq of potassium chloride [9]. California Department of Corrections from 226A, "Lethal Injection—Execution Record," consists of a table listing "operations," including injection of each drug, cessation of respiration, flat-lining of the cardiac monitor, and pronouncement of death, with columns for time, heart rate, and respiration rate. Such execution records were available for 9 of the 11 lethal injections performed in San Quentin California State Prison from 1996 to 2006 [9,10]. One record was incomplete and contradictory and is not reported here. In the remaining 8 executions, respiration rate ceased from 1 min (inmate WB1966) to 9 min (CA2006) after the injection of thiopental (Figure 2). Cessation of respiration was noted coincident with (WB1966, SW2005, CA2006) or up to 3 min after (SA2002) injection of pancuronium bromide. Flatlining of the cardiac monitor occurred 2 min (DR2000) to 8 min (JS1999) after the last injection of potassium chloride. The records indicate that a second dose of potassium chloride was used in the execution of SA2002, and the California warden has said that additional doses were used in two

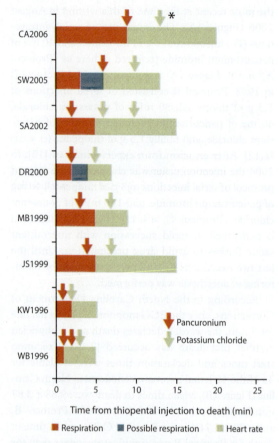

Figure 2 Lethal Injection Executions in California

Depicted are duration of respiration and heart rate after initiation of the thiopental injection at time 0. Injection of pancuronium bromide is indicated by the red arrow, potassium chloride by the green arrow. Note that additional injections were given of potassium chloride in SA2002 and of pancuronium bromide in WB1996. SW2005 was noted to be breathing 3 min after thiopental, but not at the time of pancuronium bromide injection; the exact time respiration ceased was not recorded. DR2000 was noted to have chest movements 2 min after respiration was noted to have ceased. *A second dose of potassium chloride was administered to CA2006, but not noted on the log. A third, unidentified inmate was also given a second dose of potassium chloride, according to the warden (see text).

DOI:10.1371/JOURNAL.PMED.0040156.G002

other executions, one being CA2006 and the other unknown [16]. Eyewitness reports document "sudden and extreme" convulsive movements 3–4 min into the execution of MB1999 [17] and more than

30 heaving, convulsive movements of the chest and abdomen of SA2002 [18].

DISCUSSION

Most US executions are beset by procedural problems that could lead to insufficient anesthesia in executions. This hypothesis has been supported by findings of low postmortem blood thiopental levels and eyewitness accounts of problematic executions. Herein we report evidence that the design of the drug scheme itself is flawed. Thiopental does not predictably induce respiratory arrest, nor does potassium chloride always induce cardiac arrest. Furthermore, on the basis of execution data and clinical, veterinary, and laboratory animal studies, we posit that the specified quantity of thiopental may not provide surgical anesthesia for the duration of the execution. Thus some inmates may experience the sensations of pancuronium-induced paralysis and respiratory arrest.

In the United States and Europe, techniques of 10 animal euthanasia for clinical, laboratory, and agricultural applications are rigorously evaluated and governed by professional, institutional, and regulatory oversight. In university and laboratory settings, local oversight bodies known as Animal Care and Use Committees typically follow the American Veterinary Medical Association's guidelines on euthanasia, which consider all aspects of euthanasia methods, including drugs, tools, and expertise of personnel in order to minimize pain and distress to the animal. Under those guidelines, lethal injections of companion or laboratory animals are limited to injection by qualified personnel of certain clinically tested, Food and Drug Administration–approved anesthetics or euthanasics, while monitoring for awareness.

In stark contrast to animal euthanasia, lethal injection for judicial execution was designed and implemented with no clinical or basic research whatsoever. To our knowledge, no ethical or oversight groups have ever evaluated the protocols and outcomes in lethal injection. Furthermore, there are no published clinical or experimental data regarding the safety and efficacy of the three-drug lethal injection protocol. Until the unprecedented and controversial use of bispectral index monitoring in the last two North Carolina lethal injections [19], no monitoring for anesthesia was performed. Given this paucity of knowledge and documentation, we sought to evaluate available data in order to determine the efficacy of the three-drug protocol.

The designers of lethal injection intended that each of the drugs be fatal independently and that the combination provide redundancy [2]. Moreover, in legal challenges to the death penalty, the leading expert witness testifying on behalf of the states routinely asserts that 3 g of thiopental alone is a lethal dose in almost all cases [14]. The data presented here, however, suggest that thiopental alone might not be lethal. First, extrapolating from clinical use, the lowest dosages used in some jurisdictions would not be expected to kill. Calculated dosages in North Carolina executions using 3 g of thiopental ranged from 10 to 45 mg/kg. Assuming inmates are roughly the same size across jurisdictions, the dose range would be 17–75 mg/kg in California, where 5 g of thiopental is used, and 6.6–30 mg/kg in Virginia and other jurisdictions, which use 2 g. Thus, at the lowest doses, thiopental would be given near the upper range of that recommended for clinical induction of anesthesia (3–6.6 mg/kg)—clearly not a dose designed to be fatal [20]. Second, the calculated doses used across lethal injections are only 0.1–2 times the LD_{50} (dose required to kill 50% of the tested population) of thiopental in dogs (37 mg/kg), rabbits (35 mg/kg), rats (57.8 mg/kg), and mice (91.4 mg/kg) [21, 22]. Third, intravenous delivery of thiopental alone is not recommended by the Netherlands Euthanasics Task Force, which concluded "it is not possible to administer so much of it that a lethal effect is guaranteed" [23], even in their population of profoundly ill patients.

The most compelling evidence that even 5 g of thiopental alone may not be lethal, however, is that some California inmates continued to breathe for up to 9 min after thiopental was injected. This observation directly contradicts testimony of that state's expert witness, who asserted that "this dose of thiopental sodium will cause virtually all persons to stop breathing within a minute of drug administration" and that "virtually every person given 5 grams of thiopental sodium will have stopped breathing prior to the administration of the pancuronium bromide" [24]. The witness has made identical statements regarding 3 g of thiopental [14]. Indeed, the clinical literature is replete with examples of patients experiencing respiratory failure after even low doses of thiopental [25]. Others, however, experience merely transient, nonfatal apnea. Of course, for inmates who did not stop breathing with thiopental alone, it is impossible to know whether the thiopental solution was correctly mixed, whether the entire dose was administered intravenously, or whether the apparent resistance was due to bolus dosing or individual variation. It remains possible, however, that bolus dosing of 5 g of thiopental alone might not be fatal in all persons. Indeed, nonhuman primates given as much as 60 mg/kg (the mass equivalent of 6 g for a 100 kg man) experienced prolonged sleep, but ultimately recovered [26].

If thiopental does not reliably kill the inmates, then perhaps death is effected by potassium chloride. Rapid intravenous or intracardiac administration of 1–2 mmol/kg potassium chloride under general anesthesia is considered acceptable for euthanasia of large animal species; thus the 1.11–2.35 mmol/kg doses given in North Carolina's lethal injections ought to be fatal. If potassium chloride contributes to death through cardiotoxicity, however, cardiac activity ought to cease more quickly when potassium is used than when it is not. Indeed, such is the principle behind the animal euthanasia agent, Beuthanasia-D Special, in which the cardiotoxic effects of phenytoin synergize with the central nervous system–depressive effects of pentobarbital, accelerating death over pentobarbital alone [27]. In contrast, our analysis shows that use of potassium chloride in North Carolina's Protocol C did not hasten death (defined as flatlining of the ECG) over Protocol A, which used thiopental and pancuronium alone. Moreover, in California executions, ECG flatlining was noted from 2 to 9 min after potassium chloride

administration. This observation contrasts sharply with reports of accidental bolus IV administration of concentrated potassium chloride solution, in which patients experienced complete cardiopulmonary arrest almost immediately upon injection [28]. The North Carolina and California data together suggest that potassium chloride might not be the lethal agent in lethal injection.

Given that neither thiopental nor potassium [15] chloride can be construed reliably to be the agent of death in lethal injection, death in at least some inmates might have been due to respiratory cessation from the use of pancuronium bromide. The typical use of 0.06–0.1 mg/kg pancuronium bromide under balanced anesthesia produces 100% neuromuscular blockade within 4 min, with approximately 100 min required for 25% recovery [29]. The doses used in North Carolina were some 3–11 times greater than the typical intubation dose, and thus would be expected to produce more rapid paralysis of many hours duration and complete respiratory arrest [30]. Indeed, pancuronium might have been the agent of death even in inmates who ceased breathing coincident with or shortly after injection of pancuronium, rendering permanent the thiopental-induced apnea. In addition, because pancuronium bromide is effective even when delivered subcutaneously or intramuscularly, pancuronium is likely the sole agent of death when IV catheter misplacement or blowout impairs systemic delivery of the other two drugs. In such cases death by suffocation would occur in a paralyzed inmate fully aware of the progressive suffocation and potassium-induced sensation of burning. This was likely the experience of Florida inmate Angel Diaz, whose eyes were open and mouth was moving 24 min into his execution and who was pronounced dead after 34 min. Findings of two 30-cm burns over both antecubital fossae prompted the medical examiner to conclude that the IV lines were misplaced and the drugs were delivered subcutaneously [31].

Executions such as Diaz's, in which additional drugs were required, constitute further evidence that the lethal injection protocols are not adequate to ensure a predictable, painless death. Court documents and news reports indicate that at least Virginia [32], California [10], and Florida [31] have administered additional potassium chloride in multiple executions when the inmate failed to die as expected. If a Virginia execution takes too long and if the inmate fails to die, the protocol indicates that additional pancuronium and potassium chloride should be injected, although there is no provision for additional thiopental [32]. In cases such as Diaz's, additional drugs may have been required due to technical problems with delivery, but it remains possible that in others, the standard drug protocol failed to kill.

Given the uncertainty surrounding the mechanism of death and low postmortem blood thiopental levels in some executed inmates [7], one must ask whether adequate anesthesia is maintained to prevent awareness and suffering. Medical experts on both sides of the lethal injection debate have asserted that 3 g of thiopental properly delivered should reliably result in either death or a long, deep surgical plane of anesthesia [13,14]. In support of this contention, continuous or intermittent thiopental administration was formerly used for surgical procedures lasting many hours. In one study, 3.3–3.9 g given to patients over 25–50 min resulted in sleep for 4–5.5 h [33]. Depth and duration of thiopental anesthesia depends greatly upon dose and rate of administration, however, and bolus dosing results in significantly different pharmacokinetics and duration of efficacy than administration of the same quantity of drug at a lower rate [22].

In the modern practice of anesthesia, thiopental is used solely to induce a few moments of anesthesia prior to administering additional agents. Anesthesiologists are taught to administer a small test dose while assessing patient response and the need for additional doses [20]. Such stepwise administration and evaluation has been the practice from the first reports of thiopental usage in 1934, due to the known potential for barbiturate-induced respiratory arrest [34]. It was early recognized that age, body composition, health status, anxiety, premedication, and history of substance abuse clearly influence response to thiopental, with some individuals showing marked resistance to standard doses [35] and others fatal sensitivity [25]. Thus the historical and modern clinical use of thiopental results from its cautious application to prevent respiratory arrest both in the typical patient and the abnormally susceptible. In consequence, there is almost no information about duration of anesthesia following large bolus doses of thiopental in unpremedicated patients, and there are few living anesthesiologists with clinical experience relevant to lethal injection protocols.

Unlike in clinical medicine, however, bolus injection of thiopental is regularly practiced in laboratory animals and veterinary medicine. Standard texts specify from 6 to 50 mg/kg thiopental, depending on the species, for 5–10 min of anesthesia [36], including 18–22 mg/kg for 10–15 min of anesthesia in dogs, pigs, sheep, and swine [37]. Such dosages are conservative guidelines based on average responses of animals in experimental trials (Table 1), with the assumption that respiration and depth of anesthesia will be assessed in individual animals prior to onset of the procedure. (In addition, thiopental is not recommended for painful procedures in animals.) Withholding or administering additional dosages would compensate for individual variation in response.

Although species differences complicate pharmacological comparisons from animals to humans, animal studies are the basis for virtually all human drug trials. According to FDA guidelines, toxicity endpoints for drugs administered systemically to animals are typically assumed to scale well across species when doses are normalized to body surface area (i.e., mg/m^2) [38]. Calculating the human equivalent dose (HED) as recommended by the FDA [39] gives a more conservative estimate of thiopental equivalencies across species than does using simple mg/kg comparisons (Table 1). Swine in particular are regarded as an excellent model of human cardiopulmonary and cerebrovascular physiology, with comparable

Table 1
Reported Duration of Sleep or Anesthesia after Bolus IV Injections of Thiopental in Experimental Animals

Species	Dose (mg/kg)	n	Mean Duration of Sleep[a] (min)	Mean Duration of Anesthesia[b] (min)	Reference	Calculated HED[c] (mg/kg)
Mouse	30		4.7–6.4		[43]	2.4
Rat	20	32	4.0–7.0		[43]	3.2
	25	7	22.6		[43]	4
	18		9.3–10.5		[44]	2.88
	22		30.0 ± 6.0		[44]	3.52
Rabbit	20	1	0	0	[45]	6.4
	21	10	28		[21]	6.72
	22	16	14.8–15.2		[44]	7.04
Dog	10.2	5	10.8	1.8	[46]	5.51
	10.9	5	11.4	1.4	[46]	5.89
	15	8	26	8.5	[47]	8.1
	25	22	74.4 ± 7.1		[47]	13.5
Sheep	20	4	30–45	18.3 ± 5.10	[48]	18.1
	25			15	[49]	22.6
Goat	12.7–13.9	4		12.0 ± 5.20	[48]	8.8–9.6
Swine	13.8–25.0	4		5.5 ± 2.7	[48]	12.3–22.4
Cattle	20	4		32.25 ± 14.36	[46]	28.8
Nonhuman primate	60	1	95		[43]	16.5

[a] From loss to return of righting reflex or voluntary movement.

[b] Typically corneal areflexia.

[c] Human equivalent dose was calculated as HED = animal dose(mg/kg) × (animal weight[kg]/human weight[kg])$^{0.33}$ [35,36].

doi:10.1371/journal.pmed.0040156.t001

size, body composition, and brain perfusion rates [40]. Comparing the HED for thiopental anesthesia in swine to lethal injection dosages, we conclude that at least some inmates at the lower end of the thiopental dose range might have experienced fleeting or no surgical anesthesia, while others at the higher end of the range might have received doses predicted to induce more prolonged anesthesia (Table 1). Such a prediction is impossible to evaluate, however, because any evidence of suffering would be masked by the effects of pancuronium.

Our study is necessarily limited in scope and interpretations. Given the secrecy surrounding lethal injections, we were able to analyze only a small fraction of the 891 lethal injections in the United States to date. Indeed, the majority of executions actually take place in states such as Texas and Virginia, where the protocols and procedural problems are likely similar to the ones described, but where the states are unwilling to provide information [7]. Not only are available data limited, however, medical literature addressing the effects of these drugs at high doses and in combination is nonexistent, emphasizing the failure of lethal injection practitioners to design and evaluate rigorously a process that ensures reliable, painless death, even in animals. In consequence, the adequacy of anesthesia and mechanism of death in the current lethal injection protocol remains conjecture.

Despite such limitations, our analysis of data from more forthcoming states along with reports of problematic executions and judicial findings [41] together indicate that the protocol of lethal injection for execution is deeply flawed. Technical difficulties are clearly responsible for some mishandled executions, such as Diaz's. Better training of execution personnel and altering delivery conditions may not "fix" the problem [41, 42], however, because the drug regimen itself is potentially inadequate. Our analysis indicates that as used, thiopental might be insufficient both to maintain a surgical plane of anesthesia and to predictably induce death. Consequently, elimination of pancuronium or both pancuronium and potassium, as has been suggested in California [41], could result in situations in which inmates ultimately awaken.

With the growing recognition of flaws in the lethal injection protocol, 11 states have now suspended the death penalty, with nine of those seeking resolution of issues surrounding the process [42]. In California and Florida, commissions of experts have been charged with evaluating and refining lethal injection protocols. As deliberations begin, we suggest that the secrecy surrounding protocol design and implementation should be broken. The available data or lack of data should be made public and deliberations should be open and transparent.

SUPPORTING INFORMATION

Alternative Language Abstract S1. Translation into Spanish by Francisco López-Muñoz

Found at doi:10.1371/journal.pmed.0040156.sd001 (24 KB DOC)

ACKNOWLEDGMENTS

Author contributions. TAZ, JPS, DAL, and LGK conceived the study. TAZ and JPS obtained protocol information and execution data. TAZ, DAL, and LGK analyzed the data and published literature. DAL, LW, and RW provided clinical insights. TAZ, JPS, and FLM provided historical perspectives and references. All authors contributed to writing and editing the manuscript.

REFERENCES

[1] Denno D (2002) When legislatures delegate death: The troubling paradox behind state uses of electrocution and lethal injection and what it says about us. Ohio State Law J 63: 63–260. Available at: http://moritzlaw.osu.edu/lawjournal/issues/volume63/number1/denno.pdf. Accessed 16 March 2007.

[2] Fellner J, Tofte S (2006) So long as they die: Lethal injection in the United States. Human Rights Watch. Available at: http://hrw.org/reports/2006/us0406. Accessed 16 March 2007.

[3] Oklahoma Statute Title §22-1014(A) Available at: http://www.lsb.state.ok.us/osstatuestitle.html. Accessed 16 March 2007.

[4] United States District Court, Western District of Oklahoma (20 July 2005) Complaint and Motion to Dismiss, Anderson v. Evans. Case Number 5-825. Document Number 1, pp. 25–34.

[5] US District Court, Western District of Oklahoma (6 September 2005) Complaint and Motion to Dismiss, Anderson v. Evans. Case Number 5-825. Document Number 26, pp. 3–4.

[6] Dundee JW (1960) Alterations in response to somatic pain associated with anaesthesia. II. The effect of thiopentone and pentobarbitone. Br J Anaesth 32: 407–414.

[7] Koniaris LG, Zimmers TA, Lubarsky DA, Sheldon JP (2005) Inadequate anaesthesia in lethal injection for execution. Lancet 365: 1412–1414.

[8] North Carolina Department of Correction (2007) News regarding scheduled executions. Available at: http://www.doc.state.nc.us/dop/deathpenalty/execution__news.htm. Accessed 19 March 2007.

[9] United States District Court, Northern District of California (20 January 2006) Exhibit A to Motion for TRO,

Morales v. Hickman. Case Number 6-219. San Quentin Operational Procedure No. 770. Available at: http://www.law.berkeley.edu/clinics/dpclinic/Lethal%20Injection%20Documents/California/Morales/Morales%20Dist%20Ct.Cp/Ex%20A%20to%20TRO%20motion%20(Procedure%20No.%20770).pdf. Accessed 16 March 2007.

[10] United States District Court, Northern District of California (20 January 2006) Exhibit 2 to Exhibit C in Motion for TRO, Morales v. Hickman. Case Number 6-219. Document Number 15-2. Available at: http://www.law.berkeley.edu/clinics/dpclinic/Lethal%20Injection%20Resource%20Pages/resources.ca.html. Accessed 16 March 2007.

[11] United States Supreme Court (6 March 2007) Brief for Amicus Habeas Corpus Resource Center, Hill v. McDonough. Case Number 05-8794. Available at: http://www.law.berkeley.edu/clinics/dpclinic/Lethal%20Injection%20Documents/Florida/Hill/2006.03.06%20amicus%20hcrc.pdf. Accessed 16 March 2007.

[12] United States District Court, Eastern District of North Carolina (31 October 2005) Polk Deposition, Page v. Beck. Case Number 5:04-CT-4. Document Number 98.

[13] United States District Court, Eastern District of North Carolina (3 November 2005) Second Heath Affidavit, Page v. Beck. Case Number 4-04. Document Number 102.

[14] United States District Court, Eastern District of North Carolina (27 September 2004) Affidavit of Dershwitz, Perkins v. Beck. Case Number 04-643. Document Number 7, pp. 22–31.

[15] United States District Court, Eastern District of North Carolina (7 April 2006) Order, Brown v. Beck. Case Number 5:06-CT-3018-H. Available at: http://deathpenaltyinfo.org/Brownorder.pdf. Accessed 16 March 2007.

[16] United States District Court, Northern District of California (25 January 2006) Second Declaration of Dr. Mark Heath, Morales v. Hickman. Case Number 06-219. Document Number 22-1.

[17] United States District Court, Northern District of California (20 January 2006) Declaration of Patterson, Morales v. Hickman. Case Number 06-219. Document Number 14. Available at: http://www.law.berkeley.edu/clinics/dpclinic/Lethal%20Injection%20Documents/California/Morales/Morales%20Dist%20Ct.Cp/Ex%20B%20to%20TRO%20Motion.pdf. Accessed 16 March 2007.

[18] United States District Court, Northern District of California (20 January 2006) Declaration of Rocconi, Morales v. Hickman. Case Number 06-219. Document Number 15-4. Available at: http://www.law.berkeley.edu/clinics/dpclinic/Lethal%20Injection%20Documents/California/Morales/Morales%20Dist%20Ct.Cp/Ex%203%20to%20Heath%20Decl%20(Rocconi%20Decl%20re.%20Anderson%20execution).pdf. Accessed 16 March 2007.

[19] Steinbrook R (2006) New technology, old dilemma— Monitoring EEG activity during executions. N Engl J Med 354: 2525–2527.

[20] Abbott Laboratories (1993 November) Pentothal for injection, USP (Thiopental Sodium) Reference 06-8965-R10. A similar document is available at: http://www.rxlist.com/cgi/generic/thiopental.htm. Accessed 16 March 2007.

[21] Werner HW, Pratt TW, Tatum AL (1937) A comparative study of several ultrashort-acting barbiturates, nembutal, and tribromethanol. J Pharmacol Exp Ther 60: 189–197.

[22] Robinson MH (1945) The effect of different injection rates upon the AD50, LD50 and anesthetic duration of pentothal in mice, and strength-duration curves of depression. J Pharmacol Exp Ther 85: 176–191.

[23] (1994) Administration and compounding of euthanasic agents. The Hague: Royal Dutch Society for the Advancement of Pharmacy.

[24] United States District Court, Northern District of California (20 January 2006) Declaration of Dershwitz, Morales v. Woodford. Case Number 06-219. Document Number 15.

[25] Harris WH (1943) Collapse under pentothal sodium. Lancet 242: 173–174.

[26] Taylor JD, Richards RK, Tabern DL (1951) Metabolism of ^{35}S thiopental (pentothal): Chemical and paper chromatographic studies of ^{35}S excretion by the rat and monkey. J Pharmacol Exp Ther 104: 93–102.

[27] (2005) Freedom of Information Summary. Original Abbreviated New Animal Drug Application. Euthanasia-III Solution. Rockville (Maryland): Food and Drug Administration. Available at: http://www.fda.gov/cvm/FOI/200-280020305.pdf. Accessed 6 March 2007.

[28] Wetherton AR, Corey TS, Buchino JJ, Burrows AM (2003) Fatal intravenous injection of potassium in hospitalized patients. Am J Forensic Med Pathol 24: 128–131.

[29] Gensia Sicor Pharmaceuticals (2003 October) Pancuronium bromide injection (prescribing information and material safety data sheet). Available at: http://www.sicor.com/products/1044.html. Accessed 16 March 2007.

[30] Mehta MP, Sokoll MD, Gergis SD (1988) Accelerated onset of non-depolarizing neuromuscular blocking drugs: Pancuronium, atracurium and vecuronium. A comparison with succinylcholine. Eur J Anaesthesiol 5: 15–21.

[31] Tisch C, Krueger C (14 December 2006) Second dose needed to kill inmate. St Petersburg Times.

State/Suncoast edition. St. Petersburg. p. 1A. Available at: http://www.sptimes.com/2006/12/14/State/Second__dose__needed__to.shtml. Accessed 16 March 2007.

[32] United States Supreme Court (6 March 2006) Brief for Amicus Curiae, Darick Demorris Walker, Hill v. McDonough. Case Number 05-8794. Available at: http://www.jenner.com/files/tbl__s69NewsDocumentOrder/FileUpload500/674/Brief__Amicus__Curiae__Walker.pdf. Accessed 16 March 2007.

[33] Brodie BB, Mark LC, Lief PA, Bernstein E, Papper EM (1951) Acute tolerance to thiopental. J Pharmacol Exp Ther 102: 215–218.

[34] Heard KM (1936) Pentothal: A new intravenous anesthetic. Can Med Assn J 34: 628–634.

[35] Mallison FB (1937) Pentothal sodium in intravenous anaesthesia. Lancet 230: 1070–1073.

[36] Kohn DF, Wixson SK, White WJ, Benson GJ, editors (1997) Anesthesia and analgesia in laboratory animals. New York: Academic Press. 426 p.

[37] Plumb DC (2005) Veterinary drug handbook. 5th Ed. Stockholm (Wisconsin): PharmaVet. 929 p.

[38] Mordenti J, Chappell W (1989) The use of interspecies scaling in toxicokinetics. In: Yacobi A, Kelly J, Batra V, editors. Toxicokinetics and new drug development. New York: Pergamon Press. pp. 42–96.

[39] Center for Drug Evaluation and Research (2005) Guidance for industry estimating the maximum safe starting dose in initial clinical trials for therapeutics in adult healthy volunteers. Rockville (Maryland): Food and Drug Administration. Available at: http://www.fda.gov/CDER/GUIDANCE/5541fnl.htm. Accessed 16 March 2007.

[40] Hannon JP, Bossone CA, Wade CE (1990) Normal physiological values for conscious pigs used in biomedical research. Lab Anim Sci 40: 293–298.

[41] United States District Court, Northern District of California (15 February 2006) Memorandum of Intended Decision; Request for Response from Defendants, Morales v. Tilton. Case Number C 06-219, C06-926. Available at: http://www.deathpenaltyinfo.org/CalifLethalInjection.pdf. Accessed 16 March 2007.

[42] Koniaris LG, Sheldon JP, Zimmers TA (2007) Can lethal injection for execution really be "fixed"? Lancet 369: 352–353.

[43] Mirsky JH, Giarman NJ (1955) Studies on the potentiation of thiopental. J Pharmacol Exp Ther 114: 240–249.

[44] Richards RK, Taylor JD, Kueter KE (1953) Effect of nephrectomy on the duration of sleep following administration of thiopental and hexobarbital. J Pharmacol Exp Ther 108: 461–473.

[45] Gruber CM, Gruber JCM, Colosi N (1937) The effects of anesthetic doses of sodium thio-pentobarbital, sodium thio-ethamyl and pentothal sodium upon the respiratory system, the heart and blood pressure in experimental animals. J Pharmacol Exp Ther 60: 143–147.

[46] Ramsey H, Haag HB (1946) The synergism between the barbiturates and ethyl alcohol. J Pharmacol Exp Ther 88: 313–322.

[47] Wyngaarden JB, Woods LA, Ridley R, Seevers MH (1948) Anesthetic properties of sodium 5-allyl-5-(1-methyl-butyl)-2-thiobarbiturate (surital) and certain other thiobarbiturates in dogs. J Pharmacol Exp Ther 95: 322–327.

[48] Sharma RP, Stowe CM, Good AL (1970) Studies on the distribution and metabolism of thiopental in cattle, sheep, goats and swine. J Pharmacol Exp Ther 172: 128–137.

[49] Komar E (1991) Intravenous anaesthesia in the sheep. Proc Int Congr Vet Anesth, 4th. Utrecht (The Netherlands). pp. 209–210.

Reading Questions

1. What are the researchers able to suggest by comparing the human equivalent dose (HED) of thiopental anesthesia in swine to lethal injection doses?

2. According to the researchers, what does the lack of research concerning the effects of the drugs used as part of the execution protocol suggest about the protocol overall?

Rhetoric Questions

3. What elements of the study's structural components are designed to lessen any appearance of bias on the part of the researchers?

4. The study is published with an abstract and an editors' summary at the beginning. Why do you suppose both of these are offered to readers, and in what context is one likely to be more useful to readers than the other?

5. According to the editors' summary, the study's results "suggest that current protocols used for lethal injection in the United States probably violate" (par. 7) the Eighth Amendment of the U.S. Constitution, which prohibits cruel and unusual punishment. Do you agree with the editors' assessment?

6. Identify the unique challenges you believe researchers face when they study controversial issues like capital punishment. How might researchers address those challenges?

ACADEMIC CASE STUDY • CAPITAL PUNISHMENT   APPLIED FIELDS

The Nexus between Attribution Theory and Racial Attitudes: A Test of Racial Attribution and Public Opinion of Capital Punishment

ADAM TRAHAN AND KALEIGH LAIRD

Adam Trahan is an associate professor and the director of graduate programs in the College of Health and Public Service at the University of North Texas. He studies several topics related to criminal justice, including capital punishment and the effects of incarceration on families. His co-author, Kaleigh Laird, is a teaching associate at Indiana University of Pennsylvania. In the following study, Trahan and Laird explore the factors that appear to impact whether people support the death penalty.

ABSTRACT

Research has shown that attribution theory and racial attitudes are among the most consistent attitudinal predictors of capital punishment opinion. This study explores the overlap of these two constructs, racial attribution, and its ability to account for support and opposition to the death penalty. Using data from the 1972–2016 cumulative data file of the General Social Survey, three logistic regression models were used to analyze the effect of internal and external racial attribution on capital punishment opinions for (a) the aggregate sample, (b) White respondents only, and (c) Black respondents only. Respondents were asked whether racial inequalities were due to structural disadvantages or personal deficiencies of Black Americans. Findings showed that respondents in all three models were more likely to support the death penalty when they attributed racial inequalities to personal deficiencies of Blacks and less likely to support the death penalty when they endorsed structural disadvantages, although the effects were somewhat muted for Black respondents. These findings suggest that ongoing public support for capital punishment in the United States is based at least in part on a fundamental attribution error in which Whites and some Blacks alike blame Blacks for their own deprivation.

Keywords: capital punishment opinion, race, racial attitudes, attribution

INTRODUCTION

Public opinion of capital punishment influences the administration of the death penalty in a variety of ways. Support from a majority of the public is likely requisite to maintaining capital punishment systems in the United States in general (Bohm, 2014; Ellsworth & Gross, 1994). Although support has waned somewhat in recent years, data from the 2016 Gallup poll show 60 percent of respondents supported and 37 percent opposed capital punishment (Jones, 2016). Without widespread public support, capital punishment systems could become unsustainable for legislators and executives. This is not the only avenue through which public opinion can influence capital punishment laws, however. The Supreme Court has recently demonstrated in two separate cases a willingness to make major changes to the administration of capital punishment based principally on public opposition.

In *Atkins v. Virginia* (2002) and *Roper v. Simmons* (2005) the Court exempted intellectually disabled persons and juveniles, respectively, from execution. The Court's rationale in both cases was based on the Eighth Amendment's evolving standards of decency doctrine (*Trop v. Dulles*, 1958). In the *Atkins* ruling, the Court observed that, beginning with Georgia in 1986, 21 states and the federal government had outlawed execution of the intellectually disabled. The majority of the justices thus ruled that a national consensus, reflected by state legislative activity, had developed against executing people with intellectual disabilities. In *Roper*, a majority of the justices identified a national trend away from subjecting persons who were under the age of 18 at the time of their crimes to the death penalty. Specifically, they observed that since 1989 when they had last visited the issue five states had abolished execution for juveniles and none had established the practice. Further, only six of the 20 states that retained the death penalty for juveniles had actually executed a juvenile capital offender. In both cases, the Court reasoned that society's standards of decency had evolved to a point where the public no longer approved of executing juveniles and the intellectually disabled.

Public opinion also drives the administration of capital punishment via its influence on the everyday decisions of local prosecutors and judges. People in these positions are directly elected or appointed by elected officials. Whether they fear political consequences or believe their role is to carry out the will of the people, they are generally averse to taking action that is not consistent with the preferences of the majority of their constituents (Bright, 2003; Dieter, 1996). This can be especially true regarding prominent emotive "law and order" issues like capital punishment (Bohm, 2014). Understanding the landscape of public opinion is thus important to understanding the administration of capital punishment at a broad, national level and in the everyday, seemingly common choices of practitioners of law and criminal justice.

The demographic correlates of support and opposition are well established. Supporters of capital punishment are disproportionately White (Bobo & Johnson, 2004; Cochran & Chamlin, 2006; Johnson, 2001), male (Cochran & Sanders, 2009; Robbers, 2006; Stack, 2000), Protestant (Grasmick & McGill, 1994; Young, 1992), politically conservative (Longmire, 1996; Young, 1991, 1992), and married (Bohm, 2014; Fox, Radelet, & Bonsteel, 1990–1991). These findings have been consistently observed in nearly every modern study of capital punishment opinion. The empirical record is quite clear as to "who" tends to support capital punishment. We know relatively less about why people support or oppose the death penalty. Two additional characteristics—racial attitudes and attribution style—have, to date, shown quite consistent and substantial effects on capital punishment opinion (Green, Staerkle, & Sears, 2006; Robbers, 2004; Unnever & Cullen, 2009). The study presented here was designed to extend this literature by exploring the overlap between racial attitudes and attribution style—racial attribution—and its ability to predict support and opposition to capital punishment.

LITERATURE

Research on the underlying sources of capital punishment opinion has shown that support and opposition are not based on the rational, pragmatic effects of the policy itself. Rather, people's attitudes toward the death penalty are linked to their personal value systems (Bohm, 2014; Vollum, Longmire, & Buffington-Vollum, 2006). The empirical record on what these values are is still developing. To be sure, people often cite pragmatic reasons, such as deterrence, when asked why they support or oppose the death penalty (Bohm, Clark, & Aveni, 1991). Several studies have shown, however, that death penalty opinions are generally immutable (Bohm & Vogel, 2004; Bohm, Vogel, & Maisto, 1993; Vollum, Mallicoat, & Buffington-Vollum, 2009). Subjects who claim they support the death penalty for its deterrent value tend to be unaffected when presented with information showing the death penalty does not deter crime (Lee, Bohm, & Pazzani, 2014). The conclusion is that death penalty opinions are expressions of people's underlying personal values. The results of these studies have been imperative to answering various research questions, most notably those pertaining to Marshall hypothesis[1] (see Bohm, 2014).

Findings suggest that supporters of capital punishment, and punitive sentences in general, are disproportionately authoritarian (Carroll, Perkowitz, Lurigio, & Weaver, 1987; Hagan, 1975) and autocratic (Valliant & Oliver, 1997). Results regarding the relationship between extraversion and capital punishment support are mixed, with some finding a positive association (McKelvie, 1983; McKelvie & Daoussis, 1982; Robbers, 2006) and others finding no significant relationship (Lester, Hadley, & Lucas, 1990; Lester, Maggioncalda-Aretz, & Stark, 1997). Several findings suggest people who score high on a neuroticism scale are more likely to support the death penalty (Lester et al., 1990; Robbers, 2006). Lastly, openness (i.e., interest in theoretical and philosophical debate and alternative thinking) and agreeableness (i.e., high levels of interpersonal skill and sympathy) have been associated with opposition to capital punishment (Robbers, 2006).

Two other characteristics are singular in the consistency with which they have been linked to death penalty opinions and the magnitude of their effect on the same. First, racial attitudes, specifically White racism, have been found to significantly predict support for capital punishment across various methodological designs (Unnever & Cullen, 2009; Unnever, Cullen, & Jonson, 2008). Second, attribution style, i.e., how lay persons think about the causes of events, has consistently separated supporters from opponents of the death penalty (Green et al., 2006; Robbers, 2004). Specifically, these studies show that subjects with dispositional attribution styles, who believe that internal, personal characteristics cause people's behavior, are significantly more likely to support the death penalty than those with

a situational attribution style. People with a situational attribution style believe that external, environmental characteristics cause behavior and are more likely to oppose the death penalty (Robbers, 2004).

Racial attitudes

Research on racial attitudes was prompted by the persistent finding that Whites support the death penalty at considerably higher levels than Blacks (Ellsworth & Gross, 1994; Young, 1991). In one of the earliest analyses, Barkan and Cohen (1994) explored univariate relationships between support for capital punishment among Whites and antipathy to Blacks and endorsement of Black stereotypes. Both relationships were significant such that respondents who scored higher in personal antipathy toward Blacks and those who endorsed more Black stereotypes were more likely to support capital punishment. Other studies using different sources of data, measures of racial attitudes, and methodological designs have shown that racial animosity is one of the most robust predictors of capital punishment support among Whites (Bobo & Johnson, 2004; Borg, 1997; Soss, Langbein, & Metelko, 2003).

In one of the most notable studies on the topic, Unnever and Cullen (2007a) explored whether White racism could account for the gap between White and Black support for capital punishment. Respondents to the National Election Study were asked to indicate their level of agreement with four disparaging statements about Blacks. A dichotomous measure of capital punishment opinion was regressed on a scale summed from these four items. Their findings showed that one-third of the racial divide in support for capital punishment could be attributed to White racism. The association was so robust that support among non-racist Whites was similar to Blacks.

The effect of racism on support for capital punishment has been observed across various populations. Unnever et al. (2008) analyzed data gathered in Great Britain, France, Spain, and Japan and found that animosity to racial or ethnic minorities predicted support for capital punishment in each nation. Butler (2007) found that racism was positively associated with support for capital punishment among a sample of venirepersons in Florida. Particularly concerning, the positive association between racism and support for capital punishment was stronger among the venirepersons who met the eligibility criteria to serve on capital juries.

Attribution style

Past research has shown an association between attribution style and public opinion of punitiveness in general (Cullen, Clark, Cullen, & Mathers, 1985; Grasmick & McGill, 1994; Sims & Johnston, 2004). That attribution style might also influence capital punishment opinions was a logical extension of these findings. In fact, studies have consistently shown that dispositional attribution is associated with support for capital punishment and situational attribution is associated with opposition.

Robbers (2004) explored the relationships between religiosity, attribution style, and death penalty opinion among a sample of students attending a religiously affiliated university. She measured attribution using a seven-item scale developed by Cullen et al. (1985). All seven items in this scale measured criminal attribution. That is, respondents were asked whether criminals commit crimes because of personal characteristics (dispositional) or environmental stressors (situational). Results of their analysis showed that dispositional attribution style predicted support for capital punishment.

Cochran, Boots, and Heide (2003) measured the relationship between attribution style and attitudes toward capital punishment for juveniles, the mentally incompetent, and the intellectually disabled. They administered a survey to 697 persons called for jury service which included eight Likert-type measures of attribution style developed by Grasmick and McGill (1994). The Grasmick and McGill scale is also based on criminal attribution. Results of their analysis showed that dispositional attribution style was significantly and positively associated with higher levels of support for capital punishment for each defendant condition. Situational attribution style was

significantly and negatively associated with support for capital punishment for juveniles but not mentally ill or mentally retarded offenders.

Cochran, Boots, and Chamlin (2006) subsequently examined whether attribution style could explain why conservatives and Republicans so consistently support capital punishment at higher levels than liberals and Democrats. They posited that conservatives and Republicans are more likely to support the death penalty precisely because they are more likely to adopt a dispositional attribution style which stresses the personal culpability of criminal offenders. Again using the Grasmick and McGill (1994) scale of criminal attribution, their results showed support for their thesis. Specifically, attribution style fully mediated the effects of political ideology on support for the adult and juvenile death penalty.

Racial attribution

Except for the work of Green et al. (2006) described below, research on capital punishment opinion has treated racial attitudes and attribution style as separate concepts. Attitudes about other racial groups and the ways we think about the causes of events and behavior are not entirely isolated, however. The nexus between racial attitudes and attribution style is commonly referred to as racial attribution. Racial attribution refers to whether people attribute differences between racial groups to dispositional or situational factors. For example, people may attribute racial differences in standardized test scores to organic intellectual deficiencies (dispositional) or inequalities in access to quality education (situational). Given the strength with which racial attitudes and attribution can separately account for capital punishment opinion, it seems plausible that the locus of their overlap might be an important source of attitudes toward the death penalty. Only one study has measured whether and how the nexus of racial attitudes and attribution is associated with capital punishment support.

Green et al. (2006) tested whether racial attribution could predict Whites' support for punitive and preventative crime policies among a sample of 849

White respondents to the Los Angeles County Social Survey. To measure racial attribution, they employed the Symbolic Racism 2000 Scale developed by Henry and Sears (2002) which measures internal and external racism. Items referring to internal (i.e., dispositional) racism were measures of (a) work ethic and individual responsibility and (b) making excessive demands of society. External (i.e., situational) racism was measured with items that tapped (a) denial of discrimination, and (b) undeserved advantage. Their findings showed that internal racism predicted support for capital punishment net of standard controls.

The research on racial attitudes, attribution style, and the one study of racial attribution have been imperative. We feel, however, this literature has two shortcomings. First, studies on racial attitudes have measured only the racial attitudes of White subjects. This is true of research on racial attitudes as well as the Green et al. (2006) study of racial attribution. A focus on White racism is understandable given what we know about race and the administration of capital punishment. Time and again, studies have shown that the death penalty is applied disproportionately to Black offenders, particularly those who kill Whites. A logical extension then is that the disproportionately high levels of support consistently observed among White respondents for a policy that discriminates against Blacks might be accounted for by White racism. This assumes however that Blacks cannot harbor generalized negative attitudes toward their own race. Burgeoning research on intersectionality has shown significant intragroup variation of attitudes and opinions within racial groups (Mallicoat & Brown, 2008; Unnever & Cullen, 2007b). It is possible, for example, that wealthier Black respondents might endorse (some) Black stereotypes in explaining the inequalities experienced by their poorer Black counterparts. The notion that intra-group prejudice might explain support for capital punishment among Black respondents is worth measuring at least.

Second, research on attribution style has focused solely on attributions of criminal behavior. That is, the measures of attribution used in the extant research tapped whether respondents believed dispositional or situational factors cause people to commit crime. Attribution theory is a much broader model about how people evaluate cause and effect. Fiske and Taylor (1991, p. 23) described attribution theory as "deal[ing] with how the social perceiver uses information to arrive at causal explanations for events. It examines what information is gathered and how it is combined to form a causal judgement." Despite the important contributions of the research on criminal attribution, we know little about whether and how attribution style in other domains may drive capital punishment opinions. One such domain is racial attribution. Racial attribution relates to how laypersons think about the causes (attribution) of racial differences (racial attitudes).

The current study is designed to contribute to this literature by analyzing the relationship between racial attribution in ways that address the shortcomings noted above. We imposed models on the data that regressed capital punishment opinion on racial attribution among White and Black respondents separately and in the aggregate. Moreover, the measures we include of racial attribution are not crime-specific. Respondents were asked whether they think racial inequalities in society are due to inherent differences between Blacks and Whites (dispositional) or structural factors (situational).

DATA AND METHODS

Data for the current study come from the cumulative 20 data file of the NORC General Social Survey (GSS). This file is comprised of 31 independent surveys conducted annually or biennially from 1972–2016. Surveys were administered to full-probability samples of English-speaking adults living in the continental United States. Measures of the dependent and independent variables were included in 20 iterations of the survey, including the most recent.[2] These include 45,125 total respondents. Prior to conducting any analyses, all missing data were imputed using a multiple chained equations imputation in order to retain as many cases as possible and mitigate bias that might result from missing data.

Capital punishment opinion

Response categories for the item that asked whether respondents favored or opposed the death penalty for convicted murderers included "favor," "oppose," and "don't know." A dichotomous variable was created to indicate whether respondents favored (0) or opposed (1) capital punishment. "Don't know" responses, which accounted for approximately six percent of the sample, were coded as missing.

Racial attribution

A total of four items were used to measure racial attribution. Respondents were first told that "on the average Blacks have worse jobs, income, and housing than White people." They were then asked whether they think these differences are (a) mainly due to discrimination; (b) because Blacks have less in-born ability to learn; (c) because most Blacks don't have the chance for education that it takes to rise out of poverty; or (d) because most Blacks just don't have the motivation or will power to pull themselves up out of poverty. The first and third items asked whether situational factors account for racial inequalities. The second and fourth items asked whether dispositional factors account for racial inequalities. Response options for all four were dummy coded for "yes" (0) and "no" (1). "Don't know" responses were coded as missing.

Controls

Several demographic variables were included to control for the effects of known correlates of death penalty support. These include respondents' age as measured in years, race (White = 0, Black = 1),[3] education (high school or less = 0, post-high school = 1), sex (male = 0, female = 1), marital status (currently married = 0, other = 1), religious affiliation (protestant = 0, other = 1), and religious salience. Religious salience was measured using a scale for how often respondents attended religious services, ranging from "never" (0) to "more than once a week" (8). Lastly, a seven-point scale that measured political ideology from "extremely liberal" (1) to "extremely conservative" (7) was included to control for the known association between political conservatism and capital punishment support.

Several attitudinal measures were also included in the model to control for confounding effects. Given that prior research suggests that support for capital punishment is linked to a "just deserts" perspective (Cook, 1998; Wiecko & Gau, 2008), a measure of the respondents' punitiveness was included. This measure reflects whether the respondents felt that courts deal with criminals "too harshly" (1), "about right" (2), or "not harshly enough" (3). Fear of crime has also been found to be positively associated with capital punishment support (Keil & Vito, 1991). Thus, a variable that asked whether respondents were afraid to walk alone at night (yes = 0, no = 1) was included.

Analytical strategy

Because the dependent variable is dichotomous, binary logistic regression was used to analyze relationships between variables. We imposed three models on the data. The first model includes data for all respondents and race is used as a control variable. This model shows the effects of racial attribution on death penalty opinions net of controls for all respondents. The second model includes only White respondents and the third model includes only Black respondents. These two models allowed us to measure the effects of racial attribution for Blacks and Whites separately. Due to coding "don't know" responses to the independent and dependent variables and racial groups "other" than Black and White as missing, listwise deletion paired the final sample to 35,277 for the first model, 30,118 for the second model, and 5,159 for the third model. Lastly, we tested the difference in regression coefficients for the independent variables between the second and third model. To do so, we calculated z-scores using the formula in Brame, Paternoster, Mazerolle, and Piquero (1998). This allowed us to determine whether the

Table 1

Descriptive Statistics for Independent Variables and Controls by Opposition to the Death Penalty

	Oppose Death Penalty (%)	n		Oppose Death Penalty (%)	n
Overall	28.9%	42,387	Attend Weekly	32.1	13,286
Race			Political Ideology*		
Black	52.4	5,670	Liberal	41.1	11,243
White	24.1	33,828	Moderate	26.6	14,467
Education			Conservative	21.1	14,274
High School or Less	26.4	20,386	Punitiveness		
Post High School	31.1	22,001	Too Harsh	57.5	3,673
Sex			About Right	40.6	6,270
Males	23.9	19,033	Not Harsh Enough	23.4	32,444
Females	32.9	23,354	Fear of Crime		
Marital Status			Yes	31.3	16,075
Currently Married	24.6	21,109	No	27.4	26,312
Other	3.1	21,278	Discrimination		
Religion			Yes	39.0	16,076
Protestant	26.5	23,382	No	21.9	24,705
Other	31.8	19,005	Ability		
Age*			Yes	22.8	5,280
< 35	30.4	12,710	No	29.8	35,934
35–44	27.7	8,859	Educational Opportunities		
45–60	28.8	11,115	Yes	35.0	20,112
> 60	28.0	9,701	No	22.8	21,180
Religious Salience*			Motivation		
Never Attend	27.1	11,277	Yes	21.5	20,900
Attend Annually	25.5	10,678	No	37.0	19,491
Attend Monthly	30.6	6,710			

*The response categories for these three covariates are collapsed in this table. Age was collapsed by calculating quartiles and rounding to the nearest multiple of five.

effect of the independent variables on capital punishment opinion was significantly different for Black and White respondents.

RESULTS

Table 1 shows basic descriptive statistics for the independent variables and covariates. The number of respondents in each category and the percent that opposed the death penalty are provided. To act as a baseline measure, we also calculated the percent of opposition to capital punishment for the entire sample. Almost 29 percent of the sample opposed the death penalty and approximately 71 percent voiced support. Several patterns start to emerge regarding the relationship between the independent variables and capital punishment opinion. Respondents with a situational racial attribution style opposed the death penalty at higher rates than respondents who rejected situational explanations. Specifically, opposition among respondents who believed that discrimination and a lack of educational opportunities could account for racial inequality was approximately 17 and 12 points higher, respectively, compared to opposition among respondents who felt that these situational factors could not explain inequality. Conversely, respondents with a dispositional racial attribution style opposed the death penalty at lower rates than respondents who rejected dispositional explanations. Opposition among respondents who believed that less in-born ability to learn and less motivation and will power could explain racial inequalities opposed the death penalty at a rate approximately 7 and 15 points lower, respectively, compared to opposition among

respondents who felt that these dispositional factors could not explain inequality.

Table 2 presents the standardized logistic regression coefficients and odds ratios for all three models. Given standing interest in the demographic correlates of capital punishment opinion, the effects observed for some control variables are worth noting. The direction and magnitude of effects for control variables in Model 1 are generally consistent with extant research. Respondents who attended religious services less often, did not fear crime in their neighborhoods, had a high school education or less, Whites, men, married persons, protestants, conservatives, and those who are more punitive were each significantly more likely to favor capital punishment than their counterparts. The results of Model 2 and Model 3

Table 2

Results of Logistic Regression Analyses of Capital Punishment Opinion on Racial Attribution

	Model 1		Model 2		Model 3	
	Whole Sample		Whites Only		Blacks Only	
	Beta	Odds	Beta	Odds	Beta	Odds
Race	.966**	2.628	—		—	
Education	.149**	1.161	.185**	1.203	−.018	.982
Sex	.437**	1.548	.439**	1.551	.403**	1.496
Marital Status	.155**	1.167	.158**	1.171	.110	1.116
Religion	.327**	1.387	.348**	1.416	.121	1.128
Religious Salience	.070**	1.072	.078**	1.081	.045**	1.046
Political Ideology	−.206**	.814	−.241**	.786	−.065*	.937
Punitiveness	−.649**	.522	−.704**	.495	−.468**	.626
Fear of Crime	−.058*	.943	−.067*	.935	−.024	.976
Discrimination	−.329**	.720	−.352**	.703	−.195*	.823
Ability	.138*	1.148	.172*	1.188	.039	1.040
Educ Opportunities	−.223**	.800	−.232**	.793	−.127*	.880
Motivation	.429**	1.536	.456**	1.577	.291**	1.338
R^2	.207		.176		.078	
n	35,277		30,118		5,159	

** $p < .001$.

* $p < .05$.

show that the magnitude of effect for several covariates are different for White and Black respondents. Marital status, religious affiliation, education and fear of crime had a significant effect on Whites' capital punishment opinions but showed a non-significant effect among Black respondents.

Regarding the independent variables, the results of Model 1 show that dispositional racial attribution decreased the odds of opposing the death penalty, whereas situational racial attribution increased the odds of opposition. Specifically, respondents who believed that discrimination was the source of racial inequalities in work, income, and housing were approximately 28 percent more likely to oppose the death penalty than respondents who saw no connection between discrimination and inequality. Respondents who believed that a lack of educational opportunities was responsible for racial inequalities were approximately 20 percent more likely to oppose the death penalty than those who rejected this explanation. Respondents with dispositional attribution styles were more likely to support the death penalty. Those who believed that inborn disabilities to learn and a lack of motivation and will power were responsible for racial inequalities were approximately 15 percent and 54 percent more likely to support the death penalty, respectively, than their counterparts.

The results of Model 2 show that racial attribution significantly predicted White respondents' capital punishment opinions. Moreover, the effect size of the independent variables on capital punishment opinion among Whites were similar to those found among the aggregate sample. White respondents who believed that less in-born ability to learn and a lack of motivation among Blacks could explain racial inequalities were approximately 19 percent and 58 percent more likely to support the death penalty, respectively. White respondents who believed that discrimination and a lack of educational opportunities could explain racial inequalities were approximately 30 percent and 21 percent more likely to oppose the death penalty, respectively, than those who rejected these explanations.

The results of Model 3 were somewhat different. The measures of situational attribution style used here—i.e., whether racial inequalities in work, income, and housing are due to discrimination or a lack of educational opportunities—predicted opposition to capital punishment among Black respondents, but the magnitude of the effect was smaller compared to Whites and the aggregate sample. Black respondents who believed that discrimination and a lack of educational opportunities could explain racial inequalities were approximately 18 and 12 percent more likely to oppose the death penalty than their counterpart who rejected these explanations. One of the two measures of dispositional attribution—whether racial inequalities are a result of Black people having less in-born ability to learn—failed to predict Black respondents' capital punishment opinions within a range of statistical significance. However, Black respondents who believed that a lack of motivation and will power was the reason why Blacks generally have poorer jobs, incomes, and housing were approximately 34 percent more likely to support capital punishment than their counterparts who rejected this argument.

Testing the difference between regression coefficients showed significant differences for the effects of three of the four independent variables on capital punishment opinion for White and Black respondents. Beliefs that discrimination ($z = 2.19$), a lack of educational opportunities ($z = 2.85$), and a lack of motivation and will power ($z = 2.34$) could account for racial inequalities had significantly different effects on Black and White respondents' capital punishment opinions. Believing that less in-born ability to learn ($z = 1.26$) could account for racial inequalities did not meet the standard threshold of 1.96, suggesting that this variable had similar effects on capital punishment opinions among White and Black respondents.

DISCUSSION

The findings of the current study contribute to the literature on the sources of capital punishment opinion in general and to the literature on capital punishment opinion and racial attitudes and attribution style, specifically. Extant research has shown that White racism (Barkan & Cohen, 1994; Unnever & Cullen, 2007a) and dispositional criminal attribution (2006; Cochran et al., 2003) are significantly and positively associated with support for the death penalty. The findings reported here show that the nexus between racial attitudes and attribution style, i.e., racial attribution, can predict capital punishment opinion. Attributing racial inequalities in work, income, and housing to an inborn disability or lack of motivation and will power each predicted support for capital punishment in all three models. Conversely, attributing racial inequalities to discrimination or a lack of educational opportunities predicted opposition in all three models. Only one variable in the third model failed to predict capital punishment opinion. Black respondents who felt inborn ability could explain racial inequalities were not significantly more or less likely to support capital punishment.

The current study addresses several shortcomings in the literature on racial attitudes and attribution style. As noted, extant research has measured racial attitudes among White respondents and one form of attribution, i.e., criminal attribution. Our findings suggest that the existing focus on White racism may be unwarranted. All four measures of racial attribution significantly predicted capital punishment opinion among Whites in the theoretically expected direction. Three of these four measures also predicted capital punishment opinions among Black respondents. Some Black respondents felt racial inequalities in work, income, and housing were due at least in part to a general lack of motivation and will power among Blacks. These respondents were significantly more likely (34 percent) to support the death penalty than Black respondents who rejected this argument. Moreover, some Black respondents attributed racial inequalities to discrimination and a lack of educational opportunities, and these respondents were significantly more likely (18 percent and 12 percent, respectively) to oppose the death penalty.

This finding suggests that we should be less rigid in our thinking and research on racial attitudes and how they influence opinions of capital punishment, as well as other criminal justice initiatives. Our

rigidity manifests in at least two ways. First, we tend to adopt the stereotypical view that racial attitudes, particularly negative ones, are directed only toward other groups. That is, we ignore intragroup racism, or racism toward members of one's own group (Clark, 2004; Johnson, 2014). Second, we tend to ignore variation within racial groups based on other powerful, identity shaping characteristics. For instance, we can be certain that the Black respondents observed here are comprised of men and women, poor and wealthy, Christians and Muslims, and various other subgroups. Many of these characteristics are likely to influence capital punishment opinions even among Black respondents. These variations may be what is driving the finding that Black respondents who felt racial inequality was due to less motivation and will power among Blacks were more likely to support capital punishment. It may be, for instance, that wealthier, more affluent Black respondents tend to hold their poorer Black counterparts personally responsible for the deprivations they experience. That is, more affluent Blacks may feel they succeeded through hard work while poorer Blacks could have succeeded as well if they worked harder. This is speculative, but virtually all of the research on capital punishment attitudes have shown that attitudes toward the death penalty are more complex than we assume. This seems similarly true of racial attribution and capital punishment opinion.

The current study also includes measures of attribution not tied to criminality. Past research has measured whether respondents believe people commit crime because of some characteristic unique to them or to their environment, and whether these beliefs could predict capital punishment opinion. We feel the notion that criminal attribution can predict capital punishment opinion is somewhat tautological. Dispositional attribution, in the context of crime, refers to a belief in personal criminal culpability and blameworthiness. Thus, the observed association between dispositional criminal attribution and support for capital punishment amounts to finding that people support the harshest punishment when they believe offenders are culpable. Here we find that a tendency to assign personal responsibility to the event of racial inequality, something that has no inherent tie to criminality, is associated with support for the death penalty. This is arguably a theoretically richer finding in that the results are not tangled in the notion that supporting harsh punishment is based on a belief people can be blamed for their actions.

The findings of the current study also contribute to the literature on the values underlying capital punishment opinion. The empirical record has reached a point where most scholars accept that capital punishment opinions are expressions of underlying value systems (Bohm, 2014; Ellsworth & Gross, 1994). As noted previously, we know relatively little about exactly what these values are and how they drive capital punishment opinions. The results reported here help shed some light on the value orientations that separate supporters from opponents of the death penalty. Scholars of attribution theory use a concept called "fundamental attribution error" that refers to the phenomenon wherein people overestimate the extent to which dispositional characteristics drive outcomes and underestimate the role of situational, environmental stimuli (Ross, 1977). That is, people tend to neglect the extent to which environmental advantages and disadvantages shape people's life experiences and instead attribute successes and failures to individual characteristics. Essentially, then, dispositional attribution represents biased, inaccurate thinking (see Gilbert & Malone, 1995; Moran, Jolly, & Mitchell, 2014). As mentioned previously, public support for capital punishment is arguably the primary requisite for maintaining capital punishment systems in the United States. Thus, we conclude that the administration of capital punishment persists in part because of an attribution error in which Whites and Blacks alike blame Black people for their own deprivations.

Future research should explore other forms of attribution and their impact on death penalty opinion. Attribution theory has the ability to explain how lay persons think about a variety of potentially important phenomena. For instance, it may be interesting and fruitful to analyze whether respondents believe that recent events involving police misconduct and use of force are problems associated with individual police officers or police culture, a "bad apple" or "bad barrel" problem, and whether these can predict capital punishment opinion. Moreover, the current study focused on explanations of racial deprivation but future research might explore gender deprivation. Doing so may be fruitful considering gender is second only to race in terms of demographic predictors of support and opposition to capital punishment (Cochran & Sanders, 2009; Fox et al., 1990–1991; Gross, 1998; Whitehead & Blankenship, 2000).

Future research should also explore attribution and capital punishment opinion across different demographic intersections. Our findings suggest that certain groups may be driving some of the results we observe in aggregate samples. Specifically, in model two and three, which disaggregated the sample by race, we saw that the measure of inborn ability was predictive of capital punishment for Whites but not Blacks. This suggests that the association between inborn ability and capital punishment opinion observed in the aggregate sample was skewed by the responses of White subjects. This type of trend can result in a muting of the opinions and perspectives of minority groups. It would be plausibly fruitful then to disaggregate samples into as many demographic intersections as possible. Consider, for instance, the possibility that the association between racial attribution and capital punishment opinion found among Whites in the current study may be a function of White male responses. That is, if we were to further disaggregate the sample, the results may be different for White men and White women. Doing so was beyond the scope of the current study.

One additional implication of the findings that should be addressed in future research relates to the likelihood that different social groups support and oppose the death penalty for different reasons. Our results show that only four of the eight control variables, which were included here because of the consistency with which they have been associated with capital punishment opinion in extant research, exhibited a significant relationship with capital punishment opinions among Black respondents. Moreover, the entire model could only account for less than 8 percent of the variation in Black respondents' capital punishment opinions. Thus, supposedly standard correlates do not seem to influence the capital punishment opinions of Blacks. Something qualitatively different must be driving Black people's attitudes toward the death penalty. Research to date has focused disproportionately on explaining the capital punishment opinions of Whites to the detriment of Black and other minority voices. Future research should remedy this bias and attempt to uncover the different underlying factors that drive support and opposition among different segments of the population.

The most conspicuous limitation of the current study relates to the single-item, dichotomous dependent variable. The evolution of capital punishment opinion research has detailed the complexity of people's opinions and the difficulty in accurately measuring them. Dichotomous "favor or oppose" questions fail to offer alternatives such as life without parole, life with parole, or restitution. However, these single-item, dichotomous measures have certain benefits (Ellsworth & Gross, 1994). Most notably, the legal status of the death penalty is dependent upon generalized public support. The Supreme Court's Eighth Amendment jurisprudence makes clear that capital punishment must reflect society's evolving standards of decency. Most recently, the Court ruled that executing juveniles (*Roper v. Simmons*, 2005) and the mentally retarded (*Atkins v. Virginia*, 2002) is unconstitutional due to the fact that a national consensus has developed against it. The results of dichotomous measures that ask respondents to take a clear position for or against capital punishment can be beneficial to gauging the general landscape of public support.

NOTES

1. In a concurring opinion in *Furman v. Georgia*, (408 U.S. 238, 1972) Justice Thurgood Marshall hypothesized that support for the death penalty would diminish if the public were better informed about the practical shortcomings and flaws in the administration of the death penalty, such as race

and gender discrimination, the lack of a deterrent effect, and increased costs.

2. These include the GSS surveys from 1977, 1985, 1986, 1988, 1989, 1990, 1991, 1993, 1994, 1996, 1998, 2000, 2002, 2004, 2006, 2008, 2010, and 2012.

3. The GSS data include only one additional racial category, "other." Given that this category is comprised of persons with diverse racial identities and that it only accounts for 4.9% of the GSS sample, this category was coded as missing.

REFERENCES

Barkan, S.E., & Cohn, S.F. (1994). Racial prejudice and support for the death penalty by whites. *Journal of Research in Crime and Delinquency, 31*(2), 202–209.

Bobo, L.D., & Johnson, D. (2004). A taste for punishment: black and white Americans' views on the death penalty and the war on drugs. *Du Bois Review, 1,* 151–180.

Bohm, R.M. (2014). American death penalty opinion: past, present, and future. In J.R. Acker, R.M. Bohm, & C.S. Lanier (Eds.), *America's experiment with capital punishment: reflections on the past, present, and future of the ultimate penal sanction* (3rd ed.) (pp. 39–75). Durham, NC: Carolina Academic Press.

Bohm, R.M., Clark, L.J., & Aveni, A.F. (1991). Knowledge and death penalty opinion: A test of the Marshall hypotheses. *Journal of Research in Crime and Delinquency, 28,* 360–387.

Bohm, R.M., & Vogel, B.L. (2004). More than ten years after: the long-term stability of informed death penalty opinions. *Journal of Criminal Justice, 32,* 307–327.

Bohm, R.M., Vogel, B.L., & Maisto, A.A. (1993). Knowledge and death penalty opinion: A panel study. *Journal of Criminal Justice, 21,* 29–45.

Borg, M.J. (1997). The southern subculture of punitiveness? Regional variation in support for capital punishment. *Journal of Research in Crime and Delinquency, 34,* 25–46.

Brame, R., Paternoster, R., Mazerolle, P., & Piquero, A. (1998). Testing for the equality of maximum-likelihood regression coefficients between two independent equations. *Journal of Quantitative Criminology, 14*(3), 245–261.

Bright, S.B. (2003). The politics of capital punishment: the sacrifice of fairness for executions. In J.R. Acker, R.M. Bohm, & C.S. Lanier (Eds.), *America's experiment with capital punishment: reflections on the past, present, and future of the ultimate penal sanction* (2nd ed.) (pp. 127–146). Durham, NC: Carolina Academic Press.

Butler, B. (2007). Death qualification and prejudice: The effect of implicit racism, sexism, and homophobia on capital defendants' right to due process. *Behavioral Sciences and the Law, 25,* 857–867.

Carroll, J.S., Perkowitz, W.T., Lurigio, A.L., & Weaver, F.M. (1987). Sentencing goals, causal attributions, ideology, and personality. *Journal of Personality and Social Psychology, 52*(1), 107–118.

Clark, R. (2004). Interethnic group and intraethnic group racism: perceptions and coping in black university students. *Journal of Black Psychology, 30*(4), 506–526.

Cochran, J.K., Boots, D.P., & Chamlin, M.B. (2006). Political identity and support for capital punishment: A test of attribution theory. *Journal of Criminal Justice, 29*, 45–79.

Cochran, J.K., Boots, D.P., & Heide, K.M. (2003). Attribution styles and attitudes toward capital punishment for juveniles, the mentally incompetent, and the mentally retarded. *Justice Quarterly, 20*, 65–93.

Cochran, J.K., & Chamlin, M.B. (2006). Can information change public opinion? Another test of the Marshall hypothesis. *Journal of Criminal Justice, 33*, 573–584.

Cochran, J.K., & Sanders, B.A. (2009). The gender gap in death penalty support: an exploratory study. *Journal of Criminal Justice, 37*, 525–533.

Cook, K.J. (1998). A passion to punish: abortion opponents who favor the death penalty. *Justice Quarterly, 15*, 329–346.

Cullen, F.T., Clark, G.A., Cullen, J.B., & Mathers, R.A. (1985). Attribution, salience, and attitudes toward criminal sanctioning. *Criminal Justice and Behavior, 12*(3), 305–331.

Dieter, R.C. (1996). Killing for votes: the dangers of politicizing the death penalty process. Retrieved June 17, 2017 from https://deathpenaltyinfo.org/node/379

Ellsworth, P.C., & Gross, S.R. (1994). Hardening of the attitudes: Americans' views on the death penalty. *Journal of Social Issues, 50*, 19–52.

Fiske, S.T., & Taylor, S.E. (1991). Attribution theory. In S.T. Fiske & S.E. Taylor (Eds.), *Social Cognition* (pp. 22–41). New York: McGraw-Hill.

Fox, J.A., Radelet, M.L., & Bonsteel, J.L. (1990–1991). Death penalty opinion in the post-*Furman* years. *New York University Review of Law and Social Change, 18*, 499–515.

Gilbert, D.T., & Malone, P.S. (1995). The correspondence bias. *Psychology Bulletin, 117*(1), 21–38.

Grasmick, H.G., & McGill, A.L. (1994). Religion, attribution style, and punitiveness toward juvenile offenders. *Criminology, 32*, 23–46.

Green, E.G.T., Staerkle, C., & Sears, D.O. (2006). Symbolic racism and whites' attitudes towards punitive and preventative crime policies. *Law and Human Behavior, 30*(4), 435–454.

Gross, S.R. (1998). Update: American public opinion on the death penalty—It's getting personal. *Cornell Law Review, 83*, 1448–1479.

Hagan, J. (1975). Law, order, and sentencing: A study of attitudes in action. *Sociometry, 38*(3), 374–378.

Henry, P.J., & Sears, D.O. (2002). The symbolic racism 2000 scale. *Political Psychology, 23*, 253–283.

Johnson, D. (2001). Punitive attitudes on crime: economic insecurity, racial prejudice or both? *Sociological Focus, 34*, 33–54.

Johnson, T.R. (2014). *Black-on-black racism: The hazards of implicit bias.* Retrieved January 25, 2018, from https://www.theatlantic.com/politics/archive/2014/12/black-on-black-racism-the-hazardsof-implicit-bias/384028/.

Jones, J.M. (2016). *U.S. death penalty support at 60%.* Retrieved May 19, 2017, from http://www.gallup.com/poll/196676/death-penalty-support.aspx?g_source=Death%20penalty&g_medium=search&g_campaign=tiles.

Keil, T.J., & Vito, G.F. (1991). Fear of crime and attitudes toward capital punishment: A structural equations model. *Justice Quarterly, 8*(4), 447–464.

Lee, G.M., Bohm, R.M., & Pazzani, L.M. (2014). Knowledge and death penalty opinion: the Marshall hypotheses revisited. *American Journal of Criminal Justice, 39*, 642–659.

Lester, D., Hadley, R.A., & Lucas, W.A. (1990). Personality and a pro-death attitude. *Personality and Individual Differences, 11*(11), 1183–1185.

Lester, D., Maggioncalda-Aretz, M., & Stark, S.H. (1997). Adolescents' attitudes toward the death penalty. *Adolescence, 32*(126), 447–449.

Longmire, D.R. (1996). American's attitudes about the ultimate weapon: capital punishment. In T.J. Flanagan & D.R. Longmire (Eds.), *Americans view crime and justice: a national public opinion survey* (pp. 93–108). Thousand Oaks, CA: Sage Publications.

Mallicoat, S.L., & Brown, G.C. (2008). The impact of race and ethnicity on student opinions of capital punishment. *Journal of Ethnicity in Criminal Justice, 6*(4), 255–280.

McKelvie, S.J. (1983). Personality and belief in capital punishment: A replication and extension. *Personality and Individual Differences, 4*(2), 217–218.

McKelvie, S.J., & Dauossis, L. (1982). Extraversion and attitudes toward capital punishment. *Personality and Individual Differences, 3*(3), 341–342.

Moran, J.M., Jolly, E., & Mitchell, J.P. (2014). Spontaneous mentalizing predicts the fundamental attribution error. *Journal of Cognitive Neuroscience, 26*(3), 569–576.

Robbers, M. (2004). Extremists or believers? Religious salience, literalness, attribution styles and attitudes toward the death penalty among students: an empirical examination of main and moderating effects. *Journal of Crime and Justice, 27*, 119–149.

Robbers, M. (2006). Tough-mindedness and fair play. *Punishment and Society, 8*(2), 203–222.

Ross, L. (1977). The intuitive psychologist and his short-comings: distortions in the attribution process. In L. Berkowitz (Ed.), *Advances in experimental social psychology* (pp. 173–220). San Diego, CA: Academic.

Sims, B., & Johnston, E. (2004). Examining public opinion about crime and justice: A statewide study. *Criminal Justice Policy Review, 15*(3), 270–293.

Soss, J., Langbein, L., & Metelko, A.R. (2003). Why do white Americans support the death penalty? *Journal of Criminal Justice, 27*, 467–474.

Stack, S. (2000). Support for the death penalty: A gender-specific model. *Sex Roles, 43*, 163–179.

Unnever, J.D., & Cullen, F.T. (2007a). The racial divide in support for the death penalty: does white racism matter? *Social Forces, 85*(3), 1281–1301.

Unnever, J.D., & Cullen, F.T. (2007b). Reassessing the racial divide in support for capital punishment: The continuing significance of race. *Journal of Research in Crime and Delinquency, 44*, 3–37.

Unnever, J.D., & Cullen, F.T. (2009). Empathic identification and punitiveness: A middle-range theory of individual differences. *Theoretical Criminology, 13*(3), 283–312.

Unnever, J.D., Cullen, F.T., & Jonson, L. (2008). Race, racism, and support for capital punishment. *Crime and Justice, 37*(1), 45–96.

Valliant, P.M., & Oliver, C.L. (1997). Attitudes toward capital punishment: A function of leadership style, gender, and personality. *Social Behavior and Personality, 25*(2), 161–168.

Vollum, S., Longmire, D.R., & Buffington-Vollum, J. (2006). Confidence in the death penalty and support for its use: exploring the value-expressive dimension of death penalty attitudes. *Justice Quarterly, 21*, 521–546.

Vollum, S., Mallicoat, S., & Buffington-Vollum, J. (2009). Death penalty attitudes in an increasingly critical climate: value expressive support and attitude mutability. The *Southwest Journal of Criminal Justice, 5*(3), 221–242.

Whitehead, J.T., & Blankenship, M.B. (2000). The gender gap in capital punishment attitudes: an analysis of support and opposition. *American Journal of Criminal Justice, 25*(1), 1–13.

Wiecko, F.M., & Gau, J.M. (2008). Every life is sacred . . . kind of: uncovering the sources of seemingly contradictory public attitudes toward abortion and the death penalty. *The Social Science Journal, 45*, 546–564.

Young, R.L. (1991). Race, conceptions of crime and justice, and support for the death penalty. *Social Psychology Quarterly, 54*(1), 67–75.

Young, R.L. (1992). Religious orientation, race and support for the death penalty. *Journal for the Scientific Study of Religion, 31*, 76–87.

CASES CITED

Atkins v. Virginia, 536 U.S. 304 (2002).
Furman v. Georgia, 408 U.S. 238 (1972).
Roper v. Simmons, 543 U.S. 551 (2005).
Trop v. Dulles, 356 U.S. 86, 101 (1958).

Reading Questions

1. According to Trahan and Laird, what is "racial attribution"?

2. What are two of the recommendations that the authors make for future research that could be conducted as a follow-up to their study?

Rhetoric Questions

3. At the beginning of the article, the authors include keywords for their research. These keywords serve as search terms for others to locate the article. Take a look at the keywords that Trahan and Laird chose to include. What do they tell you about who the authors see as their audience? What keywords would you have included that they do not include?

4. The authors cite several prior research studies in lists within in-text citations, including multiple citations in the same set of parentheses. Why might the authors have chosen to cite so many sources in this way? Choose one of the citations and look up the sources in the References list. When you read the titles of the articles and the journals in which they appear, what do you notice about them that is similar or different?

Response Questions

5. The article reports the results of an analysis of existing survey data. In other words, the two authors did not collect the data in the surveys but rather used data that had already been collected by others. What reasons can you imagine that researchers might choose to analyze existing data instead of collecting new data?

6. The article ends with a paragraph that describes one of the limitations of the study. What did you think when you saw that the article ended there? Was it a satisfying conclusion to you?

Writing Project **Evaluative Rhetorical Analysis**

Begin this assignment by locating a popular news article that explores an issue related to crime, punishment, or justice in America. Alternatively, you might choose to focus on one of the articles written for a popular audience included in the chapter offerings. After carefully reading the article, compose an evaluative rhetorical analysis in which you assess the likely effectiveness of the article in light of its intended audience.

As part of your introduction, identify the source of publication for the piece you selected (Where was it published?) and its likely intended audience (Who is likely to read the piece, given its publication source?). Then identify the specific values, beliefs, or desires you think the intended audience members likely share with one another. With these common values in mind, offer your evaluation of the likely effectiveness of the rhetorical strategies used in the article as your thesis. How effective is the writer at crafting the text, via its rhetorical elements, specifically for the intended audience?

Develop the body of your analysis by addressing the following two questions as support for your position or evaluation of the writer's rhetorical decisions:

- What does the writer successfully do that likely appeals directly to the intended audience's values, beliefs, or desires?

- What other decisions could the writer have made to appeal even more directly or successfully to the intended audience's values, beliefs, or desires?

As part of your conclusion, reflect on the piece's overall potential for connecting with, or for moving, the intended audience. Given what you've shown, what effects do you think the piece will have on its intended audience?

Introduction to Documentation Styles

You've likely had some experience with citing sources in academic writing, both as a reader and as a writer. Many students come to writing classes in college with experience only in MLA format, the citation style of the Modern Language Association. The student research paper at the end of Chapter 7 is written in MLA style, which is the most commonly required citation style in English classes. Although MLA is the citation style with which English and writing teachers are usually most familiar, it is not the only one used in academic writing—not by a long shot.

Some students don't realize that other citation styles exist, and they're often surprised when they encounter different styles in other classes. Our goal in this appendix is to help you understand (1) why and when academic writers cite sources and (2) how different citation styles represent the values and conventions of different academic disciplines. This appendix also provides brief guides to MLA, APA (American Psychological Association), and CSE (Council of Science Editors) styles—three styles that are illustrated in student papers found in Part Two of this book. Near the end of this appendix, you'll find a table with other citation styles commonly used in different disciplines, including some of the applied fields discussed in Chapter 10.

Why Cite?

There are several reasons why academic writers cite sources that they draw upon. The first is an ethical reason: academic research and writing privilege the discovery of new knowledge, and it is important to give credit to scholars who discover new ideas and establish important claims in their fields of study. Additionally, academic writers cite sources to provide a "breadcrumb trail" to show how they developed their current research projects. Source citations show what prior work writers are building on and how their research contributes to that body of knowledge. If some of the sources are well respected, that ethos helps to support the writers' research as well. It demonstrates that the writers have done their homework; they know what has already been discovered, and they are contributing to an ongoing conversation.

These two values of academic writing—the necessity of crediting the person or persons who discover new knowledge, and the importance of understanding prior work that has led to a specific research project—shape the choices that academic writers make when citing sources. Anytime you quote, summarize, or paraphrase the work of someone else in academic writing, you must give credit to that person's work. *How* academic writers cite those sources, though, differs according to their academic discipline and writing situation.

Disciplinary Documentation Styles

Citation styles reflect the values of specific disciplines, just like other conventions of academic writing that we've discussed in this book. When you compare the similarities and differences in citation styles, you might notice that some conventions of particular citation styles that seemed random before suddenly have meaning. For example, if we compare the ways that authors and publication dates are listed in MLA, APA, and CSE styles, we'll notice some distinctions that reflect the values of those disciplines:

MLA	Greenwell, Amanda M. "Rhetorical Reading Guides, Readerly Experiences, and WID in the Writing Center." *WLN: A Journal of Writing Center Scholarship*, vol. 41, no. 7–8, Mar.–Apr. 2017, pp. 9–16.	• Author's full name • Year of publication listed near the end
APA	Greenwell, A. (March–April 2017). Rhetorical reading guides, readerly experiences, and WID in the writing center. *WLN: A Journal of Writing Center Scholarship*, *41*(7–8), 9–16.	• Only author's last name included in full • Year included toward the beginning, in a place of importance
CSE	Greenwell A. 2017 Mar–Apr. Rhetorical reading guides, readerly experiences, and WID in the writing center. WLN. 41(7–8):9–16.	• Only last name given in full, and first and middle initials are not separated from last name by any punctuation. • Year also has a place of prominence and isn't distinguished from the name at all, emphasizing that timeliness is as important as the name of the author.

MLA lists the author's full name at the beginning of the citation, emphasizing the importance of the author. Date of publication is one of the last items in the citation, reflecting that a publication's currency is often not as important in the humanities as it is in other disciplines. By contrast, APA and CSE list the date of publication near the beginning of the citation in a place of prominence.

Interestingly, CSE does not use any unique punctuation to distinguish the author from the date other than separating them by a period, reflecting that they are of almost equal importance.

Citation styles reflect the values of the respective disciplines. In a very real sense, citation styles are rhetorically constructed: they are developed, revised, updated, and used in ways that reflect the purpose and audience for citing sources in different disciplines. Some rules in documentation styles don't seem to have a clear reason, though, and this is why it's important to know how to verify the rules of a certain system. Our goal is to help you understand, on a rhetorical level, the way three common citation styles work. Memorizing these styles is not always the most productive endeavor, as the styles change over time. Really understanding how they work will be much more useful to you long term.

Modern Language Association (MLA) Style

What Is Unique about MLA Style?

MLA style is generally followed by researchers in the disciplines of the humanities such as foreign languages and English. One of the unique aspects of MLA style, when compared with other styles, is that the page numbers of quoted, summarized, or paraphrased information are included in in-text citations. While other styles sometimes also include page numbers (especially for exact quotations), the use of page numbers in MLA allows readers to go back to find the original language of the referenced passage. In the disciplines that follow MLA style, the way in which something is phrased is often quite important, and readers might want to review the original source to assess how you are using evidence to support your argument.

We offer some basic guidelines here for using MLA style, but you can learn more about the style guides published by the Modern Language Association, including the *MLA Handbook*, at www.mla.org. For an example of MLA paper format, see the Insider Example in Chapter 7.

In-Text Citations in MLA Style

When sources are cited in the text, MLA style calls for a parenthetical reference at the end of a sentence or, if multiple sources are cited in a single sentence, at the end of the information being cited. The page number(s) of the reference appear in parentheses with no other punctuation, and then the end-of-sentence punctuation appears after the parenthetical reference. The source author's name is either included in a signal phrase or within the parentheses.

> According to Döring and Wansink, the frequency with which customers ordered dessert at restaurants can be correlated with the BMI of the waitstaff (198).

The frequency with which customers ordered dessert at restaurants can be correlated with the BMI of the waitstaff (Döring and Wansink 198).

Works Cited Citations in MLA Style

The citations list at the end of an academic paper in MLA style is called a Works Cited page. Citations are listed on the Works Cited page in alphabetical order by the authors' last names (or by title for works with no authors).

> Döring, Tim, and Brian Wansink. "The Waiter's Weight." *Environment and Behavior*, vol. 49, no. 2, 2017, pp. 192–214.

1. **Author** Author's name is listed first, with the last name preceding the first name and any middle initials. The first name is spelled out and followed by a comma, and then the second author is listed with the first name preceding the last name. For three or more authors, use "et al." after the first author's name.

2. **Title of Source** Article titles and book chapters are given in quotation marks. All words in the title are capitalized except for articles, prepositions, coordinating conjunctions, and the *to* in infinitives (unless they are the first words). Include a period after the title, inside the last quotation mark.

3. **Title of Container Where the Source Was Found** Book, journal, magazine, and newspaper titles appear in italics. A comma follows the title.

4. **Other Contributors** If the container has editors, translators, or other contributors, those would be listed directly after the title of the container.

5. **Version** If the source is an edition or specific version of a text, that information would be listed next.

6. **Number** For a journal, the volume number follows the title of the journal, preceded by the abbreviation "vol." If the journal has an issue number, that would then be listed after the volume number, preceded by the abbreviation "no." Use commas to separate the volume, issue number, and any information that follows.

7. **Publisher** If a specific publisher is listed, give the name of the publisher next.

8. **Publication Date** The year of publication is listed next, followed by a comma. For journals, include the month and/or season before the year.

9. **Location** Inclusive page numbers are provided in the MLA citation of a journal article, preceded by "pp." and followed by a period. If you are citing an online source, give a permalink or DOI (digital object identifier) if a source has one. If a source does not have a permalink or DOI, provide the full URL. (Unless you want a live link, you may omit the protocol, such as "http://".)

Citing Different Types of Sources in MLA Style

Comparison of different kinds of sources in MLA style

Type of Source	Example of Works Cited Entry	Notes
Book	Davies, Alice, and Kathryn Tollervey. *The Style of Coworking: Contemporary Shared Workspaces.* Prestel Verlag, 2013.	When more than one author is listed, only the first author's name is reversed in MLA style.
Book Chapter	Ludvigsen, Sten, and Hans Christian Arnseth. "Computer-Supported Collaborative Learning." *Technology Enhanced Learning*, edited by Erik Duval et al., Springer International, 2017, pp. 47–58.	Be sure to list both the book chapter and the title of the book when citing a chapter from an edited collection.
Scholarly Journal Article	Waldock, Jeff, et al. "The Role of Informal Learning Spaces in Enhancing Student Engagement with Mathematical Sciences." *The Journal of Mathematical Education in Science and Technology*, vol. 48, no. 4, 2017, pp. 587–602. *Taylor Francis Online*, https://doi.org/10.1080/0020739X.2016.1262470.	If more than two authors are listed, use *et al.* after the first author's name. If the source was found in an online database, list the database or website as a second, external, container.
Magazine or Newspaper Article	Goel, Vindu. "Office Space Is Hard to Find for Newcomers." *The New York Times*, 2 Apr. 2015, p. F2.	Periodical articles can differ in print and online, so be sure to cite the correct version of the article.
Website	Goodloe, Amy. "TIPS—Composing and Framing Video Interviews." *Digital Writing 101*, 2017, digitalwriting101.net/content/composing-and-framing-video-interviews/.	If a permalink or DOI is not available for online sources, include the exact URL for the source as the location, excluding http:// or https://, unless you want to provide a live link.
Website with No Individual Author Listed	Sage One. "Eight Ideas for Designing a More Collaborative Workspace." *Microsoft for Work*, Microsoft Corporation, 10 Jul. 2014, blogs.microsoft.com/work/2014/07/10/eight-ideas-for-designing-a-more-collaborative-workspace.	When no author is listed, you can begin the citation with the title of the article or site. If an organization or some other entity is sponsoring the article (as in this case), that can be listed as the author.

SAMPLE MLA WORKS CITED PAGE

Works Cited

Davies, Alice, and Kathryn Tollervey. *The Style of Coworking: Contemporary Shared Workspaces*. Prestel Verlag, 2013.

Goel, Vindu. "Office Space Is Hard to Find for Newcomers." *The New York Times*, 2 Apr. 2015, p. F2.

Goodloe, Amy. "TIPS—Composing and Framing Video Interviews." *Digital Writing 101*, 2017, digitalwriting101 .net/content/composing-and-framing-video-interviews/.

Ludvigsen, Sten, and Hans Christian Arnseth. "Computer-Supported Collaborative Learning." *Technology Enhanced Learning*, edited by Erik Duval et al., Springer International, 2017, pp. 47–58.

Sage One. "Eight Ideas for Designing a More Collaborative Workspace." *Microsoft for Work*, Microsoft Corporation, 10 Jul. 2014, blogs.microsoft.com/work/2014/07/10/ eight-ideas-for-designing-a-more-collaborative-workspace.

Waldock, Jeff, et al. "The Role of Informal Learning Spaces in Enhancing Student Engagement with Mathematical Sciences." *The Journal of Mathematical Education in Science and Technology*, vol. 48, no. 4, 2017, pp. 587–602. *Taylor Francis Online*, https://doi.org/10.1080/0020739X .2016.1262470.

American Psychological Association (APA) Style

What Is Unique about APA Style?

Researchers in many areas of the social sciences and related fields generally follow APA documentation procedures. Although you'll encounter page numbers in the in-text citations for direct quotations in APA documents, you're less likely to find direct quotations overall. Generally, researchers in the social sciences are less interested in the specific language or words used to report research findings than they are in the results or conclusions. Therefore, social science researchers are more likely to paraphrase information from sources than to quote information.

Additionally, in-text documentation in the APA system requires that you include the date of publication for research. This is a striking distinction from the MLA system. Social science research that was conducted fifty years ago may not be as useful as research conducted two years ago, so it's important to cite the date of the source in the text of your argument. Imagine how different the results would be for a study of the effects of violence in video games on youth twenty years ago versus a study conducted last year. Findings from twenty years ago probably have very little bearing on the world of today and would not reflect the same video game content as today's games. Including the date of research publication as part of the in-text citation allows readers to quickly evaluate the currency, and therefore the appropriateness, of the research you reference. Learn more about the *Publication Manual of the American Psychological Association* at www.apastyle.org. For an example of APA paper format, see the Insider Examples in Chapter 8.

In-Text Citations in APA Style

When sources are cited in the text, APA style calls for a parenthetical reference at the end of a sentence or at the end of the information being cited (if in the middle of a sentence). The author's name and the year of publication are included in parentheses, separated by a comma, and then the end-of-sentence punctuation appears after the parenthetical reference. Page numbers are included for summaries and paraphrases from long sources such as books and for direct quotations.

> The frequency with which customers ordered dessert at restaurants can be correlated with the BMI of the waitstaff (Döring & Wansink, 2017).

Often, the author's name is mentioned in the sentence, and then the year is listed in parentheses right after the author's name.

> According to Döring and Wansink (2017), the frequency with which customers ordered dessert at restaurants can be correlated with the BMI of the waitstaff.

References Page Citations in APA Style

The citations list at the end of an academic paper in APA style is called a References page. Citations are listed on the References page in alphabetical order by the authors' last names.

Döring, T., & Wansink, B. (2017). The waiter's weight. *Environment and Behavior, 49*(2), 192–214.

1. The author's name is listed first, with the last name preceding first and middle initials. Only the last name is spelled out, and the initials are followed by periods. With two or more authors, separate the names with commas. Include names for up to twenty authors, with an ampersand (&) before the last author's name.

2. The date of publication directly follows the name, listed in parentheses and followed by a period outside the parentheses. For books, give the year. For other types of publications, give the month and day of posting or publication, if available.

3. Article titles and book chapters are listed with no punctuation other than a period at the end. Only the first word in the title and any proper nouns are capitalized. If there is a colon in the title, the first word after the colon should also be capitalized.

4. Journal titles appear in italics, and all words are capitalized except articles and prepositions (unless they are longer than four letters or are the first words). A comma follows a journal title.

5. The volume number follows the title, also in italics. If there is an issue number, it is listed in parentheses immediately following the volume number, but not in italics. This is followed by a comma.

6. Inclusive page numbers appear at the end, followed by a period.

Citing Different Types of Sources in APA Style

Comparison of different kinds of sources in APA style

Type of Source	Example of References Page Entry	Notes
Book	Davies, A., & Tollervey, K. (2013). *The style of coworking: Contemporary shared workspaces.* Prestel Verlag.	In APA, multiple authors are linked with an ampersand (&).
Book Chapter	Ludvigsen, S., & Arnseth, H. C. (2017). Computer-supported collaborative learning. In E. Duval, M. Sharples, & R. Sutherland (Eds.), *Technology enhanced learning* (pp. 47–58). Springer International Publishing.	Be sure to list both the book chapter and the title of the book when citing a chapter from an edited collection.
Scholarly Journal Article	Waldock, J., Rowlett, P., Cornock, C., Robinson, M., & Bartholomew, H. (2017). The role of informal learning spaces in enhancing student engagement with mathematical sciences. *The Journal of Mathematical Education in Science and Technology, 48*(4), 587–602. https://doi.org/10.1080/0020739X.2016.1262470	In APA, the journal number is italicized with the journal title, but the issue number (in parentheses) is not. Include the DOI (digital object identifier) if the source has one.
Magazine or Newspaper Article	Goel, V. (2015, April 2). Office space is hard to find for newcomers. *The New York Times,* F2.	Periodical articles can differ in print and online, so be sure to cite where you found your version of the article.
Website	Goodloe, A. (2017). TIPS—composing and framing video interviews. *Digital Writing 101.* digitalwriting101.net/content/composing-and-framing-video-interviews/	
Website with No Individual Author Listed	Sage One. (2014, July 10). Eight ideas for designing a more collaborative workspace [Web log post]. Microsoft. http://blogs.microsoft.com/	When no author is listed for a web-based source, you can begin the citation with the title of the article or site. If an organization or some other entity is sponsoring the article (as in this case), that can be listed as author.

SAMPLE APA REFERENCES PAGE

7

References

Davies, A., & Tollervey, K. (2013). *The style of coworking: Contemporary shared workspaces*. Prestel Verlag.

Goel, V. (2015, April 2). Office space is hard to find for newcomers. *The New York Times*, F2.

Goodloe, A. (2017). TIPS—composing and framing video interviews. *Digital Writing 101*. digitalwriting101. net/content/composing-and-framing-video-interviews/

Ludvigsen, S., & Arnseth, H. C. (2017). Computer-supported collaborative learning. In E. Duval, M. Sharples, & R. Sutherland (Eds.)*, Technology enhanced learning* (pp. 47–58). Springer International Publishing.

Sage One. (2014, July 10). Eight ideas for designing a more collaborative workspace [Web log post]. Microsoft. http:// blogs.microsoft.com/

Waldock, J., Rowlett, P., Cornock, C., Robinson, M., & Bartholomew, H. (2017). The role of informal learning spaces in enhancing student engagement with mathematical sciences. *The Journal of Mathematical Education in Science and Technology, 48*(4), 587–602. https://doi.org/10.1080/ 0020739X.2016.1262470

Council of Science Editors (CSE) Style

What Is Unique about CSE Style?

As the name suggests, the CSE documentation system is most prevalent among disciplines of the natural sciences, although many of the applied fields of the sciences, like engineering and medicine, rely on their own documentation systems. As with the other systems described here, CSE requires writers to document all materials derived from sources. Unlike MLA or APA, however, CSE allows multiple methods for in-text citations, corresponding to alternative forms of the reference page at the end of research reports. The three styles—**Citation-Sequence**, **Citation-Name**, and **Name-Year**—are used by different publications. In this book, we introduce you to the Name-Year system.

For more detailed information on CSE documentation, you can consult the latest edition of *Scientific Style and Format: The CSE Manual for Authors, Editors, and Publishers*, and you can learn more about the Council of Science Editors at its website: http://www.councilscienceeditors.org. For an example of CSE paper format, see the Insider Example: Professional Research Proposal in Chapter 9.

In-Text Citations in CSE Style

When sources are cited in the text, CSE style calls for a parenthetical reference directly following the relevant information. The author's name and the year of publication are included in parentheses with no other punctuation.

> The frequency with which customers ordered dessert at restaurants can be correlated with the BMI of the waitstaff (Döring and Wansink 2017).

References Page Citations in CSE Style

The citations list at the end of an academic paper in CSE style is called a References page. Citations are listed on the References page in alphabetical order by the authors' last names.

> Döring T, Wansink B. 2017. The waiter's weight. Envir and Behav. 49:192–214.

1. The author's name is listed first, with the full last name preceding the first and middle initials. No punctuation separates elements of the name.
2. The year directly follows the name, followed by a period.
3. Article titles and book chapters are listed with no punctuation other than a period at the end. Only the first word in the title and any proper nouns

are capitalized. If there is a colon in the title, the first word after the colon should not be capitalized.

4. Journal titles are often abbreviated, and all words are capitalized. A period follows the journal title.

5. The volume number follows the title. If there is an issue number, it is listed in parentheses following the volume number, but not in italics. This is followed by a colon. No space appears after the colon.

6. Inclusive page numbers appear at the end, followed by a period.

Citing Different Types of Sources in CSE Style

Comparison of different kinds of sources in CSE style

Type of Source	Example of References Page Entry	Notes
Book	Davies A, Tollervey K. 2013. The style of coworking: contemporary shared workspaces. Munich (Germany): Prestel Verlag. 159 p.	Listing the number of pages is optional in CSE, but useful.
Book Chapter	Ludvigsen S, Arnseth HC. 2017. Computer-supported collaborative learning. In: Duval E, Sharples M, Sutherland R, editors. Technology enhanced learning. Gewerbestrasse (Switzerland): Springer International Publishing. p. 47–58.	
Scholarly Journal Article	Waldock J, Rowlett P, Cornock C, Robinson M, Bartholomew, H. 2017. The role of informal learning spaces in enhancing student engagement with mathematical sciences. Journ of Math Ed in Sci and Tech. 48(4):587–602.	Some journal titles in CSE are abbreviated.
Magazine or Newspaper Article	Goel V. 2015 Apr 2. Office space is hard to find for newcomers. New York Times (National Ed.). Sect. F:2 (col. 1).	
Website	Goodloe A. 2017. Tips — composing and framing video interviews. Digital Writing 101; [accessed 2018 Jan 10]. http://digitalwriting101 .net/content/composing-and-framing-video -interviews/.	CSE calls for the exact URL and an access date for web-based sources.
Website with No Individual Author Listed	Sage One. 2014. Eight ideas for designing a more collaborative workspace [blog]. Microsoft at Work. [accessed 2015 Apr 2]. Available from http://blogs.microsoft.com/work/2014/07/10 /eight-ideas-for-designing-a-more -collaborative-workspace/.	

SAMPLE CSE REFERENCES PAGE

Running head 7

References

Davies A, Tollervey K. 2013. The style of coworking: contemporary shared workspaces. Munich (Germany): Prestel Verlag. 159 p.

Goel V. 2015 Apr 2. Office space is hard to find for newcomers. New York Times (National Ed.). Sect. F:2 (col. 1).

Goodloe A. 2017. Tips—composing and framing video interviews. Digital Writing 101; [accessed 2018 Jan 10]. http://digitalwriting101.net/content/composing-and -framing-video-interviews/.

Ludvigsen S, Arnseth HC. 2017. Computer-supported collaborative learning. In: Duval E, Sharples M, Sutherland R, editors. Technology enhanced learning. Gewerbestrasse (Switzerland): Springer International Publishing. p. 47–58.

Sage One. 2014. Eight ideas for designing a more collaborative workspace [blog]. Microsoft at Work. [accessed 2015 Apr 2]. Available from http://blogs.microsoft.com/work/2014/07/10 /eight-ideas-for-designing-a-more-collaborative-workspace/.

Waldock J, Rowlett P, Cornock C, Robinson M, Bartholomew H. 2017. The role of informal learning spaces in enhancing student engagement with mathematical sciences. Journ of Math Ed in Sci and Tech. 48(4):587–602.

Other Common Documentation Styles

Many disciplines have their own documentation styles, and some are used more commonly than others. The following chart lists a few of the most popular.

Name of Citation Style	Disciplines	Website
American Chemical Society (ACS)	Chemistry and Physical Sciences	http://pubs.acs.org/series/styleguide
American Institute of Physics (AIP)	Physics	http://publishing.aip.org/authors
American Mathematical Society (AMS)	Mathematics	http://www.ams.org/publications/authors
American Medical Association (AMA)	Medicine	http://www.amamanualofstyle.com/
American Political Science Association (APSA)	Political Science	http://www.apsanet.org/Portals/54/files/APSAStyleManual2006.pdf
American Sociological Association (ASA)	Sociology	http://www.asanet.org/documents/teaching/pdfs/Quick_Tips_for_ASA_Style.pdf
Associated Press Stylebook (AP Style)	Journalism	https://www.apstylebook.com/
Bluebook Style	Law and Legal Studies	https://www.legalbluebook.com/
Chicago Manual of Style (CMoS)	History and other humanities disciplines	http://www.chicagomanualofstyle.org/
Institute of Electrical and Electronics Engineers (IEEE)	Engineering	https://www.ieee.org/documents/style_manual.pdf
Linguistic Society of America (LSA)	Linguistics	http://www.linguisticsociety.org/files/style-sheet.pdf
Modern Humanities Research Association (MHRA)	Humanities	http://www.mhra.org.uk/Publications/Books/StyleGuide/StyleGuideV3.pdf

Tracking Research

There are many useful, free digital tools online that can help you track your research and sources. Three of the best are personalized research-tracking tools and social applications that enable you to find additional resources through other users of the application:

- **Diigo (https://www.diigo.com/)**   Diigo is a social bookmarking application that solves two dilemmas faced by many writers. First, you can access all of the bookmarks that you save in a browser on multiple devices. Additionally, you can tag your sources and share them with others. That means you can search using tags (not very different from searching with key words in a database) and find other sources that users of Diigo have tagged with the same words and phrases that you have chosen.

- **Zotero (https://www.zotero.org/)** Zotero is a robust research tool that helps you organize, cite, and share sources with others. You can install Zotero into your web browser and quickly save and annotate sources that you're looking at online. Zotero can help you generate citations, annotated bibliographies, and reference lists from the sources that you have saved.

- **Mendeley (http://www.mendeley.com/)** Similar to Zotero, Mendeley is a free reference manager and academic social network that allows you to read and annotate PDFs on any device.

Your school may also have licenses for proprietary tools such as RefWorks and EndNote, which are very useful research-tracking applications. Most of these applications can help you generate citations and reference lists as well. However, you need to understand how a documentation style works in order to check what is generated from any citation builder. For example, if you save the title of a journal article as "Increased pizza consumption leads to temporary euphoria but higher long-term cholesterol levels," a citation builder will not automatically change the capitalization if you need to generate a citation in MLA format. You have to be smarter than the application you use.

Glossary

academic disciplines Areas of teaching, research, and inquiry within higher education.

active voice A sentence structure in which the subject of the sentence is the agent—the person or thing doing the action.

annotated bibliography List of citations formatted in a consistent documentation style that includes summaries of source material.

applied fields Academic disciplines that are generally focused on practical application.

argument The process of making a logical case for a particular position, interpretation, or conclusion.

audience The recipient or consumer of a piece of writing.

author The person who produced a piece of writing.

claims Arguable assertions that are supported with evidence from research.

closed-ended question A question that can be answered by *yes* or *no*.

close reading The careful observation of a text in the pursuit of understanding and engaging with it fully.

content/form-response grid An organizational format used to generate ideas when interpreting a text.

conventions In the context of academic writing, the customs associated with how to organize findings, use language, and cite sources.

counterarguments The objections of those who might disagree with you.

disciplinary discourse Writing or speaking that is specific to different disciplines.

discourse communities Groups that share common values and similar communication practices, both socially and professionally.

ethos An appeal based on credibility or character.

freewriting Writing in a free-flow form, typically for a set amount of time.

genres Approaches to writing situations that share some common features, or conventions, relating to form and content.

hedging The action of adding qualifiers to a sentence to limit the scope of a claim in a way that allows for other possibilities.

humanities Academic disciplines that ask questions about the human condition using methods of inquiry based on analysis, interpretation, and speculation.

hypothesis A proposed explanation or conclusion that is usually either confirmed or denied following examination.

idea mapping A brainstorming technique that creates a visual representation of ideas and their connections.

interdisciplinary field An area of study in which different disciplinary perspectives or methods are combined into one.

jargon A specialized vocabulary used by a particular community.

listing A brainstorming technique to help generate and record ideas, often in response to a prompt.

literacy narrative A reflective genre that examines how someone has developed reading and writing skills over time.

logos An appeal based on elements of logic and reason.

natural sciences Academic disciplines that ask questions about the natural world using methods of inquiry based on experimentation and quantifiable data.

open-ended question A question that provokes a fuller response beyond *yes* or *no*.

paraphrasing Translating the author's words and sentence structure into your own.

passive voice A sentence structure that eliminates or subordinates mention of the agent.

pathos An appeal based on emotions.

peer review The process of evaluating a peer's writing during the drafting phase to provide feedback.

plagiarism Failure to attribute source material to its original author.

popular sources Research produced for a general, public audience.

prewriting/invention The step in the writing process that involves brainstorming and organizing ideas.

primary audience The targeted recipient or consumer of a piece of writing.

primary sources Direct, first-hand evidence that helps support arguments.

purpose A reason for producing a piece of writing.

quoting Directly pulling the words of a source verbatim.

rebuttal A measured response to a counterargument that strengthens your own position.

research questions A question or set of questions that requires further investigation in order to answer.

revision Making content-level and organizational changes to a piece of writing.

revision plan A list of the big-picture changes the writer would like to make.

rhetoric The study of how language is used to communicate.

rhetorical analysis Close, critical reading of a text or image, examining the elements of author, audience, topic, and purpose.

rhetorical appeals Persuasive strategies within a piece of writing, including ethos, logos, and pathos.

rhetorical context Considerations of author, audience, topic, and purpose that are fundamental to each writing situation.

scholarly sources Research produced for an audience of other academics.

search terms Key words and phrases used to differentiate and locate specific research materials.

secondary audience An implied recipient who may be interested in a piece of writing.

secondary sources Evidence that offers commentary, description, or analysis of primary sources.

social sciences Academic disciplines that ask questions about human behavior and society using methods of inquiry based on theory building or empirical research.

structure, language, and reference (SLR) Categories that offer a guideline for analyzing the conventions of genres at a deeper level.

summarizing Condensing a piece of writing to its main ideas.

text Any object that can be "read" and transmits some kind of informative message.

thesis statement The central claim of an argument.

topic The subject of the writing.

transitional words or phrases Language used to signify shifts between and among the different parts of a text.

writing process The steps and methods used to produce a piece of writing.

Acknowledgments

Text Credits

Barbara L. Allen. "Environmental Justice, Local Knowledge, and After-Disaster Planning in New Orleans." *Technology in Society,* Volume 29, Issue 2, April 2007, pp. 153–59. Copyright © 2007 Elsevier. Republished with the permission of Elsevier Science and Technology Journals; permission conveyed through Copyright Clearance Center, Inc.

Gustavo Arellano. "Taco USA: How Mexican Food Became More American Than Apple Pie." *Reason Magazine,* June 2012. © 2012 Gustavo Arellano. Reproduced with the permission of the author.

Aziz Aris and Samuel Leblanc. "Maternal and Fetal Exposure to Pesticides Associated to Genetically Modified Foods in Eastern Townships of Quebec, Canada." *Reproductive Toxicology,* Volume 31, Issue 4, May 2011, pp. 528–33. Copyright © 2011 Elsevier. Republished with the permission of Elsevier Science and Technology Journals; permission conveyed through Copyright Clearance Center, Inc.

Jimmy Santiago Baca. "Coming into Language." *PEN America,* March 3, 2014. https://pen.org/coming-into-language/. Used with permission.

Jada E. Brooks and Darren D. Moore. "African American Young Adult Women's Stories about Love: What I Want in a Long-Term Partner." *Journal of Black Studies,* Volume 51, Issue 4, 2020, pp. 295–314. DOI: 10.1177/0021934720908487. © 2020 Sage Publications Inc. Republished with permission of Sage Publications Inc.; permission conveyed through Copyright Clearance Center, Inc.

Mike Brotherton. Excerpt from "Hubble Space Telescope Spies Galaxy/Black Hole Evolution in Action." From press release on mikebrotherton.com, June 2, 2008. Reproduced with the permission of the author.

Mike Brotherton, Wil van Breugel, S. A. Stanford, R. J. Smith, B. J. Boyle, Lance Miller, T. Shanks, S. M. Croom, and Alexei V. Filippenko. Excerpt from "A Spectacular Poststarburst Quasar." *Astrophysical Journal,* August 1, 1999. Copyright © 1999 The American Astronomical Society. Reproduced with the permission of the authors.

Ellen Byron. "How the Definition of an American Family Has Changed." *Wall Street Journal online,* December 15, 2019. *Journal Reports: Decade in Review.* Copyright © 2019. Republished with permission of Dow Jones & Company, Inc; permission conveyed through Copyright Clearance Center, Inc.

Wanda Cassidy, Karen Brown, and Margaret Jackson. "'Under the Radar': Educators and Cyberbullying in Schools." *School Psychology International,* Volume 33, Issue 5, October 2012, pp. 520–32. Copyright © 2012 by the Authors. Reprinted by permission of SAGE Publications, Ltd.

Inimai Chettiar. "The Many Causes of America's Decline in Crime." *Atlantic Magazine,* February 11, 2015. Copyright © 2015 Inimai M. Chettiar. All rights reserved. Used with permission.

Ta-Nehisi Coates. "The Paranoid Style of American Policing." *The Atlantic,* December 30, 2015. © 2015 The Atlantic Media Co., as first published in *The Atlantic Magazine.* All rights reserved. Distributed by Tribune Content Agency, LLC.

Nicki Lisa Cole. "Understanding the School-to-Prison Pipeline." *ThoughtCo,* August 28, 2020. thoughtco.com/school-to-prison-pipeline-4136170.

Christopher Collins. "Final Meals: The Theatre of Capital Punishment." *Theatre Annual,* Volume 62, 2009, pp. 88–103. Copyright © 2009 by The College of William and Mary.

Gregory Colson and Wallace E. Huffman. "Consumers' Willingness to Pay for Genetically Modified Foods with Product-Enhancing Nutritional Attributes." *American Journal of Agricultural Economics,* Volume 93, Issue 2, pp. 358–63. Copyright © 2011 by the Author. Published by Oxford University Press on behalf of the Agricultural and Applied Economics Association. All rights reserved. doi: 10.1093/ajae/aaq103.

Robin Dembroff and Daniel Wodak. "If Someone Wants to Be Called 'They' and Not 'He' or 'She,' Why Say No?" *The Guardian,* June 4, 2018. Copyright Guardian News & Media Ltd 2020.

Francis Dizon, Sarah Costa, Cheryl Rock, Amanda Harris, Cierra Husk, and Jenny Mei. "Genetically Modified (GM) Foods and Ethical Eating." *Journal of Food Science,* Volume 81, Issue 2, 2016, pp. R287–91. Copyright © 2015 Institute of Food Technologists. Wiley Publishers. doi: 10.1111/1750-3841.13191.

EBSCO Health. "Sample Discharge Orders." From www.ebscohost.com. Reproduced with permission from EBSCO Information Services.

Gavin Fairbairn and Alex Carson. "Writing about Nursing Research: A Storytelling Approach." *Nurse Researcher,* Volume 10, Issue 1, October 2002, pp. 7–14. Copyright © 2002. Republished with permission of RCN Publishing Co.; permission conveyed through Copyright Clearance Center, Inc.

Dana Gierdowski and Susan Miller-Cochran. Poster presentation. "Diversifying Design: Understanding Multilingual Perspectives of Learning in a Flexible Classroom." Used with permission.

by permission of Random House, an imprint and division of Penguin Random House LLC. Reprinted by permission of HarperCollins Publishers Ltd. All rights reserved.

Adam Trahan and Kaleigh Laird. "The Nexus between Attribution Theory and Racial Attitudes: A Test of Racial Attribution and Public Opinion of Capital Punishment." *Criminal Justice Studies,* Volume 31, Issue 4, pp. 352–67. Copyright © 2018 by Taylor & Francis Group. Reprinted by permission of the publisher Taylor & Francis Ltd. http://www.tandfonline.com.

Brian Wakamo. "Student Athletes Are Workers; They Should Get Paid." *Inside Sources,* October 29, 2019. Copyright © 2019 by Inside Sources. Used with permission.

Grant Alexander Wilson and David Di Zhang. "The Marketing of Genetically Modified Food with Direct and Indirect Consumer Benefits: An Analysis of Willingness to Pay." *Journal of Commercial Biotechnology,* Volume 24, Issue 2, April 2018, pp. 27–39. Doi: 10.5912/jcb838; http://www.commercialbiotechnology.com.

WPA Outcomes Statement. Ratified in July 2014. Reproduced with permission by The Council of Writing Program Administrators.

Teresa A. Zimmers, Jonathan Sheldon, David A. Lubarsky, Francisco López-Muñoz, Linda Waterman, Richard Weisman, and Leonidas G. Koniaris. "Lethal Injection for Execution: Chemical Asphyxiation?" *PLOS Medicine,* Volume 4, Issue 4, 2007, p. 156. © 2007 Zimmers et al. http://www.plosmedicine.org/article/info%3Adoi%2F10.1371%2Fjournal.pmed.0040156. CC Attribution 4.0 International.

Vikram Zutshi. "What 'Indian Matchmaking' Tells Us about Love." *Fair Observer,* August 5, 2020. Copyright © 2020 by Fair Observer. All rights reserved.

Index

Q

qualitative research methods, 168–69, 219–20
quantitative research methods, 167–68, 219–20
questions
 developing research questions, 260
 why, what, and *how* questions, 140–42
quoting, 552
 in academic research, 84
 others' interpretations of texts, 126
 in the social sciences, 185
 summarizing and paraphrasing others' writing, 185

R

Ramirez, Cristina (writing studies), on writing in the
 humanities, 149
Rathunde, Kevin (social sciences), 166
 on having multiple perspectives on a question, 166
 "Middle School Students' Motivation and Quality of
 Experience: A Comparison of Montessori and
 Traditional School Environments," excerpts
 from (with Csikszentmihalyi), 167–68, 169,
 173–74, 175–79, 180, 181
 on research questions, 166
Ray, Sarah (student), "Till Death Do Us Part: An
 Analysis of Kate Chopin's 'The Story of an
 Hour,'" 154–61
reading and writing rhetorically, 33, 37–41
rebuttal, 57, 58, 552
recency of research, 223
reference conventions
 American Psychological Association (APA), 151,
 183–84, 541–42
 Chicago Manual of Style (CMS), 151–52, 548
 Council of Science Editors (CSE), 88, 227, 545–46
 in different disciplines, 108–9
 in the humanities, 150–52
 Modern Language Association (MLA), 151–52,
 537–40
 in the natural sciences, 227
 for a research proposal, 240
 in the social sciences, 183–85, 240
 summarizing and paraphrasing others'
 writing, 185
reflective writing, 19, 24–25
RefWorks, research-tracking application, 549
replicability, 222
replicable and quantifiable research methods, 219
reports, lab, 247–58
research
 developing questions, in the humanities, 140–42

in the humanities, 123–32
in idea mapping stage, 17
issues, researchable, 69
in the natural sciences, 163, 181
primary and secondary, 70–72
researchable subject in academic research, 69
research methods
 institutional review boards (IRBs) format,
 170
 mixed-methodology studies, 169
 qualitative, 168–69
 quantitative, 167–68
research papers, structure of, 223–25
research process
 designing a research study, 219–20
 hypotheses, 216, 218–19, 220
 methods section, 224
 observation, 216, 228–38
 sections in, 224
 speculation, 218–19
 statistical data and findings, 54–55
 study, designing, 219–20
research proposal, 239–46
 methods section, 240
 strategies for writing a, 239
 Writing Project, 240–45
research questions, 140–42, 552
 content/form-response grid, 142
 developing, 68–70
 in the humanities, 140–42
 natural sciences, 218–19
 open-ended questions, 142
 popular sources, 79–81
 in the social sciences, 164–65
results, 175–76
review of scholarship. *See* literature review
revising, 552
 of drafts, 19
 in idea mapping stage, 17
revision plan, 23, 552
rhetoric, 552
 in the applied fields, 261–62
 principles of, for college writing, 9–10
rhetorical analysis, 42, 44–47, 103, 552
rhetorical appeals, 49–50, 552
"Rhetorical Appeals in 'Letter from Birmingham Jail'"
 (Ahamed), 61–66
rhetorical contexts, 34, 42, 81, 552
 to analyze academic writing, 103–5
Richter, Michelle (criminology)
 on choosing a career in criminal justice, 278
 on quantitative and qualitative research, 55

Ritchison, Gary, "Hunting Behavior, Territory Quality, and Individual Quality of American Kestrels (*Falco sparverius*)," 240–46

S

scene writing, 26–27, 29
scholarly articles and engaging with other scholars, 150–51
scholarly sources, 79–81, 552
scientific writing process, 214–15
scope in academic research, 69
search engines, 73–76
search terms, 73–76, 552
secondary audience, 34–35, 552
secondary sources for academic research, 71–72, 552
short story, analyzing, 136–39
SLR (structure, language, and reference) for analyzing genres, 107–121, 552
social literacy, 28–29
social sciences, 162–213, 552
  charts and figures, 177–79
  conventions of writing
    abstracts, 180
    acknowledgments, 180
    appendices, 181
    conclusion, 180
    Introduction, Methods, Results, and Discussion (IMRaD) format, 172–79
    references, 183–85
    structural, other, 180–81
    titles, 181
  Discussion section, 179
  genres of writing
    literature review, 185–98
    poster presentation, 210–12
    source synthesis chart, 187
    theory response essay, 198–209
  introduction to, 162–63
  language conventions
    active and passive voices, 182
    hedging, 182–83
  observing behavior, 163
  others' experiences, 200
  personal experiences, 198
  reference conventions, 183–85
    in-text documentation, 184–85
    Publication Manual of the American Psychological Association (APA), 183–85
    summary and paraphrase, 185

  research in, 163–71
    bias, addressing, 170
    institutional review board (IRB) policies, 170
    methods, 166–70
    mixed-methodology studies, 169
    neutrality, 170
    qualitative research methods, 168–69
    quantitative research methods, 167–68
    questions and hypotheses, 164–65
    statisticians, role in, 167–68
    theories of human behavior and human systems, 164
    theory, role of, 163–64
  results, 175–76
  scholars in, 6
  structural conventions, 171–79
  synthesizing sources, in the social sciences, 188–89
  titles, for articles, 181
  visual representations of data, 177–79
  writing about others' experiences, 200
  writing about personal experiences, 198
sources
  evaluating, 79–81
  citing, 535–36
  journal databases, 76–78
  peer-reviewed articles, 76, 78
  primary and secondary, 70–72
  scholarly *versus* popular, distinguishing between, 79–81
  searching for, 73–78
  summarizing, paraphrasing, and quoting, 81–85
  synthesizing, in the social sciences, 188–89
source synthesis chart, 187
"Spectacular Poststarburst Quasar, A" (Brotherton, Van Breuge, Stanford, Smith, Boyle, Miller, Shanks, Croom, and Filippenko), 109–10
speculative writing, 217–18
statistics
  data and research findings, 54–55
  procedures, 167–68
  role in social sciences, 167–68
Stegner, Jack (student), draft of literacy narrative, 21–23
"Story of an Hour, The" (Chopin), 136–38
Stout, Sam (student), on academic writing, 9
"Strategies of Forbidden Love: Family across Racial Boundaries in Nineteenth-Century North Carolina, The" (Milteer), 82, 366–83
structure
  conventions in social sciences, 171–79
  in the humanities, 139–46
  in the natural sciences, 223–25